33⅓ REVOLUTIONS PER MINUTE

33 ⅓
REVOLUTIONS
PER MINUTE

A Critical Trip Through the Rock LP Era, 1955–1999

Mike Segretto

Backbeat
Books

Guilford, Connecticut

Backbeat Books

An imprint of Globe Pequot, the trade division of
The Rowman & Littlefield Publishing Group, Inc.
4501 Forbes Blvd., Ste. 200
Lanham, MD 20706
www.rowman.com

Distributed by NATIONAL BOOK NETWORK

British Library Cataloguing in Publication Information available

Library of Congress Cataloging-in-Publication Data
Names: Segretto, Mike, author.
Title: 33 1/3 revolutions per minute : a critical trip through the rock LP
   era, 1955–1999 / Mike Segretto.
Description: Guilford, Connecticut : Backbeat Books, 2022. | Includes
   bibliographical references and index. | Summary: "A loose history of the
   rock album told through critiques of a personal selection of nearly 700
   albums released from 1955 to 1999"— Provided by publisher.
Identifiers: LCCN 2021044621 (print) | LCCN 2021044622 (ebook) | ISBN
   9781493064595 (paperback) | ISBN 9781493064601 (ebook)
Subjects: LCSH: Rock music—History and criticism. | Rock
   music—Discography. | LCGFT: Discographies.
Classification: LCC ML3534 .S437 2022 (print) | LCC ML3534 (ebook) | DDC
   781.6609—dc23
LC record available at https://lccn.loc.gov/2021044621
LC ebook record available at https://lccn.loc.gov/2021044622

CONTENTS

ACKNOWLEDGMENTS

First of all, a big thanks to John Cerullo for green-lighting yet another one of my book projects and another one to Robert Rodriguez for introducing me to the world of Backbeat Books quite a few years ago. My sincere appreciation to Andrew Grant Jackson for encouraging me to recycle my Psychobabble content (read his books on the music scenes of 1965 and 1973—they're great!). Many, many thanks to Laurel Myers for all of her assistance and encouraging feedback. Thanks too to the design team who cooked up the snazzy cover. I'd also like to express my appreciation to Barbara Claire, Bruce Owens, and Meaghan Menzel for their editorial assistance and a special thanks to Uncle Rob Busch, who worked his proofing magic on this book as he did on my first one, *The Who FAQ*. Thanks to my wife, Elise, for letting me borrow her phone so I could take all the album cover photos that litter this book (and for being all-around fab) and my son, Desmond, an aspiring author who will surely put my work to shame someday. And thanks to my kitten, T. Rex, for ceasing to bite me long enough to allow me to write these acknowledgments (he resumed biting me as soon as I was finished).

Most of all, I'd like to thank the many loyal readers who have visited my blog Psychobabble over the years and inspired me to keep writing the material that ultimately found its way into this book.

FRONT COVER

When I was in a small-time Long Island punk band in the early nineties, my greatest ambition was to record an album. Performing onstage was great fun and the optimal way to commune with the people who liked our music (all three of them), but an album is the ultimate expression of a musician's imagination as far as I was concerned. After working out a dozen or so songs in a notebook and perfecting their performances onstage, musicians really summon their songs into existence by recording them in a studio and transferring them to the tangible plastic discs you can drop on a turntable or wing across a room.

I thought my band and I might get our chance to make our own disc when we scored a meeting with a guy who'd recently started his own independent label. The meeting did not go as I expected. The guy lived in squalor and didn't seem to have the resources to release music. Even more disturbing than his ominous warning not to use the toilet (I assumed he meant the one in the bathroom and not the disconnected one sitting in the middle of his living room) was that he didn't seem to like music. His agenda was primarily political; he apparently believed that releasing vinyl singles out of a ranch house in Lindenhurst would somehow fell the corrupt corporate major-label behemoth. He explained that his label would release only singles because—and I quote—"no one has ever made a good album. All of them only have one or two good songs. The rest are shit."

This did not go down well with someone who'd come of age with *Revolver*, *Who's Next*, and *Purple Rain*. Self-described patriots had their flag; I saluted *The Kinks Are the Village Green Preservation Society*. Religious types had the Bible; I had *Doolittle* and the gospel according to Black Francis, Kim, Joey, and David. The *Mona Lisa* never meant a thing to me; *Exile in Guyville* meant everything. Basically, the rock album was the most potent and meaningful symbol, text, and artistic medium that my twenty-year-old self could imagine, and I suspected that a lot of other twenty-year-olds felt the same way.

A single? A single is a mere trailer. A long-playing record is a film. *The Cars* is a big Hollywood blockbuster. *Electric Ladyland* is a special effects–charged sci-fi extravaganza. *Tumbleweed Connection* is a western. *All Things Must Pass* is a biblical epic. *What's Going On* is a message picture. *Gentlemen* is a harrowing relationship drama. *Ogden's Nut Gone Flake* is a farce. *The Piper at the Gates of Dawn* is one of those fantasies full of magical creatures and talking animals. *The Marble Index* is the scariest horror movie ever made. *Doolittle* is a David Lynch movie. *The B-52's* is an Ed Wood movie. *Dirty Mind* is a porno.

The LP can be a disjointed collection of scenes, but at its most effective, it tells a sort of sonic story by the way it moves from track to track toward a nebulous yet satisfying conclusion. In the case of concept albums, song cycles, and rock operas, the conclusion is more explicit but not necessarily more profound. You can have a record playing in the background while you clean your room or do your homework, but ideally, you shut out the lights, slip on headphones, and give that album all the attention you'd afford *Citizen Kane* or *2001: A Space Odyssey*. If the album is thoughtfully written, performed, produced, arranged, and packaged, it might reward your attention. If not, it might at least rock your socks off.

Even during the days when making music was a lot more important to me than writing about it, I had a borderline academic fascination with the rock album. I ate up books like Tim Riley's *Tell Me Why* that explained the cultural, artistic, and historical significance of music. A few years after that meeting with the little punk label, I started writing my own critical history of the rock album's development in a marble notebook. That project didn't go far, but my love for writing about music lingered well beyond my days performing it.

When I became a professional writer, I paid the bills writing educational texts instead of music criticism, but I still found an outlet for that topic much closer to my heart when I started my pop-culture blog Psychobabble in 2008. One of my first posts was a list of what I thought were the ten best albums of 1979. That piece developed into a series that I megalomaniacally dubbed "The Great Albums," as if one tremendously flawed person has the authority or supernatural insight to decide which albums do or don't belong in the "canon." The albums weren't *the* great albums; they were just my favorites. Granted, a lot of them are pretty great, but I was always aware of how personal the selections were. The series wrapped up after ten years in 2019.

Looking for a way to keep myself busy—and perhaps make a little bread amid the COVID-induced economic downturn of 2020–2021—I decided to compile my old "Great Albums" posts into a proper book along with most of the other album reviews I'd posted on Psychobabble over the years. Assembling all of this material chronologically, I noticed a linear story emerging—the story I intended to tell in that marble notebook twenty-five years earlier. It was the story of how the rock and roll album went from a vehicle for singles and filler aimed at kids with an excess of pocket money to a legit, self-contained art form. I started noticing the factors that caused the rock album to develop into art and looking for other causes I had not yet considered. I also realized that these write-ups might provide clues to explain why the rock album had lost so much of its influence and power by the end of the twentieth century. There were still some glaring holes in the story that I filled with a wealth of new historical details and eighty-five or so new entries on additional favorite albums and historically important ones, some of which I don't necessarily love. Such entries should be recognizable by my relative lack of enthusiasm. Like that breed of journos you might identify as "critics," I can be critical, but unlike a lot of them, I don't get off on ripping artists to shreds. So I tried to keep such obligations to a minimum. I figured the book would work just fine without anything by, say, Kiss, the Grateful Dead, the Eagles, or Lynyrd Skynyrd, none of whom do it for me to say the least.

There is also a slant that most definitely prevents this book from being a definitive history of the rock album. My preference is for early rock and roll, British invaders, sixties soul, psychedelia, punk, New Wave, eighties college rock, and nineties alternative rock. These are the genres I grew up with, the ones I fell in love with, the ones I've listened to most, read about most, lived with most. I did my best to include enough information on other genres to fashion what I hope is a reasonably satisfying and wholesome history of the rock album, but my ignorance would be extra clear if I'd overreached myself. My apologies to fans of disco, metal, hip-hop, reggae, or any of the other important subgenres I shortchanged.

Conversely, if I tend to overstate the importance of artists such as P. P. Arnold, the Damned, Guided by Voices, and Suzanne Vega, it's just because I personally love them and personally believe they deserve greater attention. Then there are the albums that the critic half of my brain maybe knows aren't so hot but the human side loves for expressly extrinsic reasons. A critic is not supposed to give an album a five-star review simply because it reminds them of the day they bought it and fell in love with the checkout clerk or the magical Christmas morning they first received that objectively subpar record, but these are the factors that get tangled up with our love of particular albums, and they do indeed have value. Albums are not just random objects to collect or vessels for good tunes. They are the bookmarks of our lives.

So always bear in mind that despite the historical thread that weaves through many of its entries and its plethora of factoids, this book is just one individual's entirely subjective trip. Additional apologies if I'm being overly explanatory or even defensive, but the responsibility that goes along with writing a book of this sort in the twenty-first century is not lost on me. To quote Z-Man in *Beyond the Valley of the Dolls*, "this is my happening and it freaks me out."

The importance of the Beatles cannot be overstated regardless of your personal opinion of them (believe it or not, there are people who don't like the Beatles, and they usually like to make a big show of that contrarian stance). I've still gone a bit overboard on this crucial album group by including every installment of my Psychobabble series on the American versions of their albums in this book. My "Beatles in America" entries also serve an important function in explaining the history of the rock album: they show how record label geniuses often senselessly edited and jumbled the work of important artists in the days before the rock album was considered to be important art and explain how the Beatles changed that attitude.

Some of the odd, not-quite-essential albums by artists such as the Rising Storm, the Fox, Ultimate Spinach, Judee Sill, and Murray Head are here simply because I reviewed them for Psychobabble and didn't think it would hurt to include as much available material as possible. I hope some potentially excessive tangents involving such non–LP-related topics as rock and roll festivals, movies, and even TV shows ("Hey, hey . . .") will also shed some light on the rock and roll album's evolution.

While I organized the original "Great Albums" posts according to a hierarchy of personal preference on Psychobabble, I reorganized them alphabetically by artist for this book to make them easier to locate for those who'd rather flip around for their favorite discs than read this whole thing from cover to cover.

So what is this thing you're reading? It's a bit of a compendium of personal recommendations (and a few condemnations) from someone who has listened to a lot of music and spent way too much time thinking about it. It's a bit of a loose and winding history of the rock album—perhaps too loose and winding, which is why I prefer to think of it as a trip rather than a history. You'd have to read almost every entry to connect all the historical dots, but if you're anything like me, you're probably more apt to dip in and out of this book as you would with the *Rolling Stone* or *Trouser Press* record guides. Feel free to use it as you please. It's pretty thick. Prop open your front door with it and let in some fresh air. Thump it in time to Ringo's drum solo in "The End." Bonk some sense into a Republican with it. Whatever works for you.

What this book isn't is some megalomaniacal critic's attempt to establish his personal favorite albums as some sort of canon. I'm sure I don't have to say this, but you won't always agree with my opinions, which are (and I don't think I have to say this either, but I will) just my opinions. Feel free to disagree. You may think I'm crazy for naming *Their Satanic Majesties Request* my favorite Rolling Stones album or think I'm a schmuck for dismissing *Never Mind the Bollocks, Here's the Sex Pistols* or think this book should never even have been published without entries on *The Joshua Tree* and *Appetite for Destruction*. That's okay. To quote that other Z-man, "I ain't lookin' for you to feel like me, see like me, or be like me." Go ahead and yell at this book whenever you get frustrated with me. Kick it across the room. Singe it with your Zippo. Get your back up and ready to defend your own favorite albums. That's how you know you're a true rock and roll fan.

Yet this book isn't an act of mindless hero worship. It certainly isn't an academic analysis of a medium that should be approached only in a spirit of healthy impudence, disorderliness, vulgarity, and fervor. Because those who approach rock and roll in any other way don't understand a damn thing about rock and roll.

Above all, I hope this book is fun because that's what rock and roll is when it's getting the job done, whether Little Richard is inspiring you to spring out of your seat to do the shimmy or Syd Barrett is transporting you to wonderland or Marc Bolan is letting you wear his hub-cap diamond-star halo or Cyndi Lauper is giving you the green light to dip your head into a tub of magenta Manic Panic. And we can dissect the artistic merits of *The Dark Side of the Moon* until the atom heart mothers come home, but a single, crucial truth must always rise above the blather: all those people bought all those copies of Pink Floyd's mega-selling masterwork because strapping on a set of headphones and going along for the rocket ride is fun.

Maybe this book will inspire you to check out some gem you've never heard or revisit a chestnut like *Dark Side* with fresh ears or decide that *Their Satanic Majesties Request* really isn't so bad after all. If you're one of those nuts who thinks albums are nothing more than two good tracks and a bunch of shit, as the world's least qualified record label owner did back in the early nineties, maybe this book will get you to rethink that too.

Let's go trippin'.

ROCK AND ROLL:
THE FIRST EIGHT YEARS

An immediate and punchy by-product of the nastiest electric blues and the pithiest country and western (C&W) rave-ups, rock and roll was not born for long playing. It was for blasting out on popshop jukeboxes and hip radio stations. It was meant to be snagged for the stray cents snuggled in the lint of an average teen's blue jeans pocket. According to the January 8, 1955, issue of the music industry magazine *Billboard*, the cost of an RCA Victor single was 89¢ (11¢ less than the year's minimum-wage rate of $1 per hour). The relatively new and more expensive long-playing record (LP)—$3.98 as of January 1955—was intended for a more adult audience, which is why classical music was the format's preferred genre in its earliest days (in the sixties, the stereo LP would hold out at roughly $3.98, while the mono one generally sold for $1 less).

RCA Victor had rolled out the first twelve-inch LPs in 1931, but the privations of the Great Depression threw a bucket of cold water on the project. That was all for the best since the discs were less than perfect. They were made of a vinyl compound RCA dubbed "Victorlac," which was not sturdy enough to handle the heavy pickups phonographs used at the time. After a number of plays, those Victorlac discs would be severely damaged. Columbia attempted to market ten-inch-long players in 1932 but ran into similar issues.

Peter Carl Goldmark, an engineer at Columbia, led a team in perfecting the LP in 1948. The new version made of melted and pressed polyvinyl chloride (PVC) pellets offered longer playing times (twenty-one minutes per side before sound quality diminishes) than the brittle shellac 78-RPM discs (just five minutes per side of a twelve-inch disc) then dominating the market by shrinking the 78's groove width from 0.01 to just 0.003 inch. That groove size necessitated a smaller stylus, which means a lighter stylus. The microgroove stylus, also developed at Columbia, was a tidy alternative to those weighty pickups that had been massacring Victorlac discs eighteen years earlier. Columbia's first vinyl LP, a recording of conductor Bruno Walter having his way with Felix Mendelssohn's Violin Concerto in E Minor, was the label's first LP and typical of the kind of stuffy stuff the first LPs tended to deliver.

At that very same time, some new sounds were bubbling up well beyond the classical scene's periphery vision. In 1948, Chicago bluesman Muddy Waters released a 78 of his composition "I Can't Be Satisfied" that revolutionized the blues with electricity. Waters was not the first blues artist to plug in—Floyd Smith led his 1939 "Floyd's Guitar Blues" on electric guitar, and T-Bone Walker achieved genuine stardom in 1942 by slinging an electric—but Muddy's disc was something else. His tone stung with his amplifier's natural distortion. It was nasty (as was Muddy's "I'm gonna shoot my cheating woman" lyric, the kind of typical blues sentiment that so influenced the misogyny that would plague rock and roll). It was dirty. It was—well, not quite rock and roll yet. The sound was there. The attitude was there. The rhythm, however, was still a bit too swinging, a bit too shuffling. His instrumental "Muddy Jumps One" is closer to the hopping and bopping mark, and its rhythm guitar is still pretty distorted.

That disc has nothing on one released in 1951 when Jackie Brenston & His Delta Cats (née Ike Turner and His Rhythm Kings) launched their phallocentric "Rocket 88." Producer Sam Phillips's decision to go ahead and use an amp that busted on the way to the session resulted in distortion as fuzzy and extreme as the sound Keith Richards would coax from his Gibson Maestro FZ-1 Fuzz Tone pedal fourteen years later. So "Rocket 88" had it all: rock and roll's distortion, fierce beat, and dirty mind. It even came out on Chicago-based Chess Records, *the* key rock and roll label that would introduce such genre luminaries as Chuck Berry, Bo Diddley, and the Flamingoes (not to mention rockin' blues legends such as Muddy Waters, Etta James, Howlin' Wolf, and John Lee Hooker) to the world. One thing "Rocket 88" did not have was a home on an LP, and even when artists started specifically identifying themselves as rock and rollers in the mid-fifties, their beat spun primarily at 45 RPM. It would be close to a decade before rock and roll really started to matter at 33⅓ too.

That doesn't mean there weren't great albums in rock and roll's infant years, though it's likely most artists didn't consciously set out to make great albums the way Hendrix, the Beatles, and the Beach Boys would when the genre matured in the mid-sixties. At first, the rock LP was little more than an extravagant souvenir, a special Christmas or birthday gift, and, more often than not, a couple of singles and a whole lotta filler. Some albums held more than a couple of great singles, and those are the discs that tended to be the greatest in this primordial period. A lot of the best early rock and roll albums were basically greatest-hits packages. Others were the products of artists so good that they transcended the limitations of their era. Such discs were the first serious hints that the genre had the potential to spawn genuine works of art.

1955

Bill Haley and His Comets: *Rock around the Clock*

Appropriate for the very, very beginning of a new movement, Bill Haley and His Comets are transitional artists. Haley's background as a C&W yodeler and the Comets' big-band professionalism were straight out of the pre-rock era. They sang about rocking as much as that other key transitioner, Muddy Waters, but this septet of guys in their late twenties weren't even as rock and roll unruly as middle-aged Muddy, whose electrified blues tethered the new genre back to old-fashioned rural blues and made it clear exactly what he meant when he howled about rolling and tumbling.

In contrast to Waters's pelvic rocking, Haley's is as harmless as an invitation to the prom, though teenagers read enough into Billy Gussak's thumping (not even as primal as what their parents heard on their Gene Krupa records) and Danny Cedrone's speedy yet precise jazz licks that they were inspired to tear up cinema seats as "Rock around the Clock" blared over the opening credits of the juvenile delinquency melodrama *Blackboard Jungle*. Tellingly, those riots occurred only in the United Kingdom, where rock and roll would become much more serious business than it was in America in the next decade.

This combination of wanton youthful rebellion and hot rhythms may not be the very, very beginning of rock and roll (to reiterate, that honor belongs to Jackie Brenston & His Delta Cats), but there's no question that "Rock around the Clock" was the record that made the genre a household term when it became a number one hit on its use in *Blackboard Jungle* a year after its disappointing initial release.

Bill Haley and His Comets' record is not just a document of historical significance or a lazy signifier of the fifties to be spun over the credits of *Happy Days*. It's a crazy-making piece of rock and roll. Don't hold the square spit curl or the fact that he looked more like a traveling salesman than an instigator of teenage rebellion against him; Haley led his band through one hot piece of wax.

Try this little exercise: forget every time you've ever heard "Rock around the Clock." Forget hearing it on corny oldies radio. Forget the Fonz, Potsie, and Ralph Malph. Forget Haley's pudgy uncle face. Don't wait for "Rock around the Clock" to just pop up in a TV ad or on the supermarket sound system. Put it on deliberately. If you don't have the record, pull it up on YouTube or Spotify or whatever. Now listen. Really let it hit you. Key into that suspense-building intro. Feel the band kick in after twelve o'clock, feel how they pound out that relentless rhythm in unison, feel how they *work*. That beat never lets up. It doesn't slow down. It doesn't speed up. Let it hypnotize you. Let it carry you along. Allow yourself to dig it. Stomp your foot. Bang your head. Smash a drinking glass. Let Danny Cedrone's gibbering guitar solo melt you down completely.

Basically, I'm asking you to listen to this cobwebby antique like you're hearing it for the first time. Hear what those greaser kids heard in 1955. Hear what made them rip up their cinema seats. Hear what made young, clean-cut, culturally invisible Perry Como fans let their crew cuts elongate into ducktails, race to record shops with nothing but sixty-five cents in their pockets, send the first rock and roll record to number one, and feel their own power for the very first time. I'm asking you to let it make you crazy the way it once made you or your mom or your grandpa or your great, great-granny crazy (how the hell old are you anyway?). And feel free to do the same for any other red-hot nugget that overplaying has similarly cooled: maybe "Johnny B. Goode" or "Tutti Frutti" or "She Loves You" or "(I Can't Get No) Satisfaction." Hear rock and roll with fresh ears. Lose your cool.

The Comets' other 45s of this period are pretty smoking too with driving tracks like "Razzle, Dazzle," "Thirteen Women," "Dim, Dim the Lights," and "Rock-A-Beatin' Boogie" that serve as bridges between rock and roll and its swing jazz roots. Only "ABC Boogie" is strictly cornball city, but it indicates that the rockers were still trying to work out how young, exactly, their audience was.

These singles make up Haley and His Comets' second full-length album. Haley did not set out to make an album called *Rock around the Clock*, just as he didn't set out to make rock and roll's first album, *Rock with Bill Haley and the Comets*, a 1954 compilation of singles he had cut for Essex Records. *Rock around the Clock* is another compilation of singles (all released on Decca). All of them had already been compiled on the difficult-to-define *Shake, Rattle, and Roll*, a ten-inch, twenty-minute disc of only eight tracks that is too substantial for an EP (extended-play record, usually no longer than six tracks) and too slight for an LP, although it did spin at 33⅓ RPM like an LP instead of the single's 45. However, *Rock around the Clock* is typical for what passed for a proper album in the earliest days of rock and roll and indicative of how strong the thoughtfully produced rock albums of the near future could be.

1956

Johnny Burnette & the Rock 'n Roll Trio: *Johnny Burnette & the Rock 'n Roll Trio*

If Bill Haley brought swinging spirit and pro-theatrics to rock and roll and Elvis Presley supplied the voice (more on that guy shortly), then Johnny Burnette & the Rock 'n Roll Trio continued to build the genre by introducing its ratty, fuzzy, straight-from-the-garage noise. Kids may have swung to Haley, but few of them likely heard what Danny Cedrone was doing and thought, "Hell, I could do that!" Girls and boys alike fainted when Elvis shifted his hips, but few probably thought, "Hell, I could be that sexy!" I wonder how many heard Johnny Burnette and said, "Shit, I could scream and grind and make a funky noise like that!" because a lot of them probably could, and the unpolished accessibility of rock and roll has always been one of its most appealing and exciting features.

That wildness is evident in every track of *Johnny Burnette & the Rock 'n Roll Trio*. Plenty of bands cut their teeth on "The Train Kept A-Rollin'," and it is still one of the most propulsive, hypnotic, and hysterical rock and roll records, but tracks such as "Honey Hush" and "Sweet Love on My Mind" also introduced a scary homicidal rush to the sonic mania. Unapologetic misogyny makes these songs hard to hear without serious reservations today, and that will be a running issue with so much of the twentieth century's rock and roll. Joyous nonsense like "Rock Billy Boogie" can be enjoyed without any complications, though, man, does Johnny Burnette sound *mean* on this one. His meanness can be heard in his grungy guitar plucking even before his threatening voice enters. All he's singing about is doing a dance, but his song feels more like a punch in the face followed by another punch in the face.

Elvis Presley: *Elvis Presley*

"Rock around the Clock" is rock and roll's first iconic record. Elvis Presley, of Tupelo, Mississippi, is its signature artist for all eras. Without question, Elvis Presley deserves more credit for popularizing rock and roll than any other artist in the genre's history. At a time when mainstream (i.e., white) media steered clear of the African American artists who really invented rock and roll like Jackie Brenston & His Delta Cats and Muddy Waters (more on him to come), he was the genre's acceptable (i.e., white) face, and though he could shout the blues with a certain authenticity, he also had the natural ability to croon like the singers Mom and Dad love. Parents still found Elvis's rhythms and suggestive dance moves genuinely threatening.

Yet his greatest influence on rock and roll is the inspirational role he played for a new breed of musicians whose music bore little similarity to his. He may have dazzled Lennon and Jagger and Townshend and Dylan and the rest, but most of those artists appropriated few of his records' signatures. The 2/4 beat of Elvis's Sun recordings is evident in much of Dylan's mid-sixties electric work, but it was hardly pervasive beyond the fifties. On the odd occasion a singer seemingly attempted to mimic his honking baritone—as Lennon did on "(Just Like) Starting Over" or Robert Plant did on "Candy Store Rock"—the results sound more like parody than tribute. That Elvis was never a songwriter further limits his personal impact. As a rock and roll icon, he is without peer.

Elvis's first few albums are pretty good, but he is best represented on this 1976 compilation of his essential Sun Sessions. Author's collection.

Elvis's records fully lived up to his iconic image only when he was making raw C&W and rhythm and blues (R&B) wonders for Sun Records at the very beginning of his career. A collection of that work would constitute his greatest record when RCA released the *Sun Sessions* compilation in 1976, but there are enough of those raw and haunting early sides on Elvis's proper debut to make it a killer collection too.

Indeed, Sun sessions dating back to 1954 and 1955 provide some of the best material here—"Just Because," "I Love You Because," "Trying to Get to You," "I'll Never Let You

Go," and the eternally spooky "Blue Moon," on which Elvis links the verses with strange falsetto wails—but Elvis's really unhinged takes on Carl Perkins's "Blue Suede Shoes," Ray Charles's "I Got a Woman," and the Drifters' "Money Honey" he cut at RCA Victor recording studios in 1956 are strong too.

While *Elvis Presley* couldn't be confused with *Elvis's Greatest Hits*, it certainly isn't what we'd consider a "proper" album with its tracks cut at various studios for various labels over various years. But that was the Elvis LP formula for his first several releases, and it must have packed some sort of chemical magic because those are his best.

1957

LaVern Baker: *LaVern Baker*

The sad fact of rock and roll's first—*yikes*—thirty-five or so years is that women were shunted to the sidelines completely, and even when there were a lot more women with guitars in the nineties, they were often categorized according to their gender. If you knew where to look, there were naturally great women rockers a long time before *Exile in Guyville* and *Dry*. One of the very best was LaVern Baker.

Although she would shift more into gospel territory in a few years, Baker was a straight belter without any of gospel's melisma on her early rock and roll hits. The tone of her biggest was wide-eyed, bluebirds-on-her-shoulder, smiling-sunshine joy. Good luck digging up songs happier than "Jim Dandy," "Tra La La," and "That's All I Need." For pure peppiness, nothing beats "Tweedlee Dee." LaVern Baker and her tweetering backup singers sound like a line of robins rocking around the forest. If they don't charm you to your core, your core is probably full of shit.

On the second side of *LaVern Baker*, darkness starts to creep in with the slow and emotionally wrecked "Play It Fair," and the LP hits a disturbing final note with the violent and deeply sad "How Can You Leave a Man Like This," which slips into the traditional blues formula of matching tragic lyrics with joyful music. Complexity might not be what one was expecting from the singer of "Tweedlee Dee," but LaVern Baker sucker punches you with it on her second album.

Chuck Berry: *After School Session*

All of the artists in this book own condos in the architecture that Chuck Berry built. He brought the pace with rhythms revved up like a 1957 Thunderbird, gunning along on power chords accelerated with a pinky swing to the sixth. With his limber riffing, he took rock and roll's most essential tool and zapped it to life like Dr. Frankenstein. He also brought literate flair to rock and roll. Berry didn't spew moon and June clichés; he spun yarns. Saying he loved a girl wasn't adequate for the duck walker; he needed to convey his frustration about being unable to undo her seat belt while fumbling in the front seat of his car. He needed to protest being inundated with bills, fast-talking salesmen (you listening, Jagger?), schooling, the military, and all the other monkey business. He needed to create fully fleshed characters: the road-bound daddy distraught because he can't get a phone call through to his daughter back home, a prehistoric monkey who raises the ire of all the other animals in the jungle, the hot-picking country boy with dreams of being the "leader of a big old band." Berry's tall tales were the seeds that sprouted "(I Can't Get No) Satisfaction," "Like a Rolling Stone," "Janie Jones," and too many others.

With *After School Session*, Chuck Berry also made a great album that did all of the things all future great albums would do. It does not excessively lean on singles. It is full of diversity, which is especially impressive for an artist who often seemed to be recycling the same two songs over and over. There is Santo & Johnny–style mood music ("Deep Feeling"), loose-lipped rapping ("Too Much Monkey Business"), pure blues ("Wee Wee Hours," "No Money Down"), Latin flavors ("Berry Pickin'"), traditional balladry ("Together We Will Always Be," "Drifting Heart"), calypso ("Havana Moon"), and haunted proto–horror rock ("Down Bound Train"). There is also plenty of that patented Chuck Berry speed and sparkle on the classics "School Day" and "Brown Eyed Handsome Man." *After School Session* may have come out a good five or six years before the rock and roll LP came into its own, but it would rate as one of the great albums in any era.

Johnny Cash: *Johnny Cash with His Hot and Blue Guitar!*

Johnny Cash's first recordings for Sun Records weren't too different from Elvis Presley's. They were basically acoustic country pieces with a bit of twangy, tangy electric guitar and rock and roll rhythm. While Elvis already sounded like he was pitching his star power across the theater, Johnny sounded like he was perched next to a creek serenading the carp. Both made great Sun records, but there is a special allure to Johnny Cash's lonesome country boy aura that the pretty boy usually couldn't match no matter how spooky Elvis's "Blue Moon" is. Even the cat who wrote the liner notes to Cash's debut album, *Johnny Cash with His Hot and Blue Guitar!*, was tuned in to this quality, noting Cash's "big, hollow voice" and—with no shortage of public relations hyperbole—suggesting that one might think Cash "invented the word" "loneliness." Yet Johnny Cash exudes solitary strength across a debut album that surely ranks among the best. At twenty-five, he was already com-

The cover of *Johnny Cash with His Hot and Blue Guitar!* boasts some boss mid-century design work. Author's collection.

posing seasoned classics like "I Walk the Line" and "Folsom Prison Blues" while also arguably cutting the definitive version of the immortal and much-covered "Rock Island Line." Not bad for a first go.

Fats Domino: *This Is Fats*

A bunch of pieces of the rock and roll puzzle fell into place when Antoine "Fats" Domino Jr. bounded onto the stage. With his New Orleans R&B and barrelhouse background, he brought the traditional soul that linked rock and roll to one of its main roots. With Little Richard and Jerry Lee Lewis, Domino also helped establish the piano as every bit a central rock and roll tool as the guitar, though his smooth-rolling style reminiscent of another Fats (Waller) surely wasn't as out of control as Richard's or Lewis's pounding. Fats Domino also brought true sweetness to rock and roll without the cloying flavor of the teen-pandering pretenders. You can hear it in his mouth-full-of-candy voice and his eighty-eight-key rhythms. He could kick up the tempo on "What's the Reason (I'm Not Pleasing You)," but that sugary flavor is still there (though some atypically dissonant guitar work keeps "Trust in Me" from doing the same). Fats was most at home in a slow stroll, and the perennials here take their time. "Blueberry Hill" and "Blue Monday" drag the tempo right down, achieving an intense yearning that makes them as sexy as they are sweet.

The Everly Brothers: *The Everly Brothers*

Elvis, Fats, Johnny, LaVern, and Chuck were all extraordinary solo singers. Brothers Phil and Don Everly set another brick in the pop infrastructure with their uncannily blended harmonies.

The first two Everly Brothers albums mostly spotlight the duo's two sides in an extreme fashion that would be more organically blended on their subsequent albums. *The Everly Brothers* largely frames Phil and Don as rockers with covers of raw material like "This Little Girl of Mine," "Leave My Woman Alone," "Keep A-Knockin'," "Be-Bop-A-Lula," and "Rip It Up." The sweet-voiced duo can't break a sweat like Ray Charles, Gene Vincent, or Little Richard, but they pull this material off by rearranging it to suit their cheerier style.

More significantly, *The Everly Brothers* contains two of their sprightliest hits. "Bye Bye Love" is as immaculately structured and timeless as a folk standard. "Wake Up Little Susie" gave the clean-cut duo some rock and roll cred when radio stations banned it for its suggestive lyrics. Parents were terrified that the libidinous drive of rock and roll was going to transform their sweet little Larry Talbots into a pack of drooling, fornicating Wolf Men (and, of course, Wolf Women). Poor Susie and her beau knew this all too well because when they woke up after a long night of conversing, the kids knew what everyone would think. Phil and Don sweat out the kids' plight over a tune catchy as crabs and rolling as a game of backseat bingo.

The Crickets: *The "Chirping" Crickets*

If Elvis was the captain of rock and roll's high school football team, Buddy Holly was its valedictorian, and we all know which one of those guys is better primed for long-term success. When the smoke clears, Elvis may have his face plastered on more T-shirts, commemorative plates, and toilet seat lids, but Buddy is the finer artist by a mile. He did for early rock and roll melody what Chuck Berry did for the genre's lyrics, and it's hard to imagine the major Merseybeat and folk-rock innovations of the sixties without the boy from Lubbock, Texas.

Buddy Holly was not as fleet-fingered on the frets as Berry. His lyrics didn't display as much panache. He was a moon and June guy, not a storyteller. But whereas Berry was content to repeat the same tune, guitar riff, and chord progression over and over and over again, Buddy was a restless composer and musical innovator. No two Holly songs sound the same, and the same cannot be said of any other rocker of his generation. He made rock and roll the one thing its early proponents never expected it could be: eclectic. He could pump out a Bo Diddley beat on "Not Fade Away." The fatalistic "That'll Be the Day" is a soulful swing. "I'm Looking for Someone to Love" is euphoric, finger-snapping pop.

Unlike a lot of fifties rock, "Oh, Boy!," "Not Fade Away," "Maybe Baby," "Tell Me How," "That'll Be the Day," "I'm Looking for Someone to Love," and almost everything else on Holly's first album with his group the Crickets would have sounded just as fresh, contemporary, and relevant had they been released in the middle of the British Invasion. That there was so much production progression between his first and next albums suggests Buddy Holly could have already been in *Sgt. Pepper's* territory by 1964 if he had not died at such a tragically young age.

Little Richard: *Here's Little Richard*

Chuck brought the wit, Buddy brought the craftsmanship, and Bo brought the rhythm, but rock and roll would reside in Nowheresville without cuckoo energy. Little Richard was the architect responsible for that crucial construction. Whenever you hear a song veer out of control, whenever a singer can't hold back a whoop or a shriek or starts speaking in tongues (**"A-WHOMP-BOMP-A-LOO-BOP, A WOMP-BAM-BOOM!" "BAMA LAMA BAMA LOO!"**), there's probably more than a little Richard Penniman in their bloodstream.

Parents who were terrified of rock and roll would have been grossly overreacting if it were not for this man, though he started his career as a relatively conventional soul singer whose voice bore a startling resemblance to Nina Simone's. Then came his most electrifying work, which he did for Specialty Records in a tight two-year period. This was the reign of "Long Tall Sally," "Ready Teddy," "Slippin' and Slidin'," "Rip It Up," "She's Got It," and "Jenny Jenny," all of which appear on *Here's Little Richard*.

Yet Little Richard is no one-shriek pony on his debut. Bringing down the tempo but not the mania on "True, Fine Mama" and "Miss Ann," he coinvents a new form of gut-busting soul with James Brown that would send seismic waves through the sixties, setting the careers of Wilson Picket and Otis Redding on track. Even on the relatively restrained "Oh

Little Richard doing what he does best: screaming his pompadour off. Author's collection.

Why?," on which Richard reveals what a good traditional singer he is, he can't hold back a couple of wild whoops. At its best, rock and roll is unbridled excitement. *Here's Little Richard* is unbridled rock and roll at its best.

Little Richard

Little Richard is basically just another clutch of bone-shaking singles, but these are some of Little Richard's wildest: the skull-demolishing "Keep A-Knockin'," the crazed "Good Golly Miss Molly" (on which his screams cross the line from merely libidinous to horror-movie murder scene), the bugs-under-the-skin shimmy of "Heeby-Jeebies," the squealingly gleeful "Ooh! My Soul," the atypically sweet "Send Me Some Lovin'," and the more sophisticatedly arranged "The Girl Can't Help It," which earns extra credit for bringing to mind images of Little Richard abusing his keys in the first great rock and roll movie.

Carl Perkins: *Dance Album*

C&W was as important an element in rock and roll as R&B, and while Elvis Presley and Chuck Berry were mixing the two styles in nearly equal proportions, Carl Perkins stripped out as much R&B as he could without giving in to pure C&W completely. Even on the quintessential rocker statement of purpose, "Blue Suede Shoes," his guitar is extra twangy, and there's more than a little hick in his hiccup. Yet the dance in this *Dance Album* is no square one. Kids could kick up some serious hay to "Blue Suede Shoes," "Movie Magg," "Gone Gone Gone" (a close cousin to Johnny Burnette's patented style), "Honey Don't" (on which he throws in some exotic guitar work unheard of in trad C&W), and the nutty "Wrong Yo Yo." On tracks such as "Sure to Fall" and "Tennessee," Perkins gets more explicit about his origins, adding some extra authenticity and variety to an album that still would not have been generic rock and roll without them.

Gene Vincent and His Blue Caps: *Gene Vincent and His Blue Caps*

Little Richard made a career of losing his cool. Gene Vincent made one of being just barely able to restrain it. He wasn't an unfettered screamer or whooper, but he always sounded like he was just on the precipice of wailing, weeping, or swallowing his tongue. He pants and pleads and sweats through his ducktail across twenty-eight heart-halting minutes of *Gene Vincent and*

His Blue Caps. His Blue Caps have no restraint at all, lurching forward like a locomotive or shrieking in cacophony behind their leader on this solid set of rockabilly mania. Even when they bring it down on the slow-crawling "Blues Stay Away from Me," there is the underlying sense that everyone's about to lose it. *Gene Vincent and His Blue Caps* has the extra-novel hook of not including a single single. So in a sense, one could make a solid argument that the album era actually begins here.

1958

Bo Diddley: *Bo Diddley*

The great rock and roll pioneers had their specialties: Elvis had the image, Fats had the soul, Chuck had the lyrics, Little Richard had the mania, Buddy had the melody, and the Everlys had the harmonies. Bo Diddley specialized in pure rhythm. Perhaps no other pop artist is so associated with a particular rhythm: the shave-and-a-haircut Afro-Cuban funk instantly recognizable as the "Bo Diddley Beat." That beat was the man's claim to well-deserved fame, but like all of our other essential pioneers, he wouldn't be so essential if he could be reduced so easily. Ellas McDaniel was equally adept at hard Chicago blues ("I'm a Man," "Diddy Wah Diddy"), John Lee Hooker–style ticktock ("Bring It to Jerome"), slinky country blues ("Before You Accuse Me"), Latin jingling ("Dearest Darling"), and doo-wop ("Say! [Boss Man]"). It's still the classic Diddley beat that will keep you vibrating long after *Bo Diddley* ceases spinning, and "Who Do You Love?," "Pretty Thing," "Bo Diddley," and "Hush Your Mouth" are the best examples of that shuffle you'll ever hear.

Buddy Holly: *Buddy Holly*

Buddy Holly's innovations are all over his second long player. Dig how the echo keeps clipping on and off Jerry Allison's tom-toms on "Peggy Sue." Kids too scared to get on roller coasters could find a pretty good substitute in this song. The rhythm rolls all over the track, goes through the loop-de-loop. Buddy gets real into doing his hiccup shtick. The simplest guitar solo in guitar solo history busts out like a guy plummeting out of his roller-coaster car while it goes through the loop-de-loop. Revel in those dreamy double-tracked Buddies on "Listen to Me." Listen to him invent the folk-rock sound with "Words of Love." Fifties rock and roll tends to chug, pound, bounce, and brawl. We don't generally think of it jangling until the Beatles helped twelve-string Rickenbackers fly off music-shop shelves in the mid-sixties. So, as he often was, Buddy Holly was ahead of his times when he recorded "Words of Love." A fine cover by the expected suspects naturally followed in 1964. Listen to him invent twee pop with that totally un–rock and roll yet totally perfect Celesta on "Everyday." Hear him invent punk pop with "Rave On." Some tracks aren't especially innovative; they're just great: "I'm Gonna Love You Too," "Look at Me," and "Mailman, Bring Me No More Blues," a surprisingly convincing take on Little Richard's "Ready Teddy."

Buddy Holly got to release only one more proper album before he died in that tragic plane crash that also took the lives of Ritchie Valens and J. P. "The Big Bopper" Richardson (and let's not forget pilot Roger Peterson), but the innovations he continued to make on sophisticated productions such as "True Love Ways" and "Raining in My Heart" let us know that pop lost a legit innovator on February 3, 1959. Had he lived, would he have taken the next steps that defined sixties rock before his followers could? Miles from the prude his image implied, he might have led the psychedelic brigade before John Lennon's and George Harrison's dentist spiked their coffee with LSD in early 1965. Or maybe he would have put his zeal for instrumental experimentation and studio trickery to use as a producer. Most likely, he would have continued writing and singing and perform- ing and recording. And though he may not have remained consistently at the top of the charts, he would have remained consistently popular and influential. And we don't need "maybes" or "what ifs" to qualify that last point because it's the stone truth. It's in the hiccups of Ronnie Spector and Joey Ramone. It's in the thump of Keith Moon's cardboard kit on "See My Way" and the heavy, black frames on Elvis Costello's face. It's in the Everly Brothers' "True Love Ways," the Rolling Stones' "Not Fade Away," the Beatles' "Words of Love," Blind Faith's "Well . . . All Right," Blondie's "I'm Gonna Love You Too," and the Raveonettes' "Everyday." Buddy Holly did not live to experience his own legacy, as his fellow pioneer Chuck Berry did, but it exists and it persists, never to fade away.

Muddy Waters: *The Best of Muddy Waters*

The term "rock and roll" wasn't on anyone's lips in 1948 when Muddy Waters released the malicious "I Can't Be Satisfied." With its pulsing rhythm and a title that the Rolling Stones would alter to create a genre- defining disc seven years later, it's hard not to view "I Can't Be Satisfied" as the birth of something. The connection between Muddy's blues and the rockers who worshipped him would get even sharper when he plugged in for records such as "Rollin' Stone" and "Honey Bee." Keith stole his sting. Mick stole his yowl.

One thing that wasn't too rock and roll about Muddy Waters's earliest records was the format. While the 45 would become *the* rock and roll format in the fifties, Waters's discs rotated at 78 RPM like the majority of pre–rock and roll discs. In 1958, Chess Records glued together twelve of those cuts and shipped them back out on LP for the first time.

The Best of Muddy Waters remains a bracing listen both for the power of Waters's voice and guitar and for the eerie atmosphere that transcends the usual notions of 1950s

When young Keith Richards saw Mick Jagger toting this album and Chuck Berry's *Rockin' at the Hops*, he realized they might have a bit in common. That led them to strike up the partnership that would lead them through sixty wonderful years of ripping off Muddy Waters and Chuck Berry together. Author's collection.

rock and roll. Most potent of all is an explicit sexiness that burns hotter than perhaps anything any other artist produced in rock or the blues. Muddy Waters expresses what Jagger and Robert Plant can only pretend to feel.

1959

Chuck Berry: *Chuck Berry Is on Top*

If you wanted to amass Chuck Berry's biggest smashes in 1959, there was no way to go but up on top. "Almost Grown," "Carol," "Maybellene," "Sweet Little Rock and Roller," "Roll Over Beethoven," "Johnny B. Goode," "Little Queenie," and "Around and Around" are poured onto a piece of wax that would be a greatest hits in everything but name if it weren't for the oddities that fill it out. Some of these showcase Chuck's unfortunate proclivity for ethnic stereotypes, and the pseudo-Italian mugging of "Anthony Boy" and the

This 2011 reissue features Chuck Berry's two best albums as far as I'm concerned. Author's collection.

Speedy Gonzalez drawling of "Hey Pedro" aren't just offensive—they support some pretty corny music. "Blues for Hawaiians," a cover of Floyd Smith's milestone "Floyd's Guitar Blues" in all but name and a rhythmic retread of Berry's own "Deep Feeling" from *After School Session*, is inessential for other reasons. Still, the humor, energy, vivid characterizations, and joyful musicianship of the hits on *Chuck Berry Is on Top* inspired generations of musicians to pick up their Gibsons and pens for the first time. Those tracks are as fundamental to a musical education as the ABCs are to an academic one.

The Fleetwoods: *Mr. Blue*

Cool defines fifties rock and roll. The Fleetwoods are anything but. They are two identically groomed, soda-sipping prom queens and a crew-cut square in a Navy cap. Their voices are as placid as Little Richard's is out of control. The Fleetwoods may not have worn leathers or screamed about girls who can't help it, but they do click another essential rock and roll element into place: it can be intensely lush and beautiful. The hits "Come Softly to Me," "Confidential," and "Mr. Blue" are soft as down and incandescent as an October moon. I can hear swirls of the Kinks in their music, streaks of the Beach Boys, grace notes of Donovan. *Mr. Blue* backs up the hits with a healthy crop of odd yet enchanting tracks: the

No one ever said the Fleetwoods were hip. Author's collection.

clamoring "Three Caballeros" (unfortunately marred by more of the casually racist vocal shorthand that makes certain tracks on Chuck Berry's latest a drag), the gently unspooling "Raindrops, Teardrops," and the ghostly near a cappella take on "Unchained Melody."

Elvis Presley: *For LP Fans Only; A Date with Elvis*

Despite whatever a title like *For LP Fans Only* implies, the grab-bag formula of *Elvis Presley* continues with Elvis's next two LPs. *For LP Fans Only* and *A Date with Elvis* are hashes of vital Sun sessions ("Mystery Train," "I'm Left, You're Right, She's Gone," "You're a Heartbreaker," "Blue Moon of Kentucky," and "Milk Cow Blues Boogie") and more recent recordings in his tamer style ("Playing for Keeps," "I Was the One," "Young & Beautiful,"

"You're So Square," "I Want to Be Free," and "Is It So Strange"). That style is what made Elvis the crossover rocker he became, but placing those mild cuts alongside the early recordings is like plopping a cocker spaniel in a cage with a pit bull.

That these two albums are so skimpy—each comes in at just ten tracks and under twenty-four minutes—also lends them the whiff of rip-off. Still, *For LP Fans Only* and *A Date with Elvis* remain extremely important because of their high count of Sun recordings, which remain as ready to rumble as any early rock and roll. In 1959, grabbing these two discs was the handiest way to amass those essential recordings.

Howlin' Wolf: *Moanin' in the Moonlight*

With its sophisticated electric instrumentation and the relatively plush facilities of Chess Studios, the Chicago blues was a less rough and rustic affair than its southern counterpart. Chester Burnett—better known as Howlin' Wolf—was on the Chess roster, but all the fancy Fender guitars and recording consoles in the world couldn't citify this Mississippi native. Wolf's records are swampy and distorted in intended and unintended ways. His voice is a Buzz Buzzard growl. Certain sides, such as "I Asked for Water (She Gave Me Gasoline)," which is held together only by a primordial percussive thump, are downright ramshackle. In other words: magic.

Like almost all of the artists of his generation, Howlin' Wolf cut singles, not albums, so despite the absence of "Greatest Hits" or "Best of" in its title, his first album is really a singles compilation. *Moanin' in the Moonlight* sports many of Wolf's best-known hits, including the hypnotic title track, the boogied-up "How Many More Years," and the wailing "Evil." The endless/timeless groove of "Smokestack Lightnin'" launched a thousand British Blues Babies.

This picture looks so funky because I left the shrink-wrap on the cover. Carefully opening a new LP along the right-hand edge with an X-Acto knife is a time-honored practice among music geeks determined to provide their record covers with as much protection as possible. Gatefold sleeves force us to make some hard choices. Author's collection.

1960

The Everly Brothers: *It's Everly Time*

"LP's Top Singles in Unit Sales for First Time," blared a headline in the February 15, 1960, issue of *Billboard* magazine, as Bob Rolontz reported that LP sales account for 55 percent of all record sales for the first time ever in 1959. "50 Million Album Sales Foreseen," boasted another article in the September 26, 1960, issue of *Billboard*, as LP sales neared 50 million units sold in a single year for the first time. The unattributed writer attributed this milestone to the growing popularity of classical stereo discs and comedy mono ones by the likes of Shelley Berman, Jonathan Winters, Mike Nichols and Elaine May, and Bob Newhart (who'd released his smash hit *The Button-Down Mind of Bob Newhart* that year), among many others. The writer goes on to predict industry sales figures for the decade ahead.

Rock and roll is not referenced in either article; their writers could not have possibly known that rock and roll artists would be the ones driving album sales by the end of the decade. Had that writer taken notice of *It's Everly Time*, the idea that the LP could become a meaningful format for rock and roll artists may have been more apparent.

Whether they were going for the tear ducts on "So Sad" and "Sleepless Nights" or the heart on "Memories Are Made of This" and "That's What You Do to Me" or even the crotch on "Just in Case," Phil and Don Everly's voices seemed to rise from the same throat. John Lennon and Paul McCartney—who allegedly considered going by the name of the "Foreverly Brothers" before settling on the "Beatles"—were listening. The Everly Brothers weren't just integral to the sweetest side of pop; Pete Townshend cottoned to their tight harmonies *and* Don Everly's distinctively aggressive acoustic guitar rhythms.

Perhaps all of those great British LP makers were also paying attention to how seriously the Everly Brothers took their own LP making. *It's Everly Time* is no Elvis-style hash or Chuck-style greatest hits. It was recorded as a unified work over two consecutive weeks in March 1960, and like most classic mid-sixties albums, it only leans on one hit single and includes not one piece of filler. This is the future of the rock album.

A Date with the Everly Brothers

The Everly Brothers' second LP of the sixties isn't as pure of an affair as their first. *A Date with the Everly Brothers* was not recorded in a tight time span. It dug up a relatively old hit, "Cathy's Clown," to hook it. A cover of "Lucille" was fated to harmonious failure when measured against Little Richard's cacophonous original. Still, that hit is one of the Everlys' most buoyant, and if nothing else, that cover shows how radically the guys could reinvent rock and roll essentials. They also debut one of their essential future hits on *A Date with the Everly Brothers*: the heart-rending "Love Hurts." The rest of the album does not live up to the hits or many of the LP exclusives on *It's Everly Time*, but the rumbling "Made to Love," the characteristically dreamy "That's Just Too Much," the authentically bluesy "Baby, What You Want Me to Do?," and "So How Come (No One Loves Me)" are all ace cuts.

Wanda Jackson: *Rockin' with Wanda*

Wanda Jackson positioned herself to push back at rebel rockers like Gene Vincent and Johnny Burnette and annihilated the latter's misogyny with some of the most explicitly violent lyrics of their time. Johnny probably hid under his leathers when Wanda started raging, "Well you can talk about me, say that I'm mean/I'll blow your head off baby with nitroglycerine." She could play nice too on the tame-Elvis-like "Did You Miss Me," but *Rockin' with Wanda* lives up to its name for the vast majority of its run time. "Rock Your Baby," "Honey Bop," "Cool Love," "Mean, Mean Man," and the incendiary "Fujiyama Mama" are fierce. She mixes up the rockabilly with the Latin-style "Don'a Wan'a,"

The album is called *Rockin' with Wanda* and the photo shows Wanda Jackson posed in front of a rocking chair. A lot of early album covers are pretty stupid. Author's collection.

which repeats Chuck Berry's ugly Latin minstrel show but skates on some very tasty music, and "I Gotta Know," which mixes up tempos and styles, bouncing between lazy C&W and hot-rod rock and roll from bar to bar in a manner alien to fifties rock and roll. If it wasn't for the sexist record industry's tendency to exclude women with guitars, who knows how many other great female rockers like Wanda Jackson we'd have?

1961

Gary "U.S." Bonds: *Dance 'til a Quarter to Three with U.S. Bonds*

Unpolished recordings were common in the lo-fi indie and alternative rock age of the eighties and nineties. Gary "U.S." Bonds did it first. Hearing his records is like failing to make it through the velvet rope, getting locked outside the hot rocking club and left to press your ear up against the wall with just a muffled impression of the music. The listening experience is an acquired taste, but it makes the Louisiana jump of the classics "Quarter to Three," "New Orleans," and "School Is Out," as well as excellent LP mates such as "Cecilia," "That's All Right," "Minnie the Moocher," "Not Me," and "One Million Tears," atmospheric and exciting. Perhaps no other artist had such a knack for boiling the essence of an off-the-hook party down to 45 RPM.

Del Shannon: *Runaway with Del Shannon*

Del Shannon was one of the most important transitional artists to emerge during the years between the reign of rock and roll's primary titans and the British Invasion. Born Charles Westover, Shannon had his feet in fifties pop clichés but his gaze on a more progressive future. Before bands started touting the sitar or the Mellotron as the latest novel addition to the guitar/drums lineup, Shannon went all in on the Musitron, an electronically modified Clavioline that produced a ghostly, shrill sound. It is the spotlight instrument on Shannon's best-known hit, the stunningly theatrical "Runaway." It's also all over his debut album, though most of the material on *Runaway with Del Shannon* is not as worthy of that odd instrument or Shannon's own odd instrument: an emotive voice that sometimes breaks into its own ghosty, shrill wail. His ballads are strictly for squares, but rockers such as a cover of Elvis's "His Latest Flame" and Shannon's own "Lies" cut the mustard, and the title hit is obviously phenomenal.

Frankly, though, there is little evidence of Del Shannon's significance on the LP that includes his most significant song. That would crystallize in the years to come as Shannon proved to be perhaps the only early rock and roll star to move with the times without embarrassing himself. Although his biggest songs ("Hats Off to Larry," "Little Town Flirt," "Keep Searchin'") would all successfully recycle the "Runaway" formula, singles such as "Break Up," "Move It on Over," and "Show Me" sounded as legit gnarly as any mid-sixties garage rock. His "I Go to Pieces" was a big hit for Peter and Gordon in 1965, though those guys' weightless reading is no match for Shannon's emotion-fraying version. In 1968, he recorded the genuinely credible psychedelic LP *The Further Adventures of Charles Westover*, which went nowhere on its release but has been rediscovered as a lost classic in more recent years. The trajectory of Del Shannon's career suggests the kind of career the similarly visionary Buddy Holly may have had had he not died so young. Sadly, Shannon cut his own life short when he committed suicide after a long bout with depression in 1990.

1962

The Beach Boys: *Surfin' Safari*

Who would have thought the Beach Boys would develop into one of pop's most innovative and influential acts? They started as a makeshift band of three talented brothers (bassist/leader Brian Wilson, lead guitarist Carl Wilson, and drummer Dennis Wilson), one cousin of dubious abilities (singer Mike Love), and a family friend (rhythm guitarist Al Jardine, soon replaced by David Marks when Jardine decided dentistry suited him better than rock and roll) and cut a cheap single cashing in on California's surfing trend. "Surfin'" is a forgettable song, but its style and topic were novel when it was released. With their surf and sun–focused early recordings, the Beach Boys probably seemed likely to be little more than a novelty themselves. As it turned out, they were one of the very, very few pop bands to claim a genuine genius in their ranks, and Brian Wilson's production, composition, and arranging innovations would completely reshape rock and roll. The dichotomy between Wilson's apparent simplicity (he is known for his inarticulateness and all-American passions for burgers, girls, and sports) and intellectual complexity (he is graced with a futuristic imagination and cursed with deep psychological scars stemming from a turbulent relationship with the domineering, abusive father who also managed the Beach Boys in their early days) makes him one of rock's least likely but most potent major artists.

While there is a good deal of evidence of Wilson's simplicity on the Beach Boys' execrable debut album, there is little evidence of his revolutionary genius. *Surfin Safari* is notable only for housing two good singles (the title song and "409") and a whole lot of dreck, such as a horrid rendition of the offensive children's ditty "Ten Little Indians" and dreary novelties like

"Chug-a-Lug," "Cuckoo Clock," and "The Shift." *Surfin' Safari* is the worst debut album by a major band, but the Beach Boys would start to get on track with their next LP.

Bob Dylan: *Bob Dylan*

Bob Dylan belongs with the Beatles and Jimi Hendrix in that very small and select group of artists that most profoundly molded the sounds and ideas of the sixties. With atypically imaginative and poetic lyrics that supercharged the evolution of the rock and roll song, simple melodies, acidic attitude, and anyone-can-sing voice, the man born Robert Zimmerman remolded himself as a sardonic troubadour, inspired everyone who heard him, and was surpassed by few.

Although his most strident early followers wore their hatred of rock and roll as a badge of honor, Dylan was not against the new genre, though his first few albums are more in the folk tradition with their topicality, perceptiveness, and poeticism. His arrangements are as spare as Pete Seeger's: sweetly unspooling, fingerpicked acoustic guitar and winded harmonica. His voice of "sand and glue," as David Bowie would later describe it, is pretty rock and roll from the get-go, and it would actually never be more so than it is on his first album.

Dylan's debut is primitive, but wouldn't all of his finest future music be kind of primitive too? Aren't the stomp and thrash of "Subterranean Homesick Blues," the repetitive chords of "Desolation Row," and the wheezing Salvation Army band of "Rainy Day Women" primitive?

There are no classic compositions on *Bob Dylan* to entice longtime fans. The only two originals are the generic "Talkin' New York" and the more distinctive yet naive "Song to Woody." However, once new discoverers hear Dylan's versions of "In My Time of Dying," "House of the Risin' Sun," "Pretty Peggy-O," "Fixin' to Die," and "Baby, Let Me Follow You Down," they will wonder how they haven't been spinning them alongside "The Times They Are A-Changin'" and "Like a Rolling Stone" all along.

Anyone who was shocked to hear Dylan go rock and roll in 1965 wasn't listening to his nasty grunts and growls on *Bob Dylan*. Although it fails to show off Dylan's greatest

Whoever owned this album before me really did a number on it. Author's collection.

strength—his songwriting—*Bob Dylan* is still an electrifying way to begin a career and a new musical era. The sixties start here.

Roy Orbison: *Crying*

Artists before him used sadness and melodrama to appeal to maudlin teenagers, but Roy Orbison brought something else to the glummer side of pop: genuine sophistication. Formerly a rock-a-billy raver, an image that never really suited his reserved demeanor or bel canto tenor, Orbison expanded his vocabulary of chord changes and arrangements and created grand expressions of emotion devastating enough to transcend the era in which he created them. His music is not that of a fifteen-year-old flopping onto his bed to cry tears of unrequited love into his pillow. There is experience in that operatic voice. There is refinement in arrangements that commingle rock and roll strings with classical ones. There is nothing adolescent in "Love Hurts," the paranoid "Running Scared," or "Crying," the *ne plus ultra* of romantic anguish. These records sound like the next logical step after Buddy Holly's late-career work and ground the first album Orbison made in his most natural style, *Crying*.

While Orbison's vocal style—and the light orchestrations and corny backing singers that muck up some of the records' lesser tracks—suggest that he could have just as easily committed to entertaining parents, he was definitely a rock and roll artist. Dig the fat fuzz bass on "Lana" grunging up rock three years before Richards could on "Satisfaction" or McCartney could on "Think for Yourself." "Dance" and "Night Life" kick up some dust too, but Roy Orbison was rarely completely convincing when trading in "yeah yeahs" and "ay-yi-yi-yi's" (although there are exceptions: "Lana," "Dream Baby," "Oh! Pretty Woman," "Mean Woman Blues"). He was at his greatest when playing the great dramatist at both the writing desk and the mic and balancing his blues foundations with his sophistication. *Crying* provides ample evidence that pop artists could hit more mature notes and that rock and roll might not be the fad critics insisted it was.

1963

Albums weren't a huge concern in the rock and roll world of 1963. Until that point, Elvis Presley and Ricky Nelson were the only rock and rollers to have number one albums in the United States. The single continued to be the preferred medium, and it would remain in that position until 1967, the first year a group of electric-guitar pickers had the number one album of the year (though *More of the Monkees* was the one album the Monkees released that year on which they didn't do much guitar picking).

There had been great rock and roll LPs before 1963, though most were more like singles compilations fattened with filler than thoughtfully conceived statements. However, in 1963, artists such as Phil Spector, Sam Cooke, Roy Orbison, and Bob Dylan set the changeover in motion with truly fine LPs conceived to be just that.

Yet no element of 1963 was as alchemically integral to zooming the rock LP into the future as the arrival of the very first Beatles album. Moving forward, we shall pay special attention to this band, and if you don't already know why, then this book may actually have some value after all.

But it wasn't just the Beatles pushing rock and roll forward, up the hill, and to the cliff's edge of art. Not everyone of their countrypeople the Beatles dragged along with them would play an integral role in the evolution of the rock and roll album (sorry, Gerry and the Pacemakers; forgive me, Freddie and the Dreamers; sincerest apologies, Herman's Hermits), but the ones who would—naturally, I'm thinking of fellow A-list British invaders such as the

Rolling Stones, and the Who—would impact the art in ways the Beatles did not always think to do first. The guys in these groups were not only among rock and roll's biggest superstars but also its highest-profile record geeks. The Beatles snapped up all the latest and most obscure American records that reached the shores of Liverpool and snagged even more when they hooked up with manager Brian Epstein, who also managed the record department of his father's music shop, NEMS, where the boys discovered songs by the likes of Barrett Strong and the Donays that would fill out their own LPs. They worked hard to make their album tracks gems and omitted singles from most of their albums because they felt ripped off whenever they bought albums laden with filler and songs they already owned. Down in Dartford, Mick Jagger had the brain wave of placing mail orders with Chess Records, and he and Keith Richards totally geeked out when Richards spotted Jagger toting his latest acquisitions by Chuck Berry and Muddy Waters, which reignited a childhood friendship and led them to form their own band. Pete Townshend had his own bout of drooling after his American roommate at art school, Tom Wright, was deported for pot possession and left behind his enviable collection of blues and jazz discs.

Rock and roll may have straight up ceased to be if it wasn't for these geeks. Following a period when many of the first wave of rockers were out of commission—jailed, drafted, or fiddling with born-again salvation— America had Roy Orbison, Del Shannon, Dion, and the Beach Boys but few other new rockers of depth. Chuck Berry eventually managed a respectable return with "Nadine," "No Particular Place to Go," and "You Never Can Tell" in 1963. Back from the army, Elvis still produced tremendous work on occasion, such as "His Latest Flame" or "Little Sister," but his spark was largely gone. The charts were dominated by old-fashioned crooners and vapid teen idols: Shelley Fabares, Connie Francis, Bobby Rydell, Bobby Vinton, Neil Sedaka, Tommy Roe, Steve Lawrence, and Bobby Vee. By far the most vital American music of the period was coming from the soul and R&B artists enjoying their initial successes on new labels like Tamla/ Motown and Stax or with wunderkind producer Phil Spector and his fabulous roster of artists, particularly Darlene Love and the Ronettes.

In Great Britain, young musicians were listening intently to their more soulful neighbors. Americans tended to stereotype England as a tiny, quaint burg of manners and repression. Yet no white American rockers of the period captured the spontaneity, excitement, and commitment of their R&B countrypeople with the authenticity of the new wave of singers emerging in the United Kingdom. Although none of them had anything on, say, Otis Redding or Wilson Pickett, they were still capable of delivering their own impressive brand of fierce R&B.

However, with that white appropriation of the sounds that black artists originated came one of rock and roll's more troubling shifts. A form of music that grew naturally out of black rhythm and blues started to become predominantly white. A lot of commentators lay the blame on Elvis Presley, who fashioned his act by appropriating the sounds and dance moves of black artists and who became a superstar not because he was a better artist than Chuck Berry or Little Richard but because of the way he looked. Pat Boone's lack of melanin also explains why his utterly lifeless renditions of "Ain't That a Shame" and "Tutti Frutti" outsold Fats Domino's and Little Richard's vital originals. The Beatles were great songwriters and studio innovators, but they too got their start performing the songs of Chuck Berry, Little Richard, Smokey Robinson, Ray Charles, the Shirelles, and many other artists they outsold by vast quantities. When a quintet of white kids from London called the Rolling Stones began recording in 1963, they ransacked the art of black artists even more fervently than Elvis had. In 1965, *Billboard* revived its "Hot R&B" chart after fourteen months of dormancy during which rhythm and blues records were so popular with white rock and roll fans that the magazine deemed a segregated chart redundant. Black singles would continue to place on the magazine's central "Hot 100" chart, but the perceived need for a separate chart suggested that there was no longer a place for black musicians in "mainstream" guitar-based rock and roll. When African American rock guitarists such as Jimi Hendrix, Prince, and Vernon Reid broke into the increasingly white rock world in the coming years, the industry often treated them as novelties, interlopers, or nonentities. Prince's lightning licks rarely electrified rock radio stations during his 1980s heyday. Living Colour, who could run rings around every single white hard-rock band of their day, had a hell of a time getting signed because of their race and their willingness to deal with issues of race in their songs. Even some of those who worshipped Hendrix had no compunction about describing him in freakish terms. In a 1968 interview with *Rolling Stone* magazine, guitarist Mike Bloomfield celebrated Hendrix as a "super spade" and stated that Hendrix deliberately built the threat of rape into the image he'd constructed. The mind boggles; the gag reflexes kick in.

Understandably, most black musicians turned their backs on that pivotal form of music they created to fashion new forms, such as soul, reggae, disco, and hip-hop. White musicians would infiltrate all of these forms with some success but failed to take them over as they took over guitar-based rock and roll. As popular as, say, Vanilla Ice or Michael Bolton were during their respective fifteen minutes of fame, no self-respecting music writer would have ever spoken of them in the same breath as, say, Snoop Dogg or Sam Cooke. The same could not be said of, say, the Rolling Stones and Chuck Berry.

As new forms of guitar-based rock and roll emerged—from heavy metal to punk to grunge—there was rarely any place for black musicians at all. Meanwhile, artists such as England's Rolling Stones would be praised for the "authenticity" of their Chicago-influenced blues and R&B recordings and chastised when experimenting with more English idioms on controversial albums such as *Between the Buttons* and *Their Satanic Majesties Request*. The mind continues to boggle.

Despite the overwhelming whiteness washing over rock and roll, 1963's best albums were still pretty varied. Live albums, proto–concept albums, holiday albums, and the usual singles collections all shared space on the shelves. The rock LP era had not arrived as a significant artistic and commercial force yet, but as of 1963, it was just a matter of time.

THE BEACH BOYS: *SURFIN' USA*

The common misconceptions of those skeptical of the artistic value of the Beach Boys' music and the cult it inspired is that the group didn't show signs of progress until *Pet Sounds*, and in the words of *Rolling Stone* magazine's Dave Marsh, "Brian Wilson became a Major Artist by making music no one outside his own coterie ever heard" (Marsh was talking about *SMiLE*; more on that later).

This is wholly untrue, and evidence of Wilson's "Major Artistry" (those are Marsh's smugly mocking caps, by the way) is apparent as early as the Beach Boys' second album, *Surfin' USA*. For those who don't think the hit title song is enough to qualify Wilson as an important artist, there's "Lonely Sea." In this one largely forgotten ballad is all of the harmonic inventiveness and heartfelt pathos that would help make *Pet Sounds* a formidable classic. Unlike *Pet Sounds*, the arrangement is as sparse as could be. Some lightly brushed drums, barely-there bass, and a gently picked, heavily tremeloed guitar are the only decorations that backdrop Brian's chilling lead vocal and the guys' gossamer harmonies. Gentle vocal tracks such as "Farmer's Daughter" and "Lana" are also excellent, but *Surfin' USA* as a whole suffers from too many pure surf instrumentals, and with all due respect to the velvet-voiced Carl Wilson, he was no Dick Dale.

SURFER GIRL

Despite its weaknesses, *Surfin' USA* is an improvement over *Surfin' Safari*. *Surfer Girl* is significantly better. Filler is on short order, though there is some pretty poor material, such as "South Bay Surfer," which cribs the melody of "Old Folks at Home," and the generic, sloganeering "Surfer's Rule." The instrumentals are inessential at best, though a version of the Dick Dale's "Let's Go Trippin'" is sufficiently spirited. The rest of the album is not only first rate but also a very early indication of Brian Wilson's extreme inventiveness. He cribs a more fittingly magical tune ("When You Wish upon a Star") and renders it in complexly constructed harmonies on the title track, waves a harp like a magic wand over "Catch a Wave," sprinkles pizzicato strings over "The Surfer Moon," and expresses the personal perspective that would flower in his best work with "In My Room." "Little Deuce Coupe" and "Hawaii" perfect the uncomplicated, summery rock and roll for which the Beach Boys were already loved.

THE BEATLES: *PLEASE PLEASE ME*

The Beach Boys were innovative, but no band reshaped pop music as radically and peerlessly as the Beatles did. A scruffy quartet from the drab port town of Liverpool, England, John Lennon, Paul McCartney, George Harrison, and Ringo Starr got their education from the American soul and C&W records imported into town and honed their skills with marathon performances at home and in Hamburg, Germany. Lennon and McCartney developed a fruitful songwriting partnership with each other and a tremendously creative record-making relationship with producer George Martin, who signed them to Parlophone, the branch of EMI Records he ran. Their personal politics of universal love embodied by songs such as "The Word" and "All You Need Is Love" would help shape the current generation's attitudes and set it in stark relief against their parents' hawkishness and acceptance of the status quo. So would their personal style of long hair and flamboyant clothing, which blurred established gender roles and made that older generation more than a little uncomfortable. Most importantly for our purposes, the Beatles developed the rock and roll album into a genuine work of art with nearly each of their successive releases (unconsciously at first and then with more acute self-awareness mid-career). As we shall also see, the disrespectful treatment their albums received in the crucial American market forced the Beatles to revise their contract with the American label, Capitol Records, as a veritable Rock and Roll Bill of Rights allowing them the control over their LPs that officially decreed the medium's artistic legitimacy.

Perhaps their first album in the United Kingdom, *Please Please Me*, no longer sounds as if it is heralding in the most important artists of the rock album era, but it must have been pretty revelatory in 1963. Their combination of pumping Chuck Berry riffs, girl-group harmonies, and a peculiarly English use of melody and chord structure was totally original.

Not all of the material is fantastic. "Love Me Do" lacks dynamics or an interesting lyric or melody. Harmonically, it is as primitive as a nursery rhyme, and it most likely went to number one in the United States in 1964 because nearly everything the Beatles released that year went to number one.

Elsewhere, their songwriting genius is already budding with the brisk title track with its coy sexuality and tension-building "come ons," Lennon's first brushes with self-pity ("Misery") and introspection ("There's a Place"), and McCartney's opening salvo of filthy rock and roll ("I Saw Her Standing There") and the traditional craftsmanship that would make it not ridiculous to speak of him in the same breath as Cole Porter or Hoagy Carmichael ("P.S. I Love You").

Rock and roll artists always filled out their LPs with covers in those days, but few did it with the imagination of the Beatles. By adapting girl-group and R&B hits such as "Boys," "Chains," "Baby It's You," and "Twist and Shout" to their four-British-guys-with-guitars format, they made recordings completely unlike the originals. Their performances are as committed on the covers as they are on John and Paul's songs. The Beatles also toy with non-rock material by tackling Bobby Scott and Ric Marlow's "A Taste of Honey," which began life as incidental music for the play of the same name. It may not be exciting, but it does underscore the breadth of the band's eclectic interests and abilities.

Please Please Me did not change the album overnight, and its impact in America was watered down when Vee-Jay Records lopped off the Capitol single "Love Me Do"/"P.S. I Love You" and released the LP as *Introducing . . . The Beatles* in early 1964. By that point, the Beatles had already taken command of England and released their second album there, but that is more a matter of history than artistry. In retrospect, *Please Please Me* is still a great album by the greatest album group, and it's hard not to look back on its release as the dawning of a new era.

WITH THE BEATLES

Like *Please Please Me*, the Beatles' second British LP is a sampler of their live set and Lennon and McCartney's incipient songwriting efforts. Not all of these reveal the guys' supernatural talents. "Little Child" and "Hold Me Tight" are pleasant but insubstantial, while a speedy take of a nothing song called "I Wanna Be Your Man" cowers in the presence of the Rolling Stones' savage version. The Beatles' other songs are all considerably better, though the fact that "All My Loving" is the only one that really gets tossed among the classics leaves *With the Beatles* feeling thin compared to what came before it and certainly what would follow.

That also means there are some great things for novice fans to discover, such as the pounding "It Won't Be Long," the sincerely soulful "All I've Got to Do," and the wounded "Not a Second Time." Although a lot of critics thumb their noses at George's debut contribution, I've always loved the bratty, sulky, snarly "Don't Bother Me." *With the Beatles* packs some exceptional covers too. John gets to scream off some of his personal baggage on rowdy renditions of "Please Mr. Postman" and "Money" and gets to really unveil the depth of his vocal talents on "You Really Got a Hold on Me." To perform a Smokey Robinson song without embarrassing comparisons to the master is a true feat.

BOB B. SOXX & THE BLUE JEANS: *ZIP-A-DEE DOO DAH*

As well known as George Martin is, the Beatles would always receive most of the credit for the albums he produced. Phil Spector was the rare producer to overshadow his acts. Eccentric, ingenious, abusive, volatile, and deeply disturbed (he was convicted of murdering actress Lana Clarkson in 2009), Spector was a toxic person who treated his artists abysmally but forged a new sound by approaching rock and roll the way Nelson Riddle approached adult pop. Spector was never content with the usual guitar, bass, and drums lineup. He'd orchestrate his records with a muscular mass of strings, horns, mallets, and clattering castanets, building it up to an echoing din affectionately known as "The Wall of Sound."

Despite his concentration on constructing hit singles, Spector produced several exceptional LPs. The purpose of each is pretty different. Bob B. Soxx & the Blue Jeans' *Zip-a-Dee Doo Dah* seems motivated by a spirit of experimentation. This is by far the weirdest of the albums on Spector and partner Lester Sill's Philles label. The title track, a bizarrely mechanized cover of a tune from a racist Disney movie *and* a top-ten hit, telegraphs this. Such unlikely covers as "The White Cliffs of Dover" and "This Land Is Your Land" do too, though the presence of the perfectly accessible hit "Why Do Lovers Break Each Other's Hearts" shows that Spector's pop savvy is still in full effect. So is Darlene Love's stunning voice, which powers "Why Do Lovers," the overlong though deeply soulful "My Heart Beat a Little Bit Faster," and the squirmy "I Shook the World."

A member of the singing group the Blossoms whom Lester Sill recommended when Spector needed to rush record a version of Gene Pitney's "He's a Rebel" before producer Snuff Garrett could, Darlene Love was

I got this original copy of *Zip-a-Dee Doo Dah* on Philles Records out of a $2 bin at the Jersey City Record Riot a few years ago. According to the web music marketplace Discogs.com, it's worth between $77 and $600. *Cha-ching*! Author's collection.

the most professional, powerful, and expressive singer in Spector's stable of artists and arguably the greatest soul-pop singer of the sixties. Love tended to outshine the group's namesake Bobby Sheen, but he still manages to keep pace with the wacky "Dear (Here Comes My Baby)" and the groovy shuffle "Everything's Gonna Be Alright." The album gets its off-kilter feel from Spector's gears-and-cogs arrangements of "Zip-a-Dee Doo Da," "The White Cliffs of Dover," and "Let the Good Times Roll." "Baby (I Love You)" (not the Ronettes' classic) sounds like it was recorded at the bottom of a bottomless pit, and there's a kooky instrumental featuring neither Bob B. Soxx nor Blue Jeans named after Spector's shrink—a guy who clearly was not very good at his job.

JAMES BROWN: *LIVE AT THE APOLLO*

For pure adrenaline, James Brown had no peer. His voice is a rough shriek, and his songs often barely qualify as songs at all, but his performances are legendary. A wiggly-ankled, spring-loaded dancer and knee-dropping dramatist, James Brown choreographed performances that floored and elevated audiences. No one could top him onstage.

So it is fitting that Brown's most enduring LP is a live one. *Live at the Apollo* is a valiant effort to capture his show for the home audience, though the fact that so much of his greatness was in his shimmying ankles and drop-to-the-floor shtick means that these two vinyl discs still aren't ideal. The Fabulous Flames vamp endlessly while Brown steps away from the mic to no doubt do something fabulous, but the lack of essential visuals leaves a couple of stretches of *Live at the Apollo* a little tedious, and ten-plus minutes of "Lost Someone" is a lot of time to spend listening to a slow jam.

Live at the Apollo really earns its place as the ultimate James Brown album in its pithier moments. He and the Flames lay waste to the recorded versions of "I'll Go Crazy," "Try Me," "I Don't Mind," and "Please, Please, Please." A hyperventilating version of "Think" implies that James Brown might also be the Godfather of Speed Rock.

SAM COOKE: *NIGHT BEAT*

Sam Cooke's voice was every bit as sweet as James Brown's shriek was corrosive. The polished crooner from Clarksdale, Mississippi, was known for light pop soul hits like "Wonderful World" and "Saturday Night at the Movies," but he could also tap into his deep blues roots with striking authenticity.

Sam Cooke is also an underrated innovator at 33⅓ RPM. *Night Beat* proves that some artists really were thinking deeply about the LP format in 1963. It is a completely successful attempt to make an LP with a specific sustained mood with carefully selected songs and soft-glow, dusky arrangements cooked up during three late-night sessions with such stellar session men as keyboardist Billy Preston and Phil Spector's go-to drummer and guitarist Hal Blaine and Barney Kessell. There is little of the pop that won Cooke his biggest hits on *Night Beat*. Instead, he interprets the blues using his full range of gospel tools without ever indulging in showiness. Cooke's vocals are some of the most emotive and beautiful on record, and on "Lost and Lookin'," it is some of the most intensely controlled too. The one misstep is a version of "Shake, Rattle, and Roll" that is too subdued to compete with other versions of that warhorse yet still too peppy to sit comfortably with the hushed material that makes *Night Beat* enchanting.

THE CRYSTALS: *HE'S A REBEL*

While *Zip-a-Dee Doo Dah* smacks of an artist's first inkling that an album era was dawning, *He's a Rebel* is singles-era exploitation at its purest. It's not only a shameless repackaging of quite a few recordings previously released as singles, but it's also nearly identical to the first Crystals album, *Twist Uptown*, sharing *nine* songs with that eleven-track album. Nine!

Despite the group name on the record label, not every track is by the Crystals. The title track is a Phil Spector hoodwink meant to capitalize on that group's successful name in the days when Darlene Love was not yet household-name material, but her voice is as unmistakable as Spector's signature clangor, which was rarely more exhilarating than it is on "He's a Rebel." Gene Pitney composed this rather moving declaration of allegiance to a boy who isn't nearly as bad as the naysayers say. Love could wring premium emotion out of "Zip-A-Dee Doo Dah," so when she's given a lyric of greater meaning to sing, the effect could be emotionally overwhelming.

Love was not expecting a solo career when she recorded "He's a Rebel" as a session singer. The session for "He's Sure the Boy I Love" was a different story. Although Spector promised this would be the first record credited to *Darlene Love*, even signing a contract agreeing he'd do just that, he pulled a last-minute switcheroo for fear that Love's name would not move as many units as the Crystals'. She was rightfully incensed, but that doesn't make "He's Sure the Boy I Love" any less powerful. Love testifies that her boyfriend might not be rich, good looking, or successful, but he's sure good enough for her in a tempestuous voice that could never be mistaken for anyone else's.

The presences of "He's a Rebel" and "He's Sure the Boy I Love" guarantee *He's a Rebel*'s superiority over *Twist Uptown*, though the inclusion of the divisive "He Hit Me (and It Felt Like a Kiss)"—either a sympathetically grim representation of singer Little Eva's abuse at the hands of her monstrous boyfriend or a big steaming heap of misogyny, depending on your perspective—may make you prefer *Twist Uptown*. Despite its flaws, *He's a Rebel* still has a lot to recommend it because of those two Love songs, the dramatic "Uptown," "There's No Other (Like My Baby)," "Oh Yeah, Maybe Baby," and "On Broadway," and even very fun throwaways like "Frankenstein Twist."

BOB DYLAN: *THE FREEWHEELIN' BOB DYLAN*

Bob Dylan reached the pinnacle of his explicitly political phase on his finest acoustic album. Just two LPs into his career, he mastered his style with a voice aged beyond its years, nimble fingerpicking technique, and songwriting far beyond where Wilson, Lennon, McCartney, or anyone else on the outskirts of Dylan's scene was in 1963. At a wee twenty-one years old, he had written the enigmatic, purely poetic, yet completely grounded "A Hard Rain's a-Gonna Fall," "Blowin' in the Wind," and the vitriolic "Masters of War." The latter two songs are actually interpretations of traditional folk songs, but if anyone ever proved that great artists steal, Dylan did so with the songs on which he took ownership of "Scarborough Fair" (the captivating "Girl from the North Country") and Paul Clayton's "Who's Gonna Buy You Ribbons" (the breathtaking "Don't Think Twice, It's All Right"). Both are

That's Dylan with his then girlfriend Suze Rotolo. Author's collection.

timeless love songs that indicate that Dylan was already thinking beyond current events.

There are also flashes of his impish humor on "Bob Dylan's Blues" and a giddy version of "Honey, Just Allow Me One More Chance" and the crazed psychedelic wordplay that would blossom in 1965 on "I Shall Be Free." On a cover of "Corrina, Corrina," he even plays with a band! Of course, Bob carries most of the album with nothing more than his voice, harmonica, and guitar, and this is the rare album of that sort that never gets monotonous.

THE MIRACLES: *THE FABULOUS MIRACLES*

No label churned out hits like Motown/Tamla did in the sixties. That may be because no rock label was governed by a specific philosophy the way Motown was. Founder Berry Gordy Jr. used only the best session musicians, a group informally known as the Funk Brothers. I got my first Motown album, *The Four Tops' Greatest Hits*, partially because I liked the Tops and largely because I played bass and hoped to learn something from Motown's legendary house bassist James Jamerson. Mimicking his style was not easy, and I didn't even know yet that he plucked all those agile, rhythmically perfect bass lines using only his index finger! If I knew that and tried to do what he was doing on things like "Reach Out, I'll Be There" with just one finger, I probably would have packed it in.

Gordy used as much taste and rigor when it came to his singers. He'd run them through a sort of finishing school to ensure they fit in with the white media that usually shunned African American artists. Seemingly every artist Gordy signed became a phenomenal superstar: the Supremes, the Four

Tops, the Temptations, the Marvelettes, Mary Wells, Stevie Wonder, the Jackson Five, Gladys Night & the Pips, Marvin Gaye, and the Miracles. Gordy's system produced some of pop's finest hit singles.

Motown was not necessarily known for its LPs, at least not until Marvin Gaye and Stevie Wonder started taking the medium seriously in the seventies. That's actually a good thing for you, fellow record collector, because now you can start discovering some of those Motown albums from the sixties and delighting in how unexpectedly wonderful many of them are. They aren't all wonderful. You'd probably do well to stay away from any album that leans too heavily on Broadway standards or rock and roll songs made famous by other artists, but there are way more excellent Motown long players from the sixties than the label usually gets credit for. As we continue our trip together, I'll be pointing out some of my faves as well as a couple that are a bit less essential but still worth a mention for one reason or another.

The Fabulous Miracles, I regret to say, is actually one of those less essential types, but it is worth a mention, especially when considering how early in the rock LP era we currently are. Smokey Robinson was Motown's most graceful singer and one of its core house songwriters. That artistry is not quite evident yet on *The Fabulous Miracles*, though the album is a solid representation of the soft Tamla sound that would give way to a heavier beat a year or two later. A few of Robinson's songs are a bit too typical of his label's early sound, and the mere ten tracks leave the package feeling thin. Yet his butterfly voice never stops fluttering with elegance and tonal perfection. The spellbinding "You've Really Got a Hold on Me" is perfect in both performance and composition. Apparently, this ballad about a bad relationship the singer just can't shake was almost relegated to the B-side of a single with the bluesy boogie "(Have a) Happy Landing" in the coveted spot. Alas, wiser heads prevailed, and the Miracles got their first big hit in two years. The tougher, Sam Cooke–style blues of "Won't You Take Me Back," the joyous yet easygoing stroll of the minor hit "A Love She Can Count On," and the darting woodwinds of "Whatever Makes You Happy" mix things up nicely on the LP, but bigger things are definitely on the way for the Miracles and Hitsville U.S.A.

ROY ORBISON: *IN DREAMS*

When the Beach Boys and Beatles matured, both were celebrated for making "concept" albums, though each group really only completed one apiece, and neither *Pet Sounds* nor *Sgt. Pepper's* is more unified in concept than Roy Orbison's *In Dreams*.

Orbison fixates on his R.E.M.s with exquisite covers of Johnny Mercer's "Dream," the Everly Brothers' "All I Have to Do Is Dream," and Steven Foster's "Beautiful Dreamer." He also manages to create dreamy visions by describing landscapes the Texan surely never visited on the sumptuous "Shahdaroba" and stirring nightmarish claustrophobia on "House Without Windows." The title track is both high drama and high pop poetry, the singer expressing the agony

Roy Orbison's music rarely sounded as jolly as he looks on the cover of *In Dreams*. Author's collection.

of a man in love who can touch the woman of his dreams only after a visit from that candy-colored clown they call the sandman. On his realization that his grand romance is nothing more than a nocturnal fantasy, Roy's cosmic voice rises to a pained pitch. Hearts all around the world split in two.

Elsewhere, Orbison sings of nocturnal fancies on "Lonely Wine" and "My Prayer," while "Sunset" is sort of the upbeat flip side of "In Dreams"— we keep waiting for another "it was all a dream" punch line that gratefully never comes. Some of the tunes don't fit the concept, but that's okay when they are as fine as Hank Williams's "No One Will Ever Know" with a "Running Scared"–revisited arrangement and the magical "Blue Bayou," which is as dreamy a musical creation as there ever was.

VARIOUS ARTISTS: *A CHRISTMAS GIFT FOR YOU FROM PHILLES RECORDS*

Like so many visionaries, Phil Spector refused to grow up. Perhaps this was the cause of so many of the problems—his infantilizing of ex-wife Ronnie Spector, his daddy issues, and his fatal obsession with playing with guns—but it is also the source of his art. His favorite toys were the ones in a recording studio, and his favorite time of year was Christmas. In 1963, Spector attempted to capture the essence of the holiday several months before December 25 in the less-than-seasonal setting of Gold Star Studios in sunny Los Angeles.

How would his thunderous Wall of Sound work with corny kiddie songs like "Rudolph the Red-Nosed Reindeer" and "Frosty the Snowman" or the hymn carol "Silent Night" or the easy-listening standard "Winter Wonderland"? Brilliantly, of course, though it has taken longer than Spector wished for this to become common knowledge. As the often-told tale goes, the release of *A Christmas Gift for You from Philles Records* is not the first thing that comes to mind when most people recall November 22, 1963. At 12:30 p.m. that day, John Kennedy's motorcade was driving through Dealey Plaza in Dallas, Texas, when the president was assassinated. How this affected *A Christmas Gift for You* depends on whom you ask. By most accounts, it was a simple matter of national mourning displacing holiday merrymaking. In her autobiography *My Name Is Love*, Darlene Love wrote that her producer decided to "yank" the album from distribution out of respect for the grim times.

Whatever the circumstances, *A Christmas Gift for You from Philles Records* was a flop, and the British Invasion that rocked American shores in the first months of 1964 would do even more damage to Phil Spector's dominance of the pop scene. Although he'd continue to score some huge hits with the Righteous Brothers through 1966, radio now belonged to Motown and the Beatles. Spector would get a creative and commercial second wind at the end of the decade by hooking up with that band and its ex-members, but there's no question that late 1963 was as dark a time for him as it was for everyone else.

The original release of *A Christmas Gift for You from Philles Records* gave all due credit to the great roster of singers who brought it to life . . .

. . . for its 1972 reissue on Apple Records, *A Christmas Gift for You* received a more self-aggrandizing title and a photo of Phil Spector as a terrifying Santa straight out of a *Vault of Horror* comic. Both: author's collection.

Today, *A Christmas Gift for You from Philles Records* sits in the classic spot it should have earned fifty years ago. Hip holiday fans with no patience for church choirs or Andy Williams feel no embarrassment when giving this disc a spin. Surely no other Christmas record rocks so hard, is so soulful and powerful, and yet translates that indescribable holiday feeling so authentically. *A Christmas Gift for You* is snow and sleigh bells and fur-fringed red suits. It's also a rowdy office party, a make-out session under the mistletoe, and, in at least one instance, the gut-shredding anguish of spending Christmas all alone. With incalculable support from the expressive voices of the Crystals, the Ronettes, Bob B. Soxx & the Blue Jeans, and—whoa, hold onto your Santa hat—Darlene Love, as well as the instrumental might of the Wrecking Crew, Spector not only made the never-will-be-challenged greatest Christmas record but also made one of the greatest rock and roll records of any season.

JOHNNY "GUITAR" WATSON: *JOHNNY "GUITAR" WATSON*

The artists of the fifties weren't necessarily known for their eclecticism, but Johnny "Guitar" Watson was a true exception. Toying with blues, soul, pop standards, jazz, and rock and roll, he bucked limitations at the very start of his career. As a singer, he could grit it up like Stax's nastiest renegades or spread on the sweet butter like Tamla's smoothest stars. Even the specificity of his nickname couldn't keep him from having his way with keyboards, percussion, and saxophone. As the decades progressed, he always moved with the times, scoring hits in the funk era with "Superman Lover" and "A Real Mother for Ya" and convincingly laying claim to the invention of rap. You could even argue that his "Posin'" pioneered voguing when Madonna was barely toilet trained.

A dozen of Johnny "Guitar" Watson's early sides are represented on his eponymous compilation for King Records. While blues rules, the tracks play with the form enough so that you never feel like you're hearing the same thing twice. I'm not sure if I've ever heard a pretty string arrangement sweeten hard blues as successfully as it does on "Cuttin' In." When Watson strays from the blues, as when he dives into the Great American Songbook and swims up with "Embraceable You," he kicks up enough vocal debris that it doesn't sound out of place among its grittier company.

1964

If March 22, 1963—the day the Beatles released *Please Please Me*—was the rock album era's date of conception, then 1964 was its year of infancy. As the British invaded and the singles charts remained central for kids, a higher-quality crop of LPs started to sprout too. Two artists were particularly reliable, but Bob Dylan and the Beatles were not the only makers of excellent albums in 1964. A number of the year's best were the very first efforts from some of the decade's defining stars. And if most of the following albums don't stand as their artists' defining long-playing statements, all are noteworthy for appearing before a lick of self-conscious artistry sneaked into the music. In the year before "Yesterday," "Desolation Row," and "California Girls," the defining sound was simple, exuberant, electrifying pop.

THE BEACH BOYS: *ALL SUMMER LONG*

The Beach Boys survived the British Invasion by shipping out wave after wave of great singles, but as the Beatles quickly made clear, it was going to take more than great 45s to compete. *Surfin' USA*, *Surfer Girl*, and *Little Deuce Coupe* were very good albums for their time, but none were completely solid. A sprinkle of spectacular tracks aside, *Surfin' Safari* and *Shut Down Volume 2* were pretty lousy.

The Beach Boys really entered the game with *All Summer Long*. On this album, they solidified their lineup: following one too many run-ins with overbearing manager Murry Wilson, Dennis Marks quit the band, and Al Jardine, who would mature into a fairly important collaborator and sing lead on the group's second number one single, returned. The album still contains some filler—the instrumental "Carl's Big Chance," the generic Mike Love cheers "Drive-In" and "Do You Remember?," and the time-wasting babble "Our Favorite Recording Sessions"— but the rest of the album is great. "All Summer Long" and "Wendy" are radiant Brian

All Summer Long was the Beach Boys' first unimpeachable album. Well, maybe you could impeach "Our Favorite Recordings Sessions." Author's collection.

Wilson production pieces, and with their mingling of bells, woodwinds, and maxed-out reverb, we hear early traces of the *Pet Sounds* sound. The spine-melting "We'll Run Away" introduces themes that would mature in "Wouldn't It Be Nice": a pair of lovesick teens rhapsodize about ditching their folks to get married. In the innocent world of the early Beach Boys, "getting married" is code for being old enough to have sex—a quaintly fifties concept at odds with the wanton shouts of fifties rockers like Little Richard and Chuck Berry who were never concerned about tying the knot before indulging in a bit of wop bomp-a loo-bomp, a-wop bam-boom. As chaste as the lyric is on its surface, Brian's moaned vocal absolutely sweats sexual longing. "Little Honda," "Don't Back Down," and "I Get Around" are the group's hardest-rocking early tracks, and the latter number became their first number one single. Brian Wilson gallops closer to Lennon and McCartney with an album of almost 100 percent original material (the only cover is "Hushabye," and it's a terrific one). Within a year or so, those horses would be neck and neck.

THE BEATLES: *A HARD DAY'S NIGHT*

Press goon: "Don't you ever get a haircut?"

George Harrison: "I had one yesterday."

Everyone: *hysterics*

If the Beatles could break up a room by drolly delivering middling quips like this, just think what they could do mouthing the words of a professional screenwriter! After all, they've already sent millions into a frenzy doing nothing more than twanging their electric ukuleles, bashing their Ringo bongos, shaking their freakish wigs, and screeching "Yeah, yeah, yeah!" Look at all the cash raked in on those awful Elvis films. Quickly, quickly! Get a writer! Get a director! Any will do! No budget is too small! Just get "The Beatles" up on the marquees before time runs out on this fab fad.

Rock and roll wasn't supposed to last, and rock movies were even more ephemeral. *The New York Times* said *The Girl Can't Help It* was "as meager and witless as a cheap pin-up magazine joke." So what if Frank Tashlin infused it with the color and energy of a Tex Avery cartoon? So what if Little Richard, Gene Vincent, Fats Domino, and the Treniers pitched the pace into hyperdrive with their elation-inducing performances? *The Times* knew well they were just "grab[bing] the spotlight and beat[ing] out their agonized tunes . . . the way alert bullfighters rush into the ring when a companion is gored." No one would remember the picture beyond 1957, but it doubled its budget at the box office. No one would remember a Beatles movie beyond 1964, but that sort of thing was guaranteed cash in the bank.

The Beatles didn't seem to think much of the Elvis pictures, but they did catch *The Girl Can't Help It*. Lennon was particularly turned on by the sights of Little Richard screaming while beating his piano standing up and Gene Vincent and his Blue Caps shaking off their blue caps during "Be-Bop-a-Lula" (a record that he first heard from his mother, that the Beatles often covered in their early days, and that opened Lennon's *Rock 'n' Roll* LP in 1975). *The New York Times* may have been quite happy to forget all about *The Girl Can't Help It*. The Beatles weren't. On September 18, 1968, they even delayed the night's "White Album" session—and put their severe personal problems on hold—to convene at Paul's place to watch the movie's BBC debut. Perhaps rock and roll movies weren't so fleeting. Perhaps they could have profound impacts, inspiring fledgling musicians to change the world and patch up damaged relationships. Perhaps a visionary director such as Frank Tashlin could make a difference.

Few affected John Lennon's art like that first wave of rockers, but his mother, friends, and favorite writers (particularly Lewis Carroll) seasoned his work as well. He was particularly taken with the absurdist comedy trio of Peter Sellers, Spike Milligan, and Harry Secombe, known as the Goons. Knowing that George Martin had produced that group helped seal their working relationship. Another goon collaborator was American Richard Lester, who'd directed and starred in a short film with Sellers and Milligan called *The Running, Jumping & Standing Still Film* in 1960. Producer Walter Shenson had worked with Lester on that short and *The Mouse That Roared* (1963), also starring Sellers. Lester had music-film credentials, having made *It's Trad, Dad!*, a 1962 cash-in on the British "trad jazz" (Dixieland is the American term) craze that made a star of Acker Bilk and gave the Who their start. Lennon didn't choose Lester to direct his band's film. Shenson brought his old colleague on board, but the fit was just as right as the George Martin/Beatles pairing. Another director may have scoffed at fashioning a cinema cash-in for the faddish Beatles. Lester crowed, "I'll do it for nothing!"

Television writer Alun Owen (*Armchair Theatre, Corrigan Blake*) cooked up the script for the tentatively titled *Beatlemania*. The fabs' quips were sharper when scripted (Press goon: "What would you call that hairstyle you're wearing?" George Harrison: "Arthur."). Wilfrid Brambell (*Steptoe & Son*) as Paul's "very clean" grandfather and the wonderful Welsh multitalent Victor Spinetti as a priggish TV producer were comedic aces in the hole in the event the Beatles' humor didn't translate well to the big screen. Lester could just shoot the film in workmanlike fashion, and United Artists could make a tidy profit (the budget was miniscule enough that Shenson answered Lester's cry of "I'll do it for nothing!" with "Don't worry about that, Dick, we're all going to do it for nothing"). But that wasn't the approach the still-new filmmaker took.

Lester was excited by the prospect of directing the Beatles. He unstrapped his imagination to a degree the band hadn't even dared yet. He broke rules of continuity ("Hey Mr., can we have our ball back!" Paul shouts outside the train he was riding in the previous frame), editing (the proto-music video "Can't Buy Me Love"—notice how John disappears from the scene without explanation), and filmmaking 101 (he shoots directly into a lamp during the "And I Love Her" sequence, a big no-no at the time that has since become standard, even overused, as it was during Otis Redding's performance in *Monterey Pop*). And let's not underplay the Beatles' contributions to a film that ultimately rested on their shoulders. Paul is charming and atypically cynical. George's shrugging naturalism makes his meeting with a smarmy ad man one of the film's most memorable scenes. John's flashes of quintessential madness ("My name's Betty!") make the whole thing seem spontaneous, anarchic. Ringo's underplayed pathos raises the film above a mere larf, imbues it with genuine emotion, and signals that he might be the Beatle with a real film career ahead of him. But it was Lester who transformed the rock and roll movie into art as assuredly as the Beatles transformed the rock and roll LP into art.

With the film's sound track album, the Beatles created the closest thing to an art LP to date. Lennon and McCartney had progressed to the point where they could provide all of their own material. Unlike *All Summer Long*, there isn't a single bum track on *A Hard Day's Night*. The album is a full plunge into the joy of Beatlemania undiluted by Motown or Chuck Berry interpretations. For the first time, we really hear the Lennon and McCartney personas at work in their work. Paul is the optimistic expert craftsman of "Can't Buy Me Love," "And I Love Her," and "Things We Said Today." John is the more personal, acerbic, self-pitying artist behind "If I Fell," "I'll Cry Instead," "You Can't Do That," and "I'll Be Back."

BEATLES FOR SALE

Although the overwhelming temper of *A Hard Day's Night* is joyous, a melancholic streak is entering the work too, and the Beatles expand their electricity with country and folk flavors and subtler acoustic instrumentation on nearly half the tracks. This is the sound that would govern their next three albums.

The first of these often gets bad press because it takes a major step back from the complete originality of *A Hard Day's Night*. The Beatles sound weary on covers of "Rock and Roll Music" and "Everybody's Trying to Be My Baby." Much of the new material is downbeat, but that is what makes *Beatles for Sale* compelling. The bleakness of "No Reply," "I'm a Loser," "Baby's in Black," and "I Don't Want to Spoil the Party" contribute as much to the album's autumnal atmosphere as their largely acoustic backing tracks do. The mood even consumes some of the happier material. John sings Paul's happy-to-be-in-love "Every Little Thing" as if he's contemplating suicide. "Eight Days a Week" is the only original to recapture the ecstatic *A Hard Day's Night* vibe, and its quality earned the band another number one in America. Paul brings additional substance with "I'll Follow the Sun," an old song he once performed in ragtime style and now treated wistfully, and "What You're Doing," a trivial composition with some neat interplay between heavy bass and drums and twelve-string guitar. There are also a few really good covers here, with the guys harmonizing angelically on Buddy Holly's "Words of Love," John shrieking torment on Dr. Feelgood's "Mr. Moonlight," and Ringo doing Carl Perkins's "Honey Don't" with bubbly humor, but the Beatles' reliance on covers was about to fade out.

THE BEATLES IN AMERICA: *INTRODUCING . . .*
THE BEATLES

"*. . . Fah!*"

A mistake. That's how Americans first heard the most influential artists of the rock album era when *Introducing . . . The Beatles* was released in 1964. Blame the engineer at the Universal Recording Corporation of Chicago. It has become something of a cliché to include the four-count at the beginning of a recording of a blazing track (just ask Bruce Springsteen). This was not the case in 1963 when that engineer heard a new song called "I Saw Her Standing There." He assumed its inclusion on the tape was a mistake, and in an attempt to fix it, he sloppily snipped off Paul McCartney's shouts of "One, two, three . . ." just short of that climactic "*. . . fah!*"

That a mistake begins the Beatles' long-playing introduction to America is appropriate considering how messy their presentation would be throughout their first three years in the country. It isn't the only difference between the Beatles' American and British debuts. In Britain, Parlophone released *Please Please Me* as a fourteen-track album. Because such a generous number of tracks would have necessitated paying more publishing royalties than stingy American record companies wanted to hand out, American LPs usually only had eleven or twelve tracks. They also tended to include hit singles to draw in more customers. For extra value, the Beatles often left singles off their later British LPs to save consumers from repurchasing tracks. In this way, *Introducing . . . The Beatles* was more similar to one of those British releases. The Beatles' second British single was the first to be released in America. After EMI tasked entertainment lawyer Paul Marshall with dumping the Beatles on an American label, he hooked them up with Vee-Jay Records, which put out "Please Please Me" b/w "Ask Me Why" on February 22, 1963. These were the two songs initially clipped from *Introducing . . . The Beatles*.

The album was supposed to follow that single by just a few months, but it was delayed after Vee-Jay's president Ewart Abner stepped down after using company cash to pay off his own gambling debts. So *Introducing . . . The Beatles* was not introduced until January 10, 1964. This was just ten days before EMI finally took advantage of the cash cow in its stable and its Capitol Records released *Meet the Beatles*, twenty-seven days before the boys had their first American number one single with "I Want to Hold Your Hand," and just one month before Beatlemania exploded with the band's stateside television debut on *The Ed Sullivan Show*. EMI used its ownership of "Love Me Do" and "P.S. I Love You" to legally block Vee-Jay from distributing further copies of *Introducing . . . The Beatles*. The impoverished label would not see their one opportunity to earn taken from them and replaced those two forbidden tracks with "Please Please Me" and "Ask Me Why." So much for British-style value. Thus, *Introducing . . . The Beatles* could be sold until October 15, 1964, when Vee-Jay's right to distribute its small cache of Beatles songs expired, according to a settlement between that label and Capitol.

The retraction of *Introducing . . . The Beatles* would not be the norm for the Beatles in America. In fact, the albums they intended to make would not see official release in the United States until their compact disc editions came out in 1987. Until then, most Americans would know nothing about albums such as *Please Please Me*, *With the Beatles*, and *Beatles for Sale*. The Rolling Stones and the Who would have to wait until the *next century* to have all of their unadulterated British LPs released in America.

MEET THE BEATLES!

Calling the Beatles' second American album *Meet the Beatles!*—essentially claiming that this was their *real* debut—was an arrogant move considering how Dave Dexter Jr. had been treating the band. Capitol's artists and repertoire (A&R) man had rejected the Beatles time and again, believing that American record buyers wouldn't cotton to the Liverpool lads with the weird haircuts. After Dexter passed on the surefire smash "I Want to Hold Your Hand," the Beatles' manager Brian Epstein passed on him and pled his case directly to label president Alan Livingston, who displayed greater savvy by finally giving the Beatles the green light on Capitol.

And now Dexter was pretending that *Introducing . . . The Beatles* didn't exist, that he had dibs on the guys all along. Granted, the Vee-Jay LP wasn't the ideal introduction to the Beatles. Key songs had been clipped. An engineer had botched the count-in of "I Saw Her Standing there." The cover was ugly. But these alterations were nothing compared to how Dexter fiddled with the Beatles' first disc on Capitol. Its closest cousin is Parlophone's *With the Beatles*. That record contained fourteen tracks. Six were covers, and none were singles. On *Meet the Beatles!*, Dexter replaced five of those covers with both sides of the band's first Capitol single, "I Want to Hold Your Hand" b/w "I Saw Her Standing there" (it's count-in fully intact) and the Parlophone B-side "This Boy." "I Want to Hold Your Hand" and "This Boy" were subjected to lousy duophonic mixes (highs equalized to one channel, lows equalized to the other, and the channels run slightly out of sync in a poor simulation of stereo) as a mono alternative. Dexter brightened the sound a bit overall—either to prevent the bass frequencies from causing the needle to hop off the vinyl or to give the sound more bite—and layered extra echo onto "I Want to Hold Your Hand."

So Dave Dexter Jr.'s vision for *Meet the Beatles!* was quite different from the Beatles and George Martin's *With the Beatles*. Which album is better is a valid point of contention. Purists will insist that there is no comparison. *With the Beatles* is the record the Beatles wanted to release and is therefore intrinsically superior. For many Americans who grew up with *Meet the Beatles!*, *With the Beatles* lacks something. Hearing so many Lennon/McCartney originals (plus the very

When I got into the Beatles at the age of thirteen, my mom passed her old copy of *Meet The Beatles!* along to me. She'd really beaten the shit out of it. Author's collection.

first Harrison one!) gathered in one place is exhilarating, and the three appended to the Capitol record are three of the very best they'd penned to date. The excised covers are well honed after many stage performances, but such a level of original songs on one album was rare on a rock and roll album in early 1964. Sure, it was a cagey farrago, but most American kids didn't know that. Without a monumental track such as "I Want to Hold Your Hand" or "I Saw Her Standing There" to anchor it, *With the Beatles* feels inconsequential in comparison. The decision to retain the corniest cover—the show tune "Till There Was You"—makes for a less thrilling inclusion than "Please Mr. Postman" or "Roll Over Beethoven" would have, and "Not a Second Time" isn't as rousing a conclusion as "Money" had been on *With the Beatles*, but Lennon and McCartney's beautiful original does make for a wistful, anticipation-stoking finale.

The wholesomeness of *Meet the Beatles!* may be debatable, but its commercial success is not. A week after 73 million viewers took in that *Ed Sullivan* appearance on February 9, 1964, the album was perched at the top of the *Billboard* charts and would stay there for the next eleven weeks. The Beatles were now transatlantic stars.

THE BEATLES' SECOND ALBUM

Not even three months passed between the releases of the Beatles' first and second Capitol LPs. On March 2, they started shooting their first feature film, which would prove the guys' prowess across media. So would John Lennon's book of fanciful gobbledygook, *In His Own Write*, published on March 23. It would sell a reported 90,000 copies in the United States in its first print. During that period, American shops were flooded with official and unofficial Beatles merchandise: shirts and suits and badges and dolls and wigs.

With such mad demand for anything and everything Beatles, one could hardly expect Capitol to keep its hugest property in reserve—certainly not when everyone believed all Beatlemania would flash out as quickly as it began. Bundling up the five leftover covers from *With the Beatles* that didn't make it to *Meet the Beatles!*, both sides of their second American number one single, side B of their third one, side B of their third British single, and side A of the soon-to-be-released *Long Tall Sally* EP (marking the first time fresh Beatles material would reach the states before Britain), Dave Dexter Jr. had enough material for an all-new grab bag.

The imaginatively titled *The Beatles' Second Album* showed all the signs of its hasty assembly. It is the Beatles' first American album with no British equivalent. For the first and final time, covers would outnumber originals on LP. All the five originals are strong—and at least "She Loves You" and "You Can't Do That" are crucial—but the fact that John is the prominent voice on all of them and the sole composer of two ("You Can't Do That" and "I Call Your Name") sketches an imbalanced picture. There is none of the stylistic variety of *Please Please Me*, *With the Beatles*, or *Meet the Beatles!* There are no show tunes or light ballads.

So as *Meet the Beatles!* showcased John, Paul, and George as new pop craftsmen, *The Second Album* celebrates them as house-burning rock and rollers. While I personally feel its preponderance of covers makes it less interesting than *Meet*, *Second* has its share of devotees. AllMusic's Bruce Elder declared it the Beatles' "best pure rock and roll album." Back in the nineties, MTV executive Bill Flanagan pleaded with Neil Aspinall to release it—if no other Capitol album—on CD. The head of Apple Corps. apparently never even heard of the album, scoffing, "You mean Capitol actually put out an LP called *The Beatles' Second Album*?" No one has ever defended that title.

If anything reins in *The Beatles' Second Album*, it is Dexter's usual monkeying. He boosts the treble and the reverb. Duophonic mixes of "I'll Get You" and "She Loves You" are used on the stereo LP. "You Can't Do That" is slowed down rather painfully (the British mix falls squarely in the key of G; the U.S. one falls in the crack between F# and G). At least Dexter didn't shuffle the Beatles' fiery recordings with a bunch of Muzak instrumentals. That wouldn't happen for another two months when United Artists Records got in on the free-for-all, further muddling the Beatles' presentation in the United States.

A HARD DAY'S NIGHT

Since there was no reason to believe John, Paul, George, and Ringo would outlast any other pop sensation, a cash-in flick had to be rushed into production. Expectations were low, but *A Hard Day's Night* was a smash, and the Beatles' immutable charisma translated from vinyl to celluloid without a hitch. The apparently effortless brilliance of the Beatles' screen work extended to the accompanying sound track. Released on July 10, 1964, *A Hard Day's Night* housed thirteen wonderful new Lennon/McCartney tunes undiluted by the R&B covers that filled out their first two LPs. It is one of pop's most thoroughly joyous records even as Lennon fully allows his own cynicism to come to the fore of numerous tracks. The sounds are consistently fortifying. Several years before the LP became the primary rock and roll conveyance with the boys' own *Sgt. Pepper's*, they had already made a record that demanded to be left as is.

Not a chance. In fact, the Beatles' finest early album received the shabbiest treatment. *Please Please Me* had merely lost a couple of tracks when Vee-Jay pruned it down to *Introducing . . . The Beatles*. *With the Beatles* was altered with a much heavier hand, but both of the resulting two albums— *Meet the Beatles* and *The Beatles' Second Album*—had genuine merit in their own rights. The record released in the United States as *A Hard Day's Night* was a completely different story. United Artists distributed the film, and therefore the company had dibs on the sound track. Whereas Parlophone's album was split between the seven songs composed for the film and six additional fresh tracks, the United Artists record offered only the movie songs plus an extended edit of "I'll Cry Instead," which was originally intended for the climactic romp scene (Lester found it too grumpy and reused "Can't Buy Me Love" instead). Four pieces of George Martin's incidental music occupied the rest of that valuable vinyl real estate.

Martin's music isn't terrible, but it is terribly dated. Each of his four tracks are adaptations of Lennon/McCartney songs, each performed in a slightly different—though very un–rock and roll—style by a studio band. The title number is done as a sort of Dave Brubek pastiche with bursts of big-band bombast. That latter style runs all the way through "I Should Have Known Better." "This Boy" is an exercise in elevator Muzak retitled "Ringo's theme" because of its use during the drummer's debauched "parading" in the film. When issued on 45, it hit number fifty-three on the *Billboard* Hot 100 chart—and more appropriately number seven on the Middle-Road (now Adult Contemporary) one. The best of these road bumps is a loungy, moody, Nelson Riddle–esque take on "And I Love Her," but it isn't likely that any fans were happier with this than a proper Beatles song.

SOMETHING NEW

Fans were either allowed a more appealing option or ripped off again less than a month later when Capitol decided that United Artists had its fun and released *Something New*. This was an ironic title considering how half its tracks had been issued on *A Hard Day's Night*. As inept as that album had been, it still went to number one and stayed there longer than any other album in 1964. *Something New* just missed that top spot, held at bay by *A Hard Day's Night*. This must have been one of the only times in *Billboard* history that the top two albums had so much material in common. One can imagine the disappointment of the kids who excitedly grabbed *Something New* out of the bin, plopped their five bucks on the counter, raced home, and dropped it on the turntable only to discover they already had most of these tunes.

For those who hadn't contributed to *A Hard Day's Night*'s zoom up the charts, *Something New* was unquestionably the LP to get. Yes, it had to be augmented with the "A Hard Day's Night" and "Can't Buy Me Love" singles, and "Komm Gib Mir Deinde Hand"—"I Want to Hold Your Hand" sung in German—was filler, but the all-Beatles *Something New* is still a more listenable alternative to United Artists' *A Hard Day's Night*. In fact, it was the third noncompilation Beatles album I chose to buy (the first two being *Sgt. Pepper's* and *Abbey Road*, incidentally). I convinced my mother—an original Beatlemaniac who'd seen them at Shea Stadium and passed her well-abused copy of *Meet the Beatles!* down to me—to give me a ride to the Pathmark supermarket, which had a small but decent record department, by agreeing to release a garter snake I'd caught in our backyard. She was scared of snakes, and I was a little shit.

For the record buyers of the sixties, *Something New* was also overkill. Released a bit beyond 1964's halfway mark, the year had already seen *four* new Beatles albums. Beatlemania was in danger of bankrupting the kids who saved their pocket change to purchase every new record. Fortunately, they'd get a breather, and a new album of Beatles music (distinct from the cash cow that was Capitol's double-disc documentary *The Beatles Story*) would not appear until so late in 1964 that it's title portended the year to come.

BEATLES '65

Because of its preponderance of cover songs, *Beatles for Sale* has often been painted as a lesser Beatles album. However, the richness and emotional depth of the album's originals find the band progressing toward the maturity of *Help!* and *Rubber Soul*. The joyful "Eight Days a Week" is the only original song that sounds like it could have fit on an earlier Beatles record. That was one of the songs clipped when Capitol went to town on *Beatles for Sale* to refashion it as *Beatles '65*. "Eight Days a Week" was held aside for single release (coupled with another casualty, "I Don't Want to Spoil the Party"). Commercially, the move paid off when "Eight Days a Week" became the Beatles' seventh number one hit in the United States in early 1965. In its stead on the latest Capitol record were both sides of the band's sixth number one, "I Feel Fine" b/w "She's a Woman." The inclusion of these two souped-up walls of electricity might have made *Beatles '65* a less dour affair than *Beatles for Sale* if the very *Beatles for Sale*–style *A Hard Day's Night* leftover "I'll Be Back" had not been included.

Ultimately, it's a bit of a wash. As different as the lineups of *Beatles for Sale* and *Beatles '65* are (the fourteen-track Parlophone album and the eleven-track Capitol one have only eight songs in common), they still share the same shadowy feel. Because "I Feel Fine," "She's a Woman," and "I'll Be Back" are all such strong tracks, *Beatles '65* ends up being a strong album in its own right. Of course, Dave Dexter Jr. still had to ruin those particular tracks with some of the heaviest application of echo on any Capitol Beatles LP. Had the mass of covers been set aside to allow "Every Little Thing," "Eight Days a Week," "What You're Doing," and "I Don't Want to Spoil the Party" to find homes on *Beatles '65* instead of "Rock and Roll Music," "Mr. Moonlight," "Honey Don't," and "Everybody's Trying to Be My Baby," it most certainly would have been a better album than *Beatles for Sale*—and possibly the Beatles' best pre–*Rubber Soul* album, period. But then that would have left the Beatles' next Capitol LP in pretty sorry shape.

BOB DYLAN: *THE TIMES THEY ARE A-CHANGIN'; ANOTHER SIDE OF BOB DYLAN*

Bob Dylan made his finest preelectric album in 1963 by giving voice to both his political and his romantic sides (and writing some of the best melodies of his career). These two sides split the following year. Neither *The Times They Are A-Changin'* nor *Another Side of Bob Dylan* are as momentous as *The Freewheelin' Bob Dylan*, but both find his work progressing. The title track of the more topical *The Times They Are A-Changin'* is a much better anthem than "Blowin' in the Wind" from *Freewheelin'*, employing a tougher, less singsongy melody and powerfully stormy imagery to match. His commentaries get startlingly specific, whether he's decrying poverty and racism with original fiction ("The Ballad of Hollis Brown") or reportage (the outraged "Lonesome Death of Hattie Carroll" and "Only a Pawn in Their Game"). Dylan allows himself ample space to cry his messages, making for an unusually epic album in a year overrun with ultracompact pop songs. His songs on *Another Side of Bob Dylan* would be no briefer, but his romantic stance was a lot more in line with the kind of stuff John and Paul were singing in 1964.

The Times They Are A-Changin' looks outward. *Another Side* is completely internal. Dylan dissects his relationships on "To Ramona," "I Don't Believe You (She Acts Like We Never Have Met)," and "Ballad in Plain D," though his nastiness can make one long for the days when fans were a bit more ignorant of his personal issues. He deals with romance without the cynicism on "Spanish Harlem Incident."

Dylan also continues to tighten his craft, and a slew of pop covers follows. The Byrds practically built their career on this album. Dylan's most stubbornly folkie followers regarded his self-obsession as a betrayal. He'd finish off alienating those close-minded few with his next two albums on which he'd go pop in a much more radical way.

THE KINKS: *KINKS*

The Kinks had one of the most unusual careers of any sixties band. The sound that defined the North London quartet at the outset of their career—at least once they stopped messing with Merseybeat and hacked out a more personal style—was the vicious crunch of Dave Davies's power chords. Confoundingly, this proto–heavy metal outfit rapidly matured as brother Ray Davies developed a peculiarly English style of social criticism and personal reflection. After falling out of favor despite the extraordinary quality of their music, the Kinks worked their way out of scrap heap city by revisiting their heavier days in the late seventies, but the refined and beautiful records they made from 1966 through 1973 are what make them one of pop's top groups.

Still, there's a lot to be said for their power-chord days, and the chemical formula of all pre-1965 British pop LPs catches fire on *Kinks*. Take a few

Chuck Berry covers, a few blues nuggets, a snatch of originals by a budding songwriter, and one monumental single, and you have everything necessary to convince teens to part with five bucks. Unlike the Rolling Stones or the Beatles, the Kinks do not keep their Britishness in check when doing those Berry and blues songs, so things like "Beautiful Delilah" and "Too Much Monkey Business" sound more poppy, if not necessarily more polite, in their hands. Dave Davies's naturally ravaged voice makes the former track sufficiently rude, but Ray's grinning sigh is already audible on the latter one. He sounds a lot more at home on his own material, as he screams through the psychotic "You Really Got Me," pumps through the Mersey-beat style of "I Took My Baby Home" and "I Just Can't Go to Sleep," and chokes up throats with "Stop Your Sobbing." In light of what would come later, *Kinks* is fairly weak, but "Stop Your Sobbing" and the epochal "You Really Got Me," which is regularly lauded as the first heavy-metal record, are essential, and the fact that *Kinks* is the first album by one of the crucial groups of the rock LP era makes it a legit milestone.

OTIS REDDING: *PAIN IN MY HEART*

Otis Redding is the greatest soul singer of the sixties. He could consume any song no matter how associated it was with its original artist and spit it back out as something wholly his own. And he took on material by some of the most cover-proof artists of his age: the Beatles, the Rolling Stones, Sam Cooke, the Temptations. His voice was raw but tremendously sensitive. His character was powerful but as cuddly as a teddy bear. His music was fiery but welcoming. He also made some of the best albums of all time, elevating the soul LP to an art form right from the very start of his brief but fabulous career.

By all accounts, Redding was a sweet, good-natured guy, but he pulled things from his soul that made the pain he conveyed 100 percent authentic. The title track, "These Arms of Mine," "That's What My Heart Needs," "Security," and an astonishing cover of Sam Cooke's "You Send Me" will turn your

The original edition of *Pain in My Heart* featured an odd photo of Redding on the cover that made him look more like an evangelical preacher than a pelvic-thrusting singer. Pictured here, Atco's CD reissue of 1991 uses an era-inappropriate but much more exciting shot of him from 1967's Monterey Pop Festival. Author's collection.

knees to jam. There's joy on *Pain in My Heart* too, as Redding invites you to dance the Rufus Thomas way on "The Dog" and reduces your skull to rubble with his own "Hey Hey Baby." If "Pain in My Heart" is the heart of this record, then "Hey Hey Baby" is its wiggling legs.

THE ROLLING STONES: *THE ROLLING STONES*

A love for American blues birthed many a British band, but none took that particular ball and ran farther with it than the Rolling Stones. Because they were so adaptable, they outlasted most of their peers. They radiated personality with a singer who made up for any vocal deficiencies with a natural charisma and a knack for mimicry and an instrumental front line that favored well-finessed simplicity. Grooving came just as naturally to guitarist Keith Richards, drummer Charlie Watts, and bassist Bill Wyman as moving came to Mick Jagger. Their secret weapon was Brian Jones, who could pick up any instrument and effortlessly coax cool sounds out of it. The Stones' youthful manager, Andrew "Loog" Oldham, understood the importance of image in the pop world and molded his charges into the dark, dirty shadow of the cheery Beatles.

Mick Jagger and Keith Richards would eventually write great songs too, but *The Rolling Stones* is almost entirely dependent on the material of others. The only Jagger/Richards original on their first album is "Tell Me," which is much more memorable for its cavemen-play-"Earth-Angel" approach than the song itself. Of all the important British rock debuts, none are more dependent on performance than *The Rolling Stones*. The Stones rampage through warhorses like "Route 66," "Walking the Dog," and "I Just Want to Make Love to You" like Attila's Huns. They get more creative with the blues, transforming Bo Diddley's "Mona" into cosmic mood music and Slim Harpo's "I'm a King Bee" into a sexed-up slip down a playground slide.

The one weak point of *The Rolling Stones* is that its most celebrated contributor hasn't matured yet. Mick Jagger's adenoidal attempts to sing soul render "Can I Get a Witness" and "You Can Make It If You Try" weak (the weakest overall track is a sped-up instrumental version of "Witness" that sounds like it should be playing under Keystone Cops footage). Mick would catch up soon enough, he and Keith would start writing classics, and Brian Jones would hang up his harp and guitar and pick up his sitars, Mellotrons, and dulcimers. The Stones would start making their greatest records in a couple of years. Until then, there's this proof that before they were consummate record makers, Brian, Keith, Bill, and Charlie were a great band.

THE RONETTES: *PRESENTING THE FABULOUS RONETTES FEATURING VERONICA*

Coming at the end of a year dominated by the Beatles and their British brethren, the Ronettes and their Spectorian sistern were on a downward curve in popularity. The year before, both were on top when "Be My Baby" nearly topped the Hot 100. It is a perfect record produced with a master's touch, sung with a skin-rippling combo of coquettish charm and from-the-gut desire and written so directly that it could be translated into any language. "Be My Baby" is an exemplar of simplicity, as encapsulated in Hal Blaine's iconic opening drumbeat and an intricate work layered with choral harmonies, heavenly strings, and percussion that sounds like a musical trans-lation of the goose bumps that arise on the discovery of first love. Ronnie Spector has taken some guff for not being a singer as expert as Darlene Love, but her New Yawk coo conveys the sex and sincerity roiling in Jeff Barry and Ellie Greenwich's song beau-tifully. And when her voice escalates for the aching "Whoa oh oh's" that say as much as the English-language lyrics, sit down sucker, or you're gonna faint.

There's nothing like a nice concise album title. Author's collection.

It's too bad that the Ronettes' one and only album was not the smash its centerpiece was because simply owning that single and the others—and everyone who didn't own "Baby I Love You," "Walking in the Rain," "Do I Love You," and "(The Best Part of) Breaking Up" at the time needed to do some serious work on their 45 collection—was not enough.

Presenting the Fabulous Ronettes Featuring Veronica is more than a greatest hits album in all but name. Nearly everything on it is great. Ronnie Spector's earnestness is irresistible. A dour rendition of the corny "Chapel of Love" is a trifle, but the crazed, faux-live version of "What'd I Say," the percussive workout "How Does It Feel?," the fifties throwback "When I Saw You," Ellie Greenwich and Jeff Barry's starry-eyed "I Wonder," and the ecstatic "You, Baby" all make *Presenting the Fabulous Ronettes* truly fabulous.

THE SUPREMES: *WHERE DID OUR LOVE GO*

No group embodied the elegance of Motown better than the Supremes. Diana Ross, Florence Ballard, and Mary Wilson looked fabulous with their plastered-on smiles and plastered-on evening wear, but there is real emotion in their music, and the restraint of it is as emotionally affecting as any Otis Redding wail. Ross's elongated "Mmmmms" on the title track of her group's second album marinates in longing, sadness, and the underlying eroticism at the core of all the Supremes' hits. "When the Lovelight Starts Shining Through His Eyes" allows that eroticism to bust through their wigs and gowns. Pure joy.

As excellent as album cuts like "Long Gone Lover" and "I'm Standing at the Crossroads of Love" are, the main strength of *Where Did Our Love Go* is its reliance on singles. When it came out in August 1964, half of it had already been released as A-sides (another two were Bs). Along with the title track and "When the Lovelight Starts Shining Through

I cannot tell you how happy I was when I found this in the dollar bin at my local record store. Crate diving is the only sport worth a damn. Author's collection.

His Eyes," there is "Baby Love," "Come See About Me," "Run Run Run," and "A Breathtaking Guy." So, like *Presenting the Fabulous Ronettes*, *Where Did Our Love Go* is a product of a time when a singles compilation could still get passed off as something it wasn't. That would change soon.

1965

The single hadn't quite passed the medal to the album yet in 1965, but a transition was inevitable in the year the Beatles stopped putting cover songs on their albums, Mick Jagger and Keith Richards whipped their song-writing skills into shape, Brian Wilson started seeing the album as a huge canvas to fill with his multicolored imagination, and Bob Dylan viewed it in nearly novelistic terms. It was also the last year unsympathetic record labels overtaxed such artists, and it would be rare for artists to release more than one album in a single year going forward. Debut albums by the Who, the Lovin' Spoonful, and the Byrds indicated that artists who'd cut their teeth on the Beatles, Dylan, the Beach Boys, the Kinks, and the Stones under-stood the value of long-form music making from the very beginning. Even hit-oriented Motown artists started creating albums that were more than singles collections.

While 1964 unlocked the doors of the sixties as Motown and all things British consumed the charts, 1965 swung them wide open to allow the major developments that would make the decade so creatively significant to cross the threshold. The year 1965 was the one when Dylan plugged in and the Stones got topical. It was the year George Harrison picked up the sitar and John Lennon got personal. It was when Brian Wilson expanded the Beach Boys sound after quitting the road a week before the year began. It was the year he and John and George and Ringo and Keith and Brian took their first doses of lysergic acid diethylamide, the hallucinogen partially responsible for inspiring them to expand the possibilities of performing, recording, and composing lyrics. It was when Pete Townshend took a stand for his g-g-generation, hippie poet Allen Ginsberg planted the seeds of flower power, the Velvet Underground hooked up with Warhol and Nico, Otis Redding broke out, and the Byrds married folk and rock. Such artistic efforts reflected the year's more profound revolutionary actions in the civil rights movement that sought to correct America's historic abuse of its black citizens, the women's liberation movement intent on eliminating sexism, and the antiwar movement determined to squelch America's escalating and unjust military action in Vietnam.

THE BEACH BOYS: *THE BEACH BOYS TODAY!*

Commentators make a big deal out of how the Beatles went from the basic Merseybeat sound of "I Want to Hold Your Hand" to the wild experimentation of *Sgt. Pepper's Lonely Hearts Club Band* in just three years. That the Beach Boys went from "Fun, Fun, Fun" to *The Beach Boys Today!* in little over a year receives less attention. The celebrated production innovations of *Pet Sounds* were just a short leap from what Brian Wilson had already accomplished on this record released in early 1965 when the Beatles' greatest studio innovation was strumming acoustic guitars.

Wilson used Phil Spector's Wall of Sound as a jumping-off point for his own distinctive style (and often hired the very same session musicians Spector used). The major difference is that Wilson's productions breathe in a way that Spector's claustrophobic cacophony rarely does. You can hear each shimmering guitar lick, each pulsing thud of the bass, every click and crack of percussion, every stroke of vibes. The harpsichord hops out of "When I Grow Up (to Be a Man)."

The album is divided between rockers (side A) and ballads (side B), but regardless of rhythm and tempo, each song is finely detailed. The songwriting has also progressed immensely. Sensitive lyricism buoys tracks such as "When I Grow Up," "Please Let Me Wonder," and "In the Back of My Mind," a sort of psychocentric flip side to "In My Room." Conflicted and self-pitying but buoyed by a palpable romantic hopefulness, "In the Back of My Mind" skirts standard pop structure to unwind in a jazzier, more mercurial fashion. This is the kind of thing that someone like Frank Sinatra could have sung, but as it happens, little brother Dennis Wilson takes the complicated lead, which he handles with a masterful blend of sensitivity and gravelly intensity.

SUMMER DAYS (AND SUMMER NIGHTS!!)

Because of the excessive demands for new product Capitol put on them, the Beach Boys were doomed to follow up *Today!* with an album that could never be as consistent even though two massive hits—a more finished production of "Help Me, Rhonda" (the group's second number one single) than the one on *Today!* and "California Girls," which Brian wrote under the influence of acid and on which he worked the usual sun and bikinis themes into a sort of psychedelicized variation on the Wall of Sound—are the backbones of *Summer Days (And Summer Nights!!)*. Although Brian Wilson produced much of it with his usual imagination, there is a good deal of filler elsewhere: the pointlessly faithful cover of "Then I Kissed Her" (given gender reassignment surgery), the Mormon-pandering drivel "Salt Lake City," the seasonal Muzak "Summer Means New Love." He did no such thing when producing the demo-like "I'm Bugged at My Ol' Man," the record's least listenable yet most interesting morsel of filler because of its oddly childish take on Brian's serious conflicts with his controlling and abusive father. Brian had finally ousted Murry from his managerial role the year before, but the Wilson patriarch stopped back in the studio to make the recording of "Help Me, Rhonda" hellacious with his overbearing and incoherent directions to lead singer Al Jardine (a recording of that cringe-worthy incident in which Brian finally banished his dad from the studio once and for all has been widely bootlegged).

With the dopey "Amusement Parks USA," a rewrite of the equally super-fluous "Drive-In" (or is it "County Fair"?), those filler tracks constitute nearly half of *Summer Days*. The other half contains the most accomplished assortment of pre–*Pet Sounds* Beach Boys music. In addition to "Rhonda" and "California Girls," there's "The Girl from New York City," a tough answer to an Ad Libs hit; "Let Him Run Wild," a production feat that would have sounded perfectly at home on *Pet Sounds*; "And Your Dreams Come True," a sumptuous example of the group's unadorned harmonies; "You're So Good to Me," another semi-psychedelic pop song; and "Girl Don't Tell Me," a wistful folk-rock number on which the band provides all of the instrumentation and Carl Wilson's heart-rending voice ceases to be the most underused tool in the Beach Boys' box.

BEACH BOYS' PARTY!

When Brian Wilson heard the Beatles' *Rubber Soul*, its consistent quality and mood blew him away and drove him to create his defining work, *Pet Sounds*. Had that album followed *Summer Days*, it might have started to seem as though the Beach Boys' work was finally progressing more naturally. Instead, Capitol demanded more product for the coming holiday season. So the Beach Boys gathered in the studio with a couple of acoustic guitars, bongos, and a bunch of covers. They later dubbed on some chattering and beer-glass clinking to give the impression that the tracks were cut at one of the guy's houses during a party instead of at Western Recorders Studio in Hollywood.

Beach Boys' Party! hardly rates among the band's greatest albums, but a project that began as a sloppy stopgap before becoming a full-fledged gimmick has had a pretty impressive life. Not only did it spawn the last of the old-style Beach Boys hits with a cover of the Regents' "Barbara Ann" (with a prominent vocal from Dean Torrence of Jan and Dean, who'd cut the song three years earlier), but it was also a genuine predecessor of the "unplugged" fad of the nineties. And though *Party!* was a definite backward step after *Today!* and the best of *Summer Days*, its ace trilogy of Beatles covers, Al Jardine's sincere take on "The Times They Are A-Changin'," and Mike and Brian's angelic harmonies on "Devoted to You" are probably easier to appreciate today than they were when *Rubber Soul*, *Highway 61 Revisited*, *Otis Blue*, and *My Generation* were new releases.

THE BEATLES: *HELP!*

A *Hard Day's Night* was a smash experiment: a rock and roll film that functioned more as cinema than LP advertisement. Its success was largely due to its magnetic stars and its inventive director. Yet the union between Beatles and Richard Lester was not flawless. They next settled for a James Bond–derived script not as imaginative as the secret agent's films but just as casually racist. Of course, *Help!* has its moments. Lester designed terrific set pieces around "You're Gonna Lose That Girl" (elegantly shadowed Beatles sink into smoke) and "Ticket to Ride" (stoned Beatles go skiing). His proto–Monty Python "intermission" joke is priceless. The colors are vibrant, and the Beatles' semidetached lair is a hipster's dream habitat. The supporting players are top notch (Eleanor

Bron, John Bluthal, Leo McKern, *Hard Day's Night* vet Victor Spinetti, Patrick Cargill, who does a funny Ringo impersonation), but the freshness is gone. *A Hard Day's Night* vibrated. *Help!* feels overlong at a mere ninety-two minutes.

Just as the brilliance of *A Hard Day's Night* the film shone down on *A Hard Day's Night* the album, the indifference of Lester's *Help!* is reflected in the Beatles' sound track. All those gigs, TV appearances, recording dates, press appointments, and movie shoots had to catch up with the guys eventually. The group who'd made one of the greatest pop movie sound tracks the year before had now recorded an album that mingled classics with some pretty halfhearted new songs. "The Night Before," "Another Girl," and "You Like Me Too Much," easily the weakest thing George Harrison ever slipped onto a Beatles record, lack spark. Buck Owens's "Act Naturally" is a clever vehicle for Ringo, but the Beatles had outgrown covers regardless of whether or not they worked. A strained cover of Larry Williams's "Dizzy Miss Lizzy" confirms that.

When the Beatles are inspired, they refine their strengths. Lennon digs through his intestines on the title track's sunny-sounding cry for help. With "You've Got to Hide Your Love Away" he allows his wordplay to take charge without masking the raw emotions beneath. "Ticket to Ride" and "You're Going to Lose That Girl" are less personal but no less committed, forceful, or tuneful.

The Beatles' pose on the cover of *Help!* does not spell "help" in semaphore. It spells "nujv" because photographer Robert Freeman thought it was a more interesting looking pose. Why the Beatles didn't rename their album and its accompanying feature film *Nujv!* remains a mystery. Author's collection.

McCartney's work is less consistent than Lennon's, though he contributes the most important song of his career. "Yesterday" is significant not just for its obvious quality but also for George Martin's strings arrangement, which opened up new instrumental avenues the band was eager to explore with all albums to come. It also verified that young people's pop could be as artful and adult as any form of music.

RUBBER SOUL

Fully exploring the smoky, dusky, acoustic ballads they'd introduced on *Beatles for Sale* and *Help!*, *Rubber Soul* feels conceptual even though it still contains roughneck tracks like "Drive My Car" and Harrison's sneering "Think for Yourself," on which McCartney leads the groove with acidic fuzz bass. Yet the only songs that really feel out of place here are Ringo's goofy hoedown "What Goes On" and "Run for Your Life," which spoils the album's meditative mood with violent misogyny.

Otherwise, *Rubber Soul* is the Beatles' most consistent album yet in terms of style, sophistication, and quality. Lennon and McCartney had never before composed songs so thoughtful and evocative. On "Norwegian Wood (This Bird Has Flown)," Lennon stealthily documents his extramarital activities, and Harrison contributes rudimentary lick on his sitar, a twenty-one-stringed Indian instrument that captured his imagination when he heard it used in the incidental music of *Help!* Lennon's poignant "In My Life," his self-chastising "Nowhere Man," and McCartney's cynical "I'm Looking Through You" are all excellent additions. Harrison's songwriting blooms on "Think for Yourself" and the gorgeously chiming "If I Needed Someone," which finds the Byrds influencing the Beatles just as the Beatles influenced the Byrds. With "The Word," Lennon first moved away from romantic aspects of love toward a more universal love philosophy that would have a tremendous and nearly immediate impact on the values of his generation and the burgeoning antiestablishment, antiwar hippie movement. Songs such as "Tomorrow Never Knows" on the Beatles' next album ("Love is all and love is everyone"), the single "All You Need Is Love," and many of his solo recordings would further establish Lennon as the face and voice of the peace movement often at odds with his often nasty, sometimes violent personal behavior.

Like most Beatles records, *Rubber Soul* rearranged the face and mind of pop music. Brian Wilson took the album as a tossed gauntlet and composed *Pet Sounds* as his riposte. The Rolling Stones were inspired to create their own shadowy versions of the record's folk rock on *Aftermath* and *Between the Buttons*. Everyone who was anyone rushed to antique shops in search of sitars. Little did they realize that the Beatles were still just warming up to blow minds even more profoundly with their next album.

THE BEATLES IN AMERICA: *THE EARLY BEATLES*

When Capitol reissued Vee-Jay's stash of *Please Please Me* tracks as *The Early Beatles* (complete with incongruously recent cover photo torn from the back of Parlophone's *Beatles for Sale*), it was missing three tracks from the Beatles' British debut. The absence of "I Saw Her Standing There" was a given since Capitol had already used it on *Meet the Beatles!* More consequently, two Lennon/McCartney originals—the girl-group parody "Misery" and the mature, introspective "There's a Place"—would not be released on a Capitol LP until the *Rarities* compilation in 1980. This was a major blunder considering that a couple of the lesser covers, such as "Chains" and "Baby It's You," would have made much more sensible omissions.

The *Early Beatles* also fiddled with the running order of *Please Please Me.* "Love Me Do," which Vee Jay's subsidiary Tollie sent to number one in the United States in May 1964, was moved to the top position even though this lightweight folk-blues ditty made for an infinitely less forceful opener than the wild "I Saw Her Standing There." The even more out-of-control "Twist and Shout," plumped out with a bit of extra echo (as was "P.S. I Love You"), was shipped from the climactic position on *Please Please Me* to the number two spot on *The Early Beatles*, diminishing the track's impact.

BEATLES VI

The Beatles' rapid progression had been fully evident on their previous American LP, *Beatles '65,* so *The Early Beatles* did not sound of its time when released in early 1965 and was treated largely as a closet-cleaning platter by Capitol. Less than three months later, Capitol issued a much more contemporary collection of leftovers and tracks that had not yet been issued in the United Kingdom. A month before they appeared on Parlophone's *Help!,* "Tell Me What You See," "You Like Me Too Much," and a cover of Larry Williams's "Dizzy Miss Lizzy" debuted on *Beatles VI.* A cover of Williams's "Bad Boy" became the only track the Beatles recorded exclusively for the American market (though it would be included on the British comp *A Collection of Beatles Oldies* in time for Christmas 1966). The inclusion of the gorgeously melancholy B-side "Yes It Is," the only track to suffer from duophonic reverb excess this time, also helped to make *Beatles VI* the most unique Beatles LP Capitol slapped together since *Second Album.*

All the remaining six tracks were remnants from *Beatles for Sale.* Since those tracks lean more toward trad rock and roll than Lennon and McCartney's new sullen brand of folk rock, *Beatles VI* sounds like a bit of a step backward after *Beatles '65.* Only "I Don't Want to Spoil the Party," "Every Little Thing," and "Tell Me What You See" fall in line with that record's folkier feel.

HELP!

If that melancholy mood implied the guys were tiring of their work schedule, their next project suggested they'd found a way to stop caring. That way was pot, and their stoned disinterest was evident in some of the songs they wrote for their second film. However, the film's incidental music is much more interesting than the Muzak George Martin composed for *A Hard Day's Night*. His personality clashes with director Richard Lester while making that movie caused Martin to decline work on *Help!* The job went to Ken Thorne, who'd previously scored Lester's *It's Trad, Dad!*, an early pop picture featuring Del Shannon, Gary "U.S." Bonds, and Gene Vincent. Thorne was a year away from winning his one and only Oscar for scoring *A Funny Thing Happened on the Way to The Forum*, three years from writing the rousing "Plus Strings" that closes the Monkees' film *Head*, and four years from contributing music to the Ringo Starr vehicle *The Magic Christian*. For *Help!*, Thorne displays great resourcefulness, creating an exciting variation on Monty Norman's "James Bond Theme"; adapting Wagner's Act III prelude to *Lohengrin* for a piece titled "In the Tyrol"; adapting such Lennon/McCartney numbers as "From Me to You," "You Can't Do That," and "A Hard Day's Night"; and most significantly of all, introducing raga (a melodic structure for improvisation in Indian classical music) to George Harrison. Thorne's "The Chase" features some of the most frantic sitar playing on pop wax.

Following the format of United Artists' *A Hard Day's Night* sound track, Capitol's *Help!* intersperses the seven Beatles songs that appear in the film with incidental music. Thanks to Thorne's creativity, Capitol's *Help!* is a more listenable sound track record than United Artists' *A Hard Day's Night*.

RUBBER SOUL

If Capitol's *Help!* is a disappointment, the label arguably made up for that half-baked collection with its next concoction. In the United Kingdom, the Beatles had released their most consistent line up of original material yet, though a couple of tracks did not fit the majority's folk feel: the jarring C&W of "What Goes On" and the skidding rock and soul of "Drive My Car." That issue would be resolved when Capitol rejiggered *Rubber Soul*. Two appropriately rustic *Help!* leftovers replaced "What Goes On" and "Drive My Car." "I've Just Seen a Face" would now begin the album, easing the listener in with a jaunty but totally acoustic tune. The moody rasp of

"It's Only Love" would start side B in a manner much more appropriate to its surroundings than Ringo's electrified monotony "What Goes On."

With these two replacements, *Rubber Soul* started sounding nearly conceptual. With the additional loss of the Beatles' very first song to eschew love themes completely, Lennon's empathetic "Nowhere Man," Capitol's *Rubber Soul* could pass as a concept record lyrically too—not that most pop albums weren't solely comprised of love songs in 1965.

The competition was listening. It was the complete musical coherence of the American version of *Rubber Soul* that pricked up Brian Wilson's ear. "I'd never heard a collection of songs that were all that good before," he told *The Times of London*. "It's like a collection of folk songs, and they're all just really, really great songs." Capitol's *Rubber Soul* is the album that inspired him to make *Pet Sounds*—the album that would then impel McCartney to captain *Sgt. Pepper's Lonely Hearts Club Band*.

The significance of Capitol's *Rubber Soul* doesn't end there. It is the one American album sometimes rated superior to the British original, which is saying a lot considering that the British *Rubber Soul* is certainly one of the Beatles' best LPs. Musical coherence is the sole reason that preference for the Capitol record persists. "What Goes On" is a weak track, but the other casualties—"Drive My Car," "Nowhere Man," and "If I Needed Someone"—are all superb and superior to at least "It's Only Love." But the way Lennon's old *Help!* track—a song he later told *Playboy* was "lousy" and "abysmal" and he "hated" (even McCartney marked it as "filler")—brings the whole project together and helps evoke a mood that writer Ron Schaumburg evocatively likened to "wood and smoke."

THE BYRDS: *MR. TAMBOURINE MAN*

In 1963, the Beatles revolutionized pop with a distinctly English ear for melody and harmony and an uncompromised big beat yanked from the Yanks. That same year, Dylan rearranged the face of folk with a ragged edge that brought the sanitized harmonies of the Kingston Trio and Peter, Paul, & Mary to Earth and a surreal way with words that kicked it back into the cosmos. As dissimilar as their styles were at the time, there was already some cross-pollination between folk and rock happening. As early as 1962, Dylan rocked up his hootenanny with the obscure "Mixed-Up Confusion," and the Beatles' debut single "Love Me Do" was more folk than pop with its turgid beat, absence of electric six-strings, and wheezy harmonica. Once Dylan and the Beatles became aware of each other, such heavy petting was

over, and the marriage was officially consum-
mated as Dylan's influence loomed all over
"I'll Be Back" and much of *Beatles for Sale*
and the Beatles' beat inspired Dylan to plug
in—though his stripped-down, thumping
sound was always more Stones than Beatles.
It took the Byrds of Los Angeles to pointedly
fuse Dylan's far-out poetry and the Beatles'
clean jingle-jangle, officially putting a face on
the new folk-rock genre.

The Byrds are often credited
with making the first psychedelic
record with "Eight Miles High."
The fish-eye lens photo on the
cover of *Mr. Tambourine Man*
arguably makes it the first psychedelic album cover. Author's
collection.

In 1965, the Byrds were America's most
credible response to the Beatles. Although
the Beach Boys and the Beatles shared a
genuine artistic competition, those two bands
shared little when it came to sound. After the
field trip to a cinema showing *A Hard Day's
Night* that inspired them to go electric, the
Byrds picked up on the Beatles' beat and
tight song structure and made the sound their own by filtering it through
their traditional folk sensibilities and brightening it with twelve-string guitars and nasal harmonies. However, they owed their greatest debt to Bob
Dylan, whose songs were so integral to the Byrds' success. There are four
of them on the Byrds' first album.

The Byrds' debut practically plays like a *Greatest Hits* album. So many of
their best songs are collected here that it's hard to believe they hadn't completely exhausted their resources with *Mr. Tambourine Man*. With their
big-beat version of the title song (allegedly originally offered to British R&B
combo the Pretty Things, who'd turned it down), the Byrds established a
tradition of radical interpretations of Dylan's music, which were ripe for
such tinkering because they are melodic yet fluid in form. One doesn't
necessarily miss the multitude of verses the band excised from "Mr. Tambourine Man" because the Byrds restructured it to the point where it nearly
became a different song. Dylan's arrangement is spartan: voice, two guitars,
and harmonica; the Byrds' features velveteen vocal harmonies, Roger (*née*
Jim) McGuinn's ringing twelve-string Rickenbacker, swooping bass, and a
rock-steady backbeat (full disclosure: studio musicians are responsible for
all but the voices and McGuinn's guitar on the hit version). In their hands,
"Mr. Tambourine Man" became an entirely different animal incomparable
to the original. The Byrds' version did not best Dylan's and vice versa. Both
are perfectly wonderful for their own reasons.

The Byrds pull off similar feats with Dylan's "Spanish Harlem Incident," "All I Really Want to Do," and "Chimes of Freedom," all culled from *Another Side of Bob Dylan* and all superior to Dylan's primitive originals. While mainly a cover act at this point, the Byrds still supply a handful of terrific originals. The best of them, "I'll Feel a Whole Lot Better," is forceful enough to call their laid-back, L.A. folky image into question. Dylan had already glued folk to rock on *Bringing It All Back Home*, but with *Mr. Tambourine Man*, the Byrds fashioned the genre's trademark jangle that became the sound of 1965.

DONOVAN: *FAIRYTALE*

Glasgow's Donovan Leitch got a lot of press and a fair share of guff for being a Dylan-patterned folkie, but he spent a pretty brief portion of his career in his little fisherman's cap and harmonica harness. The better of his two pure folk discs is *Fairytale*, a showcase for his liquid fingerpicking and harmonica wheezing. The album points to the sounds that would define the rest of his career as he dabbles with calypso and jazz. The aromatic "Sunny Goodge Street" features a marvelous arrangement that draws on baroque music as much as it does jazz. Still, guitar and voice lead *Fairytale*. Donovan would soon welcome electric instrumentation as enthusiastically as Dylan already had though with a more fantastical and far less cynical posture, leaving *Fairytale* as the final word on Donovan's Dylan phase.

BOB DYLAN: *BRINGING IT ALL BACK HOME*

Bob Dylan's literate and sly way with words had already been a strong influence on rock and roll musicians. Now the influence went the other way, as he gave in to his boyhood love of Elvis Presley and superimposed his fanciful folk over a hard, Rolling Stones beat. His most rigid listeners grumbled about the love songs on *Another Side of Bob Dylan*. They accused him of nothing less than sedition when he "went electric." The infamous cries of "Judas" stung, but they seemingly made him more determined to follow his muse than ever. The work Dylan created over the next couple of years would have a titanic influence on sixties rock. If the Beatles set the sonic and philosophical rules for psychedelic rock with things like "Norwegian Wood" and the universal love–championing "The Word," Dylan determined its lyrical possibilities with the records he made during his electric phase. Many pop songwriters left love songs behind and made a mad dash for their thesauruses.

Dylan could not have drawn a more explicit line between his acoustic and electric periods than he did when spotlighting each phase on a selected side of his latest album. Side A is a storm of electric guitars, bass, and drums with Dylan's mangled voice shouting in a tumultuous new era. His lyrics had never been more tongue-twistingly clever than on "Subterranean Homesick Blues," more defiant than on "Maggie's Farm," or more outright hilarious than on "Bob Dylan's 115th Dream."

On side B, it's just Dylan and his acoustic guitar for what will be the last time in a decade. Here are some of his most darkly

There was a rumor that the woman on the cover of *Bringing It All Back Home* is Dylan in a dress and wig (it's actually Sally Grossman, the wife of Dylan's manager Albert). Some people have way too much time on their hands. Author's collection.

intense songs: "Gates of Eden," "It's Alright Ma (I'm Only Bleeding)," and "It's All Over Now, Baby Blue." "Mr. Tambourine Man" is one of his most fanciful. Dylan topped this achievement with his next record, but *Bringing It All Back Home* still stands as the most balanced portrait of his brilliance.

HIGHWAY 61 REVISITED

The thunder-crack drum fill that kicks off *Highway 61 Revisited* is like the final bullet blasted through the acoustic-wielding folkie Bob Dylan once was. His budding fascination with rock and roll has won for good. *Highway 61 Revisited* is Dylan's hardest-rocking, most electrifying album. "Like a Rolling Stone" is a mountain of clashing, thrashing organ, guitars, and drums. From the eye of the hurricane, Dylan observes and chastises a generation losing its way. In contrast to straight-talking compositions like "Masters of War" and "Talkin' World War II Blues," he strains his reportage through a sieve of wacko imagery and weird wordplay.

The new approach caused a lot of unimaginative critics to fear that Dylan had sold his soul and social conscience to the demons of pop gibberish. Songs like "Tombstone Blues," "Ballad of a Thin Man," and the epic "Desolation Row" certainly require more decoding than the earlier material that got him labeled a "protest singer." When decoded, the messages of his new songs are just as socially and politically focused as anything on *The Freewheelin' Bob Dylan*. The crazy words ("The sun's not yellow; it's chicken!" . . . the only rock lyrics that have actually made me laugh out loud) reveal that Dylan has decided to greet the imminent apocalypse with a stoned smirk.

THE FOUR TOPS: *FOUR TOPS SECOND ALBUM*

The Four Tops were Motown's most versatile male vocal group of the sixties. Levi Stubbs's gruff voice was made for the shouting and emoting that made early Tops singles such as "Sad Souvenirs" and "Baby I Need Your Loving" so powerful, but he could also croon the more traditional Broadway and pop standard material that Berry Gordy Jr. hoped would broaden his products' appeal. Considering the relatively low chart placings of standards-heavy albums like *On Top* and *On Broadway*, Gordy's gambit didn't really work, and the Tops always sounded best when playing to the young pop crowd by interpreting the new classics of Holland–Dozier–Holland.

Lamont Dozier and brothers Brian and Eddie Holland were as responsible for the iconic Motown sound as the labels' star singers and house band. Holland–Dozier–Holland wrote the vast majority of material on *Four Tops Second Album*. Their sun-bright singles "I Can't Help Myself," "Something About You," and "It's the Same Old Song" are among the Four Tops' most recognizable songs. The singers and composers also comport themselves well on the lesser-known tracks. None stretch the Tops' sound very far, but they all have substance. The often-anthologized "Helpless," the Temptations-like "Stay in My Lonely Arms," and Eddie Holland's collaboration with Cleo Drake and George Fowler "I'm Grateful" are as good as the hits, which makes *Four Tops Second Album* one of the most solid early Motown LPs.

THE KINKS: *KINDA KINKS*

Kinks was important almost solely because it's the record with "You Really Got Me." Aside from that concrete-cracking single "Stop Your Sobbing" and "Just Can't Get to Sleep," there just wasn't enough quality original material.

On the Kinks' second album, Ray Davies supplies ten of the dozen tracks, and almost all of them are terrific. "Tired of Waiting for You" is another two-chord riff in the "You Really Got Me" tradition, but it brings the temper down to sighing resignation, which would be a central Kinks stance in the years to come. "So Long," "Don't Ever Change," and "Something Better Beginning" continue that tone, while "Come On Now," "Look for Me Baby," "You Shouldn't Be Sad," and "Got My Feet on the Ground"—notable as the first Kinks track with a Dave Davies credit—are simple yet fiery Merseybeat-style numbers. The acoustic blues "Nothin' in the World Can Stop Me Worryin' About That Girl" is a tantalizing refusal to follow through on the emotional climax it seems to promise.

In 1969, Marble Arch reissued *Kinda Kinks* with an era-inappropriate shot from the *Village Green Preservation Society* photo shoot on the cover. Author's collection.

Kinda Kinks only stumbles when it fills out its running time with a shambling and skeletal version of "Dancing in the Streets" (Martha and the Vandellas' original recording is renowned for its majestic production) and a dreary run through of Jimmy Anderson's "Naggin' Woman." Those stumbles are actually good news for the Kinks, who could now be confident that they'd never need any writers but Ray and Dave Davies again.

THE KINK KONTROVERSY

The Kinks first truly cohesive record could have been torpedoed by Shel Talmy's murky production, but the muddy sheen actually gives *The Kink Kontroversy* a unique allure and never mutes the sparkling melodies of "I'm On an Island," "Where Have All the Good Times Gone?," "The World Keeps Going 'Round," and "You Can't Win." The murk also reflects Ray Davies's consistently pessimistic worldview. That downbeat tone even infuses romantic reveries like "Ring the Bells," which could have been a wedding standard if Ray Davies didn't sing it as if he was in mourning. "Till the End of the Day" and a deranged cover of Sleepy John Estes's "Milk Cow Blues," on which bassist Pete Quaife finally steps out of the deep background to discharge some electrifyingly jittering runs, provide "You Really Got Me" punkiness, but *The Kink Kontroversy* mostly highlights Ray's increasing maturity as a songwriter, which would fully bloom in the second half of the sixties.

THE LOVIN' SPOONFUL: *DO YOU BELIEVE IN MAGIC*

Unlike a lot of their peers, New York's Lovin' Spoonful leaped onto the field sprinting at high speed. *Do You Believe in Magic* ranks with *Mr. Tambourine Man, Love,* and *Music from Big Pink* as one of the sixties' best American debut albums. The Spoonful's blend of rock and roll electricity and homemade washboard folk funk is already in full effect here. Their original material is ripe: the transcendent title track, the sly "Did You Ever Have to Make Up Your Mind," the creepy yet dreamy "Younger Girl," and the ramshackle rocking "On the Road Again." The Spoonful's readings of Fred Neil's "The Other Side of This Life," the Ronettes' "You Baby," and the multiple traditional folk and blues songs they cover are equally integral to the album's greatness.

At a time when it was hippest to rail against the squares invading your cloud or poseurs limiting their acid tripping to the weekend, the Lovin' Spoonful revel in positivity. Mick Jagger would have trouble making up his mind between two women because both are so beneath him; John Sebastian can't do it because both are so groovy. The title track is an unabashed, sincerely moving celebration of music in all its forms. Even Jagger and Lennon must have felt uplifted after hearing it.

THE PRETTY THINGS: *GET THE PICTURE?*

Could the Pretty Things have achieved more than cult success in America if their manager didn't have the lack of vision to book them on a New Zealand tour instead of taking them to the United States in the early days of their career? Did this possibly fatal decision allow the Rolling Stones to swoop in and swipe the title of rock's dirtiest, nastiest band in the world's biggest pop market, leaving the Pretty Things doomed to cult act status? I kind of doubt it. Just hold up photos of the two bands circa 1965 side by side. See how relatively short the Stones' hair is. See how nattily they dress, even if they aren't wearing matching suits like those fit-for-grandma Beatles did. See how long and unkempt the Pretty Things' hair is, and I don't just mean singer Phil May's celebrated mane. Dick Taylor's facial scruff looks like it reeks of beat clubs and pot stench and stage sweat. And no one in rock and roll was more outrageous than drummer Viv Prince, who allegedly once entertained passersby with a dead crawfish on a leash while wearing pee-soaked trousers. Had this mob appeared on American shores in 1965, they probably would have been tossed into the nearest zoo.

But could they have made it here if radio played their records more aggressively? I doubt that too. Unlike the Stones, who had good noses for pop hits, the Pretties were too uncompromising in their devotion to the hardest blues. They were so unwilling to bend to the strictures of radio that they not only recorded an obscure R&B song called "Come See Me" as aggressively as possible but also left in the line about laying a girl and had the sheer madness to put it out as a single. Naturally, American stations refused to play it. By the time the Pretty Things went psychedelic with "Defecting Grey," a "song" that sounds like it was pieced together from bits of tape during arts and crafts hour at the local psych ward, the possibility that they'd ever hit it big in America had long since gone AWOL.

Although virtually unknown in the United States, the Pretty Things were public enemies in the United Kingdom at the start of their career, and their debut album went top ten there, but they very quickly fell out of favor. Just seven months after *The Pretty Things* peaked at number six on the British LP charts, *Get the Picture?* didn't even register. Perhaps that's only fitting for one of the rawest, nastiest beat records of the sixties. *Get The Picture?* is a storm of roiling R&B (the title track), proto-psych (the haunting "Can't Stand the Pain"), garage punk ("Buzz the Jerk"), pleading blues ("Rainin' in My Heart"), and slash-and-burn pop ("You Don't Believe Me"). By their next album, 1967's *Emotions*, the Pretties went in the freaky folk-psych direction that set the groundwork for their masterstroke, *S.F. Sorrow*, leaving *Get the Picture* to stand as the greatest piece of recorded evidence of why the Pretty Things scared the knickers off of British society.

OTIS REDDING: *OTIS BLUE/OTIS REDDING SINGS SOUL*

With his best lump of material yet, Otis Redding made an album to shame a lot of the ones his pop peers were putting out in late 1965. He is often hailed as a great soul singer and a brilliant writer, but Redding was also a genius interpreter. He takes "(I Can't Get No) Satisfaction," the Rolling Stones' most iconic hit, and transforms it into something completely his own. Gone are the tightly controlled angst and most of the caustic lyrics of the original—in floods unbridled, manic frustration. Redding can't express himself with anything more than tortured screams and growls by the track's conclusion. Jagger had to tell you he can't get satisfaction. Redding makes you understand this by *sounding* like he can't get it. His readings of Sam Cooke's "A Change Is Gonna Come" and "Wonderful World," Solomon

Burke's "Down in the Valley," B.B. King's "Rock Me Baby," and William Bell's "You Don't Miss Your Water" are less unfettered but just as good.

Otis's own songs are in short order on *Otis Blue*, but the three he supplies show how much his compositional skills have flourished. "Ole Man Trouble" emphasizes the blues in R&B. "I've Been Loving You Too Long" is a dramatically paced soul ballad with a mature lyric about the complex feelings that arise at the tail end of a long-term romance. "Respect" is a desperate plea that would evolve into a righteous feminist message when Aretha Franklin discovered it. *Otis Blue* is sure proof that, had Redding survived, he would have joined Stevie Wonder and Marvin Gaye in creating some of the

Putting traditionally pretty blonde ladies on the covers of albums by black artists was a marketing maneuver popular with labels looking to appeal to the more racist music aficionado. Author's collection.

most visionary soul records of the seventies. He certainly made some of the most visionary ones of the sixties.

SMOKEY ROBINSON AND THE MIRACLES: *GOING TO A GO-GO*

Going to a Go-Go is not a nonstop soul rave-up in the spirit of its manic title track. It starts with the most profoundly sad soul hit of 1965, and the tracks of Smokey's tears will have you weeping so hard you might not be up for going to a go-go when the title track immediately follows it. More likely, you'll just marvel at our host's phenomenal range of expression because whether he's demanding you shimmy on "Go-Go" and "From Head to Toe," smashing your heart with a sledgehammer on "Tracks of My Tears" and "Ooo Baby Baby," or strutting through less extreme emotions on "Choosey Beggar" and "My Girl Has Gone," Smokey Robinson is masterful all the way through *Going to a Go-Go*. And I'm not just talking about that maple syrup voice. He writes or cowrites all but one of the outstanding tracks on the first album credited to Smokey Robinson and the Miracles.

Smokey Robinson may have fully taken command with *Going to a Go-Go*, but the Miracles do more than provide heavenly harmonies. Bobby Rogers, Ronald White, and Mickey Stevenson helped write some of the album's finest songs. So despite that new extension of the Miracles' name, *Going to a Go-Go* is very much a group effort.

THE ROLLING STONES: *ROLLING STONES NO. 2*

The Rolling Stones was a fine representation of what the Stones were in 1964: enthusiastic and instinctively rhythmic blues and rock and roll purists who couldn't really write a song and had a front man who needed some serious seasoning. The Stones started to smooth out those wrinkles on *Rolling Stones No. 2*. The enthusiasm and rhythm is still strong, but there is also some good original material. For "Off the Hook," Mick Jagger takes his first stab at storytelling, and Keith Richards works out an original riff. Mick's voice is the biggest development since the debut album. Any attempt to tackle something as formidable as Solomon Burke's "Everybody Needs Somebody to Love" a year earlier would have been laughable. The version cut in early 1965 is marvelously dynamic and enriched with Jagger's first great soul vocal. Not to be outdone, Keith reaches new peaks with his fleet-fingered work on the album's most exciting cut: a hopped-up version of Don Raye's "Down the Road Apiece." Both Mick and Keith shine on "Time Is on My Side," while Brian Jones reminds us why he ruled the band in the first place with his whiplash slide work on "I Can't Be Satisfied." The

My personal pick for the very best Stones album of 1965 is the American compilation *Rolling Stones, Now!* It uses the same idiotic liner notes as *Rolling Stones No. 2*. Obsessed with *A Clockwork Orange*, Andrew Oldham cluelessly urged kids to beat up and rob blind men to get the cash necessary to purchase the Stones' latest in pseudo Nadsat—the Russian-based language Anthony Burgess invented for *Clockwork*'s "droogs." The liner notes were removed from certain later pressings of the album, and the Stones never did star in that adaptation of *A Clockwork Orange* Oldham dreamed of making. Author's collection.

only thing hindering *Rolling Stones No. 2* is a soppy version of "Under the Boardwalk" that they probably recorded only to satisfy producer Andrew Oldham's ambition to follow in idol Phil Spector's footsteps. The Stones almost make up for that error in judgment with the snarling punk of "Susie Q" and their own vicious mess "Grown Up Wrong."

OUT OF OUR HEADS

After two albums almost totally dependent on seething blues and Chuck Berry covers, the Stones mixed up the formula a bit in late 1965 but not when it came to writing. While their peers in the Beatles, the Kinks, and the Beach Boys had already made LPs of mostly original material, the Stones still relied on covers. However, sweet soul standards prevail over tough rock and blues on *Out of Our Heads*. This was a daring choice considering how disastrous their cover of "Under the Boardwalk" had been on *Rolling Stones No. 2*. Nothing on *Out of Our Heads* is nearly so bad as that, though Jagger still has trouble navigating some of the new selections. He wasn't going to make anyone forget Sam Cooke, Otis Redding, Marvin Gaye, or Solomon Burke with his attempts at "Good Times," "That's How Strong My Love Is," "Hitchhike," and "Cry to Me." Songs with so much heart never really suited Jagger, who sounds much more at home with his own "Heart of Stone," interpreting a hard-hearted lyric with newfound sensitivity that exposes the self-doubt of the callous lothario.

Such original material is what makes *Out of Our Heads* really worthwhile. The Stones get satirical on "The Under Assistant West Coast Promotion Man," spacey on "I'm Free," and breezy "Gotta Get Away." They also get off a couple of good covers—a slowed-down and sexed-up take on Chuck Berry's "Talkin' 'Bout You" and a lurching, gleeful rendition of Don Covay's "Mercy Mercy"—and one great one. Their TNT detonation of Larry Williams's "She Said Yeah" is the best cover they ever did as far as I'm concerned.

THE SONICS: *HERE ARE THE SONICS!!!*

While solo artists and swinging big bands ruled fifties rock radio, homegrown rock groups took over in the sixties. All across America and elsewhere, quartets of pimply kids gathered in basements and garages to bash out two or three chords. This movement was under way well before the Beatles arrived, but that group's popularity sparked a gold rush for the next big thing that saw amateurish bands who never would have been signed under normal circumstances getting the chance to cut records for major and minor labels.

The garage-rock movement produced a slew of nasty, unforgettable hits: The Kingsmen's "Louie Louie," Question Mark & the Mysterians' "96 Tears," the Syndicate of Sounds' "Little Girl," the Castaways' "Liar Liar," the Music Machine's "Talk Talk," the Swingin' Medallions' "Double Shot (of My Baby's Love)," the Music Explosion's "Little Bit O' Soul," and on and on. Some of these guys, such as the Sonics, even managed to sustain their rough magic across twelve inches too.

These maniacs from Tacoma, Washington, are rock and roll traditionalists who bleed every bit of lunacy lurking in the Chuck Berry, Contours, Barrett Strong, Richard Berry, Little Richard, and Rufus Thomas classics they attack on their debut. That approach was becoming old-fashioned in 1965, yet there's nothing old-fashioned about *Here Are the Sonics!!!* The Sonics take chestnuts like "Do You Love Me" and "Louie Louie" and beat them into a pulsating pile of gore. Gerry Roslie screams like he's gonna puke up his own spleen. Bob Bennett gives his drums the "Hulk smash" treatment. Larry and Andy Parypa overdrive the beats with atomic bass and guitar, and Rob Lind blows the ceiling off with his monster sax. Imagine if the Stones had cut every cover on *Out of Our Heads* the way they cut "She Said Yeah," and you'll start to get the picture. There are also a few incredible originals on *Here Are the Sonics!!!*, and for "Psycho," "Strychnine," and "The Witch," Gerry Roslie supplies lyrics every bit as monstrous as the accompaniment. There are no murderers or monsters in "Boss Hoss," but the driver of that song's hot rod must be one of Big Daddy Roth's bug-eyed ghouls. *Here Are the Sonics!!!* is must listening for any hot rodder, monster kid, punk, juvenile delinquent, psycho, or bug-eyed ghoul.

THE STRANGELOVES: *I WANT CANDY*

If scientists could distill a beer-drenched party down to its essence, melt it like wax, and remold it into 33⅓ revolutions of rock and roll revelry, the results would probably sound like *I Want Candy*. We all know the stomping title tune, and if that's your cup of malt liquor, the rest of this record won't disappoint you. With the exception of one token ballad, which doesn't even make it to the two-minute mark, there isn't a moment of respite as the Strangeloves bash out their basic beats on originals such as "Cara-Lin," "No Jive," and "Night Time," which scored a spot on Lenny Kaye's essential garage-rock compilation *Nuggets*. This trio of New York City producers (*not* Australian sheep farmers as their press releases would have you believe) deliver equally electrifying covers of "Hang On Sloopy," "New Orleans," "Willie and the Hand Jive," and "(I Can't Get No) Satisfaction," which adds on the beefy horn section Keith Richards always wished for that song. Turn it up loud and do some keg stands.

THE SUPREMES: *MORE HITS BY THE SUPREMES*

With that title and a lineup that includes "Stop! In the Name of Love," "Back in My Arms Again," and "Nothing but Heartaches," the Supremes' sixth album seems more like a hits compilation than a proper release. The nine tracks that didn't command the top twenty support that flavor because Holland, Dozier, and Holland had yet to exhaust their vault of riches when *More Hits by the Supremes* appeared in the summer of 1965. Future albums like *I Hear a Symphony*, *A-Go Go*, and *Reflections* would rely too much on Holland–Dozier–Holland tunes that had already been hits for other Motown artists or tired covers like "Up, Up and Away," "Hang on Sloopy," and "Yesterday." *More Hits* is a thoroughly original collection and feels unified even though some tracks date back to the previous year. That barely matters since the dramatic and beautifully arranged "Ask Any Girl," the snappy almost-a-single "Mother Day," the sweet "Honey Boy," the elegant "Who Could Ever Doubt My Love," and the simmering "I'm in Love Again" are well worthy of sitting side by side with the hits. Those hits are some of the Supremes' very best. "Stop! In the Name of Love" may be their definitive record, but the propulsive "Nothing but Heartaches" and "Back in Love Again," with its supercool self-references to Mary and Flo and their humming exclamations that vibrate like a struck wine glass, are even better.

The back cover of my personal copy of *More Hits by the Supremes* was pasted on upside down. Author's collection.

THEM: *THE ANGRY YOUNG THEM*

A few years before striking out on his own with a sound that stirred pop, folk, jazz, and soul into a totally potent potion, Van Morrison was making hard-hitting garage rock no one would ever associate with him after "Brown Eyed Girl." Yet listen to the animal passion and feral improvisation of solo numbers like "Listen to the Lion" and realize that Morrison hadn't hung up everything he'd learned while fronting Belfast garage band Them. The big difference is that in his solo years, he no longer received backing as raw as what Peter Bardens, Billy Harrison, Ala Henderson, and John McAuley supplied on *The Angry Young Them*. This album is as legit a punk predecessor as *My Generation* or *The Seeds* with Van barking one- and two-chord wonders like "Don't Start Crying Now," "Baby Please Don't Go," the satanic "Mystic Eyes," and "Gloria," a garage classic attempted by every future punk group worth its piss-soaked salt. Morrison even sounds like a cranky Rottweiler on a lot of the slow soul numbers, though there are occasional flashes of his future sensitivity on things like "Don't Look Back." For the mass of its run time, though, *The Angry Young Them* lives up to its title.

THE TURTLES: *IT AIN'T ME BABE*

Although they scooped up a bundle of smash 45s such as "Elenore," "You Showed Me," "It Ain't Me Babe," and the perennial "Happy Together," the Turtles of Los Angeles never quite garnered the reputation for being a great album group. That's unfortunate because the Turtles' albums tend to be as effervescent, memorable, and weird as their singles.

However, the L.A. sextet are in total folk-rock mode on *It Ain't Me Babe*. They cover Dylan with almost as much enthusiasm as the Byrds did on their own debut. The Turtles shred through a couple of bitter treats by Dylan aspirer P. F. Sloan and thoughtful originals such as "Wanderin' Kind" and "Let the Cold Winds Blow" by their own Howard Kaylan. While there are none of the gumdrops that would soon come tumbling out of the Turtles' shells, a bubbly version of "Your Maw Said You Cried" and the band's decision to cover a tune by Tin Pan Alley team Barry Mann and Cynthia Weil is an early clue that times would soon be changing for the less politicized.

THE WHO: *MY GENERATION*

The Who wasn't the first band to turn up their amps to the max and give their instruments the what for, but *My Generation* still feels like something entirely new. The Sonics played it loud and noisy but without the unique finesse of the Who's three instrumentalists. Pete Townshend could throttle unearthly howls out of his Rickenbacker, but he could also strum it with the nimble rhythmic perfection of a seasoned flamenco guitarist. No drummer cascaded across the skins as relentlessly or rapidly as Keith Moon did, and no rock bass player even imagined of using the bass as a lead instrument as John Entwistle did on the epoch-defining "My Generation." The first time I saw the anarchic Who history film *The Kids Are Alright* and realized that it was the *bass player* fingering the solo and not the guitar player picking it, it reshuffled my mind and changed the way I played bass completely. I've spent the subsequent three decades trying to master that solo as Entwistle played it in *The Kids Are Alright*. I think I almost have it.

The Who's interplay—bass and drums functioning as veritable lead instruments while rhythm guitarist holds it all together while occasionally indulging in a frustratedly dispensed blast of lead or making some unearthly noise with pick or pickup—was utterly unique in a time when it was more common for groups to play with such unity that it was almost impossible to discern the different instruments. The Beatles, the Rolling Stones, the Funk Brothers, and the Kinks were all playing for the team. The three instrumentalists in the Who sounded like they were at war with each other. That's probably because they were (well, not Moon and Entwistle; they were best buddies).

Only the bands in the very top of pop's tier—the Beatles, the Beach Boys, the Kinks, the Rolling Stones—had a songwriter of Townshend's caliber. He hasn't quite matured yet on the Who's first album, but "The Kids Are Alright," "It's Not True," "Much Too Much," "A Legal Matter," and "The Good's Gone" are all great tunes and unusually complex and varied takes on the love song. Roger Daltrey's singing takes some critical knocks because it lacks subtlety on the band's first records, but he sounds perfectly in sync with the tough but sensitive stance of the early Who.

The back cover of the American equivalent of *My Generation* suggests that if you like the Who's bludgeoning squall, you might also enjoy records by Ricky Nelson, the Kingston Trio, Len Berry, and Brenda Lee. Oh boy. Author's collection.

Between their earsplitting music, eye-popping pop-art fashion (the Union Jack jacket and the target tee!), and iconic windmilling, guitar-smashing, microphone-swinging, cymbal-chucking act, the early Who were simply awe-inspiring onstage. *My Generation* is the only Who album that even attempts to capture that mania on vinyl, which it does most admirably.

THE ZOMBIES: *BEGIN HERE*

With their rich and cool vocals and emphasis on jazzy electric piano instead of raunchy guitars, the Zombies were the most sophisticated-sounding band to come out of the British Invasion. Their graceful first hit, "She's Not There," is the centerpiece of *Begin Here*, and the Zombies are most convincing when traveling similar territory on that debut album. They get moody with a swirling version of "Summertime," "I Can't Make Up My Mind," the enchanting nearly a cappella "The Way I Feel Inside," the adult blues "Can't Nobody Love You," the cavernous and spooky "I Remember When I Used to Love Her," and "What More Can I Do," which strikes the right balance between brooding and passionate. Rockers such as "Roadrunner," "Sticks and Stones," "Woman," and "I Got My Mojo Working" are less characteristic, and Colin Blunstone is no natural screamer, but the Zombies make the material work. Moving forward, they'd commit more fully to their innate style and make some of the loveliest and most inspired music of the pop era.

1966

Before 1966, the 45 was rock and roll's defining medium. Aside from notable exceptions courtesy of Dylan and the Beatles, LPs were second-class citizens cobbling together recent hits, stray originals, and covers. By the end of 1965, long players such as *Rubber Soul* and *Highway 61 Revisited* had created a don't-look-back situation. Albums would now be labored over with the same level of care and invention as singles, and a surprising number of artists were up to the task of supplying an LP's worth of strong originals. Some made the transition with less ease but with ample promise to make classics in the near future.

American artists such as Dylan, Otis Redding, and the Supremes created some of the year's most phenomenally influential music, but the American West Coast proved to be the country's most fecund zone. In L.A., Brian Wilson was transforming pop while the Beach Boys were on the road, and groups such as the Doors, Love, and Buffalo Springfield were getting together. Up north in San Francisco, Jefferson Airplane (featuring Grace Slick), Big Brother and the Holding Company (featuring Janis Joplin), and the Grateful Dead were cutting their first recordings. Most of these bands were expanding their consciousnesses with hallucinogens, their performances with the kind of extended improvising usually reserved for jazz musicians, and their lyrics with poetic, political, and personal content previously unheard of in pop music.

Across the pond, London, England, was the nexus of creativity. The April 15 issue of *Time* magazine declared it "the Swinging City," and that city's ingenuity was evident in the fashions, films, pop art, and music that flooded from it. Swinging London fixtures such as the Beatles, the Rolling Stones, the Who, the Kinks, the Yardbirds, and Donovan and newcomers such as the Jimi Hendrix Experience made the records the world danced, partied, screwed, and did drugs to. While the Beatles and Dylan tended to lead the way at the exclusion of all others in previous years, there was a great deal more healthy cross-pollination happening in 1966. Now, the Who, the Kinks, and the Stones were influencing the Beatles just as the Beatles had influenced those bands in years earlier. The countercultural ideas that the year's LPs espoused—the Beatles slyly championed drug experimentation, the Kinks mocked consumerism and capitalism, the Stones mocked sexual repression, the Who mocked everything—helped stimulate the hippie movement that became the definitive cultural and political youth movement of the sixties.

The rock album and perspectives of the rock album were growing up in tandem. Fans, fellow musicians, and a mushrooming serious rock press began listening to rock albums in the same way they pored over poetry or decoded European art films. In January 1966, Paul Williams's *Crawdaddy!* became the first magazine to feature reviews with greater insights than the usual "big beat; should sell!" piffle. In August 1967, Pauline Rivelli's *Jazz* magazine acknowledged the maturation of rock and roll and officially changed its name to *Jazz & Pop*. In November of that year, Jann Wenner and Ralph Gleason founded *Rolling Stone* in the United States. The new critics, such as Williams and Wenner (and later Lenny Kaye, Dave Marsh, Lester Bangs, John Swenson, Patti Smith, etc.), started calling the tunes a lot of the artists danced to—and not always to positive ends.

The new youthful press was not the only contingent arguing that rock and roll artists were capable of creating true art. In April 1967, no less a respected musician than Leonard Bernstein hosted *Inside Pop: The Rock Revolution*, a documentary for CBS TV in which he explained why pieces such as "Penny Lane," "Love You To," "Paint It Black," "Pretty Ballerina," and "I'm a Believer" deserved to be heard with open ears to a presumably adult audience. Brian Wilson's stunning solo performance of the astoundingly complex "Surf's Up" spoke louder than Bernstein's analyses.

As an ironic side note, 1966 also saw the eight-track tape rise in popularity because of its convenient, car-friendly portability, but the format did a disservice to the year's increasingly arty rock LPs. To balance the run time of each of a tape's tracks, carefully devised track listings were disarrayed and songs were faded out and faded in *in medias res*. So eight-track buyers lived in a world where "Sad Eyed Lady of the Lowlands" immediately followed "Stuck Inside of Mobile with the Memphis Blues Again" on *Blonde on Blonde*, and "Tomorrow Never Knows" faded out mid-song and wasn't the climactic track on *Revolver*. Needless to say, the vinyl LP remained the ultimate rock medium, just as it still is today.

THE BEACH BOYS: *PET SOUNDS*

An overabundance of Beach Boys albums obscured Brian Wilson's startling artistic development. Cut out contractual obligation releases like *Shut Down Vol. 2* and *Party!*, and it becomes clear that he had been working toward something since the very beginning. From *Surfin' USA* to *Surfer Girl* to *All Summer Long* to *Today!* to select tracks on *Summer Days (And Summer Nights!)*, Brian was honing his skills as a composer and producer of unparalleled sensitivity and imagination.

Wilson reached his peak with *Pet Sounds*, one of the most influential albums ever produced. He took the complex orchestrations of his idol, Phil Spector, and made them weirder with unusual instruments (bass harmonica, Theremin, harpsichord, banjo, a vast variety of percussion) and more delicate by allowing the arrangements to breathe. He'd have dissimilar instruments play in unison to create completely new sounds. On "Wouldn't It Be Nice," twelve-string guitar injected directly into the mixing desk sounds like an ice cream truck's chimes. Running a guitar through an organ's rotating Leslie speaker on the title track makes it waver as if it was recorded beneath the ocean waves Wilson romanticized.

As adventurous as the vocal and instrumental arrangements are on *Pet Sounds*, the songs tend to be relatively straightforward in structure. One major exception is "Here Today," which bounces between taut, staccato verses and megalithic oompah choruses before winding off into the strato-sphere for an instrumental passage that sounds like "Eye of the Tiger" segueing into incidental music from a carnival spook house. More than any other track on *Pet Sounds*, "Here Today" indicates the bizarre paths the Beach Boys were preparing to beat with "Good Vibrations" and *SMiLE*.

Because Brian Wilson was so in command of the sessions and did most of the work while the rest of the Beach Boys were touring Japan, *Pet Sounds* feels more like a solo project than a group effort. However, his collaborators brought a lot to the record. Brian was determined to make his lyrics as special as his music and hired an unlikely collaborator, ad-jingle writer Tony Asher, to translate his musings on maturing and romance more poetically than Mike Love ever could have. Lyrically, Wilson and Asher's most profound piece is "I

Just Wasn't Made for These Times," the song that best represents where Brian's head was while making his most renowned work. He felt his more outré ideas would not be welcomed by others in his camp and rightfully so considering the guff he received from his fellow Beach Boys when they returned from that tour of Japan to hear what he'd been cooking up in the studio. Anyone else would consider possessing Brian's genius a blessing, but the grief he received from his band and record label made it a burden. That's why this song's "I'm ahead of my time" message is more lament than Lennonesque boast à la "And Your Bird Can Sing." A song originally titled "Hang On to Your Ego" would have been even more unusual, but Mike Love objected to lyrics he small-mindedly believed glorified acid and bullied Brian into allowing him to rewrite it as the more philosophically prosaic "I Know There's an Answer."

When I got my first CD player, I had the brilliant idea to sell about 115 of my vinyl albums—every Beatles album, every Stones album, *Pet Sounds, etc.*,—for $100 so I could spend my earnings on CDs. In 1990, $100 would get you about seven or eight CDs. As an adult, I've spent at least $500 rebuying most of the records I practically gave away in '90s. I wish I could go back in time and punch myself in the face. Author's collection.

"God Only Knows" is the album's most completely extraordinary creation and a song so associated with its chief creator that the efforts of Brian's collaborators are often unfairly sidelined. Carl's vocal is so transcendently gorgeous that it is mind-boggling Brian didn't have his little brother sing more songs before it. Still, it is meaningful that Brian would have Carl sing many of his finest songs from this point on. Ethereal as Brian's falsetto is, he tended to belt more when singing in his lower range. Carl maintained his delicacy remarkably when singing in the deeper tones "God Only Knows" required. It is so delicate that listeners often miss Asher's cruel tease that opens the song ("I may not always love you . . ."). Of course, he will continue to love you "long as there are stars above you." That means forever, folks. "God Only Knows" is desperately romantic, bordering on the neurotically needy. Without peer, it is the most beautiful love song ever written, and I fall to pieces whenever I hear it.

The group's harmonies are perfect throughout the record, but that has more to do with Brian's choral arrangements and unrelenting work ethic than the particular qualities of the guys' voices. In a rare move likely to let his brothers feel more involved in the production, Brian allowed Dennis and Carl Wilson to play on the bed track of "That's Not Me."

Mike Love's lack of vision made his cousin's achievement bittersweet. The singer didn't support the Beach Boys' move away from juvenile surf and hot-rod themes and played a major role in sabotaging Brian's next project, which would have bested *Pet Sounds* had it been completed. But in a world without *SMiLE*, *Pet Sounds* stands as the Beach Boys' greatest completed album. Pop would never be the same.

THE BEATLES: *REVOLVER*

The innocent joy of Beatlemania had worn off for the Beatles as far back as *Beatles for Sale*, but it positively curdles on *Revolver*. The band's greatest album is also their most disillusioned. Lennon's hallucinogenic experiments find him unable to pull himself out of bed on "I'm Only Sleeping," questioning his sanity on "She Said She Said," experiencing delusions of grandeur on "And Your Bird Can Sing," singing the praises of his dealer on "Doctor Robert," and plummeting into madness on "Tomorrow Never Knows." A pre-spiritual George Harrison laments his dwindling bankroll on "Taxman" before confessing his inability to communicate on "I Want to Tell You." His "Love You To," a tribute to free love, contains the most cynical lyric in any Beatle song ("There's people standing 'round who'll screw you in the ground, they'll fill you in with all their sins, you'll see"). Ever the romantic, McCartney provides a couple of moments of genuine light ("Good Day Sunshine" and "Here, There, and Everywhere") but spends much of the record in similar disorder: elegizing a dead relationship on "For No One" and turning paranoiac and obsessive on "Got to Get You into My Life," a love song in which the object of Paul's affection is pot. "Eleanor Rigby," which eschews romantic themes altogether, is a grim account of loneliness and death. Even the merry "Yellow Submarine" is nothing if not an escapist fantasy.

Its cynicism adds additional layers of complexity to *Revolver*, but its combination of perfect songwriting, energetic musicianship, and unbridled experimentation are what make the album wonderful. Unlike the

Klaus Voormann's Aubrey Beardsley-esque illustration/collage kicked off a vogue for illustrated album covers, and it's never been topped as far as I'm concerned. Voormann couldn't get George's eyes right so he just pasted photos of them onto his drawing of George's face. The result has been creeping out Beatlemaniacs for decades. Author's collection.

handful of tracks on *Sgt. Pepper's* that are relatively inconsequential when separated from the album's overall concept, every song on *Revolver* stands on its own. The album overflows with moments integral to Beatles lore and launched an endless parade of imitations: the octave-hopping bass line of "Taxman," the slashing string octet of "Eleanor Rigby," the backward guitar lines of "I'm Only Sleeping," the full Indian orchestration of "Love You To," the languid warmth of "Here, There, and Everywhere," the sound effects and psychedelicized kiddy naïveté of "Yellow Submarine," the clinging vine guitars and wild drumming of "She Said, She Said," the old-timey good vibes of "Good Day Sunshine," the ecstatic harmonizing and intricate riffing of "And Your Bird Can Sing," the baroque waltz of "For No One," the filthy guitar lick and funky backbeat of "Doctor Robert," the off-kilter piano line of "I Want to Tell You," the chunky brass of "Got to Get You into My Life," the tape loop frenzy of "Tomorrow Never Knows." *Revolver* is the Beatles at their least self-consciously experimental, and hearing them create such incredible music is so thrilling that it's easy to miss how demented these songs are. The cover's damn creepy too.

THE BEATLES IN AMERICA: *YESTERDAY AND TODAY*

More than six months had passed since *Rubber Soul*. Despite the massive artistic bounds the Beatles had taken with their latest record, Capitol remained tone-deaf to the fact that they were more than just another pop group. The Beatles were not exclusive victims to Capitol's nearsightedness. Execs were so skeptical of the Beach Boys' recent fun and sun-shunning *Pet Sounds* that the label didn't wait two months before following it with the more commercial *Best of the Beach Boys*. The move was tantamount to a slap in the face to Brian Wilson, who'd put so much of his heart and soul into the album that he admitted *Rubber Soul* had inspired.

Only such clueless individuals could not be anticipating what the Beatles had in store after their finest record yet. The follow-up to *Rubber Soul* is the record now widely regarded as their best. *Revolver* both seems a companion piece to *Rubber Soul* (in the *Beatles Anthology* documentary series, George Harrison said he considers the records a sort of two-volume set) with its like-minded freshness, Swinging London sophistication, and winking drugginess and a leaps-and-bounds progression past the pop romanticism of *Rubber Soul*. *Revolver* is far more experimental, far more lyrically and musically varied, darker, weirder, and wilder.

While the Beatles were taking too long with their latest pop record for Capitol's liking, it was time to get some new product in American shops. In the vaults were a couple of leftovers from *Help!* ("Yesterday" and "Act Naturally"), four from *Rubber Soul* ("Drive My Car," "Nowhere Man," "If I Needed Someone," and "What Goes On"), and two from that album's companion single ("Day Tripper" and "We Can Work It Out"). With the latest single ("Paperback Writer" and "Rain"), the tally came to ten tracks—not quite enough for a proper LP.

Bizarrely, that new major single was not under consideration for Capitol's making-time record of the summer of 1966. Instead, Brian Epstein had to hand over three of the six completed tracks from the Beatles' current sessions. As Robert Rodriguez explains in *Revolver: How the Beatles Reimagined Rock 'N' Roll*, "It was George Martin's unenviable task to choose which songs to throw onto the cobbled-together *Yesterday and Today*." Rodriguez speculates that Martin selected the particular tracks because "Taxman" was so obvious a record starter, and "Tomorrow Never Knows" and "Love You To" would have sounded wrong alongside numbers as ancient as "Act Naturally" and "Yesterday." So Martin slipped the remaining completed tracks to Capitol: "Doctor Robert," "And Your Bird Can Sing," and "I'm Only Sleeping." Because they were not mixed for stereo, they appear on *Yesterday and Today* in awful duophone, echoing as if they'd been piped into a cavernous tiled bathroom.

A cover also had to be shot. This is where *Yesterday and Today* veers from *Beatles VI*–style curio to full-blown "bigger than Jesus" infamy. Australian photographer Robert Whitaker draped the Fab Four in butcher smocks and raw meat, gave them some dirty baby doll parts to play with, and told them to say "cheese." What did it all mean? According to Rodriguez, Whitaker had succumbed to his artistic pretensions. The guy who'd shot the chummy "Beatles for All Seasons" pics on the cover of *Beatles '65* was now drawing inspiration from his dreams and conceiving a triptych called "A Somnambulant Adventure," one panel of which would show the world's most popular band posing with dolls and pork. Ringo was under the impression the photo had more personal connotations, that it was a statement on the way Capitol chopped up the Beatles' "babies" (their LPs). Paul liked to believe it was some sort of criticism of the Vietnam War. John said it was a protest against boring photo shoots. George just thought it was gross.

So did the retailers and radio stations that received advance shipments of *Yesterday and Today*. The outcry was so overwhelmingly negative that Capitol went into crisis mode, pasting an innocuous Whitaker shot of the guys posing around a steamer trunk over about 750,000 copies of the controversial cover. Instant collector's item.

And so we have the one and only Beatles album more famous for its cover than its music. But what of its music? Sure, *Yesterday and Today* is a mishmash culled from three fairly different albums. It is still a charming artifact of the Beatles in the midst of their most astounding progression. *Help!*, *Rubber Soul*, and *Revolver* are all well removed from the "Yeah, yeah, yeah" early days of Beatlemania. They precede the self-conscious artiness of *Sgt. Pepper's*, *Magical Mystery Tour*, "The White Album," and *Abbey Road*. As different as the albums that constitute *Yesterday and Today* are, they all find the Beatles

The cover in which *Yesterday and Today* actually reached shops was somewhat less remarkable than the scrapped butcher sleeve. The image of Paul in a case still hit the spot for a lot of Paul-Is-Dead conspiracy theorists. Author's collection.

advancing naturally and with great humor. "A string quartet on 'Yesterday'?" says Paul. "Sure, let's give it a shot." "Oh those backwards vocals sounded so groovy on 'Rain'," says George. "Let's see what happens if we do the same thing to my guitar on 'I'm Only Sleeping.'" "Ha!" laughs John. "I'm gonna write a song about my drug dealer!"

Charming it may be, but *Yesterday and Today* is still an odd duck. It is the only Beatles single-disc LP with two lead vocals by Ringo and the only one that initially lost money (because of the cover debacle). It has no British counterpart whatsoever. It was created for purely commercial purposes. By absorbing three key *Revolver* tracks, it single-handedly hobbled the Beatles' best album for millions of Americans. That all three of the songs sacrificed were John Lennon's rendered the most balanced of the Beatles' British albums totally unbalanced in the United States.

REVOLVER

Capitol's *Revolver* is the only Beatles album on which George Harrison contributes more songs than Lennon. John only sings twice as many as Ringo. The grandest collaboration of the Fabs' career ends up sounding like the Paul and George show. Paul's romanticism envelops the record. George suddenly seems like he's become the cynical one. John's two songs are left to close each side, giving them pride of place but making them seem like they've swooped in from a different, crazier record. Had John lost his mind? Was he able to come up with only two new songs during a period that was so clearly a creatively fertile one for his bandmates? And these are the songs he came up with? He hadn't even bothered to come up with more than one chord for "Tomorrow Never Knows"!

Capitol's *Revolver* is an intrinsically great record because all its eleven songs are great. Dave Dexter Jr. finally conceded that George Martin knew what he was doing and refrained from laying on the echo. Comparatively speaking, Capitol's *Revolver* is sorely inadequate once we know what we've lost. John's three missing songs don't just make the Parlophone record more balanced; they make it rock harder. Without the soaring guitar duel of "And Your Bird Can Sing," the grungy licks of "Dr. Robert," and the backward leads of "I'm Only Sleeping," the lasting sonic impressions of *Revolver* are its strings, sitars, French horns, clavichords, and brass bands. John's songs bring extra color to a dark record, even though his sly nastiness still encrusts each song. The loss of them makes the Beatles' most perfect album less perfect. Had Americans known *Revolver* as the Beatles intended it to be known, *Sgt. Pepper's Lonely Hearts Club Band* may have never built a reputation as the Beatles' most far-out disc.

What must have the Beatles thought when they consciously set out to make their artiest statement? What injustices would Capitol rain down on *Sgt. Pepper's Lonely Hearts Club Band*? Would Dave Dexter drown "A Day in the Life" in even more echo? Would he lop off "Fixing a Hole" so he could put it out on a new record called *The "Hole" Beatles*? Maybe he'd remove "With a Little Help from My Friends" for *The Friendly Beatles* or another one for *Getting Better with the Beatles*?

Luckily for that record's reputation, Capitol demoted Dexter in 1966. The Beatles officially forbade any other exec from tampering with their art when they renewed their contract with Capitol in January 1967. So the only alteration Capitol made was removing the two-second loop of gobbledygook from the run-out groove of side B of *Sgt. Pepper's*. Otherwise, Americans finally received the same Beatles record as their British friends. Never again would Capitol mess with a Beatles LP at all, and this trend quickly spread throughout the rock and roll universe. Groups that had formerly seen their albums chopped up as ruthlessly for the American market as the Beatles' had been mostly no longer had to worry about such desecration of their art, though there would still be some odd exceptions in the days that immediately followed the release of *Pepper's* (Capitol Records massacred Pink Floyd's epochal *The Piper at the Gates of Dawn* in the United States) and occasionally well into the future (LPs by such key artists as Elvis Costello and the Attractions and XTC would be significantly altered after crossing the Atlantic in the seventies and eighties). The Beatles' EPs, however, remained fair game.

THE BYRDS: *FIFTH DIMENSION*

Fifth Dimension is hit or miss, but the hits are so strong that the album still ranks as one of the Byrds' best. It contains what may be their greatest recording, an account of jetting into London usually mistaken for a drug song called "Eight Miles High." Chris Hillman's simple bass line is a mighty launchpad for the wild flurry of John Coltrane–inspired noodling Roger McGuinn elicits from his twelve-string. The harmonies are the Byrds' most ethereal *and* forceful. This is one of the most exciting rock songs ever recorded, and its presence guarantees that *Fifth Dimension* would have been a classic even if the other ten tracks were junk. There are a couple of throwaways that drag down side B (the sub–Booker T. instrumental "Captain Soul" and the irritating "2-4-2 Fox Trot"). However, "I See You" (another frenetic track along the lines of "Eight Miles High"), the swirling "5D (Fifth Dimension)," and the delightfully goofy bluegrass "Mr. Space-man" are classics. The latter two tracks introduce McGuinn's fascination with space travel that would continue on the Byrds' next two albums.

Their first album without a single Dylan song, *Fifth Dimension* makes room for the Byrds to spin out their two best traditional folk covers: "Wild Mountain Thyme," which features an august string arrangement, and "John Riley." The stark "I Come and Stand at Every Door" sets Nâzim Hikmet Ran's poem about the victims of the Hiroshima bombing against a haunting backbeat. The group's version of "Hey Joe (Where You Gonna Go)," which features more of McGuinn's crazed guitar picking and an overdose of cowbell, may be the only non-Hendrix version of this over-covered song that doesn't feel totally redundant.

CREAM: *FRESH CREAM*

Cream introduced the term "supergroup" to the pop lexicon. Eric Clapton had already made a name for himself with the Yardbirds and John May-all's Bluesbreakers. Jack Bruce and Ginger Baker came from the Graham Bond Organization. That group's lack of commercial success stretches the "supergroup" designation, but the label stuck anyway and would be more legitimately applied to future groups like Crosby, Stills, and Nash and Blind Faith, which included two-thirds of Cream.

Artistically, none of the more legit supergroups would top Cream. *Fresh Cream* would have made good on Cream's super status regardless of the guys' past associations. No album was as heavy in 1966. Cream's weight came largely from Ginger Baker's muscular yet precise drumming and Jack Bruce's snarly, active bass. Bruce's shivering tenor and Eric Clapton's vibrato-charged (yet thin and, frankly, overrated) guitar work fills the ether.

Fresh Cream does not parade out the classics like *Disraeli Gears* would the following year, but it is a much more cohesive album. Cream is in full-on blues mode on their debut, but the distinctiveness of their four basic elements keeps clichés at bay. An ambling version of Robert Johnson's "Four Until Late" is pedestrian in Clapton's slow hands, but Bruce and Baker transform standard blues fare such as "Sleepy Time Time" and "Spoonful" into haunting, engrossing powerhouses. A jittery, speed-freak version of Muddy Waters's "Rollin' and Tumblin'" verges on punk hysteria. Any indication that "I'm So Glad" was a traditional blues number in Skip James's hands is stripped away in

This 1974 reissue of *Fresh Cream* includes "Wrapping Paper" and "The Coffee Song," which had only been included on the original release in Scandinavia. Author's collection.

Cream's bubbly reading. Cream rarely got as poppy as they did on "N.S.U.," "Dreaming," "Sweet Wine," and "I Feel Free," the group's stunning breakthrough single available only on the American edition. Ginger Baker's "Toad" is a boring drum solo (is there any other kind?), but the rest of the album makes for a fresh listen.

THE CYRKLE: *RED RUBBER BALL*

The major beats of the Cyrkle's career were limited to 1966. That year, they toured with the Beatles during the Fabs' final live performances, released their sole hit singles, and recorded their only two albums. The second of these, *Neon*, was not released until 1967, by which time the Cyrkle was basically forgotten. The first, released in 1966, housed the hits while dishing up a neat variety of mid-sixties pop styles bridging the gap between the bubble gum of the Paul Simon–penned "Red Rubber Ball" and the tougher, more psychedelic "Turn Down Day," which flaunts superb interplay between the bass guitar and the sitar and presages summer of love sentiments by half a year.

Red Rubber Ball offers plenty of other first-rate tracks in the garage-raga ("Cry"), breezy Britpop ("Why Can't You Give Me What I Want," "Baby You're Free"), proto-punk ("There's a Fire in the Fireplace"), and moody Merseybeat ballad ("How Can I Leave Her") styles that scream 1966. The misogyny of a lot of these tracks tamps down the pleasure, "Big Little Woman" bears an all-around terrible lyric, and a version of Larry Williams's "Boney Moronie" is sickly cute, but *Red Rubber Ball* still sums up the year in pop nicely.

DONOVAN: *SUNSHINE SUPERMAN*

Sunshine Superman is Donovan's most consistently enchanting album and one of the few sixties pop records to really explore India music outside of a single token number. The prevailing sounds—chiming acoustic guitars, sitars, harpsichords, strings, and stand-up bass—make it a sort of chamber/jazz/raga/rock record. Donovan never leans too heavily on his precious tendencies, as he sometimes would later in his career, and nearly every song is strong. "Legend of a Girl Child Linda" is overlong, but "Three Kingfishers" and "Guinevere" are two of Donovan's eeriest raga-folk articles. "Ferris Wheel" and "The Fat Angel" are two of his most inviting. "Bert's Blues" lays the groundwork for the jazzy *Mellow Yellow*. The megahit "Sunshine Superman" is a groovy and disarmingly adult pop song percolating with Jimmy Page's neat guitar swells. "Season of the Witch" is one of Donovan's most timeless and timely songs: a sinister, seductive premonition of the troubled days to come that would put the optimism of hippies like Donovan to the test.

BOB DYLAN: *BLONDE ON BLONDE*

The great paradox of Bob Dylan's career is that when he tried to escape that "voice of his generation" tag by ditching his acoustic guitar for an electric and writing bafflingly cryptic lyrics, he only broadened his legend. *Blonde on Blonde* is the apex of his mid-sixties electric period, which alienated his folkie purist followers but won him legions of new rock fans. It is a sprawling double album's worth of stoned poetry, giddy giggling, pseudo-profundities, cynical love songs, and sheer nonsense.

Despite his too-cool-to-care pose, Dylan was clearly embittered when his old fans deserted him (see "Positively 4th Street"), but on *Blonde on Blonde*, he really does seem to be past the point of caring about anything at all. The closest thing to topicality is "Leopard Skin Pillbox Hat," a put-down of the wealthy class, but that track fits equally well into the album's main theme of puncturing pomposity. Sometimes that attitude is tough to take, as when Dylan resorts to the patronizing platitudes of "Just Like a Woman." It's more fun when he gleefully lays into Lennon on the pretty "4th Time Around," mocks love song clichés with the swirling "I Want You," or hands his more academic fans a load of nonsense to ponder with "Stuck Inside of Mobile with the Memphis Blues Again." True glimpses of sincerity occasionally gleam through the sarcasm, as when Dylan cryptically bares his heart on the mesmerizing "Visions of Johanna" and "Sad Eyed Lady of the Lowlands," a valentine to his future wife Sara Lownds.

A couple of the blues numbers are comparatively inconsequential, and "Sad Eyed Lady of the Lowlands," which takes up an entire side of the album, is not nearly as interesting an epic as "Desolation Row," but *Blonde on Blonde* is still a towering testament to Dylan's abilities as a not-so-straightforward rocker and a dramatic finale to his most important period.

THE HOLLIES: *FOR CERTAIN BECAUSE . . .*

Too smart to qualify as bubble gum, too sweet to scare the teenyboppers, the Hollies had broad appeal and a bunch of hits. Lead singer Allan Clarke's desire to keep it sweet and guitarist/vocalist Graham Nash's need to mature would eventually cause discord in the band, but all seemed right with the world when they were harmonizing on fresh 45s like "Bus Stop" and "Carrie Anne."

Although they were primarily a singles act, the Hollies did put together a few strong albums during their mid-sixties salad days. One of the best is *For Certain Because . . .*, which is their first album of all original material. Released at the end of 1966, *For Certain Because . . .* is a remarkably confident and eclectic bag, storming in with the assaultingly cheerful "What's Wrong with the Way I Live?" before cascading into the trippy waltz "Pay You Back with Interest." Elsewhere, there are mildly exotic and thoroughly groovy numbers like "Tell Me to My Face" and "Stop, Stop, Stop," a hit single about a guy who gets so horny in a belly-dance club that he has to be dragged out by security—not your typical pop-hit fare in 1966. As is the case with every Hollies album, there is one unbearably corny track ("High Classed"), but the rest of *For Certain Because . . .* is among the class of 1966's finest pop.

THE INCREDIBLE STRING BAND: *THE INCREDIBLE STRING BAND*

While the American hippies were digging up the blues and country roots buried in their home soil, their British counterparts were getting back in touch with their own past. Thus, archaic ballads, weird legends, and a creepy gothic sensibility came billowing out of the cauldron that some branded "acid folk." The endless Jerry Garcia jams yawning across the pond could sound only staid and boring in comparison.

The guiding light of the late-sixties British underground folk movement was the Incredible String Band, which melded the sitars, keyboards, and bells of the current psychedelic sound with Olde Scottish balladry. I'd be surprised if Mike Heron and Robin Williamson didn't spend their off hours burning cops in wicker men.

Their debut is more scaled back than the LPs that would follow. The group tosses in the occasional violin, mandolin, banjo, or whistle, but *The Incredible String Band* centers mostly on Heron and Williamson's acoustic guitars and elfin voices. The droning opener "Maybe Someday" is the only hint of the more international direction the Scots would take on their second album.

THE KINKS: *FACE TO FACE*

Welcome to Daviesland, a kurious little nook of England where the Kinks secreted themselves a year after being unofficially banned from touring the United States. Since that unfortunate event, in which Ray socked an insult-spewing musician's union representative, the boys enjoyed a steady string of top-ten hits in their homeland, but managed to sneak into the American top twenty only twice with "A Well Respected Man" and "Sunny Afternoon."

Unable to promote themselves properly in the world's biggest rock and roll market and apparently satisfied with all they'd achieved thus far, the Kinks resigned themselves to more modest, domestic ambitions. The U.S.-friendly heavy riffing of their early smashes blared one final bang in late

1965 with "Till the End of the Day," which flitted in and out of *Billboard*'s top fifty in the wink of an eye. Afterward, Ray Davies, Dave Davies, Pete Quaife, and Mick Avory seemingly set out to become the most English of all English bands. The first unfiltered evidence of the Kinks' new modus operandi arrived in early 1966. "Dedicated Follower of Fashion" is a boisterous knees-up, name-checking, Swinging London's sartorial mecca Carnaby Street without any concern for whether or not Yank listeners would get the reference or cotton to the record's music-hall camp. Not surprisingly, it barely peaked into the American top forty. The similar "Sunny Afternoon" did, but the failure of such a perfectly formed pearl to get closer to *Billboard*'s top spot hinted that America's affair with the Kinks might be over for good.

Of course, it wasn't, but some four years would pass before the Kinks would reclaim their former stateside glory with the hard-rocking "Lola." In the interim, their music became more modest, quieter, and very, very English. By retreating from the world outside of their U.K. microcosm from 1966 through 1970, they developed a personal voice quite unlike that of any of their peers and created the most splendid music of their career.

Face to Face is the Kinks' first great album. The butterflies that swath its cover are its perfect metaphor. This is the album on which the Kinks fully metamorphosed from purveyors of primitive garage rock to subtle scrutinizers of British culture and the human condition. Only "I'll Remember" (which is pretty) and "You're Looking Fine" (which is mediocre, although it somehow became a Kinks concert staple for many years) sound out of date, and indeed, both were recorded the previous year. The new Kinks combined refined pop with music hall, and every Brit from the Beatles to the Stones was quick to cop their sound. Ray Davies's masterly ability to express disdain, admiration, humor, and wistfulness simultaneously infuses many of the trenchant yet pithy character profiles that populate *Face to Face*. "Sunny Afternoon" stars a layabout antihero. "Rosy Won't You Please Come Home" is a sad tale of teenage rebellion told from the parents' point of view (more than six months before the Beatles' "She's Leaving Home"). "Session Man" gives

Although Ray Davies was not a fan of it, the groovy artwork on the cover of *Face to Face* reflects the light psychedelia of tracks such as "Little Miss Queen of Darkness," "Fancy," and "Rainy Day in June" and the butterflies that flit through "Rainy Day" and the period single "Dedicated Follower of Fashion." Author's collection.

mildly mocking credit to the pop musicians denied the perks of pop stardom. "Dandy" admires and admonishes a womanizer. "Most Exclusive Residence for Sale" tracks the downward slope of a materialist. These tragicomic characters are so lifelike their fingerprints can be felt between every vinyl groove.

It's unfortunate that the Powers That Be at Pye Records were not farsighted enough to allow Davies to execute *Face to Face* exactly as he originally intended, which would have involved using sound effects to link the tracks, but stray remnants of this concept pop up on vividly visual numbers such as "Party Line," "Rainy Day in June," and "Holiday in Waikiki."

Face to Face was the first link in a chain of albums that established the Kinks as the most unashamedly British rock group of their era, and we probably wouldn't have bands like the Jam, Madness, or Blur without it.

LOVE: *LOVE*

Take the Stones' backbeat, layer on a contemptuous garage-rock vocal topped with some Byrdy twelve-string guitars, and you have the formula for Love's first album. *Love* is not as experimental as the music the L.A. band

would soon create; it's just a great garage/folk-rock record. The band never sound limited by their basic guitar/bass/drums lineup. The variety of styles and tones Love strikes on their debut is outstanding, whether it's bullish ("Can't Explain," "My Flash On You"), sensitive ("Message to Pretty," "Softly to Me"), dogged ("No Matter What You Do," "You I'll Be Following"), or sparse and doomy ("Mushroom Clouds," "Signed D.C.").

Arthur Lee's penchant for morose, morbid meditations is already present on *Love*, as is his tendency to approach universal topics by addressing his friends by name. The subject of the withered anti-smack tale "Signed

Man oh man, Love loved that stone structure. They'd pose in front of it again on the cover of their second album, *Da Capo*. Author's collection.

D.C." is Lee's pal, Don Conka. Yet this is a far less insular record than *Forever Changes* or even *Da Capo*. Love also handle a couple of covers: yet another version of "Hey Joe" and a nervy arrangement of the Bacharach/

David number "My Little Red Book" that deservedly become a garage-band standard.

THE LOVIN' SPOONFUL: *DAYDREAM*

By 1966, most bands had finally slowed down the breakneck release sched-ules more common in the earlier years of rock and roll and started sweating over magnum opuses such as *Pet Sounds* and *Revolver*. The Lovin' Spoon-ful arrived to the game a bit late and had to make up for lost time. Their most prolific year was 1966. The band put out four LPs during the twelve-month period between November 1965 and November 1966. Released just a few months after *Do You Believe in Magic*, *Daydream* is nearly as uniformly spectacular. The easygoing title track, the dreamy "Didn't Want to Have to Do It," the sumptuous "You Didn't Have to Be So Nice," and the fuzzy, funky "Jug Band Music" are among the group's best numbers. "It's Not Time Now" is a slinky blueprint for the future classic "Nashville Cats," and "Warm Baby" shimmers with John Sebastian's autoharp scrapes. The moving "Butchie's Tune," featuring the wistful and underrated voice of drummer Joe Butler, is the album's hidden gem, and it would be used to moving effect thirty-six years later in a pivotal episode of TV's *Mad Men*.

WHAT'S UP, TIGER LILY?

The Lovin' Spoonful's intense release schedule was clearly taking a toll on their art, and their next album is their least essential. Their sound track to Woody Allen's goofy dubbing experiment *What's Up, Tiger Lily?* consists largely of instrumentals and failed to yield a hit. It's better approached as a sound track than a proper Lovin' Spoonful album, although "Pow," "Fishin' Blues," and "Bespoken" are decent vocal tracks, and the instrumental "Lookin' to Spy" provides a first glimpse of the haunting "Coconut Grove." Most of the rest is just okay, but the Spoonful more than made up for this album's superfluousness with their next one.

HUMS OF THE LOVIN' SPOONFUL

Psychedelia was already pretty pervasive by the time *Hums of the Lovin' Spoonful* was released later in the year, but Moonshine seems to be the

Spoonful's drug of choice when they dig into the bluesy, backwoods groove "Voodoo in My Basement" or strike up their good-timin' country shuffle on "Darlin' Companion." *Hums of the Lovin' Spoonful* is radical in its refusal to play into the trends of its time. "Henry Thomas"—a wacky ode to a cat led by slide whistle, Ozark harp, and banjo—and the Grand Ole Opry–celebrating "Nashville Cats" are funny yet oddly sincere unlike, say, the Stones' more parodic takes on C&W. There's a moment in "Full Measure" where the group seems like they're about to drift off into an acid improv. Psych! They slam back into the song's stately, earthy rhythm, barely missing a beat. The Spoonful drifts toward more contemporary territory on the mysterious, wispy "Coconut Grove" and "Summer in the City," a Spectorian tone poem that shatters the album's rural reveries with sweaty, urban paranoia.

Hums of the Lovin' Spoonful may have sounded quaint when it was released at the same time Lennon was writing "Strawberry Fields Forever" and Wilson was immersed in *SMiLE*, but considering the retreat to rustic simplicity that would immediately follow the psychedelic age, *Hums* is both behind *and* ahead of its time.

THE MONKEES: *THE MONKEES*

The Monkees shattered any number of rock and roll's rules. Mike Nesmith, Micky Dolenz, Peter Tork, and Davy Jones were not neighborhood buddies who graduated from jamming in the garage to club gigs to superstardom. They were carefully selected from auditions to play the roles of musicians on TV's first rock and roll sitcom, not be musicians on the same playing field as organically formed groups like the Beatles and the Stones. Of course, that is what they became.

The TV series for which they the Monkees was assembled was equally unusual. Without any parental supervision (the only recurring adult in their world was their greedy landlord, Mr. Babbitt), Mike, Micky, Peter, and Davy were free to expose the phoniness of their medium, satirize other shows, break the fourth wall to address the audience directly, and indulge in plenty of pure surrealism. All of this was highly unusual in an age of dim-witted, formulaic fare: *F Troop*, *My Three Sons*, *The Beverly Hillbillies*, *Gilligan's Island* (which aired opposite *The Monkees*), *I Dream of Jeannie* (which aired after it).

Stylistically, *The Monkees* had more in common with the sly pop-art parody *Batman*, which had debuted on ABC the previous January. More subtly, it tread in the footsteps of *The Twilight Zone*. Like Rod Serling, *Monkees* creators Bob Rafelson and Bert Schneider used their series to smuggle politics on the air in a seemingly harmless package. Just as Serling knew sci-fi and fantasy were not taken seriously enough to scrutinize, Rafelson and Schneider apparently understood that sitcoms—particularly those as silly as *The Monkees*—could sneak below the censorship radar. *The Monkees* rarely ran aground of NBC's bowdlerizers. When it did, it was for innocuous things, such as showing a woman in a bikini (which was blurred out of "Too Many Girls" in reruns) or using the word "Hell (which was bleeped out of "The Devil and Peter Tork"). This left the producers, writers, *and* stars of *The Monkees* to get on with communicating their collective statement and radicalizing American television.

The Monkees was the first TV series to bring antiestablishment, long-haired young people into American living rooms on a weekly basis. Unlike the shaggy, "commie" criminals Friday and Gannon apprehended every week on *Dragnet* or the daft Beatles parodies that appeared on episodes of *The Munsters* or *The Flintstones*, hippies were the protagonists of *The Monkees*, and they often imparted their message of peace. That may not seem very radical, yet such messages are regarded as downright anti-American during wartime. This is not some dated attitude limited to the Vietnam era. Recall that after George W. Bush invaded Iraq in 2003, Warner Bros. altered an image of Amanda Bynes flashing the peace sign from advertisements for the banal teen comedy *What a Girl Wants* for fear it would be viewed as a war protest.

Although stylistically radical, the season 1 *Monkees* scripts did not delve deeply into political content. That was reserved for the unique candid interview segments used to both fill out short episodes and give viewers a more intimate portrait of their new idols. Halfway through that debut season, Rafelson was picking the Monkees' brains about prejudice against long-haired men (Tork invoked "the civil rights act" when harassed about his shaggy locks) and the recent teen protests ignited by an imposed 10 p.m. curfew on the Sunset Strip. Dolenz was among the protestors at the media-dubbed "riot," where the worst act of violence was a single overturned car. As he explained, "In actuality, since I was there, they've been demonstrations. But I guess a lot of journalists don't know how to spell 'demonstration,' so they use the word 'riot' because it only has four letters." That's a prickly statement to come from a supposedly vacuous puppet with "nothing to do or say" and air on TV in the first month of 1967. For the first time, a network sitcom was giving direct voice to young people and standing unequivocally on their side. The hippies, heads, peaceniks, and commies had taken over television.

The show's subversiveness was particularly cagey since it was aimed at TV's most impressionable viewers: preteens. *The Monkees* helped dose its adolescent viewers with a healthy—and necessary—tab of antiestablishment sentiment. "Question your leaders," the Monkees told their viewers. "Peace *is* an answer," they said. "Your individuality is *your* individuality." Nesmith's "no statement *is* a statement" line is contradicted by one in the series' otherwise dopey theme tune: "We're the young generation and we've got something to say." The subversive messages tucked inside *The Monkees* may have assisted an even younger generation to develop the desire to have something to say too.

While other groups were parroting messages of freedom and revolution, the Monkees were actively applying them to their own lives. Just five months after the series debuted, Mike Nesmith dropped the bomb that his group did not play the instruments on their records, instructing the *Saturday Evening Post* to "tell the world we're synthetic because, damn it, we are."

Before long, the Monkees were granted freedom to write, choose, and record their own music (more on that later, Monkeemaniacs). The move resulted in the two best albums of the Monkees' career: *Headquarters* and *Pisces, Aquarius, Capricorn, & Jones, Ltd.* They didn't just use their new-found freedom to up the quality of their records; they upped those records' political content. This further radicalized their TV show, as the Monkees now romped to songs decrying war ("Zor & Zam," Tork's "For Pete's Sake," which served as the closing theme throughout the second season), chronicling the Sunset Strip protests (Nesmith's "Daily Nightly"), satirizing drug dealers ("Salesman") and the establishment (Dolenz's "Randy Scouse Git"), presenting scandalous sexual situations ("Cuddly Toy," "Star Collector"), sneering at the police and celebrating pot (the group composition "No Time"), and criticizing suburban conformity (the big hit "Pleasant Valley Sunday"). Released after the show went off the air in 1968, Micky's "Mommy and Daddy" ("Ask your mommy and daddy why doesn't that soldier care who he kills . . .") was even more pointedly political.

The Monkees was also a brilliant advertising vehicle for the group's albums, as it gave them a means to plug not only their latest singles but also their album cuts, which no doubt helped push the four LPs they released at the height of the series' popularity to the number one spot on *Billboard's* album charts. With the possible exception of the Beatles, no group was getting that much mainstream airtime for their album cuts in the mid-sixties. The popularity of the entire enterprise enabled the Monkees to wrangle greater control over the extramusical content of their show, increasing the level of improvisation and bizarre in-jokes ("Save the Texas prairie chicken!" "Frodis!") while often appearing visibly stoned on camera (watch Jones closely in "The Monkee's Paw"). Rafelson and Schneider gave Tork and Dolenz permission to direct episodes. Dolenz's "Mijacogeo," which he also scripted, is a scathing criticism of television's brain-deadening effects. The hero of the piece is a giant, alien marijuana plant with a football for a head and a weirdly touching peace philosophy. Appropriately, this most radical of *Monkees* episodes was the last one to air in the series' original run. Rafelson and his boys were now free to get even further out with the one and only Monkees movie. Cowritten by Jack Nicholson, *Head* took an even sharper blade to TV and continued the massacre to slice up the war in Vietnam, American conservatism and consumerism, and the Monkees' manufactured image (more on that later, too).

Despite their numerous achievements, the Monkees couldn't buy themselves a lick of praise from the press or the increasing snobby rock audience. Yet the company they kept further validated the guys' hip credentials. As has often been repeated, they introduced the Jimi Hendrix Experience to mainstream America by inviting the band to open for them during their 1967 tour (the preteen audience was not receptive, and Hendrix and his band soon booked). They did the same for Frank Zappa and Tim Buckley by giving the musicians guest spots on their TV show. The Monkees were championed by tastemakers, such as Zappa, John Lennon, Jerry Garcia, and Eric Burdon, and were reportedly scheduled to appear on an early episode of the Who's proposed TV show *Sound and Picture City* alongside fellow guests Bob Dylan and Lulu. The Byrds only criticized the contrived way the Monkees were assembled with "So You Want to Be a Rock and Roll Star," but they respected the Monkees themselves and even invited Nesmith to sit in with them onstage at the Berkeley Community Theatre in August 1968. Byrds bassist Chris Hillman accurately described the Monkee as "a great songwriter and singer" in a 1973 interview with *Zigzag* magazine. Neil Young and Dewey Martin of Buffalo Springfield played on several Monkees recordings. The Springfield also selected longtime friend Tork to introduce them at the Monterey Pop Festival. George Harrison recruited Tork to play banjo on the score he composed for the 1968 film *Wonderwall*. Lennon invited Nesmith to the recording of the orchestra on "A Day in the Life," and the Monkee appears in a filmed document of the session. Perennial genius Brian Wilson was the first signee on a petition calling for their induction into the cliquey Rock and Roll Hall of Fame.

Alternately, *The Monkees* TV show could be embarrassingly status quo at times, particularly with its habitual portrayal of women as personality-devoid sex objects and the cringe-inducing stereotypes of "The Monkees Chow Mein," "Son of a Gypsy," and "It's a Nice Place to Visit." Of such things, Nesmith, Dolenz, Tork, and Jones had no more control than the Beatles had of the depiction of "filthy Easterners" in *Help! The Monkees* did not exist entirely outside of its era, but it certainly subverted it more radically than any comedy program before it.

The reason I'm going on so much about this group that my fellow rock writers belittled and dismissed for some many decades is because I may not have even been a rock writer if not for them. When the Monkees became a media-saturating phenomenon all over again amidst their twentieth anniversary, they sparked my obsession with sixties pop because their jangling guitars, unaffected drums, and pristine harmonies sounded much more organic—much more *real*—to me than Starship, Phil Collins, and all the other synthesized, sanitized stuff clogging the airwaves when I was just the right age to get into music. Reading Erik Lefcowitz's *The Monkees Tale*, the first book to actually take the Monkees seriously, sparked my interest in writing about music. On a more personal note, the Monkees' left-leaning stance on their TV show heavily influenced my own political views when I was growing up in a middle-of-the-road household on decidedly right-leaning Long Island. All of this also explains why I'll be spending so much of the text on the coming pages diving deeply into the work of a band most others would not put in the same league as the Beatles, Dylan, and Hendrix.

That being said, I will admit that some of the future criticisms of the Monkees' music does hold water on their debut album. Admittedly, the primary goal of the "Monkees" project was to sell records, not establish Mike, Micky, Davy, and Peter as artists, yet Mike, who had yet to become a proven hit songwriter (his first smash, the Stone Poney's "Different Drum," was still a long way off), was allowed to write and produce two tracks, even though one was the product of a forced collaboration with Gerry Goffin and Carol King. The result of that uneasy union is "Sweet Young Thing," a truly far-out merger of thumping garage rock and wild Zydeco that sounded utterly unlike anything in the charts. Nesmith's solo composition, the joyous Tex-Mex rave-up "Papa Gene's Blues," was nearly as unique.

The rest of *The Monkees* is more conventional, although quite a bit skirts the group's bubblegum image. "Saturday's Child" is startlingly heavy, and "Tomorrow's Gonna Be Another Day" is a pretty convincingly bluesy garage rocker. "Let's Dance On," a transparent clone of "Twist and Shout," falls short as a composition but cooks as a performance. "Take a Giant Step" features a mid-song psychedelic freak-out. "This Just Doesn't Seem to Be My Day" shifts between dissonant Turk-rock and powdered-wig chamber music. "Last Train to Clarksville," a chiming pop tune about being shipped off to Vietnam, became the Monkees' first massive hit. The rest of the album is either sappy or corny, but *The Monkees* is a better debut than anyone could have expected considering its contrived origins, and the Monkees would quickly develop into one of the sixties' grooviest groups.

QUESTION MARK & THE MYSTERIANS: *96 TEARS*

The definitive garage-rock band began when three sons of Mexican American migrant farmers—Larry Borjas, Bobby Balderrama, and Robert Martinez—began jamming on surf-rock instrumentals around the Bay Area in the early sixties. The Mysterians found their sound when Martinez's brother Rudy changed his name to punctuation (and claimed to be from Mars) and Frank Rodriguez Jr. plugged in his Farfisa. With that, a new mélange of soul rhythm, keyboard riffing, and punk attitude was born.

Question Mark & the Mysterians would deserve a place in any rock book worth its salt if they'd made nothing more than their number one smash "96 Tears," a paragon of bubblegum melody and snotty posturing. The album that hit anchors is solid enough to earn a place in this book as the Mysterians wrangle up a respectable roster of such memorable originals in the "96 Tears" style as "I Need Somebody," "8 Teen," "Upside," and "Midnight Hour" (not the Wilson Pickett classic) as well as a sugary version of T-Bone Walker's blues standard "Stormy Monday."

WILSON PICKETT: *THE EXCITING WILSON PICKETT*

Wilson Pickett did not have the voice of an average-sized man in his mid-twenties. He sounds large and lived in. Scream yourself hoarse for a week, and you still couldn't rasp like Wilson. You sure wouldn't have it in you to replicate his force, freedom, or ingenuity. A gospel singer when he was a boy, Wilson Pickett developed a raw, weathered, sexy style. Just twenty-five when he recorded his third album, he growls effortlessly, agedly, commandingly. *The Exciting Wilson Pickett* lives up to its name and then some. The rhythm section jitters, and the horns cackle and crunch. The lineup of songs is staggering. "Land of 1,000 Dances," "634-5789 (Soulsville, U.S.A.)," "In the Midnight Hour," and "Ninety-Nine and a Half" are some of his definitive songs, and all were hits. His versions of Chris Kenner's "Dances" and "Something Got You," Don Covay's "Mercy Mercy," the Falcons' "You're

So Fine," the Valentino's "She's So Good to Me," and Robert Parker's "Barefootin'" smoke the originals. His own originals "Danger Zone" and "I'm Drifting" are just as hot. The token slow song "It's All Over" is the most nondescript number, but you need it to catch your breath after all the excitement that precedes it.

OTIS REDDING: *THE OTIS REDDING DICTIONARY OF SOUL: COMPLETE AND UNBELIEVABLE*

That title may be unwieldy, but it doesn't lie. The *Otis Redding Dictionary of Soul: Complete and Unbelievable* doesn't get the respect that *Otis Blue* receives, but I think it's a superior album. There's a much wider selection of Redding originals, and each one is fabulous, whether he's in ranting-and-raving mode ("Sweet Lorene," "She Put the Hurt on Me"), sweet-pleading mode ("Fa-Fa-Fa-Fa-Fa [Sad Song]," "My Lover's Prayer"), or somewhere in between ("I'm Sick Y'all").

The final album Otis Redding deliberately recorded during his lifetime. Author's collection.

Redding's excellent originals share vinyl with some of his most masterful and whimsically selected covers. Who would have imagined the king of soul would record the definitive versions of hoary standards like "Tennessee Waltz" and "Try a Little Tenderness"? As he did with the Stones' "Satisfaction" on *Otis Blue*, Redding again takes on the British Invasion, completely revolutionizing the Beatles' "Day Tripper" by losing most of the song's recognizable elements. The M.G.'s only hint at the iconic riff during the chorus. Lennon and McCartney's melody and lyric are essentially exorcised to allow Otis room to vamp in his inimitably funky way. Complete and unbelievable for sure.

PAUL REVERE AND THE RAIDERS: *MIDNIGHT RIDE*

Because of their goofy persona and embarrassing Revolutionary War stage gear, Paul Revere and the Raiders are rarely ranked among the best second-tier bands of the sixties. That's unjust since they made tough, terrific singles and some really consistent albums. The first couple they made with producer Terry Melcher rely too heavily on covers that can't top the originals and make the mistake of democratizing the vocal chores when the group really only had one great singer. And don't let his little ponytail and bowl cut fool you: Mark Lindsay is one of the sixties' best pop soul howlers.

He gets to show off that ability on the Raiders' breakthrough album, which ups the ante of original material without diluting the band's garagey spirit. Okay, the sappy-crap instrumental "Melody for an Unknown Girl" dilutes it to a puddle of nothing, but "There's Always Tomorrow," "Get It On," and "Take a Look at Yourself" kick. Outsiders wrote the two most well known tracks—Barry Mann and Cynthia Weil provide the just-say-no smash "Kicks," and Tommy Boyce and Bobby Hart supply "(I'm Not Your) Steppin' Stone," which would soon be overshadowed by the Monkees' definitive version—but the best track on *Midnight Ride* is Lindsay and keyboardist Revere's own "Louie, Go Home," an earlier song they remake with a perfect balance of garage ferocity and psychedelic freakiness.

THE SPIRIT OF '67

That spirit of garage ferocity and psychedelic freakiness spreads across *The Spirit of '67*, possibly the Raiders' best record. The terrific hits "Hungry," "The Great Airplane Strike" (which I always suspected was directly inspired by the Stones' similarly themed and similar sounding "Flight 505"), and "Good Thing" (ditto the Beach Boys' "Good Vibrations"), which sports harmonies worthy of the Beach Boys, are simple, stomping anthems. They belt out a bit more of the bluesy pop that was their forte on "Louise," "In My Community," and "Our Candidate" and stretch themselves to create tongue-in-cheek parodies of Scott Walker–esque melodrama ("All About Her," "Oh! To Be a Man"), raga rock ("Why? Why? Why?," "1001 Arabian Nights"), and "Eleanor Rigby" chamber pop ("Undecided Man"). *Revolver* for wiseasses.

THE ROLLING STONES: *AFTERMATH*

After three cover-heavy LPs, *Aftermath* completed the Rolling Stones' journey toward self-actualization. If they were to compete with Brian Wilson, Lennon and McCartney, Bob Dylan, Ray Davies, and newcomer Pete Townshend, Mick Jagger and Keith Richards had to finally show they could write an album's worth of strong originals. They also had to hack out a definitive sound for their band. Their first shot was an assortment of dark folk songs and psychotic rockers like "19th Nervous Breakdown" and "Think," but Decca Records refused to release an album with the "sacrilegious" title *Could You Walk on Water?*

During the long period spent negotiating a release with their priggish label, the Stones continued recording, rethought the track lineup, and settled on the record they would put out as *Aftermath* (as in the "aftermath" of the *Could You Walk on Water?* fiasco). The record is sprawling and eclectic. There are remnants of the early Stones' rock and blues influences on "Doncha Bother Me," "Goin' Home," "It's Not Easy," and "Flight 505," a rollicking number about a plane crash. They explore morose English folk with alluring results on "Lady Jane," "Mother's Little Helper," and "I Am Waiting." "Under My Thumb," "Out of Time," and "Stupid Girl" are Motown-style soul numbers that further darkened the Stones image with their nasty misogyny (Brian Jones's history of violence against women fulfilled the horrid promise of that image in the worst way). "High and Dry" is silly C&W. At its most uncharacteristic, the Stones ape Roy Orbison melodrama ("Take It or Leave It") and white-bread Beach Boys harmonies ("What to Do"). Brian Jones keeps things interesting with his marimbas, dulcimer, and keyboards. Such fate-to-the-wind eclecticism shows that the Stones had found their sound: a fluid reworking of the popular sounds of their time strained through a dark sensibility and grounded with a rock-solid swing and Mick Jagger's iconic poses. On *Aftermath*, the Rolling Stones became *The Rolling Stones*.

SAM & DAVE: *HOLD ON, I'M COMIN'*

Sam Moore and Dave Prater were the greatest male duo in the history of soul. With Otis Redding, they were *the* voices of Stax Records, cutting such exuberant, iconic singles as "Hold On, I'm Comin," "Soul Man," and "I Thank You" for the label from 1965 through 1969. Sam & Dave also released a string of strong long players for Stax. Their first, *Hold On, I'm Comin'*, is the hardest, rawest record in their repertoire. Over Booker T. & the M.G.'s' salty bedrock, Sam & Dave explore all the possibilities of duo singing: harmonizing, trading lines, contrasting each other with distinctly different approaches and ranges, dropping encouraging asides off mic, and bouncing off each other in fleet counterpoint, as they do on the magnificent "Ease Me."

DOUBLE DYNAMITE

Also released in 1966, *Double Dynamite* builds on *Hold On* by introducing some unexpected rhythms into the mix with the herky-jerky funk of "Said I Wasn't Gonna Tell Nobody," the stately bounce of "Sweet Pains," the breezy skate of "I Don't Need Nobody (To Tell Me 'Bout My Baby)," and the low-flame pulse of "Home at Last." As is the case with each of these albums, the leadoff track is a big hit single, and hearing "You Got Me Hummin'," it's confounding that radio censors took issue with the mildly suggestive title of "Hold On, I'm Comin'" but apparently didn't have a problem with this track's erotic moaning.

THE SEEDS: *THE SEEDS*

They couldn't claim a string of international hits, but the Seeds were L.A. garage-rock royalty. Sitting on the throne was yowling, howling spaceman Sky Saxon. He and his horde—rippling electric pianist Daryl Hooper, fuzz-faced guitarist Jan Savage, and cro-mag drummer Rick Andridge—spun out two-chord songs simple as nursery rhymes and scary as Grimms' fairy tales. Although they've been accused of recording the same song over and over, there's enough blood running through *The Seeds* to make it a killer record in the *Ramones* vein, and tracks such as the single-minded "Pushin' Too Hard," the mesmeric "Evil Hoodoo," and the chanting "No Escape" are as punk as anything the Ramones and their ilk would do a decade later. The debut single "Can't Seem to Make You Mine" contrasts the prevailing speed and stomp with a dreamy pace, but it also has Saxon's most intense vocal as he erupts into anguished primal screams. I wonder if John Lennon was listening.

SIMON & GARFUNKEL: *PARSLEY, SAGE, ROSEMARY, AND THYME*

Since it's a-wop-bomp-a-loo-bomp beginning, rock and roll seemed to have little space for intellectuals. Yet Paul Simon is the archetypal New York intellectual, and though the folk duo he led got their dose of rock and roll without his knowledge when producer Tom Wilson had studio musicians add electric guitars and drums to their plaintive "The Sound of Silence," Simon and singing partner Art Garfunkel went along with the gambit and became superstars.

Simon & Garfunkel completed their trip from folk to folk rock on *Parsley, Sage, Rosemary, and Thyme*. There's still much less rock in their folk rock than there is in Dylan or the Byrds. Aside from the gnarly "Big Bright Green Pleasure Machine" and the embarrassingly clueless Dylan spoof "A Simple Desultory Philippic (or How I Was Robert McNamara'd into Submission)," this is a delicate record that often confronts somber subject matter. This is true of two other tracks that have aged poorly: "7 O'Clock News/ Silent Night," which superimposes the grimmest mid-sixties headlines over the titular Christmas carol with heavy-handed irony, and "The Dangling Conversation," a minor hit that surveys the communication breakdown between a pair of pretentious intellectuals, falling into its own pit of pretentiousness in the process.

"The Dangling Conversation" is still an exquisitely arranged and sung track with the attention to detail that defines *Parsley, Sage, Rosemary, and Thyme*. "Homeward Bound" and "For Emily, Wherever I May Fine Her" capture a sense of movement through open spaces that is a Simon & Garfunkel specialty. The candlelit "Scarborough Fair/Canticle" couldn't sound more intimate. Elsewhere, Simon & Garfunkel get taut and neurotic ("Patterns"), lighthearted and mildly corny ("The 59th Street Bridge Song [Feelin' Groovy]"), and adrenalized ("Poem on the Underground Wall," which conveys the thrill of spraying graffiti in a New York subway). Everything hangs together due to the duo's consistently expressive and graceful harmonies and the equally intricate arrangements Simon helped concoct.

SMALL FACES: *SMALL FACES*

British mod culture was defined by rigorous rules of style and musical tastes. Razor-sharp mohair suits were donned for shaking all night to the latest Northern soul (any American soul records popular in Northern England) while pilled to the clouds on bennies and dexies. Small Faces were the quintessential homegrown mod band, and their eponymous debut is easily one of the best debuts of the British Invasion era. Even the Who's *My Generation* wasn't quite this raw, probably because Roger Daltrey had yet to perfect his primal scream. Steve Marriott sounds like he shrieked his way out of the womb. The band's songwriting is still rudimentary, but the bone-pulverizing performances of "What'Cha Gonna Do About It," "Come On Children," "E Too D," and "You Better Believe It" make up for any compositional shortcomings. There are also potent covers of Sam Cooke's "Shake" and Willie Dixon's "You Need Love" (shiftily retitled "You Need

Loving" and credited to Marriott and Ronnie Lane, a con that Led Zeppelin would later double down on by renaming it "Whole Lotta Love" and claiming the composition as their own). The big British hit "Sha La La La Lee" and "Sorry She's Mine" point toward the poppier path on which Small Faces would soon embark, but even those tracks are pretty wild. Perhaps no group was ever as simultaneously heavy and swinging as Small Faces was on their first record.

THE STANDELLS: *DIRTY WATER*

The Standells of Los Angeles is another band that helped define sixties garage rock. They also gave Boston its signature song when they recorded former Four Prep Ed Cobb's "Dirty Water." With its sneering delivery, greasy riff, and show of solidarity with "muggers and thieves" (cool people, all), the track defined the band as bad boys even though Larry Tamblyn, Dick Dodd, Tony Valentino, and Gary Lane insisted that they were nice, clean-cut guys. Going that route would do them no favors, and the Standells were at their best when playing the roles of druggies ("Medication"), rabble-rousers ("Riot on Sunset Strip"), and letches (the widely banned "Try It").

The Standells pulled off that masquerade without fail on their debut album. *Dirty Water* is a nasty collection of menace and mayhem. The title track and the minor classic "Sometimes Good Guys Don't Wear White" are widely acknowledged as fabulous, but so are relative oddities like the sexy/stoned "Medication," the lascivious "Little Sally Tease," and the fuzzy "Rari." A cover of "19th Nervous Breakdown" won't cost Mick Jagger any sleep, but it is right at home here. Even the token ballad "Pride and Joy" is tough.

WHY PICK ON ME/SOMETIMES GOOD GUYS DON'T WEAR WHITE

The Standells' follow-up, *Why Pick on Me/Sometimes Good Guys Don't Wear White*, goes too soft on tracks like the Italian-language "Mi Hai Fatto Innamorare" and the almost Four Seasons–like "The Girl and the Moon." Still, the sophomore album with the name I don't have the energy to type again has enough grungy smashes to redeem it. "Black Hearted Woman," "Mr. Nobody," "I Hate to Leave You," and the two singles for which it is named do exactly what you want Standells tracks to do, though "Sometimes Good Guys Don't Wear White" is a pointless rerun after its appearance on *Dirty Water*.

THE SUPREMES: *THE SUPREMES A' GO-GO*

Motown's biggest stars made some of the label's best LPs, but 1966's *The Supremes A' Go-Go* is not one of them. It leans way too hard on remakes of past hits by other artists. Not only are the Supremes' versions of "This Old Heart of Mine," "Shake Me, Wake Me," "Baby, I Need Your Loving," and "Get Ready" redundant by nature, but Diana Ross's tepid vocals also pale in comparison to the Isley Brothers', the Four Tops', and the Temptations' committed performances. Mary Wilson does a more convincing job of holding her own against performances past with her lead on "Come and Get These Memories," but it still doesn't measure up to Martha Reeves.

The Supremes recorded a bunch of other covers during sessions for the covers-heavy *Supremes A' Go-Go*, including "Satisfaction," "It's Not Unusual," "Mickey's Monkey," and "Heat Wave," a version of which would find a home on their next and arguably best album. Author's collection.

Nevertheless, *The Supremes A' Go-Go* is a milestone album because it is the first album by an all-female group to top the *Billboard* chart, and it did so on the strength of two of the Supremes' very best hits: the jubilant "You Can't Hurry Love" and the grinding "Love Is Like an Itching in My Heart." There are also a couple of interesting covers that don't invite unflattering comparisons with past Motown hits. Ross still sounds like she's checking her watch on a version of "These Boots Are Made for Walking," but the arrangement is very cool with its *Twilight Zone* guitar riff that runs through the whole thing. She rouses herself sufficiently for a set-closing take on "Hang on Sloopy." A chunky version of Barrett Strong's "Money" is the one Motown remake on which the arrangement is sufficiently distinctive and Ross gets herself sufficiently worked up.

THE TURTLES: *YOU BABY/LET ME BE*

Everyone knows about the backlash Bob Dylan suffered when he made his transformation from topical folkie to absurdist rocker (queue squeals of "Judas!"). Less legendary is the similar path the Turtles took at the beginning of their career. The group best known for sugar-schlock ditties like "Happy Together" and "Elenore" once had a following of serious folk fans who'd gravitated to the band after the Turtles scored a hit with Dylan's "It Ain't Me Babe." When they recorded P. F. Sloan's "You Baby," a wad of bubble gum thick enough to clog the Mariana Trench, the folkies' screeched of betrayal and headed for the exit.

Thus were the Turtles free to develop into the hit-making machine we know and love today, but the shift was not a sudden one. Their second album, *You Baby/Let Me Be*, is nearly as striking a transitional album as Dylan's own *Bringing It All Back Home*. Its title even name checks both the last of their folk-rock hits and the wonderfully poppy piffle that gave them their second wind. The rest of the album is no less muddled, trading off sardonic rallying cries like the anti-conformity conga line "Down in Suburbia" and the bluesy "Pall Bearing, Ball Bearing World" with frivolous, frantic garage-rock–like "Flyin' High" (featuring one of Al Nichol's hottest guitar riffs) and the Kinky "Almost There" as well as the pure pop of "You Baby," "I Know You'll Be There," and "Just a Room." Regardless of what the Turtles attempt on *You Baby/It Ain't Me Babe*, they invariably get it right with their impeccable harmonies, tough backbeat, and budding songwriting skills.

TURTLES '66 (RELEASED 2017)

During a commercial low point between their previous top-twenty hit ("You Baby") and their first number one ("Happy Together"), the Turtles recorded another album's worth of material with producer Bones Howe in 1966. "Grim Reaper of Love," "Outside Chance," "Can I Get to Know You Better," and a version of Vera Lynn's "We'll Meet Again" were all released on singles, and they all flopped. The rest of the tracks were shelved, relegating what would have been the band's second album of 1966 to the "lost" pile along with albums like the Rolling Stones' *Could You Walk on Water?* and the Beach Boys' *SMiLE*.

While the Turtles' album would not have been nearly as momentous as either of those releases, it certainly would have been as solid as any of their own earlier records. "Grim Reaper" and "Outside Chance" are two of the Turtles' coolest recordings. "Can I Get to Know You Better" is a classic bubblegum bridge between "You Baby" and "She'd Rather Be with Me." Their version of "We'll Meet Again" is a more suitably kooky *Dr. Strangelove* tribute than the reserved one that ended the Byrds' *Mr. Tambourine Man*. A few of the other album tracks are weak, but "I Can't Stop" is a good hunk of garage rock, "I Get Out of Breath" is a neat recall of the Turtles' early folk-rock sound, and "Wrong from the Start" is a fine saunter into country-pop territory. "So Goes Love" is eerie and pretty, and so is "She'll Come Back," which sounds like it inspired the Monkees' "Words"—it probably didn't, even though future Monkees producer Chip Douglas was playing bass with the Turtles during these sessions.

THE WHO: *A QUICK ONE*

The Who's non-songwriting triad were nearly bankrupt by the time the band recorded their sophomore album. Manager Kit Lambert's solution was to commission two songs each from Roger Daltrey, John Entwistle, and Keith Moon to provide the guys with a little extra revenue. The results could have been disastrous. Instead, Moon turned out two infectiously wacky numbers: the Beach Boys homage/Beatles parody "I Need You" and a crazed instrumental polka called "Cobwebs and Strange" (actually nicked from incidental music from the NBC-TV series *Man from Interpol*). Daltrey was capable of completing only a single song, but "See Me Way" is a rolling little Buddy Holly–influenced tune that is all the sweeter for its brevity.

The real shocker—in more ways than one—is John Entwistle, who emerged as a writer with great flair and genuine originality. The bassist's macabre wit and monstrous riffing come to the fore on the deathless "Boris the Spider" and the underrated "Whiskey Man."

Pete Townshend was tasked with filling out the rest of the record but had only three completed numbers on hand. The best of these was the definitive power-pop marvel "So Sad About Us." Lambert had another stroke of genius: he suggested that Townshend string together several of his unfinished compositions to create a single piece that would fill up half of side B. Townshend later said he was initially skeptical, thinking, "Rock songs are two minutes fifty by tradition!" A little cajoling from Lambert awakened Townshend's latent pretentiousness, and the writer set to work on formulating the piece he would later refer to as his first "mini opera" and "*Tommy*'s parents." Indeed, "A Quick One, While He's Away" is of historic importance because it is rock's first extended narrative (boy goes rambling, girl commits infidelity with lecherous engine driver in boy's absence, boy returns home, and all is forgiven) and plants the rock-opera seeds that would grow into *Tommy*, thereby solidifying the Who's career in commercial (and, arguably, artistic) terms.

That's all well and good, but the real appeal of "A Quick One" is its delightful melodiousness, its schoolboy dirty humor, and the rounds of "You are forgiven!" that provide its orgasmic climax. Onstage, the Who would push "A Quick One" into a harder direction, giving them a live tour de force they'd never

For some reason, pop artist Alan Aldridge depicted bassist John Entwistle playing a twelve-string guitar. He's playing it lefty for reasons of symmetry. Author's collection.

parallel (their performance of it in *The Rolling Stones Rock and Roll Circus* is the best live performance I've ever heard). Yet I still prefer the studio version, which is more of a power-pop epic and retains verses and instrumental passages lost during live renditions. The studio version also allows Entwistle to sing the role of Ivor the Engine Driver without any obnoxious interruptions from Daltrey. Bonus points for that, too.

The rewards of "A Quick One, While He's Away" would be far reaching, not only providing the Who with their greatest live vehicle but also establishing seeds that would blossom into the rock opera that would make them international superstars. "A Quick One" is also a thrilling nine-minute ride full of dirty schoolboy humor and concluding with a fittingly operatic volley of harmonies that provides what may be the most spellbinding moment in the entire Who discography.

THE YARDBIRDS: *YARDBIRDS (AKA: ROGER THE ENGINEER)*

The Yardbirds' reputation as an academy for prominent British blues guitarists—Eric Clapton, Jeff Beck, and Jimmy Page all passed through their ranks—tends to overshadow their achievements as a band. The guys made some tough blues rock, but they also played with odder forms, especially after Clapton left the band, when they started to stray from their basic blues origins and started experimenting more. A more visionary guitarist than Clapton, Jeff Beck was the perfect commander for this phase.

This is also when the Yardbirds released their only official studio album in their British homeland. Their debut *Five Live Yardbirds* was a live album (duh), and both *For Your Love* and *Having a Rave Up* were U.S.-only singles compilations. The group finally released a proper album in 1966, and *Yardbirds* (known informally as "Roger the Engineer" because of guitarist Chris Dreja's cover illustration of, *errr*, Roger the Engineer) is a powerhouse showcase for Jeff Beck's innovative guitar work and the group's swinging blues and Asian- and African-influenced brand of psychedelia. The album's most spectacular melding of both these influences is the Yardbirds' final hit single, "Over, Under, Sideways, Down," but "Lost Woman," "He's Always There," and "Rack My Mind" are nearly as exciting. "Ever Since the World Began" and "Turn to Earth" find the Yardbirds at their most ominous.

Because the title of Chris Dreja's illustration "Roger the Engineer" appears so prominently on the cover of the Yardbirds' eponymous album, most people think the album is actually called *Roger the Engineer*. This reissue from 1983 includes both sides of the fab "Happening Ten Years Time Ago" b/w "Psycho Daisies" single as bonus tracks. Author's collection.

Yardbirds is terrific, but it still feels transitional in the same way a lot of 1966 LPs do. Mainly a singles band, the Yardbirds couldn't come up with quite enough material for a masterpiece. The instrumentals "The Nazz Are Blue," "Hot House of Ormagarishid," and "Jeff's Boogie" (an uncredited cover of Chuck Berry's "Guitar Boogie") are all fun but a touch flimsy. Beck left shortly after making *The Yardbirds*, leaving the group in the hands of Jimmy Page, who led it through its most uninspired period before stripping it down and rebuilding it into the New Yardbirds, better known as Led Zeppelin.

1967

The rock LP had been etching out its position as rock's chief artistic vehicle for over a year. The Beatles had stopped filling out their albums with covers when they released *Rubber Soul* in late 1965. That album directly inspired Brian Wilson to create an even more cohesive piece with *Pet Sounds* in 1966. The Beach Boys' album would serve the same inspirational role when the Beatles got back into the studio at the end of that year to begin work on the album that would give the LP its ultimate foothold in 1967, the year that rock LPs started outselling both singles and "adult pop" LPs (albums by Sinatra and his ilk) for the first time.

The influence of *Sgt. Pepper's Lonely Hearts Club Band* was immediate. In February 1967, the single release of "Strawberry Fields Forever," a track recorded at the very beginning of the album's sessions, revealed just how far the Beatles were taking the possibilities of the recording studio. They embellished a basic band track consisting of guitar, drums, bass, and Mellotron (an early synthesizer that used actual analogue tapes to replicate the sounds of other instruments) with a totally different take featuring studio musicians on cellos and trumpets. Through a fortuitous feat that required slightly slowing the speed of the orchestral track, George Martin edited the two tracks together to complete the ultimate expression of compositional and studio creativity, a recording I personally believe to be the best ever produced. Brian Wilson was apparently so devastated by "Strawberry Fields Forever" that he started having second thoughts about his own *SMiLE*, an album he partially conceived as a riposte to the Beatles' recent experimentation and one that may have been *the* record of 1967 had he completed it.

Less paranoid artists took healthier inspiration from "Strawberry Fields" and tales of the Beatles' studio exploits. Such *Pepper*-esque platters as *Their Satanic Majesties Request* and *Axis: Bold as Love* were under way even before the May 26 release of *Sgt. Pepper's*. Tellingly, several others—*Forever Changes, After Bathing at Baxter's, Pisces, Aquarius, Capricorn, & Jones, Ltd.*—were started in June. Some were created in parallel, as fellow Abbey Road occupiers Pink Floyd may have taken inspiration from the sounds bleeding beneath the Beatles' door (and vice versa). A great deal of great music was born throughout those magical post-*Pepper* months of 1967. From that point on, the album would be regarded as more than a souvenir for record buyers with money to burn. It would be rock's central mode of expression.

THE ACTION: *BRAIN* (RELEASED IN 1995)

During the mid-sixties, the Action was one of the leading mod combos in Britain, bashing out Northern soul covers with silky voiced front man Reg King. As tastes began to change during the psychedelic era, even the rootsiest bands were expected to progress with the times. This resulted in some embarrassing music (for example, all of the Animals' forays into psychedelia), but the Action was more than up to the task. Instead of jumping headlong into weirdness-for-the-sake-of-weirdness, they prodded their tight rhythm section toward more open vistas and wrote an impressive and thoughtful selection of songs. Reg King's voice remained as clear and expressive as it had been when the Action was playing Motown covers.

After the Action released singles on Parlophone for a couple of years, that label's George Martin signed them to his own imprint, AIR, so they could finally cut their first LP. The Action completed an album's worth of demos and one fully orchestrated Martin production before EMI decided the record was not worth releasing. The universally ecstatic reviews that greeted the sessions' release decades later show just how wrongheaded EMI was. *Brain* (now better known as *Rolled Gold* after its release on Reaction Recordings in 2002) is superb even though the arrangements are much simpler than the lavish ones Martin surely would have concocted had a proper album been green-lit. Perhaps that is for the best because this disc sounds progressive *and* raw. One could imagine brass or sitars or Mellotron on gnarly tracks like "Love Is All," "Strange Roads," "Brain," and "Look at the View," but they don't necessarily need such trimmings. The Action never got the chance to get a taste of the success most other artists in this book enjoyed, but it would have been a veritable tragedy if we'd never gotten to hear the wonderful music reconstructed on *Brain* at all.

THE BEACH BOYS: *SMILE* (RELEASED IN 2011)

After completing *Pet Sounds*, Brian Wilson began reimagining the very process of producing rock records. Traditionally, a band would perform a song straight through while putting it to tape. Sometimes producers would edit sections of different takes to create the best possible finished product, but those sections were generally pulled from complete performances. Brian Wilson started deliberately recording pieces of music section by section without necessarily having a specific idea of how those pieces would fit together. The first major product of that approach, "Good Vibrations," was a phenomenally time-consuming and expensive project, but the success was undeniable. The Beach Boys got their third number one hit single and blew many a mind with its combination of jazzy bass, mystical lyricism, powerhouse choruses, and the sci-fi whistle of the Theremin, an odd instrument that requires the player to manipulate its pitch manually without actual physical contact.

When Wilson schemed to make an entire album using the same collage-like method that produced "Good Vibrations," we imagined the first rock album as art piece. This was years before *The Dark Side of the Moon*, years before *Tommy*. It was even before Paul McCartney devised his loose concept for *Sgt. Pepper's Lonely Hearts Club Band*. *SMiLE* was to be an album of segues and suites rather than the usual dozen individual songs. One cluster of songs would trek through American history, observing the arrival of Europeans and how they would change the country's terrain with little regard for ecological balance. The second would be an oblique perspective of the relationship between parents and children. The final would be a programmatic representation of the four natural elements.

To put a voice to his complex ideas and weird music, Brian Wilson hired former child actor and poet Van Dyke Parks, whose lyrics are the perfect melding of recognizable imagery and his own inimitable psychedelic jibber-jabber ("columnated ruins domino"). Songs such as "Heroes and Villains," "Cabin-Essence," and "Surf's Up" are brilliantly conceived, picturesque, self-contained suites.

As Brian Wilson toiled away on *SMiLE*, the burgeoning rock press became aware of this project that promised to be unlike anything the world had ever heard. Wilson alternately portrayed it as an avant-garde comedy album and a "teenage symphony to God." Dennis Wilson vowed that it would "make *Pet Sounds* stink" during a late 1966 interview with *Hit Parader*. The teasers were plentiful, but the Beach Boys' *SMiLE* never materialized. The reasons were just as diverse and plentiful as the descriptions of what it might have been. The release of the Beatles' monumental and highly experimental single "Penny Lane"/"Strawberry Fields Forever" left Brian feeling like an also-ran, as did the subsequent release of *Sgt. Pepper's* as he struggled to figure out how to piece his own album together. Simple-minded Mike Love had sabotaged it with his "don't fuck with the formula" demands (though both Love and Wilson insist that Mike never specifically said those infamous words). Brian Wilson thought the music was inappropriate for the Beach Boys' audience. He had "lost his mind."

In place of *SMiLE* was a thin interloper called *Smiley Smile*, which sounded more like a collection of hastily made demos than the operatic record Brian Wilson had been making for close to a year. Over the next several years, bits of the original sessions started to leak out. "Cabin-Essence" and "Our Prayer" appeared on 1969's *20/20*. There was the title track of 1971's *Surf's Up*. In the eighties, bootlegs began bobbing to the surface. If the Beach Boys were never going to release the largely unfinished music Wilson recorded during the *SMiLE* sessions, fans were going to get their hands on it by other means and assemble their own versions of the album. This is the main reason *SMiLE* is so unique: it is the first album that forced fans to interact with it directly. We had to make our own edits and running orders on cassettes. They enjoyed debates on how it was supposed to be heard and what tracks were really intended to be included in the mythic "Elements" suite that supposedly would have climaxed the album.

Years before I became aware of the bootlegs and the cult and the myriad fan mixes, I first heard about *SMiLE* in *The Beach Boys: An American Band*. And what did I do as soon as I finished watching that 1985 documentary? I took my only two post-surf/hot-rod Beach Boys records—*20/20* and *Good Vibrations: The Best of The Beach Boys*—and made my own "SMiLE" tape. The result, which mostly consisted of non-*SMiLE* era stuff like "I Went to Sleep" and "Friends," had little to do with the Beach Boys' lost album, but it shows how hungry even new fans such as myself were for that magical, spooky, thrillingly experimental album we'd never really get to hear. Sure there are the bootlegs, the thirty minutes of *SMiLE* tracks on 1993's *Good Vibrations: Thirty Years of the Beach Boys* box set, the 2004

solo album *Brian Wilson Presents Smile*. All
consolation prizes.

The *SMiLE Sessions* set that Capitol
Records officially released in 2011 is really
another consolation prize. Although the producers offer their own high-tech *SMiLE*
mix tape featuring complete original sessions, unfinished backing tapes, and elements pulled from demos and recordings
completed after the final official *SMiLE*
sessions in May 1967, it isn't what the Beach
Boys would have released that year had Brian
Wilson been able to complete his vision. But
as consolation prizes go, it is beyond anything
SMiLE obsessives could have ever expected.
Content-wise, it is more than we could have
ever hoped for. The set contains some of
the most dazzlingly imaginative music ever
made. Brian takes the experimentalism of
the earlier *Pet Sounds* past the point of sanity, and the results are mystical, magical,

I used to store my records in
stacked plastic crates. Shortly
after I finally got my copy of the
fabled *SMiLE Sessions*, the crates
buckled under the weight of all
those records. The only one that
got damaged was *SMiLE*. I guess
I had it coming, but I still wish
my copy of *Rollin'* by the Bay
City Rollers had gotten creased
instead. That album sucks.
Author's collection.

mesmerizing—a jigsaw puzzle in which none of the pieces should fit, but
they do in a way that almost makes it all sound like pop music.

In a reissue-crazy environment that sees rarities and re-creations
released regularly, the release of *The SMiLE Sessions* is something else. It
is not merely an opportunity to hear some amazing music for the first time.
The SMiLE Sessions is more like discovering that the Loch Ness Monster
exists or finding proof that whirring UFOs actually do abduct yahoos and
spirit them into the sky. *The SMiLE Sessions* is mythology made real.

SMILEY SMILE

But *The SMiLE Sessions* is a triumph for 2011. Tripping back in the summer of 1967, things were looking bleak for the Beach Boys. While their
chief rivals the Beatles were dropping jaws with *Sgt. Pepper's Lonely
Hearts Club Band*, Brian Wilson terminated his struggle to create *SMiLE*.
After accepting an invitation to perform at the taste-making Monterey Pop
Festival, the Beach Boys pulled out supposedly out of fear that they would
look pathetically unhip sharing a stage with the likes of Hendrix, the Who,

and Jefferson Airplane. Unable to follow up on the smash commercial and artistic success of "Good Vibrations," the Beach Boys floundered.

If the Beach Boys could not (or would not) keep up with pop's rapid progress, they would at least keep working. In the waning months of this ignominious year, they released two albums. While *Smiley Smile* is a pale shadow of the grand *SMiLE*, it was at least weird enough to sound fairly contemporary. And along with the two momentous singles that ground *Smiley Smile*—"Good Vibrations" and "Heroes and Villains"—it has some pretty little sketches, such as the psychedelic doo-wop of "With Me Tonight" and the heavenly Hawaiian sojourn "Little Pad."

WILD HONEY

The Beach Boys' final album of 1967 was much stronger than *Smiley Smile*, eschewing weird psych trends for an earthy soul sound exemplified by the divine minor hit "Darlin'," the funky title track, and an unexpectedly terrific cover of Stevie Wonder's "I Was Made to Love Her." Ten days before Dylan got all the credit for popping the psychedelic balloon with *John Wesley Harding*, the Beach Boys had done it first with *Wild Honey*.

THE BEATLES: *SGT. PEPPER'S LONELY HEARTS CLUB BAND*

No album would do more to establish the LP as a singular art form than *Sgt. Pepper's Lonely Hearts Club Band*. The Beatles' seventh album would impact the pop world even before its release, and after it detonated on May 26, 1967, it immediately affected nearly every release that followed it in 1967 and continued to influence albums for decades to come. As the first rock album to include its lyrics printed on the sleeve, *Sgt. Pepper's* emphasized that rock artists now had more to say than "Tutti Frutti Oh-Rooti."

Despite its unquestionable importance, a great deal of the *Sgt. Pepper's* legend is due to right circumstances/right time. After their achievements on *Rubber Soul* and *Revolver*, the Beatles were possibly the only pop group widely acknowledged as genuine artists. The progress they made with those albums caught the world's ear. The compositional and recording innovations of their "Penny Lane" b/w "Strawberry Fields Forever" single released in February 1967 increased anticipation for what the Beatles might do next.

No Beatle was more aware of the band's high-stakes position than Paul McCartney, who ensured that their next album would be something special.

He brought the project together, writing most of its songs, coming up with the loose "concept" (he imagined each song as the product of a different, wacky hippie band), and giving the album its mouthful title (a tribute to the longwinded names American West Coast bands like Big Brother and the Holding Company and Quicksilver Messenger Service were adopting). The lack of silent pauses between tracks (banding) abets the illusion that the LP is a singular artistic statement. Some tracks segue into each other. With such built-in mystique and self-conscious "artistic value," *Sgt. Pepper's Lonely Hearts Club Band* was instantly hailed as the greatest rock album ever made—and likely the greatest rock album that ever *would be* made.

Much to its benefit, *Sgt. Pepper's* is no longer saddled with its unrealistic—and frankly undeserved—status. As undeniably influential as it is, it's not even the greatest Beatles album. There's too much of an emphasis on oompah beats, and a few of the songs are not sufficiently earthshaking ("Fixing a Hole," "Good Morning Good Morning," "She's Leaving Home," "Within You Without You"). For all the album's supposed innovation, there isn't much on *Sgt. Pepper's* that the Beatles hadn't already done. We'd already heard the brass that permeates the record on "Got to Get You into My Life" and "Yellow Submarine." "Within You Without You" revisits the raga rock of "Love You To" without the vital aggression. The tape loops of "Being for the Benefit of

Naturally, the most famous album of all time also has the most famous album cover. Pop artist Peter Blake designed the life-size collage and Michael Cooper took the photo. Author's collection.

Mr. Kite" sound tame after "Tomorrow Never Knows." "She's Leaving Home" is "Eleanor Rigby" with more musicians and less bite.

Held up to reasonable standards, *Sgt. Pepper's* is a great album, and even those aforementioned slight songs display the group's melodic and lyrical sophistication and George Martin's production brilliance. The great songs—of which there are many—are excellently executed in every respect. The title track squashes accusations that the album is devoid of punchy rock and roll, even if it does veer off into big-band pomp. "With a Little Help from My Friends" is the ultimate Ringo vehicle, and its genial message is tarted up with enough weird Lennon wit to skirt sentimentality (the "it" Ringo sees when he turns out the light is supposedly his penis). "Lucy in the Sky with Diamonds" projects Lennon's most endearingly whimsical pictures over ethereal verses and robust choruses. "Getting Better" seems like the record's most straightforward track until Indian tambouras intrude on the simple four-piece rock-band arrangement and the complex lyrical back-and-forth between McCartney and Lennon. "Being for the Benefit of Mr. Kite" and "Lovely Rita" are fanciful, colorful characterizations and two of the album's most underrated and fun numbers.

And then the Beatles break the whimsical spell of *Sgt. Pepper's Lonely Hearts Club Band* for a big, big comedown. Roadwork needs to be done. A man dies in a car crash. Time to get up and go to work. This is the mundane stuff songs like "Lucy in the Sky with Diamonds" and "Being for the Benefit of Mr. Kite" did not address. The arrangement is anything but mundane. It is a horror show of Ringo's cavernous drumming and an orchestra's apocalyptic mushroom cloud. The final note is pure doom. "A Day in the Life" is the track that makes good on *Sgt. Pepper's* promise as the most progressive pop album of all time even if its others do not.

THE BEATLES IN AMERICA: *MAGICAL MYSTERY TOUR*

And so Dave Dexter Jr. was banished to the land of the Blue Meanies, and *Sgt. Pepper's Lonely Hearts Club Band* had rescued the Beatles—and pop music—from ever being treated with anything less than respect again. However, since they chose to release the sound track to their homemade TV movie *Magical Mystery Tour* on a format that was on its way out in the United Kingdom (the *Magical Mystery Tour* double-EP set was released just days after the EP chart was discontinued in the United Kingdom, causing it to miss the number one spot it would had taken if it wasn't being held from the top spot of the singles chart by the Beatles' own "Hello Goodbye") and nearly unsellable in America, Capitol was forced to do some more tinkering.

In earlier years, the EP was a very viable medium in England, functioning as a more affordable alternative to the LP. Songs such as "Twist and Shout" and "Yesterday," which headed hit singles in the United States, performed similar roles on EPs in England. In the summer of 1964, the Beatles bopped to number one with *Long Tall Sally*, their first EP consisting of tracks unavailable in any other format in the United Kingdom. By the beginning of the following year, it would sell a million copies all over the world.

One market that did not cotton to *Sally* was the United States. The extended play simply did not sell there, and only two Beatles EPs—*Four by the Beatles* and *4 by the Beatles*—would ever chart there (an EP would not go to number one in America until the release of Alice in Chains' *Jar of Flies* CD in 1994).

That was 1964. Three years later, the EP was even further out of favor in America. That might have changed had the *Magical Mystery Tour* EP been released in the United States and not been available in any other format. Certainly, American fans would have broadened their horizons if an EP had been the only way to obtain "Magical Mystery Tour," "Your Mother Should Know," "The Fool on the Hill," "Flying," and "Blue Jay Way" (the set's most noteworthy track, "I Am the Walrus," was available on the back of the number one smash "Hello Goodbye"). That would not be an issue since Capitol took no chances and leaned on their old format of compiling recent tracks with songs the Beatles intended to release only on 45.

This time, it worked quite splendidly. While there are those who prefer the American *Rubber Soul* to its British counterpart or think *Meet the Beatles!* is a stronger album than *With the Beatles*, only the purest purist could prefer the *Magical Mystery Tour* EP to Capitol's LP. Beyond the minor irritation of having to lift the needle and flip the record every few minutes—beyond the bummer of shrinking a groovy LP-sized booklet of photos, comics, lyrics, and stories to EP size (perhaps less of a crime was shrinking the front cover, which is surely the Beatles' ugliest)—there's the fundamental issue of the content. Unlike *A Hard Day's Night* or *Help!*, films for which the Beatles produced mostly excellent new material, some of the *Magical Mystery Tour* sound track selections are weak. Much of it recycles the *Pepper* sound with Paul grafting the brass that decorated the title track of his last album to another title song that isn't nearly as strong. "Your Mother Should Know" revisits the nostalgia jazz of "When I'm 64" with a flimsier, more repetitious song. "Blue Jay Way" is very repetitious too, though its fazed-out atmosphere has a definite allure. "The Fool on the Hill" is a good ballad, but "Flying"—funky as it is and mesmerizing as its tape-loop finish may be—is straight-up filler.

There are reasons why this wasn't the Beatles' best crop of tunes. They'd spent so much creative energy on *Sgt. Pepper's*—and their last five years of near-constant work—and needed time to recoup their inspiration. Instead, Paul pushed them to keep working so he could complete a film that wasn't an ambition his bandmates shared. John and George could force out only one song each, and those two tracks were arguably the best ones on the EP set. The recent death of manager and friend Brian Epstein made matters a lot more complicated. The guys were severely saddened, which is not the ideal mood for creating the kinds of jolly numbers their frivolous film required.

By bolstering a selection of pretty okay songs with such phenomenal singles as "Strawberry Fields Forever" and "Penny Lane" and good ones such as "Hello Goodbye," "Baby You're a Rich Man," and "All You Need Is

Love," the whole project becomes stronger. No longer do so-so tracks like "Your Mother Should No" and "Flying" constitute such a large percentage of the entire platter. They are merely passing moments on the way to "I Am the Walrus," "Strawberry Fields Forever," and "Penny Lane." On the downside, the LP was rushed into stores so quickly (even beating the British EP by eleven days) that proper stereo mixes of "Penny Lane," "Baby You're a Rich Man," and "All You Need Is Love" could not be completed, leaving these tracks in lousy duophonic mixes on the stereo LP (a complete stereo mix would not appear until 1971). It was almost as if Dave Dexter never left.

Capitol's *Magical Mystery Tour* was a big hit on the commercial level too. No matter that the TV movie advertised on the album cover hadn't even been released in the United States and wouldn't be until a one-off showing at a fund-raiser for the underground Liberation News Service at the Fillmore East in August 1968. *Magical Mystery Tour* enjoyed the biggest sales of any LP in the United States to that point, moving 8 million copies in the first three weeks of its release. It even performed fabulously in the United Kingdom, where it went as high as thirty-one on the charts as an import in January 1968. As the EP continued to evaporate, the Capitol album was officially released in the United Kingdom in 1976. When the Beatles' albums were released on compact disc for the first time in 1987 and the British versions of these albums finally standardized around the world, *Magical Mystery Tour* was the only Capitol album canonized alongside *Please Please Me*, *With the Beatles*, *Beatles for Sale*, and the rest. As its contents were almost completely unique (only "All You Need Is Love" appeared elsewhere on the *Yellow Submarine* sound track), it made more sense to put this one American album out intact instead of shuffling its contents into the *Past Masters* compilations. This continued to hold true for the 2009 remaster series and the 2014 *Beatles in Mono* vinyl box set. For one man, the *Magical Mystery Tour* album has been standard going back a lot further than 1987: in 1974, John Lennon himself rated it as one of his favorite Beatles LPs "because it was so weird."

CAPTAIN BEEFHEART AND HIS MAGIC BAND: *SAFE AS MILK*

Less than two years before releasing *Trout Mask Replica*, the album that would forever endear them to defiantly intellectual rock critics, Captain Beefheart and His Magic Band put out a record that was actually listenable.

Despite its comparative poppiness and wholesome title, *Safe as Milk* isn't exactly *Up, Up and Away*. Don Van Vliet's pre–Tom Waits frog howl is still way out there, and the Magic Band's fuzzed-up and freaked-out interpretation of the blues is still intense. What really puts this album over the top is its totally consistent, totally eclectic songwriting. The group takes a mud dive into garage rock ("Zig-Zag Wanderer"), thereminized psychedelia ("Electricity"), hippity-hoppity country pop ("Yellow Brick Road"), pseudo–Native American percussive madness ("Abba Zaba"), irascible murk ("Autumn's Child"), and slow-grind soul ("I'm Glad," a song I'm convinced former neighbors of mine fucked to on repeat every Sunday morning) and come up dirty every time.

BLOSSOM TOES: *WE ARE EVER SO CLEAN*

Blossom Toes come in at the more extreme end of British psychedelia. With their crazed and campy lyrics and cacophonous arrangements, they make Syd Barrett's Pink Floyd sound like the Association. On repeated listens, the melodiousness under the madness starts to emerge. No acclimation is necessary for instantly appealing pop like "Telegram Tuesday," "When the Alarm Clock Rings," "What's It For," the Move-esque "I Will Bring You This and That," and "I'll Be Late For Tea," a marvelous Kinks imitation that fuses that band's early heaviness with their mid-sixties pastoralism. Borderline grating pieces such as "Track for Speedy Freaks" (snippets of all the album's tracks played simultaneously)," "The Remarkable Saga of the Frozen Dog" and "Look at Me I'm You," which sounds like William Burroughs diced up and randomly reassembled the master tapes of *Revolver*, take more getting used to but reward the work (well, maybe not "Track for Speedy Freaks").

BUFFALO SPRINGFIELD: *BUFFALO SPRINGFIELD AGAIN*

They released only three albums and earned only one hit song (the indelible "For What It's Worth," a protest song about protests), but Buffalo Springfield is renowned as the band that launched the careers of Stephen Stills—a folk-pop songwriter with a mellow voice and fiery guitar style—and Neil Young—a more committed rocker with a withering voice and guitar style. Their smooth and curdled contrast made Stills's song sound more interesting and Young's more palatable when set side by side on vinyl.

The principal Buffalo Springfield sound may have been laid back, but relationships in the band were anything but. Neil Young was always a mercurial guy, and his constant comings and disappearances made the recording of the band's second album tense. Stephen Stills and the rest of the band couldn't complain too much because when Young did show up, he always pushed the band into the challenging territory that kept them from getting left behind in the post–*Sgt. Pepper* age. The three songs he brought to *Buffalo Springfield Again* are the album's most audacious. Each one is totally different from the other: the raging "Mr. Soul," the dreamy and uplifting "Expecting to Fly," and the fractured, avant-garde "Broken Arrow." Instead of trying to compete with Young's wild imagination, Stills kept up by doing some of his best work in his established folk-rock style. "Bluebird" and "Rock and Roll Woman," allegedly a tribute to Grace Slick, are two of his best songs. Richie Furay's work is more varied as he dabbles in country, soul, and jazz, but really, it is Neil Young who makes *Buffalo Springfield Again* a work of art.

THE BYRDS: *YOUNGER THAN YESTERDAY*

The Byrds were on the edge of turmoil when they recorded *Younger Than Yesterday* in late 1966. David Crosby's erratic and narcissistic behavior was a major source of this growing discord, and he'd be out the door before they released their next album (Crosby claims that reports he was kicked out specifically because of his rants about the JFK assassination onstage at the Monterey Pop Festival is exaggerated though).

Such tumult is barely evident on *Younger Than Yesterday*, which song for song is the Byrd's best LP. Roger McGuinn had developed into a consistently excellent songwriter by this point, and Chris Hillman's first songwriting efforts revealed great budding talent. Crosby was far less disciplined than his two bandmates, but his "Everybody's Been Burned" is a haunting, moody love song with jazz overtones—a sort of psychedelic "Cry Me a River." The tuneless, rhythmless, pretentious "Mind Gardens" was a bone of contention among the Byrds, and it has not aged as well as the rest of the album. For some listeners, it will be a quaint artifact of the kind of experimentation that was going down in the wake of "Tomorrow Never Knows."

Such trippy production frills are used liberally but tastefully throughout *Younger Than Yesterday*, and with the exception of "Mind Gardens," they never overwhelm the songs. The sarcastic "So You Want to Be a Rock and Roll Star" (featuring Hugh Masekela on trumpet) was one of the Byrds' last hit singles. "C.T.A.-102" looks back to the psychedelic space travel obsessions of *Fifth Dimension* and forward to the straight country of *Sweetheart of the Rodeo*. "Have You Seen Her Face," "Time Between," and "The Girl with No Name" are similarly appetizing country-rock morsels.

With such a stellar lineup of original material, I almost regret to admit that the album's most extraordinary track is its sole cover. Of course, one of the things that made the Byrds was their brilliant interpretations of Dylan songs, so it's fairly fitting that their version of "My Back Pages" is such a standout track on their standout album. However, the inclusion of yet another Dylan cover irked Crosby and would only heat up the Byrds' interpersonal problems that would boil over while making their follow-up.

THE CHOCOLATE WATCHBAND: *NO WAY OUT*

The Chocolate Watchband was San Francisco's top garage band, a group that continued bashing out Stones and soul covers with maximum chutzpah and minimum frills even after their neighbors had started dazing off into marathon jams. At times, this was the band that appears on the records with the "Chocolate Watchband" label. At other times, it was this band fronted by a session singer. Sometimes, the real Watchband had nothing to do with their recordings at all. Producer Ed Cobb and engineer Richie Podolor brought in studio singer Don Bennett and a cast of studio musicians to cut bizarre psychedelic opuses under the banner of the Chocolate Watchband.

Understandably, Cobb and Podolor's tampering shocked and revolted the group, who came to consider their albums entities completely unrelated to the real Chocolate Watchband. They continued playing their Stones and soul covers onstage and left the experimentation to producers making albums to which the band contributed little.

As is the case with the Monkees' first couple of records, the synthetic creation of *No Way Out* and *The Inner Mystique* does not render the music unworthy. In fact, their records are pretty vital and unpretentious in spite of their contrived creations. Yes, that is Bennett singing "Let's Talk About Girls," the pulsing nugget that kicks off *No Way Out*, but with all apologies to Dave Aguilar, the band's rightful singer, a great track is a great track. Still, it is strange that Cobb felt it necessary to replace Aguilar with Bennett on several of the album's vocal tracks since Aguilar's commanding soul roar is more accessible than Bennett's strange, twenty-fathom bass. One certainly doesn't miss Bennett when the band's real singer does his convincing Jagger impersonation on a psych-tinged reading of Chuck Berry's

"Come On," the menacing singles "Are You Gonna Be There (At the Love In)" and "No Way Out," and the Bo Diddley raga "Gone and Passes By." Credit where credit is due: Cobb and Podolor's bandless instrumentals are pretty groovy psychedelic-era mood music undulating with spaghetti western guitars, overzealous echo, celestial organs, percussion, and ample fuzz.

CREAM: *DISRAELI GEARS*

Deeper into the psychedelic era, Cream started working with the bizarre sounds and lyricism of the day without totally shedding the pure blues of their first album. As a result, *Disraeli Gears* is a two-faced album. It splits time between earthy blues exercises such as "Outside Woman Blues" and "Take It Back" and cosmic psych weirdoes such as the Homeric nightmare "Tales of Brave Ulysses," the swirling "Dance the Night Away," and the dramatically swelling "We're Going Wrong."

On occasion, these two poles fuse. "Strange Brew" weds a backing track for Buddy Moss's "Hey Lawdy Mama" to producer Felix Pappalardi's acid imagery (though these are certainly his least daffy lyrics on the album). "SWALBR" (allegedly an acronym for "She Walks Like a Bearded Rainbow" or "She Was Like a Bearded Rainbow") matches a basic garage lick with poet Peter Brown's gibberish. "Sunshine of Your Love" smothers Brown's psychotropic lust with a heavy blues riff. Many a novice guitarist would murder that riff.

Its dueling extremities and negligible tracks, such as Ginger Baker's goofy "Blue Condition," the novelty sing-along "Mother's Lament," and a couple of middling blues numbers, render *Disraeli Gears* inconsistent, but its best tracks are some of the most vibrant of rock's most vibrant year.

THE CREATION: *WE ARE PAINTERMEN*

They never got a hit like a lot of the other British bands that American producer Shel Talmy handled, but some rock cultists—such as Talmy—insist that the Creation was every bit as good as the Kinks and the Who. With mighty, multicolored records such as "Making Time," "Nightmares," and "How Does It Feel to Feel," the Creation's creations were easily as good as what the Kinks and the Who were doing in 1966.

The Creation's one official album could have been a lot better. It's poorly sequenced, and the tracks are poorly chosen. *We Are Paintermen* could have been a complete assault of spectacular original material, but whoever compiled the record decided to include irrelevant versions of "Like a Rolling Stone" and "Hey Joe" (their cheeky take on the Capitol's "Cool Jerk" is the one worthwhile cover). There were plenty of superior original tracks in the can that could have made *We Are Paintermen* one of the greatest albums of all time. As it stands, it's merely a great album. Any record that includes ear-bursting mod anthems like "Making Time," "Try and Stop Me," and "Biff Bang Pow" and corrosive psychedelia like "Nightmares" and "Through My Eyes" can withstand a couple of mediocre covers.

DANTALIAN'S CHARIOT: *CHARIOT RISING* (RELEASED IN 1996)

It doesn't matter how much of a blues purist a musician was; every one of them went psychedelic in 1967. Some wore it well. Eric Clapton ran his B.B. King licks through an LSD stomp box on *Disraeli Gears,* and the Stones went full fantasy on their cult classic *Their Satanic Majesties Request.* Others didn't adapt as convincingly, as former greats such as Eric Burdon and the Animals hacked out pretentious drivel and puny tunes.

Zoot Money and His Big Roll Band were among Britain's blues purists in the early sixties, but they never had the success Clapton, the Stones, or the Animals had, so there was a lot less riding on their Summer of Love metamorphosis into the flower-twirling Dantalian's Chariot. Their sole album didn't even get released for thirty years. When *Chariot Rising* finally came out on Wooden Hill Records in 1996, it indeed proved to be a lost classic in the *Disraeli Gears/Satanic Majesties* vein rather than a miscalculation in the "San Franciscan Nights"/"Monterey" one. The album is a charming and largely consistent artifact of the height of psychedelia with its backward tape loops, sitars, wacky lyrics, forceful rhythms, and distinctively British whimsy.

Today, Dantalian's Chariot's biggest claim to fame is the fact that future Policeman Andy Summers was a member, but his guitar work does not stand out as much as his and Zoot's songwriting does. Fans of this fragrant period can kick off their shoes and stretch back into the daisy-strewn lawns of "Madman Running Through the Fields" (released as a single—the only vinyl the band put out during their brief existence), "Sun Came Bursting Through the Clouds," and "World War Three." A couple of picturesque instrumentals are reminiscent of Chocolate Watchband's lush *Inner Mystique.* Only "Flying Bird"—with its fussy guitar solo and Burdon-esque

references to people with flowers in their hair and San Francisco—deserves
a cringe or two. The rest of *Chariot Rising* is dated in only the very best
way.

DONOVAN: *MELLOW YELLOW*

Two of Donovan's raunchiest tracks bookend
his third album, *Mellow Yellow*: the bumping,
grinding title tune and the name-dropping,
Swinging London reportage "Sunny South
Kensington." In between lies the songwriter's
most graceful selection of baroque folk and
rainy jazz, which his band executes with
stand-up bass, lightly brushed drums, piano,
and occasional woodwinds. Donovan's fluidly
picked acoustic guitar leads the way.

    Mellow Yellow is also the most credible
support for Donovan's claim that he's a
poet above all else. "Writer in the Sun" is an
empathetic faux autobiography of an author
whose best days are behind him. "Museum"
is a cheeky, picturesque love letter. "An
Observation" finds Donovan at his most bit-

Sheena McCall's painting on the
cover of *Mellow Yellow* reflects
the psychedelic' generation's
fascination with art nouveau.
Author's collection.

ing, as he transforms the frustration of "(I Can't Get No) Satisfaction" into
outright spite. "Young Girl Blues" is a tart portrait of a party girl with the
kind of explicit sex and drug references that one would expect from Lou
Reed. *Mellow Yellow* is Donovan's most authentically artistic statement and
a handsome, sometimes gritty snapshot of pop's most mythical era.

A GIFT FROM A FLOWER TO A GARDEN

Mellow Yellow was one of the most adult pop records of 1967, but Donovan
was also enamored with children's music, and he indulged his inner child
on rock's first double-LP box set. The first disc of *A Gift from a Flower to
a Garden* is intended for the parents, though innocent tracks such as the
pastel hit "Wear Your Love Like Heaven," "Mad John's Escape," "Skip-
a-Long Sam," "Oh Gosh," "Little Boy in Corduroy," and "The Land of
Doesn't Have to Be" seem as though they were aimed at the little ones. The

more pointedly childlike (or is it childish?) second disc is the one actually labeled "For Little Ones," and it's a more hit-or-miss assemblage of sparely arranged folk music. Some of the songs, such as "Song of the Naturalist's Wife" and the overlong "Epistle to Derroll," are a bit shapeless and more likely to put the kids to sleep than get them singing along. "Isle of Islay" is too gloomy for wee ones. "The Mandolin Man and His Secret," "Lay of the Last Tinker," and "The Tinker and the Crab," an impressionistic vignette that suggests a fairy tale without stooping to convey a coherent story, are the best tracks.

THE DOORS: *THE DOORS*

Because of their extreme cult popularity, the Doors seem like the quintessential sixties L.A. band even though that scene's main style is the pithy, punchy rock of groups like the Standells and Love. Of course, neither of those bands was as successful as the Doors, whose spooky, jazzy organ/guitar interplay and shameless artsy fartsiness became tremendously influential beyond the Sunset Strip. Regrettably, so was Jim Morrison's unpalatable doggerel.

He manages to keep that in check for a good deal of the Doors' landmark debut. Guitarist Robbie Krieger wrote the album's big hit, and "Light My Fire" is a worthy classic with Ray Manzarek's catchy Bach-inspired organ lick and his and Krieger's most memorable extended improvising. Its flip side, "The Crystal Ship," is a ballad beautiful enough to make up for its nonsensical lyrics. "Break on Through" crams Morrison's philosophical "insights" into an agreeable pop song. The group's blues numbers are credible, and their rakish cover of Brecht and Weill's "Alabama Song" is phenomenal.

Morrison makes us pay for all these nice songs when he unleashes his full pretentious powers across eleven outrageous minutes of "The End." This Oedipus-complex "shocker" is the number most responsible for his tiresome iconic status. It gave him the ultimate excuse to act out onstage and sports the most god-awful rhymes this side of a box of ninety-nine-cent Valentine's Day cards.

STRANGE DAYS

Strange Days follows a similar format to *The Doors*, and again, it's mostly successful. "People Are Strange" and the bluesy "Love Me Two Times" are two more good singles. The misty "You're Lost Little Girl" and the spry "Moonlight Drive" are two of the band's best album tracks. "Unhappy Girl" and "I Can See It in Your Face" are effectively creepy, and the title track is their best "weird song." "When the Music's Over" is another dopey epic, and "Horse Latitudes" is further evidence that Morrison is no poet, so *Strange Days* continues to build the case that the Doors work best as a pop band and worst as Beatnik Gods.

BOB DYLAN: *THE BASEMENT TAPES* (RELEASED IN 1975)

The Byrds' release of "Eight Miles High" in early 1966 is often cited as the official beginning of the psychedelic age that would rule pop music with weird lyrics and discordant music for the next two years. As the Byrds' main guiding light and a master of weird lyrics and discordant music, Bob Dylan may have been a sort of psychedelic pioneer, but he didn't like the music. Instead of engaging in the craziness of pop's craziest year, he went into retreat to recover from a bad motorcycle accident and make stripped-down, sepia-toned country and folk music that couldn't have been more of a contrast to the rainbow abandon of *Sgt. Pepper's* and *Satanic Majesties*.

While most of their peers were spending 1967's overly romanticized "Summer of Love" in a psychedelic fog, Bob Dylan and the Hawks (soon to be the Band) were gathering at each other's Woodstock homes with a rudimentary recording setup and a stash of exceptional songs and basically having fun. Dogs and children wandered in and out, noisy furnaces caused a little easily overcome trouble, everyone mellowed out with a joint or got their pulses racing with the high-octane coffee Dylan guzzled all day long. The atmosphere of low-key domesticity complimented the rustic music the guys made with their mandolins and acoustic basses.

Even before rock geeks obsessed about such great, lost recordings as the Beatles' "Get Back" tapes and the Beach Boys' *SMiLE*, they frothed over those tapes Bob Dylan and the Band casually cut over the summer of 1967. This is likely because some of the recordings were gathered on the first widely distributed rock bootleg. The sessions, which both Dylan and the ex-members of the Band would come to regard as relatively minor points in their respective careers, yielded a wealth of great songs, some of which would be made famous by Manfred Mann ("Quinn the Eskimo"), Julie Driscoll and Brian Auger ("This Wheel's on Fire"), the Byrds ("Nothing Was Delivered," "You Ain't Going Nowhere"), and the Band themselves ("Tears of Rage," "I Shall Be Released"). The tapes were never intended to be released, and only in 1975 did a scoop of them appear on the officially issued double LP *The Basement Tapes*, but Dylan still got his chance to make his rootsy retreat clear in 1967.

JOHN WESLEY HARDING

The acoustic guitar, bass, drums, and harmonica arrangements of *John Wesley Harding* make the album sound defiantly simple even as it smuggles in some of Dylan's weirdest and most complex lyrics. The rampant biblical allusions are an early indication of his bizarre embrace of Christianity in the coming decade. In light of the lyrical flights of *Highway 61* and *Blonde on Blonde*, the album's most radical moves are the two shockingly simple and sincere love songs that finish off *John Wesley Harding* and map out Dylan's plans for his next few records.

As was always the case, the entire rock world followed Dylan like a parade of little goslings, and *John Wesley Harding* quickly inspired the lot to abandon their sitars, Mellotrons, and acid for rustic textures, making one of the final albums of 1967 the most influential one of 1968.

THE FOUR TOPS: *REACH OUT*

The Four Tops' *Reach Out* is a sort of course correction following an ill-advised attempt to appeal to the over-thirty set that was all too common of Motown in the mid-sixties. After *On Top*, which split time between a side of the foursome's classic soul power and a side of Muzak, and the frilly show tunes of *4 Tops on Broadway*, *Reach Out* stiffs the oldsters to play solely to kids. A look at the track list might give you pause since it's so dependent on covers of contemporary pop and bubblegum hits by the likes of the Monkees, the Left Banke, and the Association, but nearly every track is wonderfully realized. The Tops redecorate "I'm a Believer" and "Last Train to Clarksville" as classic Motown dance numbers and nearly equal the Left Banke's version of "Walk Away Renee." They even work their magic on Tim Hardin's folk ballad "If I Were a Carpenter," a hit for Bobby Darin in 1966 and an unlikely resident of Hitsville USA.

These excellent covers are topped by the finest lineup of Holland–Dozier–Holland tunes on a tops LP. "Reach Out I'll Be There," "7 Rooms of Gloom," "Bernadette," and "Standing in the Shadows of Love" compliment the covers well since they take so many of their cues from the latest pop with their harpsichords, spacey percussion, trippy lyrics, and brooding tones.

The only thing that fails to make the grade is a version of "Cherish." The Association rendered this ode to romantic misery flaccid with their bland harmonies. Levi Stubbs should have let it rip to exploit the songs' strong emotional core, but he never breaks a sweat, and the Tops' harmonies are even stiffer than the Associations'. That little bump doesn't prevent *Reach Out* from being what may be the Four Tops' best. It's certainly their best since 1965's *Second Album*.

ARETHA FRANKLIN: *I NEVER LOVED A MAN THE WAY I LOVE YOU*

Aretha Franklin grew up singing sacred songs at her Baptist church in Detroit, Michigan, and cutting a couple of religious records for JVB in the fifties. She resigned herself to secular soul when she signed with Columbia in 1960, though she retained the deep, expressive, mildly melismatic style she developed while belting gospel.

Most of Franklin's early records favored pop standards and gospel. She took on more contemporary material with 1967's *Take It Like You Give It* and perfected the approach that would bring in the hits with her breakthrough LP *I Never Loved a Man the Way I Love You*. The burning title track will stop you in your tracks. Her smash remake of Otis Redding's "Respect" will get you moving again, and sung by a woman, the lyrics became a potent feminist message.

The rest of the album is strong as well, as Franklin cajoles vowels like a master trumpeter on "Soul Serenade" and eases into the blues on "Drown in My Own Tears." She cowrites some of the record's best songs, such as the gently shimmying "Don't Let Me Lose This Dream," the sweet "Baby, Baby, Baby," and "Save Me." She ends it all with a mighty interpretation of Sam Cooke's "A Change Is Gonna Come" that builds to a climax over which she sets off all the vocal bottle rockets that made her soul's most influential singer.

THE JIMI HENDRIX EXPERIENCE: *ARE YOU EXPERIENCED?*

When he invaded the pop scene in 1966, Jimi Hendrix had the same effect on guitarists that Dylan had on lyricists and the Beatles had on four-piece combos. Eric Clapton and Pete Townshend fretted over their apparent and sudden irrelevance. Everyone else simply marveled at Hendrix's ability to draw unearthly sounds from his Stratocaster. Employing Noel Redding and Mitch Mitchell as his rhythm section allowed him a lot of room to maneuver onstage, and he gained fame by knocking audiences sideways with his unpredictability and skill.

I always preferred the fish-eye lens photo of the Experience in their wacky garb on the cover of the American edition of their debut to the drab band photo on the British one. Author's collection.

Harnessing that kind of flamboyance on record can be tricky, but *Are You Experienced?* accomplishes it by complimenting the instinctive improvising that made the Experience explosive onstage with futuristic touches that could be painted only in the studio. At this early point, Hendrix is a good songwriter capable of greatness, which is best showcased on the singles "Purple Haze" and "The Wind Cries Mary." These tracks, as well as his 1966 hit version of "Hey Joe," were included on the American edition of *Are You Experienced?* The British version suffers because of their absence (and its less interesting jacket). There's still plenty of stunning stuff: the panic-inducing metal riff of "Manic Depression," the sleazy mania of "Fire," the neurotic "I Don't Live Today," the looming "Love or Confusion." "Remember" and "May This Be Love" show that Hendrix can do delicate just as well as heavy. The band, producer Chas Chandler (former Animals bassist), and engineer Eddie Kramer take the experimentation of "Tomorrow Never Knows" to the breaking point (the title track) and beyond ("Third Stone from the Sun"). Hendrix would sharpen his songwriting considerably on his next record, but the Experience would never make a more combustible record than their first.

AXIS: BOLD AS LOVE

Having established himself as a peerless guitar pyrotechnician on his debut album, Jimi Hendrix was ready to perfect the rest of his craft on his second. *Axis: Bold as Love* expands on the far-out production of *Are You Experienced?* while venturing down new songwriting avenues. Hendrix had never before—and perhaps never since—written a lyric on the level of "Castles Made of Sand," which addresses his part Cherokee heritage via a triad of complex character vignettes. He balances the gravity of his lyrics with ethereal chord structures. "Little Wing" soars on jazzy figures and a heartfelt lyric. "If Six Was Nine" overcomes its trite hippie provocations with a whimsical structure (Hendrix's piercing puffs through a recorder are annoying though). "Up from the Skies" is all buoyant, mellow sweetness. "Spanish Castle Magic" and "Little Miss Lover" are slabs of metal that haven't been beaten to death like "Foxy Lady" or "Purple Haze" have. The title track is a psychedelic soul rainbow. "Wait Until Tomorrow" and "You've Got Me Floating" are two of Hendrix's most straightforward and seductively funky songs, and both make great use of Noel Redding's backing vocals. Even Redding's poppy original "She's So Fine" is pretty great. *Axis* isn't the pioneer its predecessor was or the grand artistic statement its follower would be, but it may be the Experience's most consistent LP.

THE HOLLIES: *BUTTERFLY*

"We're as psychedelic as a pint of beer with the lads," said Hollie Alan Clarke in 1966. That didn't stop Britain's premier champions of delightfully airy pop songs from hopping on the acid-spiked gravy train the following year.

The Hollies did not forsake their collective gift for melody even when dabbling with raga-rock paraphernalia on "Maker" or slathering fashionable backward tape loops over "Try It." That particular track is marred by inept acid lyrics, as is "Elevated Observations," and a couple of tracks suffer from overdoses of preciousness ("Wish You a Wish" and "Charlie and Fred"). The majority of the album is fairly inventive and thoroughly refreshing. The middle section of the single "Dear Eloise" features the Hollies at their most exuberant; the intro and outro bookend that middle with an acid sea shanty. "Away, Away, Away" and "Step Inside" are neat pop. The colorfully orchestrated title

The American release *Dear Eloise/King Midas in Reverse* loses three of the more psychedelic tracks on *Butterfly* and adds the Who-esque older track "Leave Me Be" and the excellent single "King Midas in Reverse." That cumbersome title and the photo of the band in front of a news agent (which includes some prominently displayed nudie magazines) are a lot less psychedelic too. Author's collection.

track is very pretty despite more silly, pseudo-psych lyrics. "Would You Believe" is a ravishing, uplifting love song.

Graham Nash would soon split from the group, irritated with their refusal to push further into artier territory. *Butterfly* displays the pluses and minuses of the Hollies' artistic ambitions, but it mostly validates Nash's desires.

JEFFERSON AIRPLANE: *SURREALISTIC PILLOW*

Jefferson Airplane was the only band to emerge from San Francisco's improvisation-addicted hippie rock scene with a true grasp of rock's menace and power. After cutting a strong debut album, original vocalist Signe Anderson left the band to raise a family with husband and Merry Prankster Jerry Anderson. The Airplane quickly swiped Grace Slick from the ramshackle Great Society and became a very different band. Although Slick was a ringer for Anderson when belting, she could also descend to a near whisper that granted a creepy, icy undertone to the Airplane's unconventional ballads. The group also began stretching out more onstage, fully exploring the jazzy yet metallic interplay between guitarist Jorma Kaukonen, drummer Spencer Dryden, and ace bassist Jack Casady.

Doing such things on vinyl was unacceptable in the pre-*Pepper* days of 1967, and producer Rick Jarrad made sure Jefferson Airplane cooked up some digestible potential hits for their second album. The scheme worked, even if *Surrealistic Pillow* doesn't showcase the Airplane at their most piquant or visionary. The first single, "My Best Friend," is a piece of pop piffle that failed to further the band artistically or commercially, but the next two singles, which Slick brought with her from the Great Society, struck an alchemic balance between the band's outré tendencies and the hit parade. The scathing "Somebody to Love" and the needling "White Rabbit," which implicates fantastical children's lit as a sort of gateway drug, were two of the most memorable—and, in the case of "Rabbit," unlikely—top-ten smashes of 1967. Both songs have been a bit tarnished by overplay. Lazy filmmakers may have abused "White Rabbit" as the go-to sound track for on-screen acid trips, but in 1967, it was the most musically and lyrically radical hit of the year.

Although Slick hooked the record, *Surrealistic Pillow* is hardly a one-woman show. Jorma Kaukonen thrills with the odd, winding "She Has Funny Cars" and his soaring solo acoustic guitar piece "Embryonic Journey." Marty Balin delivers the Airplane's two most haunting ballads

("Today" and "Comin' Back to Me") and two good songs that would develop into monsters on stage ("3/5 of a Mile in Ten Seconds" and "Plastic Fantastic Lover"). The polite production mutes the dynamic rhythm section of bassist Jack Casady and drummer Spencer Dryden, and Paul Kantner doesn't get much to do, but both of those wrongs would be righted on the band's next album.

AFTER BATHING AT BAXTER'S

Surrealistic Pillow was a major commercial success, but it didn't represent how Jefferson Airplane really sounded in 1967. On that record, they were a lightweight folk/rock group. Live, they were a five-headed monster with jazzy but growly bass, stinging guitar, stormy drums, and the most gloriously undisciplined three-part harmonies in rock. No doubt, RCA Records expected the Airplane to follow up their breakthrough smash with a similar album. The label certainly didn't expect the band to spend five months (an unusually long time back then) recording the stark-raving *After Bathing at Baxter's*.

Baxter's is the Airplane's first record to capture their live sound and completely take advantage of the studio techniques *Sgt. Pepper's* made possible. It is a free-floating mix of heavy rock, cutting-edge improvisation, evil jazz, spidery folk, and hammering blues assembled as a series of loose suites. While the suites are little more than a gimmick to give the record a conceptual whiff, the individual songs are the best on any Airplane record. "Martha," "The Ballad of You & Me & Pooneil," "Watch Her Ride," "Won't You Try/Saturday Afternoon," and "Wild Tyme" are all cracked classics and give a clearer idea of what the hippie movement was about than any amount of rap ever could. Grace Slick's "Rejoyce," which does for James Joyce what "White Rabbit" did for Lewis Carroll, is the Airplane's most spellbinding undiscovered gem. *After Bathing at Baxter's* was nowhere near the hit *Surrealistic Pillow* was, but it pummels its predecessor to pieces.

THE KINKS: *SOMETHING ELSE BY THE KINKS*

With klassic Kinky irony, the band's waning international popularity occurred just as their unique influence took hold of their more popular peers. The Beatles scored their first hit of 1967 with the "Penny Lane"/"Strawberry Fields Forever" single, two tracks that make specific references to English locales as so many Kinks records do. The Rolling Stones, Britain's highest-profile proponents of American blues and rock and roll, dipped into music hall on *Between the Buttons* and scored their fourth number one hit in the United States with "Ruby Tuesday," an airy pastoral fit for *Face to Face*. Kinky anglophilia was so rampant in these days that a studio creation called the New Vaudeville Band managed a massive, Grammy-winning hit in late 1966 with the gimmicky "Winchester Cathedral." Yet the band that inspired the whole wave couldn't cash in. Not that the Kinks really tried to.

When futuristic psychedelia started to dominate the pop scene in 1967, the Kinks immersed themselves deeper in a world that pined for the past, where depressive housewives, unemployed newlyweds, conservative cricketers, window-gazing loners, and dead clowns fail to assimilate into the libertine Swinging London scene, much like Ray Davies, who'd recently found himself domesticated with a new wife and daughter.

The real protagonists of these songs are often unnamed observers. Golden Boy David Watts is far less compelling than the narrator who so covets his status. The reclusive singer of "Waterloo Sunset" is more complexly drawn than carefree Terry and Julie. The few love songs are similarly complex: paranoid ("No Return"), melancholically nostalgic ("Afternoon Tea"), utterly mysterious ("Funny Face"). "Funny Face" is one of three examples of Dave Davies's emergence as a writer to rival his older brother. "Death of a Clown" reveals Dave's Dylan fixation and the allure of his strangled voice. Ray's wife Rasa lends her haunting soprano to several of the tracks.

Something Else by the Kinks is one of the least psychedelic, least 1967-sounding albums released by a major group between *Sgt. Pepper's* and *John Wesley Harding*, Bob Dylan's late 1967, back-to-the-roots game changer. Yet the album could not have been made during any other time because it is a reaction to 1967, an uncomfortable shrug against the radical changes happening in the pop world.

Something Else was the Kinks' first album to fail to come within a hair of the British top twenty and miss the American top 150 altogether, the band's first significant international commercial letdown. Creatively, it was the Kinks' greatest triumph to date. Ray's ousting of Shel Talmy (who received coproducer credits on the original album for contractual reasons) resulted in a clarity that serves the delicate creations far better than that American producer's booming wall of noise would have. The Kinks show they can still pummel on "Love Me till the Sun Shines," but the playing consistently veers toward the delicate, even on ostensible rockers like "Situation Vacant" and "David Watts." Ray's personal frustrations drive him to compose his most perceptive and consistent material to date—not a single piece of past-due filler in the batch. Robert Christgau of *The Village Voice* famously christened "Waterloo Sunset" "the most beautiful song in the English language." Meanwhile, dark-horse Dave prances to center stage with rookie compositions that flaunt a master's touch. The lightness of the material prevents drummer Mick and (particularly) bassist Pete from making many audacious contributions, but this is no longer an audacious Kinks. This is not the power-chording Kinks of yore. This is a new age for the band, and what they may have been losing in power and popularity they gained in grace, insight, and beauty.

THE LEFT BANKE: *WALK AWAY RENEE/PRETTY BALLERINA*

On their superb debut album, *Walk Away Renee/Pretty Ballerina*, New York anglophiles the Left Banke one-up many of their British heroes by creating one of the most consistently wonderful—and one of the most English—records of the sixties. Here the Left Banke invent the kind of melodramatically mopey pop the Smiths would make twenty years later and Belle & Sebastian would make a decade after that. The obvious influence here is the Zombies, but the Left Banke takes such fey, baroque pop and shuts the lights off completely. Are there any songs from the sixties more anguished or exquisite than "Walk Away Renee," "Pretty Ballerina," and "Shadows Breaking over My Head"? Even when the Left Banke rocks on "She May Call You Up Tonight," "I've Got Something on My Mind," "Evening Gown," and "I Haven't Got the Nerve," the tearful tones of singer Steve Martin crank up the pain.

This is music way ahead of its time, even as it is most certainly of its time (the harpsichord was very in style in late 1966/early 1967, and it's all over this album). Production whiz kid, chief songwriter, and keyboardist Michael Brown deserves much of the credit for making *Walk Away Renee/Pretty Ballerina* such an exceptional album, but it's the plaintive voice of Martin that will haunt listeners long after needle lifts off vinyl.

LOVE: *DA CAPO*

Love's second album is frustrating because it doesn't follow through on its tremendous promise. Side A of *Da Capo* may be the best run of Love songs the band ever recorded. Side B's sole occupant is a jam misleadingly titled "Revelation" that is fun for about three minutes. It rides out the rest of the record with sixteen minutes of time-wasting filler either inspired by or an inspiration for the Stones' similarly interminable "Goin' Home." *Da Capo* may have been the best pre-*Pepper* album of 1967 and possibly the best Love album if side B had some songs on it, but the incredible strength of side A still sets it well above the majority of its contemporaries.

The first half of *Da Capo* bridges Love's garagey debut and the more refined *Forever Changes*. Since those albums are so diametrically unlike, *Da Capo* sounds totally different from either of them. The songs are tough, tricky, and inspired. Saxophone, twittering harpsichord, Arthur Lee's wildly soulful shouting, and the dime-stopping rhythm section coalesce perfectly on "Stephanie Knows Who" and the shuddering "The Castle." "¡Que Vida!" is as reflective as anything on *Forever Changes*. Bryan MacLean's "Orange Skies" presages that album's mood if not its introspection. "7 and 7 Is" is a galloping demon—Hendrix on amyl nitrate instead of acid. "She Comes in Colors" is a mysterious ballad that would influence the Stones' "She's a Rainbow" as much as their "What a Shame" influenced Love's "Can't Explain." Perhaps Love poured so much into side A that there was nothing left for side B, but their next album would be dramatically consistent and their most enduring classic.

FOREVER CHANGES

Da Capo pushed Love's hard rock as far as it could go. They could never make a wilder recording than "7 and 7 Is" or a more indulgent one than "Revelations." The pendulum swung far from their second record when they made their third one. *Forever Changes* is one of 1967's quietest rock records. Even when electric guitars whip up a gale on "A House Is Not a Motel," the results are not nearly as unhinged as most of *Da Capo*. Acoustic guitars, whispered vocals, and elegant string arrangements command *Forever Changes*.

Under these dulcet sounds, fury and terror percolate. In 1967, Arthur Lee became obsessed with the idea he'd die soon, and his lyrics are morbid, often twisted, sometimes

Bob Post's iconic painting adorns *Forever Changes*. Author's collection.

hostile. The hippie gentility of the music creates an ironic and disturbing counterpoint.

Forever Changes is largely Lee's show, but Bryan MacLean supplies its most memorable song, "Alone Again, Or." It is a sumptuous opening chapter to a gorgeous and troubling record that reveals new mysteries with every spin.

THE MONKEES: *MORE OF THE MONKEES*

On a schedule that would have even been extreme in 1964, the second Monkees album hit shops just three months after their debut. From the point of view of Colgems, such rapid releasing must have seemed necessary since no one knew when Monkeemania was going to suddenly end. It was possible because an army of producers were constantly holding sessions in the desperate hope that they'd cut a track that would end up on an album guaranteed to sell zillions. So there was a mass of material at the ready to fill out *More of the Monkees*, and, as was the case with *The Monkees*, most of it was more fabulous than anyone should have expected it to be. Or maybe it should have been expected since Tin Pan Alley pros such as Goffin and King, Boyce and Hart, and Neil Diamond were contributing songs.

Despite the hasty and totally inorganic way it was put together, *More of the Monkees* contains the best-known Monkees double-sided hit—"I'm a Believer" b/w "(I'm Not Your) Steppin' Stone"—and their best-known album tracks: Boyce and Hart's pounding "She," Goffin and King's wistful "Sometime in the Morning," Diamond's euphoric "Look Out (Here Comes Tomorrow)," and Mike Nesmith's supercool "Mary Mary." Each is a pop gem polished to perfection, and "Steppin' Stone," "She," and "Mary Mary" are tough enough to give the impression of a real garage band at work even though this was not the case. Nesmith's clattering and joyful "The Kind of Girl I Could Love" and the driving baroque pop tune "Hold on Girl" are pretty terrific too.

The music on *More of the Monkees* is not the only thing that made Mike Nesmith furious. He also hated the cover photo, which showed the band modeling tragically unhip JCPenney's fashions. Author's collection.

The rest of the album is more of an acquired taste. Fans tend to love or hate Peter Tork's fart sounds on "Your Auntie Grizelda." Most just seem to hate the lurching, goofy "Laugh" (I'm in the minority of fans who find it catchy fun), and a serious gag suppressant is required to make it through the mushy "The Day We Fall in Love," easily the worst piece of trash ever to score a place on a Monkees LP. One could only imagine Nesmith's disgust when he heard this particular track and totally sympathize with his battle to win the Monkees the right to make their own records.

HEADQUARTERS

When critics roasted the Monkees on discovering they didn't "play their own instruments," Mike Nesmith and Peter Tork, the most serious musicians in the group, felt humiliated and angered. Just a few months into their existence, at which point they were already the biggest-selling act on the pop scene, Nesmith led a revolt. He convinced Peter and Micky Dolenz to take a concerted stand against "music supervisor" Don Kirshner. When he insisted that he and the guys, who had already been performing as a live band for months, should be allowed to play on their recordings, Herb Moelis of Colgems Records reminded Nesmith that he was under contract and had no say in the production of the Monkees' disks. Reaching the limits of flower-power pacifism, Nesmith put his fist through a wall and allegedly told Moelis, "That could have been your face, motherfucker." Sympathetic with Nesmith and Tork's artistic ambitions—and afraid they'd walk out on their contract—the TV show's producers, Bob Rafelson and Bert Schneider, decreed that a real Monkees recording would appear on the group's next single. Irritated with having his authority questioned and perhaps finding it hard to respect a Monkee who made physical threats while also accepting a $250,000 check for earnings on an album that so enraged him, Don Kirshner had other plans.

Without any real artistic ambitions, Davy Jones was ambivalent about Nesmith's crusade, but he turned out to be instrumental in the Monkees' victory when Kirshner lured him into the studio to record Neil Diamond's "A Little Bit Me, A Little Bit You" and Jeff Barry's "She Hangs Out." When Kirshner released these two songs on a single despite Rafelson and Schneider's decree, the producers canned Kirshner, withdrew the single, and rereleased "A Little Bit Me, A Little Bit You" with the Monkees' own recording of Nesmith's tonic "The Girl I Knew Somewhere" on the B-side. Nesmith had hired former Turtle Chip Douglas to produce it.

And so the Monkees had mounted and won pop's most unexpected and successful revolution. They had not only scored a triumph over the record industry that would be unthinkable today but also went on to make one of the great pop albums of the sixties. *Headquarters* doesn't sound radically different from the first two Monkees records, but it displays the energy of a young band thrilled to be making music in an organic manner those earlier records lack. There is the occasional missed drum fill or piano flub, but that only adds to the record's charm. Playing bass on most tracks as well as producing, Chip Douglas is the only non-Monkee on most of the tracks (Nesmith's pal John London plays bass on a couple of songs, Jerry Yester plays bass on another two, and a guest French horn player and cellist contribute to "Shades of Gray"). The Monkees chose their own material and were smart enough to write and select songs superior to the ones Don Kirshner foisted on them but close enough to the established Monkees sound to not alienate fans.

The country-pop sound with which Nesmith had already been experimenting rules *Headquarters*. This is most apparent on his three contributions: "You Just May Be the One," which features a tricky Peter Tork bass riff; the pumping boogie "Sunny Girlfriend"; and "You Told Me," which is more country rock than country pop. The sound is also apparent in the sweet "I'll Spend My Life with You," Peter Tork's hippie anthem "For Pete's Sake," and the pedal steel runs on the somber ballads "Mr. Webster" and "Shades of Gray," on which Peter's grave baritone offsets Davy's syrupy chirp perfectly. Davy also holds his own with "Forget That Girl" and the eerie "Early Morning Blues and Greens," both of which are more mature than the songs he'd been assigned on the previous albums (the same cannot be said of "I Can't Get Her Off My Mind," the record's one bubblegum blunder). Micky Dolenz not only serves up a blister-raising vocal on the Little Richard–esque jam "No Time" but also pens the record's most fabulously experimental song. "Randy Scouse Git" somehow combines music-hall piano lines, jazz scatting, orchestral timpani swells, surreal reportage, and pre-punk pandemonium without sounding like anything less than perfect pop.

PISCES, AQUARIUS, CAPRICORN, AND JONES, LTD.

Irritatingly, *Headquarters* did little to change critical opinion of the Monkees during their time, but those hip enough to dig them now know that it's one of the most refreshingly tuneful records of the sixties. However, with a schedule filled to the brim with live appearances, TV show filming, and getting baked, the Monkees didn't have the time to slog through more recording sessions, and as terrific as *Headquarters* turned out, the sessions were a slog. Only Peter Tork really wanted the Monkees to carry on as a band. The other guys were content to welcome studio musicians like drummer "Fast" Eddie Hoh back into the fold. Consequently, *Pisces, Aquarius, Capricorn, & Jones, Ltd.* struck the perfect balance between Monkee musicians and studio pros.

Mike Nesmith dominates more than ever. He has relatively few songwriting credits but more lead vocals on this album than he does on any other Monkees disc. There isn't a trace of bubblegum cutesiness in the dry twang he lends to "Salesman," a wry putdown of drug pushers; "Love Is Only Sleeping," a tough psych number with a haunting riff in 7/8 time; the joyous yet callous "What Am I Doing Hangin' 'Round?"; and Douglas and Bill Martin's beauteous, Heinlein-inspired "The Door into Summer," which I personally consider to be the finest thing the Monkees ever recorded.

Pisces is also notable as the first pop album to really spotlight the newly invented Moog synthesizer, which adds sci-fi blips and bleeps to Nesmith's "Daily Nightly," a surreal poem about the Sunset Strip curfew demonstrations of 1966 with a serpentine bass hook, and "Star Collector," an unfortunately nasty slam at groupies (blame writers Gerry Goffin and Carole King). That cynical edge recurs throughout the record on the bitter love song "Words," which features excellent dialoging between Dolenz and Tork; "Cuddly Toy," a malicious Harry Nilsson lyric about a "Hell's Angels gang bang" in a subversively cutesy-pie crust; and Goffin and King's "Pleasant Valley Sunday," which wraps everything that made Monkees music fabulous into a tidy hit package.

Not everything on the album is outstanding, but the best tracks are as great as anything the Monkees' peers made in 1967.

This is the first vinyl album I ever owned all to myself (to find out what my first co-owned album was, flip ahead to the 1983 chapter). During the sixteen-hour wait for my mom to finish shopping in some store in the Massapequa Mall, my grandma and I were chatting about our mutual appreciation for the Monkees and I told her I dug their song "She Hangs Out." She said that if I could find the album that contains that song at Record World, she'd buy it for me. She kept her word and I began building my record collection. Author's collection.

While *Headquarters* may be remembered more fondly because of the way it was created, *Pisces, Aquarius, Capricorn, & Jones, Ltd.* is the Monkees' grooviest record.

THE MOODY BLUES: *DAYS OF FUTURE PASSED*

Birmingham's Moody Blues underwent one of pop's most radical metamorphoses when they transitioned from the soul-beat group that recorded a drama-packed version of Bessie Banks's "Go Now" into the dreamy psychedelic pop unit that pioneered what would become known as progressive rock in the mid-sixties.

Progressive rock is most associated with complex and extended structures, virtuosic musicianship, and time signatures that reach beyond rock's usual four bangs to the beat. The Moody Blues' brand of prog is more wrapped up with grand arrangements than ambitious songwriting and performing. The grand arrangements of *Days of Future Passed* were actually conceived for practical rather than progressive purposes. Executives at Decca Records thought a combination of pop instrumentation and classical orchestration performing Dvorak's "New World Symphony" would be a good showcase for stereophonic mixing. The label earmarked the Moody Blues for this project. Instead, the band adapted some of their own songs for this project on the sly. The magical "Tuesday Afternoon" and "Nights in White Satin" somehow transposed the emotional intensity of the Moodies' early hit "Go Now" over a landscape of Mellotron and orchestra. "Peak Hour" rocks reasonably, but most of the rest of the album leans too hard on its symphonic gimmick and fills space with some truly ghastly spoken word passages. Nevertheless, the *Days of Future Passed* formula rejuvenated the Moody Blues' career, and along with Procol Harum's debut album, it gave progressive rock its first big push.

VAN MORRISON: *BLOWIN' YOUR MIND*

Following his stint fronting Them, Van Morrison went solo in the hopes of carving out a very singular artistic niche for himself. Instead, he sat back in horror as producer Bert Berns took his strange, fluid songs and tried to mold them into pop hits. The smash "Brown Eyed Girl" solidified his career, and concise numbers like the Latin-tinged "Spanish Rose" and the blistering "Ro Ro Rosey" were not the kind of music he yearned to make.

There was no way that cracked pieces such as "He Ain't Give You None" and "T.B. Sheets" (a sweaty epic expressing a man's attempt to flee a loved one's sickbed) could have ended up as anything less than bizarre, but the recordings still did not completely align with his vision.

Morrison was incensed when Berns randomly assembled eight tracks from sessions that yielded twice as many and released it on his Bang Records under the fatuous and highly inappropriately psychedelic title *Blowin' Your Mind* (Morrison would mock that title in a track called "Blowin' Your Nose" in an infamous contractual obligation recording session).

Although this is not the record Van Morrison wanted to make, *Blowin' Your Mind* is still a strong and unusual LP for 1967, with its intense, personal perspective of relationships sexual and otherwise. Fortunately for Van the artist, he'd soon wrestle his way out of commitments to Bang and record an album that truly reflected his desires.

NICO: *CHELSEA GIRL*

Former model Nico never really belonged in the Velvet Underground, and the band never really wanted her even though she got to voice some of the most important tracks on the most important pre-*Pepper* album of 1967. She parted ways with the band amicably enough to continue working with Lou Reed and John Cale outside its confines.

Oddly, Nico's first solo album would be even less representative of her very individual artistic ambitions than *The Velvet Underground & Nico* had been. Its folky songs mostly written by Reed, Cale, and future MOR star Jackson Browne and arranged tastefully with strings, flutes, and finger-picked guitars were too pretty for an artist who longed to challenge and disturb. Things like "The Fairest of the Seasons," "These Days," "Little Sister," "Winter Song," "and "Somewhere There's a Feather" may not have been Nico's cup of arsenic, but they are winsome, like skeletal trees standing strong against the bitter winter winds of her frosty vocals. It is interesting that Nico had long burned to record Dylan's "I'll Keep It with Mine" because it is the most conventional track on *Chelsea Girl*, but it is also a tremendously stirring piece. The title track pairs a jovial tune with a disturbing lyric about the squatters in Warhol's factory.

The lengthy, dissonant "It Was a Pleasure Then," which matches its unpleasant lyric with equally off-putting discordance, gives a better idea of where Nico's solo career was headed, and her next album would be fearlessly uncompromising. *The Marble Index* would be Nico's greatest album, but chances are you'll enjoy listening to *Chelsea Girl* a lot more.

HARRY NILSSON: *PANDEMONIUM SHADOW SHOW*

Although *Sgt. Pepper's* is hailed as a monument of art rock and psyche-delia, the album's predominant sound is Paul McCartney's old-timey music-hall pop. So ironic singer-songwriter Harry Nilsson's second album, *Pandemonium Shadow Show*, sounds much more Peppery than, say, *Their Satanic Majesties Request* or the majority of albums dismissed as *Pepper* pretenders. And not only did the Beatles inspire Nilsson, but he also pays direct tribute to them when he covers "She's Leaving Home" and cheekily mangles a variety of their songs in the hilarious mingle-mangle "You Can't Do That."

"River Deep—Mountain High" has been covered by too many people who aren't Tina Turner, Nilsson's version of "Cuddly Toy" is just margin-ally better than the Monkees', and "Ten Little Indians" was a good song in the hands of neither its creator nor the Yardbirds, who recorded the most famous rendition during their Jimmy Page period. The rest of *Pandemo-nium Shadow Show* is phenomenal. "Sleep Late, My Lady Friend" is the lullaby Bacharach and David always wanted to write. Gil Garfield and Perry Botkin's show-tuney "There Will Never Be" is an instant standard. Sparsely arranged with cello, bass, and flute, "Without Her" is a haunting marriage of baroque and jazz balladry. The knockout of *Shadow Show* is "1941," an elegiac lament documenting Nilsson's abandonment by his father, which would be a recurring theme in his work that did not prevent him from pull-ing the same shit on his own firstborn. That theme endeared him to John Lennon, who also learned to be a dodgy dad from his own one. Lennon and the rest of the Beatles' support was the ultimate endorsement. Three of them personally called Nilsson to tell him how much they loved his first record.

PINK FLOYD: *THE PIPER AT THE GATES OF DAWN*

At the same time the Beatles were recording *Sgt. Pepper's Lonely Hearts Club Band*, Pink Floyd was down the hall at Abbey Road, translating the bizarre sounds and pictures pirouetting through Syd Barrett's mind to tape. As wonderful as *Sgt. Pepper's* is, it is self-conscious in a way that most albums with high-art ambitions are. There's nothing self-conscious about *The Piper at the Gates of Dawn*. It is well known that Syd Barrett not only was an ego-annihilating acid enthusiast but also may have also been schizophrenic. The bizarre images and fractured sounds that permeate *Piper* seem to have sprung naturally from the whimsical wellsprings of Barrett's head.

Fans have over romanticized Barrett's alleged mental illness, but there is a less dicey influence at play as well: his lifelong love of Kenneth Grahame (who coined the album's title phrase), J.R.R. Tolkien, Edward Lear, and Lewis Carroll's very British brand of natural-world whimsy. Gnomes, living scarecrows, demonic cats, friendly mice, and unicorns gambol at the Gates of Dawn.

Barrett is most definitely in charge of Pink Floyd at this point, but Rick Wright's space-jazz keyboard work is vital to the album's sound, and though Roger Waters's one composition is the record's weakest, his bass playing is his best on wax. So Pink Floyd's debut is not a depressing portrait of a guy losing his grip on reality; it's the work of a fantastically unorthodox artist indulging his every fanciful impulse with fine support from a band willing to follow him down any rabbit hole. If there's anything depressing about it, it's that the rest of the band would soon shunt Barrett aside and that Pink Floyd would never make an album as delightful and unselfconscious as *The Piper at the Gates of Dawn* again.

THE PRETTY THINGS: *EMOTIONS*

Even in the months before *Sgt. Pepper's* landed, the old rock quartet lineup was looking primitive thanks to pre-*Pepper* items like "Strawberry Fields Forever," "Ruby Tuesday," and "Good Vibrations." For the Pretty Things, primitive was as much a way of life as it was for Alley Oop, so it's no wonder why they were beside themselves when producer Steve Rowland slathered their latest batch of songs with Nelson Riddle–esque strings and brass.

While such a move would have been an unequivocal disaster had it been perpetrated against their earlier blues and booze romps, the tracks on *Emotions* already found the Pretties in less surly territory. In fact, the brass blurts work quite well on the Kinky character portrait "Death of a Socialite" and the intense, psych vamp "My Time." Brass adds extra punch to the already hard-driving "There Will Never Be Another Day." "The Sun," an elegant stroke of baroque pop, is unimaginable without its complementary strings. At times, the embellishments don't work as well, although that may be as much the fault of middling material like "Children" and "Tripping" as it is Rowland's fault.

Emotions is controversial and a bit uneven, but it reveals great growth in the songwriting partnership of Phil May and Dick Taylor, which would flourish fully the following year on an album that would be a genuine rock milestone.

PROCOL HARUM: *PROCOL HARUM*

Procol Harum invented what would become known as "goth rock" with their debut album. Bach-influenced funereal dirges get in bed with rock and roll for the first time. Lyricist Keith Reid, who was considered an official member of the band even though he didn't sing or play an instrument, is obsessed with figurative and literal death. The lazy blues "Something Following Me" is a surreal tragic/comic tale of a man who keeps encountering his own tombstone. "Conquistador" views the death of a conqueror past his prime through the eyes of a disillusioned onlooker. The incongruously titled "Salad Days (Are Here Again)" mourns a relationship. Even the goofy music-hall throwaway "Mabel" begins with a grotesque line about a family decimated by food poisoning.

Procol Harum's lineup was just as unique in 1967 as their gloomy fixations were. The emphasis is on majestic keyboards rather than shrieking guitar, which is ironic considering that Robin Trower would soon establish himself as a career Hendrix impersonator. Gary Brooker's Ray Charles croon keeps the band soulful and their pretensions in check.

Procol Harum were dissatisfied with their debut, which they were rushed into the studio to make in order to capitalize on their hit single "A Whiter Shade of Pale" (the hit was not included on the British version of *Procol Harum*). The elaborate arrangement of "Conquistador" on the *Procol Harum Live with the Edmonton Symphony Orchestra* album may indicate what the band had in mind for their debut. Perhaps they were better off with fewer resources because the simplicity of this album gives it a raw strength

Dickinson's cover illustration always reminded me of the penultimate shot in Georges Franju's elegant 1960 horror movie, *Eyes without a Face*. Dickinson later married Procol Harum's in-house lyricist, Keith Reid. Author's collection.

that superfluous orchestrations may have diluted. So much of the music released in the post-*Pepper* days 1967 was presented in self-conscious Technicolor. *A Whiter Shade of Pale/Procol Harum* is cast in the black and white of an early Mario Bava horror show.

PAUL REVERE AND THE RAIDERS: *REVOLUTION!*

Paul Revere and the Raiders sure look dorky in their Revolutionary War costumes on the cover of *Revolution!*, but the swampy blues/soul/pop/psych noise on the record dispels that silly image. That image is really the extent of the band's involvement in a record that was basically a Mark Lindsay solo product cooked up with producer Terry Melcher.

Despite a somewhat prefab creation, *Revolution!* is the most consistently thrilling album credited to the Raiders, even as it marks the point at which their commercial viability began to decline. "Him or Me (What's It Gonna Be)" was the group's last radio smash (before they shortened their name to the Raiders in the seventies and recorded the cheesy MOR hit "Indian Reservation"), and it is all pilled-up adrenaline and grimy swagger. The Stonesy rocker "Mo'reen" is nearly as exciting. "Make It with Me" has so much bottom that it sounds like the studio floor is about to cave in under the band. "Reno" and the ridiculous "Ain't Nobody Who Can Do It Like Leslie Can" (a tribute to Paul Revere's maid; his vocal is the only contribution to the album from a Raider other than Lindsay) are the best pure blues recordings on a Raiders record. The haunting "I Hear a Voice" is the best psychedelic one, and it twinkles like a sky speckled with very strange stars.

THE RISING STORM: *CALM BEFORE . . .*

The artists that make the most concerted effort to be futuristic often end up with the product that most fails to stand the test of time. *Calm Before . . .* , the debut of "Bosstown" (DJ Dick Summer's term for the Boston rock scene) band the Rising Storm, commits such unhip-in-1967 crimes as loading up on soul and blues covers. Yet the way this group of high school kids effortlessly transform warhorses like "In the Midnight Hour" and "Big Boss Man" into their own creations is more legitimately progressive than anything on many of the year's psychedelic pretenders. With their low-fi recording techniques and Velvet Underground–light style, the Rising Storm can't help but make atmospheric music. A version of Love's "Message to

Pretty" would fit seamlessly onto the Velvet's eponymous third album. The group makes its most striking music when handling its own compositions, whether they're rocking "She Loved Me" or painting "Frozen Laughter" and "The Rain Falls Down" in acid watercolors.

The Rising Storm only printed up 500 copies of their self-released album, selling half and either giving away or keeping the rest. *Calm Before . . .* is one of those forgotten albums that lives up to the myth building.

THE ROLLING STONES: *BETWEEN THE BUTTONS*

The Rolling Stones are the great, dark mirror of rock and roll. As distinctive as their sound is, they were rarely innovators. Whether mimicking their favorite blues artists on their early records or aping disco on things like "Miss You" and (*gag*) "Hot Stuff," the Stones rarely let a popular sound pass them by.

Between the Buttons is an amalgam of the paramount pop styles of late 1966 when the record was recorded. Some have criticized it for shamelessly drawing on *Blonde on Blonde*–era Dylan ("She Smiled Sweetly," "Who's Been Sleeping Here?"), *Rubber Soul*–era Beatles ("Yesterday's Papers," "Back Street Girl"), the Kinks ("Cool, Calm, and Collected," "Something Happened to Me Yesterday"), the Beach Boys ("Complicated"), the Yardbirds ("All Sold Out"), and the Who ("Please Go Home"). Yet these are all terrific tracks infused with the Stones' patented dark sensibility and increasingly complex lyrics that add character studies, surrealism, and tales of legal woes to the usual misogynistic trash.

Despite such reliance on the Stones' contemporaries for inspiration, a couple of the tracks are without precedent. I certainly have never heard anything quite like the sprightly country-rock "Connection," which pulses like a heart monitor, or the swirling, carnival-psych "My Obsession" (Brian Wilson's fave Stones song; he was also present for its production). Charlie Watts gets a chance to take center stage by supplying the main hooks of "My Obsession," "Please Go Home," and "Complicated," while the rest of the group expands the essential Stones sound with vibes, accordion, recorder, kazoo, Dixieland horns, and, for the first time, a harmonica that wheezes like Dylan's instead of whining like Little Walter's. Without a single regularly anthologized track on the album, *Between the Buttons* tends to slip between the cracks. As such, it's a treasure trove of obscure gems by one of rock and roll's most familiar groups.

THEIR SATANIC MAJESTIES REQUEST

For the band's least dogmatic fans, *Their Satanic Majesties Request* is also such a treasure trove. It is the Rolling Stones' most controversial album, even though it was inevitable that rock's biggest fad hoppers would get in on the post–*Sgt. Pepper's* "my art is artier than your art" pissing contest. Yes, *Satanic Majesties* would never have been made without the Beatles' psych monolith. That's inarguable. However, I contend that the Stones' album is more beguiling than the Beatles', and despite its obvious pretensions, it's a perfect encapsulation *and* a perfect critique of psychedelia.

While every other band copped the Beatles' colorful whimsy, no one but the Stones could have created a record that so grippingly captured the alienation, terror, and mystery of the psychedelic experience. "Sing This All Together (See What Happens)" seems an indulgent mess on first listen. Try listening with the lights off. It is blood curdling. The same goes for the extended improvisation on "Gomper," the Fritz Lang future-shock heavy rock of "Citadel," and the album's masterpiece, "2000 Light Years from Home," which is as funky, creative, and foreboding as anything the funky, creative, and foreboding Rolling Stones ever conjured. The moments of hippie-dippy sloganeering come off as mocking parodies when placed among such nasty material, yet moments such as the lovely "She's a Rainbow" remain wonderful at face value. "Sing This All Together" has silly, pseudo-mystical lyrics (supposedly inspired by the Taoist text *The Secret of the Golden Flower*), but it also features the most mesmerizing improvisation on the record.

The self-described "Touch of the Arabian Nights" contributed by Brian Jones (who had recently returned from Morocco with an intense affinity for its traditional music) deepens the album's enchantment. His crafty hand is apparent in so much of the Mellotrons, marimbas, bells, whistles, clangs, and bangs that augment the basic rock backdrop. Keith Richards's guitar work is consistently dirty and bluesy. Tortured riffing invades "Citadel," "2000 Man," "The Lantern," and "Sing This All Together (See What Happens)," keeping the album rooted in the Stones' usual rock and blues. Charlie Watts lays down powerful beats on "She's a Rainbow" and "Citadel," provides "2000 Light Years from Home" with its shuffling funk, and trips up the fluid folk opening of "2000 Man" with one of his most intricate rhythms (that's a 3/4 time beat under a 4/4 melody). The obscure occult references in Mick Jagger's lyrics indicate he's done his homework. Even Bill Wyman distinguishes himself with his first and only songwriting contribution to a Stones album, and "In Another Land" is as visual, dreamy, and gritty as any of the album's other demonic carnival sideshows. At its most effective, art is transporting: it ships you to another world where everything temporal melts away. When I listen to *Satanic Majesties*, I am pulled away from the day's news, whatever is on my "to-do" list, whatever pressures and problems exist in grinding reality, and into a land of sci-fi citadels, meandering spacecraft, river nymphs, ladies faire, surreal dreams, and metaphysical journeys. I never felt overly compelled to indulge in psychedelics because I had *Their Satanic Majesties Request*.

No amount of praise will force listeners who cannot accept the Rolling Stones as anything but purveyors of earthy blues rock to succumb to the bounteous allures of my favorite Rolling Stones album. It certainly has never been a cool Stones album to admit to loving. I first became fascinated with it after falling for "She's a Rainbow" and "2000 Light Years from Home" when I heard them on *Through the Past Darkly (Big Hits Vol. 2)*, the compilation that really made me a Stones freak. When I saw that those two songs were on that bizarre-looking album with the fantasy group portrait on the cover, my curiosity about *Satanic Majesties* was piqued. At the time, I was taking guitar lessons, although my reluctance to do my homework had basically degenerated those lessons into paid hour-long rap about music sessions with my teacher, Joseph. During one of our discussions, I played the Monkees song "Writing Wrongs" for him because I wanted him to help me to understand if it

Michael Cooper shot the cover of *Their Satanic Majesties Request* with an innovative 3D camera. The Stones helped make the quaint fantasy props and quite agreeably dressed up as goofy wizards and minstrels. Long replaced by a run-of-the-mill 2D photo from the same session, the original lenticular 3D cover image was reinstated for this two-LP/two-CD fiftieth anniversary edition of *Satanic Majesties*. Author's collection.

was complex beyond my fourteen-year-old ability to get it or just a bad song. Joseph assured me it was a bad song and said that it reminded him of *Their Satanic Majesties Request*. Well, I had actually already made up my mind about "Writing Wrongs" (bad or not, it fascinated me), and his comment just further stimulated my curiosity about that one Stones album that really did not look like a Stones album to me. He assured me that *Satanic Majesties* is bad too and offered to lend me his own copy (which he kept just for its valuable 3-D cover) so I could hear how bad it was for myself.

I wanted to hate it. I really did. I wanted to hate it because I thought I was *supposed* to hate it. But I didn't. It mesmerized me. And I played it over and over all week long until Joseph came back for the next lesson and I thrust his record at him and said with faux outrage, "Get this thing out of my house." I didn't want him to know that I loved *Their Satanic Majesties Request* or that my musical tastes were starting to go off the rails.

Fuck that. My tastes were just fine. And so are yours regardless if you think *Satanic Majesties* is the cat's meow or a load of rubbish or you'd simply rather listen to Coldplay than the Rolling Stones. We like what we like. Don't let the critics in your life dictate your taste because if I'd been so stubborn that I didn't go out and buy my own copy of *Satanic Majesties* as soon as I handed Joseph's back to him, if I didn't let that album into my life, my life would not have been nearly as rich as it's been.

SAM & DAVE: *SOUL MEN*

Sexy stuff like "You Got Me Hummin'" was a long way from Sam & Dave's roots as gospel crooners. So was the guys' next and biggest smash, "Soul Man," but that single's accompanying album was a retreat from the raucous raunch of *Hold On, I'm Comin'* and *Double Dynamite*. A version of the standard "Let It Be Me" and "Just Keep Holdin' On" indicate how Sam & Dave might have sounded had they stuck with sacred music in 1967. While *Soul Men* is a smokier, mellower record than the ones it followed, the down-tempo vibe allows the guys a freer playing field to improvise. For sheer singing, *Soul Men* might be Sam & Dave's most impressive showcase, even if it isn't their most electrifying.

SMALL FACES: *SMALL FACES*

Maybe Small Faces felt like a totally reborn band after moving from Decca Records to Andrew Oldham's label Immediate. Maybe they were just so happy with their name and the title of their debut album that they decided to call their second one *Small Faces* too. This would be a lot more confusing if the group didn't sound so different this time around. Steve Marriott still shouts with the same soul fury, and there is a strong current of R&B running though these songs, but there is also a superior level of songwriting and playing as well as a noticeable dose of hard psych. Small Faces augments their primal rock lineup with percussion, Mellotron, and horns, but the trippier strain in their music has more to do with delivery than arrangement. "Green Circles," "Things Are Gonna Get Better," and

"Feeling Lonely" are dulcet pop pieces quite unlike anything the band had tried yet. Small Faces plays with greater subtlety too, which is good because these excellent songs deserve to breathe. "My Way of Giving," "Get Yourself Together," "Talk to You," and "Happy Boys Happy" pack major wallops even as the band executes them with sensitive dynamics. With "Tell Me (Have You Ever Seen Me)," Steve Marriott turns the cute line "Pretty flowers are breaking through the concrete" into a scream of triumph, and Kenney Jones wrecks his drum kit in a way he never did

Small Faces loved to name their albums *Small Faces*. Author's collection.

with the Who. *Small Faces* flaunts Small Faces' ability to progress without ever sounding pretentious, a skill that would make their next release one of the best concept albums ever made.

THE SMOKE: . . . *IT'S SMOKE TIME*

The Smoke scored a hit in their native England with the acid-championing "My Friend Jack." They never returned to the charts after that stomping blast of mod psych, so they were not allowed to make more than a single LP. Released only in Germany, *It's Smoke Time* is a hand grenade of pop executed with snarling attitude and buttery vocals curdled by rumbling undercurrents of guitar noise. The hit kicks things off, and nearly every song that follows is just as exceptional. "Waterfall" glistens. "You Can't Catch Me" is all slithery melody and searing feedback. "High in a Room" bounces like Herman's Hermits, but the lacerating guitar slashes would have given

Only the Germans were lucky enough to get this fabulous disc in 1967, but it has since been reissued on CD with oodles of bonus tracks. Author's collection.

Peter Noone the fear. Had they scored another hit after "My Friend Jack," the Smoke may have given the Who and Small Faces a run for their money. Still, one great album is a lot more than most bands achieve.

THE SUPREMES: *THE SUPREMES SING HOLLAND–DOZIER–HOLLAND*

The covers-laden *Supremes A' Go-Go* was significant because it was the first LP by an all-female group to top the *Billboard* charts, but *The Supremes Sing Holland–Dozier–Holland* is a much greater musical achievement. The hits—the saturnine "You Keep Me Hangin' On," the ethereal "Love Is Here and Now You're Gone"—are among the Supremes' finest and might be Motown's first official acknowledgment of the psychedelic era. Many of the non-hits are nearly as wonderful. Diana, Flo, and Mary are at their most ecstatic on the shoulda-been-a-hit "There's No Stopping Us Now," their most dramatic on "Remove This Doubt," and their rawest on "Going Down for the Third Time." The other songs that weren't made famous by other Motown artists are groovy too, and the redundant covers are kept to a relatively minimal three. So don't be fooled by its generic title and cover. Only the slightly cornball "Love Is in Our Hearts" is a bit flimsy. The *Supremes Sing Holland–Dozier–Holland* is essentially the Supremes' *Revolver*: eclectic, a bit dark, a bit freaky, but always inviting.

THE TEMPTATIONS: *WITH A LOT O' SOUL*

As terrific as *The Supremes Sing Holland–Dozier–Holland* and the Four Tops' *Reach Out* are, they still rely on too many outdated album-making methods to sound truly in step with 1967. *With a Lot O' Soul* may have been a hint that Holland–Dozier–Holland and Smokey Robinson were saving all their best untouched songs for the Temptations.

With a Lot O' Soul isn't just a solid collection of songs that hadn't already been made famous by Rodgers and Hart or the Monkees—it's a great soul album track after track, showing off how fabulously the Temps conveyed sweetness ("All I Need," "It's You That I Need," "You're My Everything") and paranoia ("I'm Losing You," "Ain't No Sun Since You've Been Gone," "No More Water in the Well"). None of it sounds particularly in tune with its era's psychedelic sensibilities, as the Supremes' contemporaneous hit "Reflections" did, nor does it hint at how the Temptations would soon launch themselves into Lysergic Land with things like "Could Nine." It's simply the most rock solid Motown album of the sixties.

TRAFFIC: *MR. FANTASY/HEAVEN IS IN YOUR MIND*

The release of *Sgt. Pepper's* ushered in an era of rock-album-as-art and (mostly) brought an end to the one in which British LPs were hacked to pieces in the United States for purely commercial reasons. Oddly, an exception in this new era was one of its most genuinely artful records, and its pond-crossing alterations were some of the most convoluted. In the United Kingdom, Traffic's debut was titled *Mr. Fantasy*, contained no tracks previously released as singles, and favored several solo compositions by guitarist Dave Mason. In the United States, *Heaven Is in Your Mind* lost two Mason tracks, both examples of his delightfully naive and exotic psychedelic pop, and gained the singles "Paper Sun" and "Hole in My Shoe" as well as "We're a Fade, You Missed This." The latter track is a clear attempt to give the American album a sort of *Pepper*-esque reprise, as it is a brief sample of the extended fade from an alternate version of "Paper Sun." The almost subliminal snatches of the single "Here We Go Round the Mulberry Bush," used to link most of the tracks, are also used for conceptual unity. In other words, *Mr. Fantasy* was butchered in the United States for reasons both commercial *and* artistic. To muddle the story further, the American LP was eventually rereleased as *Mr. Fantasy*, yet the altered track listing remained.

Messing with British albums for the U.S. market will always be a controversial practice. For the most part, Americans received inferior products. In some odd cases, they received albums arguably stronger than their purer British counterparts (*Rubber Soul*, perhaps? *The Rolling Stones Now!* vs. *Rolling Stones No. 2*, maybe?). *Mr. Fantasy* vs. *Heaven Is in Your Mind* is a bit of a case of "six of one/half dozen of another." *Heaven Is in Your Mind* may have beaten *Mr. Fantasy* had it lost some of its less spectacular tracks, such as the jazzy jam "Giving to You," but the Mason tracks lopped off it are as strong as the two singles included. There's a specific reason Mason's tracks were the ones that were sacrificed, though; he'd left the band since its creation, hence his absence from the cover of the American disc.

So what Americans were left with was a drastically changed album (the running order was juggled too) that may have been more in tune with the post-*Pepper* era than the band intended it to be. Questions of purity aside, *Heaven Is in Your Minds* is an excellent product of its time with all the idioms represented. Acoustic psychedelia? Check. Baroque folk? Check. Sweeping psych anthems? Check. Raga rock? Check. Mellotrons and harpsichords and woodwinds and whimsical narration and sitars and the aforementioned reprise and jazz and music-hall gestures? Check, check, check,

check, check, check, check, and check. There's also Steve Winwood's soul wail to tether the sundry celestial debris to Earth.

THE TURTLES: *HAPPY TOGETHER*

The year 1967 was a breakthrough one for the Turtles. It's when they released the hit singles that really defined their career and their most commercially successful LP. Losing most of the folk leanings of their first two albums, the Turtles made a more typically wacky album. "Happy Together" and "Me About You" are too moody to really categorize as bubblegum music, but "She'd Rather Be with Me," "Guide for the Married Man," "Makin' My Mind Up," and "Person Without a Care" deliver the Bazooka Joe goods. The Turtles also start exploring their inner zany for good ("The Walking Song") and ill (the unlistenable "Rugs of Woods and Flowers").

VARIOUS ARTISTS: *MONTEREY INTERNATIONAL POP FESTIVAL* (RELEASED IN 1992)

Capturing rock and roll at a less self-indulgent and drab phase than Woodstock would, the Monterey Pop Festival is arguably rock's ultimate multi-day, multi-artist extravaganza. The concert that took place from June 16 through June 18 at the outset of the mythologized "Summer of Love" made room for soul (Otis Redding and Booker T. & the M.G.'s, Lou Rawls), raga (classical sitarist Ravi Shankar), jazz (Hugh Masekela), singer-songwriters (Laura Nyro), blues (Big Brother and the Holding Company), pacific pop (Simon & Garfunkel, the Mamas & the Papas) proto-punk (the Who), and, of course, psychedelic rock (the Animals, Country Joe and the Fish, Jefferson Airplane, the Jimi Hendrix Experience) artists. The performances were as electric as they are eclectic. The bands and artists were in a great mood. No one had to stand in mud or rain.

Sure there were some boring local groups like the Grateful Dead and the Quicksilver Messenger Service, but most of the performances captured for posterity in D. A. Pennebaker's essential concert film *Monterey Pop* and the *Monterey International Pop Festival* box set belatedly released in 1992 mostly highlight the best of the show.

As the liner notes state, not every artist who was recorded agreed to be included on the 1992 box. Such refusers must include Laura Nyro, Simon & Garfunkel, and Buffalo Springfield, all of whom had performances captured on film. This is unfortunate since all of the aforementioned artists made some good noise at the festival (and don't listen to the much-repeated rap that Nyro embarrassed herself: one listen to her breath-snatching performance of "Poverty Train" on the DVD of Pennebaker's *Monterey Pop* concert film quashes that myth).

The first disc of *Monterey International Pop Festival* has the most variety, with the Association comporting themselves very well for a token lightweight pop act, Lou Rawls proving that Otis wasn't soul's only breakout performer at the fest, and Big Brother and the Holding Company ripping the ceiling down for the disc's best set. Performing the funky "Not So Sweet Martha Lorraine," Country Joe and the Fish are better represented here than they are in Pennebaker's film, which features the atmospheric drivel "Section 43" instead. Eric Burdon and the Animals don't fare as well, with their good, fiddle-driven cover of "Paint It Black" being passed over in favor of the embarrassing "San Franciscan Nights." Canned Heat play some so-so white-guy blues.

An overabundance of white-guy blues makes the first half of the second disc kind of a drag. The worst offenders are the Butterfield Blues Band, who are represented by five dreary tracks and followed by a few cuts by the Steve Miller Band and the Electric Flag that are only marginally better. The disc gets legitimately interesting with Hugh Masekela's "Bajabula Bonke (Healing Song)," which careens from discordant screams to a meditative jazz sigh. Then we get a full set from the Byrds, whose playing and singing are unbelievably sloppy. They do bring a bit of much-needed garage-band chutzpah to the disc, and David Crosby's between-songs hippie rants are hilarious. Finally, there's a Ravi Shankar raga edited down to a mere six minutes and a looooong but relatively lively jam from the Blues Project that veers closer to Motown soul than the dull blues that began the disc. Diagnosis: needs less Butterfield, more Shankar.

The third disc is the set's unadulterated gem with monumental sets from Jefferson Airplane, Booker T. & the M.G.'s, Otis Redding, and the Who. No complaints here, just committed performances from some of the era's greatest stage acts. Getting to hear the Who perform a rare live performance of the fabulous single "Pictures of Lily" is a particular treat, and hearing a tech trying to get the mic working after the band smashes the place to pieces is the uproarious icing on the cake.

The fourth disc is split between just two groups, and the Jimi Hendrix Experience and the Mamas & the Papas couldn't be more different. Hendrix's set needs no talking up. He transformed "Like a Rolling Stone" and "Wild Thing" into aural Star Destroyers. He fucked his amp and set his guitar on fire. He dressed like Clarabell the Clown and mumbled a stream of psychedelic nonsense between songs. Awesome. After him, the pleasant pop of the Mamas & the Papas could only be anticlimactic, and a bass player who apparently never heard any of their songs before further hinders the group. Despite an apparent lack of rehearsal, the Mamas & the Papas still put on a good show, bringing three nights of electric lunacy to a pleasingly mellow conclusion.

THE VELVET UNDERGROUND: *THE VELVET UNDERGROUND AND NICO*

The New York sound of the mid-sixties was the folky lilt of Simon & Garfunkel, the garage thump of Blues Magoos, or, at its most outré, the piss-taking of the Fugs. Nobody sounded like the Velvet Underground, the defiantly unlovable quartet of hipsters who served as the house band of Andy Warhol's Factory clique. Although there are wispy traces of Paul Simon folkiness in the Velvet's lighter moments—"I'll Be Your Mirror," "Sunday Morning," "Femme Fatale"—garage energy in their noisy attack, and Fugs-style sex and drugs (sans the jokiness) in Lou Reed's story songs, the Velvet Underground sounds nothing like any of those bands. Their nightmare obsessions with death, S&M decadence, hard drugs, and grungy street life made the darkest Stones records seem wholly inauthentic. The Velvets unleashed squalls of noise that went far beyond anything in the Who's vocabulary. Nico's Teutonic dron-ing and the unrelenting bleakness would have dispersed one of Procol Harum's black masses. The *Velvet Underground and Nico* is the album Jim Morrison would have made had he been half the visionary Lou Reed or John Cale (or even Morrison's occasional girlfriend Nico) was.

The Velvet Underground and Nico would be indispensably influential on glam, punk, New Wave, and indie rock. If it didn't exist, there would be no Modern Lovers, no Patti Smith, no Talking Heads, no Television, no Siouxsie and the Banshees, no Pere Ubu, no Cure, no R.E.M., no Jesus & Mary Chain, no Sonic Youth, no Pixies, no Nirvana, no My

The banana on original copies of *The Velvet Underground & Nico* peeled away to reveal a pink fruit beneath. I'm pretty sure Andy Warhol didn't intend it to be a phallic symbol though. Author's collection.

Bloody Valentine, no Yo La Tengo, no. . . well, you get the picture. While every rock band of the first half of 1967 looked forward to the midyear game changer the Beatles were reportedly creating, *Sgt. Pepper's* arguably wouldn't have as enduring an effect on rock as an album barely anyone heard during its time would.

WHITE LIGHT/WHITE HEAT

White Light/White Heat, however, is the album that separates the dabblers from the truly committed acolytes. Nico's harsh baritone may be gone, but the Velvets don't need her to crank up the harshness on a most unrelentingly noisy set. The power of tracks such as the title one, "I Heard Her Call My Name," and the endless "Sister Ray" is undeniable. The Velvets manage to mold their feedback racket into something truly dreamy for "Lady Godiva's Operation."

 White Light/White Heat is renowned for its abrasiveness, but its most distinctive feature may be its humorousness. "Lady Godiva's Operation" and the spoken word "The Gift" are laugh-out-loud funny. After a good ten minutes or so, "Sister Ray" becomes a patience test, but "too busy sucking on my ding-dong" is the most incongruously and uproariously juvenile refrain imaginable from a group with the Velvet Underground's grave persona. "Here She Comes Now" is the only number that scales back the noise, and its pensive hum would be the defining sound of the Velvet's next curve ball.

THE WHO: *THE WHO SELL OUT*

Americans didn't know how good they had it in the sixties. In 1964, the Federal Communications Commission's FM Non-Duplication Rule, which officially decreed that AM and FM radio stations in the same geographic location must not broadcast more than 25 percent of the same programming, as well as the proliferation of car and transistor radios, resulted in a wealth of diverse radio programs, 90 percent of which featured music of all genres by 1967. DJs such as Murray the K in New York often eschewed the overplayed hits of top-forty FM stations for groovy album tracks that became known as "FM cuts." It would not be unusual to hear something as radio unfriendly as Dylan's epic "Desolation Row" on such programs.

In Britain, the stodgy old BBC was less varied, so hip music listeners had to rely on illegal offshore signals to hear groovy DJs and groovier music. When the Beeb wiped out the pirates for good in 1967, the Who's managers Kit Lambert and Chris Stamp conceived *The Who Sell Out*, a tribute that used fake advertisements and promos to link dazzling songs.

Too much is made of this gimmick, and even more is made of the fact that it isn't used between every song on side B (which always rang true to me; the radio shows I used to listen to always featured "rock blocks" of uninterrupted songs). Yes, the ads are clever and fun. Fabulously, some of the full-length songs are actually extended ads, such as the heavenly deodorant commercial "Odorono." This song unfolds as one of Townshend's funniest, most suspenseful dramas: a pretty ingénue has just retired to the dressing room following her triumphant stage debut. The man of her dreams, a certain Mr. Davidson, comes calling to praise her performance, but—alas!—he flees after catching a whiff of her B.O. If only she'd used Odorono. Revealing itself to be an ode to antiperspirant only with its final line, "Odorono" is a terrific practical joke on the listener, but it's also a truly lovely piece of music with the Who's lush harmonies soaring over Townshend's elliptical guitar riff. Advertisements like this might keep more people from hitting the "mute" button during station breaks.

And as clever as the album's concept is, the quality of songs such as "Odorono" and the band's thoughtful performances are its real draws. The Who brush out a sound that is dense yet ethereal. This is beautiful music with little of their usual thunder, though they do retain their wiseass humor through "Odorono," the flamencofied "Mary Anne with the Shaky Hands" (a sweet song about getting jerked off by a prostitute), and John Entwistle's Edwardian chant "Silas Stingy." "Tattoo" is a delightful combination of silly humor, traditional storytelling, and ethereal elegance as well as a return to the teen concerns of *My Generation*. Two brothers decide to commemorate their impending manhood by getting tattoos, each triggering disastrous results when Mom and Dad get a load of them. My pick for "most perfect song Pete Townshend ever composed," "Tattoo" is a tragicomic portrait of adolescence, an inspired example of otherworldly production (the descending guitar riff channeled through a revolving Leslie speaker is a beautiful touch), and a monument to Townshend, Daltrey, and Entwistle's superb three-part harmonies. Daltrey provides one of his most sensitive lead vocals, proving he could do a lot more than bluster. As the only song from *The Who Sell Out* that would regularly feature in live Who performances throughout the band's career, "Tattoo" possesses a magic that clearly was not lost on the men who created it. Jokiness is dropped on the most romantic songs Townshend ever wrote ("I Can't Reach You," "Our Love Was," and his jazzy solo piece "Sunrise")—lush beauty is not.

For those who prefer the Who at their more incendiary, there's the thrashing midsection of "Relax" and the controlled tumult of "I Can See for Miles," which was the group's biggest hit in the United States (although the fact that it didn't hit number one in Townshend's home country irked him for years). On the enigmatic "Rael," Townshend takes the Wagnerian aspirations of "A Quick One, While He's Away" to their extremes and ends up with one of the most enigmatic story-songs in the Who's catalog. Initially, he intended "Rael" to be a full-blown opera about a postapocalyptic conflict between Israel and Red China with protégé Arthur Brown (who'd soon have a huge international hit with "Fire") in the lead role. When management reminded him that the band was in greater need of a new hit single than another unwieldy concept, Townshend edited "Rael" mercilessly, boiling away the plot until he was left with an indecipherable but breathtaking six-minute piece still too long for a single in 1967. Although "Rael" does not provide the satisfying storytelling of "A Quick One, While He's Away," it is a more unified piece of songwriting, its multiple sections flowing into one another fluidly, its harmonies tighter and denser, its musicianship flawless. Townshend did not drop the rock-opera issue with "Rael," and he even recycled some

If a record was not selling well, shopkeepers would saw a notch in the cover's spine, punch a hole in a corner, or just clip the corner off with scissors and drop it in bargain or "cut out" bins to be sold at a drastic discount. *The Who Sell Out* was a regular occupant of cut out bins after its unsuccessful American release. As you can see from the clipped lower right-hand corner, my own copy was a victim of the bin. Author's collection.

of its instrumental passages on the Who's next album, but nothing on *Tommy* bested "Rael" in terms of musical complexity or operatic grandeur. He'd also reuse the midsection of "Sunrise" and the "see, feel, or hear you" refrain of "I Can't Reach You" on *Tommy*. Such pieces hardly needed to be salvaged. They'd already found perfect homes on an album not as well known as *Tommy* but much more timeless. The Who would never again strike such a flawless balance of supernatural splendor, muscle, cartoon comedy, and stark romanticism as they did on *The Who Sell Out*.

THE YOUNG RASCALS: *COLLECTIONS*

While the Velvet Underground was the East Coast's most uniquely progressive band, the Young Rascals was its most expertly old-fashioned. The New Jersey quartet played soul and pop with the professionalism of a wedding band, the natural spirit of a Stax act, and the catching joy of the early Beatles.

On their second album, the Young Rascals also began developing into fine songwriters. The elating "What Is the Reason" and "Love Is a Beautiful Thing" are the best things they wrote in their original soulful style. However, *Collections'* combo of covers and originals was way too old-fashioned for the year of the art album. Relying on only a single cover, the Young Rascals got their act together for their second LP of 1967.

GROOVIN'

Felix Cavalerie and Eddie Brigati's originals make *Groovin'* the best Rascals album yet. That they could whip together a bunch of smashes that ranged from their usual fresh soul ("A Girl Like You") to threatening garage punk ("You Better Run") to adult pop ("How Can I Be Sure" with its crushing Brigati vocal) to a great little hippie idyll (the title track) makes one wonder why they weren't doing their homework from the very beginning.

The non-hits are terrific and eclectic too as the guys show off how well they can drone ("Find Somebody"), spray sunshine ("I'm So Happy Now"), groove ("If You Knew"), and trip out ("It's Love"). On *Groovin'*, the group that would soon drop the "Young" from their name grew up, and unlike a lot of their peers, they did it without giving up a crumb of their innate pop gifts.

1968

After a year of bold and ambitious artistic statements, the LP was firmly established as rock's most meaningful art form. This was reflected in stereophonic sound taking precedence over monophonic. While mono was still the chief format for singles in the days before most radio stations began broadcasting in stereo, the LP began favoring two-channel sound in 1968. Stereo was originally considered to be an audiophile format for lovers of "adult" jazz, classical, Broadway, and easy-listening sounds. Although albums by artists such as the Teddy Bears and Elvis Presley were mixed in stereo shortly after the format debuted in 1958, young rock and roll fans continued to favor the mono records, which were less expensive and could be played on less sophisticated equipment. Following a $1 price drop in 1968, stereo became the principal rock format just one year after *Sgt. Pepper's* forced the rock LP into maturity once and for all. Yet George Martin and the Beatles paid so little mind to stereo in 1967 that they spent just three days on *Pepper's'* stereo mix after lavishing three weeks of attention on its mono one. In 1969, the Beatles, the Stones, Dylan, and many other major artists would not even bother to mix their latest releases in mono, though "fold downs" (a combination of a stereo mix's two channels into a single monophonic one) still appeared in certain markets. The industry seemed to be encouraging this shift of preference, as many labels raised the shelf price of mono LPs to that of stereo ones in mid-1967.

As psychedelia waned over the course of 1968, groups stopped falling over each other to prove they were the artsiest artists of all and just settled into making mature, strong works. This does not mean that mad experimentation drained out of rock completely, and Nico, Jimi Hendrix, and the Monkees (yes, *The Monkees*) made some of the strangest albums of the sixties in 1968. However, the controlling theme of the year was the anti–freak show "back to the roots" trend that Dylan initiated when he issued the stripped *John Wesley Harding* from his tree-lined retreat in Woodstock, New York, at the end of the previous year. That record, as well as another by Dylan's neighbors and collaborators the Band, completely shifted rock and roll from the cosmos to the farm in 1968, and pretty soon, hippies across the nation were rambling about "getting it together in the country."

It's ironic that Dylan was such a leader in this movement since he both hated being thought of as a leader and hated hippies. In fact, he'd essentially abandoned the leftist politics that won his original following to become pretty conservative—perhaps not incidentally, the prevailing political stance of pre–hippie influx Woodstock—following the lead of manager Albert Grossman into an odd-bedfellow balance of rustic living and materialism and even privately voicing support for segregationist George Wallace. Nevertheless, the hippies flooded Woodstock, tried their best to get to Dylan, and would stage the most famous outdoor festival in rock history in 1969.

Meaningfully, the movement away from overly fussy and complex recordings arrived in a year of traumatic complexity that left a lot of people longing for simpler times. On January 30, the conflict in Vietnam reached its boiling point after a sneak attack during what was supposed to be a Tet holiday truce caught the U.S. military with its pants down. On March 16, American soldiers acted out in the most horrendous way imaginable when they raped, mutilated, and massacred hundreds of citizens in My Lai. Two weeks later, civil rights leader Martin Luther King Jr. led a march through Memphis that ended with the death of a teenage boy and the injury of sixty other people. King himself would be murdered on April 4. On April 23, the police brought a violent end to a demonstration at Columbia University, and on May 6, student demonstrators in Paris engaged in their own revolutionary conflict against gas grenade–hurling cops. Andy Warhol was shot on June 3. Robert Kennedy was shot two days later and died on the June 6. Cops beat protesters at the Democratic National Convention in Chicago on August 28. Cops and soldiers murdered protestors in Mexico City on October 2. And then, on November 5, Richard Nixon was elected president of the United States, ensuring many more dark days to come.

P. P. ARNOLD: *FIRST LADY OF IMMEDIATE*

Pat Arnold was opening for the Rolling Stones as an Ikette in the Ike and Tina Turner Review when she struck up a friendship with Mick Jagger. Jealous Ike gave Pat her pink slip, but the Stones' savvy manager, Andrew "Loog" Oldham, quickly signed her up to his label, Immediate Records.

As P. P. Arnold, she released "Everything's Gonna Be Alright," a smooth bubblegum soul production that was equal parts Phil Spector and Motown, but the record's real gem—and the real indicator of the Arnold agenda—was the flip side. "Life Is Nothing" is a moody, acoustic ballad with tasteful strings that is more reminiscent of the Beatles than anything Aretha Franklin would have cut. That's what really set P. P. Arnold apart from her soul peers: she essentially transformed British pop numbers into achingly soulful workouts every time she layered on her emotionally wrenching cracked rasp. Frankly, all I have to do is *think* about that voice, and I get a lump in my throat. You don't want to be around when I actually hear it.

What P. P. Arnold was doing was not dissimilar to the records of her label mates, Small Faces, so when she eventually started recording with them, it was a match made in Northern Soul Nirvana. She shreds her vocal cords beyond the call of duty on her greatest record, which was written by Small Faces Steve Marriott and Ronnie Lane and saddled with the laughably dated title "(If You Think You're) Groovy." Her most famous record is the definitive reading of Cat Stevens's "The First Cut Is the Deepest." Such singles hooked *The First Lady of Immediate*, though all twelve tracks do their part in making it a flawless soul-pop debut. "Am I Still Dreaming" would have prodded Spiro Agnew to leap off his ass and do the pony.

P.P. Arnold's excellent first two albums are tough to come by these days, but this 2001 compilation is a nifty way to obtain all of her *Immediate*-era work on CD. *The First Lady of Immediate* and *Kafunta* really deserve proper vinyl reissues though. Author's collection.

KAFUNTA

Arnold's second album, the more conceptually produced *Kafunta*, is weakened by too many polite arrangements of overly familiar covers. Andrew Oldham may have been the man who sculpted the Stones' "bad boy" image, but his real ambition was to be Phil Spector, and he overproduces *Kafunta* to a near fault. Arnold salvages much of it by fully committing to her versions of "As Tears Go By," "Eleanor Rigby," and "Yesterday." They're still pretty inessential, but her reading of Spector's own (and the Ronettes') "Is This What I Get for Loving You, Baby?" is excellent, and "God Only Knows" is astounding, especially since the original features what might be the most beautiful pop vocal ever recorded. That it's not irrelevant is a major feat. That it's one of P. P. Arnold's best is practically miraculous. That she also sang a spectacular version of "Angel of the Morning"—a song that more famously got the sap treatment from the likes of Juice Newton, Merilee Rush, and Olivia Newton John—is equally unfathomable. Careening from P. P. Arnold's throat, "Angel of the Morning" is an exemplar of mighty assuredness, and John Paul Jones's exquisite baroque-soul arrangement is the LP's best.

THE BAND: *MUSIC FROM BIG PINK*

In 1968, Bob Dylan's backing band got together at a house (known as "Big Pink") in Saugerties, New York, and wrote a batch of songs that developed on the mystic Americana themes of their boss's *John Wesley Harding*. The resulting album introduced the Band as a group far less generic than their name suggests. Garth Hudson's shimmering, creeping organ fills; Robbie Robertson's tortured guitar lines; and Levon Helms's solid funk beats blend into a totally unique brew. There certainly is no equivalent to the group's ramshackle harmonies: three voices working together beautifully—each one rough and distinct.

An original Bob Dylan painting is featured on the cover of *Music from Big Pink*. Author's collection.

That seemingly casual approach travels through every performance on *Music from Big Pink*, but the songs, though unconventional, are crafted with great care. There is one marvelously interpreted traditional number ("Long Black Veil"), and Dylan lends a helping compositional hand to three arresting tracks ("Tears of Rage," "This Wheel's on Fire," and "I Shall Be Released"), but the Band do just fine on their own with the outstanding originals "Caledonia Mission," "We Can Talk," "Chest Fever," and "The Weight." They would need no outside assistance at all on their next and greatest record.

THE BEACH BOYS: *FRIENDS*

The Beach Boys went through a weird period after abandoning SMiLE. As a possible reaction to the failure of what would have been an elaborately produced magnum opus, they released *Smiley Smile* and *Wild Honey*, two skeletally produced albums. With *Friends*, the Beach Boys started to regain their ambitions. The songs retain the offhand simplicity of their previous two albums, but the arrangements are more intricate and varied than those on *Smiley Smile* or *Wild Honey* (though still far from the density of the *Pet Sounds/SMiLE* era).

The Beach Boys augment their lush harmonies with organ, bells, strings, jazzy guitar, various harmonicas, woodwinds, brass, ukulele, and just about anything else they (and the studio musicians who did the bulk of the instrumental work) could get their hands on. The group sounds completely refreshed after their recent troubles, and though some of the material is lightweight, all of it sounds as gorgeous as their best work.

And much of the material *is* great. There's the warm and odd title track (with its instrumental break that reminds me of "The Chipmunk Song"), the sincerely positive "Wake the World," and the sincere yet surreal tone poem "Diamond Head." "Busy Doin' Nothin'" is an oddity in the Beach Boys' body of work because of its breezy samba rhythm, its total lack of choral harmonies, and its status as a track composed solely by Brian Wilson. Always confident at the piano, Brian was less comfortable as a lyricist and tended to rely on people such as Mike Love, Tony Asher, and Van Dyke Parks to supply the words. Lyrically, "Busy Doin' Nothin'" is idiosyncratic in a way distinct from Mike Love's surf/cars/girls obsessions, Tony Asher's romanticism, and Van Dyke Parks's cosmic weirdness. Brian composed his tale of time wasting in an awkwardly plainspoken manner that essentially ditches pop lyric conventions, such as rhyme and regular meter. Unusual as it is in the Beach Boys' oeuvre, Brian's lyric is absolutely charming. His arrangement of light percussion, woodwinds, and acoustic bass is exquisite. Less effortlessly lovable is "Transcendental Meditation," an invigorating reminder of how out-there the Beach Boys could get. In 1967, they became the second most famous pop band to fall in line behind the Maharishi Mahesh Yogi and start practicing his patented meditation technique. In tribute, they recorded this discordantly freaky jazz rocker with the heaviest sax work this side of Captain Beefheart. Experimental. Dennis Wilson, he of the rough larynx and pinup puss, emerges as the most promising new writer in the bunch. His "Be Still" is pretty yet slight, but "Little Bird" is a taught mini-masterwork with an inventive rhythm and a catchy "nya nya

nya" chorus. It also marks the beginning of the ecological concerns that would dominate the band's best early seventies work.

THE BEATLES: *THE BEATLES*

As if the Beatles hadn't already earned their crown as popular music's ultimate group, they followed their triumphant *Sgt. Pepper* with the single greatest encapsulation of popular music ever blasted onto four sides of vinyl. The *Beatles* (aka "The White Album") is like an encyclopedia of popular music. The Beatles didn't set out to achieve this self-consciously. They just dug a wide variety of sounds and wrote a titanic wealth of songs during a Transcendental Meditation retreat in India with guru Maharishi Mahesh Yogi.

The Beatles and producer George Martin debated whether to put out *The Beatles* as a double album. Most of the group favored the double; Martin fought for a single (and for the rest of his life, he continued to insist they should have pruned it). Fortunately, the band won out because *The Beatles* wouldn't be *The Beatles* if it didn't include all of the zany toss-offs and gimmick songs that make it so fascinatingly sprawling, delightfully indulgent, and deliriously diverse. Nearly every type of existing pop subgenre is present on this thirty-track crazy quilt: straight rock and roll, surf, psychedelia, hard rock, ska, doo-wop, chamber pop, folk, baroque, C&W, blues, heavy metal, jazz, soul, musique concrète, and Hollywood schmaltz. If hip-hop was around in 1968, they would have had Ringo beat boxing and Lennon freestyling about his smack habit.

The Beatles wouldn't be so enduring if it were nothing more than an exercise in variety. So many of the Fabs' greatest songs are here: "Happiness Is a Warm Gun," "While My Guitar Gently Weeps," "Everybody's Got Something to Hide Except for Me and My Monkey," "Long, Long, Long," "Cry Baby Cry," "Dear Prudence," "Glass Onion," "Martha My Dear." Scattered amongst the meat and potatoes are nutso experiments and parodies such as "Wild Honey Pie," "Piggies," "Goodnight," "Rocky Raccoon," "The Continuing Story of Bungalow Bill," and "Revolution 9," which is hated by many Beatle fans but provides *The Beatles* with its necessary—and really scary—climax. Losing it would be like editing the star-gate sequence out of *2001: A Space Odyssey*. The Beatles released albums that were more consistently strong than their eponymous magnum opus, but the inconsistencies of *The Beatles* make it all the more enthralling and enveloping.

JEFF BECK: *TRUTH*

Leaving the Yardbirds in Jimmy Page's capable hands, Jeff Beck put together his own group and went to work on his first solo record. The overall sound is fiery British blues, but the territory is far more expansive. Beck refreshes his own history by revisiting the Yardbirds' classic "Shapes of Things" as a swaggering behemoth. He brings similar flavor to "Let Me Love You" and Willie Dixon's "I Ain't Superstitious," essentially giving birth to the exact kind of heavy blues Led Zeppelin would make massively popular in the early seventies.

But *Truth* isn't all boozy dick swinging. Renditions of the standards "Greensleeves" and "Ol' Man River" are sensitive pastorals. A version of the folk standard "Morning Dew" seesaws between simmering menace and animal adrenaline. The extended blues jam "Blues Deluxe" is as dull as those types of things tend to be, but the instrumental "Beck's Bolero" (originally released as the B-side of Beck's solo British hit "Hi-Ho Silver Lining" in early 1967) is maniacal, mostly due to the antics of a timpani player credited as "You Know Who" (Keith Moon playing hooky from Track Records). Throughout the record, Rod Stewart shows what he was capable of before he fell in love with pink satin pants.

BIG BROTHER AND THE HOLDING COMPANY: *CHEAP THRILLS*

Janis Joplin got her revenge on the conformists who made her Texas childhood a living hell when she moved up to San Francisco and received carte blanche to let her freak flag fly. Life certainly improved for her, but the pain of her past lingered, and she directed those emotions into some of rock's rawest vocal bloodletting.

Joplin did not always get the best band or material to match the power of her voice, but when everything aligned, she was capable of greatness. Her most important band is Big Brother and the Holding Company, and their most notable album is *Cheap Thrills*, but it is a hit-or-miss affair. The ramshackle "Combination of the Two" was exciting at the Monterey Pop Festival, but its embarrassingly dated lyrics and lack of structure or tune make it weary at-home listening. The lesser-known tracks are indistinct. Big Mama Thornton's "Ball and Chain" was Monterey's ultimate showstopper, so its vinyl version can only suffer in comparison. However, a suitably humid rendition of George Gershwin's "Summertime" is magical seasonal mood music, and the remake of Erma Franklin's "Piece of My Heart" may be Joplin's definitive record. The stage is where she really shined, though.

THE BYRDS: *THE NOTORIOUS BYRD BROTHERS*

The Byrds started to unravel when drummer Michael Clarke quit and David Crosby got fired while recording their fifth album. Under such tumultuous conditions, the band somehow recorded what may be their most placid and beguiling album. The *Notorious Byrd Brothers* gets off to an uncharacteristically strident start with the shrill, brassy, amphetamine-celebrating "Artificial Energy," but then the mood settles down for a string of light-psychedelic creations. The sweet waltzes "Get to You" and "Tribal Gathering," the ecologically minded "Dolphin's Smile," and Goffin and King's "Goin' Back" and "Wasn't Born to Follow" are all peaceful pieces. The Byrds' placid harmonies and

When the Byrds kicked David Crosby out of the band, they replaced him with a horse on the cover of *The Notorious Byrd Brothers*. Apparently the horse was a much more agreeable collaborator. Author's collection.

chiming guitars alleviate the antiwar angst of "Draft Morning." Even its machine-gun sound effects are strangely serene. Only the synth-saturated oddity "Space Odyssey" raises the temper back up a bit.

SWEETHEART OF THE RODEO

Personnel changes continued to upset the Byrds after *The Notorious Byrd Brothers*, and before making their next record, they acquired a new member who'd remake their sound radically. Although the band had dabbled in country on most of their previous albums, *Sweetheart of the Rodeo* is such a complete excursion into the genre that it may as well have been credited to a totally different band. Thank Gram Parsons.

The Byrds were 100 percent at home in their rustic digs. Parsons's croon on "I Am a Pilgrim" and "Hickory Wind" is more authentically soulful than the Byrds' earlier attempt to ape Stax on "Captain Soul." When Roger McGuinn steps in, his mock drawl withers that authenticity. He remolds the Louvin Brothers' absurdly pious "The Christian Life" into an uproarious comedy number, and his version of Dylan's "You Ain't Going Nowhere" is as droll as it would be when the writer later recorded his own version. For many major acts, 1968 was a year of retreat from all things trippy. No one took that "return to your roots" attitude further than the Byrds did with *Sweetheart of the Rodeo*.

CREAM: *WHEELS OF FIRE*

Like George Harrison's *All Things Must Pass*, *Wheels of Fire* is an album that can be fully valued only if certain parts are ignored. *All Things Must Pass* is a phenomenal double album that includes a completely disposable bonus record full of boring jams. *Wheels of Fire* is Cream's best studio album, but it also includes a live disc that displays some of their worst tendencies.

The live portion is not a complete washout. "Crossroads," which has been mercifully edited down from its original length, is a succinct and spirited blues rocker, but only the most masochist listener will sit through all 17:39 of Ginger Baker's drum solo.

Baker atones for the punishment he doles out on "Toad" with his contributions to the studio half of *Wheels of Fire*. He comes into his own as a writer on "Passing the Time," which splits time between a magically starry verse and a ferocious mid-song vamp. His odd "Pressed Rat and Wart Hog" makes good use of his off-key vocals and *Wind in the Willows* whimsy. Baker is also the engine behind the dramatic and absurd hit "White Room," though Jack Bruce makes it beautiful. "As You Said" is simply beautiful. Cream are in rare unplugged mode, and Bruce's tenor is at its most spine tingling.

Really, every studio track on *Wheels of Fire* is excellent. The group had never put together such inventive arrangements. Bruce and Baker's bass/drum interplay is as frenzied as their personal relationship. The playing on the live side is strong, but with barely any songs, it's best left in its sleeve.

DONOVAN: *THE HURDY GURDY MAN*

In an era defined by wild diversity, Donovan made exceptionally cohesive albums. From the man with a guitar folksiness of his first two albums to the Swinging London raga folk of *Sunshine Superman* to the jazziness of *Mellow Yellow* to the spare children's ditties of *A Gift from a Flower to a*

Garden, each of Donovan's albums followed a tonal theme. On *The Hurdy Gurdy Man*, he started to boggle up those sounds a bit. There is raga-rock drone ("Peregrine," "The River Song," "Tangier"), jazz ("Get Thy Bearings"), light pop ("The Sun Is a Very Magic Fellow"), "There Is a Mountain"–style calypso ("West Indian Lady"), floral balladry ("Jennifer Juniper"), and one acid-rock smash that may not be the Led Zeppelin audition tape it is rumored to be (John Paul Jones is the only Zeppelinite to play on "Hurdy Gurdy Man"), but it sure sounds like it is.

Another groovy art nouveau creation for a Donovan record. This one's by David Richards. Author's collection.

THE DOORS: *WAITING FOR THE SUN*

Without any of the fatuous epics of their first two albums and with the band's bubblegummiest hit—the Kinks rip-off "Hello, I Love You"—*Waiting for the Sun* feels like the Doors' poppiest LP. Although its songs are compact, they're actually the group's weirdest assortment. "Not to Touch the Earth" (mercifully whittled down from Morrison's biggest brain wave yet: a sidelong drivel fest called "Celebration of the Lizard") is dissonant and only marginally listenable. "My Wild Love" is the kind of a cappella Native America chant only a bunch of white hippies could devise.

The rest of the album constitutes the Doors' best work. The chilling "Unknown Soldier" makes effective use of firing squad sound effects and features Morrison's most well earned screaming fit. The eerie "Spanish Caravan" features Robbie Krieger's best guitar playing on disc. "Love Street" is charmingly goofy, and "Five to One" is one of the few Doors songs that makes good on the band's confrontational image. The Doors aren't known for their restraint, but they give a perfectly controlled performance on the smoky "Yes, the River Knows." Jim Morrison's vocal is his most touching. The interplay between Robby Krieger's dusky guitar and Ray Manzarek's jazzy piano is simply beautiful. Then it all reaches an unexpectedly powerful climax in the final refrain. "Yes, the River Knows" breaks my heart. Even throwaway numbers like "We Could Be So Good Together," "Wintertime Love," and "Summer's Almost Gone" are good.

FAMILY: *MUSIC IN A DOLL'S HOUSE*

Few albums encapsulated 1968's multiplicity better than *Music in a Doll's House*. It is as down-home as *Music from Big Pink*, as eclectic as "The White Album," as progressive as *Shine On Brightly*, and as concise and tune-packed as *Village Green Preservation Society*. Mellotron-infused grandeur, raga rock, slinky British blues, militaristic psychedelia, and mood pieces anxious and ethereal all vie for space on Family's track-packed debut. Roger Chapman's inimitable voice is the unifying element. His vibrato will shatter every champagne flute in your cupboard.

Dave Mason's organic production keeps the whole thing grounded, so no matter which untraveled corridor Family explores, it never turns pretentious or inaccessible. The production helps *Music in a Doll's House* hang together. Short link tracks give it a vague conceptual tang, but the album is mainly a treasury of marvelous unrelated songs.

The Beatles originally intended to call their 1968 album *A Doll's House*, but they had to rename it because of this little number by Family. Author's collection.

GEORGE HARRISON: *WONDERWALL MUSIC*

For a goofy little period-piece film that few people saw, George Harrison composed some pretty music that mostly spotlights his raga obsession but also dallies with baroque pop, acid rock, music hall, psychedelia, Mellotron mood music, Moody Blues romanticism, tape loops, and avant-garde collages. *Wonderwall Music* is tough to view as George's proper solo debut since it relies so much on outside help. John Barham, a fellow student of Ravi Shankar, is largely responsible for bringing the project together, and George doesn't sing a single note on the album (incidentally, Monkee Peter Tork supplies banjo). *Wonderwall Music* is still a charming encapsulation of all the things that made mid-sixties music wonderful.

THE JIMI HENDRIX EXPERIENCE: *ELECTRIC LADYLAND*

Jimi Hendrix's abilities as a musician came together immediately. On his very first album, he was already manipulating the strings like a master puppeteer. It took him a little longer to fully develop as a songwriter and record maker.

In the United Kingdom, the cover of *Electric Ladyland* featured a David Montgomery photo of a bunch of naked women. Obviously that was not going to go down well in uptight America, so Reprise issued the album with this blah profile instead. Hendrix, who favored a Linda Eastman (soon to be McCartney) shot of the band and some kids hanging out by the Alice in Wonderland sculpture in NYC's Central Park, did not like either cover. Author's collection.

Hendrix fully ripens with two LPs of *Electric Ladyland*. It is the sound of an artist of limitless imagination exploring and exploiting his every idea. Everything great about Jimi Hendrix froths from the grooves of *Electric Ladyland*. Hendrix the interpreter was never better than when teaching Bob Dylan how it's done with "All Along the Watchtower." Hendrix the singer reaches heights never before hinted at with his Curtis Mayfield falsetto on "Have You Ever Been (To Electric Ladyland)." Hendrix the bluesman stretches from the Mississippi Delta to Neptune on "Voodoo Chile." With "Burning of the Midnight Lamp," Hendrix the pop craftsman pulls one of psychedelia's bubbliest nuggets from his cauldron. Hendrix the doobie-sucking jazzbo lays back and grooves on "Rainy Day, Dream Away." Hendrix the town crier shouts of racial injustice in "House Burning Down." Hendrix the acid prankster forges ". . . And the Gods Made Love," and Hendrix the hippie Walt Disney animates "1983 (A Merman I Should Turn to Be)"/"Moon, Turn the Tides . . . Gently, Gently Away." Hendrix the guitarist, of course, shines and burns and glows on every track.

Soon, the hallucinogen consumption that inspired Hendrix to create such an untamed work of imagination would intensify conflicts in the Experience, and the band would break up the following year, leaving *Electric Ladyland* as what may be rock's wildest farewell.

TOMMY JAMES AND THE SHONDELLS: *CRIMSON AND CLOVER*

When bubblegum hit machine Tommy James and the Shondells took their whole-hog plunge into psychedelia, it had the potential to be asinine, yet it's a pretty short leap from the utter nonsense of "My baby does the hanky panky" to the utter nonsense of "Crimson and clover, over and over." By jettisoning the faux intellectualism that defined so much psych, the group frees themselves to get down to cranking up crazy sounds and hooks as candy-sweet as any of their earlier hits.

The title track is a monument of inspired insipidness and one of the greatest singles of the sixties with its mind-melting tremeloed backing vocals and warped wah-wah guitars. The amphetamine exultation "Crystal Blue Persuasion" (sorry, Tommy, I refuse to believe this song has anything to do with the Bible) and "Sugar on Sunday" were memorable singles too, although the party-anthem throwback "Do Something to Me" sounds out of place here. It's still a pretty exciting track, though.

The album-only cuts are nearly as good as the hits. "Kathleen McArthur" is a pretty psychedelic ballad. "Breakaway" is hard-driving funk, and "Smokey Road" is light-headed pop soul. But the real undiscovered gem is a fabulous explosion of acid-steeped insanity on which James finally reveals his true self: "Hello, banana, I am a tangerine." Just what I suspected all along.

JEFFERSON AIRPLANE: *CROWN OF CREATION*

Jefferson Airplane had been making records for only two years when they released *Crown of Creation*, but they sound like a completely different band here than they did on their debut. *Jefferson Airplane Takes Off* was mainly a showcase for Marty Balin's romantic folk rock. *Crown of Creation* is a tour de force for each member of the group. It is also the group's darkest, creepiest, and most cynical album. One might be surprised to learn that the freakish "Lather," which Grave Slick wrote about her aging boyfriend Spencer Dryden, was intended to be affectionate. She had no such intentions when composing "Greasy Heart," a blood-drawing screed against a vain society girl and her self-deluded artist boyfriend. Her version of David Crosby's "Triad" is an eerie number about a threesome that he desperately wanted the Byrds to release (McGuinn would have no part of it). Paul Kantner's similar-sounding "In Time" addresses a less complex romantic relationship but with more poetic imagery. He also comes up with the classic agit-prop title track, which stands as one of his best songs and one of the most devastating examples of Jack Casady's bass clawing. Jorma Kaukonen contributes two mid-tempo rockers with "Star Track" and "Ice Cream Phoenix." Marty Balin delivers two of his best songs with the ominous "Share a Little Joke" and the grooving "If You Feel." Spencer Dryden out-weirds the song he inspired with the brief, scary instrumental "Chushingura." Nearly as frightening is "House at Pooneil Corners," the apocalyptic monstrosity that closes this uneasy album.

J.K. & CO.: *SUDDENLY ONE SUMMER*

With its backward tape loops, distorted guitars, bleary-eyed lyricism, and airiness, *Suddenly One Summer* rolls the spirit of 1967 over into 1968. The album's morbid concept about an addict's slow death belies the fact that Jay Kaye was a mere fifteen-year-old when he wrote and recorded it. Tracks like "Nobody" (in which Kaye moans "My happiness is in a needle"), "Magical Fingers of Minerva," and "Dead" are chilling. Even the sprightly love ballad "Christine" and the incongruously spry "O.D." are spooky and somber. Perhaps J.K. and his company of session men were so dour because they sensed that *Suddenly One Summer* would be both their first and final album. It's a potent sole statement and one of the few genuinely focused concept albums.

THE KINKS: *THE KINKS ARE THE VILLAGE GREEN PRESERVATION SOCIETY*

As I suggested in my defense of my second-favorite album, *Their Satanic Majesties Request*, the greatest works of art transport the appreciator to fully realized, finely detailed, perfectly inhabitable worlds, whether they're the films of Kubrick and Lynch, the literature of Poe and Melville, or my favorite album, *The Kinks Are the Village Green Preservation Society*.

Each remarkable song is like a visit to a different nook of the Welsh coastal community Ray Davies conjures like a wizard of imagery, character-ization, and pathos. Stop at a café to catch up with an old friend with whom you sadly no longer have anything in common. Hurry down to the Main Street drag strip to see tough but sensitive biker Johnny Thunder racing his motorcycle through town. Then it's on to the abandoned engine yard to look nostalgically on the rusting last of the steam-powered trains. Watch the sunset while sitting by the river, but be sure to make it home before dark lest you get lost in the woods and have a puzzling encounter with the mystical Phenomenal Cat or fall prey to local broomstick rider Wicked Annabella (you may want to pay Monica a visit under her street lamp if you're looking for some after-hours thrills, though). All the while, the Big Sky hovers overhead, indifferent to everyone dashing about His world like ants. Davies captures all of these wonderfully drawn settings and characters in brief songs that are economically arranged and absurdly tuneful.

The Kinks Are the Village Green Preservation Society is a perfect album and one that would cause its chief creator as much joy and disappointment as he expresses in its songs. Ray Davies spent a long time preparing the album, originally imagining it as his solo debut. Recording began back in 1966 with "Village Green" (a more elaborately orchestrated production than anything else that ended up on the record) when the Kinks were still a fairly commercial property on both sides of the Atlantic, having recently scored a big hit with "Sunny Afternoon." By the time *Village Green* emerged as a Kinks record in late 1968, the band had been all but forgotten in both America and England. Pye Records knew the Kinks could not sell enough copies to justify the twenty-track, double-LP set Ray invisioned and rejected that version, instead shipping out a single LP featuring the wistful single "Days" and the cheery outtake "Mr. Songbird." Ray convinced his label to withdraw that twelve-track disc (which landed in shops only in France, Sweden, Norway, and New Zealand) and strike a compromise. Instead of a puny twelve-track album or a copious twenty-track one, *Village Green* would be a fifteen-track album without "Days" and "Mr. Songbird" but with "The Last of the Steam Powered Trains," "Big Sky," "Sitting by the Riverside," "Animal Farm," and "All My Friends Were There." The fruits of all those negotiations mattered little at that time. Record buyers and the press almost unanimously ignored the album when it was released on the same day as the Beatles' illustrious eponymous double album, but a small and vocal minority cottoned to its enchantments. In his review for *Rolling Stone*, charter Kinks Kultist Paul Williams wrote, "I can't sit here and come up with phrases to argue genius, I can only shout, as modestly as possible, about how deeply I'm affected. I'm thinking, only genius could hit me so directly, destroy me and rebuild so completely, but that's ontology, proving has nothing to do with making you believe. I've never had much luck turning people on to the Kinks. I can only hope you're onto them already.

"If you are, brother, I love you. We've got to stick together."

Over the years, that kult of which Williams wrote grew and grew, and *The Kinks Are the Village Green Preservation Society* is now widely regarded as an impeccable example of British pop and one of the greatest rock albums ever produced. The first time I heard it, I was struck with the uncanny sensation that I'd been listening to it my entire life (I'm not alone in this: Williams wrote of experiencing a similar sensation in his review). This is quite appropriate considering the album's timelessness and fixation on the draws and pitfalls of nostalgia. The Kinks rarely fell vic-

Best album ever. Author's collection.

tim to the trends of their day, and though there are traces of 1968 on the album (the heavy blues of "The Last of the Steam Powered Trains," the wisps of psychedelia in "Sitting by the Riverside" and the bizarre "Phenomenal Cat," the touches of raga rock in "Big Sky," the fuzzed-out acid rock of "Wicked Annabella," which features one of the most gloriously corroded guitar sounds on wax), it still sounds as though it could have been recorded yesterday—or, say, 1868. The *Kinks Are the Village Green Preservation Society* is not as flashy as *Sgt. Pepper's Lonely Hearts Club Band* or as tumultuous as *Beggars Banquet*, but many who have gone out of their way to hear it regard it as the finest album ever made for its own peculiarly Kinky reasons.

THE LEFT BANKE: *THE LEFT BANKE TOO*

Michael Brown was basically the Left Banke's own Brian Wilson–style head boy, but he had departed the band by the time they recorded their second album. The inclusion of 1967's "Desiree," a magnificent single that actually manages to up the angst level of "Walk Away Renee" while also laying down a spiraling, intense riff that shudders from 7/4 to 4/4 to 6/4 time, is the only evidence of his brilliance on *The Left Banke Too*.

Without Brown, the rest of the group had to step up their creativity just as the other Beach Boys had to when Brian checked out. Steve Martin, Tom Finn, and George Cameron comport themselves very well with an album's worth of intricate baroque pop. "Dark Is the Bark" and "My Friend Today" (featuring a young Steven Tyler on backing vocals) are spectacular specimens of pitch-black gloom pop. The rest of the album is more lighthearted.

"In the Morning Light," "Nice to See You," and "Sing Little Bird Sing" glisten. "Bryant Hotel" and "There's Gonna Be a Storm" set their respective scenes marvelously.

The Left Banke Too isn't as consistent as the band's first album, but that's a high hurdle. It's still one of the great underappreciated pop albums of the late sixties.

THE LOVIN' SPOONFUL: *EVERYTHING PLAYING*

After working on the so-so sound track to Francis Ford Coppola's medio-cre proto-*Graduate* comedy *You're a Big Boy Now* and a high-profile drug arrest, eccentric guitarist Zal Yanovsky left the Lovin' Spoonful and returned home to Canada. The Spoonful replaced him with Jerry Yester, formerly of the Association. John Sebastian would follow soon after, but first he recorded one last record with the Spoonful. *Everything Playing* is not a classic on the level of *Do You Believe in Magic, Daydream,* or *Hums.* The band's new democratic approach results in a few misfires. Bassist Steve Boone is responsible for one poorly sung track and one Muzak instrumental that would have fit better on one of the band's sound tracks. Yester closes the record on a sour note that he should have saved for *Farewell, Aldeba-ran,* his bizarre 1969 collaboration with wife Judy Henske. *Everything Playing* still has its share of first-rate tracks: the powerful "Six O'Clock," the insightful "Younger Generation," the lazy blues "Boredom," and "Money," which introduced cash-register percussion six years before its Pink Floyd namesake.

TAJ MAHAL: *THE NATCH'L BLUES*

As leader of the Rising Sons, Taj Mahal was a fixture on the mid-sixties L.A. scene. He made a name for himself as a modern bluesman after that group disbanded in 1966. Two years later, he released both his debut album and his sophomore one, *The Natch'l Blues.* That album's most magnetic track, "Ain't That a Lot of Love," takes the Spencer Davis Group's "Gimme Some Lovin'" and gives it a mud bath, but it is not really representative of *The Natch'l Blues,* which is more rustic blues than modern soul.

Taj Mahal's blues is stripped down to dobro, bass, drums, barrelhouse piano, and the man's rock crusher rasp, yet it's as sunny as daybreak. Taj Mahal uses the blues to get outside his sadness, and "Good Morning Miss

Brown," "Ain't Gonna Let Nobody Steal My Jellyroll," the epic "Done Change My Way of Living," and the standard "Corrina" are as uplifting as they are genuine.

THE MONKEES: *THE BIRDS, THE BEES, & THE MONKEES*

After winning their artistic freedom, the Monkees made two excellent albums with Chip Douglas at the helm. The results of their hard-earned successes may have made the guys a bit bigheaded because they then decided to let Douglas go. Each Monkee then produced his own tracks without the slightest regard for what the others were doing. Any semblance of cohesion is now gone. *The Birds, the Bees, & the Monkees* is largely split between some of Davy Jones's sappiest tracks and Mike Nesmith's freakiest.

As a whole, the LP doesn't really work, though there are some great things on it. The best of the bunch is a new song Mike cowrote with Keith Allison of the Raiders. "Auntie's Municipal Court" is both traditional sounding with its folk-country melody and twangy guitar licks and extravagantly psychedelic. Richard Dey's bass arches out of the mix like a rainbow. Mike's "Tapioca Tundra"—a peculiar concoction of psych, country, and the twenties jazz that had recently caught his fancy—is also terrific and somehow became one of the Monkees' most successful B-sides on the charts. The wonderfully authentic "Magnolia Simms" gave his jazz fixation full attention, but the nightmarish, nearly prog "Writing Wrongs" is most definitely an acquired taste. Sitting it next to the cheery smash "Daydream Believer" has to be one of the most subversive moves in the history of LP programming.

Which brings us to the album's biggest problem. "Daydream Believer," the elegant "Dream World," and the relatively tough-rocking "Valleri" are all catchy enough, but Davy's other contributions stink. "The Poster" is juvenile, and Davy's claim that it was based on the spooky "Being for the Benefit of Mr. Kite" implies that he may have liked the Beatles, but he probably didn't understand them. "We Were Made for Each Other" is a crime of saccharine writing and

That crease in the upper left-hand corner is why you shouldn't carry brand-new albums home on your bikes, kids. Author's collection.

arranging. A Byrds-like backing track for the song that Chip Douglas produced highlights what a bad move firing him was.

Because he didn't have Mike and Davy's drive, the original voice of the Monkees feels like a sideman on *The Birds, the Bees, & the Monkees*. Micky Dolenz's most personal contribution is also his sketchiest since "Zor and Zam" is a queasy Jefferson Airplane counterfeit, but his vocal contributions to "Auntie's Municipal Court," Boyce and Hart's cleverly produced "P.O. Box 9847," and a superior remake of the *More of the Monkees*–era outtake "I'll Be Back Up on My Feet," which featured in a couple of episodes of their TV series, are terrific.

HEAD

After the *Monkees* TV series was canceled early in 1968, cocreator Bob Rafelson seemed determined to put the final nail in the project's coffin with a withering film called *Head*. However, this may seem to be case only in retrospect. At the time, there clearly was enthusiasm for a film that no one but the most acid-blitzed, ego-stroked, multimedia megastar could have thought would be anything but a resounding flop. "Our film is going to astound the world," Nesmith declared in the April 1968 issue of *NME*. "The Monkees are dead. We've been gently moving away from the prefabricated image of the four of us in the last few TV episodes. . . . We want to be thought of as real people. We are still largely victims of the monsters we helped create, and people still expect us to act our TV parts in real life."

The fact is, no one was astounded by *Head* in 1968 because no one saw it. Legend has it that the picture opened and closed in the same weekend. The Monkees never would completely lose their image as prefab bubblegum peddlers Nesmith wished the film to annihilate. The audience that had made them superstars in 1967 was growing up and out of the Monkees in 1968. Most of these kids would never even get the chance to see the guys graphically French kiss a willing and rather empowered woman on the big screen or see them wail through Nesmith's blazing rocker "Circle Sky" as a real band playing real instruments or see their antics juxtaposed with shocking images of the real murder of a Vietcong operative or see Mike, Micky, Davy, and Peter end their very first movie by committing suicide together. Most straggling Monkees fans didn't even know that *Head* was a Monkees movie. Although the group was featured prominently in the film's theatrical trailer, they were nowhere to be seen in the print or TV ads that simply superimposed the title over the face of promotion man and future literary agent John Brockman's head.

Davy Jones, the Monkee with the least avant-garde sensibilities, took issue with *Head* because, as he often retrospectively said, he thought his group should have made a movie "like *Ghostbusters*"—in other words, a ninety-minute version of their old sitcom. Instead, they went as far out as is imaginable, stapling together a plotless, surreal, often grotesque compilation of clips unified by the dreary reality that the Monkees will never escape their prefabricated image. Micky's suicide attempt ends with him being rescued by mermaids only so he can be sexually rejected. The mass suicide attempt that climaxes the film ends with all four Monkees trapped in a box and not for the first time in *Head*. That ominous black box is the demonic shadow of the monolith in *2001: A Space Odyssey*. While Kubrick's slab of polished black rock brought evolutionary leaps in intelligence and ability to a race of monkey men, the black box of *Head* denies our Monkee Men such boons, constantly imprisoning them back in the black box of 1960s TV ruled by stupidities such as *The Beverly Hillbillies*, *Dragnet*, and *The Flying Nun*.

Peter Tork, the Monkee with the hippiest sensibilities, would later come to dislike the movie for what he perceived as Bob Rafelson's cynicism toward Peter and his mates, yet Rafelson really attacks only the group's public image in the film. The guys reveal the lies behind the venomous "Ditty Diego" chant—"Hey, hey, we are the Monkees! You know we love to please! A manufactured image with no philosophies!"—by refusing to please their audience easily (*Head* is no *Ghostbusters*, to put it mildly) and revealing an anti-media, anti-manufacturing philosophy throughout the myriad sketches and vignettes. Rafelson also portrays the Monkees as a real rock and roll band playing the best music of their career in electrifying live sequences and innovative music videos. Peter gets more of his own songs on the sound track than he ever did on a previous Monkees record, and considering that *Head* featured only six songs, that's a hefty percentage of the whole. Just as significantly, Peter gets to address his image as "the dummy" in a scene that plays quite poignantly to anyone familiar with how uncomfortable the intelligent fellow was with the role he was forced to play on the TV show.

Head is mostly cynical about television, a medium that puts the silliness of sitcoms and the revolting graphic violence of the evening news on a level playing field. America's newly preferred way of receiving entertainment and information is revealed to be a stupefying fake. Micky gets shot with arrows in a cavalry movie and slaps them out of his torso wearily and rips through the fake southwestern backdrop. He gets lost in the desert during a

Lawrence of Arabia parody before coming on another Kubrickian stand-in, a monolithic Coke machine that is out of bottles, then blows up the product that fails to deliver on its Madison Avenue promise ("Things go better with Coke!") with a tank canon. We pull back on Davy Jones serenading girlfriend Annette Funicello tenderly to reveal a film crew, and a random hand reaches into the frame to wipe a glycerin tear from Annette's cheek. Unseen forces manipulate the Monkees into starring in a dandruff shampoo commercial. Peter punches out a waitress who had been raking the Monkees over the coals, but when Rafelson wraps the scene, she pulls back her wig to reveal that she's actually a male actor. Peter expresses distress over being forced to hit a woman on-screen to a filmmaker who couldn't care less about his chattel's input. Here, Rafelson (who appears on-screen with cowriter Jack Nicholson) portrays himself as the villain in the film. As the filmmaker, Rafelson once again treats Peter with great sympathy. We feel his discomfort with the scene and the crushing feeling of being ignored and patronized. The beautiful "As We Go Along" is the next song we hear, further heightening the unexpected poignancy of the sequence.

Rhino's 1984 vinyl reissue of *Head* replaced the truncated album version of "Porpoise Song" with the full-length single version. Both the Rhino reissue and original editions of *Head* were released in reflective sleeves so you could view your very own head in *Head*. This particular head belongs to me. Author's collection.

Poignant, funny, frightening, pointed, and brimming with great songs, *Head* has recovered well since it was dropped into a landscape of war, social unrest, and political assassinations forty-five years ago today and closed a few days later. Today, it is rightly regarded as a cult classic, and the film's accompanying sound track shows just how musically innovative the Monkees could be. Half of the album consists of weird and witty sound collages that co-screenwriter Jack Nicholson stitched together from the film's dialogue. The rest comprises the six original songs featured in the film that is the most consistently fine selection of songs the group ever recorded. Davy Jones perhaps doesn't interpret Harry Nilsson's "Daddy's Song" with adequate nuance, but "Porpoise Song" is majestic and the Monkees' greatest single. Mike Nesmith's "Circle Sky" is as exciting as rock and roll gets, and, contrary to popular opinion, I will forever insist that this propulsive studio version massacres the film's live version on which Micky Dolenz's drum fills keep tripping up the beat. Peter Tork delivers his two best songs with the whirling-dervish "Can You Dig It?" and the punky rocker "Long Title: Do I Have to Do This All Over Again?" Micky gives an extraordinarily sensitive performance on the beauteous ballad "As We Go Along," which features Neil Young on guitar.

The sound track's sole flaw is that it contains only six Monkees songs, so it's more like an EP than a proper LP. However, as far as avant-garde EP/LPs recorded by rapidly disintegrating prefabricated pop stars go, *Head* is most definitely the best.

THE MOODY BLUES: *IN SEARCH OF THE LOST CHORD*

For their second album as a psych group, the Moody Blues cooked up some actual material to supplement the singles, and though *In Search of the Lost Chord* is not remembered as fondly as *Days of Future Passed*, it is a much better album. What the leadoff single "Ride My See-Saw" lacks in crafts-manship or lyricism it makes up for in fire. It's the rockingest of all Moody Blues records with a dirty, hypnotic guitar lick. By scaling back the poetry, the Moodies make the occasional spoken passages more palatable. In fact, I contend that the only way to hear "Ride My See-Saw" is with the brief, crazed poetic prologue that ignites it.

Nothing else on *Lost Chord* is as powerful as "See-Saw," but almost all of it is very good. The two-part "House of Four Doors" may ramble on too long, but the hippity-hoppity "Dr. Livingston, I Presume," the loony Timothy Leary eulogy "Legend of a Mind," the splendid single "Voices in the Sky," and the ethereal "Visions of Paradise" and "Om" are all dated in the best way.

VAN MORRISON: *ASTRAL WEEKS*

With his stifling days with Bang Records behind him, Van Morrison longed to dispense with rock instrumentation and make a record rooted in acoustic jazz, folk, and blues—a statement entirely personal and unique. There are all sorts of legends about how *Astral Weeks* was recorded, but the truth is that it was laid down live in the studio over the course of three sessions in the autumn of 1968.

Astral Weeks could not have been made any other way. The sound is autumnal. The musicians are clearly playing off of each other and follow-ing Morrison's every dynamic move and soulful whim. Even with Richard

Davis's supple stand-up bass and John Payne's magically capricious flute, the greatest instrument on *Astral Weeks* is Morrison's voice, as brassy and full-blooded as Miles Davis's trumpet. Even when he whispers, which he does often on this record, Morrison sings with torrential power and rich emotion. When he cuts loose, step back and get stunned. Just as extraordinary are Morrison's poetic lyrics, which explore a life from childhood through death, emphasizing how sex, desire, and bemused confusion shape the individual. Van Morrison would make many more great records throughout his career but never one as miraculous as *Astral Weeks*.

THE MOVE: *MOVE*

Delivering childlike, singsongy tunes with the vivid, pop-art explosiveness of the early Who, the Move of Birmingham, England, released three of the liveliest singles of 1967 but were slow to produce their first album. Finally appearing in March 1968, *Move* included both sides of their previous two British hits ("Flowers in the Rain" b/w "[Here We Go Round] the Lemon Tree" and "Fire Brigade" b/w "Walk upon the Water"), a handful of newly recorded originals, and a triad of covers. The covers range from red-hot (Eddie Cochran's "Weekend") to inessential (a too-faithful version of Moby Grape's "Hey Grandma") to bloody awful (the schlock-o-la standard "Zing Went the Strings of My Heart" with its vocal by tone-deaf basso profundo drummer Bev Bevan).

The rest of the new recordings are much worthier of sitting alongside the hits. "Yellow Rainbow" and "Useless Information" have all the melodiousness and mod ferocity of the Move's singles. The ballad "Mist on a Monday Morning" may be less electrifying, but its overwrought arrangement of harpsichords, strings, and woodwinds render it as spectacularly unsubtle as the rockers. "Cherry Blossom Clinic" mashes such orchestral elements with electric instruments for a heady climax.

When the Move began recording albums more seriously, they favored epic, indulgent experimentation, leaving the stitched-together *Move* as one of their few long players to really show off what a great singles act they were.

OS MUTANTES: *OS MUTANTES*

The Tropicália movement blended traditional Brazilian art with the avant-garde to denounce the military dictatorship that came to power in 1964 and that would rule Brazil for the next two decades. Tropicália encompassed all of the performing arts, but it made its first and biggest splash in music. Artists such as Tom Zé and Gilberto Gil got it started, but the cartoon trio Os Mutantes really animated Tropicália with their synthesis of kitchen-sink psychedelia, rock and roll, and jazz. "Panis et Circenses," the first track on their first album, superimposes Wagnerian bellowing, cacophonic *Yellow Submarine* bleating, and a kooky "Strawberry Fields" parody over cherubic psych pop. *Os Mutantes* doesn't get any less wacky as Rita Lee, Sérgio Dias, and Arnaldo Baptista chew up fuzzy go-go rock, contrapuntal hymn harmonies, doo-wop, vaudevillian goof pop, samba, and a bastardized *Batman* theme and spew it back out for their seemingly random yet politically pointed purposes. You don't have to understand Portuguese to get the humor, the melodies are irresistible, and there's always another layer of instrumental filigree to discover on repeat listenings.

NAZZ: *NAZZ*

Like the Left Banke, Nazz was one of the first and best anglophile groups. While the Left Banke drew on the lighter British Invaders like the Kinks and the Zombies, Nazz was influenced by those types of groups as well as harder rockers like Yardbirds, Cream, and the Who. Both styles are present in all their dueling glory on Nazz's debut album. On one end of the spectrum is moody pop, such as "See What You Can Be," "Crowded," "If That's the Way You Feel," and "Hello, It's Me," which would become a hit for Nazz guitarist/chief songwriter Todd Rundgren when he went solo in the seventies. On the other end are the acid rockers: "Back of My Mind," "When I Get My Plane," "Wildwood Blues," and "Lemming Song." These songs are more generic than the lighter ones, but their power is still flooring.

The record's best and best-known moment grafts the two disparate styles together.

My wife once called me and told me someone was giving away a ton of albums with covers that had suffered some superficial water damage. When I arrived at the address, there were albums sitting all over this person's lawn and the sidewalk in front of the house. I collected armloads: Elvis's Christmas album, *McCartney*, Neil Young's *Harvest*, *The Supremes & The Temptations-TCB*, the very roughly used copy of *Nazz* you see here, and many, many more. In retrospect, I wonder if the person was really giving away these albums or just leaving them out to dry. If the owner of those records is reading this and wants them back, give me a ring. Author's collection.

"Open My Eyes" is one of the last great psych singles of the sixties, a 2:45 distillation of everything great about that decade's music: the Beach Boys' harmonies, the Who's power riffing, groovy *Magical Mystery Tour* phasing, and all the youthful brio of the best garage bands. *Nazz* is a little inconsistent, but as a nostalgically retro-sixties record released before the decade was even over, it's a constant delight.

NICO: *THE MARBLE INDEX*

Nico's folk debut *Chelsea Girl* was pretty, but it was as inauthentic an expression of her true vision as *Blowin' Your Mind* was of Van Morrison's. Unlike Morrison, whose *Astral Weeks* is endearing and enduring, Nico set out to purposely alienate fans with her ghoulish new look and shocking music to match it.

Nico ejects melody almost completely and sinks into a gothic horror-scape on *The Marble Index*. Her wheezing harmonium and the clattering rogue's gallery of classical and rock instruments that producer and former Velvet Underground bandmate John Cale overdubbed blend and jar against each other for a shattering sound experience. Listening to *The Marble Index* all the way through makes me physically anxious, like I've been given a heavy dose of nasty medicine. Producer Frazier Mohawk claimed he snipped a couple of songs off the record because he feared listeners would start killing themselves if they had to hear more than half an hour of this stuff.

I see his point, yet there are some incredibly beautiful things here too. "Ari's Song" is a sweet lullaby to Nico's son albeit one sung over a disorienting backing track pierced with something that sounds like a screeching teakettle. The spare strings and vocal of "No One Is There" have a stately grace, and Nico's multitracked wails toward the end of the track are captivating. "Julius Caesar (Memento Hodie)" enchants with its woozy duet of viola and harmonium. "Frozen Warnings," the artist's personal favorite of her songs, is as icy as its title suggests yet also ethereal, haunting. However, "Lawns of Dawns," "Facing the Wind," and especially "Evening of Light" are flat-out terrifying.

Beautiful former model Nico decided to remold herself as an overall scarier artist with her second album. I'd say she accomplished that quite well, wouldn't you? Author's collection.

Listen to *The Marble Index* on the most overcast day in the most forebodingly empty landscape. You'll crap your pants.

HARRY NILSSON: *AERIAL BALLET*

Harry Nilsson's second album is less comic than *Pandemonium Shadow Show* and more personal. The previous album had been evenly divided between covers and Nilsson originals. *Aerial Ballet* contains only a single cover, a version of Fred Neil's "Everybody's Talkin'," a song without the burlesque of his Beatles medley or the redundancy of his versions of "She's Leaving Home" and "River Deep—Mountain High" on *Shadow Show*. It is the ultimate vehicle for his sensitive voice and would become one of his hallmark numbers after filmmaker John Schlesinger used it in *Midnight Cowboy*. Nilsson's own composition "One" would become an even bigger hit when Three Dog Night covered it the following year. Another ode to his wayward father, "Daddy's Song," would be included on first editions of *Aerial Ballet* only because the Monkees paid for the exclusive use of the song, which was featured in their film *Head*. This is an ironic fate both since *Head* was a flop and Nilsson's reading of this very personal song is the definitive one.

PINK FLOYD: *A SAUCERFUL OF SECRETS*

Pink Floyd is one of the few groups that didn't allow the loss of its key member to impede its career. While I personally think the band never eclipsed the artistic heights of their Syd Barrett phase, they certainly became more successful after Roger Waters took over. *A Saucerful of Secrets* marks that transition of power as Barrett fades into the shadows and Waters commences his rise.

No single member of the group is in command yet on *A Saucerful of Secrets*, and the results are shockingly good considering how much Barrett monopolized *The Piper at the Gates of Dawn*. Each member of Pink Floyd makes his presence felt both instrumentally and compositionally. At this point, Rick Wright seems like he might be Barrett's most logical successor. His "Remember a Day" and "See Saw" come closest to recapturing Barrett's childlike whimsy. Rick is also a vocal ringer for Syd. However, it is Roger Waters who takes the band farthest into challenging territory with two defining whooshes of space rock—"Let There Be More Light" and

"Set Your Controls for the Heart of the Sun"—and the crazed *Sgt. Pepper's* burlesque "Corporal Clegg." The entire group, new boy David Gilmour included, collaborated on the extended, experimental title track, which hacks out the somewhat meandering path the band would follow through their next few albums. Barrett manages to have the last word with his shattered "Jugband Blues," the final song on the album and the final song he'd ever place on a Pink Floyd record.

THE PRETTY THINGS: *S.F. SORROW*

Many bands have laid claim to inventing the rock opera. The Who have taken most of the credit since their *Tommy* was the first and biggest hit in that form. They do deserve that credit but not for *Tommy*. They'd actually invented the rock opera with the nine-minute "mini-opera" they recorded in late 1966. The first full-length rock opera came out two years after "A Quick One, While He's Away" and several months before *Tommy*.

Phil May's concept for the Pretty Things' *S.F. Sorrow* follows its title character from birth through a traumatic life tainted by his experiences in World War II and the tragic death of his girlfriend and then on to his own death. *S.F. Sorrow* is historically notable for its novel structure, but it's the songs that make the album. In their early days, the Pretty Things were one of the loudest, most raucous R&B bands going. They carried all that grit and power into their psychedelic phase too. Dick Taylor's guitar stings and Twink's drumming whip up such power on "She Said Good Morning," "Balloon Burning," and "Old Man Going" that you'll feel like you've been zapped into the middle of a typhoon. But the band also developed their songwriting and harmonies to the point they could artistically compete with their A-list peers. "Private Sorrow" and "Death" will spook you out. "Trust" and "I See You" will elevate the hairs on your neck. "Bracelets of Fingers" is a mini-symphony worthy of Brian Wilson. Commercially, *S.F. Sorrow* tanked, which is a sad fate for an album so innovative and superbly crafted—but being a rock geek wouldn't be half as much fun if there weren't obscure nuggets like it to discover and cherish.

Phil May didn't just conceive the plot of *S.F. Sorrow*; he also illustrated its cool cover. Author's collection.

PROCOL HARUM: *SHINE ON BRIGHTLY*

It irks me when Procol Harum get lumped in with prog-rock bands, but even I'll admit that *Shine on Brightly* makes a pretty good case for that label. Side B houses rock's first jumbo, multisectional, time signature–defying opus. What sets "In Held 'Twas in I" apart from many of the epics that followed is its absurd humor. "In Held 'Twas in I" is a parody of prog rock's ridiculous pretensions before prog rock really even existed. Procol Harum always had a sort of clairvoyance, though. Their first album anticipated goth rock by a decade.

While not necessarily superior to *Procol Harum*, *Shine on Brightly* is more varied. Shades of the debut are apparent in the swirling organs and panoramic drumming of "Quite Rightly So" and the title track, but "Wish Me Well" is a ragged blues number, "Skip Softly (My Moonbeams)" is a sort of nightmarish polka-out-of-bounds, and "Magdalene (My Regal Zonophone)" is a regal portent of the kind of material that would feature on *A Salty Dog*. The humor that infuses "In Held 'Twas in I" is present throughout the entire album, whether in the coda of "Skip Softly (My Moonbeams)," the voices imitating horns on "Magdalene," or the zaniest lyrics Keith Reid ever composed. If all prog records were as fun, funny, and self-effacing as this, the genre would have an entirely different reputation.

THE RASCALS: *ONCE UPON A DREAM*

Following the *Sgt. Pepper's* phenomenon, every band in late 1967/early 1968 was expected to whip up their own psychedelic freak fest. To the Rascals' credit, they did not abandon their soul strengths for overreaching artiness even as *Once upon a Dream* expands their sound with the usual post-*Pepper* trappings (weird sound effects, tape experiments, orchestrations, sitars, trippy segues). While this is the Rascals' first album to lack major hits (the groovy "It's Wonderful" barely poked its head into the top twenty), it hangs together as a complete listening experience better than any of their earlier records just as it's their most eclectic release yet. There's a little rustic blues ("Easy Rollin'"), a little urban blues ("Singing' the Blues Too Long"), a little New Orleans soul ("I'm Gonna Love You"), a little shifty rock and roll with jazz aspirations ("Please Love Me"), a lot of Brian Wilson–style orchestral grandeur ("Rainy Day," "My Hawaii," the title track), and a rare raga rocker that delivers the raga *and* the rock in equal proportions ("Bells/Sattva"). These disparate elements add up to a minor masterwork that should delight fans of the cosmic and the earthbound alike.

PAUL REVERE AND THE RAIDERS: *GOIN' TO MEMPHIS*

Probably the weakest Raiders album is a record Mark Lindsay cut with a bunch of Memphis session men. The songs on *Goin' to Memphis* aren't distinguished, and the covers of the classics "Boogaloo Down Broadway" and "Soul Man" won't make anyone forget the formidable originals. Still, Lindsay was one of the more expressive pop-soul singers of the sixties, and there are a few good songs. "One Night Stand" recaptures some of the feel of *Midnight Ride*'s "All I Really Need Is You" by tripping from 4/4 time to an exaggerated 3/4. "My Way" draws power from a heavy horn arrangement, and "Peace of Mind" does the same from the support of Darlene Love and the Blossoms. As a song, "Peace of Mind" isn't as memorable as the Raiders' earlier hits, and its poor performance on the charts wasn't undeserved. With its underlying twang, *Goin' to Memphis* kind of foreshadows Mike Nesmith's 1969 Nashville sessions, which yielded that landmark of country soul, "Listen to the Band."

SOMETHING HAPPENING

Paul Revere and the Raiders got back a bit of their chart mojo with *Something Happening*, and with the actual band backing Lindsay this time on the hard garage and light-psych material that was their forte, this sounds more like a proper Raiders record. The problem is that it's their most uneven one since *Just Like Us*. The frustrating thing is that the poor cuts could have been whipped into shape with a producer less given to self-indulgence than Lindsay. "Happens Every Day" and "Love Makes the World Go Round" aren't bad songs, but overly cutesy touches sink them. "Communication" is presented in two parts when one would have been plenty, and no one needs to hear that minute and a half of obnoxious drag-racing noise at the start of the otherwise decent "Get Out of My Mind." The rest of the record is quite good, as the guys work it out on the near acid rock of "Too Much Talk" and the classic Raiders raver "Don't Take It So Hard" and get pretty on the light-psych "Observation from Flight 285 (in ¾ Time)."

THE ROLLING STONES: *BEGGARS BANQUET*

Beggars Banquet isn't my favorite Rolling Stones album, but I do believe
it is their best. Everything that made the Stones great is here: their cynicism, their greasy rhythms and filthy funk, their willingness to disturb, their
reverence for country and Delta blues, their uncanny ability to strike seemingly authentic poses, and their undervalued way with words.

Beggars Banquet may be best known as the album that returned the
Stones to solid earth after their cosmic experiments on *Their Satanic Majesties Request*, but they were smart enough to retain many of the details
that made their unfairly maligned psychedelic masterwork so interesting.
"Street Fighting Man" is such a thrashing rocker that listeners often miss
the droning sitar, tamboura, and shehnai (an Indian reed instrument that
Traffic's Dave Mason adds to the track) in its coda or the fact that an acoustic guitar drives the rhythm. Mellotron is still amply used, but it appears in
the more organic settings of "Jigsaw Puzzle," "Stray Cat Blues," and "Factory Girl."

Beggars Banquet is the most rustic and raw of the Stones' albums, its
songs rooted in country, blues, folk, and basic rock. Jagger regularly trots
out his Dylan impersonation in obvious tribute to *John Wesley Harding*,
the album that sent groups scrambling back to their acoustic guitars in early
1968. Mick Jagger also recast himself as some sort of working-class every-
man. It's a pose as absurd as any of his others, yet it's impossible not to get
sucked into his tribute to the faceless crowd on "Salt of the Earth" and the
blue-collar romance he describes on "Factory Girl" or marvel at his delirious portrait of societal collapse on "Jigsaw Puzzle" or feel every bit of the
poor-boy angst and powerlessness he expresses on "Street Fighting Man."

Perhaps the only way the egomaniacal Jagger could balance such lowly
masquerades was to embody the devil himself. "Sympathy for the Devil"
is rock's greatest historical portrait and, as far as I'm concerned, its finest
lyric. Every aspect of the song is working for it from its frenzied percussion
to Keith Richards's jittery bass line to his guitar solo, which he slashes out
like a stiletto-wielding hooligan.

The Stones really figured out their act with *Beggars Banquet*, which is
one reason why it is their most accomplished piece of work but also why
their future work would suffer. The Stones constructed the album so perfectly that they started using it as a framework for most of their albums to
follow, and working within that framework would blunt their former inspiration. The calculated scandalousness of "Parachute Woman" and "Stray Cat
Blues" (in which he deliberately tries to out-shock the Velvet Underground

with a nasty fantasy of sex with a teenage run-away) would ossify into a string of lazy gross-outs. Jagger would write stuff like "Brown Sugar," "Star Star," and "Some Girls" as a kid wields a turd at the end of a stick. He would inevitably be rewarded with the public revul-sion and massive sales he desired, but all of that stuff betrayed a lack of imagination and inspiration. Sixties tracks such as "My Obses-sion," "2000 Light Years from Home," and "Paint It Black" didn't need cheap shocks to provoke; those recordings *sound* evil (so does "Stray Cat Blues" for that matter). They also sound completely unlike each other or

The Stones conflict with the record label over this charming photo of a toilet delayed the release of their latest and great-est album for several months. Author's collection.

anything else the Stones ever did. Moving forward, Richards would match Jagger's tacky tedium with interchangeable blues and Berry riffs, rendering the Stones' sound formulaic. There might be the occasional disco beat or choir, but the unpredictability of the band that dabbled with sitars, marimbas, and electric dulcimers was largely gone. That might be because *Beggars Banquet* is also the Stones' last album with their most versatile member. Exasperated with his unpredictability, Jagger and Richards fired Brian Jones while working on their next album (and he was still playing in the instrumental toy box, having added autoharp to "You Got the Silver"). He drowned a month later.

SAM & DAVE: *I THANK YOU*

The wildness of Sam & Dave's first two albums and the elegant pol-ish of their third mesh on their final Stax LP. For a CD reissue of the album, annotator Tony Rouse hypothesized that *I Thank You* is actually a mix of new cuts and older outtakes, though the entire album sports a contemporary-for-1968 sheen. For the first time, the essential backing of bass, drums, guitar, and horns expands with strings, vibraphone, and a variety of keyboards and percussion. The tracks are the duo's most eclectic with the unpredictable "You Don't Know What You Mean to Me" sitting alongside the symphonic "Everybody's Got to Believe in Somebody" and the tougher-than-tough "Ain't That a Lot of Love" (which Taj Mahal would immortalize before the year's end). The album also features one of soul's greatest double-sided singles: "I Thank You" b/w "Wrap It Up."

SIMON & GARFUNKEL: *BOOKENDS*

Bookends is Simon & Garfunkel's best record, but it's actually kind of a phony one. Only side A consists of material specifically recorded for the album. Side B is a dumping ground for singles, some dating back two years. The thing is that side A is a meticulously constructed suite of insightful songs about aging, and the singles on side B are uniformly superb. The pretentiousness that marred some of the duo's earlier work is absent here. In its place is an adult literacy rare in rock. "America," "Mrs. Robinson," "Save the Life of My Child," "At the Zoo," and "Fakin' It" are novels packed into three-minute songs. Supremely evocative mood pieces sail the range from jolly resignation ("Punky's Dilemma") to mellow reflection ("Old Friends") to utter hopelessness ("A Hazy Shade of Winter"). This is one of the most sophisticated albums of the sixties—so detailed, beautifully realized, and thematically consistent that it hardly seems cobbled together at all.

SMALL FACES: *OGDEN'S NUTGONE FLAKE*

As we've seen time and again, no one was immune to gratuitous experimentation in the post–*Sgt. Pepper's* pop world, not even the rowdy lads in Small Faces. True to form, their experiments are just as humorous, boozy, and hard-hitting as their early R&B interpretations, making *Ogden's Nutgone Flake* one of rock's least pretentious concept albums. Side A is made up of unrelated tracks, each one played and sung with typical gusto whether they're bone-crushing rockers or chipper music-hall treats. Only on the side-closing "Lazy Sunday" does the band expand their basic sound, but the embellishments are perfectly chosen and placed sound effects that enhance the picturesque lyrics rather than draw attention to themselves.

The real experimentation takes place on side B, a song cycle about a goofball's attempt to find the missing portion of the half-moon. Here's where Small Faces get crazy, dabbling with pseudo-Renaissance folk ("Happiness Stan"), fanciful psychedelia ("The Hungry Intruder"), and barroom sing-alongs ("Happy Days Toy Town") while still setting aside a spot to rock their socks off on the Hendrixy

Ogden's Nut Gone Flake was originally packaged in a revolutionary circular sleeve. Author's collection.

"Rollin' Over." The individual episodes of Happiness Stan's Saga are linked by comedian Stanley Unwin's ludicrous double-spoken pieces. Oh, what a mind blast.

THE SUPREMES: *REFLECTIONS*

Reflections reflected everything great and out of date about Motown in 1968. The tracks on side A implied that the image-conscious label's artists were capable of true progression. The title tune, a Summer of Love hit the previous year, is the Supremes' best single—a perfect marriage of stylish soul and moody psychedelia. "Forever Came Today" is another refined single, and "In and Out of Love" is simpler yet still contemporary. The resolute and sad "I'm Gonna Make It (I Will Wait for You)" is the Supreme's best album track, and "Bah-Bah-Bah" is more mature than its title implies. Pound for pound, side A of *Reflections* is the best side of any Supremes album.

Things get watery on side B with too many covers of current MOR sap ("What the World Needs Now Is Love," "Up, Up, and Away") and one of those redundant covers that fill out too many Motown albums (an inferior take on the Vandellas' "Love [Makes Me Do Foolish Things]"). Ironically, the Supremes finish the disc with a version of Bobbie Gentry's "Ode to Billie Joe"—the song that prevented this album's title track from claiming the top spot on *Billboard*'s singles chart in September 1967. Only two terrific Smokey Robinson songs elevate side B of *Reflections*, but side A is some of the most convincing evidence yet that the label could grow up, which it would do in the coming decade when artists such as Marvin Gaye and Stevie Wonder really explored the outer limits of adult soul.

TOMORROW: *TOMORROW*

Tomorrow stormed onto the scene with the single "My White Bicycle," dropped their sole album, and peddled off to oblivion, freeing Steve Howe to cofound Yes and drummer John "Twink" Adler to hook up with the Pretty Things. Tomorrow made some extraordinary music during a career that lasted a little over a year (well, longer if you count the period they worked as a mod band called the In Crowd). They had much of the character, humor, and energy of groups like the Move and the Creation, and in Steve Howe, they had an instrumental ringer few other bands possessed.

His sitar playing on the spring-loaded "Real Life Permanent Dreams" shreds.

Tomorrow was less about proggy showboating than about whipping up witty pop songs such as "My White Bicycle" (a song I first heard on my local classic rock station immediately following a broadcast of a Who concert, so I assumed it was some obscure John Entwistle song), "Shy Boy," and "The Incredible Journey of Timothy Chase" and jazzing them up with delightful psychedelic garnishes. Such overindulgences only get the better of the kitchen sink–containing "Revolution," but that little bump does no real damage to a wonderful record.

THE TURTLES: *THE TURTLES PRESENT THE BATTLE OF THE BANDS*

Produced by former Turtle Chip Douglas, 1968's *The Turtles Present the Battle of the Bands* houses a concept that allows the band to indulge every idiosyncratic side of their personality. The album makes good on the supposed concept beneath *Sgt. Pepper's*: the Turtles pretend to be a different band on each track, mocking soul combos ("The Battle of the Bands"), psych groups ("The Last Thing I Remember"), corny C&W pickers ("Too Much Heartsick Feeling"), surf bands ("Surfer Dan"), jazz fusionists ("Food"), Booker T. & the M.G.'s ("Buzz Saw"), *errr* "world music"? (the racist "I'm Chief Kamanawanalea"), and themselves ("Elenore"). "Earth Anthem" is a rare flash of sincerity that suggests the Turtles still cared about their world, could create work of tremendous beauty, and were rather prescient in their ability to foresee the coming environmental movement of the seventies. Anyone baffled by how the guys who sang "Happy Together" ended up working with Frank Zappa should listen to *Battle of the Bands*.

ULTIMATE SPINACH: *ULTIMATE SPINACH*

At the forefront of the "Bosstown" movement (see the entry on the Rising Storm's *Calm Before . . .*) was Ultimate Spinach, a psychedelic conglomerate led by an acid muncher named Ian Bruce-Douglas and supported by a bunch of squares. Although the group is known only by the most hardcore psych acolytes today and they never even tried to score a hit single, Ultimate Spinach's eponymous debut album did surprisingly well, even climbing to number thirty-four in the LP charts, and is remembered fondly by a dedicated few.

Hearing *Ultimate Spinach* today, it is definitely dated, but if you're going to be dated to a particular date, 1968 is pretty great date to be dated to. Much of *Ultimate Spinach* is kitschy enough to provoke a chuckle, but it is capable of earning a sincere gasp or two too. The druggy imagery and ham-fisted social commentary are pretty hard to take seriously, but things like "Ego Trip" and the harpsichord tinkling "Plastic Raincoat/Hung Up Minds" are still effectively evocative of a grand era.

Bruce-Douglas has major issues with his first album because of its "mid-rangey, bubblegum" production, and he is not wrong that the *Ultimate Spinach* lacks Popeye's punch. However, it is the more bubblegum moments that hold up best. When the aim is progressiveness, things get tedious. The album's most legendary track, the eight-minute-plus "Ballad of the Hip Death Goddess," is a totally listless jam, though Barbara Jean Hudson's vocals, which recall Dorothy Moskowitz's ultracool work with the United States of America, are preferable to Bruce-Douglas's less assured singing. His subpar pipes torpedo the otherwise intense "Your Head Is Reeling." There are times when everything comes together beautifully, as they do on "Pamela," which has the most exquisite keyboard breaks since "She's a Rainbow."

THE UNITED STATES OF AMERICA: *THE UNITED STATES OF AMERICA*

With a serious background as a doctoral student in ethnomusicology at UCLA, Joseph Byrd brought an intellectualism to pop music that would have confounded John Lennon or Brian Wilson even as they likely would have marveled at the sounds he created. The *United States of America*, the album that would have been Byrd's doctoral thesis had he stuck with the program, might be the most psychedelic album I've ever heard. Everything is coated with spacey noise and experimental tape loops and filtered through distortion and phasing effects. With an exotic lineup of violin, synthesizer, harpsichord, calliope, fretless bass, an assortment of percussion, and the ultracool voice of Dorothy Moskowitz, the United States of America forgot to add one integral element of all psych—and all rock—albums: the electric guitar. The complete absence of six-string may be the most radical quality of *The United States of America*, but like all great psych efforts, the songs are more important than any unconventional instrumentation or swathes of freaky effects.

The United States of America is loaded with tracks that leap into all the various nooks of the psychedelic fun house. There's floaty, Floydian atmospherics ("The American Metaphysical Circus," the astonishing A. A. Milne adaptation "Cloud Song"), free-form freak-outs ("Hard Coming Love," which features a distorted violin every bit as raunchy as Hendrix's axe), bracing energy rushes ("The Garden of Earthly Delights"), music-hall goofs (the defiantly weird "I Won't Leave My Wooden Wife for You, Sugar"), pseudo–Gregorian chants ("Where Is Yesterday"), and avant-garde epics ("The American Way of Love (Parts I–III)." There is so much to dazzle the ear on *The United States of America* that it can probably be heard hundreds of times before revealing all of its intricate and outrageous layers.

THE ZOMBIES: *ODESSEY AND ORACLE*

The Zombies were responsible for two of the best singles of 1964 ("She's Not There" and "Tell Her No"), but they'd basically been forgotten by 1967. With their commercial prospects at an end, they decided to make one final album before breaking up. The Zombies may not have realized it, but they were making the most enduring work of their brief career.

Odessey and Oracle is a monument of baroque British pop that covers a marvelous spectrum of colors and styles over the course of its slim thirty-five minutes. The jazzy soulfulness of the group's early hits is present in the album's most famous track, "Time of the Season," which would become a huge posthumous hit in 1969. The prevailing sounds of *Odessey and Oracle* are soaring harmonies, glistening piano lines, Mellotron, and exotic percussion. The lyrics can be highly ingenious. Rod Argent's "Care of Cell 44" conveys the euphoria of a man whose sweetheart is finally being released from prison. Chris White's "Butcher's Tale (Western Front 1914)" is an intense, haunted portrait of World War I. Most of the others are love songs, but they are some of pop's finest. Every track on *Odessey and Oracle* is a miniature work of art. Every band should go out on a note as high as this one.

When artist Terry Quirk misspelled "odyssey" in its cover painting, the Zombies' most perfect album was saddled with an imperfect title. Author's collection.

1969

The years from 1966 to 1968 saw an era of experimentation and imagination that generated such monuments as *Revolver*, *Pet Sounds*, *Blonde on Blonde*, *The Who Sell Out*, *Are You Experienced*, *Astral Weeks*, *The Kinks Are the Village Green Preservation Society*, and *Beggars Banquet*. Like all golden ages, it wasn't meant to last, and when artists started feeling as though they'd worked themselves into a psychedelic corner, they decided to "return to their roots." *Beggars Banquet*, *Astral Weeks*, and numerous other 1968 releases signaled this change in the weather, and by 1969, any band still relying on their sitars and tape loops were in danger of sounding out of date even as "out of date" became the new ethos. The year 1969 was a renaissance for acoustic folk and country, electric blues, and fifties-style rock and roll. New artists such as Creedence Clearwater Revival, the Band, and Led Zeppelin got massive by mucking around in rootsy rhythms. Thirty-three artists—including Creedence, the Band, Hendrix, Jefferson Airplane, Janis Joplin, the Who, and Sly and the Family Stone—convened on a dairy farm in Bethel, New York (forty miles from Woodstock), to indulge in the new communal spirit for three days in mid-August while the audience literally played in the mud. Talk about returning to the roots.

Experimentation had not vanished, but its spirit did seem a bit broken. Consequently, 1969 wasn't quite as exciting a year as the three preceding it. Quite a few spectacular albums were still released that year, though.

THE BAND: *THE BAND*

Perhaps no album defines the spirit of 1969 as the Band's second one does. *The Band* encapsulates the year's retro focus with its earthy Dixieland, American folk, waltz, and country sounds. Much of that was present on *Music from Big Pink*, but *The Band* beats that debut with a flawless lineup of completely original material sensitively arranged. The Band layers old-fashioned mouth harp, tuba, accordion, and mandolin over their rustic songs. The lyrical concerns are straight out of the past too: the fall of the Confederate army on the uncomfortably empathetic "The Night They Drove Old Dixie Down," mountain romance on "Up on Cripple Creek," farming woes on "King Harvest (Has Surely Come)," and the emigration of Canadian pioneers on "Across the Great Divide." Even the sepia cover photo of the shaggy group looks like it was shot a hundred years before the record was recorded. The guys sound even looser and more confident than they did on *Music from Big Pink*. On "Rockin' Chair" and "The Unfaithful Servant," they achieve an unparalleled dignity. The gruff harmonies of Richard Manuel, Garth Hudson, and Rick Danko tussle and tangle and intertwine like no other.

THE BEATLES: *YELLOW SUBMARINE*

The Beatles' final year as a functioning band got off to an odd start when Apple finally issued the sound track to the 1968 pop art nouveau animated feature *Yellow Submarine*. The record was put off to avoid competing with "The White Album," and by the time it appeared, its psychedelic whimsy must have seemed pretty out of date. That it featured only four new Beatles tracks—one being Paul McCartney's execrable "All Together Now"—guaranteed that no one would rate *Yellow Submarine* as their favorite Beatles record.

It's unrealistic (or at least unfair) to rate *Yellow Submarine* as a proper Beatles record at all. Like one of those old American sound tracks for the first two Beatles pictures, half of the tracks are incidental music, but this time, they're totally enjoyable. George Martin's inspired compositions reflect the film's childlike phantasmagoria perfectly.

And though *Yellow Submarine* is the least essential Beatles LP, it still has some essential tracks. Many have criticized George Harrison's *Sgt. Pepper's* outtake "Only a Northern Song" for being monotonous and sloppy, but its anything-goes arrangement and Ringo Starr's jittery drum fills make it trippy fun. Expansive and arresting, George's "It's All Too Much" is one of the few genuinely underrated Beatles songs. John Lennon's biting "Hey Bulldog" is the one new track that pretty much everyone agrees is great. Its anxious blend of gonzo wordplay and cynical sincerity is invigorating. Paul's bounding bass work is some of his best.

ABBEY ROAD

A more thoroughly essential Beatles record arrived before the end of the year. It's common knowledge that *Let It Be* is the last album the Beatles released and that *Abbey Road* is the last one they actually recorded (though recent evidence that Beatles historian Mark Lewisohn uncovered indicates that they were considering cutting another LP after *Abbey Road*). They were *still* altering the face of popular music right up until the end of their career. Using a medley as a resting place for unfinished songs was a clever move that makes for a fascinating sprint through so many of the qualities that made the Beatles the most beloved band in pop history. Their irresistible melodies, divine harmonies, oddball character sketches, and Liverpudlian humor segue until "The End," on which each guy steps forward to take a final solo—even the ever-reluctant Ringo—before famously declaring, "The love you take is equal to the love you make."

But first there's a heap of stand-alone songs that point to where each Beatle would take his respective solo career. On "Come Together" and "I Want You (She's So Heavy)," John Lennon dishes out the pared-down rock and roll and bone-rattling self-exorcism that would define *Plastic Ono Band*, and the haunting "Because" presaged the delicacy and pacifistic philosophies of "Love" and "Imagine." If Paul McCartney's silly "Maxwell's Silver Hammer" indicates how he'd often diddle about during his solo career, "Oh! Darling" demonstrates that he could still commit when inspired. McCartney would also serially attempt to re-create the

A couple of weeks after the release of *Abbey Road*, the rock album devolved into urban legend fodder when a caller on DJ Russ Gibb's radio show floated the theory that Paul McCartney bit the dust in a car crash in 1966 and the Beatles replaced him with a look-and-sound alike. The caller insisted clues supporting this theory littered the Beatles' album covers and the records inside them, which sometimes needed to be spun backwards to reveal their creepy bullshit. Author's collection.

side B medley on Wings records from *Red Rose Speedway* to *Venus and Mars* to *Back to the Egg*. The masterful mini-medley "You Never Give Me Your Money" sums up all his best attributes. Ringo's "Octopus's Garden" shows that the most lovable Beatle would continue to be lovable (and lightweight). George Harrison's "Something" and "Here Comes the Sun" suggests that the quiet one might have the most promising solo career of all. Although he would expend all of that promise on his first album, the results would be the best Beatle solo album and arguably the best pop album of the seventies: *All Things Must Pass*. *Abbey Road* may be a bit too slick for its own good, but it is a far more fitting farewell than the cobbled-together *Let It Be*.

THE BYRDS: *DR. BYRDS AND MR. HYDE*

The Byrds' post–*Sweetheart of the Rodeo* work isn't their most essential, but there are still some great songs on their later records. The most consistent of them is the LP that immediately followed *Sweetheart*. Its title underscores the identity crisis that would destabilize the Byrds for the rest of their career. Were they still purveyors of jangly psych and folk rock, or had *Sweetheart of the Rodeo* forever re-created them as a woodsy bluegrass band?

As jarring as that dual nature makes *Dr. Byrds and Mr. Hyde*, the songs are mostly good. The two numbers Roger McGuinn wrote for the sound track of the sex farce *Candy* are as dated as that movie, but "Old Blue," "Your Gentle Way of Loving Me," and the satirical "Drug Store Truck Drivin' Man" are country tracks worthy of *Sweetheart of the Rodeo*. "King Apathy II" and "Bad Night at the Whiskey" are decent rockers, and "This Wheel's on Fire" is a Dylan cover that gets the job done even if it isn't nearly up to the standard of "My Back Pages" or "Mr. Tambourine Man." *Dr. Byrds and Mr. Hyde* is second-rate Byrds, but it's still worth a listen.

CREEDENCE CLEARWATER REVIVAL: *BAYOU COUNTRY*

Bizarrely, Creedence Clearwater Revival was pretty unhip back in the sixties, even though they made some of the hardest, darkest rock and roll of that period. When it was fashionable to play endless guitar and drum solos,

Creedence was at their best pumping out punchy two-minute singles that mopped the floor with their more self-indulgent contemporaries. John Fogerty occasionally proved that he could be as pretentious as any other artiste, and there are a fair share of long jams on the band's 1968 eponymous debut and *Bayou Country*, which includes their first major hit, "Proud Mary," and "Born on the Bayou," their first attempt to sell themselves as southern swamp dwellers rather than the residents of El Cerrito, California, they are.

GREEN RIVER

There'd be a few more jammy epics on records to come, but there's no evidence of that on Creedence's first great album. *Green River* follows an old-fashioned format: a clutch of classic hit singles, a few strong album tracks, and an old R&B cover thrown in to fill things out. This is basically the formula that made the Beatles' Capitol albums so much fun, yet it was hardly trendy in the days when bands were expected to jam out and compose all of their own material.

Of course, those early Beatles albums were never as dark as *Green River*. Death and apocalyptic visions hover over "Tombstone Shadow," "Sinister Purpose," the huge hit "Bad Moon Rising," and the swampy title track. "Commotion" is a lament of urban life's frantic pace, while "Wrote a Song for Everyone" and "Lodi" are aching rural soul numbers about the failure to connect. Critics who dismissed Creedence Clearwater Revival as a sort of bubblegum band must have had cotton in their ears when listening to these dark, raw songs, and anyone who failed to recognize Fogerty's exceptional craftsmanship had his head up his ass. The only problem with *Green River* is that there isn't enough of it—just nine songs in under thirty minutes. Fortunately, Creedence was a really prolific band that did not leave their audience wanting for long. *Green River* was Creedence's second album of 1969, and

Released in 1978, the *Creedence Clearwater Revival 1969* twofer was a handy way to get the band's two best albums of that year. There were also twofers comprised of the two albums that preceded (*Creedence Clearwater Revival 1968/1969*) and followed (*Creedence Clearwater Revival 1970*) the ones in this set. 1972's *Mardi Gras* was never included in a twofer because CCR's last album was an odd-number release and because it sucks. Author's collection.

there'd be *another* one by the end of the year. That ability to turn put out product so prolifically also linked Creedence to the early Beatles.

WILLY AND THE POOR BOYS

Willy and the Poor Boys would rank as a great album if all it contained was the righteously scathing single "Fortunate Son," but Creedence's fourth long player has plenty more going for it. The wave of retro rockabilly and C&W that washes through the album makes it more cohesive than any other Creedence album. It is also one of the band's more joyous records. The hit "Down on the Corner," definitive rock covers of the traditional songs "Midnight Special" and "Cotton Fields," and the Chuck Berry–like "It Came Out of the Sky" are some of the band's most buoyant tracks. John Fogerty could never tamp down his grumpiness for a whole album, and he unleashes it for "Fortunate Son," the moody but groovy "Feelin' Blue," and one of his subtlest and most insightful indictments, "Don't Look Now." "Effigy" ends the record on such a portentously pessimistic note that you'd have to restart the album to remember how merry most of it is.

NICK DRAKE: *FIVE LEAVES LEFT*

Insular singer-songwriter Nick Drake was basically unheard of during his lifetime, but he has since become a formidable cult figure. The influence of his gentle, personal, and very, very dark folk rock has profoundly affected the work of Kate Bush, R.E.M., the Cure, and the Dream Academy, who dedicated their excellent 1985 hit "Life in a Northern Town" to Drake. It is hard to imagine that Belle & Sebastian and Elliott Smith weren't listening too.

Texturally and structurally, Drake's debut album is very similar to Van Morrison's *Astral Weeks* with its harmonically sparse songs arranged for acoustic guitar, stand-up bass, and strings. *Five Leaves Left* also shares Morrison's obsession with death and romance. Where the two records diverge is *Five Leaves Left*'s complete lack of the feral eroticism that drives *Astral Weeks*. Drake's lyrics are devoid of sex; his voice is polite and resigned.

It is difficult to listen to the album without considering Drake's early death by overdose just five years after its release, especially when so many of the songs can be read morbidly (and soothsaying-minded fans like to read a lot into the album's title). Is the "River Man" Charon, the hooded figure of Greek mythology who ferries the dead across the river Styx? Is the "day" of "Day Is Done" a metaphor for life? Is the "place in the cloud" to which Drake dreams of being lifted in "Cello Song" heaven? When Drake isn't teasing death themes, he's singing of retreating into isolation ("Three Hours"), finding the opposite sex evocatively inscrutable ("The Thoughts of Mary Jane"), or both ("Man in a Shed"). Unsettled yet resigned, grim yet beautifully sung and arranged, *Five Leaves Left* is one of folk pop's most fascinating and exquisite pieces of uneasy listening.

THE END: *INTROSPECTION*

Bill Wyman pulled off an unprecedented feat when he broke Jagger and Richards's songwriting monopoly and got his "In Another Land" onto *Their Satanic Majesties Request*. Buoyed by this achievement, Wyman started writing follow-ups to the track, but there would be no repeating his accomplishment. Although the Stones recorded his "Down Town Suzie" during sessions for *Beggars Banquet*, it wouldn't make the final cut of that record (even though it's better than some of the songs that made it on there). He never again sneaked one of his songs onto a Stones album, but he may have already suspected that would happen since he started peddling songs to another band called the End in late 1967.

Wyman had actually been using the End as a creative outlet since coproducing their single "I Can't Get Any Joy" with Glyn Johns in 1965. When he corralled them back into the studio in 1967 to record two of his own cocompositions, "Shades of Orange" and "Loving Sacred Loving," he ended up producing an entire album for the band, though *Introspection* would not see release until 1969 because the End lacked an attentive manager to see it through.

By the time it appeared, *Introspection*'s swirl of Mellotrons and bleary-eyed harmonies sounded out of touch with the year's heavy blues and backwoods country rock. That doesn't make it any less fabulous. The one lapse in taste is a corny sing-along around the piano of "She Said Yeah," a Larry Williams song the Rolling Stones cut as a feedback-spewing monster in 1965. Any comparison with the Stones should end there, even though *Introspection* has often been compared to *Their Satanic Majesties Request* just because it's psychedelic and Wyman was involved in its making. *Introspection* is a lot poppier, and terrific tracks such as "Cardboard Watch," "What Does It Feel Like," and "Under the Rainbow" would have sounded perfectly at home on 1967 radio. In 1969, the album was doomed to flop, which it did. That just makes it more of a wonderful discovery for the psychedelia treasure hunters of today.

FAIRPORT CONVENTION: *UNHALFBRICKING*

Starting off in a Byrdsy mold, Fairport Convention found their sound when they acquired robust singer Sandy Denny and committed to an Olde English folk-rock sound.

Fairport Convention's first album with Denny is a bit of a patchwork. There are a couple of quirky covers—"Si Tu Dois Partir" (a Cajun-flavored, French-language version of Dylan's "If You Gotta Go, Go Now") and an amorphous rendition of the traditional folk song "Sailor's Song"—as well as definitive versions of Dylan's stately "Percy's Song" and his deliriously playful "Million Dollar Bash." Richard Thompson gets off two good originals with the quietly incensed "Genesis Hall" and the fiery "Cajun Woman," but it's Sandy Denny who supplies the classics. Her "Autopsy" recounts the death of a relationship while seesawing between swirling waltz passages and a standard-time shuffle. The defiantly Zen "Who Knows Where the Time Goes" became a modern folk standard covered by artists ranging from Judy Collins to Nina Simone to Cat Power. No matter what the Convention attempts, Denny's powerful voice, Thompson's sassy guitar licks, and a hardworking rhythm section elevate it all. *Unhalfbricking* may take a mercurial path, but it's one worth following.

LIEGE & LIEF

Liege & Lief is the first Fairport album to really own the band's obsessions with all things olde tyme. Only three of the tracks are band originals. The rest are culled from a dusty songbook of English and Scottish traditional ballads. Denny belts a hearty wake-up call ("Come All Ye"), tingles the spine on a campfire yarn about a werefox ("Reynardine"), breaks hearts while relating the unjust execution of a pacifist ("The Deserter"), trills a song of parting ("Farewell, Farewell," another original), and spins witchy tales like a proto Stevie Nicks (the medieval ballad "Tam Lin"). A successful solo career made Richard Thompson the most high profile member of Fairport Convention, and his tasteful yet forceful guitar work should not be underestimated (nor should his haunting compositions "Farewell, Farewell" and "Crazy Man Michael"), but the most underrated weapon in the group's arsenal is fiddler Dave Swarbrick, who arranged the stormy "Tam Lin" and the manic jig "Medley." *Liege & Lief* cemented Fairport Convention as the voices of the new English folk-rock movement just in time for Sandy Denny to flutter off to her new band Fotheringay, leaving the Convention deprived of their key conventioneer.

THE FLYING BURRITO BROTHERS: *THE GILDED PALACE OF SIN*

Gram Parsons's stint in the Byrds was very brief, but it really shook things up. His C&W influence was so profound on *Sweetheart of the Rodeo* that the Byrds seemed unsure how to continue without him. Unable to fully commit to country rock without his guiding hand but unable to completely go back to their jangly roots either, the band never released another great album. More positively, country rock was officially born, and once Chris Hillman resolved to bail on the Byrds too, so were the Flying Burrito Brothers.

This was the band the Byrds probably would have been had Parsons not had the moral fortitude to quit when they decided to perform in Apartheid-torn South Africa. Pure country is more present on the band's debut *The Gilded Palace of Sin* than it had even been on *Sweetheart of the Rodeo*, partially because Roger McGuinn's Deputy Dawg drawl suggested he wasn't taking the material sincerely. As the Burrito Brothers, Parsons and Hillman harmonize with heartbreaking sincerity and have the serious material to match. The finest song is the ridiculously named but heartfelt cry of betrayal "Hot Burrito #1." There is none of the harder boogying of *Sweetheart of the Rodeo* on *The Gilded Palace of Sin*, though Sneaky Pete's fuzz-pedal lap steel guitar and a pair of soul covers place *Gilded Palace* on the country-rock spectrum. The ideology of songs such as the draft-dodging "My Uncle" and "Hippie Boy," which tricks listeners into assuming it will be a goofy parody (much like the Stones' "Far Away Eyes," which it clearly influenced) but sucker punches us with tragedy and empathy, also helps distinguish this new approach to country from its conservative predecessor.

FOREVER AMBER: *THE LOVE CYCLE*

When Cambridge cover band Forever Amber recorded a cycle of love songs by new member John M. Hudson in 1968, they had very low expectations.

Spending a mere £200 on the recording and printing up just ninety-nine copies, they gave their records away or allowed their kids to throw them around. Such humble origins played a big role in the desirability of *The Love Cycle*, which became one of the rarest, priciest artifacts of the psychedelic era decades after its inauspicious release. Copies were going for as much as £1,200 by the nineties, much to the bands' shock.

The extreme rarity of *The Love Cycle* is not the only reason it became such a valuable item. The music within captures a great deal of what made its era so special. Hudson's tunes are peppered with the weird phasing, baroque touches, capricious guitar solos, and sunny harmonies that made the mid- to late sixties pop's most magical period. Hudson's songs aren't necessarily the most original—"Going Away Again" copies the melody of Dylan's "Love Minus Zero/No Limit" and "A Chance to Be Free" and the chord progression of "Like a Rolling Stone," and you should have an easy time convincing the most hard-core Bowie fan that "Mary (the Painter)" is an outtake from his Deram era—but the crude recording sets it apart from the pristine productions so plentiful in the post–*Sgt. Pepper's* period. As tempting as it is to compare Forever Amber to other bands of their day (okay, I give in, *I* think they sound most like J.K. & Co.), they may have the most in common with early Guided by Voices as they effortlessly spin out memorable melodies wrapped in weird, miniature, low-fi bundles to be distributed to an audience of no one.

SERGE GAINSBOURG AND JANE BIRKIN: *JANE BIRKIN– SERGE GAINSBOURG*

Serge Gainsbourg didn't have the most versatile voice in the world, and he generally couldn't be bothered with composing more than a verse and chorus and putting them on repeat. Because his predilection for provocation was as much a part of his life as it was a part of his art, his art sometimes played second fiddle to a life that involved such infamous moments as burning a 500-franc note and telling Whitney Houston he wanted to fuck her on TV. But he made the most of his musical limitations and lyrical advantages. Only the Velvet Underground rivaled him for creative exploitation of repetition, and only Jane Birkin rivaled him for unbridled sexiness. Since she was his personal and occasional musical partner, they made for an explosive pair on vinyl. The cracks in her limited voice draw the eroticism out of "Jane B" on their one official collaborative LP *Jane Birkin–Serge Gainsbourg*.

For those of us who do not speak French, Gainsbourg's gift for withering wordplay is lost, but there's something about his monotone, sneering delivery that conveys all the cleverness and sleaziness that made him a superstar in his home country. There's certainly no mistaking what's going on once he starts grunting and Jane Birkin starts groaning in his signature provocation, the Procol Harum–derived "Je t'aime . . . moi non plus," even if we miss the subtlety of lines like "Je vais et je viens entre tes reins (translation: "I come and I go between your kidneys"). I was so convinced that Gainsbourg was a wry comic genius and that perusing his lyrics would be more titillating than a metric ton of dirty magazines that a few friends and I tried to learn French just so we could translate his songs when I was in my twenties. We did not get far.

Fontana Records retitled the American edition of *Jane Birkin–Serge Gainsbourg* to capitalize on the singers' sexy, sexy hit. Author's collection.

JEFFERSON AIRPLANE: *VOLUNTEERS*

Jefferson Airplane started pulling apart in 1969. Founder Marty Balin was at the end of his rope, frustrated with the third-class status he'd been stuck with after *Surrealistic Pillow*. The band was feeling hindered by drummer Spencer Dryden's inability to hit as hard as guitarist Jorma Kaukonen or bassist Jack Casady.

Volunteers would be Balin and Dryden's last LP with Jefferson Airplane (at least until Balin rejoined for a bad reunion disc in 1989), leaving it as the last record by the group's classic lineup. While Dryden's lack of thrust is evident on *Volunteers*, the other members more than make up for it with Kaukonen and Casady whipping up gale winds on the anarchic "We Can Be Together," "Volunteers," and "Wooden Ships."

In light of the band's splintering, it is ironic that the themes of all these tracks are

To illustrate the revolutionary politics of their last great album, Jefferson Airplane put on their very best wax lips and lampshades and posed for this photo. Author's collection.

solidity and community against a corrupt, war-mongering system. "We Can Be Together" and "Volunteers" are rarer among hippie anthems for actually advocating violent revolution. Grace Slick takes a no-punches-pulled environmentalist stance on "Eskimo Blue Day" ("The human dream doesn't mean shit to a tree"). The band makes their political party of choice explicit by tossing in an instrumental cover of the traditional Soviet song "Polyushko-polye" (retitled "Meadowlands") and trumpeting communal values on "The Farm." Jefferson Airplane would deal with their losses and move on to make more records, but *Volunteers* was their last good one.

KING CRIMSON: *IN THE COURT OF THE CRIMSON KING*

Classically trained musicians, mathematically complex time signatures, and a general air of otherworldly elitism tend to define progressive rock. King Crimson pummeled the stereotypes with some of the hardest-hitting, noisiest, most genuinely out there prog-rock records.

"21st Century Schizoid Man" gets King Crimson's debut started like a TNT plunger. An elephantine riff provides the track's heavy-metal hook. The dizzying saxophone/guitar/bass/drum interplay in the middle section is like something from an Ornette Coleman record. "I Talk to the Wind" couldn't be a more radical change of pace, with its pastoral woodwinds, poetic lyrics, and atmosphere of autumnal reflection. "Moonchild" is even airier, although its stark spookiness keeps it from floating away completely (the interminable noodling at the end of the track is a waste of vinyl, though). The twin dirges "Epitaph" and "The Court of the Crimson King" blend heaviness and lightness masterfully. *In the Court of the Crimson King* is also uncommonly emotive for prog rock, even if its dark fairy-tale lyrics aren't relatable to anyone who doesn't spend their summers on Middle Earth.

THE KINKS: *ARTHUR (OR THE DECLINE AND FALL OF THE BRITISH EMPIRE)*

In late 1968, Ray Davies and playwright Julian Mitchell began work on a teleplay inspired by the state of post–World War II Britain and the emigration of Davies's sister Rose and her husband Arthur from England to Australia. The TV program was never produced, but the twelve songs Davies wrote for its sound track became the basis of one of the least pretentious concept albums of its time.

Unlike the Who's *Tommy* or the Pretty Things' *S.F. Sorrow* or even Small Faces' *Ogden's Nutgone Flake*, there aren't any acid trips or mystical journeys on *Arthur (Or the Decline and Fall of the British Empire)*. It's all very unhip and very British—in other words, it's very Kinks. Considering that *Arthur* was released at the height of the Vietnam War, American listeners (who took to the album more enthusiastically than British ones did) still probably heard antiwar, antimilitary statements like "Yes Sir, No Sir," "Some Mother's Son," and "Brainwashed" as completely relevant comments on the state of the world in 1969.

Musically, this is a tougher record than the Kinks' previous few releases, and the band sounds more than pleased to be able to kick up some dirt on "Brainwashed," "Australia," "Nothing to Say," "Arthur," and "Victoria" (listen to Dave Davies hooting and hollering with joy off mic). Even the tracks that don't begin as such ultimately reach a boil. "She Bought a Hat Like Princess Marina" begins as a prim minuet before exploding into a knees up of boogying guitars and daffy kazooing. "Shangri-La" starts off with delicately plucked acoustic guitar and gentle vocals before building into one of the hardest songs the Kinks recorded in the late sixties. Considering Led Zeppelin's penchant for theft, I wouldn't be surprised if the structure and climactic descending chord progression of "Stairway to Heaven" weren't lifted from "Shangri-La."

Arthur reveals its origin as sound track music when a few songs meander on too long because they were intended to play out over long scenes in the TV movie. These aimless stretches in the otherwise excellent "Australia," "Mr. Churchill Says," and "Arthur" make the album feel a bit undisciplined when precision had been a core strength of the Kinks' two best records, *Something Else* and *Village Green Preservation Society*. *Arthur* is not as immaculate as those albums. Few albums are.

LED ZEPPELIN: *LED ZEPPELIN*

It's pretty impossible to imagine today, but when Led Zeppelin released their debut, critics reviled the album, the band, and everyone juvenile enough to adopt it as the new gospel. Those critics apparently didn't understand that they were witnessing the invention of a new genre. Groups like Cream and the Jimi Hendrix Experience (and even the Beatles with "Helter Skelter") had laid the groundwork for what would become known as heavy metal, but it was Led Zeppelin that created the first full-blooded metal record. All of the elements that would define the genre are already present on *Led Zeppelin*: the mid-tempo pile-driver riffs, the grotesque

bastardization of the blues, the absurd banshee vocals and six-string histrionics, the
trouser-snake obsession, the bombast, the
doominess, even the speed (and it wouldn't
be out of line to crown "Communication
Breakdown" the first hard-core punk record).

Still, *Led Zeppelin* is more varied than
critics—and even some fans—recognize.
The head-banging blowouts "Communication Breakdown," "How Many More Times,"
"You Shook Me," and "Dazed and Confused"
and the incredible funk/hard-rock merger
"Good Times, Bad Times," which announces
John Bonham and John Paul Jones as rock's
tightest new rhythm section, sometimes overshadow the raga-folk instrumental "Black
Mountain Side" or the rousing gospel-tinged
"Your Time Is Gonna Come" or the fact that
the group was already versatile enough to
rework "Babe I'm Gonna Leave You," a song
they originally heard on a Joan Baez record.
Led Zeppelin is not the band's best album,
but it is one of rock's most important ones.

Led Zeppelin got their name
when John Entwistle and Keith
Moon considered abandoning
the ever-dysfunctional Who for
a new group that would include
Jeff Beck and Jimmy Page and
was guaranteed to "go over like
a lead zeppelin." The zeppelin
on the dramatic cover of Zep's
debut is, of course, the Hinden-
burg, which was not made of lead
but most definitely had its own
difficulties going over. Author's
collection.

LED ZEPPELIN II

Led Zeppelin "wrote" their second album in between gigs supporting their
first and recorded and mixed it at various studios in the United Kingdom
and the United States. Despite its makeshift creation, *Led Zeppelin II*
sounds just as unified as the debut. In fact, it's pretty hard to distinguish
the two albums from each other. Both feature plundered blues classics
reshaped with Jimmy Page's bludgeoning riffs and brazenly slapped with
Bonham/Jones/Page/Plant credits. Both display remnants of psychedelia's
dwindling days, peddle stupid sexual and sexist lyrics, and occasionally hint
that Page and Plant could actually write excellent original material. The
ballad "Thank You" is sappier than a sycamore, but the autumnal "Ramble
On" is one of Zep's best, and John Paul Jones's supple bass line is divine.
Scotch-taping the band's heaviest impulses to their eeriest, "What Is and
What Should Never Be" is also excellent. Although the guys apparently

hated it, "Living Loving Maid (She's Just a Woman)" is a concise and catchy pop song, and "The Lemon Song" (a cover of "Killing Floor" written by Howlin' Wolf, *not* Bonham/Jones/Page/Plant) and "Bring It on Home" (a partial cover of a song written by Willie Dixon, *not* Bonham/Jones/Page/Plant) were much more distinctive blues covers than the relatively generic "I Can't Quit You" and "You Shook Me" on the debut. There's still no excuse for their callous, immoral thievery.

Elsewhere, the monotonous but punishing "Whole Lotta Love" (Willie Dixon again) gave Zeppelin their first and biggest hit single in the United States, and "Moby Dick" gave Bonham the opportunity to pummel drums with his fists for three hours(onstage, his solos pushed into uncharted frontiers of excruciatingly boring self-indulgence). The sloppy and deliriously stupid "Heartbreaker" won over a legion of new fans more enamored with head banging than well-written songs.

Led Zeppelin II had a few undeniably superb tracks and became a tremendous smash, but its construction and lesser tracks suggested Led Zeppelin was nearing a creative dead end. They'd mix up the formula with wonderful results on their next album.

LOVE: *FOUR SAIL*

Love had released three albums rightfully regarded as classics, underwent major lineup changes, and never fully lived up to their earlier promise again. That doesn't mean they'd totally lost it. *Four Sail* sometimes gets written off as unimaginative hard rock, but the album is a lot more varied and creative than that. There is a winding, elliptical flavor to a lot of these songs, but none are directionless. "August" is a fabulous opener with astounding rhythm guitar work. "Robert Montgomery" is another fuzzy rocker that follows a mercurial path. "Your Friend and Mine—Neil's Song" could pass for the Lovin' Spoonful, and "I'm with You" sounds like electrified Forever Changes. "Always See Your Face" doesn't boast the poeticism of "You Set the Scene," but it's still a grand finale. *Four Sail* definitely isn't the first Love album you should check out, but it definitely should be the fourth.

THE MONKEES: *INSTANT REPLAY*

Peter Tork had had it with the Monkees by 1969. The series was off the air. *Head* was a flop. The *33⅓ Revolutions per Monkee* special that was the group's last gasp on TV was wretched. There was little chance the band would work as a studio unit again. Peter didn't get along with Mike Nesmith. Music coordinator Lester Sill had vetoed all of the songs Peter recorded for *The Birds, the Bees, & the Monkees*, even though his madcap "Tear the Top Right Off My Head," the infamously expensive production "Lady's Baby," the scintillating version of "Seeger's Theme," and the sweet go at Jo Mapes's "Come On In" were all way better than several tracks that ended up on the record. Buying out his contract and basically bankrupting himself, Peter left the Monkees, which continued as a trio.

Although the public's demand for Monkees material had disappeared since the series' cancellation, Colgems kept up high demand for it. Just two and a half months after the *Head* sound track was released to an indifferent public, new music coordinator Brendan Cahill assembled a collection of old outtakes and a few more recently recorded numbers. Because of its piecemeal nature, *Instant Replay* is highly inconsistent. All three Nesmith numbers are graceful, and his version of Gerry Goffin and Carol King's "I Won't Be the Same Without Her" sports an enchanting contrapuntal vocal arrangement. That it dates back to the earliest Monkees sessions isn't obvious, but it is obvious that the pointless "Last Train to Clarksville" clone "Tear Drop City" is ancient, and the decision to release it as a single was a cowardly move that didn't pay off with a hit.

A far better Boyce and Hart relic is a majestic version of "Through the Looking Glass" cut in late 1967, and it's without question Micky Dolenz's best contribution to *Instant Replay*. His two compositions are odd ducks. "Just a Game" is insubstantial. "Shorty Blackwell" is too substantial—a bizarre, multisectional meditation on the dreadful music industry that is overblown to the point of absurdity. When I first heard it on the *Hit Factory* compilation, "Shorty Blackwell" freaked me out so severely that I called Record World to ask if I could return the cassette. Naturally, they shut me down, so I stuffed a couple of spitballs into the cassette's holes (ask your parents what that means, kids) and recorded "The Door into Summer" and "Love Is Only Sleeping" over it.

The big surprise is Davy Jones's development as a writer. His "You and I" is not only one of the album's best cuts but also its most cutting. Neil Young contributes the slicing guitar solo. "Don't Listen to Linda" and "The Girl I Left Behind Me" are passable generic Jones ballads, but the B-side "A Man Without a Dream" is a terrific, powerful production that would have made a much better A-side than "Tear Drop City."

THE MONKEES PRESENT

Released less than eight months after *Instant Replay*, *The Monkees Present* is a more consistent collection, and since it grabs only two tracks from the vault—the mediocre "Valleri" retread "Looking for the Good Times" and the horrid novelty "Ladies Aid Society"—it gives a better impression of where Mike, Micky, and Davy were in 1969. Davy's new songs are as light as ever, but they're more adult. His rainy "French Song" is an atmospheric gem. Mike's vigorous country-rock contributions are the album's most commercial tracks, and "Listen to the Band" and "Good Clean Fun" were selected to be his first A-sides. Micky seems to have developed a yen for light jazz, and "Little Girl" with its breathtaking Louie Shelton guitar licks, "Bye Bye Baby Bye Bye," and "Pillow Time," a lullaby his mom cowrote, are all nice numbers in that manner. "Mommy and Daddy," a crazed, scathing, oompah tirade against the older generation's callousness and hypocrisy, probably freaked out the few teenyboppers who bought *The Monkees Present*.

MONTAGE: MONTAGE

Keyboardist/composer Michael Brown had been the mastermind behind the Left Banke. When he wanted to retire from touring to take a more Brian Wilson–like studio role, the rest of the band balked and went their separate ways (they also wanted to distance themselves from Brown's father, who was trying to step in as the group's manager). Brown barely paused before glomming onto a group called Montage and working his magic on their sole album.

Arranging the vocals, providing his trademark elegant piano work, and cowriting all but one track, Brown essentially turned *Montage* into a Left Banke album. In fact, some critics regard it as a worthier successor to the Banke's classic debut, *Walk Away Renee/Pretty Ballerina*, than their proper second album. I think this is unfair to the underrated *Left Banke Too*, which includes the definitive version of "Desiree," but *Montage* is a fine album that indeed sounds very much like a Left Banke record. Singer Vance Chapman is even a vocal doppelgänger of the Left Banke's Steve Martin.

There are a couple of weak moments within the LP's brief twenty-five minutes. "An Audience with Miss Pricilla Gray" is a music-hall jaunt out of step with an otherwise moody collection of songs, and Brown misguidedly directed Chapman to deliberately sing sour notes in "Men Are Building

Sand" to reflect the song's anti-deforestation message (an earlier recording Brown credited to the Left Banke is the definitive version of that song), but "Grand Pianist," "I Shall Call Her Mary" (an outlet for Brown's major crush on Mary Weiss of the Shangri-Las),, and the "Eleanor Rigby"–like "She's Alone" are exquisite. *Montage* may not be the Left Banke album that never was, but it will surely appeal to anyone who digs that group.

NAZZ: *NAZZ NAZZ*

As far as Todd Rundgren was concerned, *Nazz Nazz* was not supposed to be Nazz's second album. He'd plotted a double-vinyl opus called *Fungo Bat*, but certain members of the group felt putting out a double disc so early in their career was too risky and balked at the increasingly sensitive songs Rundgren was composing. Nazz started deteriorating shortly thereafter.

With the likelihood that the band might not be around much longer, SGC Records decided to cherry-pick the *Fungo Bat* sessions for the best material and release the single-disc album we now know as *Nazz Nazz* (the remainder of the *Fungo Bat* material would end up on the band's final album, *Nazz III*, the following year). As it stands, *Nazz Nazz* is Nazz's most consistently original and exciting record, and while it failed to produce a timeless classic along the lines of "Open Your Eyes," "Forget All About It" is just as great. One might assume that getting to play stuff as bullish as that—"Rain Rider," "Hang on Paul," and the near-metal "Under the Ice"—or as hilarious as the cop-baiting Beatles homage "Meridian Leeward" should have been enough to appease Nazz's more ballad-phobic members. That those guys disliked Rundgren's ballads seems particularly clueless in light of the beauty of "Gonna Cry Today" and "Letters Don't Count."

PROCOL HARUM: *A SALTY DOG*

The witches of *Procol Harum* and wizards of *Shine on Brightly* succumb to 1969's rootsiness on their finest album. Lyricist Keith Reid's concerns are less out there on *A Salty Dog* than they'd been on Procol Harum's death-laden debut or their weirdly philosophical second album. *A Salty Dog* nearly plays as a nautical concept album, as Reid remakes himself from pop's Poe to rock's Melville, capturing that author's fascination with the sea and obsessions with death, destiny, and futility.

The band crafts majestic soundscapes to complement Reid's seascapes. Using an eclectic assortment of styles (sweeping dirges, stripped-down blues, airy folk, heavy rock, soul, classically tinged pop), instruments (various mallets, full orchestration, horns, pipes, percussion), and singers (chief Procol singer Gary Brooker shares mic time with organist Matthew Fisher, who sounds a bit like the Zombies' Colin Blunstone, and rubble-voiced guitarist Robin Trower), Procol Harum fashion a complete sensory experience through music. Close your eyes and imagine the slow agitation of the waves beneath a ship gone adrift while taking in their masterpiece, "A Salty Dog." See a

Dickinson's iconic painting on the cover of A Salty Dog is a parody of the packets that house Player's Navy Cut cigarettes. It certainly aids and abets the album's nautical themes. Author's collection.

mighty whaler being tossed and tumbled like a toy boat on a stormy sea during Fisher's breathtaking "Wreck of the Hesperus." Languish before images of a tropical island revelry while reveling in his "Boredom." Feel the balmy breeze gently roll off the ocean during the wistful "Too Much Between Us." Shudder before mightily crashing waves during "The Devil Came from Kansas," which features a simple but ingenious fill that shuffles handclaps and drums. B. J. Wilson's drumming throughout the record is among the best on any rock record, as is Gary Brooker's awesome singing, especially on the title track and the grand "All This and More." *A Salty Dog* is not the best-loved album of 1969, but as far as I'm concerned, it's the best.

PAUL REVERE AND THE RAIDERS: *HARD 'N' HEAVY (WITH MARSHMALLOW)*

Progressiveness and trend following were never major missions of Paul Revere and the Raiders, so their 1969 offering is still comfortingly loaded with mid-sixties signatures. Although they've wisely stripped off their stupid American Revolution costumes, the guys are still monkeying around like bubble gummers on the record sleeve (the decision to pose with a tank was an especially witless idea considering what was happening in Southeast Asia) and pushing their garage rock and light psychedelia inside of it. They'd rarely been more indebted to the Stones than they are on the terribly titled *Hard 'n' Heavy (with Marshmallow)*. The naugahyde-rough

"Time After Time" is brewed in the broth of 1965's "Satisfaction." The sumptuous "Cinderella Sunshine" pulls out everything in the Stones' 1966 trick bag: fat-bottomed fuzz bass, churchy organs, marimba. It sounds like an *Aftermath* outtake, as does the "Lady Jane"–esque "Trishalana." Mark Lindsay is not Mick Jagger, so all the hard rock sounds like it's been sieved through a mesh of cotton candy. There are flaccid moments too ("Out on the Road," "Hard and Heavy 5 String Banjo," "Where You Goin' Girl"), and the idea to give it a sort of linking concept with corny comedy improvs was not good. The

Light-heartedly capering with a tank at the height of the Vietnam War? Not very cool, Raiders. Author's collection.

bits before "Time After Time" and "Without You" are interminable and unfortunate since they delay the starts of two of the album's nastiest tracks.

THE ROLLING STONES: *LET IT BLEED*

Let It Bleed was a very appropriate way for the Rolling Stones to bid "fuck off" to the sixties. By the end of that decade, all of the hippie idealism that had built up since the Stones started making hits in 1964 had gone rancid with multiple assassinations, riots, police brutality, the election of Richard Nixon, and the ongoing mess in Vietnam. "Gimmie Shelter," with its horrifying refrain, distills that violence. "Midnight Rambler," a gleeful first-person peek through the eyes of the Boston Strangler, supersizes it. The other tracks are not as nasty as these two, though they are rarely less cynical. The funky "Monkey Man" is Jagger's hilarious mockery of his own cartoonish image. "Live with Me," which sports one of the Stones' best bass lines (played by Keith Richards), is a mock love song more into porno scenarios than conventional romance. The title track is a

The original title of *Let It Bleed* was *Automatic Changer*, which is a phonograph option that allows people who only need to listen to one side of an LP to stack up their records for successive play. The Stones still used Robert Brownjohn's illustrative arrangement for the cover of *Automatic Changer* (with a cake baked by Delia Smith) when they decided to call their latest *Let It Bleed* instead. Author's collection.

withering plea for companionship bloated with dirty, violent imagery. "You Got the Silver" (featuring Richards's first ragged solo vocal) and the cover of Robert Johnson's "Love in Vain" ruminate on isolation. *Let It Bleed* culminates with the operatic "You Can't Always Get What You Want," a sort of "(I Can't Get No) Satisfaction" for an audience far more jaded than the one Jagger serenaded in 1965.

The Stones sound more jaded than ever too as they pander to their audience's basest instincts. That audience has responded largely with appreciation since *Let It Bleed* is regularly rated with *Sticky Fingers* and *Exile on Main Street* as one of the band's best albums. This praise for the first Stones album that could really be called formulaic may have hindered the band's creativity. It was as if the critical hammering *Their Satanic Majesties Request* received scared them away from ever rocking the boat too much again. Each track on *Let It Bleed* has a musical or thematic twin on the far superior *Beggars Banquet*. Doubt me? Well consider the evidence. Both albums contain the following:

- one song in which Jagger plays the role of personified evil (on *Beggars Banquet*, he sings from the point of view of Lucifer on "Sympathy for the Devil"; on *Let It Bleed*, he plays the Boston Strangler on "Midnight Rambler")
- one country-blues cover (*Beggars* has the Reverend Robert Wilkins's "Prodigal Son"; *Bleed* has Robert Johnson's "Love in Vain")
- one country-blues original (*Beggars* has "No Expectations"; *Bleed* has "You Got the Silver")
- one southern-fried comedy track (*Beggars* has "Dear Doctor"; *Bleed* has "Country Honk")
- one paranoid, apocalyptic social commentary (*Beggars* has "Jigsaw Puzzle"; *Bleed* has "Gimmie Shelter")
- one glorification of libertine sex (*Beggars* has "Stray Cat Blues"; *Bleed* has "Live with Me")
- one self-mocking look at Jagger's public persona (*Beggars* has "Street Fighting Man," on which he skewers his ineffectuality regarding the rock star's ability to elicit genuine social change; *Bleed* has "Monkey Man," on which he skewers everything from his demonic facade to his goofy dance moves to his entourage of junkies)
and
- one climactic gospel number featuring prominent backing singers (*Beggars* has "Salt of the Earth"; *Bleed* has "You Can't Always Get What You Want")

The use of a choir on "You Can't Always Get What You Want" is the only time *Let It Bleed* stretches beyond the Stones' tried-and-true methods. The percentage of ordinary tracks ("Love in Vain," the country parodies "Country Honk" and "Let It Bleed," which find Jagger putting on an annoyingly "funny" voice) is too high for *Let It Bleed* to really deserve a spot among the Stones' greatest albums. Nevertheless, a record with such major ones as "Gimmie Shelter," "You Can't Always Get What You Want," and "You Got the Silver" couldn't be anything less than a classic.

SLY AND THE FAMILY STONE: *STAND!*

Sly Stone revolutionized rock and soul by forcing them to procreate and emphasizing syncopated bass/drum interplay. The progeny was a wild new hybrid called funk, and Stone's showbizzy, sci-fi stage gear inspired many black musicians to shun Motown's dinner wear and accept their inner freaks. With a big, biracial band of friends and family, Stone made some of the sixties most inspirational singles: "Dance to the Music," "Life," "Everyday People." With *Stand!*, Sly and the Family Stone began metamorphosing from a sixties-style hit machine into a seventies-style jam band.

The results are uneven since a couple of the jams don't really go anywhere. The fourteen-minute "Sex Machine" is a muddy instrumental that hints at what would come on *There's a Riot Going On* sans that album's disturbing lyricism and comparative concision. The transcendent "I Want to Take You Higher" is a much more deserving vehicle for showing off an amazing band's amazing skills. "Don't Call Me Nigger, Whitey" is a plodding thing that doesn't earn its incendiary title. It says nothing more insightful than that phrase, and, alternately, "Don't call me whitey, nigger," which undercuts the song's message since calling a white person "whitey" doesn't cut nearly as deeply as the alternative (and I am fully aware of how taboo that even typing that word is, but that's the word Sly Stone used, and it seems dishonest to either bowdlerize it or pretend that song is not a part of this record).

The rest of *Stand!* stresses the greatness of the Family's way with short songs: the rallying title track, the brick-hard funk "Sing a Simple Song," the heartbeat-pulse "Everyday People," the horn-fed "You Can Make It If You Try," and the sly, jazzy, and paranoid "Somebody's Watching You." Had those two jams been clipped to make room for more of this kind of material, *Stand!* would be a perfect record.

TOOTS & THE MAYTALS: *SWEET AND DANDY*

Beginning as a gospel-soul-ska fusion group, Frederick "Toots" Hibbert and his backing duo the Maytals (Nathaniel "Jerry" McCarthy and Henry "Raleigh" Gordon, who named the group after a Jamaican word meaning "pure and good") either slowed down ska's push and pull of on-beat drumming and offbeat guitar accents or sped up rock steady's similar rhythm for their 1968 single "Do the Reggay." By that point, they were already Jamaica's most popular homegrown act, winning the country's National Popular Song Contest with the supremely catchy rock-steady babble of "Bam Bam" in 1966 (they'd win twice more with the magnificently uplifting "Sweet and Dandy" in 1969 and "Pomps and Pride" in 1972). They were now genre pioneers too.

A year after releasing "Do the Reggay," Toots & the Maytals released a full-length collection of reggae tracks on Beverley's Records in Jamaica that contains their best-known songs: "54-46 Was My Number" (about Toots's eighteen-month stint in prison following a conviction for ganja possession), "Pressure Drop" (the group's follow-up single to "Do the Reggay" and their signature number), and the contest-winning title track, "Sweet and Dandy." "Bla, Bla, Bla," "Monkey Man," and "I Shall Be Free" are similarly strong. Producer Leslie Kong's radio-savvy wall of sound and Toots Hibbert's gruff shout keep the disc in firm soul territory, while the combo's delectable tunes are pure pop. The Maytals blend genres with such impeccable taste that it's almost disingenuous to overemphasize their importance as reggae breakthroughs. "I Shall Be Free" is nothing if not a James Brown–style soul vamp. There's still no denying the significance of these recordings in the history of reggae or how damn fun they are.

THE TURTLES: *TURTLE SOUP*

The Turtles must have been determined to make their final album exceptional. They hired Ray Davies to produce it right after he'd completed *The Kinks Are the Village Green Preservation Society*. They also wrote the most mature, well-developed songs of their career. Fans of charmingly smarmy hits like "She'd Rather Be with Me" and "Elenore" may have been disappointed that such fare was in short order on *Turtle Soup*, but that's probably neither here nor there since hardly anyone bought the album. Unlike its fellow commercial flops *Village Green*, *Odessey and Oracle*, and *Forever Changes*, *Turtle Soup* never developed a cult following.

That's a wrong that should get righted because each song on *Turtle Soup* is a perfectly crafted, witty pop song performed with big energy and arranged with Davies's ear for acoustic instrumentation and little details, such as the ticktocking percussion and strings on "John and Julie" and the Wagnerian brass bursts on "How You Loved Me" and "Love in the City," a failed single that deserved to be a hit.

Turtle Soup also gave each member of the Turtles a shot at singing and writing, and the guys contribute some terrific boogey ("Come Over," "Bachelor Mother"), twelve-string pop (the exhilarating "She Always Leaves Me Laughing"), anthems ("How You Loved Me," "Love in the City"), delicate balladry ("John and Julie"), horn-ball rock ("Hot Little Hands"), nocturnal mood music ("Somewhere Friday Night"), country waltzing ("Dance This Dance"), and classic Turtles pop ("You Don't Have to Walk in the Rain").

Despite *Turtle Soup*'s excellence, the Turtles were disappointed with Ray Davies's production. They were expecting the heavy chunk of "You Really Got Me" rather than the delicacy of "Autumn Almanac." The album's commercial failure expedited the band's end. They left a new record with producer Jerry Yester that was shaping up to be another excellent one unfinished. *Turtle Soup* still sent the guys off on a high note. Too bad that only the most devoted cultists are aware of that today.

THE VELVET UNDERGROUND: *THE VELVET UNDERGROUND*

The Velvet Underground couldn't have sounded more different from *White Light/White Heat*, the feedback freak-out that preceded it. The prevailing sound of the band's eponymous third album is shimmery acoustic guitars, lazy rhythms, and whispered vocals—many of them whispered by new guy Doug Ewell, whose boyish warble would never be mistaken for Lou Reed's grizzled grunt. The *Velvet Underground* is almost as intense an experience as *White Light/White Heat*, though it's more like spending a long, dark night of the soul over flickering candlelight than shooting speed while getting blown by a hooker in drag. Meditative tracks such as "Candy Says," "Pale Blue Eyes," "I'm Set Free," and "Jesus" are the album's defining pieces. "What Goes On" and "Beginning to See the Light" are a couple of elated rockers murky enough to not feel out of place. It all comes to a surreal conclusion with the lengthy, babbling "Murder Mystery," the strangest piece on *The Velvet Underground*, and the jaunty yet dejected "After Hours," featuring a Ringo-esque vocal by drummer Mo Tucker.

THE WHO: *TOMMY*

Tommy totally changed the Who's career. Before it, they'd been fumbling for an identity and hadn't made a significant impression in the commercially crucial American market yet. The rock opera Pete Townshend and producer Kit Lambert had been dreaming of since conceiving the mini-opera "A Quick One While He's Away" and trying to make a go of "Rael," which ended up as a short track on *Sell Out*, finally coalesced with the bizarre story of an autistic boy who loses his senses after witnessing his father murdering his mother's lover, becomes a celebrated pinball champion by sniffing the ball, regains his senses after his mom breaks a mirror, and ends up as a failed cult leader. Townshend's infatuation with Maher Baba, a spiritual leader who took a vow of silence at the age of thirty-one and coined the phrase "Don't worry, be happy," influenced the album's philosophy, which stresses the concept that the material world is illusory. That *Tommy* isn't an opera at all, as Townshend has admitted, is immaterial. Just as the Beatles fooled the world into accepting *Sgt. Pepper's* as a concept album despite its lack of a lucid concept, the Who successfully introduced the term "rock opera" into the pop-cultural lexicon despite their album's lack of staging and recitative and its extensive use of third-person narration. Some critics are more comfortable categorizing *Tommy* as a cantata than an opera, but I'm sure you'll agree that "rock cantata" doesn't have the same ring as "rock opera."

Massively popular on record and stage, *Tommy* gave the Who the conceptual hook for which they'd been searching since the days when they tried passing themselves off as mods. It also consumed them for much of the rest of their career. The Who ceased to be a great singles act and started favoring progressive heft and highfalutin concepts over the humor and pithiness that made their sixties work so amazing (not that the rock opera is devoid of humor: "Pinball Wizard," "Cousin Kevin," and "Fiddle About" are all bad-taste comedy numbers that would make John Waters jealous and "Tommy's Holiday Camp" is as silly as the Who ever got—and they could get pretty silly).

Tommy would also go on to inspire an appalling film, an appalling all-star record with the London Symphony Orchestra, and a Broadway musical that I can only assume was as appalling as everything else the rock opera birthed. The original album is difficult to assess without all the baggage that goes with it. The rock opera concept was undoubtedly revolutionary, but the story line of *Tommy* is ridiculous, and Townshend's use of physical disabilities as a metaphor for spiritual purity is wrongheaded, although the underlying implication that *Tommy* was better off without his senses may counter charges of ableism. After all, only his miserable parents seem uptight about Tommy's disabilities and desperate to "cure" him. When he does regain his senses, he becomes a total bore.

Taken as two discs of the Who's latest songs, *Tommy* is wonderful. With *The Who Sell Out*, the band best known for smashing their instruments developed a sound that was both crushing *and* ethereal. Their three-part harmonies are especially blissful on that record. *Tommy* resumes that magical sound. Inside or outside the opera's plot, "Christ-

Tommy was released in a lush package with a triptych gatefold sleeve and full-color libretto booklet. Townshend's fellow Maher Baba acolyte, Mike McInnerney, designed the Escher-like image. Author's collection.

mas," "Cousin Kevin," "Amazing Journey/Sparks," "1921," and "Go to the Mirror!" are great songs. "Sensation," the most gorgeous and least plot-heavy track on *Tommy*, would have fit nicely alongside similarly heavenly, Townshend-sung love songs like "I Can't Reach You," "Our Love Was," and "Sunrise" on *The Who Sell Out*.

There is certainly filler on this double record, but even that is quite beautiful. "Underture" is little more than an extended riff on "Sparks" (which was already an extended riff on "Rael"), and it was clearly included to bring side B up to an acceptable length. It's still hypnotic and houses some of Keith Moon's fieriest drumming. All of the time the band spent on the road before recording *Tommy* is fully evident on vinyl for the first time. Daltrey's vocals are stronger than ever, and with "Sparks," Entwistle is finally allowed to cut loose in the studio the way he always did onstage. For the Who, *Tommy* fully came to life onstage, but the pretty recording of its songs is this dinosaur's most credible legacy.

1970

From a rock and roll standpoint, the seventies began in a far neater manner than most other eras. The sixties didn't really start until the Beatles became megastars three years after the decade's calendar launch. It took the debut of MTV in 1981 to kick off the eighties, and the first year of the nineties remained a wasteland of hair bands until "Smells Like Teen Spirit," but the seventies arrived without delay.

At the very end of 1969, the Rolling Stones staged Altamont, an outdoor rock festival that descended into infamy when the Hell's Angels motorcycle gang (hired as "security") stabbed audience member Meredith Hunter to death. Just as the Stones' doomed response to blissed-out Woodstock symbolized the death of sixties hippie idealism in a manner too neat for too many rock historians to resist, 1970 found the previous decade's definitive band in ruins, and each ex-Beatle wasted no time in releasing his first solo record that year. The Stones and the Who would not break up in 1970, but both were in the process of radically redefining their sounds, and they commemorated their metamorphoses with a pair of raw live albums. Punk, the most earth-shaking rock movement of the seventies, was already in sight in the form of rabid new records by the MC5 and the Stooges, while their most significant predecessor, the Velvet Underground, released their final album (well, their final album with the last lineup that had any right to call themselves the Velvet Underground). Jimi and Janis died. The Doors played their final concert. Simon & Garfunkel released their final and biggest-selling album and would split up the following year. Diana Ross left the Supremes. Even the Monkees broke up. Amidst all this flux were a lot of great albums.

THE BAND: *STAGE FRIGHT*

The Band were responsible for one of the most influential albums of the late sixties when *Music from Big Pink* helped spark the era's "return to the roots" trend in rock and roll in 1968. They were responsible for one of the era's very best albums when they released their perfectly crafted eponymous album the following year. So the Band could be forgiven if their third album wasn't quite as fresh or electrifying. Rather, *Stage Fright* finds the quartet working in the deep groove they'd etched out with their monumental first two albums. "Strawberry Wine" is a return to the driving backwoods funk of "Up on Cripple Creek," "Sleeping" is another delicate Richard Manuel vehicle in the model of "Whispering Pines" or "Lonesome Suzie," and so on.

If the Band aren't quite stretching themselves musically the third time around, they're at least doing their thing as well as ever, and Robbie Robertson's lyrical concerns have certainly shifted. While *The Band* looked backward to America's past, *Stage Fright* looks inward for Robertson's first truly personal selection of songs. Throughout the album, he is either contemplating his own lack of motivation or looking at his band's work with alarm. The title track views live performing through a sweaty veil of anxiety. "All La Glory" is the one moment of true clarity as Robertson observes his newborn girl with awe and pens one of rock's loveliest odes to new parenthood.

So Robertson's personal investment is what really keeps *Stage Fright* sparking. The Band get themselves sufficiently worked up for a few tracks such as "Time to Kill," "Just Another Whistle Stop," and the title number, but the album could have used a bit more forceful rock and roll.

THE BEACH BOYS: *SUNFLOWER*

For many critics and fans, the democratically created *Sunflower* was the Beach Boys' return to form record after a few years of putting out sparsely arranged, quirky, homespun discs like *Smiley Smile*, *Wild Honey*, and *Friends*. Some commentators even went so far as to trumpet it as the equal of *Pet Sounds*. To my ears, it's a pretty spotty affair with fine tracks like "Add Some Music" and "Slip On Through" scattered among mediocrities like Dennis Wilson's clumsy rocker "Got to Know the Woman" and Bruce Johnston's lightweight "Deirdre" and soap opera–ish "Tears in the Morning." The album's second cut, however, is a triumph. At just under two minutes, "This Whole World" careens breathlessly through a variety of colors and levels of rhythmic intensity as Brian Wilson ruminates on romantic and universal love. Gunning off with a mean Chuck Berry riff, the song rapidly sprints through doo-wop, sparkling *Pet Sounds*–derived pop, and an a cappella tag. All the while, Carl sings as if he's holding on for dear life. However, brother Dennis's guileless, remarkably sensitive vocal on the hymn-like "Forever," is *Sunflower*'s most meaningful revelation.

THE BEATLES: *LET IT BE*

And so an era ends. On September 26, 1969, the Beatles released the last album all four Fabs intended to release. *Abbey Road* wrapped up the experience well, providing outstanding showcases for each band member: Lennon transitioned to the bloodletting of his solo career with his grungiest tracks yet, McCartney continued his obsession with lavish production with the medley that consumed side B, Harrison contributed his two most eminent compositions, and Starr comported himself well as rare composer of one track and rare soloist on another. That track was called "The End," as if the finality of *Abbey Road* needed to be made any more explicit. It was as pat a finale to the Beatles' career as anyone could imagine.

Michael Lindsay-Hogg's 1970 *Let It Be* documentary and its sound track of songs recorded in early 1969 muddied that patness. The release of those recordings was so delayed because they were such a mess. Rehearsing material for a TV special and an LP to be recorded at their first concert in three years (both aborted), the Beatles meandered through what John Lennon described in his iconoclastic 1971 interview with *Rolling Stone* magazine as "the shittiest load of badly recorded shit—and with a lousy feeling to it—ever." The statement was typical Lennon exaggeration, but it wasn't too far off. What was under consideration for release as *Get Back (with "Let It Be" and 11 Other Songs)* would have confounded fans and sent critics into a feeding frenzy had it been released in 1969. It's full of flubs, incomplete takes, lifeless takes, and dead space between tracks. Hearing it today, *Get Back* sounds like a proto–*Beatles Anthology* and is as ahead of its time as any of the most groundbreaking Beatles albums were in the sixties. *Revolver, Sgt. Pepper's,* and *Abbey Road* were all revolutionary for their recording innovations and superior quality; *Get Back* would have been revolutionary for its fearlessness in showing the most important recording innovators of their day with their pants down. It's hardly the band's most listenable work, but it would have been their most daring, and I'm pretty sure it would have been Lester Bangs's favorite Beatles album.

So manager Allen Klein passed off those roughly played, demo-like tracks and the half dozen numbers the Beatles performed live on the rooftop of Apple Corps for Lindsay-Hogg's camera to pop's most iconic producer. Lennon said that when he heard what Phil Spector did with the *Get Back* tapes, he "didn't puke." Quite the praise.

Paul McCartney felt differently when he heard the cloying strings and choirs Spector sprayed all over "Let It Be," "The Long and Winding Road," and "Across the Universe." While Spector certainly made some pretty poor recordings releasable, his heavy-handed methods are in poor taste.

Spector does the songs justice when he merely tidies up the performances and allows the fab four to play as a fab foursome. The best tracks on *Let It Be* are its most simply arranged: the Everly Brothers–esque "Two of Us," the soulful "Dig a Pony," and the startling "I've Got a Feeling," which is the strongest thing on the album by a country mile. On the usual Beatles album, most of the tracks would be up to that level of quality, but because of its shambolic production and ill-timed release, *Let It Be* was left to be the last and weakest word on the most spectacular career in rock and roll.

THE BEATLES IN AMERICA: *HEY JUDE*

If *Abbey Road* provided a sweetly polished finale to Beatlemania, then the lawyers, paper chasing, obligations, and Allen Klein's conniving were the sour end.

John, George, and Ringo's preferred manager Klein caused a lot of friction within the disintegrating band, but he is also responsible for one of the more benign obligations of the Beatles' final days. As part of his renegotiation of the group's Capitol contract in 1969, Klein promised to deliver one extra LP in the tradition of the ones the label had been conceiving since 1964, the ones I have been examining in all these "Beatles in America" entries.

As it was with *The Beatles' Second Album* or *Yesterday and Today,* the concept was songs that had yet to appear on a Capitol LP, and like most of those earlier Capitol compilations, there was little cohesiveness. Like them, there would be controversial mixes (Lennon loathed how his "Revolution" sounded in stereo). Like them, this new album would pass off singles as album tracks, and like them, it would be a huge hit, effortlessly hitting number two on *Billboard*'s album chart despite the fact that a lot of people already owned everything on it. In fact, the centerpiece of the album is the Beatles' biggest-selling single in the United States ever. The masterminds behind the album were so convinced that the song's place on the LP would move units that they changed the album's title from *The Beatles Again* to *Hey Jude*.

Unlike the previous Capitol exclusives, *Hey Jude* does not focus on a specific era, and so it also differs from *The Beatles' Second Album* or *Yesterday and Today* because it isn't trying to fool anyone into believing it's the latest batch of Beatles recordings. Perhaps it would be more at home in a discussion of compilations like *A Collection of Beatles Oldies*, *1962–1966* and *1967–1970* (all of which are actually fairly focused on a specific era). That *Hey Jude* now seems like a blueprint for 1988's *Past Masters Volume 2* makes its status as a clear-cut compilation all the more clear cut.

But *Hey Jude* is its own beast in a sense. It certainly is not a greatest hits album, even though "Can't Buy Me Love," "Paperback Writer," "Lady Madonna," "Hey Jude," and "The Ballad of John and Yoko" were all hits. It doesn't do what most greatest-hits albums set out to do, which is satisfyingly distilling a group's history down to a dozen or so essential songs. There are too many gaps in the story. There's nothing from 1965 (even though "I'm Down" could have been included and would not end up on LP until 1976's *Rock 'n' Roll Music* comp). The year 1967 is unrepresented too. *Hey Jude* is back heavy with tracks from the back end of the Beatles' career.

Of course, not every compilation is a greatest-hits album, but the worthwhile ones have a definite concept. As already mentioned, the concept of *Hey Jude* is a Capitol closet cleaning, though this does not mean all of these tracks are taking their first turns at 33⅓ RPM. "I Should Have Known Better" and "Can't Buy Me Love" had been released on United Artists' *A Hard Day's Night* sound track five years earlier.

If compiler Allan Steckler wanted to make *Hey Jude*'s masquerade as a noncompilation more convincing, he couldn't really pull it off anyway because there were too few candidates for inclusion. The upcoming *Let It Be* LP was to contain the recent past masters "Get Back" and "Across the Universe," although they would be different versions than the ones that had already been released as a single and a charity album track, respectively. Even releasing different versions of these songs might have felt like a cheat (though one in keeping with "Komm Gib Mir Deine Hand" from *Something New*). "You Know My Name (Look Up the Number)," which would be released just one month after *Hey Jude* on the B-side of the "Let It Be" single, was actually an old track from 1967. "The Inner Light," the B-side of "Lady Madonna," was a more recent piece, but its raga instrumentation makes it sound like a product of 1967. It would sound very out of place among straightforward rockers like "Don't Let Me Down," "Revolution," "The Ballad of John and Yoko," and even its own A-side, "Lady Madonna."

So what is *Hey Jude*? Is it a compilation? Is it the final sham in a six-year tradition of sham American albums? Capitol seems to opt for the latter, including it among all of its other noncomp LPs in the *US Albums* box set released in 2014. I guess it doesn't really matter because the Beatles' story on American wax has often lacked rhyme and reason. The first rock and roll group to really treat their albums like art had seen that art invaded by lounge instrumentals and jumbled so that their earliest recordings were released on their fifth LP. The Beatles had seen their masterpiece butchered, the dismembered parts lumped inside a butcher cover banned for being "offensive," and on a few occasions, their preferred versions of their albums would not be the ones a lot of fans preferred. In the end, *Hey Jude* is just another strange destination along the Beatles' vinyl trip across America.

BLACK SABBATH: *PARANOID*

Steppenwolf coined the new genre's title in "Born to Be Wild," the Beatles vulcanized its sound with "Helter Skelter," and Led Zeppelin set it in stone, but Black Sabbath was the band that really committed to heavy metal. Zeppelin's first two albums were basically metal ones, but even on those records, the band was too eclectic to fully qualify as a metal. Surely "Black Mountain Side" and "Thank You" are no one's idea of heavy metal.

Black Sabbath would have none of that folk or love ballad business. Their plodding rhythms, elemental power-chord riffs, and fixation on evil and doom won over a new generation of rock kids weary of the hippies' unrequited utopianism. Kids of all classes could drown their hopelessness with deafening volume or revel in a bit of safe rebellion against parents who overreacted to metal as histrionically as their own parents overreacted to Little Richard a dozen years earlier. No band before and few bands since have spoken to those fans as directly as Black Sabbath did. Wailing singer Ozzy Osbourne became the genre's mascot.

Sabbath's first album established their sound, but everything really coalesced on their second and best. *Paranoid* is a classic buttressed with the band's three definitive songs. Each sets a heavy-metal essential in place. The title track supplies the speed and unfocused misery. "War Pigs" supplies the anger. "Iron Man" supplies the lugubriousness and the us-against-them stance. All three house indelible riffs.

Black Sabbath experiments with subtlety on the stoned space-rock nugget "Planet Caravan," and bassist Geezer Butler and drummer Bill Ward know how to swing, but heaviness is the album's main mission. Many metal bands would fall at Black Sabbath's feet, but most would fail to pick up on the creative touches that zap *Paranoid* to life.

CREEDENCE CLEARWATER REVIVAL: *COSMO'S FACTORY*

Creedence Clearwater Revival took their LP cues from early sixties acts, slapping together their latest singles with a few early rock and roll covers the way the Beatles, the Beach Boys, and the Kinks used to. As it was for groups with writers of the caliber of Lennon and McCartney, Brian Wilson, and Ray and Dave Davies, that formula was a limited one for John Fogerty, and it peaks with *Cosmo's Factory*. Creedence's versions of Bo Diddley's "Before You Accuse Me," Roy Orbison's "Ooby Dooby," Arthur Crudup's "My Baby Left Me," and Marvin Gaye's "I Heard It Through the Grapevine" are all very well played, but the group's most consistent lineup of originals—the old-fashioned "Travelin' Band," the newfangled "Up Around the Bend," the grit-grinding "Run Through the Jungle," and the heartfelt "Long As I Can See the Light"—make the covers seem irrelevant even when the band is stretching Marvin Gaye to Grateful Dead length. The one LP-only original, "Ramble Tamble," is a much

Drummer Doug Clifford's nickname was "Cosmo," because he was into all things cosmic. Clifford's nickname for the recording studio was "the factory." Cosmo clearly enjoyed nothing more than riding his bike through the factory. Author's collection.

better use of Creedence's time, as it revs through a sweaty rock and roll dash and trips through a hypnotizing psych interlude over seven dramatic minutes.

PENDULUM

Pendulum was John Fogerty's bid to prove he could keep up with his contemporaries by moving beyond the singles/covers format of Creedence's first five albums and embracing invention and, in at least one case, indulgence. *Pendulum* has fewer recognizable Creedence classics than any of their previous albums, possibly because there is much less emphasis on the Fogerty brothers' muscular guitars. Aside from "Pagan Baby"—a long jam that would have been dull in the hands of a band lacking Creedence's seething intensity—and the fabulously frothy "Hey Tonight," electric guitar is kept to a minimum here. Acoustics drive the album's one hit, the melancholy "Have You Ever Seen the Rain?" Doug Clifford and Stu Cook's in-the-pocket rhythm section are the coal in the taut "Sailor's Lament" and the zippy Otis Redding tribute "Chameleon." Funereal Procol Harum organ is the main ingredient of the depressive "(Wish I Could) Hideaway" and the tautly beautiful "It's Just a Thought." All of these elements mingle on "Born to Move." A lot of the album's oomph comes from the Stax-style sax arrangements John Fogerty overdubbed himself. His misplaced "artistry" results in one tremendous fumble—a go-nowhere collage of crescendos without climax called "Rude Awakening #2"—but *Pendulum* still reveals that Creedence could make far more meaningful music than their more pretentious peers.

NICK DRAKE: *BRYTER LAYTER*

Lovely as it was, *Five Leaves Left* was not a big seller. Drake's girlfriend Linda Pettifer (later Linda Thompson after marrying Fairport Convention's Richard) and admirer Elton John attempted to give the shy singer a push by cutting demos of several songs from Drake's first album in the hopes of forwarding them to more commercial artists in search of material, but there were no notable takers.

Bryter Layter was another attempt to draw Nick Drake out of isolation. All the horns, backing singers, and electric guitars in the world couldn't mask his remoteness. Even when the studio band spreads sunshine on "Hazy Jane II," Drake still sounds like he's singing into his lap. Producer Joe Boyd (with a lot of help from members of Fairport Convention and John Cale) hoped *Bryter Layter* might score some hits for Drake, but the singer/writer/expert finger picker wasn't interested in success on anyone else's terms and disliked the album's arrangements.

No artist wants their visions corrupted, but the arrangements do complement Drake's most instantly pleasurable selection of songs charmingly. Whirling, autumnal guitar/piano interplay enlivens "One of These Things First" and its message of either reincarnation or opportunities missed. "Fly" is Drake's most deeply aching song. "Hazy Jane II," the smoky "At the Chime of the City Clock," the spacious "Hazy Jane I," and the atypically soulful "Poor Boy" are superb pop. The instrumental Muzak interludes strewn throughout the record are less essential, but they link the substantial tracks well enough. Each of the three albums Nick Drake recorded during his brief life is exceptional, but *Bryter Layter* is his most completely satisfying.

Nick Drake's lonesome presence on the cover of *Bryter Layter* contrasts the album's busy, guest-musician-crowded arrangements. I dig those shoes though. Author's collection.

FACES: *FIRST STEP*

A lot of groups ended with the end of the sixties, but like members of the Beatles, the Yardbirds, and Cream, Small Faces found a way to continue. The departure of Steve Marriott, one of *the* great soul singers, was a tremendous loss. Former Jeff Beck Group members Rod Stewart and Ron Wood were pretty great too, though, and the guys found a very easy place in the combo rechristened as Faces (the new guys were too tall to justify keeping the old name anyway).

A different singer, guitarist, and name weren't the only things that had changed. Small Faces was a tight group. Faces definitely, definitely was not. Everything loosened up, from the song structures to Kenney Jones's beats to their approach to record making. Each of the three proper Small Faces albums is a very individual entity: the hard-mod R&B of the first disc, the more eccentric Swinging London vibe of the second, the peculiarly British concepts of the third. Such consistency went in the loo as Faces started shuffling well-thought-out studio creations with rambling rockers, improvised instrumentals, willy-nilly covers, and even live tracks on their albums.

Faces' first disc doesn't have any of the latter, but it has a nice assortment of the formers. There's riffed-up Dylan ("Wicked Messenger"), spacey balladry ("Devotion"), crashing grooving ("Shake, Shudder, Shiver"), good-time boogie ("Three Button Hand Me Down"), honky-tonk ("Stone," which would reappear as "Evolution" on Pete Townshend's *Who Came First*), slamming blues ("Around the Plynth"), wordless romping ("Pineapple and the Monkey," "Looking Out the Window"), and about two dozen pints of Jack Daniels. Some people laughed off *First Step* as a mess, but that probably didn't bother a band more concerned with bringing smiles to faces than pleasing critics.

THE FOX: *FOR FOX'S SAKE*

Had the breaks been a little better, the Fox might now be spoken of in the same breath as Small Faces, the Creation, the Move, the Action, Traffic, and the other psych bands they resemble. Alas, the Brighton quintet made only one album because as front man Steve Brayne relates in the liner notes of a vinyl reissue of *For Fox Sake*, their management "poached" Black Sabbath and decided to put all of its eggs in that gloomy basket. Timing might have something to do with the Fox's failure since their mid-sixties sound was so out of date when they released their one and only LP in 1970.

That the Fox is all but forgotten is a drag, but there's nothing draggy about *For Fox Sake*. For lovers of the brand of refreshing British rock that the rains of Sabbath and Zeppelin washed away, this album will be a pleasure. Almost every song invites comparison to the work of more famous artists but offers enough originality to make it essential in its own right. You'd be hard pressed to find a song by a white band that used reggae offbeats earlier than "As She Walks Away," which also resembles *Larks' Tongue*–era King Crimson. Had Hendrix experimented with circus music, he may have been able to lay claim to the sound of the epic "Madame Magical." Most other tracks don't strive for such uniqueness, but why does that matter when *For Fox Sake* supplies the best Action ("Secondhand Love"), Creation ("Lovely Day"), and Small Faces ("Man in a Fast Car") songs of 1970? Only the inchoate jam "Goodtime Music" is not up to snuff.

GEORGE HARRISON: *ALL THINGS MUST PASS*

It's a sprawling boxed set of three LPs, one of which is barely listenable. It's a pop album bloated with religious dogma. It's arguably the best album by an ex-Beatle, the best album of 1970, and the best album of the 1970s.

Lennon and McCartney maintained such a stranglehold over the Beatles' LPs that George Harrison was able to amass a backlog of great songs. By some accounts, "The Art of Dying" dates back to 1966, which is funny since it's the most seventies-sounding track on *All Things Must Pass* with its heavily wah-wah'ed guitars and Chicago-esque horn section. One can only guess how it would have been arranged if included on *Revolver*.

The prevailing sounds of *All Things Must Pass*, though, are Harrison's dulcet yet expressive voice and fluid slide guitar, ringing masses of acoustic guitars, ethereal organs, and tasteful but powerful string and horn

A typical afternoon for George Harrison involved slipping on his rubber boots and hanging out with some giant garden gnomes. Author's collection.

embellishments. Phil Spector's production is full-bodied but more delicate and expansive than his classic records with the Wrecking Crew. The band is top-notch, with Badfinger supplying rhythm guitars, Billy Preston and Procol Harum's Gary Brooker on organs, Stones sidemen Bobby Keys and Jim Price on brass, the Plastic Ono Band's Klaus Voormann on bass, and old pal Ringo Starr behind the kit. That band as realized by Spector sounds magnificent, whether crawling through "Isn't It a Pity," wailing on "Hear Me Lord," stirring a cyclone on "Wah-Wah," riffing through "What a Life," partying on "Awaiting on You All," drifting into the cosmos on "Ballad of Sir Frankie Crisp (Let It Roll)" and "Beware of Darkness," or doing all of the above on "Let It Down."

None of that would matter if Harrison didn't deliver the songs, and these are some of the greatest he ever wrote. That Harrison chiefly used *All Things Must Pass* to advertise his sundry religious beliefs sounds a lot more off-putting than it actually is because his tunes are so uniformly beautiful and because he gets off at least one good zinger at the expense of the pope along the way. Some have docked *All Things Must Pass* a point or two because its third LP is a completely superfluous collection of meandering jams, but that would be like criticizing the record because you don't like the album cover (which is a totally hilarious shot of Harrison wearing huge rubber boots while hanging out with garden gnomes). Toss the jam album in the bin and take in the bounty of brilliance on the other two records for an endlessly rewarding experience.

JIMI HENDRIX: *FIRST RAYS OF THE NEW RISING SUN* (RELEASED IN 1997)

Jimi Hendrix had the chance to release only three studio albums during his lifetime. He was in the process of recording his fourth when he died from a drug overdose in 1970. Like *Electric Ladyland*, it was to be another double album but a more accessible, less experimental one full of lean, funky, potential singles, such as "Freedom," "Room Full of Mirrors," "Dolly Dagger," "Ezy Rider," "Izabella," and "Stepping Stone." "Angel" and "Drifting" were two of Hendrix's dreamiest, prettiest songs. All of these tracks signify that *First Rays of the New Rising Sun* would have been another important Jimi Hendrix record had he gotten the chance to finish it.

The cover of the 1997 compilation *First Rays of the New Rising Sun* is a Photoshop nightmare. Author's collection.

Immediately following his death, a lot of the tracks surfaced on sloppily assembled collections like *The Cry of Love* and *Rainbow Bridge*. Considering how ransacked the Hendrix archives would be, it's surprising that all of the *Rising Sun* tracks would not be thoughtfully reconstructed until 1997. Forgiving the cover, which looks like a still shot from a karaoke video, *First Rays of the New Rising Sun* is the ideal presentation of Hendrix's lost classic. The album is front-loaded with the most polished tracks to give an idea of what a perfect single disc it could have been. The less finished ones are lumped at the end, making them feel like a run of pretty good bonus tracks. Along with *Are You Experienced*, *Axis*, *Electric Ladyland*, and *Band of Gypsies*, *First Rays of the New Rising Sun* caps off the essential Jimi Hendrix collection.

JAMES GANG: *RIDES AGAIN*

Joe Walsh is most famous for jokey solo hits like "Life's Been Good" and his stint in the über-boring Eagles, but his best work was unquestionably with the Cleveland power trio James Gang. The band put out only three records with the Walsh lineup, the first and third of which being worthwhile but hit-or-miss overall. *Rides Again*, James Gangs' second LP, is a classic. A little southern twang, a little Philly funk, a little British rock ingenuity—*Rides Again* hangs together seamlessly even as it jumps genres jollily. The best-known track is the percussive trampoline "Funk #49," but there's also "Tend My Garden," which sums up the breadth of the Beatles' *Abbey Road* in one tidy six-minute package; the succinct country-pop songs "There I Go Again" and "Thanks"; and the desolate "Ashes, the Rain, and I." "The Bomber" is a heavy-rock epic that shows off Walsh's ability to mimic Jeff Beck (even quoting "Beck's Bolero" mid-song). The one misstep is "Woman," which marries a witless lyric to some so-so riffing, but the mass of *Rides Again* reveals a great band ripe for rediscovery.

ELTON JOHN: *TUMBLEWEED CONNECTION*

The hugest solo star of the seventies, Elton John sold lots and lots of albums, but the outrageously attired piano man was really a singles artist at heart. He was rarely able to fill two LP sides with consistently worthwhile material. *Tumbleweed Connection* is an exception. Perhaps devising a loose Old West concept helped John and lyricist Bernie Taupin focus because every track on the album is strong even though there isn't a single A-side in the lineup. The duo channels the rustic sound of the Band to bring their tales to life. Like most members of the Band, Taupin was a foreigner visiting a pivotal era in American history. He does not attempt Robbie Robertson's insights, but his words still snap a detailed portrait of gunslingers, Confederates, country life, and riverboats. As Robertson did with "The Night They Drove Old Dixie Down," Taupin displays an outsider's cluelessness about the South's role in the Civil War when he romanticizes the evil Confederacy in "My Father's Gun." However, John's music is consistently marvelous, and arrangements that include prominent harp on "Come Down in Time" and Leslied guitar on the atypically otherworldly "Where to Now, St. Peter" colorize the album's sepia images.

THE KINKS: *LOLA VERSUS POWERMAN AND THE MONEY-GO-ROUND*

Since cutting *Village Green Preservation Society* in 1968, the Kinks were rock's most committed storytellers. They would spend the following decade recording a string of concept albums, the most commercially successful being *Lola Versus Powerman and the Money-Go-Round*. The Kinks hadn't had a major hit at home or in the United States in years, but "Lola," a clangy number about a rube's encounter with a cosmopolitan drag queen, changed that. The album from which "Lola" was pulled recounts a young rock and roll band's rise to success and dealings with a variety of unscrupulous music publishers, agents, journalists, and TV presenters. In other words, it's the Kinks telling the story of the Kinks, and they do so with all the bitterness, humanity, sensitivity, humor, and melodiousness for which they are renowned.

Ray Davies's signature music-hall variations are present on "Denmark Street" and "The Moneygoround," and his mastery of the delicate ballad informs "Get Back in Line," "This Time Tomorrow," and "A Long Way from Home." The band also rocks harder here than they had since their power-chord heyday. Dave Davies's massive guitars tear through "Lola," "Top of the Pops," "Powerman," and "Rats." He contributes two of his best compositions with the screaming "Rats" and the cryptic "Strangers." Much of the Kinks' seventies records followed the *Lola Versus Powerman* formula closely, but none replicated its power, beauty, or ability to convey a coherent story.

LED ZEPPELIN: *LED ZEPPELIN III*

Having done things with traditional blues songs Howlin' Wolf never intended on their first album and providing more of the same to lesser effect on their second, Led Zeppelin decided it was time they stopped stealing old blues songs and relying so much on bludgeoning riffs. Neither *I* nor *II* hosted as many great originals that didn't turn out to have been written by Wolf or Willie Dixon as *III* does. Certainly no self-respecting bluesman would take credit for the mega-moronic mania of "Immigrant Song," although the lengthy dirge "Since I've Been Loving You" might have made a few envious.

The album's greatest distinction is its wealth of acoustic numbers: some serene ("Tangerine," the ecologically minded "That's the Way"), some boisterous ("Bron-Y-Aur Stomp," an ode to Robert Plant's dog), some gleefully menacing ("Friends"). The few heavy rockers deliver too, with the joyous

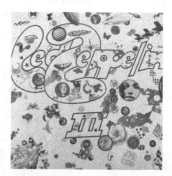

Led Zeppelin's third album featured a volvelle that alters the sleeve design when spun. This is the double-LP reissue from 2017. I got an absolutely fabulous deal on it on ebay. Author's collection.

"Out on the Tiles," the slippery "Celebration Day," and even the mega-
moronic mania of "Immigrant Song" providing as much fun as anything
Zep ever did. The two trad covers—a galvanizing, banjo-stoked version of
Leadbelly's "Gallis Pole" slightly retitled "Gallow's Pole" and a demented
version of Bukka White's "Shake 'Em On Down" retitled "Hats Off to (Roy)
Harper"—judiciously credit the boys as arrangers rather than composers
this time around. Perhaps Led Zeppelin was growing up.

JOHN LENNON: *PLASTIC ONO BAND*

If a single phrase sums up how John, Paul, George, and Ringo returned
after the Beatles split up, it must be "without compromise." Paul made no
effort to tidy up his farm-grown mess *McCartney*. George let his thoughts
on god and religion hang out further than the great, bushy beard he sports
on the cover of *All Things Must Pass*. Ringo thumbed his schnoz at the rock
and roll world that made his career with a disc of ancient standards called
Sentimental Journey.

However, no former Beatle began his solo career as uncompromisingly
as John Lennon. With *John Lennon/Plastic Ono Band*, he tossed a lit
match on the life he'd lived up until that point, tearing into religion and
former partner Paul, railing at the mother and father who'd abandoned
him and the misogynist he'd been in his younger years, and declaring that
all he needed now was himself, his wife, and maybe a little *Sesame Street*
(*"Cookie!"*).

John had recently undergone primal therapy with Arthur Janov, who
instructed patients to scream away their traumas and repressed pain. John
found a natural link between that psychological technique and the Little
Richard shrieking that had been in his repertoire all along. The primal
screaming on "Mother" and "Well, Well, Well" and cussing on "Working
Class Hero" cleared out fair-weather fans, but *Plastic Ono Band* contains
some of the strongest songs of John's solo career. "I Found Out" is nasty,
but the syncopated interplay between his guitar, Ringo's drums, and Klaus
Voormann's bass is immanently danceable. "Look at Me" and "Hold On"
are highly personal, but they're also as traditionally comely as anything on
"The White Album." "God" is intent on shattering the illusions of all acolytes, but it also features John's most committed soul vocal since the Beatles
covered "You Really Got a Hold on Me."

Without a lick of the hominess of Paul's debut, the spirituality of
George's, or the comfy familiarity of Ringo's, John made a record that was

devastating, honest, raw, and more than a little abrasive. In other words, John made a record that was very John.

MC5: *BACK IN THE U.S.A.*

Michigan's noisy, wild, and politically frank MC5 became one of the key influences on the punk movement of the mid-seventies, but their live debut, *Kick Out the Jams*, is a murky record full of songs that jam more than they kick. *Back in the U.S.A.* bounces so far across the spectrum that it sounds like a different band recorded it. The low-down muck of the former album has been replaced by tinny, harsh production, and lengthy jams are passed over for tight three-minute rockers. While the thin sound does *Back in the U.S.A.* no favors, the band's enthusiasm and the songs' retro simplicity produce total excitement. The MC5's leftist politics are limited to two tracks: "The Human Being Lawnmower," a simple antiwar statement, and "The American Ruse," which puts the shoddiness of capitalism in terms Carl Perkins could dig ("Phony stars: oh no! Crummy cars: oh no! Cheap guitars: oh no!").

The rest of the record does most of its thinking below the belt. That it's bookended by classics from Little Richard and Chuck Berry reveals *Back in the U.S.A.*'s true agenda: it is an old-fashioned, sex-crazed party album that gets its paws dirty in go-go grooves ("Teenage Lust," "High School," which rewrites the Capitol's "Cool Jerk"), slow-grind soul ("Let Me Try"), cro-mag garage rock ("Call Me Animal," "Looking at You"), and R&B (the incredible "Shakin' Street"). Awesome.

PAUL MCCARTNEY: *MCCARTNEY*

Someone had to take the fall for the Beatles' breakup. The most sniveling journalists pitched their poison pens at Yoko Ono and Linda McCartney. The rest blamed Paul. He was the first to quit and the first to release a solo record. When that record turned out to be a sketchy miscalculation (didn't he realize how the first ex-Beatle album would be scrutinized?), critics shredded it.

The reaction was not undeserved, as *McCartney* is the kind of home-made mess that is surely fun to record but offers few rewards for listeners. Most of the tracks are unfinished sketches or masturbatory jams with the title guy overdubbing all instruments himself. The melancholy "Junk" and silly yet underappreciated "Teddy Boy" are tuneful Beatles leftovers, but the album's only real song is the passionate valentine "Maybe I'm Amazed." Wisely, McCartney heeded the criticisms and put a lot of thought into his next record, but after a decade of praising everything the Beatles did, the critics had gotten a taste for his blood.

THE MONKEES: *CHANGES*

Following Peter Tork, Mike Nesmith was the next Monkee to buy himself out of his contract, and the once-formidable foursome was reduced to a duo of guys who no longer wanted to be Monkees. This is obvious on their final album, *Changes*. Micky Dolenz and Davy Jones give themselves over to producer Jeff Barry, who seems torn between the soul of his Phil Spector hits and the bubble gum of his more recent smash, "Sugar Sugar." He is responsible for several of the album's more soulful numbers—"Oh My My," "I Love You Better," "You're So Good to Me," "Tell Me Love"—but none of these songs is outstanding, and the decision to include childish crap like "Acapulco Sun," "All Alone in the Dark," and "I Never Thought It Peculiar" sinks the record. The only genuinely worthwhile tracks are "99 Pounds," a leftover from 1967 that makes me wish Davy was allowed to sing more rockers, and Micky's loose-lipped C&W ramble "Midnight Train," which gives session guitarist Louie Shelton another opportunity to scorch strings. Otherwise, *Changes* is the sound of the Monkees going out with a whimper.

VAN MORRISON: *MOONDANCE*

Astral Weeks was Van Morrison's masterpiece, a work of unimaginable depth and feeling recorded by a mere twenty-three-year old. It's also an undeniably insular record and the most un-rock record to often be lumped among the greatest rock records. *Moondance* is not a work of art on the level of *Astral Weeks*, but it opens up Morrison's sound considerably, making it accessible to listeners unaccustomed to lengthy jazz excursions without sacrificing the intense soulfulness at the heart of *Astral Weeks*. The drums are more up front, the bass is electric, and backing singers provide counterpoint to Morrison's wailing, rumbling, and mumbling. "And It Stoned Me" and the swinging "Into the Mystic" are evocative and personal but also universal in their nostalgia and good-humored soul-searching. "Caravan" is an aural party with Morrison multitracked to play the radio-loving revelers.

The title song is jazz by way of Sinatra rather than Coltrane, and "Crazy Love" is a beautiful tribute to Curtis Mayfield's falsetto. These are all Van Morrison standards, but the pumping soul of "Glad Tidings," the baroque pop of "Everyone," and the tripping-over-its-own-feet rhythms of "Come Running" are also delightful. *Moondance* showed that Morrison could get back in the top forty without diluting his distinctive brand of Celtic soul.

THE MOVE: *SHAZAM*

The Move that cut *Shazam* in 1969 was quite a different group from the one that released *The Move* just two years earlier. Acid enthusiast Christopher "Ace" Kefford had exited back in 1968, leaving bass duties to rhythm guitarist Trevor Burton, who followed Kefford out the door after beginning the sessions for the group's second album.

The Move was short on material, so they decided to beef up the few originals and a couple of covers they had on deck with zany improvisations, experiments, and allusions. In effect, *Shazam* transformed the Move into a prog band. It also throws a big custard pie in the face of charges that progressive rock is nothing but po-faced mathematics. The Move's revamped and expanded version of "Cherry Blossom Clinic" from their first album takes a series of bizarre detours that turn familiar Bach, Dukas, and Tchaikovsky

Unfortunately this album cover was never spun off into a comic book series about rock and roll's most depressed superheroes. Author's collection.

tunes into cartoon confetti. Singer Carl Wayne takes breaks to chat with passersby throughout the record. The Move makes heavy-metal hay with pop (Frankie Laine's "Don't Make My Baby Blue") and folk (Tom Paxton's "The Last Thing on My Mind") standards that King Crimson would not have touched with a twenty-foot Frippertronics stick.

After fronting *Shazam*, singer Carl Wayne was the next member to move out of the Move in search of a solo career that never quite took off. Enter Jeff Lynne, who splits songwriting, singing, producing, and guitaring duties with Roy Wood on *Looking On.*

LOOKING ON

Looking On sheds even more of the Move's early sweetness than *Shazam* had while refining that record's ideas with long songs that never sound as though a particularly merry Dr. Frankenstein had stitched them together. The Move ended up with some of their most cohesive epics. The magnificently warped "What?" and the intricately structured psych/jazz/raga fusion "Open Up Said the World at the Door" are the work of new co–band leader Jeff Lynne. Roy Wood's three concise songs—"Turkish Tram Conductor Blues," "When Alice Comes Back to the Farm," and "Brontosaurus"—are atypically playful examples of early British metal. Critics sometimes shrug off *Looking On*, but it's the first Move album that doesn't sound like it was created accidentally, and it is their first made up of entirely original material.

MICHAEL NESMITH AND THE FIRST NATIONAL BAND: MAGNETIC SOUTH

As poor Micky Dolenz and Davy Jones slogged to the bitter end with the Monkees' contractual-obligation farewell, *Changes*, Mike Nesmith gladly bought himself out of his contract and made the kind of album that newly liberated artists make. As a Monkee, Nesmith always seemed torn between his Texan C&W roots and the psychedelic mood of the times (he was even present at a recording session for "A Day in the Life"). On his first post-Monkees album, Nesmith hit on an ingenious way to structure his pure country within the kind of inventive framework *Sgt. Pepper's* made possible, so down-home tunes segue into each other, stray through picturesque soundscapes, and swirl around fanciful lyrics. Red Rhodes paints rainbow streaks over it all with pedal steel guitar that is as ear enchanting as any sitar or Mellotron.

Magnetic South wanders through an assortment of tempos and moods—jittering into a daffy samba on "Calico Girlfriend," motoring into a bluesy boogie on "Little Red Rider," slowing to a streamside stroll on the surprise hit "Joanne," zipping to the moon on the euphoric "Mama Nantucket," floating

Nes put on his most tasteful outfit for this CD reissue of his first two albums. Author's collection.

through the void on "The One Rose (That's Left in My Heart)." No matter the temper of each song, *Magnetic South* always sounds perfectly carefree. That's probably exactly how Nes felt in 1970.

PROCOL HARUM: *HOME*

Matthew Fisher, who helped define the Procol Harum sound with his majestic organ lines on "Whiter Shade of Pale," quit the band after recording *A Salty Dog*. Because of Fisher's absence and the greater reliance on Robin Trower's eclectic guitar work, many critics would have you believe that *Home* is a radical shift from Procol's previous work. Aside from "Whiskey Train," the fire-snorting blues that opens the album, *Home* actually has far more in common with the proto-goth creepiness of the band's debut album than *Salty Dog* did.

Lyricist Keith Reid's running obsession is once again death, and he handles the subject in a variety of ways. "Whiskey Train" deals with slow suicide via the bottle. "The Dead Man's Dream" is cartoonier with its grotesque Poe-inspired lyric ("And the corpses were rotten, yet each one living / their eyes were alive with maggots crawling") and a backing track that sounds like it was yanked from a Hammer horror movie. "Still There'll Be More" hilariously matches roiling rock and roll with Reid's first-person account of serial killing. "Nothing That I Didn't Know" is a moving elegy performed in the sea-shanty style of *Salty Dog*. "About to Die" is written from the perspective of Jesus' killers, and Trower's purposeful, ultra-phased guitar sets a grim tone. "Whaling Stories" is a multisectioned epic ode to the apocalypse and one of the few Procol Harum songs that makes good on the band's mostly erroneous prog rep. Through all this chilling stuff, Gary Brooker belts like the intense R&B crooner he is. These guys were always way too soulful to really qualify as prog rockers.

THE PRETTY THINGS: *PARACHUTE*

The Pretty Things were on a creative roll begun with the pioneering, pre-*Tommy* rock opera *S.F. Sorrow* when they made *Parachute*. Like its predecessor, there's a loose concept (side A focuses on the city, side B on the country) but not much of a story. That deflects no power from the songs or the Pretties' exemplary playing and singing. Their choral harmonies on

"Rain," "What's the Use," and the title track are in the same league as the Beach Boys, the Who, or the Beatles. Side A features a mini-medley obviously inspired by side B of *Abbey Road*, but the transitions between sections are more fluid than those of the Beatles. The medley then gives way to a brilliant parade of stand-alone tracks: the searing rocker "Miss Fay Regrets," the ominous "Cries from the Midnight Circus," the entrancing "Grass," the funky "Sickle Clowns," the stately "She's a Lover," and the hymn-like pair of songs that close the record, "What's the Use" and "Parachute." *Parachute* was also the Pretty Things' last great record. They spent the remainder of the seventies churning out successively more conventional rock records, but if that's because they expended so much of their inspiration reserves on *Parachute*, it was worth it.

That ugly collage is no substitute for Phil May's elegant illustration on the original cover of S.F. Sorrow, but Rare Earth's *Real Pretty* twofer was the only way you could get *Sorrow* and *Parachute* in the States from 1976 until the label reissued the albums separately in the early 2000s. Unfortunately, *Sorrow* appears in its lousy stereo mix. Author's collection.

ROD STEWART: *GASOLINE ALLEY*

As Rod Stewart was settling into his new band, he was also settling into his solo career. He'd sketched the recipe for his distinctive cocktail of British folk and Chuck Berry rock and roll on his first album. On his second, he used finer ingredients. *Gasoline Alley* has some of Stewart's best songs. The nostalgic, rustic title song is astonishingly beautiful and uplifting. "Lady Day" and "Jo's Lament" are two more handsome acoustic ballads. Yet covers make up the bulk of *Gasoline Alley*, and Stewart's interpretations of Dylan, Elton John, and Small Faces are also excellent. Renditions of the Valentinos/Stones' "It's All Over Now" and Eddie Cochran's "Cut Across Shorty" sound like parties none of the attending musicians wanted to leave. *Gasoline Alley* is Rod's first great album, and though he'd write some of his most famous songs for his next one, *Every Picture Tells a Story* isn't necessarily any better. Because the tracks on *Gasoline Alley* haven't been as overplayed as, say, "Maggie May" or "Reason to Believe," it sounds like the fresher disc today.

THE WHO: *LIVE AT LEEDS*

On February 14, 1970, the Who played a one-night stand at Leeds University that was most likely the best Valentine's Day gift anyone in the audience ever received. White hot from near constant touring in support of *Tommy*, the Who performed the rock opera, a selection of singles, a couple of stray album tracks, and a quartet of covers with incomparable fervor. They had long since earned their title as rock and roll's most electrifying, most explosive, most deafening live band, but they were rarely this *on*.

As fortune would have it, the gig was captured on tape for release as the Who's very first live record the following May 23. *Live at Leeds* presents the Who as a much heavier group than they'd ever been on record. The only track that bore any similarity to the Who's recorded sound of the sixties was a truncated rendition of "Substitute," and even that was a lot weightier in its live setting. The rest of the LP is made up of extended versions of "My Generation" (which became a sort of free-floating medley incorporating bits of "See Me, Feel Me," "Sparks," and the seeds of "Naked Eye") and "Magic Bus" and a trio of oldies the band had recorded in the studio but hadn't released.

Live at Leeds has long been considered the greatest rock and roll live album, but its greatness wasn't even fully realized until 1995 when the original eardrum-rending six-song sampler expanded to a dynamically varied fourteen-track monster with such additions as "Tattoo," "I'm a Boy," "Happy Jack," "A Quick One While He's Away," and a neat cover of Allen Toussaint's "Fortune Teller." Yet one cannot underestimate the important role the original version played in the Who's evolution as a band and the live album's evolution as a rock and roll commodity.

THE VELVET UNDERGROUND: *LOADED*

Between 1969 and 1970, the Velvet Underground moved from MGM Records to Atlantic, which insisted that the band's first album for the label contain some hits. Lou Reed not only accepted the challenge but also resolved to write a record loaded with potential hits.

It follows a perverse logic that the Velvet Underground—a group that mastered drugged-out noise rock on their first two albums and gloomy folk dirges on their third—would fall apart while making their poppiest, happiest platter. There's no trace of the rotted-out junkie poetry that made their previous albums so compelling on *Loaded*, so the album feels lightweight on first listen. All that fades when the catchiness takes over. "Sweet Jane" and "Rock and Roll" are celebrations of rock and roll that get under the skin like Lou Reed's needles. "Cool It Down" and "Head Held High" don't have the legs the aforementioned tunes do, but they're nearly as stimulating. Even down-tempo tracks like "I Found a Reason," "Oh! Sweet Nuthin'," and the novelistic "New Age" possess a sweetness missing from the band's earlier songs. With "Who Loves the Sun," the Velvet Underground could pass for the Monkees. While Lou Reed was game to make a pop record, he thought the mix went too far in taming the recordings, which would be his last with the band.

NEIL YOUNG: *AFTER THE GOLD RUSH*

The most unique member of Buffalo Springfield had the most distinguished and unpredictable solo career. Neil Young exited the sixties with two albums, both released in 1969 and both very different. His reserved first album focused on his songwriting. *Everybody Knows This Is Nowhere* was more of an outlet for his tortured guitar riffing.

Young's first solo album of the seventies finds him waking up in a new decade, hung over, mellowed a bit, but still wary, his head still muddled. *After the Gold Rush* is full of questions and concerns, even as most of the music has settled into a rainy autumn hush. The beautiful title track is the definitive turn of the decade song, casting the recent past of the sixties in romantic medieval terms and looking forward to the new decade with environmentalist unease. Young tends to pair such anguished lyricism with placid melodies, though "Don't Let It Bring You Down" disturbs with its grotesque words and a creepy melody he sings like a dying witch. The winds only really whip up on "Southern Man," a righteously ugly portrait of Red State racism on which Young gives it to his Telecaster like he had on "Down by the River" and "Cowgirl in the Sand" on the previous LP.

There are glimpses of sunlight through the storm clouds at the end of each side of *After the Gold Rush*. "Till the Morning Comes," "When You Dance I Can Really Love You," "I Believe in You," and "Cripple Creek Ferry" lighten the mood, but they don't shake the uneasy feeling that permeates the album. Mother Nature's on the run. The 1970s are here.

1971

The U.S. economy was in a state of recession as 1971 began, but it would prove to be a boom year for iconic classic rock and roll albums. The Beatles are no more, leaving the Stones to take over without their main competitors. But Led Zeppelin, Rod Stewart, and the Who all emerge as intimidating challengers, and all release the albums most fans and critics rate as their best in 1971. Some rate Marvin Gaye's LP of the year, which redefines soul as high art, as rock's best ever. Glam emerges as its sparkly new hope as both David Bowie and T. Rex make their first major statements, but progressive rock comes to the fore too. Whether we're talking about the presentation or the product, self-indulgence is king. The "Stairway to Heaven" jokes may now commence.

The market also opens up with the release of Carole King's *Tapestry*, which becomes the first album to really resonate with the female consumers who hadn't been big LP buyers in the past. According to David Hepworth in his book *Never a Dull Moment*, most of the 150,000 people buying *Tapestry* at its peak popularity were women, and the album would go on to move more than 15 million copies—the first LP by a woman to sell so spectacularly. Although King's brand of soft pop would dominate the female market for much of the seventies with similarly sedate new singers such as Karen Carpenter and Linda Ronstadt, the stage was now set for harder-rocking women like Ann and Nancy Wilson, Debbie Harry, Joan Jett, and the Go-Go's to sell big in the coming years.

THE BEACH BOYS: *SURF'S UP*

The Beach Boys were always inconsistent on LP. Capitol Records' hunger for new product and reluctance to accept Brian Wilson's maturation resulted in great records (*All Summer Long, Today*) being interspersed with limp ones (*Shut Down Vol. 2, Party*). *Pet Sounds*, an album that jolted rock and roll's evolution forward like few others, seemed to finally put the Beach Boys in the same league as the Beatles, the Stones, and Dylan, but the collapse of *SMiLE* doomed them to continue jerking back and forth while their contemporaries sprinted toward the horizon. *SMiLE* left Brian Wilson feeling dejected, and the half-baked *Smiley Smile* was a weak consolation prize. *Wild Honey* and *Sunflower* were well-realized records, and *Friends* was a great one, but 1969's *20/20* was pasted together with no greater care than their pre–*Pet Sounds* discs.

Such indifference continues to be an issue on *Surf's Up*. If the title recalls the Beach Boys' Sun & Fun early work, the somber painting of a Native American on horseback (based on James Earle Fraser's sculpture *End of the Trail*) on the cover suggested otherwise. As Brian's creativity and mental health continued to wane (he would be diagnosed with schizoaffective disorder in 1979), the other guys struggled to pick up the slack and push the group forward in fits. Al Jardine explores left-wing ideals on the ecologically minded "Don't Go Near the Water" and right-wing ones on the anti-welfare "Lookin' at Tomorrow." The cutesy toss-offs "Take a Load off Your Feet" and "Disney Girls (1957)" sit uncomfortably alongside Mike Love's "Student Demonstration Time," a politically cowardly and musically grating track that irritated a lot of people, especially Brian.

However, the Brothers Wilson rescue a potential mess. Brian channeled his distress into the haunting, fatalistic "'Til I Die" and showed Jardine how to handle environmental concerns with dramatic gravity on "A Day in the Life of a Tree" (featuring Jack Riley on lead vocals because Brian thought the Beach Boys' manager sounded like a tree, and somehow he does!). The LP's ace in the hole is its title song: the unfinished, intended centerpiece of *SMiLE*. By cobbling together a demo and backing track recorded in 1966 with newly cut passages and vocals, the Beach Boys completed a true masterpiece as dark and deep as the sea. It is indisputable proof that Brian Wilson is a composer as good as any of those wig-wearing guys from the eighteenth century and the song that caused Leonard Bernstein to gush that Wilson was one of the "greatest composers of the twentieth century." And it almost wasn't released! Brian's voice in the middle section will yank your heart out. The group's vocal interplay on the coda may induce an out-of-body experience. The complexity of Van Dyke Parks's dream-logic lyrics ("Columnated ruins domino . . .") so angered the tiny-brained Mike Love that he lobbied to get Parks fired! Pearls before swine.

The record's greatest surprise is Carl Wilson's emergence as the band's new guiding light. Not only did he oversee the completion of "Surf's Up," but he also produced two superb songs of his own: the inspirational "Long Promised Road" and the spooky, psychedelic "Feel Flows." Perhaps no other rock record displays such disparity between its great tracks and its subpar ones, and perhaps no other rock record remains so powerful despite that.

I love how the moodiness of this painting based on James Earle Fraser's sculpture *End of the Trail* offsets the seemingly sunny title of *Surf's Up*. The cover image will seem more appropriate after hearing the album's moody title track, which is my favorite song by the Beach Boys and my favorite song of the 1970s. Author's collection.

Yet the Beach Boys' power began ebbing shortly after *Surf's Up*. Carl wrote his finest song, an achingly tender tale charting the displacement and slaughter of Native Americans called "The Trader," for 1973's *Holland* but never really followed up on its brilliance in any significant way. Although Brian remained an inspirational presence on *Carl and the Passions—So Tough* and *Holland*, cowriting excellent material such as "You Need a Mess of Help to Stand Alone" and the last great Beach Boys single, "Sail On, Sailor," his issues with a combative, litigious band drove him out of the spotlight as the Beach Boys became comfortable as an oldies act, grinding out their early surf and car hits for carnival crowds while compilations like *Endless Summer* outsold new platters of warmed-over material like *15 Big Ones*, *M.I.U.*, and *L.A.* (*The Beach Boys Love You* from 1977 has a pretty committed cult following, but I've never found the charm in its silly, synth-heavy songs that make *Smiley Smile* sound like *SMiLE*). Despite having his dramatic "Wouldn't It Be Nice (To Live Again)" ousted from *Surf's Up*, Dennis Wilson seemed most likely to follow in his brother's visionary footsteps with grand creations such as "Cuddle Up" on *Carl and the Passions* and "Steamboat" on *Holland*, but he seemed to be saving his talents for a solo career.

DAVID BOWIE: *HUNKY DORY*

Many pop artists have emphasized image because their content isn't all that substantial. David Bowie was the rare one whose musical and personal aesthetic were both of the highest caliber, and both were integral to his overall artistry. His image complemented the music—it never covered for the music—and it metamorphosed along with his music throughout his complicated career.

The great shape-shifter spent his early career deciding whether he was a purveyor of corny music hall (*David Bowie*), psychedelic folk rock (*Space Oddity*), or hard-rock riffs (*The Man Who Sold the World*). After realizing he was pretty good at all these things, he made his first great album.

Hunky Dory isn't flawless—"Eight Line Poem" is a nonstarter and "Fill Your Heart" emphasizes the precious tendencies that are about to evaporate from his work—but it is far more assured than the records that preceded it. And that small handful of subpar numbers are consumed by an abundance of astonishing pieces in which Bowie sculpts a completely original amalgamation of Broadway flair and anthemic rock and roll: the curriculum vitae "Changes," the homopositive call to arms "Oh! You Pretty Things," the breathtaking sci-fi epic "Life on Mars?," the charmingly Kinky love letter to his newborn son "Kooks," the subdued "Quicksand," the eerie "Bewlay Brothers." His trilogy of peer biographies on Andy Warhol, Lou Reed, and Bob Dylan expand his sound further while checking off notable influences on his earlier work his newfound innovation rendered obsolete. With *Hunky Dory*, David Bowie took his place as the most important solo performer of the seventies.

MARVIN GAYE: *WHAT'S GOING ON*

Berry Gordy founded Motown Records to make exquisite records featuring black artists and bundles of money. Throughout the sixties, the label did exactly that. However, wonderful records like "The Way You Do the Things You Do," "Baby Love," and "How Sweet It Is (To Be Loved by You)" hardly reflected the breadth of the American black experience throughout the decade. Centuries of oppression finally gave way to the civil rights movement, and white supremacists often responded with tragic, outrageous violence.

Marvin Gaye had more to say about his world than how sweet it is to be loved by you, and he upset the Motown formula by pouring his

anguish, observations, and hopes into his
music. *What's Going On* was practically the
anti-Motown album both because of its atypically personal and political lyrics and because
it smeared away the label's concentration on
hit singles by blending its nine tracks into
an extended suite. Gaye the Hitsville hit
maker could still spin radio-ready gold, and
the gorgeous, immensely moving title track
(cowritten by Obie Benson of the Four Tops
after cops brutalized antiwar protestors at
Berkeley's People's Park in 1969) became a
massive hit and, more important, a socially
conscious standard as significant as "We Shall
Overcome" or "Blowin' in the Wind" but,

Marvin Gaye helped jolt soul
into adulthood with his brilliant
What's Going On. He also happened to be gorgeous. Author's
collection.

frankly, much more pleasant to listen to outside of a demonstration march.

Berry Gordy hated "What's Going On" on first listen, thinking it was too
jazzy for contemporary pop fans, and was reluctant to release a record with
such disregard for the Motown formula. When he took a gamble on the
record that paid off, Motown finally caught up with the times. Its social consciousness extended across an entire album of topical songs (though some,
such as the seemingly improvised "Save the Children" and the tritely pious
"God Is Love," derive much more of their power from Gaye's affecting
performances than their lyrics). Thoughtful, innovative records soon started
flowing from the label in the new decade with greater regularity, though it
would be Stevie Wonder who would take the possibilities of Motown soul
the farthest.

JOHN ENTWISTLE: *SMASH YOUR HEAD AGAINST THE WALL*

John Entwistle suffered from the worst case of George Harrison syndrome
since George Harrison. *All Things Must Pass* was the consequence of Harrison's inability to get his songs past Lennon and McCartney and onto
Beatles records. Entwistle was also desperate to get more songs on his
band's albums, but Pete Townshend's brilliance and prolificacy made that
impossible. Unsurprisingly, Entwistle became the first member of the Who
to make a solo album.

As was the case with *All Things Must Pass*, composition is paramount
on *Smash Your Head Against the Wall*. While this album could have been

nothing more than a showcase for Entwistle's superhuman bass skills, showy musicianship plays second fiddle to his songwriting, which is thoroughly unique and startlingly mature. Getting a bit of riffy heavy metal out of the way with the opening track, "My Size"—a sequel to his definitive Who song, "Boris the Spider"—the Ox mellows out and diversifies. Muscle Shoals–style soul, forlorn folk, dirges, piano-based epics, and ballads provide backdrops for Entwistle's droll takes on aging, alcoholism, simpleminded faith, and death, death, death. He certainly wasn't the only artist obsessed with death in the early seventies—Black Sabbath, the Stones, Nick Drake, and Procol Harum filled LPs with gloomy ruminations—but no other artist handled the topic with his po-faced humor. "Ted End" is a tale of a poorly attended funeral ripe for illustration by Edward Gory. "Heaven and Hell" is a pithy mockery of afterlife superstitions. "My Size" voices the murderous revenge impulses of a spider. The

Pete Townshend claimed John Entwistle was a closet romantic. Entwistle's decision to superimpose a photo of himself in a plastic mask over an X-ray of a person with heart disease seems to confirm that. Author's collection.

album's flat, murky sound complements its grave obsessions and further distinguishes it from the Who's bright, spacious albums. John Entwistle was determined to establish himself as a solo artist distinct from his band on his debut, and, like George Harrison, he succeeded brilliantly. Also, like Harrison, he never matched its success again.

THE FACES: *A NOD IS AS GOOD AS A WINK . . . TO A BLIND HORSE*

By the time Faces released their third album in late 1971, Rod Stewart had become a smash solo success, earning international hits with *Every Picture Tells a Story* and the number one single it spawned, "Maggie May." Stewart's stardom would eventually crumble his cult band while still in its infancy. But first Faces enjoyed a huge boon when *A Nod Is As Good As a Wink . . . to a Blind Horse* became their first album to crack *Billboard*'s top ten.

Faces' album may not have been better than Rod's, but they do best him in terms of diversity. Bassist Ronnie Lane mixes up the sound as he takes the lead on the lazily rocking "You're So Rude," the wistful "Debris," and the chummy "Last Orders Please," which could pass for a number by his earlier, smaller band.

Elsewhere, Faces just do what it is they do with greater confidence than before, torching the barn on "Too Bad" or settling down around the campfire to wrap their Jim Beam breath around "Love Lives Here." Even the toss-offs—an endlessly vamping version of "Memphis Tennessee" and "That's All You Need," which finishes off the record with scorching slide guitar work courtesy of Ron Wood—are pretty great. Faces' one American hit single "Stay with Me" has aged poorly because of its extreme misogyny, but *A Nod Is As Good As a Wink* is still the best thing they ever slapped together.

ROY HARPER: *STORMCOCK*

There's nothing quite like *Stormcock*. The only conceivable precedents are Bert Jansch's melancholy folk and Van Morrison's personal excursions on *Astral Weeks*. The drama and lyrical depth of the four epics that make up Roy Harper's fifth album are unparalleled. You'd need a PhD to decode these songs without the writer's help. Fortunately, he has been conscientious enough to explain that the first three tracks are exposés of the rampant hypocrisy and rot in the justice system ("Hors d' Oeuvres"), religion ("The Same Old Rock"), and our culture of violence ("One Man Rock and Roll Band"). The finale is a call for unity within and without the self ("Me and My Woman"). Harper's words are as challenging to penetrate as *Ulysses*, yet their wit, cinematic descriptiveness, and sly raunch are totally accessible.

In contrast to his dense lyrics, Harper's music unravels simply. His arrangements are desert barren—usually nothing more than his fluid acoustic guitar and achingly emotive voice. At times, tiny details sparkle through, such as the piano on "Hors d'Oeuvres" or the Mellotron on "Me and My Woman." Special guest Jimmy Page lays commanding acoustic leads over "The Same Old Rock." *Stormcock* is quiet, but no one would describe it as easy listening. It is a demanding but richly rewarding expression of controlled rage and one of rock's most unique creations.

THE KINKS: *PERCY*

Ray Davies uses irony the way Rembrandt used oils, but even Ray must have recognized the incongruity of the achingly beautiful ballads he composed for a flaccid comedy about a penis transplant. Both the *Percy* film and its sound track have drifted into obscurity. No one should mourn the disappearance of the film, but it's a shame about the Kinks' sound track because it contains some great songs. "God's Children" has received a second life on a few compilations, but the similarly beautiful chamber-pop ballad "The Way Love Used to Be" and the Beatlesque "Moments" are buried deeper in their catalog. "Dreams" is typical of the more raucous Kinks tracks of

The film *Percy* is not nearly as good as the Kinks music or this neat illustration of a naked guy. Author's collection.

its period. It ping-pongs between music-box delicacy, forceful rock and roll, and appropriately dreamy, psychedelic swirls. The Who-like instrumental "Whip Lady," the rudimentary blues "Animals in the Zoo," and the amusing Noel Coward tribute "Just Friends" are also ripe for rediscovery.

MUSWELL HILLBILLIES

The Kinks then left Pye Records and signed to RCA and became a pretty different band. The intimate quartet that recorded delicacies such as *Face to Face* and *Village Green Preservation Society* expanded to include a horn section they would fully integrate into the band for subsequent performances and recordings. The Kinks certainly sound bigger on their RCA debut, *Muswell Hillbillies*. Beginning in near silence, opening track "Twentieth Century Man" builds to a massive squall, and the energy level rarely settles down from there. The Kinks' fascination with outdated styles of music, small-town life, working-class tribulations, technological paranoia, and afternoon tea still informs their music thoroughly, but the shy waver in Ray Davies's voice is gone. That horn section further beefs up the sound with the ragtime riffs it bleats over "Acute Schizophrenia Paranoia Blues" and the Salvation Army march "Alcohol."

While the Kinks' music was changing, Ray Davies's focus on storytelling and culturally traditional concerns fell right in line with those of his other recent records. He'd decried the changing face of the little England he loved on *Village Green Preservation Society*. *Lola* depicted a world that should be ruled by art being tyrannized by shady modern businessmen. *Percy* takes a stance against body modification. *Muswell Hillbillies* depicts England as a fascist state in which every family's freedom is threatened by invasions from bureaucratic "people in grey" intent on dragging them from their homes and into council flats.

A new era of sound and arrangement notwithstanding, Ray Davies's songs are as excellent as ever: "Have a Cuppa Tea" is among his most joyous, and "Oklahoma U.S.A." is one of his prettiest. *Muswell Hillbillies* gets the Kinks' RCA era off to a ripping start, yet for many fans, it was their last truly great record.

LED ZEPPELIN: " "

Following the zonked blues of their first two records and the mystical folk experiments of their third, Led Zeppelin's mythic status was pretty well in place when they released their fourth one. The guys are well intoxicated on their grizzled bluesmen-cum-medieval warlords-cum-dime-store Satanists-cum-sexual-pillagers persona throughout *untitled* or *Led Zeppelin IV* or *Runes* or *Zoso* or whatever you want to call it.

This is the record that best sums up what made Led Zeppelin huge stars and what makes some of their stuff sound a little silly today. There're Robert Plant's simulated orgasms and Tolkien references. Its hippie yearnings date "Going to California." "Stairway to Heaven" might be rock and roll's most worshipped and mocked indulgence (honorary mention to "Free Bird," of course).

The cover of their fourth album is a monument to Led Zeppelin's mysteriousness and self-confidence. As usual, there's no image of the band on the cover, but this time their name and the album's title are absent too. In fact, the album didn't even have a title. At least they named the album's songs; otherwise, stoners wouldn't know enough to shout "Play 'Stairway'!!" while holding their Zippos aloft at Zeppelin shows. Author's collection.

Smoke a couple of bowls, and these gripes evaporate. As self-conscious as Led Zeppelin's fourth album is (right down to the band's belief that they were so godlike that they didn't even have to lower themselves to name the damn thing), a complete lack of self-consciousness when listening to it reveals why it became *the* stoner sound track of the decade. "Going to California" may be lyrically goofy, but it is very pretty. "The Battle of Evermore" is completely transporting, and guest vocalist Sandy Denny plays commanding foil to Plant. "When the Levee Breaks" still rattles the walls. "Black Dog" is all snaky intricacy and bludgeoning power. "Misty Mountain Hop" adds some much needed intentional humor. "Four Sticks" is the scariest, heaviest thing in the band's catalog. And yes, "Stairway to Heaven" earns its legendary status with its dramatic structure, legit mysteriousness, and Page's molten guitar solo. Led Zeppelin's fourth album confirms everything that inspired awe in their followers and struck terror in their detractors—though you might have to get a little toasted to fully appreciate it today.

JOHN LENNON: *IMAGINE*

John Lennon seemed determined to shed fans when he made the challenging *Plastic Ono Band*. With *Imagine*, he seemed just as determined to welcome them back. The old poppiness and a good deal of his "All You Need Is Love"–era innocence are back. While Phil Spector's bare-bones production of *Plastic Ono Band* was in no way indicative of the work that made him famous, that wall of sound is back too on *Imagine*.

Despite its musically and lyrically naive title track, which became Lennon's solo calling card, and the almost self-consciously innocent love letters to his wife "Oh My Love" and "Oh Yoko," there is still quite a bit of bite in *Imagine*. Naive it may be, but "Imagine" also had the moxie to ask 1971 radio listeners to imagine a world without religion. "Crippled Inside" is a bluesy knock against hypocrites (and, yes, Lennon did recognize his own hypocritical leanings, as we shall see in our discussion of his next album). "Gimme Some Truth" is the kind of politically pointed rant that would take his next album hostage. "How Do You Sleep?" is an unsparing and very specific attack on his former partner that spills too much venom. Did Paul really deserve this?

Spector's goopy MOR production irons too many wrinkles out of such material. Only "Gimme Some Truth," "It's So Hard," and the strident "I Don't Want to Be a Soldier Mama" have stinging music to match their lyrics. *Imagine* still houses its share of classics, and with its command of the number one spot on several album charts throughout the world, it proved that Lennon could still appeal to the masses after doing his best to put them off with his first album.

PAUL AND LINDA MCCARTNEY: *RAM*

Giddy from finally having a reason to knock a Beatle down, critics greeted Paul McCartney's second record with the same venom they spat on *McCartney*. Paul was hurt—and justifiably so. Hearing *Ram* decades removed from the national-tragedy level of hysteria surrounding the Beatles' dissolution, it's hard to see what the critics hated and impossible to miss the craftsmanship. So what if a lot of the lyrics are nonsense? Since when was profundity Paulie's objective? The tunes are his most effervescent since "The White Album." The recording is a perfect union of *Abbey Road*–style invention and *Let It Be*–style grit. Both of those albums would have benefited from such balance.

And how could listeners dip into such a diverse dish without finding something that suits their fancies? McCartney is the consummate chameleon throughout, paying homage to Brian Wilson ("Back Seat of My Car") and Buddy Holly ("Eat at Home"), playing the down-home farm boy ("Heart of the Country") and the moonshine-mad bootlegger ("Monkberry Moon Delight"), and giving us the best Beatles song since the band's breakup ("Uncle Albert/Admiral Halsey"). Those who criticized *Ram* as a cheerful exercise in style over substance ignored the spite in "Dear Boy," "3 Legs," and the flame-throwing "Too Many People." John Lennon didn't. He regarded those tracks as sucker punches from his former partner (he had a point regarding "Too Many People") and responded with the really mean "How Do You Sleep?" on *Imagine*. No one seemed to mind that Lennon's record was guilty of a lot of the criticisms lumped on *Ram*: saccharine production and puerile lyricism (though Lennon got a pass because of his stabs at political observation and self-examination). Forty years on, one of those albums still sounds 100 percent fresh, and it isn't the one on which a rich man tells us to "imagine no possessions."

THE MOVE: *MESSAGE FROM THE COUNTRY*

For their final album, the Move perfected their numerous musical pursuits and compiled them into a collection that felt eclectic rather than merely random, as *The Move* did. "Ella James" and "Until Your Mama's Gone" are examples of the heavy rock they started pursuing in the late sixties, but *Message from the Country* feels more like a return to the pithy singles of the band's mid-sixties golden era, which is a relief after the long-winded epics that took over *Shazam* and *Looking On*. "No Time" is the group's most ethereal ballad. "It Wasn't My Idea to Dance" is a warped blend of hard rock and Moroccan ornamentation (Jimmy Page and Robert Plant must have been listening). The title track and "The Words of Aaron" hint at what Wood and Lynne were planning to deliver with their soon-to-be-born Electric Light Orchestra, although ELO would rarely produce anything as tough and terse as these two tracks.

I know it's considered rock-geek heresy to prefer the American rejiggering of a British artist's album, but replacing the two Bev Bevans songs and the novelty "My Marge" with the singles "Do Ya," "Chinatown," California Man," and "Tonight" really makes *Split Ends* an improvement on *Message from the Country*. Author's collection.

THE ROLLING STONES: *STICKY FINGERS*

Commercially, the Rolling Stones were riding a high wave in 1971. They'd popped back from their controversial psychedelic period and the drug trials swirling around it to score huge critical and commercial smashes with *Beggars Banquet* and *Let It Bleed* and the massive singles "Jumpin' Jack Flash" and "Honky Tonk Women." New guitarist Mick Taylor helped refine their sound with his elegant, weaving riffs. Getting back on the road reunified the band just when they were nearest collapse.

Their personal lives were a different story. The sixties ended with the death of Brian Jones and the tragic mess of Altamont, which cast the band as villains in the press even though they had little to do with the event's planning and the Grateful Dead's manager Rock Scully bore more responsibility for the disastrous decision to hire the Hell's Angels as "security" than the Stones did. Hard drugs were slithering into the fold. Mick Jagger's girlfriend Marianne Faithfull nearly died from an overdose in 1969. Rock's highest-profile couple split up the following year.

The ambivalence of the Stones' situation is all over their first studio record of the seventies and the first on their own Rolling Stones Records imprint. "Wild Horses" conveys the push and pull of realizing a relationship is over yet not having the heart to put it to rest. "Sway" describes the undertow of self-destruction. "Moonlight Mile" is a portrait of homesickness. "Dead Flowers" is a weary junkie's kiss-off.

The music is weary too. Aside from the generic, button-pushing rockers that open each of its sides—the stale shock-schlock "Brown Sugar," which finds Jagger resorting to ludicrous racism and misogyny, cheering on a "scarred old slaver" as he physically and sexually abuses the women he has enslaved (to mask a lack of inspiration), and the monotonous "Bitch"— *Sticky Fingers* is the Stones' slowest, quietest record. Acoustic blues, country, and Western and Eastern folk are the predominant sounds. Even the electrified "Sway" and passages of the winding epic "Can't You Hear Me Knocking" feel more fatigued than furious. At times, the band sound as though they've broken down completely for better and worse. Mick and Keith's off-key wailing

The Andy Warhol–designed cover of *Sticky Fingers* is famous for its fully functioning fly. Author's collection.

renders the campfire blues cover "You Gotta Move" one of the worst things the Stones ever did. The showstopping "Sister Morphine," Marianne and Mick's terrifying account of a man who wakes up in a hospital bed after a car accident, is effectively disturbing and disturbed. The singer sounds utterly cracked.

Underneath all the pain and sleaze is a thin current of fight that makes *Sticky Fingers* harrowing. This is often attributable to the band's most stable member. Charlie Watts's drum fills shatter through the stupor of "Sister Morphine" and swell through the serene surface of "Moonlight Mile," the Rolling Stones' most beautiful recording. They would soon return to their former punkiness on *Exile on Main Street*, but *Sticky Fingers* reveals a great band struggling, and as such, it is the most inconsistent yet fascinating record from their celebrated run of records with producer Jimmy Miller.

JUDEE SILL: *JUDEE SILL*

Singer-songwriter Judee Sill's backstory is also fascinating and disturbing. The biological daughter of a man who imported exotic animals for films, she emerged from a violent home life with a stepdad who animated *Tom and Jerry* cartoons to become an armed robber, drug addict, prostitute, scam artist, and convict. Then she apparently discovered Jesus and became a recording artist.

While her lyrics take the occasional glimpse into the shadows (most fearlessly on "The Lamb Ran Away with the Crown"), Sill's first recordings fail to reflect her traumatic experiences. Her voice is full-bodied and pitch-perfect, but it does not exactly exude emotion. She sounds like she should be serenading kids on *The Magic Garden*. Her voice renders folky compositions such as "Crayon Angels" and "Jesus Was a Cross-Maker" pleasant but vapid. The religiousness of her lyrics won't appeal to everyone either. Without a doubt, the most striking song on *Judee Sill* is the heart-rending "Lady-O," which the Turtles recorded with more acute emotion in 1969.

All these songs appear on Sill's 1971 self-titled debut coproduced by Graham Nash. The inoffensive acoustic arrangements are in line with Nash's work with Crosby, Stills, and Nash's softer songs. The Paul Buckmaster–esque string arrangement on "Lopin' Along through the Cosmos" is the one potent ingredient in an otherwise bland stew.

SLY AND THE FAMILY STONE: *THERE'S A RIOT GOING ON*

Stand! was split between remarkably optimistic numbers like its title track and "Everyday People" and weird, druggy funk like "Sex Machine" and "Don't Call Me Nigger, Whitey." The latter style takes over on *There's a Riot Going On*. A style of music made for dancing and partying finally overindulges and passes out on the beanbag. Tensions within the band and Sly's deepening drug problems leech into the music, making for the first truly personal funk record. Sly's voice is low and gruff throughout. The band plays it slow and swampy in isolated overdubs instead of their usual communal jams. A drum machine often fills in for Gerry Errico. Sly's one-man band often fills in for the whole Family Stone. His lyrics deal with dysfunctional families, racism, drugs, and the downside of rock stardom.

This is also one of the first albums by an already established artist to sound, well, wrong. Gary "U.S." Bonds became big despite the fact that *Dance 'Til a Quarter to Three* sounds like it was recorded in a broom closet. *The Velvet Underground & Nico* is as high-fi as radio cross talk, but the Velvets were hardly stars. But Sly Stone was when he recorded an album that sometimes sounds

Sly Stone's decision to include a photo of his own altered American Flag on the cover of *There's a Riot Goin' On* was pretty daring considering how touchy many Americans are about the flag. Lots of them seem to care more about their symbols than they care about their fellow people. Author's collection.

like he forgot to pull the packing material off his microphone. That murky atmosphere makes the album feel all the more personal, as if the artist had created it solely for himself without any intention of letting it roam in public, not unlike *McCartney* or *Smiley Smile* but certainly more potent and less flippant than either of those albums.

There's a Riot Going On is not a fun listen, but it is a spellbinding one, and several excellent songs get caught in its nightmarish current. "Family Affair" was the big hit, but "Love N' Haight," "Brave & Strong," "(You Caught Me) Smilin'," and "Runnin' Away" are also catchy enough to stand out from the murk. Uneasy stuff like "Just Like a Baby," "Spaced Cowboy," "Time," and the torturous "Thank You for Talkin' to Me Africa" are the tracks that will linger on your fuzzy tongue.

ROD STEWART: *EVERY PICTURE TELLS A STORY*

There wasn't a ton of variation among Rod Stewart's first four albums. Each one shuffled original and cover songs interpreted with loose, largely acoustic arrangements that owed as much to traditional British folk as they did to Chuck Berry. This winning formula hit its peak on Stewart's second and third albums. *Gasoline Alley* and *Every Picture Tells a Story* are equally good, though only the latter packs a ridiculous number of Stewart standards. The May/December ballad "Maggie May" became his defining song. The exquisitely picturesque "Mandolin Wind" and the mighty "Every Picture Tells a Story"—the singer's ultimate folk and Chuck union—are tremendous songs and tremendously important to Stewart's importance. Rod's duet with Maggie Bell that rides the title track out sends chills down my spine, and Micky Waller's walloping drumming sends a kick up my ass. Anyone who doesn't believe the future face of late seventies/eighties superficiality ever had any artistic credibility need only hear these two songs.

T. REX: *ELECTRIC WARRIOR*

As Tyrannosaurus Rex, Marc Bolan and Steve Peregrine Took played hippie folk piped up from Middle Earth. When Peregrine Took drifted off and Mickey Finn drifted in and Bolan infused his freaky fantasies with stinging Les Paul riffs and hired bassist Steve Currie and drummer Bill Legend to round out the group, Tyrannosaurus Rex became T. Rex, and glam rock danced itself out of the womb.

The band's second album in their new incarnation expanded their following from a few devoted elves and trolls to the world. Throughout the summer of 1971, radios around the globe buzzed with "Get It On." Bolan's union of Chuck Berry licks, Mike Love's hot-rod-o-philia, and surrealistic witchcraft were brilliant strokes in the years after psychedelia had died the death. Kids slapped aluminum stars on their cheeks, poured themselves into patched bell bottoms, and grooved along with such inspired gobbledygook as "You've got a hub-cap diamond-star halo." Bolan hisses his weird words over an expansive universe of Phil Spectorian reverb.

Electric Warrior was rock and roll's past and its future mashed up into a confection that sweetened the teeth of soft poppers and hard rockers, fellow glam hounds and future punks, Elton John and John Lennon, David Bowie and the Damned. Marc Bolan was a mystical uniter whose nonsense spoke louder than any rhetoric. *Electric Warrior* is his mission statement and masterwork.

THE WHO: *WHO'S NEXT*

How do you follow up a career-making, genre-pioneering record like *Tommy*? Live albums are fine stopgaps, as *Live at Leeds* proved, but the Who still needed another studio release to keep the flames of their new success stoked. Pete Townshend's solution was to outdo his first full-length rock opera with a futuristic double-LP/stage/cinema project. *Lifehouse* spawned a glut of incredible songs and much head-scratching from the rest of the band. No one could quite understand what it was all about in 1971, but when Townshend finally got around to lucidly explaining the story in the liner notes of a 2000 box set devoted to the project, *Lifehouse* turned out to be a freakily prescient sci-fi epic that foretold virtual reality, the internet, and the environmental crisis that threatens our planet today.

Townshend's inability to adequately explain *Lifehouse* and a disastrous attempt to stage a free-floating concert of the material at the Young Vic theater in April 1971 put the project on permanent hiatus. The Who still needed a new album, so they salvaged eight *Lifehouse* songs, John Entwistle added a new one, and *Who's Next* was born.

The album must have felt like a devastating compromise to Townshend at the time, but its success is inarguable. Their roadwork behind *Tommy* turned the Who into a completely different sounding, heavier, more confident band. Having veteran engineer Glyn Johns behind the board cleaned up and punched up their sound. But the most dramatic advance on *Who's*

Next is Townshend's discovery of synthesizers, which add subtle textures to "Bargain" and "The Song Is Over" and transforms "Baba O'Riley" into a sparkling laser-light show.

Townshend's writing is remarkable throughout the record, and his songs don't really suffer from the loss of a cohesive story line. "Baba O'Riley" does not make much sense outside of the *Lifehouse* concept, but the self-pity of "Behind Blue Eyes," the soul-searching of "Bargain," the resignation of "The Song Is Over," the elated wanderlust of "Goin' Mobile," and the righteous mistrust of "Won't Get Fooled Again" speak for themselves. Entwistle's pile-driving "My Wife" injects the record with a dose of diabolical humor. *Who's Next* is also a triumph for Roger Daltrey. Previously considered the band's weak link, he brings staggering anguish to "Bargain," majesty to "The Song Is Over," sensitivity to "Behind Blue Eyes." I cannot improve on John Swenson's description of Daltrey's scream in "Won't Get Fooled Again" as "a moment of pure rock transcendence." The record's overexposure on classic rock radio means it no longer sounds as radical as it once did, and the current consensus among a lot of fans (including myself) is that *The Who Sell Out* is the band's best album. But heard with fresh ears, *Who's Next* is still as monumental as the monolith the guys piss all over on the record's cover.

YES: *FRAGILE*

Prog rock put a lot of asses in stadium seats in the seventies, but a disgruntled underground of future punks would soon render the willfully complex genre obsolete and leave it forever classified as self-indulgent, soulless, and embarrassing in the rock and roll history books. While the punks were welcome antidotes to an increasingly turgid scene, their complete dismissal of prog wasn't fair.

Take the genre's poster boys. Yes's songs are long, their lyrics self-consciously abstract, their playing and structures showy. They inverted the record-making process by writing and recording snippets of music and editing them into long pieces (they were capable of playing these epics live only after studying

Roger Dean is the J.R.R. Tolkien of album cover artists. If you see one of his paintings on an album cover, you can pretty much rest assured that the album inside it is a great, big, heaping helping of prog. Author's collection.

their own records!). But so what? Listen to their finest record, *Fragile*, with fresh ears. You don't need a doctorate in Euclidean geometry to get sucked into the hard and dirty "South Side of the Sky" or a powdered wig to appreciate the baroque beauty of "Mood for a Day." The punks could have learned a thing or two from the blazingly fast riffs that ignite "Heart of the Sunrise." And while bands like Genesis and King Crimson seemed to value intellect above all else, Yes knew their way around a pop hook, as the classic singles "Roundabout" and "Long Distance Runaround" display. They were also capable of scaling back their wide-screen vision to make room for pithy showpieces for each band member that link the longer tracks nicely. *Fragile* shows that a little indulgence isn't always a bad thing.

1972

With scant exceptions, the vibrancy of sixties pop fashions was nothing but a speck in the rearview by 1972. Nothing but open, earth-toned road laid ahead, and the most important artists of the decade were coming into their own. Some of the previous decade's leaders were still capable of spinning out essential works.

The shifting terrain was most apparent on the radio. As adult contemporary singers such as Melanie, Don McLean, and Carly Simon and teenybop singers such as David Cassidy and the Osmonds had a bigger influence on the top forty, rock and roll began segregating itself. That year, a program director in San Diego, California, switched KGB-FM from top forty to a new format that favored rock and roll artists who weren't making a dent in the singles charts. Ron Jacobs, the program director of San Diego's KPRI, did the same, dubbing his new format "album-oriented rock" (AOR). AOR stations played album cuts along with singles, and it steered clear of anything the programmers considered to be too commercial. As the format figured itself out in the ensuing years, it also narrowed its mind, shunning not only artists who didn't tote electric guitars but also artists who didn't happen to be white. Rock and roll was working itself into a corner and creating a racist divide that would shut out the very people who created it less than twenty years earlier.

However, a more inclusive definition of rock and roll still seemed possible at the beginning of the decade as glam and funk, reggae and power pop, transformers and exiles, pink moons and stardust all glittered in 1972.

BIG STAR: #1 RECORD

With groups like Yes and Led Zeppelin ruling the mainstream, early seventies rock was still in the thrall of post–*Sgt. Pepper's* progressive indulgence. A backlash bubbling in the underground ruled by the Stooges and the New York Dolls took its inspiration from radically regressive American garage rockers like Question Mark & the Mysterians and the Sonics. Yet few new bands seemed to be drawing on the middle ground between these two movements: the cleaner yet aggressive mid-sixties power pop of the Who and the Kinks. Even the Who and the Kinks no longer sounded anything like they did in 1965/1966.

Such sounds would make a resounding comeback in a few years with the arrival of the Jam, Elvis Costello and the Attractions, and Cheap Trick. In 1972, Big Star was one of the very few power-pop torch holders. Although co–front man Alex Chilton had achieved some fame with the Box Tops in the sixties, Big Star was virtually unknown during their time. Today, they are cult legends because their music has aged so beautifully. Great as Yes and Led Zeppelin could be, their music is tightly tied to seventies fashions. Big Star's unpretentious power pop is timeless. So is Chilton and Chris Bell's ragged small-town sentimentality, which presages the obsessions of Springsteen and Tom Petty. Tracks like "Feel," "In the Street," and "Thirteen" are disarmingly plainspoken odes to teenage loserdom. Hanging out and getting high on the street, spinning "Paint It Black" over and over as a desperate stab at rebellion, dreaming of traveling to more exotic places than the Memphis suburbs to "drink gin and tonic and play a grand piano," finding a bit of solace with a first girlfriend—this stuff is a lot more relatable to teens than battling druids or orgying with groupies or any of the other rubbish Robert Plant screeched about.

Critics loved *#1 Record*, but poor label support guaranteed it never fulfilled its title goal. After the similar *Radio City* and the breakdown document *Third/Sister Lovers*, Big Star burnt out. The inspiration they passed on to the like-minded power poppers queuing up behind them still shines on.

DAVID BOWIE: *THE RISE AND FALL OF ZIGGY STARDUST AND THE SPIDERS FROM MARS*

David Bowie really became David Bowie with 1971's *Hunky Dory*, which sustained his eclecticism across an entire LP for the first time and mapped out his shape-shifting modus operandi with the anthem "Changes." By the time he made his next album, he was already done with being David Bowie. The singer assumes his first iconic persona: the decadent, suicidal alien rock star Ziggy Stardust.

Like all worthwhile rock operas or concept albums or whatever *The Rise and Fall of Ziggy Stardust and the Spiders from Mars* is, greatness lies not in some vaguely sketched plot but in the wonderful songs that relate it. Bowie's ruminations on extraterrestrials and celebrity drama don't stick as securely as the superb songs and performances that house them. He gets the right backing from the Spiders from Mars, a mighty and unique band led by sci-fi guitarist Mick Ronson. Bowie's rockers are amazingly sharp, whether thundering ("Moonage Daydream"), boogying ("Suffragette City"), slashing ("Ziggy Stardust"), or sliding on a slick of sleaze ("Hang on to Yourself"). His ballads are dramatic without flitting toward the show-tuney lightness of his earlier records. "Five Years," "Lady Stardust," and "Rock and Roll Suicide" are just as forceful as the up-tempo numbers.

The Rise and Fall of Ziggy Stardust and the Spiders from Mars solidified Bowie's cred with an ace reservoir of material for the concerts that demonstrated how his florid dramatic ambitions could meld with throat-throttling rock and roll seamlessly. Bowie had a lot more spectacular albums up his unitard's single sleeve, but his greatest is *The Rise and Fall of Ziggy Stardust and the Spiders from Mars*.

NICK DRAKE: *PINK MOON*

Nick Drake's second LP, *Bryter Layter*, was a fine production, but the timid singer seemed lost amidst all the horns, backing singers, keyboards, and strings. Drake lost all but his voice and acoustic guitar on his final album. *Pink Moon* is stark, but its delicacy makes it powerful. The quieter Drake sings, the more methodically he plucks his guitar, the deeper his songs cut. Absorb "Road," which even reduces his poetry to a couple of sparse phrases. It is a haunting, halting performance. Drake rarely makes his dark mood explicit (the barefaced self-loathing of "Parasite" is a rare exception).

Although another shot of Nick Drake looking uncomfortable was originally planned for the cover of *Pink Moon*, Island Records decided to go with Michael Trevithick's surreal painting instead. Author's collection.

He never, ever overemotes. Yet his whispers are screams, and his fingerpicking is as weighty as the most eardrum-busting power chord. He clearly did not set out to draw attention to the soul-wracking pain he was feeling when he casually recorded *Pink Moon* in a pair of two-hour sessions, but it is palpable in every groove on the record. Even the awestruck title track huddles beneath clouds of mumbled melancholy. Those familiar with Drake's tragic trajectory often read a lot into this record, but even if he had not died of assumed suicide, *Pink Moon* would still be heartbreaking.

MURRAY HEAD: *NIGEL LIVED*

Murray Head recorded one excellent single ("She Was Perfection") for Andrew Oldham's Immediate label in 1967, but he didn't really find his unique voice until landing a role in a stage production of the hippie musical *Hair* and voicing Judas Iscariot on the album version of Andrew Lloyd Webber and Tim Rice's contrived rock opera *Jesus Christ Superstar* in 1970. Those musicals' union of pop and theater carried over to Head's first solo album in 1972.

Nigel Lived tells the story of an aspiring singer who leaves the safety of home to find stardom in the big black smoke. Instead of achieving success, Nigel succumbs to London's vices and ends up hooked on junk. Reactionary? Absolutely, but *Nigel Lived* is still one of the more successful progeny of *Tommy* because of its eclectic arrangements and styles (Head tries on funk, acoustic balladry, straight rock and roll, blues, chamber pop, and a sort of experimental pop), its excellent production values, and Head's expressive voice, which veers from a Peter Gabriel–esque croon to a soul howl.

The one thing *Nigel Lived* lacks is consistently strong songwriting. Things like "Pacing on the Station," "Ruthie," and "When You Wake Up in the Morning" are good, but a couple of the more unorthodox pieces—the pseudo-hymn "Pity the Poor Consumer" and the choppy and overlong "Junk"—are not. There are two genuinely superb standouts. Head boils downs the best of circa-1966 McCartney into "Nigel, Nigel" and recycles his own "She Was Perfection" for "Religion." If nothing else, you have to admire the guy for trying different things regardless of whether or not they always work.

THE KINKS: *EVERYBODY'S IN SHOWBIZ, EVERYBODY'S A STAR*

From *Face to Face* through *Muswell Hillbillies*, the Kinks skated on a hot streak few other bands could ever hope to lay down. It was bound to hit the curb eventually. *Everybody's in Showbiz, Everybody's a Star* is not in the same league as *Something Else* or *Village Green Preservation Society*. Ray Davies seems a bit weary, a bit low on ideas. The rock-band-on-tour concept was certainly in line with the concerns of the band that made *Lola Versus Powerman and the Money-Go-Round*, but nonstop gripes about bad food don't bite as hard as attacks on a corrupt record industry.

Everybody's in Showbiz is still a pretty great record. The concept has its roots in a tour film that never came to be. Ray's sound track focused on the things that annoyed him about road travel: the monotony, the phoniness, the suffocating hotel rooms, and the shitty food. While the lyrics aren't always his strongest, the music is a smashing extension of the big band–embellished *Muswell Hillbillies*. The hardworking "Here Comes Yet Another Day" is a perfect concert opener. "Sitting in my Hotel" is a classic Davies construction decorated with regal brass. "You Don't Know My Name" is another firm tug at the heart that Dave Davies intensifies with his ragged yowl and a twisty riff. A welcome shift in tone slips in toward the end of the album when Ray finds some solace and escape in the uplifting calypso "Supersonic Rocket Ship" and succumbs to a self-enforced attitude adjustment on "Look a Little on the Sunnyside."

Even if the preceding tracks hadn't been as good as they are, *Everybody's in Showbiz* would still be essential listening because of "Celluloid Heroes." Ray's nostalgic trek down Hollywood Boulevard leaves me with a lump in my throat. His voice had never been more fragile, his empathy never more tender. "Celluloid Heroes" ranks alongside "Waterloo Sunset," "Days," and "Animal Farm" as one of Ray's most beautiful songs and performances.

But wait—the show isn't over yet. *Everybody's in Showbiz* continues rolling on a live second disc, which cleverly illustrates the other side of rock touring with funny, loose performances of recent classics like "Lola" and "Brainwashed" and nostalgic items like "Baby Face" and "Mr. Wonderful" that take on an odd poignancy in light of "Celluloid Heroes."

JOHN LENNON AND YOKO ONO: *SOMETIME IN NEW YORK CITY*

While the most popular image of John Lennon remains the peace sign–waving peacenik who sang "Imagine all the people living life in peace," it has recently become more common to call him out as a bully, a misogynist who sang "I'd rather see you dead little girl than to be with another man," and a soft-on-revolution splash of cold water who tried to assure us "it's gonna be alright" (it wasn't).

In the early seventies, John Lennon worked to make amends for the rough man he'd been. After walking the middle of the road through much of the Beatles' career, he decided to use his booming voice for more ideologically positive purposes, championing feminist principals as early as 1970's "Well, Well, Well," moving from his plush Tittenhurst Park estate to a grubby apartment in Greenwich Village, and taking up with such high-profile activists as Jerry Rubin, Tariq Ali, and Bobby Seale.

These are the years Lennon appeared on *The Mike Douglas Show* with guests Rubin (whose no-punches-pulled rhetoric irked Douglas) and Black Panther Seale (whose nonviolent community spirit surprised and delighted the host) and *The Dick Cavett Show*, where Lennon discussed how the White House was trying to run him out of the country for his opinions and why it was so important that he be allowed to stay. These are the years Lennon railed against the unfair imprisonment of activist John Sinclair (given ten years for possessing two joints) and recorded the highly controversial *Sometime in New York City*, on which he laid out his various causes, played with revolutionary rockers Elephant's Memory, and gave Yoko Ono equal time in the musical spotlight.

The more radical messages of *Some Time in New York City* put off pop fans and annoyed the MOR rock press. Considering Lennon's past record, the left-wing press mistrusted his intentions and branded him a dilettante at best and a hypocrite at worst.

So *Some Time in New York City* ended up as Lennon's least loved album because of its hard-line revolutionary politics and because he allotted half the disc to mate and cohort Yoko Ono. The record is not the disaster it has often been labeled. While the politics may alienate middle-of-the-roaders and right-wingers, the music slams hard as Lennon draws on his rock and roll roots and Phil Spector finally delivers a production fully reminiscent of his early work. Ono's contributions can be a bit strident (her vocals on the chorus of "Sunday Bloody Sunday" and the whole of "We're All Water"), but she comports herself quite beautifully on the musically charming and lyrically horrific "Luck of the Irish" and "Sisters, O Sisters," on which she gets into the Wall of Sound spirit with a classic girl-groupish vocal. With the exceptions of strong performances of "Cold Turkey" and "Well (Baby Please Don't Go)," the bonus live LP requires a great deal more tolerance.

CURTIS MAYFIELD: *SUPER FLY*

Honey-voiced Curtis Mayfield had been the lead singer of the Impressions, the most gospel-indebted of the sixties' soul combos. He left the Impressions in 1970 to set off on the challenging, politically minded path on which Marvin Gaye and Stevie Wonder would soon join him.

So Mayfield may have seemed like an odd choice to score *Super Fly*, a film often held up as a prime example of the subcategory of exploitation flicks offensively known as "blax-ploitation." The genre is generally derided for using an African American cast to glorify violence and sexual objectification for an African American audience.

That bit on the cover with the title and Ron O'Neal in his "Super Fly" suit is a flap that reveals the track titles when folded out. Author's collection.

Gordon Parks Jr.'s film is a lot more complex than that, and so is Mayfield's sound track. Filmmaker and composer treat the characters like full-blooded humans with clear motivations and beset with real-world problems. Mayfield's voice is naturally empathetic, and songs such as "Little Child Runnin' Wild," "Pusherman," "Freddie's Dead," and "No Thing on Me (Cocaine Song)" highlight and humanize the trials and triumphs of Parks's characters. Mayfield's band lights a fire under the songs, and Joseph Scott digs his fingers into some of funk's growliest bass lines.

VAN MORRISON: *SAINT DOMINIC'S PREVIEW*

By 1972, the exploratory epic *Astral Weeks* was looking like an anomaly in Van Morrison's career. *Moondance, His Band and Street Choir,* and *Tupelo Honey* were soulful and committed, but their tightly constructed songs were nothing like the free-form excursions of *Astral Weeks*. Considering the mercurial and defiant path Van Morrison always followed, it's surprising it took him so long to get back into insular improvisations, but he eventually did with *Saint Dominic's Preview*.

Morrison cons the listener into thinking he has another *Moondance* on deck by opening the record with a compact, deliciously digestible trio of R&B pop led by the exuberant single "Jackie Wilson Said (I'm in Heaven When You Smile)." Then the curmudgeon slams down the mic and stomps offstage. In walks the lion to growl, howl, and snarl for eleven spellbinding minutes. The band rises and falls along with every bellow Morrison pushes out of his guts.

The poetry of *Astral Weeks* hasn't quite returned. The untamed emotion is back like a full-force gale. The title track is not as mysterious as "Listen to the Lion," but it too takes its time to get deep into a feeling, set a scene, and stir the soul. "Redwood Tree" is a stopover in the tidy R&B that began *Saint Dominic's Preview*. Then Van is back on the mountain, sermonizing cryptically over otherworldly backing, a synthesizer glowing through the darkness like a beacon across the sea. He sings that it's "Almost Independence Day," but independence has definitely arrived already. He's had his hits, but the untethered artist has returned, and he'd continue roaring across a new string of personal statements, never allowing listeners to predict his next move for the rest of the decade.

LOU REED: *LOU REED*

Doug Yule had the Velvet Underground's *Squeeze* in the pipeline, but that band ceased to be as soon as Lou Reed shrugged it off. In 1971, Reed signed to RCA for the inevitable solo career, releasing an eponymous debut that suggested he'd lost the focus that made each of his four Velvets albums unique. Short on new material, he recycled a bunch of songs the Velvets didn't release but recorded to better effect. Apparently, Reed was an artist who needed strong collaborators.

TRANSFORMER

Enter superfan David Bowie. The product of their collaboration is *Transformer*. The title implies that Bowie tried to remold Reed as a chameleon-like glam-slammer in his own image. The record definitely has more reptilian sinew than the flaccid *Lou Reed*, but it isn't dolled up with the celestial spangles of Bowie's recent work either. "Make Up" is the only track that panders to glam dress-ups. Otherwise, *Transformer* stinks of New York City as much as any of the earthy Velvet Underground records did. The city won a new anthem, and Reed gave himself a new signature with the jazzy, journalistic "Walk on the Wild Side." "Vicious" and "Hangin' 'Round" are tough rockers that offset lush ballads like "Perfect Day" and "Satellite of Love." The record loses some steam toward the end (the soul choir on "Wagon Wheel" succumbs to the corniness it totally side-stepped on "Wild Side"), but the classics that make up the bulk of *Transformer* are the best tracks of Reed's solo career.

THE ROLLING STONES: *EXILE ON MAIN STREET*

We've seen a lot of reinvention in 1972, when Van Morrison, Lou Reed, and David Bowie dragged their art into thrilling new places. There's nothing so radical on the Rolling Stones' *Exile on Main Street*. The album spewed out the same kind of mucky rock and roll the Stones had been rolling in since hooking up with producer Jimmy Miller back in 1968. There's just more of it this time. *Exile* sprawls across two records, but it isn't an epic poem like *Blonde on Blonde*, a wild hodgepodge like "The White Album," or a hefty concept like *Tommy*. It's a deep, dark mire. The real value of the album often cited as the Stones' greatest is that *Exile on Main Street* provides one big opportunity to sink into their dirty world, to let the stink of late-night jams and smack-addled idleness engulf you.

Miller's dense production creates a "you are there" vibe. A lot has been made of the sessions that took place in Keith's villa in the south of France while the boys were ducking Britain's taxman. Those sessions may have given the album's mythology some extra juice, but a good chunk of *Exile on Main Street* was cut in Los Angeles. Regardless of which track was cut where, everything hangs together well. In fact, it may take you several listens for the individual numbers to really rise out of the gunk. Once that happens, you will find yourself stuck with a bunch of new friends kicking around in your brain, refusing to go home, and drinking all your whiskey. The lazy lover with the uncooperative equipment of "Rocks Off" is trying to get off with some girl in your bed. The incorrigible gambler of "Tumbling Dice" commandeers the kitchen table for an all-night poker game. The lovable layabout of "Happy" is sleeping one off on the hallway floor. Sweet Virginia's in the bathroom shooting up. The drunk is out back shouting up to his angry ex, begging her to come down and give him just one more drink from her loving cup. The construction worker is heading out the door to toil down the line. The ruffians of "Rip This Joint" are smashing bottles against the living room wall. The grizzled band of "Torn & Frayed" is jamming in the den. *Exile on Main Street* is filthy and full of holes, and there are just too many damn people milling about in it, but that's what makes it a rock and roll monument.

ROXY MUSIC: *ROXY MUSIC*

More intricate than glam, sexier than prog, Roxy Music wasn't just a new band in 1972—it was a new genre. Yet Roxy Music wasn't totally unprecedented, and they had a tendency to wear their influences on their sequined sleeves. Their debut album begins with rhythmic quotes from the Velvet Underground and Chuck Berry, melodic ones from the Beatles and Wagner, and sonic ones from Charlie Parker, King Crimson, and Joe Meek. The magic lies in the way Roxy Music took such disparate influences, juggled them up, and tossed them back out as something entirely their own. Brian Eno's visionary use of synthesizers—very different from Stevie Wonder's and Pete Townshend's more rhythmic use of the new instrument—and Bryan Ferry's vibrato croon and James Bond–from–Neptune image—very different from Ziggy Stardust's brand of glamour—were entirely new to pop. And no other rock band made the oboe an integral part of the lineup.

Roxy Music is as audacious a debut as one might expect from a band like this. Each song is totally unique from the one that follows, as the thunderous "Re-Make, Re-Model" gives way to the confident stride/sci-fi rocket ride of "Ladytron," which crashes to Earth with the countryish clip-clop of "If There Is Something," which then morphs into the Move-like prog of "Chance Meeting." Roxy Music couldn't even stick to one style in a single song. It was as if they were afraid they'd never get to make another album and were intent on cramming all their ideas into their first one. Amazingly, this was only the beginning.

T. REX: *THE SLIDER*

Marc Bolan emerged from his psychedelic-folk cocoon as a glam titan when he released *Electric Warrior* in 1971. With that, the former Tyrannosaurus Rex became one of the biggest acts of the seventies. Facile but magnetic, T. Rex continued their steely attack and stream of nonsense on *The Slider*. Bolan drops some grand doozies throughout the record: "Just like a silver-studded, saber-tooth dream," "She's a Chevy Chase cheetah," "The cosmic sea was like a bumblebee," "Mice eye, dog pie, eagle on the wind." He might even inject a spew of funky gibberish into something as mundane as a count-in, transforming a simple "1 and 2 and 3 and 4" into something like "1 and 2 and BUBBLY BUBBLY BOO BOO YEAH"! Once again, he dives into fifteen years of rock and roll clichés and soups them up like restored hot rods. "Metal Guru," "Baby Boomerang," "Rabbit Fighter," "Main Man," and "Mystic Lady" are fifties gestures draped in silver lamé.

Bolan isn't stuck in the past, though. He surveys the current landscape to give it his own cherubic spin. "Buick Mackane" rivals Led Zeppelin for heavy-duty funk. He tosses respectful nods to John Lennon and Bob Dylan à la Bowie's *Hunky Dory* on "Ballrooms of Mars." He even pays tribute to himself by revamping his biggest international hit, "Get It On," as the sublime "Telegram Sam." The *Slider* is a party from start to finish. There are some unwelcome guests—shady politicians, cruel boyfriends, yappy monsters—but none of them disrupt this joyful junk because Bolan knew that when sad, the best thing to do is slide.

VARIOUS ARTISTS: *THE HARDER THEY COME*

Many audiences throughout the world had no idea what they were hearing when they first saw *The Harder They Come* on the early seventies midnight movie circuit. Hard to believe as it may now be, there was a time when reggae was unknown outside of Jamaica. Perry Henzell's film exposed that music to droves of new listeners, allegedly inspiring some to dance in movie theater aisles. Before long, everyone from Led Zeppelin to the Rolling Stones to the Police to the Clash was working reggae sounds into their music.

The film's sound track consisted mostly of old tracks, but they were so new to so many people that the record is as fresh and 1972-essential as anything actually recorded that year. The film's star, Jimmy Cliff, holds the proceedings together, flaunting reggae's

Director Perry Henzell was not thrilled with how Roger Corman's New World Pictures marketed the American release of *The Harder They Come*, which he felt made the movie seem like "*Son of Shaft.*" Perhaps the sensitivity and respect Henzell desired should not be expected from the company that gave us *Women in Cages* and *Death Race 2000*. Author's collection.

diversity by exhibiting its exuberance ("You Can Get It If You Really Want"), toughness (the title track, which is the only song recorded specifically for the film), and soulfulness ("Sitting in Limbo"). He also gets off one breathtaking non-reggae track with the gospel "Many Rivers to Cross."

A selection of classics from genre giants such as the Melodians, Desmond Decker, and Toots & the Maytals, who hijack both the film and its sound track with their double strike of "Pressure Drop" and the transcendentally happy "Sweet and Dandy," fill out *The Harder They Come*. Short on material, Island pulled the questionable trick of repeating "You Can Get It If You Really Want" and "The Harder They Come" at the end of the album, but these tracks are so wonderful that you won't mind hearing them twice.

STEVIE WONDER: *MUSIC OF MY MIND*

Stevie Wonder is one of the few pop musicians who rightfully deserve to be called a genius, and that has nothing whatsoever to do with disabilities. In my estimation, a pop genius must be a masterful innovator and executer of those innovations and a paragon of versatility. Wonder is all of these things. The synthesized funk pop he pioneered during his most meaningful years was unlike anything before it. His singing and keyboard work are extraordinary. He sometimes called on others to help him make music, but he never really needed to.

After close to a decade of delivering terrific hits like "Uptight," "A Place in the Sun," and "I Was Made to Love Her" to Motown according to the label's standard system, Stevie Wonder won a new contract granting him complete artistic freedom in 1971. Like his label mate, Marvin Gaye, Wonder used this opportunity to fashion a personal, visionary brand of soul radically different from his sixties hits. His discovery of Malcolm Cecil and Robert Margouleff's TONTO (The Original New Timberal Orchestra)—which compiled the best attributes of the Moog, ARP, Oberheim, and other distinct synthesizers—allowed him to morph into the veritable one-man band that would make his most important works.

With the first link in that chain of breakthroughs, *Music of My Mind*, Wonder reached into unexplored territories with expansive songs largely recorded alone. Most proper bands would kill to have the kind of interpersonal chemistry Wonder has with himself on long journeys like "I Love Having You Around," the emotion-throttling "Superwoman (Where Were You When I Needed You)," and the frantic "Keep on Running." There are good songs too—both "I Love Everything About You" and "Happier Than the Morning Sun" should be considered classics—but *Music of My Mind* is more of a showcase for Wonder's musicianship, singing, and technological aptitude than his compositional skills. He got to show those off more on his next album.

TALKING BOOK

On *Talking Book*, Wonder perfected his songwriting and focused his experiments. If the results aren't his best album (a case could also be made for *Innervisions* or *Songs in the Key of Life*), it's certainly his most accessible of the seventies. Even the most radio-friendly tracks take unexpected detours. The number one hit and smoochy standard "You Are the Sunshine of My Life" gets under way with guest vocals from James Gilstrap and Lani Groves. Where's Wonder? Well, once he steps in to take over, anticipation spills into euphoria. The light samba kicks into top gear. Wonder can't hold back a tickled giggle, and neither can we as we tumble into his world where love knows no shame and legs were made to shimmy.

Has there ever been a funkier rhythm than the clavinet line he clatters on "Superstition"? "Maybe Your Baby" slows the funk down to a muddy grind. "You and I" and "Looking for Another Pure Love," with its swoony Jeff Beck guitar solo, are psychedelic ballads that float beyond the stratosphere. Then earthly passion and romantic transcendence coalesce on "I Believe (When I Fall in Love It Will Be Forever)," a hypnotic finale that ranks with "God Only Knows" and "In My Life" as one of *the* great love songs. Wonder's most outré tendencies would soon get a second wind on *Innervisions*, but *Talking Book* is his most perfect balance between accessibility and invention.

1973

While it may not ring the cultural-epoch bells of 1955 (the beginning of the rock and roll era), 1964 (the British Invasion), 1977 (the punk invasion), or 1991 (cue the opening riff of "Smells Like Teen Spirit"), 1973 was a significant year for rock. Many of the sixties' biggest stars were still doing exceptional work. For some of them, it would be the last time that statement held true. In his book *1973: Rock at the Crossroads*, Andrew Grant Jackson deems the year "the zenith of classic rock," referencing an article from the poll analysis site *FiveThirtyEight.com* concluding that classic rock radio plays more songs from the year of *Houses of the Holy*, *The Dark Side of the Moon*, and *Quadrophenia* than any other.

Meanwhile, a new ruckus was rising in the more outré corners of the scene. Incalculably influential artists such as the Stooges and the New York Dolls gave come-hither glances to the ones who would revive rock toward the end of the decade. More historically, DJ Kool Herc was emceeing a party in the Bronx in when he decided to extend a beat break in James Brown's "Sex Machine" by manipulating the songs on two turntables and improvise a rap over it. Herc's brain wave would have earth-shaking effects in the next decade that would ultimately pose the most formidable challenge to guitar-based rock's domination of the pop scene.

DAVID BOWIE: *ALADDIN SANE*

On the platform heels of his space opera *Ziggy Stardust*, David Bowie abandoned storytelling and toughened up his rock and roll to make *Aladdin Sane*. Blowing out of the wings with his best Stones tribute, "Watch That Man," Bowie never lets up the intensity. The title track is both fussy and taut, creepy and gorgeous. He pumps amphetamines into "Let's Spend the Night Together"; makes "Drive In Saturday" rock's snakiest, sexiest fifties lampoon; and turns your head into a lottery hopper on the Diddley-esque "Panic in Detroit." Bowie works similar magic on the blues with "Cracked Actor" and "The Jean Genie."

Although this portrait of Bowie appears to be fairly simple aside from Pierre La Roche's elaborate makeup job, Bowie's manager, Tony Defries, schemed to make the dye transfer process as expensive as possible to ensure that RCA would promote the hell out of *Aladdin Sane*. In fact, it was allegedly the most expensive album cover ever made as of its release. Author's collection.

Much of the record's intensity steams off an unprecedented degree of creative sex. A year after Mick Jagger complained about impotence on "Rock's Off," Bowie is more than happy to take the phallic torch and thrust it into the future. On "Drive In Saturday," he eulogizes the old idol, playing the part of a postapocalyptic being who gets his mojo back watching old pornos and videos of a young Mick at work. Bowie updates "Let's Spend the Night Together" with additions more explicit than the Stones offered in 1967. Elsewhere are uncensored references to blow jobs, wanking, and picking up tricks, but they are mostly celebratory and never sleazy. *Aladdin Sane* is a great big, pansexual fuck fest, a *Rocky Horror Show* without the defusing irony, a record made for hip shaking and pelvic thrusting.

JOHN CALE: *PARIS 1919*

After Lou Reed booted John Cale from the Velvet Underground in 1968, Cale wasted little time getting on with his work, producing Nico's terrifying *The Marble Index* and the Stooges' landmark debut the following year. In 1970, he recorded his first solo album, a collaboration with minimalist composer Terry Riley that is heavy on long, instrumental, jazz-like pieces.

Church of Anthrax would not be issued until 1971, a year after Cale released *Vintage Violence*, a solo debut of relatively straightforward singer-songwriter material influenced by the Band. These two records—both interesting yet flawed—indicated that Cale's solo career would take a mercurial path, but neither hinted at the confidence and variety he'd achieve on 1973's *Paris 1919*.

Cale's third album is his most polished yet, with clear nods to such consummate pop craftsmen as Brian Wilson and Paul McCartney. *Paris 1919* is the album for people who thought *White Light/White Heat* was too scary, yet hints of the artist's less accessible tendencies are still evident in a thick Welsh accent that regularly skirts its intended notes and disturbed lyrics like "Ten murdered oranges bled on board a ship lend comedy to shame." Cale kicks up some dust on the glammy "Macbeth," but the rest of *Paris 1919* is elegant if unrestful. The dulcet "Hank Panky Nohow" is an expression of religious paranoia. The floating "Andalucia" is an aching tale of unrequited love. The chamber-pop title track is about the unresolved resolution of World War I. *Paris 1919* is a *Band on the Run* for the angsty intellectual.

GEORGE HARRISON: *LIVING IN THE MATERIAL WORLD*

George Harrison followed up the grand gesture of *All Things Must Pass* with another disc of religiosity but an increased degree of finger wagging and a relative paucity of his previous album's tremendous songcraft. Much of *Living in the Material World* resembles origami swans: plain paper folded prettily. "Give Me Love (Give Me Peace on Earth)" gave George another number one hit, but it's a flimsy song.

Substance comes in fits and starts. "Sue Me, Sue You Blues," a bitter relitigation of the Beatles' legal strife, has a cool, elliptical chord structure. The winding title track, the whispering "Be Here Now," and the swirling "Try Some Buy Some" may be George's best post-*ATMP* songs. Their placement among songs that never get going renders *Living in the Material World* a weak successor to the seventies' most majestic pop album.

ELTON JOHN: *GOODBYE YELLOW BRICK ROAD*

Although Elton John already made a perfectly cohesive, nearly conceptual LP with *Tumbleweed Connection*, *Goodbye Yellow Brick Road* still feels like his big bid for artistic credibility in the for- mat. It's an ambitious double LP that begins with a lengthy progressive suite and features a variety of styles in the "White Album" tradi- tion. Its commercial cred is mighty. *Goodbye Yellow Brick Road* became the sound track of late 1973 and early 1974, went to number one on album charts in several corners of the world (including the crucial American and British markets), and would sell more than 8 million units. Its artistic value is not quite as impressive.

The only thing that could have made this painting of Elton John in a satin jacket and platform heels more seventies is if he was giving Carroll O'Connor a piggy- back ride. Author's collection.

The cursory two weeks John spent working on this hefty project shows in the fluff scat- tered liberally throughout the two discs and clumped on dispensable side C. The proggy "Funeral for a Friend" is comparatively overcooked, but when it pours over into the bopping pop of "Loves Lies Bleeding," Elton is in his usual terri- tory and navigating it with his usual deftness. The best-known songs are the best—the Beatlesque title song, the Who-esque "Saturday Night's Alright for Fighting," the moody "Harmony," and glammy "Bennie and the Jets"— but a few of the more obscure numbers, like "This Song Has No Title" and "Grey Seal," are also excellent. "Candle in the Wind" isn't because its kitsch is not the fun variety that makes the album's upbeat pastiches so kicky.

THE KINKS: *PRESERVATION ACT I*

Ray Davies had been planning to turn *The Kinks Are the Village Green Preservation Society* into a sprawling, ambitious production with a proper story line since its inception back in 1968. In the mid-seventies, he finally brought that dream into being, though there isn't any discernible plot in *Act I.* The scene is set with the wordless "Morning Song," which wanders into "Daylight." Okay, so we're on the Village Green. Now let's meet some of its locals. The tramp who'll serve as our guide laments unrequited love on "Sweet Lady Genevieve" and the changing face of his community and world on "Where Are They Now?" He expresses contentment with his freedom on "Sitting in the Midday Sun." We meet Johnny Thunder, the rock and roll rebel without a cause of "One of the Survivors" (the one holdover from *Village Green Preservation Society*), and "Money & Corruption/I Am Your

Man" and "Here Comes Flash" introduce the villains of the piece: a fascistic moral-majority leader and a ruthless real estate developer (characters who should be recognizable to anyone aware of twenty-first-century politics). By the time we get to "Demolition," we're only beginning to get a taste of the municipal topics that will be the plot's main idea. Then *Act I* is over.

Because it's all introduction with precious little plot, *Preservation Act I* can focus on the things we actually want to hear on a record: good songs. And contrary to popular opinion, most of the songs on this album are excellent. The same cannot be said of two LPs worth of *Act II*, which gets deeper into storytelling and largely abandons Ray Davies's specialty of penning perfect, concise, stand-alone pop songs (there are still a few terrific tracks in "Artificial Man," "Money Talks," and "Mirror of Love"). The poor reputation of *Act I* stems mostly from its failure to deliver a proper plot and its link to an inferior second act. A couple of tracks are pretty weak. "Money & Corruption/I Am Your Man" is one of the few pieces that emphasize storytelling over listenable songwriting, but how anyone can resist "Daylight," "Sweet Lady Genevieve," and "Where Are they Now?" is beyond me.

I'm more understanding of anyone who can resist much of what the Kinks did after *Preservation Act I*. The band meandered through several albums that placed more emphasis on concepts than the perfectly crafted songs that made their best conceptual works so wonderful. When that reached a dead end, the Kinks further misjudged their legacy by apparently assuming their earliest work was their most important, and when Van Halen got their first chart hit by covering "You Really Got Me," the Kinks attempted to compete with the heavy-metal crowd with bigger riffs and shoutier singing. The Davies brothers' talent was strong enough that they could still create some truly beguiling work—the epic "Artificial Man," the bittersweet "Come Dancing," the simply sweet "Better Days," the ominous "Living on a Thin Line"—but they never made another album as strong as *Preservation Act I*.

LED ZEPPELIN: *HOUSES OF THE HOLY*

Houses of the Holy tends to get overshadowed by Led Zeppelin's pummeling debut, their classic-riddled fourth album, and the glut of treasures on two discs of *Physical Graffiti*. But if I were going to play a nonfan their first Zeppelin album, I'd reach for *Houses of the Holy*.

While so many of the band's albums are forged in grays and blacks, *Houses* is totally Technicolor. Only with the Floydian keyboard drones of

"No Quarter" does Zeppelin exploit their menace. Otherwise, the album is playful as a puppy. Maybe that's not what you want from your heavy-metal bands, but Led Zeppelin was always too eclectic to store in any labeled drawer. That eclecticism gets full airing on their fifth album. We bounce from the twelve-string gallop of "The Song Remains the Same" to the dramatic romance of "The Rain Song," and if your heart doesn't melt when John Paul Jones starts leaning on his Mellotron and your head doesn't bang when John Bonham finally wallops his kit, you may have been born without a heart and a head.

Then it's on to the Ren-Faire folk/metal composite of "Over the Hills and Far Away" to the freaky funk parody "The Crunge" to the seasonal pop exuberance of "Dancing Days" to the daffy reggae "D'yer Mak'er" to the sinister "No Quarter" to the classic Zep riffing of "The Ocean." No two styles are alike.

Although a couple of the tracks are throwaways, only the plodding and overlong "D'yer Mak'er" doesn't really work. Everything else is a smash, and Zeppelin sounds like they had a blast making such varied, jovial music. They made records that were weightier, scarier, and more serious. Led Zeppelin is known for all those things. They are not usually thought of as fun. *Houses of the Holy* is exhibit A that they were.

JOHN LENNON: *MIND GAMES*

After a challenging opening trio of records, John Lennon once again did the unexpected by making a poppy, jolly, melodious record worthy of old partner Paul. Perhaps *Mind Games* is a response to the critical drubbing and commercial indifference that greeted *Some Time in New York City*. With its polarizing content and an accompanying single with a title that could not be uttered on mainstream radio, that album was Lennon's first proper solo album to miss the top forty. *Mind Games* brought him back with a respectable top-twenty single and a bunch of other songs that would have sounded just as good on radio alongside Ringo's "Photograph" and Paul's "Helen Wheels."

However, Lennon seemed to catch the wave of Beatle backlash that had been slapping Paul since the start of his solo career. Critics expressed lukewarm support for his renewed poppiness at best and disgust with his peace and love sloganeering and lack of focus at worst.

Mind Games works best as a well-crafted look back on Lennon's most accessible phases. He revisits his psych days with the title track, plays the retro rocker with "Tight A$," the sensitive jealous guy with "Aisumasen (I'm Sorry)," the love-struck puppy with "One Day (At a Time)," the Spectorian rocker with "Bring on the Lucie (Freda Peeple)," and the pure popper with "Intuition." These are not Lennon's most insightful songs, but they're neither more facile nor more unsatisfying than the ones that would finally pull Paul back into critical favor.

PAUL MCCARTNEY AND WINGS: *BAND ON THE RUN*

When Paul McCartney started his solo career with a modest, homemade collection of knickknacks called *McCartney*, taking pot shots at him became the critic's favorite sport of the seventies. Granted, a lot of his records fell well short of Paul's big talent. That he could put out five minutes of smarmy "whoa-whoa-whoaing" and get a number one with it nearly justifies the hate. But some great music got lost in the anti-Paul frenzy, and the critics' knee-jerk condemnation of *Ram* was totally undeserved.

Even the most blinkered critics had to reassess their stance when Paul McCartney and his new group Wings released *Band on the Run*. It is a reminder of what he did so well when he was in the Beatles. He never had John Lennon's introspective reputation, so pointing out the trivial lyricism isn't really relevant. Paul's talent is his innate melodicism and ability to assimilate and own a wide variety of pop forms, from the trad balladry of "Yesterday" to the skull-crushing screech of "Helter Skelter." He gets similarly eclectic on *Band on the Run*, often using Beatles' classics as blueprints for his new material. The title track is a mini–*Abbey Road* medley. "Bluebird" revives the acoustic sounds and liberating aviary themes of "Blackbird." "Mamunia" revisits themes John explored in "Rain." With "Mrs. Vanderbilt," Paul goes on a "Bungalow Bill" safari. "Helen Wheels" falls in the tradition of great McCartney rockers from "I Saw Her Standing There" to "Back in the U.S.S.R.," and "Picasso's Last Words (Drink to Me)" even recalls the most far-out Beatles tracks, toying with the mantra of "You Know My Name (Look Up the Number)" and the sound collage of "Revolution 9." Most touchingly of all, he pays homage to his former partner's solo career. When John Lennon, Paul's harshest critic, gave his approval of "Let Me Roll It," that must have validated Paul more than all the praise all the critics laid on *Band on the Run*.

MOTT THE HOOPLE: *MOTT*

Mott the Hoople were rock and roll traditionalists at a time when progressiveness was paramount. The ultimate expression of their love of Chuck Berry and Jerry Lee Lewis is their penultimate album. Bouncing off the success of "All the Young Dudes," the David Bowie–penned title track of their previous record, Mott made an album of material worthy of that smash hit. Bowie's influence is very present in the album's best tracks: "All the Way from Memphis," "Whizz Kid," "Honaloochie Boogie," "Hymn for the Dudes," "Ballad of Mott the Hoople." Mott's heavier leanings bully to the fore on "Violence."

Mott the Hoople was also very self-aware and very witty, and *Mott* is early proof that punk attitude and intelligence are not mutually exclusive. "I Wish I Was Your Mother" proves that attitude and aching beauty are not mutually exclusive either.

NEW YORK DOLLS: *NEW YORK DOLLS*

They looked like a glam parody with their outfits that made Bowie and Bolan look conservative. David Johansen's pouting and strutting and Johnny Thunders and Syl Sylvain's guitar weaving suggested they could be a goof on the Stones. They quoted early sixties girl groups, covered Bo Diddley, and sang about sanitation problems and kissing. They were so extreme in their presentation and out of step with their highfalutin times that the New York Dolls were often mistaken for a straight-up joke band. When a whole generation of punks took them dead seriously, those five big-haired clowns had the last laugh.

However, *New York Dolls* should not be reduced to its role in inspiring punks. The New York Dolls' debut album doesn't necessarily deliver what a rube expects to hear on a punk album: it's groovy, funny, and almost quaint in its mythologizing of New York City's subways, drugs, and monsters. You won't hear historical significance when you spin it today—you'll hear songs that will

Just three years after Mercury Records got cold feet about putting out Bowie's *The Man Who Sold the World* in a sleeve depicting him in a dress, Mercury OK'ed this sleeve showing all five members of New York Dolls in lipstick and high heels. That's progress. Author's collection.

make you want to dance, smash, and make out. You'll want to do everything the wildest Little Richard records make you want to do. You'll want to rock and roll.

PINK FLOYD: *THE DARK SIDE OF THE MOON*

After Syd Barrett drifted off, Pink Floyd made some interesting records that often seemed more like sketchbooks than novels. While *Piper at the Gates of Dawn* and, to a certain degree, the mostly Syd-less *A Saucerful of Secrets* were satisfying, records such as *Ummagumma* and *Atom Heart Mother* were unfocused experiments. *Meddle* lost the plot with the long, boring "Echoes." *More* and *Obscured by Clouds* had a lot of good songs, but their roles as movie sound tracks made a good share of filler inevitable. However, Pink Floyd was working toward something this whole time and something very different from their Syd-era successes.

In 1973, all of their meandering sound experiments stopped meandering; all of their shapeless musical ideas took shape. Pink Floyd were richly rewarded when *The Dark Side of the Moon* became the biggest album in the solar system. It is a pretty strange record to achieve such popularity. It's almost more like a movie than an album with its orienting and disorienting sound effects, the-matic unity, carefully organized moods, and

The Super Audio Compact Disc (SACD) edition of *Dark Side* replaces the plain black background of Hipgnosis' iconic original cover with a photo of trees. The SACD was supposed to offer vastly improved fidelity over the standard CD, but frankly, I could never tell the difference. Author's collection.

seamlessness. Or maybe it's more like an album than any other album. When all is said and done, *Sgt. Pepper's* and *Tommy* work because they are collections of great songs, not because they're "concept albums" or "rock operas." You could isolate "Lucy in the Sky with Diamonds" or "Pinball Wizard," and they'd still make great pop singles. Singles were pulled from *Dark Side*, but the album needs to be heard as a single piece to hear how the chilling "On the Run" or the devastating "Great Gig in the Sky" function in the whole. *Dark Side* does have some great stand-alone songs. "Time," "Money," "Us and Them," and "Breathe" are some of the band's best, but even those need their surroundings to be fully effective. You need to hear how ingeniously yet succinctly Roger Waters boils down the factors that leave us all "hanging on in quiet desperation": the too-swift passage of time, the lust for monetary gain, the fear of otherness, the inability to simply take a moment to "breathe in the air." In essence, *The Dark Side of the Moon* is such a great and greatly appreciated album because it makes the most of its medium.

PROCOL HARUM: *GRAND HOTEL*

Procol Harum had undergone a major change between 1971's *Broken Barricades* and 1973's *Grand Hotel* when Robin Trower went solo. Losing a key member can derail a band, or it can give it a fresh lease. The latter seems to be the case for Procol Harum, as *Grand Hotel* erases many of the previous album's issues, which included meandering music and some of Keith Reid's most impenetrably pretentious lyrics.

For some fans who got off on Procol's goth poetry and persona, *Grand Hotel* will be too earthbound. Songs about breaking up with a girlfriend, eating dumplings, or getting the clap are beneath the band's usual imagination. Yet all the tracks are very good, and the production is majestic enough to elevate a song about how awesome it is to stay in a ritzy hotel above its vacuous topic. Following the successful *Live in Concert with the Edmonton Symphony Orchestra*, Procol continue working orchestral and choral parts into their arrangements, which provide a grandeur that balances the mundane lyricism.

Toward the end, Reid gets on more familiar ground with the chilling death tale "For Liquorice John," the futile war song "Fires (Which Burn Bright)" (with its haunting guest vocal from Christianne Legrand), and the pain-wracked "Robert's Box." Extra points for getting a choir to sing a line as goofy as "TV Caesar, Mighty Mouse, gets the vote in every house."

THE ROLLING STONES: *GOATS HEAD SOUP*

While the critics were cutting McCartney a break, they were getting out their razors for a band that usually got a pass. In 1980, the Rolling Stones' *Goats Head Soup* got a one-star review in *The New Rolling Stone Record Guide*. That's pretty excessive. The record may not measure up to the Stones' lauded streak from *Beggars Banquet* to *Exile*, but how long can any group keep up that kind of momentum? *Goats Head Soup* was criticized for its muddy sound and the way the band seemed to be trading in legit menace for straight-up posing. Comparing the cardboard Halloween decorations of "Dancing with Mr. D." to the epic intensity of "Sympathy for the Devil" is like pitting Cheetah the Chimp against King Kong. So what? There is too much good stuff on *Goats Head Soup* to dismiss it so completely (*one star!*). What "Dancing with Mr. D." lacks in convincing evil it makes up for with a gnarly riff and an enthralling Charlie Watts groove. Some of the band's best ballads are here: Keith's junkie valentine "Coming Down Again," the spellbinding tone poem "Winter," and "Angie," a good hit that skirts MOR territory more effectively than "Fool to Cry" would a couple of albums down the road. "Silver Train" is a first-rate Chuck Berry boogie with a slippery bass line. "Star Star" (a litany of groupie abuse originally titled "Starfucker") is mindless vulgarity, "Hide Your Love" is filler, and "Can You Hear the Music?" is a caterwauling attempt to recapture the psych alchemy of *Their Satanic Majesties Request*, but the overall murk is something to sink into rather than shower off. *Goats Head Soup*'s greatest crime is its failure to be as good as *Beggars Banquet* or *Exile on Main Street*. If every album were held up to such standards, there'd be a hell of a lot more one-star reviews.

JUDEE SILL: *HEART FOOD*

On her second album, 1973's *Heart Food*, Judee Sill taps into her troubled experiences more effectively with countryish arrangements that place her work in that genre's tradition of hard living. There are more of the grand string arrangements that were a highlight of *Judee Sill*. Most importantly, Sill lets down her guard in front of the mic. Her voice's fine quality is still very present, but by allowing it to droop into audible despair, to soar, and to bend and even crack, she creates an emotional experience rather than the merely pleasant one her first album was. The most explicitly religious thing here is an epic called "The Donor," yet it is so breathtaking that even we heathens can dig it. There's nothing as recognizable as "Jesus Was a Cross-Maker" or "Lady-O" on *Heart Food*, but it is most definitely the superior album.

RINGO STARR: *RINGO*

The reports of Ringo Starr's luck are greatly exaggerated. He wasn't some half talent along for the Beatlemania ride, as his most heartless and clueless critics insist. His solid backbeat was essential to holding the band together, and his quirky way with a drum fill was as essential to the Beatles' distinctive sound as George's ringing twelve-string or Paul's leaping bass lines.

However, there is no question that Ringo would not have had a career as a solo artist if not for his old band. While Ringo-led tracks such as "Yellow Submarine," "With a Little Help from My Friends," and "Octopus' Garden" are much more than novelty spots for the goofily charming drummer, one doesn't hear these classics and think, "Gee, this guy needs a whole album to himself."

Ringo didn't either, and when he made his first rock record in 1973 (after testing out the solo waters with platters of standards and C&W tunes), he received more than a little help from his friends. *Ringo* is

Ringo was definitely playing on fan's fond feelings for his old band when he put together his biggest album. Not only do all three of the other ex-Beatles join him on the record, but their likenesses also appear in the crowd scene on the cover, which obviously strives for a *Sgt. Pepper's* feel. Author's collection.

the only post-Beatles album that features all four Beatles, though they never work together. John Lennon supplies the cheeky "I'm the Greatest," and Paul McCartney contributes the dusky, restrained ballad "Six O'Clock," but Ringo found his most sympathetic collaborator in his fellow second banana. While "I'm the Greatest" is lively and tuneful but essentially a comedy number and "Six O'Clock" is fine but not up to the level of the material McCartney was making in 1973, "Photograph" and "Sunshine Life for Me (Sail Away Raymond)" are top-shelf George Harrison. They outshine anything George did after *All Things Must Pass*. "Photograph" is not just a great-for-Ringo track; it's one of the best tracks of the seventies, and it probably made Phil Spector more than a little green.

Nothing else on *Ringo* reaches the heart-tugging heights of "Photograph," but almost all of it is good. The only blunder is Ringo and new songwriting collaborator Vini Poncia's attempt to give the star some sort of bad-boy image with the mindless and misogynistic hard-rock tedium of "Devil Woman." Otherwise, the production earned its grand success.

THE STOOGES: *RAW POWER*

While acolytes of Dylan and the Band were "getting it together in the country" in the late sixties, the Stooges were stuck in Ann Arbor, Michigan, which was anything but a rustic retreat. In sharp contrast to the good-timing country-rock sounds of 1969, *The Stooges* was urban, angry, muscular, lean, and scary. So was Iggy Pop. His Jim-Morrison-to-the-lewdest-extreme persona found its ultimate expression in the Stooges' third album. *Raw Power* is loud, abrasive, and violent. It also has the best songs on any Stooges record. "Search and Destroy" sets out the nihilism, directionless hostility, and loudness of punk better than any song before it. "Shake Appeal" delivers punk's speed and "Your Pretty Face Is Going to Hell" its cacophony.

Raw Power isn't just unrestrained noise, though. There is shade and texture in the acoustic guitars of the seductive "Gimme Danger" and David Bowie's tinkly electric piano on "Penetration." "I Need Somebody" brings the tempo down to a bluesy bump and grind. In this way, *Raw Power* also presages punk, which was always more eclectic and creative than its ostrich-headed critics would ever admit.

THE WHO: *QUADROPHENIA*

It took a lot of ingredients to stew 1973's rock scene: the conceptualism of *Preservation Act I*, the grandeur of *Grand Hotel*, the immersive murk of *Goats Head Soup*, the craftsmanship of *Band on the Run* and *Paris 1919*, the synthesized futurism of *Innervisions*, the intensity of *Aladdin Sane*, the pure *album-ness* of *The Dark Side of the Moon*. All of those raw elements coalesce on the year's defining record. Its topic, however, spins the clock back a decade to a time when gangs of nattily attired mods roamed the Earth.

In truth, the mod angle is just window dressing—an excuse for Pete Townshend to reexamine his favorite themes: youth, identity, individuality, and spirituality. As has often been said, the sprawling and complex *Quadrophenia* couldn't sound less like the lean R&B the mods fancied. Although the songs are generally more accessible and work better on their own the ones on *The Dark Side of the Moon*, *Quadrophenia* is denser and requires more work to get into and digest, but it is rewarding work. Jimmy the Mod's journey is all our journeys: sorting out who we are and what we believe. Consequently, *Quadrophenia* is the Who's most emotionally engaging and human concept even as the banks of synthesizers make much of it sound unearthly. Sift through the synths and uncover an embarrassment of wonderful songs: "The Punk and the Godfather," "I'm One," "The Dirty Jobs," "5:15," "Drowned," "Bell Boy," "Love Reign O'er Me."

Quadrophenia has often been described as more of a Pete Townshend solo album than a proper Who record, but each member of the band makes tremendous contributions. Roger's performance has sometimes been criticized as tone-deaf bluster. His nuanced readings of "Love Reign O'er Me," "Doctor Jimmy," "Is It in My Head," "I've Had Enough," and "Sea and Sand" annihilate that complaint. Keith Moon's drumming is at its stormiest, and on "Bell Boy," he turns in a vocal that could actually be called sensitive. The MVP is John Entwistle, who painstakingly overdubbed the brass parts and whose bass playing finally achieves the full expressiveness across an entire record that he always allowed it onstage.

If *Quadrophenia* lacks one thing, it's fun, which is why I'll never spin it as much as *Sell Out* or *A Quick One* or even *Who's Next*. It is a record that demands time and attention and a particular mood, but it has never been bettered as proof of something Pete Townshend was telling us since the beginning of his career: rock and roll can be serious art.

STEVIE WONDER: *INNERVISIONS*

Innervisions lands on the perfect middle ground between the lengthy experiments of *Music of My Mind* and the sharper pop sensibilities of *Talking Book*. While there isn't a hit here as arousing as "Superstition" or a ballad as perfect as "Superwoman," it is Stevie Wonder's most consistent album. Only "All in Love Is Fair" is a bit of a sappy error in taste. The rest of *Innervisions* puts all of his strengths on display: his fusion ("Too High") and hard funk ("Higher Ground"), his psychedelic mindscapes ("Visions"), his pop ("He's Misstra Know It All") and Latin ("Don't You Worry 'Bout a Thing") leanings.

Artist Effram Wolff literalized the title of *Innervisions*. Author's collection.

The record is also a huge leap forward for Wonder's lyrical and formal skills as he moves away from the mystical love songs that led his last few discs. He digs into an antidrug public service announcement, a criticism of the Nixon administration (his first, not his final), and, in one of his most perfect and ambitious creations, racism in the American justice system. *Innervisions* would be a great album if it contained only seven high-drama minutes of "Living for the City." That Stevie made this aural movie as a one-man band makes it an almost ostentatious display of talent. If I had talent like that, I'd be flaunting it too.

1974

The first four years of the seventies were all fine for rock and roll. Perhaps they lacked some of the color and imagination of the sixties' span from 1966 through 1968, but with groundbreaking albums such as *All Things Must Pass, Who's Next, Exile on Main Street, There's a Riot Going On, Innervisions, Ziggy Stardust, Quadrophenia, The Dark Side of the Moon,* and Led Zeppelin's untitled fourth album, there were still a lot of exciting new things coming from rock's old guard.

Then came 1974. Precisely one decade after the British Invasion broke, its original invaders, who'd been carrying the seventies so far, all seemed to flag in unison. We can excuse those who didn't put out any new product that year (Led Zeppelin, the Who, McCartney). Those who did were not offering up their best work. The Rolling Stones released an album on which they seemed exasperated with having to put forth the idea that rock and roll still means something. David Bowie reached a conceptual dead end with *Diamond Dogs*, which included a couple of first-rate ersatz Stones songs (the title track and "Rebel Rebel") and a fair share of barely listenable music. Stevie Wonder, who was in the midst of a string of triumphs, put out his one boring one. That *Fulfillingness' First Finale* was still one of the year's best exemplifies the quality dip plaguing 1974. The drowsy tones of the Eagles, Jackson Browne, and Linda Ronstadt drifting from the American West Coast set the tone for rock's blandest year since the pre–British Invasion days.

Yet that quality dip is important because it gives the music history books a convenient point to preach the necessity of the punk movement that would inject fresh adrenaline into rock and roll in a couple of years. So does the preponderance of soft pap clogging the airwaves (Barbara Streisand's "The Way We Were," Terry Jacks's "Seasons in the Sun," John Denver's "Sunshine on My Shoulders," Ray Stevens's "The Streak," Olivia Newton-John's "I Honestly Love You," etc.) which really served as the sound track of 1974.

The year 1974 is also notable as the one in which disco came into force. In the early seventies, the funky dance beats that James Brown and Sly Stone pioneered tightened up to a four-on-the-floor bass drum beat and found a welcome home in urban clubs. People of all races, colors, sexualities, and economic classes soon found common ground dancing the nights away to Thelma Houston, Gloria Gaynor, Boney M., KC and the Sunshine Band, and other disco artists in jammed joints like Studio 54 (New York City), Studio One (Los Angeles), and The Pier (Washington, D.C.). Gloria Gaynor had the first disco song to go to number one on the American charts, a cover of the Jackson Five's "Never Can Say Goodbye," in November 1974.

Hard-core rock fans made a big show of how much they hated disco, missing the common ground their most reviled genre shared with John Bonham's heavy metronomic beats, Chuck Berry's celebration of class-free freedom, and Little Richard's flashiness and love of nonsensical catchphrases. Sexism, racism, and homophobia played no small role in rockers' hatred of a form of music that attracted such a diverse audience—an audience that included many of their very own idols. The Rolling Stones, Paul McCartney, Blondie, Rod Stewart, the Grateful Dead, Kiss, Queen, and the Kinks are just a few of the rock bands that would eventually dabble in disco, but few of them did anything that interesting in 1974.

Coincidentally, the year also saw the debut of *Goldmine*, a magazine ideal for record collectors frustrated with rock's present. In the pages of Brian Bukantis's monthly periodical, they could read up on collectible albums in various articles, interviews, and well-researched discographies, while audiophiles could obsess about the best-sounding pressings of particular albums. The magazine also established a system for grading used records—near mint (NM), very good (VG), poor (P), and so on—that sellers and buyers still use today on websites such as eBay, Discogs, and MusicStack. Other publications, such as *Record Collector* (founded in 1979), *Ugly Things* (1983), *DISCoveries* (1988), and *Mojo* (1993), would also cater to we geeks who often choose to look back rather than face the kind of dispiriting present rock fans faced in 1974.

BIG STAR: *RADIO CITY*

When self-consciousness was monopolizing the rock scene with complex prog and everyday-is-Halloween glam in 1972, Big Star responded with *#1 Record*, which revels in Beatlesque harmony and early Stones raunch. It doesn't have a song longer than four and a half minutes. Alex Chilton was more ambitious than that. He's running the show on *Radio City* after the departure of the more committedly pop-savvy Chris Bell and indulging in some of his stranger whims. The perfection of *#1 Record* is starting to unglue with the rambling epic "O My Soul," the shambling beat and off-key harmonica of "Life Is White," the creepy crawling "Daisy Glaze," and the unsettling and rough solo pieces that close the album.

Radio City also includes some of Big Star's most perfect moments, such as the woozy ballad "What's Going Ahn," the rolling "You Get What You Deserve," the Stonesy "Mod Lang," and the *Revolver*-esque "She's a Mover." That perfection comes to an enraptured head with "September Gurls," the decade's most heartbreaking piece of power pop. *Radio City*'s collision of sloppy experimentation and superbly crafted pop is its charm. Chilton would lose his handle on that latter element with Big Star's next and final album, *Third/Sister Lovers*.

JOHN CALE: *FEAR*

Fear boasts more of the pro-quality songwriting and eclectic style of *Paris 1919*, but it draws back some of the old grit and crazed excitement from John Cale's days with the Velvet Underground. "Fear Is a Man's Best Friend" starts off as a Bowie-like torch song before climaxing with frenzied bass noise and paranoid primal shrieks. It's scary stuff and a sharp contrast to the measured, choral beauty of "Buffalo Ballet." Reggae rhythm lays the base of "Barracuda," but Cale provides the hooks with his mumbled melody, circusy organ fills, and screechy viola solo. "Emily" is an expansive, gorgeous ballad, and like "Buffalo Ballet," "Barracuda," and the soulful "You Know More Than I Know," it makes tasteful use of backing singers. "Ships of Fools" is dizzy and romantic with a sparkling arrangement that conceals a creepy goth lyric. "The Man Who Couldn't Afford to Orgy" is as funny as its title. Critics tend to compare it to the Beach Boys, although to my ears, it sounds like a lift of Van Morrison's "Straight to Your Heart (Like a Cannonball)." The album's centerpiece is the eight-minute stomp "Gun," a sweaty-palmed tale of a criminal on the run. Lou Reed may have gotten all the press with his solo career, but I've never heard him do anything on his own as accomplished as *Fear*.

GENESIS: *THE LAMB LIES DOWN ON BROADWAY*

Yes and King Crimson were the first bands to make it big with prog rock, but neither realized the genre's full pretentious powers like Genesis. Yes and King Crimson devised unwieldy pieces but hadn't been linking those pieces to grander concepts. Their stage shows were the usual denim fests, and Yes actually had the gall to roll their eyes at key-boardist Rick Wakeman when he injected a little theatricality into the act by slipping into a spangly cape and stabbing his organ with a dagger. That was nothing compared to what Peter Gabriel was doing. Gabriel would conceive Genesis's "songs" as mini-dramas he'd act out onstage in bizarre alien headgear, fox masks, and daisy costumes.

The cover of *The Lamb Lies Down on Broadway* is just as comprehensible, unpretentious, and downright homespun as the music within it. Author's collection.

Genesis's unwieldy prog rock and Gabriel's theatrical concepts gel on *The Lamb Lies Down on Broadway*. More power to you if you can figure out this double album's story line (something about a teenage delinquent going on an erotic Lewis Carroll adventure in the New York City underground), but the songs and sparkling musicianship ring through clearly. As a whole, *The Lambs Lies Down* is an overwhelming experience. What makes it go down easy is the plethora of powerful, concise songs, such as "Fly on a Windshield," "Carpet Crawlers," "It," the title track, and the devastating "Back in NYC." The latter two tracks make the most mesmerizing use of synthesizers on a rock album this side of the Who. Gabriel's voice is equally striking. He twists it physically and electronically to heighten the phantasmagoria of tracks such as "The Grand Parade of Lifeless P" and "The Colony of Slipperman."

GEORGE HARRISON: *DARK HORSE*

After the sprawling *All Things Must Pass* and the ponderous *Living in the Material World*, *Dark Horse* is George Harrison's first lightweight album, though it's not quite lighthearted. He pitches a bit of mud at ex-wife Pattie Boyd and her new beau Eric Clapton in a jerky cover of "Bye Bye Love" and confesses his own relapse into drinking and drugging on "Simply Shady." A bout of laryngitis undermines potentially pleasant songs as he yelps and strains his way through good tunes like "So Sad," "Maya Love," and "Far East Man" (a song Ron Wood would record to much better effect the same year). The holiday single "Ding Dong, Ding Dong" is brainless, and "Hari's on Tour (Express)" sounds like a seventies sitcom theme song, so *Dark Horse* would be an uneven album even if George were in his usual voice.

KING CRIMSON: *STARLESS AND BIBLE BLACK*

The Lamb Lies Down on Broadway delivers everything a prog fan could want: an indecipherable story line, audacious theatrics, puzzling time changes, plenty of Mellotron. King Crimson's *Starless and Bible Black* has those last two elements in spades, but it also has something that most typical prog records don't: fury. Prog is usually thought of as something to be listened to studiously while sitting cross-legged on the floor as incense burns on the bookshelf. *Starless and Bible Black* has its sedate moments: the exquisite, soul-stirring "The Night Watch" (an ode to Rembrandt that makes good on prog's academic reputation), the instrumental "Trio," and the first minute and a half of "Lament." But then that song becomes unhinged and starts thrashing around. The extended improvisations "Starless and Bible Black" and "Fracture" are heavy and cacophonous. King Crimson's most exhilarating track, "The Great Deceiver," is a barrage of high-power complications. Robert Fripp's riff sounds like a malfunctioning computer. Somehow, bassist John Wetton manages to lock in with him perfectly. We listeners hold on for dear life until it slams to a stop to let Wetton sneer the anticommercialism lyric. This is prog at its proggest *and* its punkest.

JOHN LENNON: *WALLS AND BRIDGES*

One might have expected John Lennon to crawl out of his infamous "Lost Weekend" period when he was separated from Yoko Ono and subsisting on a steady diet of drugs, booze, and partying with an act of self-inflicted brutality like *John Lennon/Plastic Ono Band*. Instead, he came up with a pop album even more commercial than *Mind Games*. "Bless You" and "#9

Dream" are two of the sweetest examples of John the Cosmic Romantic. His pain is apparent on intense songs such as "Going Down on Love," "Scared," "Steel and Glass," and "Nobody Loves You (When You're Down and Out)," but his production is so polished and rich that even a track that snarls "I'll scratch your back and you knife mine" sounds radio ready. Lennon did invade that often-elusive medium with his very first number one hit single. The conspicuous presence of superstar Elton John surely played no small role in helping the invigorating "Whatever Gets You Through the Night" top the charts.

The cover of *Walls and Bridges* features two flaps that fully reveal a drawing Lennon did at age 11 when folded out. Sliding the album onto the shelf without damaging those flaps is a real challenge. Author's collection.

VAN MORRISON: *VEEDON FLEECE*

In the years following Van Morrison's most audacious artistic statement, he occasionally revisited the extended structures and improvisations of *Astral Weeks* with pieces like "Listen to the Lion" on *St. Dominick's Preview* and "Autumn Song" on *Hard Nose the Highway*, but none of his seventies records recapture the mystical mood of *Astral Weeks* as firmly as *Veedon Fleece* does.

Much of the record barely qualifies as pop with its emphasis on misty folk and jazz. The meditative "Fair Play," the hushed "Come Here My Love" and "Country Fair, and the turbulent "You Don't Pull No Punches, but You Don't Push the River" would have fit in well on *Astral Weeks*. Morrison even lets his soul go wild on the poppier material like the flop single "Bulbs" and the cheery "Cul De Sac," which he tarts up with weird growls and primal screams before he resumes snorting like a pig rooting out truffles.

Van Morrison then went into recording retreat for three years, reemerging with the slicker sound of *A Period of Transition* and

Sixteen years after posing with a couple of dog models on the cover of *Veedon Fleece*, Van Morrison complained to *Rolling Stone* that people are always asking him if he still has the dogs. FYI, people: those are adults dogs on the cover and large dogs tend to live about 13 years, which means they were totally dead by 1990. Author's collection.

continuing in that manner for much of the rest of his career. That leaves *Veedon Fleece* as a worthy bookend companion to *Astral Weeks*, enclosing his most vital period.

PROCOL HARUM: *EXOTIC BIRDS AND FRUIT*

After their opening run of four brilliant albums, Procol Harum lost their focus with *Broken Barricades*. They started getting back on track with the fine *Grand Hotel* but didn't really regain their full powers until *Exotic Birds and Fruit*. It is a flawlessly crafted pop album replete with great songs and the most professional production of any of their albums thanks to Chris Thomas.

   Exotic Birds lacks the personality of Procol's earlier LPs but makes up for that with great material expertly performed. Whether rocking out ("Nothing but the Truth," the rescued early song "Monsieur R. Monde," "Butterfly Boys"), stretching beyond rock and roll (the Weil-esque "Beyond the Pale," the angular "Thin End of the Wedge"), joking around ("Fresh Fruit"), or recapturing the classic classical Procol sound ("New Lamps for Old"), the band gets it right every time. Their stately dignity is in full effect on "As Song as Samson." Gary Brooker is at his most soulful and sincere as he wails about the small man rising above an avalanche of lies puked down by preachers, racists, capitalists, and makers of war. Procol Harum would never make an album of such consistent quality again.

THE ROLLING STONES: *IT'S ONLY ROCK 'N ROLL*

After the critics hammered *Goats Head Soup* for its uneven songs and murkiness, the Stones dealt with one of those issues by cutting longtime producer Jimmy Miller loose. Although Miller was behind the band's best-loved albums (*Beggars Banquet* through *Exile on Main Street*), he'd lost the plot with *Goats Head*, and a heavy drug problem impeded his ability to continue working even at that iffy level.

   The first Rolling Stones production credited to "The Glimmer Twins" (i.e., Mick and Keith) benefits from a renewed clarity. Inconsistent song-writing continues to be an issue. Mick and Keith's lack of focus was certainly a factor, as the former seemed interested mainly in jet-setting, and the latter was deep into his own drug problems, which were finally seriously getting in the way of his music making. Mick attempted to make light of it all by declaring, "It's Only Rock 'n Roll," scoring his genre its most noncommittal anthem. Keith didn't even play on the track, which goes back to the old Chuck Berry well once again.

It's Only Rock 'n Roll is least interesting when the guys rest on their laurels like that. When testing their abilities with grungy reggae ("Luxury"), barrelhouse blues ("Short and Curlies"), Philly funk (the paranoid "Fingerprint File," which dances on a superb Mick Taylor bass line), or jazzy mood music (the epic, gorgeous, and disarmingly self-aware "Time Waits for No One," another jaw-dropping Taylor showcase), the Rolling Stones reveal that they haven't given up completely. Mick Taylor's failure to get cowriting credit on things like "Time Waits for No One" and "Till the Next Goodbye" would cause him to give up after *It's Only Rock 'n Roll*. A full commitment to self-parody was just around the corner.

ROXY MUSIC: *COUNTRY LIFE*

Bryan Ferry was the pop star Mick Jagger couldn't bring himself to be in 1974. While Mick tried to keep up his guttersnipe image despite spending most of his time rubbing elbows with the upper crust, Ferry had no qualms about presenting himself as a tuxedoed, martini sipping, posh-o. With Roxy Music, Ferry also made the kind of on-edge, forward-thrust rock and roll Jagger knew was slipping beyond his reach. There are no Chuck Berry clichés on *Country Life*, though "The Thrill of It All" and "All I Want Is You" have all the momentum of "Too Much Monkey Business." *Country Life* is a heady mélange of sounds archaic (the medieval "Triptych"), traditional (the swinging "If It Takes All Night"), futuristic (the new-wavy "Out of the Blue"), and shockingly unlikely (the Kurt Weil–esque nightmare "Bitter-Sweet").

This controversial—and let's face it, exploitative—photo of Constance Karoli and Eveline Grunwald (the sister and girlfriend of Can's Michael Karoli, respectively) caused Atco Records to pull out all the censorship stops. Original editions were covered in semi-opaque green shrink-wrap. Reissues removed the women all together and replaced them with the back cover image of greenery and nothing but greenery. Author's collection.

STEVIE WONDER: *FULFILLINGNESS' FIRST FINALE*

After two artistic statements equaled by few artists of his day, Stevie Wonder must have felt a bit fatigued when he made *Fulfillingness' First Finale*. Although the album was a huge commercial (Wonder's first to take *Billboard*'s top spot) and critical success (it won several Grammys, including album of the year, and has been included on many "essential albums" lists), it sounds like the saggy center of Stevie Wonder's most wonderful period to my ears. *Fulfillingness' First Finale* does not offer the uniformly memorable songs or variety that *Talking Book* and *Innervisions* did. The mood is dreary and too mellow, and the somewhat nondescript tracks tend to run together. The hit "You Haven't Done Nothin'," a condemnation of disgraced president Richard Nixon, is a rhythmic retread of "Superstition." Wonder's musicianship and voice are as moving as ever, but the only songs that really stand out are the peppy "Boogie On Reggae Woman" (not a reggae song) and the cool "Creepin'," featuring Minnie Ripperton's nice harmonies.

No worries, though. Wonder's loss of mojo was temporary and to be expected considering the amount of work he'd accomplished over the course of his career: an album or two nearly every single year since 1962. He would take his time making his next one and end up with his masterpiece.

RON WOOD: *I'VE GOT MY OWN ALBUM TO DO*

On the cusp of the collapse of the Faces and his recruitment into the Rolling Stones, Ron Wood went into the studio with a few buddies and a few bottles and cut a characteristically sloppy solo record. Surprisingly, *I've Got My Own Album to Do* is more than a bundle of drunken jams. "Am I Grooving You" may be a stupid lyric slapped onto a lazy guitar lick, and "Crotch Music" may marry a dumb title with dated funk-rock fusion, but this is an otherwise solid album. Wood duets with future fuehrer Mick Jagger on the rousing "I Can Feel the Fire" (it would turn even fierier during live performances with the Faces). "Far East Man," cowritten with George Harrison, is gorgeously reeling and an improvement on George's own poorly sung version. "Mystifies Me," on which Wood goes pipe to ravaged pipe with Rod Stewart, is a neat, ragged country love song. Stewart also boosts the Chuck Berry–style rocker "Take a Look at the Guy" and masks Wood's drunkenly tuneless delivery of "If You Gotta Make a Fool of Somebody," but this is still Wood's show all the way through. Few of the albums he'd make with the Stones would improve on it.

1975

The seventies really hit their doldrums at the midpoint. Many of the decade's best artists either sat out 1975 or produced mediocre work. David Bowie created a great title track and little else for *Young Americans*. Pink Floyd had never been as boring as their critics charged they were until they put out the lethargic, overrated *Wish You Were Here*. Some of the year's most popular discs—*Fleetwood Mac*, for instance—contained a few good buoys floating in a sea of filler. A lot of the year's best albums were merely good, though there were a few genuinely fabulous ones tucked in there too.

AEROSMITH: *TOYS IN THE ATTIC*

The Rolling Stones and Led Zeppelin are among rock and roll's grandest poseurs, heisting the acts (and, in Zep's case, the songs) of legit blues and soul artists and sprinting all the way to the bank. That doesn't mean they weren't awesome. Making their career by ripping off the Stones and Zeppelin, Aerosmith was never awesome, but they certainly sound close to it on *Toys in the Attic*. Turn off your inner critic (and your ability to comprehend lyrics), and you're likely to get duped by the sleazy, bluesy "Uncle Salty," grinding "Adam's Apple," and shimmery "No More No More." No delusion is necessary to dig the album's two great singles—the proto rap "Walk This

Way" and the writhing "Sweet Emotion." One would have to be comatose to not go a bit crazy when blasted with the title track.

JOHN CALE: *SLOW DAZZLE*

Between his twin pop knockouts *Paris 1919* and *Fear* and then *Helen of Troy*, a calculated emotional-meltdown record (he wears a straitjacket on the cover [subtle]), John Cale made *Slow Dazzle*, which bridges those two phases. On the one hand, you have polished pop such as "Taking It All Away," "Ski Patrol," and "I'm Not the Loving Kind"; on the other, you have the sheer insanity of the scatological "Guts," a mannered *"I'm craaaazy!"* cover of "Heartbreak Hotel," and "The Jeweler," a spoken-word nightmare about vagina eyes. Somewhere in the middle is "Mr. Wilson," a plea to Brian that freaked out King Beach Boy despite its apparent sincerity and clear majesty, and "Darling I Need You," a bubblegum stroll about a girl-friend who runs off to join the Snake Handlers. Inconsistency is an issue with *Slow Dazzle*, but when the record is at its best ("Mr. Wilson," "Guts," "Taking It All Away," "I'm Not the Loving Kind"), it confirms that Cale had the most formidable talent of any ex-Velvet.

BOB DYLAN: *BLOOD ON THE TRACKS*

Dylan spent the years following his 1966 motorcycle crash willfully chip-ping away at the unwieldy reputation he'd built during the earliest part of his career. Releasing the acoustic *John Wesley Harding* at the height of the psychedelic craze may have been an attempt to humble him-self. However, it ended up being just as influential as his earlier work, almost single-handedly derailing psychedelia and inspiring his peers to dig their acoustic guitars out of their attics. Dylan knocked himself off his unwanted pedestal more successfully with pleasantly flimsy works such as *Nashville Skyline* and *New Morning*. He nearly self-destructed completely with *Self Portrait*, a mess of covers that earned him the worst reviews of his career.

Dicking around for nearly a decade apparently had a restorative effect, and a tough divorce provided plenty of lyric material, so Dylan was ready to get back to serious work in late 1974 when he recorded *Blood on the Tracks*. Dylan's preference for allowing his words to do most of the work is an issue with *Blood on the Tracks*. The band's lackadaisical backing drains the life from the epics "Idiot Wind" and "Lily, Rosemary, and the Jack of Hearts." It also allows Dylan's lyrics to float to the surface, and they are his most inspired since *Blonde on Blonde* and his most personal since *Another Side*. When collaboration is not an issue, Dylan carries the full load with spellbinding intensity ("Simple Twist of Fate") and tear-jerking beauty ("Shelter from the Storm," "Buckets of Rain"). "Tangled Up in Blue" is such a good song that he could have recorded it with a quartet of kazoo players and it would still be a classic.

HEART: *DREAMBOAT ANNIE*

Sisters Ann and Nancy Wilson are the heart of Heart, one of the few bands that realize Led Zeppelin's folkiness is as integral to their greatness as all that heavy riffing is. On "Crazy on You," Nancy Wilson's nimble acoustic picking strikes the match the rest of the band builds to an inferno as Ann lets loose from the diaphragm. Its riff is as pungent as any of the Zeppelin ones that inspired it. The smash "Magic Man" is all metal electricity, and the Wilsons play shoreside sprites on the multiple iterations of the acoustic title track. The lavish "Soul of the Sea" is even more ambitious as it draws as much inspiration from "A Day in the Life" as it draws from "The Rain Song."

All of those songs are great, and all of them are bunched on side A of *Dreamboat Annie*. Side B lets the quality slip considerably as Heart supplies more hard rock but without the wit and more ballads but with an unwelcome sop sheen. Few albums segregate their strong and weak tracks so dramatically, which makes listening to *Dreamboat Annie* hassle-free. Play side A and slip it back into its sleeve.

ELTON JOHN: *CAPTAIN FANTASTIC AND THE BROWN DIRT COWBOY*

No one was as sure-handed with a pop single as Elton John was in the early seventies, but with rare exception, his albums are uneven. A third of his most championed LP, *Goodbye Yellow Brick Road*, is poor.

Well, writing pop classics isn't always easy, as Bernie Taupin makes clear on *Captain Fantastic and the Brown Dirt Cowboy*. That's not because the songs aren't good; this is definitely one of his and Elton's strongest collections. It's because those songs chronicle the tribulations of becoming the decade's most popular songwriting team. *Captain Fantastic* details Elton John and Bernie Taupin's rise from poverty (the title track, "Tell Me When the Whistle Blows," the wonderful light-operatic "Better Off Dead") through the arduous process of penning hits ("Bitter Fingers," "Writing") and trying to get some attention for their hard work ("Meal Ticket"). The album's centerpiece, "Someone Saved My Life Tonight," gets even more personal as Elton frees himself from a dishonest and likely disastrous heterosexual engagement and resolves to commit to his homosexuality and dreams of pop stardom. Grand hits such as this one made all the work he and Bernie detail on this album worthwhile.

Pop-artist Alan Aldrich was supposed to create one of his surreal and busy paintings for the cover of *Captain Fantastic and the Brown Dirt Cowboy*, but Elton John decided to go with this naturalistic picture of himself and a few friends instead. Author's collection.

LED ZEPPELIN: *PHYSICAL GRAFFITI*

Led Zeppelin had a slight quandary with their sixth album. They'd recorded a bit too much material for a single record and too little for a double. Not willing to weed out any of the fine stuff they'd cut, they went vault diving and came up with enough material to fill two LPs. The band ended up with a pretty messy album, but messiness has always been a fun quality of double albums from "The White Album" to *Mellon Collie and the Infinite Sadness*.

Physical Graffiti hangs together well enough because most of its songs don't call attention to the era in which they were recorded. Okay, we can suss that "Houses of the Holy" comes from sessions for the album of the same name and that "Bron-Yr-Aur" is a leftover from the *Led Zeppelin III* sessions since its title is the name of the cottage where

Physical Graffiti arrived in a unique single-pocket sleeve wide enough to house both LPs in their sturdy inner sleeves and an extra insert. Store the insert on the outside of the inner sleeves and the album's title appears in the die-cut windows on the cover. Store the insert between the inner sleeves and you'll see the likes of Page, Plant, Jones, Bonham, Liz Taylor, Buzz Aldrin, Lee Harvey Oswald, King Kong, and others through the windows. Author's collection.

Jimmy Page and Robert Plant composed that album's material. "Kashmir" and "In the Light" are similar enough in their looming majesty and employment of synthesizers that we can tell they hail from the same sessions. However, there's none of the fourth album's gloomy mysticism in blithe stuff like "Down by the Seaside" and "Boogie with Stu" or the back-porch folkiness of *III* in the pavement-demolishing "Rover." The newly recorded "In My Time of Dying" could have been on Zeppelin's first album. The ancient "Night Flight" is a boogie as fresh as the all-new "Trampled Under Foot."

In the great double-album tradition, contempt for cohesion is the controlling concept of *Physical Graffiti*, but isn't that Led Zeppelin's controlling concept too? Stripped bare/overproduced, bluesy/folky, romantic/lascivious, mystical/prurient, anguished/joyous, *Physical Graffiti* is a two-disc summation of everything that made Led Zeppelin awesome.

JOHN LENNON: *ROCK 'N' ROLL*

In 1973, mobbed-up music publisher Morris Levy took John Lennon to task for borrowing a bit of Chuck Berry's "Too Much Monkey Business" for his own "Come Together." In all fairness, there was no more similarity between the two songs than there had been between "You Can't Catch Me" and the Stooges' "1970" or other Berry classics and T. Rex's "Get It On," Queen's "Now I'm Here," the Beach Boys' "Fun, Fun, Fun," the Stones' "Star Star," and about a million other rock and roll songs that weren't subjected to similar suits. This one was settled out of court, and Lennon's penance was to record three other songs that Levy's Big Seven published for his next album. Lennon decided to turn the obligation into a concept and record an entire album of oldies with Phil Spector producing in 1973. Spector's erratic behavior and Lennon's alcoholism turned the sessions into chaos, and a car accident that put Spector into a coma put the whole project on indefinite hiatus, which angered Levy.

Lennon resumed work without Spector in 1974, and with no shortage of additional legal and ethical hassles, *Rock 'n' Roll* finally hit the shops in early 1975. The record is not as interesting as its messy history. Some of the covers are memorable—an impassioned "Stand by Me," a crazed "Rip It Up," a fuzzy and funky "Bony Moronie"—but versions of "Be-Bop-a-Lula," "Ya Ya," and "Do You Wanna Dance" are too polite. The bloated arrangements and excess of reggae and New Orleans blues rhythms render much of the record lethargic. On some tracks, such as "Sweet Little Sixteen," "Just Because," and "Bring It on Home," Lennon manages an intense vocal that either rises above the boring backing tracks or clashes with them—you decide. The opposite is true of "Peggy Sue," on which Lennon sounds unengaged with the roaring drums and guitars. And so the Beatles' most dedicated rocker sounded like he'd lost interest in rock and roll by sleep-walking through a disc of his favorite rock and roll classics. His five-year retirement that followed seemed to support this.

RUSH: *FLY BY NIGHT*

After passing themselves off as a sort of working-class Led Zeppelin on their nondescript first album, Rush got a new drummer who brought along a lot of the elements that would make them Canada's favorite three sons and one of rock's most worshipped bands. Not all of these things are great. Neil Peart's obsession with objectivist inhumanitarian Ayn Rand politicized the band in all the wrong ways. His obsession with Tolkien contributed to the cliché that prog is strictly for Dungeons & Dragons geeks. Still, the guy could play a set of drums. Plus, as hit or miss as his lyrics could be, they displayed a level of literacy and originality sorely lacking in the beer and partying belches of Rush's first record.

Fly by Night is a transitional album, which is why a lot of it sounds particularly fresh. While most of the lyrics are less lunkheaded than the ones on *Rush*, there's still a basic rock and roll drive to this record that would get lost when grand epics and high concepts took over. The title track is a power-pop treasure, and Alex Lifeson's Who-circa-1966 chords are what won me over after years of resisting those epic concepts and Geddy Lee's banshee squawk no matter how much my Rush-crazed friends worked to convert me. "Making Memories" is the kind of breezy folk-rock that Rush bashers would never expect the group could pull off. "Beneath, Between, Behind" hits nearly as hard as "Best I Can," which could almost pass for an AC/DC single.

Sometimes an album cover can affect the way you listen to an album. I only get in the mood to listen to *Fly By Night* in the winter because of its cover (well, because of the cover and "By-Tor and the Snow Dog"). Author's collection.

Some of the stuff doesn't land as well. "Anthem" suffers from some particularly ugly Rand-inspired lyrics and an amorphous tune. "By-Tor and the Snow Dog" is Rush's goofy first pass at a conceptual epic. "Rivendell" is strictly for elves. But *Fly by Night* is Rush's first album to really sound like Rush, and that should please people who like Rush. Plus, I should repeat, the new drummer really is quite good.

CARESS OF STEEL

Neil Peart was well integrated into the band when they made their third album. His obsessions with fantasy and long-form storytelling that brought us "By-Tor and the Snow Dog" would clearly be integral to the band's destiny. Unfortunately, he still hasn't learned the best way to channel those obsessions. Two cumbersome epics occupy the bulk of *Caress of Steel*, leaving room for only a scant three concise songs. These include "I Think I'm Going Bald," a generic blues-metal riff that at least shows Peart was willing to tackle unlikely topics (what other heavy-rock band would lament aging so early in their career?); "Bastille Day," a stronger opener than "Anthem" was on *Fly by Night* though still somewhat unformed; and the nostalgic "Lakeside Park," another terrific piece of pop in the tradition of the previous album's title track and by far the best thing on *Caress*.

The album's main problem is that Peart's desire to tell a story is a lot stronger than his willingness to tell one at this point. Both "The Necromancer" and "The Fountain of Lamneth" waste a lot of grooves describing journeys on which very little happens. There are musical moments worth hearing, such as Alex Lifeson's ominous arpeggios and backward guitar shrieks that begin "The Necromancer" and Geddy Lee's catchy "Bacchus Plateau" section from "Lamneth," but most of this rambling schmutz would never have gotten through quality control if it hadn't been thumbtacked to a larger concept. Peart must have realized this himself because he really buckled down when penning his next epic, making sure to compose a purposeful plot with a clear arc and a more assured tie to the baser joys of rock and roll than any of the fantasies on *Caress of Steel*.

PATTI SMITH: *HORSES*

There's nothing about Patti Smith's status as the creator of the punk era's first album that makes sense. Punk was all about no-bullshit blasts of high-velocity venom. Patti's songs are long, capricious, and audaciously pretentious syntheses of garage rock and Rimbaud-worshipping poetry. The punks were anathema to old-timer rock critics and vice versa. Patti had been a critic obsessed with old-timers like Dylan and Keith Richards. The punks were barely out of their teens. Patti was pushing thirty when *Horses* came out in late 1975.

But what else is that album but a signpost that things were changing? The Stones thought they were pushing boundaries with the ham-fisted shocks of "Brown Sugar" and "Star Star." They didn't dare take it to the level of "Land," a terrifying flight of fancy in which a high school boy leaves his body and floats to a paradise where "Land of 1,000

Patti Smith's best buddy Robert Mapplethorpe took the iconic photo on the cover of *Horses*. Author's collection.

Dances" plays on repeat while his schoolmates rape him. If there's another image that explains the transcendent powers of rock and roll more vividly and accurately, I have no idea what it is. And what is punk but a recapturing of rock and roll's purest powers? Patti captures those powers throughout *Horses*: disturbingly with "Land," joyously with "Redondo Beach" and "Kimberly," furiously with "Free Money," ecstatically with "Break It Up." Everyone loves to blab about how many people started bands after hearing *The Velvet Underground & Nico*, but I wonder how many started them after hearing *Horses*.

BRUCE SPRINGSTEEN: *BORN TO RUN*

It wouldn't be fair to say *Born to Run* came out of nowhere. Rock and roll traditionalist Bruce Springsteen started strongly with *Greetings from Asbury Park, NJ*, and found himself with the superb *The Wild, the Innocent, & the E Street Shuffle*. *Born to Run* really just continues that upward arch, yet there is something extra special about this record. Perhaps it's the genius use of Spector's Wall of Sound as a mold to shape his latest batch of material. Perhaps it's the excellence of that material or the giddiness with which boss and band perform it. This certainly isn't innovative music—not with the clear references to Spector, Van Morrison (whom Springsteen expertly mimics on the bridge of "Tenth Avenue Freeze-Out"), Dylan, Roy Orbison, Bo Diddley, and Buddy Holly. Yet by leaning on those grassroots influences, by apparently spinning *Meet the Beatles* more often than *Sgt. Pepper's*, Springsteen really did as much to pull rock and roll away from the artistes as the punks did. A lot of them probably considered him hopelessly uncool (though Joey Ramone was a huge fan). *Born to Run* still doesn't quite feel like a cool album, but that's only because shouting about how deeply in love you are, giggling while escaping your rut, and not wasting a second on calculated cynicism have never been cool.

VARIOUS ARTISTS: *THE ROCKY HORROR PICTURE SHOW* ORIGINAL SOUNDTRACK

Jim Sharman's version of Richard O'Brien's stage musical *The Rocky Horror Show* did not invent the midnight movie phenomenon (Jodorowsky's freak western *El Topo* did). It just defines it. Everyone knows the ideal way to watch *The Rocky Horror Picture Show* is at midnight with an audience of toilet tissue–tossing wackadoos in garter belts. Still Roger Ebert was exaggerating when he said that he could think of nothing less interesting than watching the movie at home alone.

The Rocky Horror Picture Show is a good fifteen minutes too long, but it actually holds up pretty well without the TP and toast. You'd have to look to John Waters's Dreamland crew to find another cast so completely willing to commit to such transgressive, plotless material. Brad (Barry Bostwick) and Janet (Susan Sarandon) are ultraconservative newlyweds whose consciousnesses are rocked after they're stranded at the gothic castle of Dr. Frank-N-Furter (Tim Curry), a mad scientist in sexy lingerie intent on building his very own bodybuilder (Peter Hinwood) for delectable purposes.

Rock musicals usually don't work because people like Andrew Lloyd Webber don't understand the simple, primal thrust of rock and roll. The *Rocky Horror Picture Show* is a rare exception because Richard O'Brien smartly chose super-theatrical glam rock as his reference point, and his story's sexual obsessions are all thrust. He also happens to be a terrific pop songwriter. I've always found "Touch-a, Touch-a, Touch-a, Touch Me" annoying, but nearly every other number is aces. The performances particularly contribute to the authenticity because most of the

Picture discs are usually the perfect gifts for people who like records that look slightly novel but could not care less about how they sound. This *Rocky Horror* picture disc reissue from 2020 actually sounds pretty good though. Author's collection.

singers aren't traditional musical-theater types. There's nothing un–rock and roll about O'Brien's Karloff croon and metal shriek or Little Nell's bubble-gum gnawing on the timeless "Time Warp."

Naturally, Tim Curry rules the motley roost as Dr. Frank-N-Furter. He draws all the Jaggered swagger out of "Sweet Transvestite" and makes the legit inspiring "Don't Dream It, Be It" tear-jerkingly gorgeous. Although an alien transsexual who tricks the two main characters into sex is not exactly the most positive LGBTQ role model, Frank-N-Furter's transgressiveness and self-acceptance gave many people who were otherwise unaccepted in mainstream society a great sense of empowerment. Midnight showings of his movie gave them a place to feel accepted, loved, and free to look and act however they wanted to look and act. The sound track album was like a booster shot for weekdays.

THE WHO: *THE WHO BY NUMBERS*

In his autobiography, Pete Townshend claims he wasn't particularly down in the dumps in 1975. Roger Daltrey just selected Townshend's most morose new material to sing, resulting in an album that has often been likened to a suicide note. That may be true, but it's really hard to not think the man was teetering on the edge when listening to *The Who by Numbers*. Song after song, Townshend rages about his own perceived irrelevance, inability to write anything new, hypocrisy, desperation, and alcoholism. In the context of this painful material, the singsongy sex joke "Squeeze Box" comes off as the ultimate act of cynicism, Townshend's idea of what it takes to get a hit single.

Each member of the Who got a shot at overseeing an album cover design in the seventies. After Pete Townshend handled *Quadrophenia* and Roger Daltrey took care of *Odds & Sods*, it was John Entwistle's turn to illustrate the jaunty connect-the-dots cartoon on the otherwise somber *The Who By Numbers*. Keith Moon was supposed to be in charge of *Who Are You*, but he couldn't be arsed. Author's collection.

The Who by Numbers is bleak indeed, but it is also inspirational because the band plays with such intensity. Keith Moon thunders with all his facilities intact for the last time. John Entwistle had never been so brilliant in the studio, nor would he ever be again, transforming tracks such as "However Much I Booze" and "Dreaming from the Waist" into showcases for his unparalleled musicianship. His "Success Story" is a pithy, funny history lesson that follows the Who from the days when they could only dream of buying houses for their mums to the present when the grind of touring and recording ("Take 276, you know this used to be fun") has worn away their enthusiasm for rock stardom. The song features the most enthusiastically merry performance on the album, with Entwistle whipping out Chuck Berry riffs on his eight-string bass, reviving his "Boris the Spider" voice to play the band's "fairy manager," and harmonizing with Townshend like a mischievous choirboy. Daltrey's singing is confident throughout, and he uses his full range to express all of the anger, self-pity, and defiance of Townshend's lyrics even if a lot of critics dismissed it all as bluster. Townshend's tapestry of guitars and wistful singing pull "However Much I Booze" back from dourness and make it breezy and the most extraordinary track on the album. On "Blue, Red, and Grey," he steps back from all the pain to view life with beautiful optimism. Apparently, Townshend managed to tap into that optimism well enough to survive, so *The Who by Numbers* wasn't a literal suicide note, but it is the Who's last great album.

WINGS: *VENUS AND MARS*

The critics started treating Paul McCartney more kindly when he released *Band on the Run*, a collection of well-crafted, well-produced, well-played songs. Although that record was credited to Paul McCartney and Wings, it was his most solitary album since his one-man-band debut. Credited just to Wings, his follow-up was his most collaborative to date and the first convincing evidence that Wings was more than a reaction against Paul's control-freak reputation.

Venus and Mars isn't as strong as *Band on the Run* but only partly because McCartney cedes some control to the lesser talents in his band. The only song the acknowledged leader didn't write is Jimmy McCulloch's so-so "just say no" blues "Medicine Jar." Paul handed his own "Spirits of Ancient Egypt" to Denny Laine (formerly of the Moody Blues), leaving that dedicated sideman to sing its idiotic lyrics. More conscientiously, he handled the album's worst offense, the saccharine and patronizing "Treat Her Gently," himself.

Much of the rest of the album rates among Wings' best. The title track is a mysterious and tuneful prelude to the arena-quaking "Rock Show." "Love in Song" is alluringly eerie. "You Gave Me the Answer" is a pleasing revival of Paul's love for quaint forties show tunes. The comic booking "Magneto and Titanium Man" is silly fun. "Listen to What the Man Said" is a catchy single with bubbly sax work from legit jazzman Tom Scott, and the soulful "Call Me Back Again" is one of the finest artifacts of the Wings years. McCartney's democratization of Wings gave him another big hit LP and was surely healthy for the band, but it would go too far on their next album.

NEIL YOUNG: *TONIGHT'S THE NIGHT*

Tonight's the Night is a bloodletting record in the tradition of *Plastic Ono Band*. While Lennon shook out his bad vibes by screaming his head off through some pretty punky tracks, Young keeps the mood dusky even when he sounds as though he's about to weep or vomit with grief. He had much to grieve over when cutting this unsettling album. He'd recently lost two friends—bandmate Danny Whitten and roadie Bruce Berry—to drug overdoses, and references to those tragedies give the album its shaky focus. Young is too much of a craftsman to allow his pain to carry the show, and as ramshackle as *Tonight's the Night* sounds, its songs are as sturdy as those on any of the guy's records. While there is an overall sense that thunderheads are gathering, the styles below are not uniform. Young stumbles from the after-hours piano blues of "Speakin' Out" to the sure-footed country thump of "World on a String" to "Borrowed Tune," a delicate ballad in the tradition of "Birds" and "After the Gold Rush," to the rocking "Come On Baby Let's Go Downtown" and beyond.

1976

Rock and roll was in dire shape by 1976. The best work of the genre's old guard—the Who, the Stones, the Kinks, the Beach Boys, the ex-Beatles—was behind them. Diana Ross, who did so much to make the Supremes one of the most effervescent groups of the sixties, was now smarming her way through the icky "Theme from 'Mahogany.'" Other crushingly dull soft poppers like Barry Manilow, the Captain and Tennille, and the revived likes of Paul Anka and Neil Sedaka were ruling radio. Newer bands sounded stale right out of the gate, and the tired riffing and wailing of faceless groups like Journey (who'd released their debut album in 1975), Boston (who released theirs in 1976), and Foreigner (who formed that year) inspired critics to coin the term "corporate rock." Rock had otherwise splintered into prog and disco, and both genres produced their share of classics, but that old unpolished, youthful spirit of straight-from-the-garage rock and roll seemed lost forever.

Yet something had been bubbling in the underground since the Stooges and the MC5 started slashing up rock's face half a decade earlier. Stripped-down rock bands playing stripped-down songs weren't making a splash on vinyl, but they were in the clubs of London and New York City, inspiring others to pick up a guitar and make a noise. The Roxy in Covent Garden was the site of early gigs by the Adverts, the Buzzcocks, the Damned, and the Jam. Hilly Kristal's CBGB (short for Country, Bluegrass, & Blues) on New York City's infamously squalid Bowery was where Blondie, Television, the Talking Heads, Patti Smith, and the Ramones hung out and played. A scene was forming.

Punk and New Wave were still a year away from exploding, but groups like the Ramones, the Damned, Blondie, and Tom Petty and the Heartbreakers provided the first flavors of a new movement devoted to good old rock and roll. A change had come, and whether young artists were raging away with refreshing vigor or old ones were winding down, 1976 was a time of revitalization.

AC/DC: *DIRTY DEEDS DONE DIRT CHEAP*

The first half of the seventies was largely defined by post–*Sgt. Pepper's* intellectualism. Australia's AC/DC were dumb guys proud of being dumb guys. Their formula of sinewy power chords, metronomic drumming, lavatory-wall humor, and Bon Scott's leering was the perfect sound track to tooling around in a muscle car with the wind blowing through your mullet while chucking empty cans of Bud out the window. And wasn't this more the essence of rock and roll than eleven-minute odes to Tolkien? Legions of devoted fans who stuck with AC/DC through more than thirty years of releasing the same album over and over would certainly agree.

AC/DC's third version of the AC/DC album is *Dirty Deeds Done Dirt Cheap*. Produced by former Easybeats Harry Vanda and George Young— older brother of AC/DC's Angus and Malcolm—*Dirty Deeds* is particularly pleasurable because it is raw, yet the band is totally tight, and the songwriting is as diverse as anyone could expect from AC/DC. The title track is a fist pumper about a hit man who peddles his wares to high school kids (now there's a rock and roll fantasy no one had thought of before). "Ain't No Fun (Waiting 'Round to Be a Millionaire)" is long but simple and intense: equal parts Chuck Berry boogie and *Abbey Road* arpeggios. "Big Balls" is an ultra-stupid and ultra-fun ode to, well, big balls—both the kind that take place in ballrooms and the kind that dangle down the side of Angus Young's shorts. "Ride On" is that rarest of items: an AC/DC soul ballad. Maybe *Dirty Deeds Done Dirt Cheap* isn't your typical AC/DC record after all.

Outside of Australia, Hipgnosis' cool, proto-punk design replaced an ugly, ugly illustration of Bon Scott and Angus Young. Author's collection.

BLONDIE: *BLONDIE*

The apparent irony of Debbie Harry's career is that despite being in her thirties by the time she became a star, despite her classically fine voice, despite Blondie's radio-ready pop songs, she and her band got lumped in with the punks because they were part of the CBGB crowd. Their peers even criticized them as sellouts when they pumped disco sass into 1979's "Heart of Glass." Look, no one is going to mistake "The Tide Is High" for "Blitzkrieg Bop," but Harry's story is actually pretty punk. She survived in the heart of infamous mid-seventies New York City when rats and violence were in equal abundance, she survived drug addiction and sexual assault and now speaks of both nonchalantly, she survived a turbulent career at odds with her consistently massive fame, she survived getting ripped off by music-business weasels, she survived the severe illness of boyfriend and bandmate Chris Stein. Don't get taken in by how Sid Vicious's tragic trajectory is glamorized—surviving is punker than dying.

Of course, any backlash wasn't really fair since Debbie Harry and the boys wore their pop intentions on their sleeves from the word "go." As soon as Clem Burke kicks in the Hal Blaine drumbeat and Harry begins her ultracool recitation at the start of "X-Offender," Blondie's reference points are clear: the Shangri-La's, Phil Spector, sixties garage rock, and B-movies. These were the Ramones' reference points too, but that band squeezed their pop influences through a sieve of MC5 fuzz and Stooges speed. Even with Burke's Keith Moon rumble, Blondie played sweet pop cleanly. The fastest thing here is "In the Sun," which is more reminiscent of Dick Dale surf than Stooges terrorism. The meanest, "Rip Her to Shreds," is an *Aftermath* homage. "Man Overboard" even bears traces of the disco that would cause Blondie so much grief and success a few years later.

Blondie's eclecticism isn't always a good thing. The record's less successful stabs ("Man Overboard," the fussy "Look Good in Blue," the oversynthesized "A Shark in Jets Clothing") expose a new group groping for their sound. Fortunately, the vast majority of *Blondie*—"X-Offender," "Rip Her to Shreds," "In the Sun," "In the Flesh," "Little Girl Lies," the tough "Kung Fu Girls," the goofy conga line "The Attack of the Giant Ants"— show how they found it.

DAVID BOWIE: *STATION TO STATION*

When David Bowie announced he was "finished with rock and roll" in the mid-seventies, he was only half joking. In fact, he'd been deliberately moving away from the riffy electricity of his earlier career for several years, eulogizing the old guard and enjoying one final fling with the Spiders from Mars with the all-covers *Pin Ups* in 1973, then experimenting with soul on 1975's *Young Americans*. Soon he'd hook up with Brian Eno and program a series of icy, ambient, and critically celebrated records to round out his defining decade. But first: transition.

Not as rock oriented as his previous records or as frigid as the ones that would immediately follow, *Station to Station* is a modest masterwork. The record's six songs are epic without being overblown or overly reliant on instrumental flash. The album even makes room for a cover, and it's a testament to Bowie's taste and precise judgment that the version of Nina Simone's "Wild Is the Wind" that closes *Station to Station* feels very much a part of the record's sonic and emotional concept. And as cool as the Thin White Duke's voice is throughout, this is an

The cover photo was pulled from Bowie's starring appearance in Nicolas Roeg's feature film *The Man Who Fell to Earth*. Author's collection.

emotionally engaging record, achieving ultimate uplift in the vamps that climax the title track and "TVC 15," striding the balance beam between melancholia and beautiful release on "Word on a Wing" and "Wild Is the Wind," and putting a bit of jiggle in the legs on the controlled yet supernaturally funky "Golden Years" and "Stay."

BOB DYLAN: *DESIRE*

Desire continued the strength of *Blood on the Tracks*. Dylan was still smarting from his divorce, as evidenced by "Sara," a more direct message to his ex-wife than anything on the previous album. He diversified into biography with a stormy report on the unjust trial of accused murderer Rubin "Hurricane" Carter and a weepier but equally epic tribute to Joey Gallo, whom Dylan paints as a sort of morally slanted Mafioso, which stirred some controversy. The rest of the record is less dicey, with the pretty trifle

"Mozambique," the beautifully ragged "One More Cup of Coffee," the picturesque "Romance in Durango," and the frisky "Black Diamond Bay."

Blood on the Tracks and *Desire* were criticized for the restraint of Dylan's musical support (*Rolling Stone*'s Dave Marsh called the former's performances "perfunctory" and wrote that the latter lacked "a great band"). While this criticism holds water regarding *Blood*, *Desire* gains a great deal of its personality from Scarlet Rivera's fiddling, the distinctively loose rhythm section, and Emmylou Harris's raw vocal support.

THE FLAMIN' GROOVIES: *SHAKE SOME ACTION*

The Flamin' Groovies were retro before retro became cool. Their fifty/fifty split between originals and faithfully performed oldies seemed hopelessly out of date on their 1969 debut *Supersnazz*. That record was a flop and killed the Groovies' hopes of playing on the same field as their buddies in the Rolling Stones, but it did not divert them from their objective.

Shake Some Action is another hodgepodge of new and old numbers, but the band has shifted its gaze from fifties Americana to the British Invasion. The album is a neat re-creation of an early Merseybeat record. The Flamin' Groovies harmonize like the Fab Four on nuggets such as "I Can't Hide," "Yes, It's True," and "You Tore Me Down" and nearly tumble into Rutles territory with "Please Please Girl." "I'll Cry Alone" broods like something on *Beatles for Sale*, though David Wright hits a lot harder than Ringo usually did. In case any listener has missed the point, the guys toss in a hyped-up cover of "Misery."

Shake Some Action is not merely a cod-Beatles tribute record. It's also a source of Rolling Stones covers ("Don't Lie to Me," "She Said Yeah") and more obscure morsels (Gene Thomas's often-covered "Sometimes," the Lovin Spoonful's "Let the Boy Rock and Roll"). The Groovies branch out on the title track, a terrific power-pop anthem that could have fit nicely on an early Nick Lowe record. They hit dramatic heights on "I Saw Her" and "Teenage Confidential" that would have made the Shangri-La's jealous. Pure pop didn't get any sweeter than this in 1976.

LED ZEPPELIN: *PRESENCE*

Awesome as Led Zeppelin is, their persona always depended on absurd posturing. Robert Plant passed himself off as a grizzled bluesman or a

Middle Earth swashbuckler. Jimmy Page thought he was Aleister Crowley Jr.

The troubles Robert Plant suffered in 1975 were enough to humble even the goldenest god. The singer was badly injured in a car accident that forced the band to cancel a scheduled tour. He had bouts of claustrophobia while recording the latest Zeppelin disc confined to a wheelchair and took a painful spill that inspired the title of the record's first track. Combine all that with extreme homesickness, and all of Plant's iconic pretentions melted away, making way for the real human sadness that suffuses Led Zeppelin's most human album.

Presence is stark and steel gray. Not a single acoustic guitar, mandolin, or keyboard decorates the record. Aside from the fun, funky toss-off "Royal Orleans" and the rockabilly takeoff "Candy Store Rock," *Presence* reveals a serious band getting down to serious business seriously. "Achilles Last Stand" starts the record with its only mythology references, but the track is more about Page's electric chain mail than Plant's barely audible lyrics. Despite the dozen or so guitars, "Achilles Last Stand" is both lean and spacious, a high-speed race through cavernous corridors. "For Your Life," on which Plant returns to Earth to lament the damages the L.A. drug scene laid on a close friend (Page perhaps?), is contrastingly cramped and dense. This may be the most legitimately scary pair of tracks to ever open a Led Zeppelin record.

Equally disturbing is the side B opener, "Nobody's Fault but Mine," which appropriates blues clichés more genuinely than any of the band's earlier songs. In light of the events surrounding its creation, Plant's regretful cries about dealing with the devil bear no trace of parody. His eardrum-piercing harp blast halfway through the track is a primal scream. "Hots On for Nowhere," another of Page's guitar tour de forces, uses a bouncy riff to conceal Plant's harsh words for a disloyal friend (Page again?). All of the record's anguish culminates in its quietest track. "Tea for One" is an epic blues many have dismissed as a lazy rewrite of "Since I've Been Loving You," yet Plant's expression of homesickness is a far more honest piece, packing the most tortured singing and guitar work of his and Page's career.

Led Zeppelin managed only one more record before John Bonham's death, and *In*

Gets my vote for wittiest album cover. Author's collection.

Through the Out Door is a brave but spotty departure. Jimmy Page seems barely present throughout that finale. So in its own way, *Presence* is the final real Led Zeppelin album, and the band never sounded more real.

MODERN LOVERS: *THE MODERN LOVERS*

Jonathan Richman was scarcely twenty when he and the Modern Lovers started recording their first album in 1972. It's almost shocking to hear how innocent young Richman was during a time when the Stones and Led Zeppelin made cynicism and decadence fashionable. Mick certainly wouldn't have crooned, "I'm not stoned like Hippie Johnny . . . I'm straight, I'm proud to say." That's doubly true for Lou Reed, and the Modern Lovers' complete appropriation of the Velvet Underground sound as accompaniment to Richman's square declarations is borderline subversive.

Unhip as the messages "Old World," "Dignified and Old," and "Someone I Care About" impart may be, the band swaggers them out as if they are singing about more traditional rock and roll pursuits. They do that with their signature song, and "Roadrunner" is one of rock and roll's best tributes to its own recuperative powers.

Original Velvet John Cale produced most of *The Modern Lovers*, but the record's lack of polish might have made it sound rather out of place among the class of 1972. Years of record label indecision, producer turnover, and personal problems delayed the album's release until 1976. By then, the times had caught up with its punky grit, if not Richman's anti-juvenile lyrics. The original Modern Lovers lineup had essentially dissolved, leaving Jerry Harrison and David Robinson to move on to bigger things with Talking Heads and the Cars, respectively. Jonathan Richman went on to a culty solo career, but arguably none of those post Modern Lovers acts ever did anything as rapturous as "Roadrunner."

TOM PETTY AND THE HEARTBREAKERS: *TOM PETTY AND THE HEARTBREAKERS*

Although the full punk onslaught was still a year away, much of 1976's new breed indicated a shift away from the corporate and cock rockers that had overcome 1970s rock so far. Tom Petty and the Heartbreakers were sometimes ranked among the punks (and later the New Wave) simply because commentators couldn't figure out any other way to categorize the group at a time when simple "rock and roll" wasn't considered a relevant category. The Gainesville, Florida, combo wasn't concerned with relevance, which is why *Tom Petty and the Heartbreakers* must have been such an elixir in 1976. The only other writer at the time who shared Petty's zeal for earthy tales of frustrated, small-town youth was Bruce Springsteen, yet the Boss tended to aim more epic and indulgent than the pithy Heartbreakers. Most of the tracks on their first album barely clear three minutes. They worshipped the Byrds, the early Beatles and Stones, the Band, and Creedence Clearwater Revival, and *Tom Petty and the Heartbreakers* consists of songs as tight and tuneful as the records that inspired it, no matter if the Heartbreakers grumble ("Breakdown"), sprint ("Rockin' Around [With You]"), jive ("Hometown Blues"), burn slowly ("The Wild One, Forever"), or rocket into jangly transcendence ("American Girl").

THE RAMONES: *RAMONES*

Like John, Paul, George, and Ringo fifteen years before them and Kurt, Krist, and Dave fifteen years after, Joey, Johnny, Dee Dee, and Tommy did not set out to rescue rock and roll. They were just righteously fed up with the fussiness and pomp pervading the scene and decided to play the kind of spartan garage rock they dug. As bassist, chief composer, and chief wackadoo Dee Dee Ramone said in *Spin* in 1990, "I think rock 'n' roll should be three words and a chorus, and the three words should be good enough to say it all." This was barely exaggeration.

On their eponymous debut, the Ramones stripped away all of rock and roll's pretenses that had accumulated since *Sgt. Pepper's*. No orchestrations. No intellectual lyrics. No complex structures. No dynamics. The Ramones didn't even have time for guitar solos. All tracks kick off simultaneously and at top speed ("1, 2, 3, 4!"), and all have singsongy choruses. Some are nothing but choruses. Although the Ramones are famous—and were initially criticized—for their simplicity, Johnny Ramones's neck-breaking downstrokes require tremendous stamina and precision, as does the drumming of Tommy Ramone, who learned the instrument simply because the group he helped assemble needed a drummer.

The Ramones collected the raw refuse of trash culture and defiant bad taste and molded it all into a new art form. Horror movies, junk food, comic books, amusement parks, makeshift drugs, turning tricks, boneheaded shock humor, and sleazy violence all became pop fodder. They also paid tribute to a crime-ridden, skuzzy city. *Ramones* stinks of mid-seventies New

York City. Aside from the infamous "53rd
and 3rd," specific references are sparer here
than they would be on subsequent records
on which the Ramones would praise Coney
Island and Rockaway Beach, but *Ramones
sounds* like New York. The grinding gears of
a subway train. The quick snick of a switch-
blade. The expletive shout of a passing cabby.
The wicked giggle of a purse snatcher. These
sounds fester between the lines of all fourteen tracks that make up the most revolutionary record of 1976.

Hopefully Tommy Ramone was
able to buy a shirt that fits with
the money he made off of this
record. Author's collection.

The Ramones take the act a bit too far
when belching out the shock-value Nazi non-
sense "Today Your Love, Tomorrow the World," which so offended Sire
president, Ramones champion, and fairly unoffendable guy Seymour Stein
that he asked the group to change its lyric. They refused, writing the song
off as nothing more than a product of their "dark sense of humor." Is that
an adequate defense for a song in which Joey—who, we should remember,
was Jewish—plays the role of a Hitler-paraphrasing "Nazi *schätze*" ("sweetheart")? Your call.

But *Ramones* is mostly danger and menace of the cartoon variety, and
even when the guys are promoting child abuse ("Beat on the Brat"), rhap-
sodizing about bloody "massacrees" ("Chainsaw") or bodega drugs ("Now I
Wanna Sniff Some Glue"), the Ramones just sound like a bunch of dumb
kids looking for fun, and what's more rock and roll than that?

THE ROLLING STONES: *BLACK AND BLUE*

It's Only Rock 'N Roll was Mick Taylor's final album with the Stones,
and one of the main reasons for his departure was Jagger and Richards's
refusal to credit him for the songs he cowrote. Considering that those songs
included "Moonlight Mile," "Winter," and "Time Waits for No One," the
guy had a real legitimate gripe because he'd helped write a good deal of the
band's best recent material.

Taylor might have had the last laugh because his absence is sorely felt
on *Black and Blue*, which finds rock's biggest act flailing around without a
regular second guitarist and nearly no good material. The album plays as a
series of audition jams with potential new guitarists such as Wayne Perkins,

Harvey Mandel, and Ron Wood, who'd end up getting the gig. He probably didn't get it based on the strength of "Hey, Negrita," a neat riff masquerading as a song he cowrote that rambles as aimlessly as most of the album's tracks do. The pooped reggae "Cherry Oh Baby," the weightless MOR ballad "Fool to Cry," and the wretched disco "Hot Stuff," which cribs its lyrics from T-shirt slogans, are the Stones' worst exercises in those particular genres. A couple of rockers in the standard Chuck Berry mode and a much less standard jazzy collaboration with Billy Preston are decent, but only the excellent epic ballad "Memory Motel" is up to the Stones' usual standards.

RUSH: *2112*

Ever since Neil Peart replaced John Rutsey behind the kit and Geddy Lee and Alex Lifeson at the lyric-writing desk, Rush started courting bigger musical and lyrical ideas than "Hey, baby, it's a quarter to eight, I feel I'm in the mood." That kind of approach needs time to develop, and attempts to get ambitious on *Fly by Night* and *Caress of Steel* were seriously lacking in melodiousness and clarity of ideas, leaving brief songs such as "Fly by Night," "Beneath, Between, Behind," and "Lakeside Park" to represent the band more favorably.

I personally think that when Peart's ambitions coalesced on *2112*, the short songs were still the album's highlights. Rush is at their most accessible on "Lessons." "A Passage to Bangkok" and "Twilight Zone" find them at their most tuneful and funniest. Still, there's no denying that Peart, Lee, and Lifeson had developed their big ideas considerably since shapeless, shaggy-dog filler like "The Necromancer" and "The Fountain of Lamneth." The title piece of Rush's fourth album isn't their most melodic, but there is an actual story this time to justify the extended run time: in a totalitarian future society that has banned music, a guy finds a guitar, tunes it in record time, and leads a rebellion against the music-hating regime. It's a simplistic concept that would have borne serious stretch marks had it been pulled to *Tommy* length, but it gets the job done on a single side of vinyl and gave the band a centerpiece for their stage act in the same way the Who's rock opera gave them one.

WINGS: *WINGS AT THE SPEED OF SOUND*

Riding high on the success of the fairly collaborative *Venus and Mars*, Paul McCartney gave his band a lot more room on its successor, *Wings at the*

Speed of Sound. This time, his magnanimousness backfired artistically, if not commercially (it was his biggest hit album in the United States). The other band members' songs just aren't up to snuff aside from Denny Laine's two contributions: "Time to Hide," a close cousin of "Letting Go" from *Venus and Mars*, and the somber "The Note You Never Wrote," which is more effective as a recording than a composition. Jimmy McCulloch's "Wino Junko" is a tuneful enough piece of light pop, but the finger-wagging lyrics stink. Linda sings the even worse words of her "Cook of the House" amateurishly as the band boogies awkwardly behind her. There's one big surprise among these more collaborative tracks: on "Must Do Something About It," drummer-turned-singer Joe English sounds exactly like Billy Joel. Whether that's a good or bad surprise is up to you.

McCartney is working below his abilities too. The album's two huge hits are not his best, though they definitely have their winning qualities. "Silly Love Songs," which hits back at his critics with a Nerf hammer, has a terrific bass line and a complex vocal arrangement. "Let 'Em In," which is so minimalistic it's practically an anti-composition, has a contagious air of fun. These tracks are also indicative of the main problem with *Speed of Sound*: there just isn't enough good old rock and roll. Paul remembers his screaming Little Richard roots only on "Beware My Love."

WINGS OVER AMERICA

Wings recorded *Speed of Sound* during a holiday in their demanding tour schedule. If they weren't inspired in the studio, they sure were onstage. Five years after the Beatles broke up—and nine after their final gig— Paul McCartney finally came to terms with his legacy and began performing songs from his Fab days again. The move thrilled audiences who finally got a chance to hear how never-performed favorites such as "Lady Madonna" and "The Long and Winding Road" might sound live. The *Wings over the World* tour and its accompanying album also made it clear that McCartney had the material, the chops, and the innate showmanship to be one of rock's greatest live acts. Sure all

Paul did a subtle yet radical thing in the packaging of *Wings Over America*: he flipped the writing credits of the album's five Beatles songs from Lennon-McCartney to McCartney-Lennon on the record labels. Author's collection.

of his proto–hair metal "Oh yeahs!!!" were cheesier than the Velveeta factory, but all is forgiven when he starts pounding hell out of "Soily" or "Jet."

Wings over America collects three LPs worth of great musicianship and showmanship with an emphasis on tracks from Wings' two best albums: *Band on the Run* and *Venus and Mars*. McCartney's willingness to share the spotlight with Jimmy McCulloch and Denny Laine, whose rendition of his old Moody Blues hit "Go Now" is as good as anything by the show's main star, is charming. *Wings over America* is better support for the argument that Wings were more than Paulie's puppets than *Speed of Sound* is.

STEVIE WONDER: *SONGS IN THE KEY OF LIFE*

Stevie Wonder's brilliant run of albums from *Music of My Mind* to *Fulfillingness' First Finale* put enough currency into his artistic bank account to warrant the go-for-broke *Songs in the Key of Life*. Like all great double albums, *Songs* is a messy, overly ambitious sprawl that requires—and completely rewards—its listeners' patience and attention. The sun rises with "Love's in Need of Love Today," an epic that eases listeners into a strange world in which religious communion is disturbingly mechanized ("Have a Talk with God"), stately synthesizers cast sad incongruity over bleak urban landscapes ("Village Ghetto Land," "Pastime Paradise"), and pulverizing funk burbles from the tiles of socially conscious elementary schoolrooms ("Black Man").

Wonder revels in experimentation throughout *Songs in the Key of Life*, yet he still produces soul pop as deliciously accessible as his sixties hits with "I Wish" and "Sir Duke." But even the album's most popular tracks bear the stamp of Wonder's far-out ambitions. Has any hit song ever housed a trickier riff than the one that rises and falls in the center of "Sir Duke"?

As unfettered as *Songs in the Key of Life* is, Wonder displayed commendable restraint in bunching its least successful tracks on a bonus seven-inch, so there isn't much anyone should feel compelled to skip during the core album's eighty-six minutes. Maybe the fusion detour "Contusion," the sappy "Isn't She Lovely," or the slightly precious "If It's Magic." In the end, albums like *Songs in the Key of Life* are about the artist's willingness to take chances, perhaps not always achieving total success but never boring, never creating music by the numbers. When the sun sets and Wonder goes out partying with "Another Star," his listeners have completed a winding, fascinating, rocky trip without ever stepping away from their stereos.

1977

This is it. The year critics love to celebrate for giving a youth numbed by corporate rockers and disco diversions a stiff injection of punk at the peak of its vitality.

In truth, the punk movement appealed to only a very small audience (particularly in the United States), and the first wave was over almost as soon as it began. Its influence lingered longer. Not all of 1977's great records were punk products, but almost all of them were infused with the fresh spirit mined from this controversial new form of expression. Punk did not have a monopoly on freshness, though, and some of the year's disco and pop albums have aged way better than any punk would have admitted in 1977.

The year 1977 also marks a major sales peak for the rock LP era. With the emergence of new entertainments such as video games, the cassette-abetted home-taping invasion, and a new emphasis on singles rather than long players (which a certain new television channel specializing in music videos would exacerbate in a few years), album sales started trickling downward after 1977.

DAVID BOWIE: *LOW*

David Bowie's first in a trilogy of collaborations with producer Brian Eno, *Low* is atmospheric, experimental, and, well, pretty turgid for those who prefer melody to frigid soundscapes. A very vocal minority of critics have named it Bowie's—and the seventies'—best album. I always assumed there is an element of willful contrariness in all the *Low* worship, especially when there is so little Bowie in it. "Be My Wife" and "Always Crashing in the Same Car" are good songs, and "Sound and Vision" is an excellent one, but there are too few songs on *Low*.

"HEROES"

"Heroes" also splits time between vocal tracks and instrumental experiments, but it seems designed to either please both factions of Bowie's fans or ease himself back into his former songcraft. Side A is his finest run of vocal numbers since *Aladdin Sane*. "Beauty and the Beast" is as menacing as anything on *Low* and as fatally contagious as any of his past hits (though it flopped when released as the album's second single). Bowie heads out into the Berlin nightlife, ready for his beastly indulgences to overtake him like a latter-day Larry Talbot. The all-nighter is under way on "Joe the Lion," an urgently danceable call to shake off his *Low* insularity and a tribute to decadent performance artist Chris Burden. Then the breath-stealing, romantic bliss amid political chaos of the title track—quite possibly the man's most miraculous creation—and "Sons of the Silent Age." The only way to end all this physical, personal, and social turbulence is extreme overindulgence and "Blackout."

When Bowie comes to on side B, he and Eno indulge themselves with a series of atmosphere pieces that are harder rocking ("V-2 Schneider"), more dramatic ("Sense of Doubt"), and prettier ("Moss Garden") than the mass of *Low*. Our hero caps off the side with its sole pop song. "The Secret Life of

There's a record store that specializes in Latin music close to my home. The store used to have a pretty decent rock music bin, and the day after Bowie died, I was shuffling through it. When the owner saw that I liked rock, he went into the back of the store and emerged moments later with this beautiful copy of *"Heroes"* and asked if I would buy it for eight bucks. I was like, "yes, please." Author's collection.

Arabia" is a return to the *Station to Station* funk that segues seamlessly to the capper of Bowie and Eno's triptych, the even more accessible *Lodger*.

CHEAP TRICK: *CHEAP TRICK*

In the year that punk provided rock and roll with a high colonic, the new guard led by the Clash and the Sex Pistols chided the old guard of classic rockers ("No Elvis, Beatles, or the Rolling Stones in 1977") no matter how much that new guard owed to the old one. And though the best punks welcomed elements of old-fashioned, Who-inspired power pop into their music, they were careful not to stray too far from the two-chords-and-a-pissy-attitude formula (another posture that would soon fade). This is why the purists cast a skeptical eye toward folks like the Jam, Joe Jackson, and Elvis Costello, with their skinny ties and pesky melodies.

Cheap Trick never received flack for being posers the way Weller, Jackson, or Costello did because they operated on their own power-pop planet. Too polished for the punks, too snide for the classic rockers, Cheap Trick was a band bred for culthood. Robin Zander may have looked the golden god, with his pretty puss and blond mane, but his deranged yowl may have even been too much for the Zep Heads. Rick Nielsen's lead guitar work ("and when we say lead, we're not kidding: he's got thirty-five guitars," future novelist Eric von Lustbader boasted in the original liner notes) could go head-to-head with that of Jimmy Page, but his Huntz Hall getup wasn't going to get him on any centerfolds. Bun E. Carlos looked more like he should be wiping dipsticks than waving drumsticks. Only bassist Tom Petersson really looked *and* played the part of classic rocker, but who paid any attention to him?

Cheap Trick made music as paradoxical as their image. They are known to non-cultists as big, dumb rockers, a stereotype that may not necessarily be anathema to the band. But one would have to be aware of stuff like "Daddy Should Have Stayed in High School" or "He's a Whore" to suss the irony in something like "I Want You to Want Me," which too many take at face value. And how many casual listeners have really paid attention to the parodic yet oddly sincere lyric of "Surrender"? Wicked humor and taboo busting plays as key a role in Cheap Trick's greatness as hooks. That the band wasn't really able to sustain that greatness past their fourth studio LP also accounts for why they are so often dismissed by nonfanatics. But is there a trace of ironic humor in the power ballad "The Flame," the band's only number one hit? I'd find it hard to believe that there isn't considering

Cheap Trick's track record, but that doesn't necessarily forgive its surface awfulness.

But we're getting too far ahead here. Let's trip back to the back-to-basics 1977, when renewed productivity was a distinctive part of that spirit. While Fleetwood Mac was spending the better part of a year toiling over *Rumours*, bands like the Ramones, the Damned, and Cheap Trick spat out two records apiece in 1977. That kind of thing had basically been unheard of since the mid-sixties when the Beach Boys or Monkees would churn out as many as three LPs in a single year.

Cheap Trick's ability to put out their first—and best—two albums in the same year

Epic Records tended to put the two most traditionally photogenic guys on the front covers of Cheap Trick's albums and slap Rick Nielsen and Bun E. Carlos on the back. Author's collection.

is particularly appropriate since they so beautifully recapture the refreshing pop of the sixties while draining their melodies and harmonies through a grate of seventies sarcasm and snarling attitude. Their eponymous debut is the year's best power-pop album—too harmonious and intricate for the punks, too streamlined and unpretentious for the corporate rockers, too bizarre for the mainstream. No other pop group was willing to exploit pedophilia, suicide, man-whoring, and serial murder as subject matter for potential hit songs.

IN COLOR

Cheap Trick was not a hit, nor was its follow-up, which scaled back some of the lyrical mania and upped the sweetness for such near bubble-gum confections as "I Want You to Want Me," "Southern Girls," and "Come On, Come On." The guys still mined metal on "Big Eyes" and "You're All Talk" and got weird on yet another (though not their final!) ode to suicide, the marvelously moody "Downed," but *In Color* leaves a decidedly sweet aftertaste. Soon the group's wonderful songs and totally unique persona— two big-haired rock stars meet two rejects from an adult home for wayward boys—would pay off. While Cheap Trick was getting little love in their home country, pop-crazed kids across the Pacific were eating them up. A trip to Japan would yield *Cheap Trick at Budokan*. Most of the material on that triple-platinum blockbuster was pulled from their superb first two albums.

THE CLASH: *THE CLASH*

The year 1977 was rich in some of the most vital music made by some of the most important new artists to emerge since the British Invasion. So to say the Clash were the only band that mattered in 1977 is a pretty big exaggeration. Yet that famous (and, let's face it, pretty great) slogan seems so true during the thirty-five minutes it takes to spin their debut album.

This is music designed to raise fists, rally young people into the streets, enact change for the better, and shatter systems. Elvis Costello crafted his political statements to flick you in the brain. Joe Strummer whacked out his to punch you in the gut. He wanted young white kids to smash their Journey records and take a stand like the Jamaican kids who'd gone toe-to-toe against the racist police who'd been bullying them at the Notting Hill Carnival the previous year. The Clash delivered their message as directly as the Ramones impelled their followers to sniff glue and beat on brats: a few power chords, a 4/4 beat, a lot of speed, and Strummer's raspy shouting and Mick Jones's nasal pleading.

Unlike *Ramones*, *The Clash* houses a great deal of diversity. "London's Burning" brings the hysteria down to a mid-tempo football chant. The Clash weave punk's tether to reggae with their cover of Junior Murvin's "Police & Thieves." They swing between poppy arpeggios and a staccato stomp on "Remote Control." They take side trips from politics for such traditional rock and roll topics as the liberation of punching out a time card ("Janie Jones"), jamming with buddies ("Garageland"), and fucking ("Protex Blue"). No matter the message, no matter the method, every track on *The Clash* is bracing punk rock delivered with complete sincerity, complete conviction, complete control.

The Clash's 1977 debut was not issued in the United States until 1979, and that version contained the singles "Clash City Rockers," "Complete Control," "(White Man) In Hammersmith Palais," "I Fought the Law," "Jail Guitar Doors," and a rerecording of "White Riot" in place of "Deny," "Cheat," "Protex Blue," "48 Hours," and the original "White Riot." Would you lose all respect for me if I told you I prefer the American edition? Author's collection.

ELVIS COSTELLO: *MY AIM IS TRUE*

The generational shift that defined 1977 seemed to find its ultimate symbol in a bespectacled computer programmer born Declan MacManus. While the ultimate symbol of rock and roll's first wave had descended into self-indulgence—crooning and sweating in a gold-spangled jumpsuit on Vegas stages, eating and pilling himself to death while slumped on the toilet—this new Elvis was wolfish, young, and anything but complacent and conservative. That he looked more like Buddy Holly than Presley further emphasized how irrelevant facile attractiveness is when making music to feed artistic hunger instead of a bloated, superstar lifestyle.

Elvis Costello was only a punk poster boy in image. Listen to *My Aim Is True*, and hear a traditionalism that goes much further back than the early Elvis Presley bark of bands like the Clash. "Allison" is a harmonically, melodically complex neo-standard—Cole Porter smothered in a thick crust of bile. This track, which sticks out like a cowlick on *My Aim Is True*, indicates the unpredictability and ravenous diversity that would define the rest of Costello's career.

The rest of his debut is undiluted rock and roll. Only the ripsnorting "Mystery Dance" resembles punk, though it has just as much in common with Danny & the Juniors. In fact, the record's most prominent musical touchstone is the decidedly unpunk rock and roll revisionists the Band. Costello's wit draws on Lennon's and Dylan's gleeful acidity with an intense purposefulness that sets him apart from those more capricious writers. Elvis chooses each word carefully for maximum significance and maximum wordplay. Although the results are often flagrantly self-conscious, his lyrics are stimulating and truthful. His takes on sex, politics, and sexual politics are more insightful and informed than Lennon's or Dylan's. Costello would never write a song as broad as "Power to the People" or "Masters of War."

Elvis Costello's debut album arrived with "Elvis Is King" printed repeatedly across its cover less than a month before the guy known as "The King of Rock and Roll" died. Unfortunately disrespectful timing or fortuitously punk-rock timing? Author's collection.

Of course, *My Aim Is True* is no mere pop student thesis to be dissected. "Mystery Dance," "Sneaky Feelings," "Pay It Back," "Welcoming to the Working Week," and the Beatlesque "(The Angels Wanna Wear My) Red Shoes" are rock and roll as visceral as any old record by that other Elvis.

THE DAMNED: *DAMNED, DAMNED, DAMNED*

The Damned will always rank behind the Sex Pistols and the Clash in the history books. They defined neither punk attitude like Malcolm McLaren's contrivance nor its politics like Strummer and Jones's guerillas. They were four idiots bashing out idiotic garbage idiotically, encouraging their idiot fans to gob on the stage and punch each other in the face. At least, that's what the press and most of the Damned's peers would have you believe.

Always possessing much better senses of humor than their genre mates, the Damned would have the last laugh. They not only beat the rest to the record shops with the United Kingdom's first punk single and LP, but they're still at it today, putting on ferocious live shows and making good records. A lot of evolution went down in the interim. The Damned became cleverer, better musicians, and better songwriters. They embraced pop and goth and psychedelia. Band members came and went. Yet much of what made the Damned fascinating to follow for four decades was already present on their first album. The blinding singles "Neat, Neat, Neat" and "New Rose" are as catchy as the poppiest pop. Dave Vanian glowers through his vampire makeup on the spooky "Fan Club" and "Feel the Pain." The Damned could not have pulled off the musically complex (though lyrically juvenile) "Fish" if they were really as incompetent as their critics insisted. Indeed, punk's greatest drummer is already at his peak powers on his first record, and Rat Scabies is only too willing to show off his chaotic prowess. Chief songwriter Brian James would depart after the slapdash *Music for Pleasure* (also 1977), leaving the group to develop on his pop, thrash, and goth on more adventurous platters like *Machine Gun Etiquette*, *The Black Album*, and *Strawberries*, but the Damned would never sound this wild again.

FLEETWOOD MAC: *RUMOURS*

Few bands have undergone the crucial personnel and style changes Fleetwood Mac did. Rock-solid rhythm section Mick Fleetwood and John McVie have been the only constants. Starting as a British blues band under guitarist Peter Green's leadership in the sixties, Fleetwood Mac's dynamic shifted when Green left and McVie's wife Christine arrived in 1970.

The band experienced a complete makeover when romantic couple Lindsay Buckingham and Stevie Nicks joined at the end of 1974. Any trace of blues was gone as Buckingham–Nicks brought along the distinctively Californian pop brewed in Beach Boys harmonies and layered production that most people now associate with Fleetwood Mac. What had been an enduring but often nondescript blues group gained a strong new personality with Buckingham's extraordinary fingerpicked electric guitar, Nicks's abrasive voice and witchy persona, and all the personal problems those two brought with them. Fleetwood Mac became the poster band for dysfunctional lovers as members hopped from bed to bed, relationships crumbled, and the unprecedented international success of the new lineup's first album forced them to keep going for commercial reasons.

All the personal tumult would have splintered most bands. Fleetwood Mac used their songs as therapy. Christine McVie skimmed past her husband's feelings to celebrate sex with a new lover on "You Make Loving Fun" and spoke for Fleetwood's long-suffering wife Jenny Boyd with "Oh Daddy." Nicks wearily resolved to end things with the abusive Buckingham with her sad "Dreams." Buckingham sniped at Nicks with the venomous "Go Your Own Way" and cut off the band's nose to spite its face by nixing her gorgeous "Silver Springs" from the new album.

Rumours is not without optimism. Christine McVie's "Songbird" and "Don't Stop" revel in it, but they're also the disc's corniest tracks. The album's willingness to get personal, to open a vein, is what makes it spellbinding. Buckingham's stunning guitar work and Nicks's wails make it sting. An abundance of iconic songs made it a commercial phenomenon.

THE JAM: *IN THE CITY*

The Jam's British punk peers once sneered at them for being sanitized and overly indebted to sixties pop. Sure, they professed fealty to the circa-1965 Who (so did the Sex Pistols, the Clash, and the Damned). Sure, they wore sharp mod suits. Sure, Paul Weller flicked his pickup to coax Townshend-style telegraph noises out of his Rickenbacker. Those are mostly matters of image. In matters of sound, *In the City* is speed-freak fast, lean, and sweaty, all the things punk was supposed to be.

The Jam's decision not to play the punk game was very punk too. The genre's reputation for nonconformity may have held water in the United States, but the British punk scene was notoriously uncompromising. The Jam flouted conventions with their style and Weller's questionable though highly unconvincing conservatism (Weller told *Fanzine* the band was going to vote for archconservative Margaret Thatcher for prime minister just to piss off recent tour mates the Clash in 1977; he walked it back and said he'd probably vote Labour the following year). Songs like "In the City," a vicious indictment of police brutality; "Bricks and Mortar," a swipe at corporate expansion; and "Away from the Numbers," a sincere plea for nonconformity, tell a different tale. Although "Time for Truth" is known as the group's most notoriously conservative rant—Weller explicitly painting Labour Party Prime Minister James Callaghan Communist red—the target of the track's anger is once again the cops: specifically, the six who beat Liddle Towers, who'd been arrested outside the Key Club on a drunk and disorderly charge, to death in his jail cell in 1976. Tellingly, the incident inspired similar outrage from such left-leaning groups as the Tom Robinson Band and Angelic Upstarts.

In the City is not all provocative politics. "Nonstop Dancing" is a joyous ode to the title pursuit. The band pays homage to their favorite era with covers of the "Batman Theme" and Larry-Williams-by-way-of-the Beatles' "Slow Down." Soon the Jam would appropriate the lighter touch of the power-pop and soul groups of that era, and like so many other members of the class of 1977, they'd leave basic punk behind. However, *In the City* is one of the genre's most legitimate articles.

THE RAMONES: *LEAVE HOME; ROCKET TO RUSSIA*

If any band has ever painted itself into a corner with their very first album, it's the Ramones. Their image and music were so keenly sculpted that there wasn't much to do on their follow-up but more of the same. That is precisely what the Ramones did on their next two albums. The sound is a little slicker, the playing is a little less manic, and the more outré subject matter is out (no Nazis schätzes or chicken hawks this time). All the speed, catchiness, and cracked nostalgia are back, though.

The formats of *Leave Home* and *Rocket to Russia* ape *Ramones* too. Both records update early sixties treasures in the home stretch (the Riviera's "California Sun" on the second album; Bobby Freeman's "Do You Wanna Dance" and the Trashmen's "Surfer Bird" on the third). Both trade in love sincere and cynical, violence, rejects, drugs, psycho relationships, and New York City landmarks and attitude. *Rocket to Russia* goes so far as to re-create the *Ramones* album cover.

The Ramones apparently liked their first album cover so much that they practically recreated it for their third. Author's collection.

Rather than reeking of redundancy, the albums are just more of a really good thing. Played back to back to back, *Ramones*, *Leave Home*, and *Rocket to Russia* sound track an all-night party for pinheads, cretins, and punkers. We meet the new dream girls Sheena, Suzy, and Ramona. Glass-strewn Rockaway Beach becomes a destination for leather-clad beach boys. The guys mangle a bit of nonsense from the cult horror flick *Freaks* and come away with a rallying cry for their freaky fans. Gabba Gabba Hey.

RUSH: *A FAREWELL TO KINGS*

After three spotty albums that found them fumbling between beery hard rockers and intellectual prog epics, Rush cracked the nut with *2112*. The band's resident thinker Neil Peart settled in as chief lyricist, and the whole band started writing music worthy of their big concepts.

Once they had their act down, Rush started working on perfecting it. With *A Farewell to Kings*, they came pretty close. The title track, "Cinderella Man," and "Closer to the Heart"—the power ballad that launched a zillion Zippos—are miles beyond any of the short numbers on *2112*. "Xanadu" is not as ambitious as the "2112" suite, but it is more melodic and stands as one of Rush's best long songs. "Madrigal" is pretty, but the corny lyrics suggest that love songs don't fit comfortably into Rush's sci-fi and sorcery universe (no biggy), and "Cygnus X-1" is a bit of a return to the muddled narratives of *Caress of Steel*, though it's better than its mixed reputation suggests, and the middle section ("I set a course just east of Lyra . . .") rocks with that old Labatt's-fueled fury. More importantly, "Cygnus X-1" is the necessary first act of the even less penetrable yet considerably more beautiful "Cygnus X-1: Book Two" on Rush's next album.

THE SEX PISTOLS: *NEVER MIND THE BOLLOCKS, HERE'S THE SEX PISTOLS*

Critics celebrated punk for swooping into a climate of calculated, windy self-indulgence and glossy production and revolutionizing it with violent, organic energy. So it's ironic that the Sex Pistols of all bands became the movement's de facto faces.

The band's formation was only slightly more organic than the Monkees'. Svengali manager Malcolm McLaren selected Johnny "Rotten" Lydon to front the band after the weedy teen lip-synced along with a naff Alice

Cooper song. Chris Thomas, who'd worked on such punk anathema as Procol Harum's *Grand Hotel* and Pink Floyd's *The Dark Side of the Moon*, produced the Pistols' one and only LP. The production is as slick as *Abbey Road*. Instead of short, sharp attacks, the songs are obese mid-tempo clomps. There are some catchy tunes to be heard in "Anarchy in the U.K.," "God Save the Queen," "Problems," and the best of the lot, "Pretty Vacant," but Rotten often sings words that sound like some middle-aged adman's idea of punk attitude ("I wanna destroy passersby!" Scary.). As quoted in Clinton Heylin's *Babylon's Burning: From Punk to Grunge*, the Damned's Captain Sensible said that the album's lead single, "Anarchy in the U.K.," "sounded like some redundant Bad Company out-take." The clueless anti-abortion rant "Bodies" is downright conservative. Not very punk at all, boys.

As inappropriate as it is, *Never Mind the Bollocks, Here's the Sex Pistols* was punk's lightning rod. The BBC and certain shops banned the second single "God Save the Queen," giving the group the air of menace it really earned only when the genuinely dangerous Sid Vicious later joined the band. The Sex Pistols never released another proper album, but the one they did surely inspired many other groups to get together, and that is its most valuable legacy.

TALKING HEADS: *TALKING HEADS: '77*

Talking Heads was the unlikeliest band to get lumped in with the punks. The press copped out simply because David Byrne, Tina Weymouth, and Chris Franz played CBGB just like the Ramones and Richard Hell did. Hilly Kristal's piss-soaked shit hole was one of the few Manhattan clubs that welcomed groups that were neither corporation-approved mega-sellers nor cover bands. CBGB's rep may be 100 percent punk, but the bands that passed through it were often unclassifiable, and none were more impossible to pigeonhole than Talking Heads. The Heads' angular rhythms and chord structures trickled down from artists as diverse as Roxy Music, Fela Kuti, and the Meters. Their suppleness and groove slipped over from Philly soul. Their almost subliminal catchiness is pure pop, while David Byrne's eccentric lyricism betrays his art school background.

No other group before Talking Heads presented such a heady combination of influences, and no other great 1977 album was as unique as *Talking Heads: '77*. Is there a more unpunk move than opening your debut album with a mid-tempo swing seasoned with steel drums? Composing a song from the perspective of a real-life serial killer currently stalking New York

City is pretty punk, but is tripping into French arbitrarily or chummy choruses of "Fa fa fa fa fa fa fa fa fa"? Perhaps not, but they come pretty close when David Byrne runs them through the wringer of his anxiety-choked larynx. The Sex Pistols never made music this unsettling.

TELEVISION: *MARQUEE MOON*

CBGB ceased to be the home of country, bluegrass, and blues on March 31, 1974. Hilly Kristal thought his debut rock act was pretty incompetent. Little did he realize the effect Television would have on the downtown scene. Baudelaire and Jerry Garcia–style guitar solos hardly seem like the raw materials of punk, but Television's unique brand of hippie New Wave would revolutionize the New York City punk scene by opening CB's doors to the Ramones, Blondie, the Dead Boys, Talking Heads, the Heartbreakers, and the Voidoids, fronted by ex-Television channel Richard Hell.

Commanded by twin guitar heroes Tom Verlaine and Richard Lloyd, the Hell-less Television recorded an adventurous debut record that couldn't be further removed from the Ramones' dumb-guy speed rock. Soaring, poetic, agitated, magnificent, *Marquee Moon* is the sound track of rat-ridden streets illuminated by the immutable orange glow shimmering from dingy clubs. Verlaine's paranoid slur supplies the punk skuzz; his and Lloyd's weaving leads provide transcendence. A smitten Patti Smith rhapsodized that Verlaine's guitar sounded "like a thousand bluebirds screaming." The title track of *Marquee Moon* is a ten-minute testament to her description. On tracks such as this and "Venus," Television integrates their beauty and gristle seamlessly. Elsewhere, the duality pulls apart for feisty rock like "See No Evil" and "Friction" or gorgeous pieces like "Guiding Light." Yet there is always radiance glimmering through Television's toughest numbers and a thin layer of grime beneath the fingernails of their prettiest.

PETE TOWNSHEND AND RONNIE LANE: *ROUGH MIX*

On their single "1977," the Clash reserved their rage against the old guard for Elvis, the Beatles, and the Rolling Stones. The Damned were known to cover "Circles" onstage, and the Sex Pistols did a rendition of "Substitute." The Jam was often dismissed as little more than a Who cover band. When Sex Pistols Steve Jones and Paul Cook encountered Pete Townshend at the

Speakeasy and he drunkenly declared the Who were finished, a distressed Cook reportedly told him, "The Who are our favorite group."

Yes, the Who was one of the few dinosaur acts the punks revered as their forefathers, so it is typical of Townshend's disdain for trends that he chose to release *Rough Mix* in the midst of that noisy explosion. Instead of showing the youngsters Who's Who by bashing one out with the 'orrible 'oo, Townshend got together with former Face Ronnie Lane to make the gentlest record of his career.

Although the two musicians regularly clashed skulls, the music of *Rough Mix* is a pastoral ramble through English folk and American acoustic country and blues. Both shaky followers of Meher Baba, the spiritual leader whose catchphrase was "don't worry be happy" (unspoken only, as Baba took a vow of silence in 1925), Townshend and Lane walk a tightrope between spiritual devotion and earthly stumbling blocks throughout the record. Townshend dwells on his struggle to quell his self-destructive yearning on "Keep Me Turning" and empathetically profiles a series of heartsick barflies on "Heart to Hang Onto." Along with the orchestral character study "Street in the City," these are three of Townshend's loveliest songs. The most breathtaking moment belongs to Lane and his rolling "Annie."

Because Townshend and Lane rarely make distinct contributions to each other's songs, *Rough Mix* sounds more like a compilation of solo tracks than a true collaboration. Those tracks still hang together well because of their thematic and musical similarities, which are aesthetically gorgeous and emotionally rawer than the rawest punk.

VARIOUS ARTISTS: *SATURDAY NIGHT FEVER* (SOUNDTRACK)

Disco hit its peak just as rockers started saluting punk as the likeliest genre to depose disco's rule (punk was never commercial enough to do that, and disco kind of petered out on its own). As punk debuts went off like Roman candles in 1977, disco commanded cinemas when John Badham's *Saturday Night Fever* came out at the end of the year. The most disco-hating rock fans probably would have seen a lot of themselves in John Travolta's Tony Manero. He is dim, misogynistic, violent, and obsessed with music. The film has aged poorly because the character is so unpleasant, but its sound track is eternal.

Australian brother act the Bee Gees was one of many guitar groups who got in on the disco trend, and they became the year's defining superstars when producer Robert Stigwood hired them to write the sound track. The Brothers Gibb had several light-pop hits in the late sixties ("Massachusetts," "To Love Somebody," "Words," "I've Gotta Get a Message to You," etc.) but soon hit a career slump. They straightened their course with disco smashes like "Jive Talkin'" (1975) and "You Should Be Dancing" (1976). Both of those tracks were revived for the *Saturday Night Fever* sound track. "Stayin' Alive," "Night Fever," and the sultry ballad "How Deep Is Your Love" are new compositions. Yvonne Elliman sings the brothers' recherché tearjerker "If I Can't Have You." Each of these new songs was a number one single. The Trammps' "Disco Inferno" and Walter Murphy & the Big Apple Band's "A Fifth of Beethoven" were also huge hits from the sound track, and with its glut of hit singles, *Saturday Night Fever* was something of a portent of the blockbuster albums that would dominate the record market in the next decade. The Bee Gees'/Tavares' "More Than a Woman," KC and the Sunshine Band's "Boogie Shoes," and David Shire's "Night on Disco Mountain" have also become iconic in their own rights. Rockers may have hated all these delectable tunes, but they sure couldn't escape them in the late seventies.

DENNIS WILSON: *PACIFIC OCEAN BLUE*

As early as *The Beach Boys Today!*, Dennis Wilson was asserting himself as a genuine asset for the Beach Boys when he handled lead vocals on two of the album's best tracks with gruff sensitivity. When Brian Wilson began fully exploring the most outré corners of his creativity in the mid-sixties, Dennis was the Beach Boy who most supported and encouraged him. The death of *SMiLE* sent Brian into artistic and emotional retreat, making it necessary for the other guys to pick up the slack. Dennis developed into one of the band's best songwriters, composing such fine songs as "Little Bird," "Be with Me," "Celebrate the News," "Slip On Through," "Forever," and "Steamboat."

Six years before his death, Dennis Wilson recorded his only solo album, and the double-disc deluxe edition of *Pacific Ocean Blue* was one of the most ballyhooed reissues of 2008. The album is too inconsistent to fully justify the hype, but it still blows away what the Beach Boys were doing in the late seventies. "Dreamer" begins as a moody, one-chord groove before flitting off into the ether during its rhythmless bridge. Dixieland horns and a buzzing bass harmonica make the track a saucy synthesis of late seventies light funk and *Pet Sounds*–era ornamentation. The good-timey "What's Wrong" would have fit nicely on *Holland*. The majestic "River Song" is the album's acknowledged tour de force. "Pacific Ocean Blues" sounds like it was conceived under the influence of Sly Stone's (*not* Mike Love's) *There's a Riot Going On*. "Rainbows" drives along on a lazy Bo Diddley rhythm decorated with banjo, mandolins, and choral "aaahs" and "ooohs." The lyrics are generally of the simplistic "I Love You" or "Save the Earth" variety, but that's pretty par for the course for all seventies Beach Boys records. *Pacific Ocean Blue* is the decade's final work by a Beach Boy that's worth hearing.

WIRE: *PINK FLAG*

The press painted the punks as yobbos bashing out two chords while gobbing on their audience. The reality was a lot more complex. As Wire showed on their debut, punk could be raw and intellectual. *Pink Flag* is a veritable art piece, the twenty-one shards that make up its mosaic rarely clearing the two-minute mark. It all flashes by in a sustained howl on first listen. Subsequent listens reveal diversity and extraordinary songcraft from the atmospheric opener "Reuters" to the 2/4 bounce of "Field Day for the Sundays" to the robotic riffing of "Three Girl Rhumba" to the blissfully steamrolling "Ex Lion Tamer" right

While the flagpole in Annette Green's photo was a real flagpole, the pink flag was painted in later. Author's collection.

through "12 X U," the archetypal punk thrash that ends the album with a dead bang. Graham Lewis's lyrics swing past the simplistic politics of the British punks and the comic strip partying of the American ones for neurotic tales of the media constantly closing in like an all-devouring monster.

Pink Flag is all the more fascinating for its own uniqueness in Wire's catalog. The band would follow it up with longer pieces on the more psychedelic *Chairs Missing* before descending into the synthesized atmospherics of *154* and never looking back from there. Wire was so blasé about their past that they'd eventually refuse to perform any of their early material onstage, actually hiring a Wire cover band to open for them so fans could get the classics they paid to hear! *Pink Flag* may feel a little like the work of punk dilettantes in retrospect, but anyone really listening realizes how far beyond the genre's clichés Wire had already moved on their debut.

1978

The year 1977 was the one the punks inherited the Earth. The year 1978 was the one their influence was felt throughout pop music as a whole. Classic rockers such as the Rolling Stones attempted to give their careers a booster shot by speeding up their tempos and spewing their words (Zeppelin even considered releasing their punkish "Wearing and Tearing" as a seven-inch under a punky assumed name). A new wave of guitar groups tidied up punk's rawness to spearhead what would be the most important pop movement of the early eighties. Because the best records of 1978 reacted to it in one way or another, punk remained the only music that mattered for the time being, though the variety of its influence made 1978 an even more interesting year than 1977.

BLONDIE: *PARALLEL LINES*

Blondie had their Dylan-style "Judas!" moment when they had their first international number one hit with the discofied "Heart of Glass." Old pals like the Ramones accused them of selling out their integrity, missing the obvious fact that Blondie had always been a pop group first and foremost and that their breakthrough hit may have been the most scrumptious pop song of 1978, melting disco's robotic rhythm into a perfectly crafted melody and a witty lyric.

The single was featured on Blondie's best album, where disco was just one flavor in a Baskin-Robbins assortment of sweet pop styles: the steam-train pop punk of "One Way or Another," the sunshine pop of "Picture This" and "Sunday Girl," the hopped-up retro rock and roll of Buddy Holly's "I'm Gonna Love You Too," the spiky New Wave of "I Know but I Don't Know," the psychedelia of "Fade Away and Radiate," the girl groupisms of "Pretty Baby," and the arena thumping of "Will Anything Happen?" My favorite is the punk-hunk cover of the Nerve's "Hanging on the Telephone." The way the band kicks in at the end of Debbie's Harry's cold opening ("I'm in the phone booth it's the one across the *haw-wal*") slays me. Really, *Parallel Lines* doesn't have a single bum track. That's the definition of rock and roll integrity.

THE BUZZCOCKS: *ANOTHER MUSIC IN A DIFFERENT KITCHEN*

History has embalmed British punk as political (the Clash), mindlessly nihilistic (the Sex Pistols), and just plain loony (the Damned). One doesn't usually think of it as romantic, but the Buzzcocks were as concerned with the heart and its innumerable hurdles as the Ramones were across the ocean. Like the Ramones, the Buzzcocks also maximized speed and sugary tunefulness on brokenhearted anthems such as "No Reply" and "Fiction Romance." Even when a hookup manages to go down on things like "Sixteen," "I Don't Mind," and "You Tear Me Up," it just leads to disappointment or, worse, sexual revulsion, though "Love Battery" manages to keep the image of the tirelessly randy punk alive.

Pete Shelley's complex views of sex and love make *Another Music in a Different Kitchen* the wittiest and most humane album of punk's banner year. The band's machinelike cacophony makes it one of the most forward thinking. When Shelley ruminates on the annoyance and dangerousness of racing ("Fast Cars"), the frustration of idiotic consumerism ("I Need"), the confusing allure of autonomy ("Autonomy"), and—*Gasp! This from a punk band?!?*—the pleasures of maturity ("Moving Away from the Pulsebeat"), he reveals the brain above that broken Buzzcocks heart.

THE CARS: *THE CARS*

The Cars might as well have called their first album *The Cars Greatest Hits*. All but two of its tracks—the sketchy experiments "I'm in Touch with Your

World" and "All Mixed Up"—have worked their way into popular culture. You might know "Just What I Needed" and "My Best Friend's Girl" from endless plays on classic rock radio or the freaky "Moving in Stereo" from a certain scene in *Fast Times at Ridgemont High*, but overexposure should not undermine the freshness of any of those classics. Hearing them all gathered on one LP really puts the Cars' greatness into deep focus. At a time when critics felt it necessary to force every group into neat compartments, the Boston quintet was deemed pioneers of the New Wave, though the clean guitars and clean hooks that streak rainbows across their debut album make it sound like perfectly uncomplicated and perfectly perfect pop to my ears.

THE CLASH: *GIVE 'EM ENOUGH ROPE*

None of punk's defining bands moved away from the genre's defining characteristics faster than the Clash did. On their debut album, they were already fiddling with reggae and power pop, and by their second, they'd essentially freed themselves from punk's speed and leanness completely for a more anthemic sound. It is telling that a song called "All the Young Punks (New Boots and Contracts)" dismisses the clichéd ennui and ineptitude ("I knew how to sing . . . they knew how to pose") to a swirly pop backbeat. Musically, *Give 'Em Enough Rope* owes more to the Who (check out the "I Can't Explain" rip "Guns on the Roof") and the Rolling Stones ("Last Gang in Town") than the Ramones. In the jolly power popper "Julie's Been Working for the Drug Squad," Joe Strummer even quotes the Beatles, showing just how far he'd come from the "No Elvis, Beatles, or the Rolling Stones" philosophy of 1977. The full-time addition of drummer Topper Headon added extra un-punk professionalism, as did producer Sandy Pearlman, who was best known for his work with Blue Öyster Cult.

The politics remain pointed, taking on terrorism local and global and Britain's fascistic and alarmingly influential National Front party and the Association of Chief Police Officers' antidrug crusade. While *Give 'Em Enough Rope* lacks the raw vitality of the record that preceded it and the thrilling eclecticism of the one that would follow, it is a consistently great rock record with some of the Clash's best tracks ("Julie's Been Working for the Drug Squad," "Stay Free," the more trad punk of "Safe European Home" and "Tommy Gun"). All the young punks with an eye on longevity and an ear for musical growth were likely listening.

ELVIS COSTELLO AND THE ATTRACTIONS: *THIS YEAR'S MODEL*

Elvis Costello and the Attractions may have spent every waking moment gobbling amphetamines, but the singer had much more in common with Paul McCartney and Cole Porter than Johnny Rotten. No punk band shared the virtuosic skill of Costello's new band. The stamina Bruce Thomas displays on "Lipstick Vogue" is unparalleled in rock and roll.

Maybe the band's first album should be viewed through the punk lens, though. Both Elvis and the punks were coming from a lot of the same influences, and the effects of Question Mark & the Mysterians, *My Generation*–era Who, and especially *Aftermath*-era Stones are all over *This Year's Model*. Few punks recorded anything as pulse shredding as "No Action," "Pump It Up," or "Lipstick Vogue" or railed against the current culture as venomously or pointedly as Elvis does on the antifascist "Night Rally." However, the

Maybe the American edition of *This Year's Model* messed with Elvis's vision by replacing "Night Rally" with "Radio Radio," but the shot on its cover is way cooler than the one on the British disc. Author's collection.

focus of *This Year's Model* is largely inward with the sexual frustrations of "No Action," "Pump It Up," "This Year's Girl," "You Belong to Me," and "Hand in Hand." Personal yet completely relatable, virtuosic yet totally punk, *This Year's Model* is the record that best conveys the brilliance of both Elvis Costello and his new band, and in 1978, nothing could beat it.

THE JAM: *ALL MOD CONS*

After making their bids for punk legitimacy on their first two albums, the Jam fully moved on to the sixties-indebted power-pop sound that would fully convince the punks that the Jam was never one of them. There is speed and thrust behind the title track of *All Mod Cons*, "Billy Hunt," and their transitional cover of the Kinks' "David Watts." However, "To Be Someone (Didn't We Have a Nice Time)" hints at the full-on Beatles heist they'd commit two records later on *Sound Affects*. "Mr. Clean" is a Kinks-style character sketch, and "The Place I Love" pays tribute to that group with its melancholic tale of a fading era. The wistful acoustics of "Fly" and the bare-boned delicacy "English Rose" break with punk tradition completely, announcing the Jam's intentions to follow their own retro course. Then all of that beauty, social insight, and underlying agitation coalesces on the Jam's masterpiece. "Down in the Tube Station at Midnight" is a stark rejection of the conservative label many detractors slapped across the band, as Paul Weller plays the part of a man on the receiving end of a National Front hate crime with heartrending detail, wishing he could be home with his family, imagining his wife waiting with dinner. Can you believe a twenty-year-old wrote something so empathetic and emotionally devastating?

NICK LOWE: *JESUS OF COOL*

Nick Lowe was pulled into punk by sheer gravitational pull. Former Brinsley Schwarz/current Rockpile bassist Lowe was pushing thirty when he released his first solo album in 1978, and it has somehow been spoken of as a punk-related record when it's even less punk than his buddy Elvis Costello's records. Perhaps it was his stint with the indie label Stiff or his role as the producer of the Damned's debut album, but Lowe definitely drew more inspiration from Paul McCartney than the Who.

Jesus of Cool is a refreshing burst of pure pop for now people. Lowe sounds like an overexcited music geek on his first long player, sampling a little robotic proto–New Wave ("Music for Money"), Phil Spector expansiveness ("Little Hitler"), old-time rock and roll ("Shake and Pop"), reggae ("No Reason"), and, yes, punk fury (a live version of his great B-side "Heart of the City"). "So It Goes," Lowe's hit rewrite of—and improvement on—Steely Dan's "Reelin' in the Years" (something about his rhyming of "discussions" with "Russians" always tickles me) and his brilliant McCartney-style mini-suite "Nutted by Reality" reveal the craftsman at his cagiest, while the tastelessly uproarious "Marie Provost" reveal him to be one who delights in nutting pop's conventions—which is a pretty punk thing to do.

THE POLICE: *OUTLANDOS D'AMOUR*

The Police was yet another group that management and media tried to force into the punk box. This was particularly phony considering the guys' backgrounds in prog (Stewart Copeland was the drummer in Curved Air), jazz (Sting had been playing bass in fusion groups around London), and genuine 1960s psychedelia (already in his mid-thirties, Andy Summers played guitar in Dantalian's Chariot and, briefly, Soft Machine and Eric Burdon's Animals). The Police was no trio of punks; it was all a hoodwink of the first order, a crass example of bandwagon jumping as absurd as Mick Jagger (who is half a year younger than Summers!) refashioning himself punk style on *Some Girls*. Big deal. That doesn't make *Outlandos d'Amour* any less furious. "Next to You," "Peanuts," and the violently paranoid "Truth Hits Everybody" may be the greatest punk songs ever hammered out by a bunch of poseurs.

Outlandos d'Amour loosely translates as "outlaws of love." Pretentious album titles were key components of the Police's contrived image. Author's collection.

However, the main sound of *Outlandos d'Amour* is pop reggae, and no group ever did that better than the Police do on classics such as "So Lonely," "Can't Stand Losing You," "Hole in My Life," and "Roxanne." Andy Summers's spoken-word bullshit about his favorite blow-up doll is hilarious, and the high-speed rock mantra that frames it makes my skull feel like it's going to explode in the best way.

THE RAMONES: *ROAD TO RUIN*

On *Road to Ruin*, producer and former drummer Tommy Erdelyi got a lot of assistance behind the desk from Ed Stasium. Replacing him at the kit was Marc Bell, now rechristened Marky Ramone, who kicked out the beat with newfound precision.

The rest of the Ramones also try a few new tricks. Johnny rips out some atypical lead guitar work on the more-metal-than-punk "I Just Want to Have Something to Do," rings like Roger McGuinn on a cover of the Searchers' "Needles and Pins," and flashes out George Harrison–style slides and commits further blasphemy with an acoustic guitar on "Questioningly."

The changes distinguish *Road to Ruin* from the nearly interchangeable three albums that preceded it (to be clear, those three albums are all completely awesome). A few songs fall a little flat for the first time ("I'm Against It," "Go Mental," "Bad Brain"), but "Questioningly," "She's the One," and "Don't Come Close" are among the Ramones' very best, and "I Wanna Be Sedated" gave them a theme song every punk-ignorant punter knows. *Road to Ruin* is the fourth corner in a quartet of essential Ramones albums, and they'd never cut one this good again.

THE RICH KIDS: *GHOSTS OF PRINCES IN TOWERS*

Only a dope would dispute the importance of the Sex Pistols' role in establishing punk as a major force. They were the genre's poster boys and the one punk group your great-grandpa has heard of. With his spiky hair, permanent grimace, shredded attire, cockney yowl, and dentally challenged grin, Johnny Rotten gave the genre a face. Steve Jones suggested punk's danger when he told that "fucking rotter" Bill Grundy what he thought of him on live TV. Horrifically, the serially abusive Sid Vicious proved it when he (allegedly) murdered his girlfriend, Nancy Spungeon, in the Chelsea Hotel before ODing. These are historically significant incidents. Their music, though? Eh.

Far more interesting—yet far less appreciated—is the band that Glen Matlock formed after he was purportedly kicked out of the Pistols for "liking the Beatles." As spurious as that story is (Matlock says he quit just because he was sick of Johnny Rotten's assholery), the Rich Kids certainly have a greater grasp of melody and variety than the Sex Pistols ever did. I know, I know—punk is not supposed to be about melody or variety, but all the best punk groups from the Clash to the Damned to the Buzzcocks were melodic and eclectic (let's call the Ramones "the exception that proves the rule").

Ghosts of Princes in Towers fires blazing bullets like "Cheap Emotions" and "Put You in the Picture," which are much more electrifying—much more *punk*—than anything on *Bollocks*. But it also has moody dirges like "Strange One," with its twinkling organ line and massive fuzz guitars; heavy rock like "Hung On You"; and power pop like "Bullet Proof Lover" and the classic title track, which puts Matlock's purported love of the Beatles on proud display. Most of the reviews you'll read of *Ghosts of Princes in Towers* dismiss it. Never mind those bollocks. This is the real classic to come out of the Pistols' camp.

THE TOM ROBINSON BAND: *POWER IN THE DARKNESS*

Tom Robinson was an upper-class kid with a serious identity disorder. His first group was Café Society, a folk trio that by most accounts was pretty terrible, but Robinson's songs must have indicated his talent enough to charm Kinks leader Ray Davies. Davies signed Café Society to his newly formed record label, Konk, vowed to produce their debut album, and left the group to twist in the breeze while he pursued projects with his own band. Frustrated by Davies's inattention, Robinson jumped ship, adopted a cockney accent, discovered punk, came out of the closet, and put together a new band.

Right on. Author's collection.

Mind you, Tom Robinson was a street punk like Mick Jagger was a street fighting man, but the righteous fury of *Power in the Darkness* is still every bit as authentic as the most politically charged statements by the Clash (and, lest we forget, Joe Strummer was the son of a foreign-service diplomat—not exactly a gutter upbringing). The rhetoric lacks the subtlety of a bumper sticker, but that does nothing to diminish the excitement of "Up Against the Wall," "Grey Cortina," "Ain't Gonna Take It," and "The Man You Never Saw." Robinson's audacious stance as one of the first openly gay rockers lends purpose to even his most cliché-riddled cuts.

Power in the Darkness is also one of the more eclectic records to emerge in punk's earliest days. The electric piano–driven "Too Good to Be True" is moody blues rock, "The Winter of '79" borrows liberally from Springsteen's act, and the funky "Better Decide Which Side You're On" predates similar efforts by the Clash by several years. The title track is a dramatic, swaggering anthem that couldn't sound more removed from the speed-and-spit revolution even as its message will get you raising your fist like the one on the album cover.

THE ROLLING STONES: *SOME GIRLS*

While punk godfather Pete Townshend was fretting over his place in a changing scene (more on that soon), decadent jet-setter Mick Jagger was wearing garbage-bag trousers and pretending he slept in the gutter of the Bowery. Only a dolt would buy his New Yawk punk pose of 1978, but the masses still agree that *Some Girls* was the most legitimately exciting record the Rolling Stones made since *Exile on Main Street*. After the mostly sad jams and ballads of *Black and Blue*, it's good to hear the Stones revitalized with new guitarist Ron Wood, zipping through a good selection of proper songs. While Jagger may not be a street rat, his role playing isn't any more ridiculous than his previous embodiments of the Boston Strangler or the devil, so "When the Whip Comes Down" and the new-wavy rap "Shattered" still work as first-person vignettes. And there is some of the Stones' elusive authenticity to be heard amid the poses as Jagger croons a heartfelt love plea to a disco beat ("Miss You") and Keith Richards promises to stop forcing the singer to pull his drug-addled weight ("Beast of Burden") after shrugging it all off ("Before They Make Me Run").

Peter Corriston's original sleeve for *Some Girls* featured die cut face shapes and images of such famous women as Lucille Ball, Judy Garland, Marilyn Monroe, Brigitte Bardot, and Farrah Fawcett. They were soon removed for legal reasons. Author's collection.

Although it undeniably improved on *Black and Blue*, *Some Girls* isn't quite top-tier Stones, muddled by the silly lampoon "Far Away Eyes," the tossed-off punk of "Lies," and the by-numbers controversy stoking of the lazily misogynistic and racist title track. Despite its reputation as a classic, *Some Girls* is just a solid Stones album. It's the last one they'd consciously make.

RUSH: *HEMISPHERES*

As soon as they acquired resident intellectual Neil Peart, Rush developed big ambitions. Although sprawling conceptual epics were the centerpieces of album such as *Caress of Steel*, *2112*, and *A Farewell to Kings*, their short songs were still better than their long sci-fi and fantasy narratives. With their final album to contain such an epic, Rush finally got it right. As far as I'm concerned, *Hemispheres* is the first Rush album on which the long songs beat the short ones. If you put me on the rack and stretched my body until I revealed the meaning of "Cygnus X-1 (Book II-Hemispheres)," I'd end up looking like Plastic Man, but it is as dreamy, enveloping, and enthralling a musical suite as Rush would ever create. So what if the lyrics are gibberish? They sure beat the log-limbed metaphors of what may be the worst of Peart's early songs. "The Trees" imparts the message, "People bicker and complain too much! Some of them even whine about wanting equal rights!" Trenchant insights from a rich, white Ayn Rand fan.

Rush is better in the short form with the hard-edged and autobiographical "Circumstances," which boasts a wicked-tricky spiraling riff and some of Geddy Lee's most inspired wailing, but that too pales next to the album's grand finale. Considering Rush's celebrated musicianship, it is surprising that they did not record their first stand-alone instrumental until their sixth album, but "La Villa Strangiato" is well worth the wait— nearly ten minutes of Alex Lifeson's flaming Spanish guitar, lurching melodies, Geddy's wild bass flutters, and, best of all, a mighty riff based on Looney Tunes sound tracks.

The picture disc edition of *Hemispheres* is ideal for anyone who always wanted to watch that guy's butt spin at 33⅓ revolutions per minute. Author's collection.

THE RUTLES: *THE RUTLES*

In 1975, the monumentally influential British sketch program *Monty Python's Flying Circus* had recently gone off the air, and the chaps were working their way from the small screen to the slightly bigger one where they'd soon appear in the monumentally influential *Monty Python and the Holy Grail*. Meanwhile, Eric Idle was testing his extra-Python wings back on the telly with a modest comedy program called *Rutland Weekend Television* set in the rural county of Rutland, hence the title. One episode of the short-lived comedy series profiled a certain group of history-altering mop toppers. Obviously, I'm talking about the Rutles. The rest is history.

And as we all know, the Rutles were bigger than the Beatles. You know the story: they rocked the Reeperbahn where they performed to actual rats in the actual Rat Keller before being discovered by Leggy Mountbatten, who was so taken with the fit of Dirk, Nasty, Stig, and Barry's trousers that he managed them to interplanetary fame. The rest is history: they performed for the queen (of England), wrote a song for the Rolling Stones (says interviewee Mick Jagger, "It was 'orrible"), made such cinema-defining films as *A Hard Day's Rut* and *Ouch!*, and began expanding their consciousnesses and their bladders by succumbing to the mind-altering pleasures of tea (and biscuits). Ron said he was bigger than God (or at least Rod, as in Rod Stewart), and we learned by playing the groundbreaking *Sgt. Rutter's Only Darts Club Band* album backward that Stig is dead (or at least in bed). The rest is history. Of course, I already said that.

Eric Idle's cult classic documentary (with a side order of mock) *The Rutles: All You Need Is Cash* laid out this history quite thoroughly in 1978, blowing up his original four-minute film that aired on *Rutland Weekend Television* to a length considerably longer. I can still remember the first time I saw it on MTV in 1988, laughing like an out-of-sorts idiot at Leggy's mother's prim recollection of the Rutles' trousers and interviewer Idle's suggestion that Dick Jaws—the record exec who *actually* passed on the Rutles—might be an asshole as well as marveling at Neil Innes's brilliant parody/homages to classic Beatles songs. Many artists were deeply influenced by the Beatles, but few artists took the time to take the Beatles' existing songs, wipe off the lyrics, and refit them with their own words (Paul Weller being a rare exception). Innes's parodies of "Help!" ("Ouch!), "Lucy in the Sky with Diamonds" ("Good Times

The music publisher, ATV music, threatened to sue Neil Innes for copyright infringement on several Beatles songs. Innes settled out of court. The album cover is similarly too close for comfort: They clearly just removed the Beatles and the text from the covers of *Sgt. Pepper's* and *Magical Mystery Tour* to create the covers of *Tragical History Tour* and *Sgt. Rutter's Only Darts Club Band.* Author's collection.

Roll"), "I Am the Walrus" ("Piggy in the Middle"), "A Day in the Life" ("Cheese and Onions"), "Dear Prudence" ("Let's Be Natural"), and the rest are spookily authentic and not as outright comedic as the ones Spinal Tap would bash out in a few years. So *The Rutles* could almost be enjoyed as a mutant fourteenth Beatles album.

SIOUXSIE AND THE BANSHEES: *THE SCREAM*

The pioneers of the New York punk scene were a diverse lot defined more by their CBGB origins than by a particular sound. Before shattering dogma with genre-defying records like *London Calling, Cast of Thousands*, and *The Black Album*, the British punks stuck closer to the Ramones' concise speed rock. The debut albums by first wavers the Clash, the Adverts, the Damned, and the rest were unique in their own ways but very identifiable as products of the same scene.

The Scream is the one British first-wave debut to really hack out a completely individual sound. Like Talking Heads and Blondie, Siouxsie and the Banshees were punks by proximity. They huddled behind the Sex Pistols on Bill Grundy's show with the rest of the Pistols' coterie known as the Bromley Contingent. With her dramatically asymmetrical makeup, hair, and fashion, Siouxsie Sioux looked the way most punters pictured punks.

With the exception of "Carcass," which borrows heavily from the Pistols' "Problems," Siouxsie and the Banshees shun the sped-up rock that essentially defined British punk in 1978. Their sound is darker, scarier, more challenging, tougher to take on first listen, more intoxicating after multiple spins. There was nothing else like the horror-movie atmosphere of "Pure," the stomping psychedelia of "Mirage," the industrial squeals of "Metal Postcard (Mitageisen)," or the epic mood shifts of "Switch" in 1978. "Helter Skelter" is a more extreme Beatles blasphemy than even the Damned's amphetamine cover of "Help!"

Although Siouxsie has always rejected the label, we do hear smears of goth rock in her strident yet dramatic vocal, which is not emotionless as it has sometimes been criticized. Her voice is chilly yet full of legit rage. John McKay's varied guitar work showers a bit of color behind the monochrome foreground. Siouxsie and the Banshees would go on to make albums more accomplished than *The Scream*, and they'd certainly make more pleasing ones, but they'd never make a more challenging one that still rewards taking on its challenges.

PATTI SMITH GROUP: *EASTER*

After two albums of exploratory epics, Patti Smith fine-tuned her songwriting to make her best one. The jams of *Horses* and *Radio Ethiopia* give way to compact, hard-nosed rock and roll with only a stray spray of the self-conscious poetics of those earlier records. These moments are brilliantly placed, intruding on the straightforward "Space Monkey" as unexpectedly as the song's stormy, screechy finale, and functioning as an orgasmic buildup to the A-bomb "Rock N Roll Nigger." That anthem for outsiders is Smith's song that most makes good on her "Godmother of Punk" status in both sound and intent. It's three and a half minutes of tonic punk rock that makes me want to shove my head through a sheetrock wall. Its lyrics have not aged well in a world with little tolerance for white artists appropriating hateful slurs never used against them, but the music burns like nothing else Smith ever did.

Easter is not all fury and taboo breaking, though. As the title indicates, it is steeped in the weird biblical imagery of Smith's upbringing. A foreboding atmosphere hangs over eerie, haunting tracks such as "Ghost Dance,"

"We Three," and the title track. Most radical of all may be Smith's crossover collaboration with Bruce Springsteen. "Because the Night" is a shockingly traditional tune for an envelope pusher like Smith.

TALKING HEADS: *MORE SONGS ABOUT BUILDINGS AND FOOD*

Talking Heads: '77 may have been the most completely original album to come out of the CBGB scene. David, Tina, Chris, and Jerry made an even better album in 1978. *More Songs About Buildings and Food* is in some ways more of the same, especially in light of how totally individual each of Talking Heads' subsequent records would be. The sophomore one could have been called *More Angular, Sweaty, Paranoid Pop Songs for Hip College Geeks*. Yet the performances are tighter, the songs are better, and the hooks are clearer. Brian Eno's production allows each instrumental element to breathe. David Byrne delivers many of his greatest songs: the gallop of "Thank You for Sending Me an Angel," the almost bubble-gummy "The Good Thing," the serpentine "Warning Sign," the sparkling pop "The Girls Want to Be with the Girls," the twitchy "Found a Job" (featuring one of Tina Weymouth's springiest bass lines), and the panoramic "The Big Country." Byrne's songs are so good that it's almost a

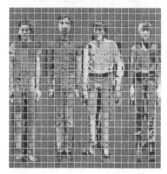

Tina Weymouth said Chris Franz is responsible for the surreal title of Talking Heads' second album. Surreally, XTC's Andy Partridge more recently published a Twitter comment in which he claimed to have given David Byrne the title. Author's collection.

shame that a cover of Al Green's "Take Me to the River" is the track that hooked the record. It zipped into the *Billboard* top thirty, as did the gold-certified *More Songs About Buildings and Food*. That commercial success further distanced Talking Heads from the punks.

VAN HALEN: *VAN HALEN*

Guitarist Alex Van Halen and his drummer brother Eddie had been kicking around in bands since the sixties. Their act started to come together when they swapped instruments. It shot off like an ICBM when they met versatile cuckoo David Lee Roth. After changing their name from Mammoth to the brothers' surname, Van Halen became America's first credible heavy-metal band. While Alex's drums sounded like an elephant stampede and Eddie's strings screamed like electrified howler monkeys (see "Eruption" for prime examples of both), the guys' grinning stage presence and Roth's incorrigible clowning made them more like heavy Faces than America's answer to Black Sabbath. Van Halen also had sharper pop instincts than the British heavy metalers. "Runnin' with the Devil," "Ain't Talkin' 'Bout Love," and "Jamie's Crying" have the molten riffs metal kids crave, but they're also catchy as all get out, and no self-respecting metal band from either side of the pond would make anything as silly as "Ice Cream Man."

THE WHO: *WHO ARE YOU*

Unlike the Rolling Stones, the Who always rejected trends—even when they were responsible for setting them. In the turmoil of the late seventies punk revolution, the Who was widely and justifiably accepted as progenitors of the movement, yet instead of catching that wave and cutting the kind of raw, noisy, terse invectives that "My Generation" inspired, they went in quite the opposite direction. *Who Are You*—with its overwhelming synthesizers and strings, ultraslick production, and overall air of weariness—is the very type of record against which the punks were revolting. Yet in its refusal to hop on an obvious bandwagon in the way artists from the Stones to Billy Joel (exhibit A: *Glass Houses*) would, *Who Are You* reveals more undiluted honesty than a lot of punk records do. Pete Townshend takes a hard look at his place in 1978 and clearly doesn't like what he sees. He is frustrated with his inability to reignite his former inspiration and irritated by his audience's complacent acceptance of "the same old song." An infamous encounter with Sex Pistols Steve Jones and Paul Cook during which Townshend drunkenly declared that the Who's responsibility was to step aside and make way for bands like the Pistols and the Clash inspired the title track.

Townshend's emotional whirlwind makes *Who Are You* a powerful statement even if the music is the least visceral the Who had made thus far. This is largely because Keith Moon's energy was so near the bottom of the incline, and he would die just three weeks after the album's release. That doesn't mean the band is on sleepwalk through the whole record. The title track is their heaviest metal, and "Sister Disco" percolates. The jazzy "Music Must Change," the tragicomic "Guitar and Pen," and the wrenchingly sad "Love Is Coming Down" are all beautiful. John Entwistle once again plays his role as a funny foil to Pete Townshend's soul-searching with songs that almost parody Pete's societal ("Had Enough") and sexual ("Trick of the Light") frustrations. The sci-fi character piece "905" (an excerpt from a larger rock opera about a future society of clones and cannibals John had in mind) mirrors the beauty of Pete's best *Who Are You* tracks.

X-RAY SPEX: *GERMFREE ADOLESCENTS*

By 1978, the Ramones were already on their fourth album, and punk was already spawning a second wave of upstarts. X-Ray Spex actually was not among them. They had been on the London scene since 1976, but they did not put out their first LP until late 1978. *Germfree Adolescents* feels like punk's next, great leap forward, expanding the usual austere arrangement with Rudi Thomson's fat-assed sax and the perspective with one of the movement's first great women: human air-raid siren Poly Styrene. By homing in on our mass-produced, overly commercialized culture—and embracing it to comically ironic effect—she also gives *Germfree Adolescents* a focus unusual for punk.

The album hits hardest when the band does tracks such as "Art-I-Ficial," "Obsessed with You," "Identity," and the classic single "The Day the World Turned Day-Glo." X-Ray Spex also counter their high-velocity with jolly mid-tempo pop ("Warrior in Woolworth's"), vintage girl-group sounds ("I Can't Do Anything"), and psychedelia (the floating title track). They would not release another studio album until re-forming and recording *Conscious Consumer* nearly two decades later, making *Germfree Adolescents* stand out that much more among the fast and first-wave punk albums.

1979

The year 1979 was a transitional one for the rock album and not just because it marked the end of a decade. Punk had been raging for the past few years, but the genre was already on the (temporary) decline, and many of the original punks that refused to evolve were facing the end of their shelf lives. Disco had been the freshest new force on radio, but it was running out of steam by decade's end, which certainly cheered cro-mag rock fans who celebrated its decline when Chicago DJ Steve Dahl organized an anti-disco rally on July 12 at Comiskey Park in Chicago. In the middle of a White Sox/Tigers double-header, attendees gathered to watch Dahl blow up a pile of disco albums. It degenerated into a full-scale riot on the field. The event symbolized an unfortunate shift in rock and roll as the music that celebrated youthful freedom and rebellion was becoming obnoxiously conservative at best and borderline fascist at worst. Like a flashlight pointed down a rat-infested alley, "Disco Demolition Night" exposed the thinking of so many rock fans who believed there was no room for anyone but white, heterosexual, male guitarists in the music world.

The old-fashioned rock and roll these ding-dongs loved was facing its own problems, as most of the biggest classic rockers of the sixties and seventies were either reaching the ends of their careers or, at least, bidding their most creative periods farewell. In the coming decade, the playing field would broaden considerably, and the electric guitar would lose a lot of its power as synthesizers, drum machines, and samples began to share the airwaves with that increasingly archaic-sounding tool. New Wave was burgeoning, power pop was on the rise, and the eighties were just a few neon months away.

THE ADVERTS: *CAST OF THOUSANDS*

Time is very kind to some albums that were initially misunderstood. *Cast of Thousands*, the record that essentially destroyed the Adverts, is one of these. Released at the tail end of punk's first wave, fans and critics were baffled by the band and producer Tom Newman's (best known for handling Mike Oldfield's decidedly unpunk prog symphony *Tubular Bells*) decision to furnish some rough rockers with acoustic guitars, keyboards, bells, and—weirdest of all—a choir (actually multitracked voices of just a few singers, including Maggie Riley, who'd sang on *Tubular Bells*). Such embellishments were highly unacceptable to blinkered listeners more concerned with the most restrictive punk ethos than the kind of unfettered self-expression that set the best bands aside from the most ephemeral. The title song, which contains the choir that so appalled former fans, is as wild as the Adverts' earlier singles but as epic and majestic as the greatest pop anthems. With T. V. Smith's feral screams on the outro vamp, "Cast of Thousands" is punk's "Hey Jude." "The Adverts" is a witty satire of advertising that naturally reads as self-promotion ("Pretty soon you'll be . . . living like the Adverts. Things could be worse") set to a driving rhythm augmented with glittering piano runs. "My Place" is a pretty union of folk rock and punk rock several years before the Violent Femmes started doing that kind of thing. "Television's Over" makes more forceful use of that powerful pseudo-choir and carnival organ. "I Will Walk You Home" is a dark, dramatic dirge with sped-up guitars mimicking mandolins. Alas, all of this shining music was tentatively tasted and puked out by punks in the late seventies. Hearing it today reveals a lost classic.

THE B-52'S: *THE B-52'S*

In the late seventies, the B-52's magnetized the pop world's attention to Athens, Georgia, where a new scene was starting to coalesce. There was no particular Athens sound. The B-52's' kitschy retro party rock was nothing like Pylons' angular avant-funk or Bar-B-Q Killer's chaotic punk or Vic Chesnutt's gritty songcraft or R.E.M.'s jangly Nuevo folk rock. But the fact that so much varied creativity was blossoming in a particular location was noteworthy and highly influential. That creativity expanded beyond pop as students and artists attracted to a bohemian oasis in the conservative state invented new ways to express themselves and hang out. They got inventive on the cheap with weird food-oriented art shows or made spectacles of themselves while people watched. Outside artists such as Matthew Sweet were drawn to the Athens to catch some of its magic.

When I went to see Matthew Sweet play at NYC's Academy in 1995, Fred Schneider was watching the show from the balcony. Before the show began, some super drunk guy in a very sharp suit noticed Schneider from the floor and started howling, "I know that guy! I know that guy!" Once he had everybody in the place's attention, he declared, "I know that guy . . . that's Iggy Pop!" Schneider waved very graciously. Author's collection.

Their surfy guitar riffs, garagey Farfisa lines, Motown beats, and demands to shake ass are straight from essential points along the rock and roll time line. Yet no other group sounds like the B-52's. Having done so much to instigate the Athens art scene, they proceeded to take over the nation with the newest-sounding New Wave of 1979. Kate Piersen and Cindy Wilson found a shiny, poppy use for Yoko Ono's ululating, but Fred Schneider's nasal sing-speak is unprecedented. Guitarist Ricky Wilson and drummer Keith Strickland had just enough chops to get the job done, and all five members had humor to beat off all comers.

The B-52's' love of B-grade sci-fi and beach movies and tatty thrift store culture garbs their eponymous debut. "Rock Lobster," "Lava," "Planet Claire" (which repurposes Henry Mancini's "Peter Gunn" riff), the intense "Dance This Mess Around," "There's a Moon in the Sky (Called the Moon)," and a deconstructed take on Petula Clark's "Downtown" are futuristic experiments *and* old-fashioned rock and roll dance numbers. "52 Girls" and "6060-842" are pure, uncomplicated fun. After the future shock of *The B-52's* wore off, the fun of the B-52's never did.

THE CARS: *CANDY-O*

The Cars' first album was loaded with hits, but like a lot of debuts, it found the band working out some kinks. The awkward progressiveness of "All Mixed Up" was the wrong way to end such a cute assortment of pop–New

Wave smashes. There's nothing like that on the perfect *Candy-O*, and even the weirder tracks—the robotic title number and "Night Spots," the Suicide-influenced "Shoo Ba Doo"—fit the mood and enhance the collection with tart contrasts to the unapologetic sweetness of the hits "Let's Go" and "It's All I Can Do." On "Dangerous Type," "Got a Lot on My Head," and "Double Life," the Cars dabble with moodier moods without sacrificing their innate pop sensibilities. The *Cars* felt like an amazing selection of singles tacked together. With its eclectic moods assuredly executed and less dependence on big hits, *Candy-O* feels like a great album.

THE CLASH: *LONDON CALLING*

For a movement that would have such a long-lasting effect on rock and roll, punk's first wave of was a mere flicker on the rock and roll time line. By 1979, groups were either dissolving or moving on to less primitive matters. As the Sex Pistols self-combusted, the Adverts were experimenting with choirs on *Cast of Thousands*, the Damned were dabbling in retro psychedelics and proto-goth on *Machine Gun Etiquette*, and the Artist Formerly Known as Johnny Rotten was putting together the first real post-punk group, Public Image Ltd. Even the devoutly primitive Ramones tentatively expanded their sound with an ill-fated collaboration with Phil Spector, who controversially added keyboards and strings atop the group's core sound on *End of the Century*. Not all of these trials worked. While Johnny Lydon went on to enjoy a far longer tenure with PiL than he did with the Pistols and the Damned continued to evolve, the Adverts broke up amidst a storm of dreadful reviews, and the Ramones scrambled to get back on track while never releasing another record as widely acclaimed as the ones they put out prior to the Spector debacle. Meanwhile, artists who were never true punks at heart—Elvis Costello, the Talking Heads, Blondie—continued progressing unabated.

The group that made the most critically and commercially successful transition from the manic tempos, stripped-down arrangements, and shouted vocals that defined early punk to a more refined sound was doubtlessly the Clash. Their movement from the ragged frenzy of "White Riot" in early 1977 to the lush *London Calling* less than three years later is as radical an evolution as the Beatles' shift from "Twist and Shout" to *Revolver* across the same time frame. *London Calling* barely sounds like the band that made either *The Clash* or *Give 'Em Enough Rope*. Yes, Joe Strummer's raw pipes remain instantly recognizable, and the reggae influences previously apparent on "Police & Thieves" and "(White Man) in Hammersmith Palais" are present and accounted for, but the sheer variety of this double album is unprecedented not only in the Clash catalog but in the entirety of punk as well. The album encapsulates rock and roll essentials as "The White Album" covered all popular music. *London Calling* reaches back to fifties rock and roll in both its cover design, which references Elvis Presley's debut LP, and its songs (a version of Vince Taylor and His Playboys' "Brand New Cadillac," a brief snippet of Lloyd Price's "Stagger Lee" on the front end of "Wrong 'Em Boyo"). The Clash then move on to the sixties with touches of British rock (the Beatlesque "Spanish Bombs"; "London Calling," which quotes the Kinks' "Dead End Street," a song that deals with the same themes of class imbalance and poverty integral to much of the Clash's most politically conscious work), Spector-style soul ("The Card Cheat"), ska ("Rudie Can't Fail"), and reggae ("The Guns of Brixton," "Revolution Rock"). "Lover's Rock" and "Train in Vain" are nods to the Rolling Stones in the seventies, and Paul Simonon's octave-hopping bass line on "Lost in the Supermarket" would not have sounded out of place on the disco floor.

One of the few major rock movements conspicuously absent on *London Calling* is the stripped-down punk that had been the Clash's previous calling card. What is still very present on *London Calling* is punk *attitude*. There is as much righteous anger packed onto its four sides as there was on the total four sides of the Clash's first two records. The apocalyptic title track stomps through current headlines: the Three Mile Island nuclear meltdown, threats of the Thames overflowing and flooding London, police violence. "Clampdown" draws parallels between the Nazism, capitalism, and violence purveyed by the racist, right-wing National Front movement. "Hateful" and "Koka Kola" are corrosive looks at drug dealers and addicts. Simonon's "The Guns of Brixton" is a chilling vision of race riots and police brutality. Yet there are also unusually personal moments, with Strummer mythologizing Mick Jones's childhood on "Lost in the Supermarket" and memorializing the punk movement he helped spearhead on "Death or Glory."

London Calling also notably strayed from punk in terms of its success. Released in the United States in early 1980, it was the Clash's first record—and arguably the first record by a "real" punk group—to crack *Billboard's*

The Clash paid homage to the design of Elvis Presley's first album cover with *London Calling*. Author's collection.

top forty, making its way to number twenty-seven. As such, it was the first album by a punk group that many kids outside the United Kingdom heard. It became a gateway into the genre's hardier, more challenging products, and it is still regarded as one of the most important rock albums ever made.

ELVIS COSTELLO AND THE ATTRACTIONS: *ARMED FORCES*

The amphetaminized garage-rock clangor of *This Year's Model* got Elvis Costello and the Attractions miscategorized as punks. No one made that mistake when *Armed Forces* followed it. Elvis was fixated on ABBA when his band recorded their second album, and the clean sheen of those Swedish hit makers is apparent in the sparkling production, expert performances, hooky melodies, and stately keyboards of *Armed Forces*. While the manic playing of *This Year's Model* is missed, Elvis's rapidly maturing songwriting remains razor sharp, and his vocals still drip sweat. Sexual and national politics mix and mingle throughout exceptional songs such as the singles "Oliver's Army" and "Accidents Will Happen," the Beatlesque "Party Girl," the nervy "Busy Bodies," and the agitating "Two Little Hitlers." "Chemistry Class" lacks a hook, and "Sunday's Best" is an irritating pseudo–circus novelty (the classic single "Peace, Love, and Understanding" mercifully replaced it on the American edition), but *Armed Forces* is still one of Elvis and the Attractions' best records.

THE DAMNED: *MACHINE GUN ETIQUETTE*

The Damned released the first British punk album, but it didn't seem likely their career would last much longer than that. Having used up his best material for their debut, Brian James composed few worthy songs for their follow-up, *Music for Pleasure*. When the guys couldn't coax Syd Barrett out of retirement to produce the record, they were stuck with Pink Floyd's drummer Nick Mason, who rendered the tracks brittle and lifeless. Stiff Records dropped the Damned, James quit, Rat Scabies followed, and the band officially broke up.

The Damned almost immediately got back together after signing to Chiswick. Scabies was back; James was not. So Captain Sensible moved from bass to guitar, and Saints bassist Algy Ward joined. While the mediocrity of *Music for Pleasure* suggested that the loss of the Damned wasn't worth mourning, the work that followed confirms that it would have been a tragedy because their first LP for Chiswick is the finest pure punk album ever made.

Machine Gun Etiquette pulls off the tricky trick of diversifying the band's sound while rarely abandoning the crisp speed and fury associated with punk. While the Clash was playing with soul and reggae, the Damned was dabbling with sixties-style garage rock and psychedelia. "Love Song" (which delivers such romantic sentiments as "You'll be the rubbish, I'll be the bin"!), the comic book homage "Melody Lee," the ripping atheist rant "Anti Pope," a breathless version of MC5's "Looking at You," "Noise, Noise, Noise," and "Liar" are as speedy and deranged as anything on the group's debut record. The Damned of *Damned Damned Damned* probably would not have dared to try anything like the trippy percussion breakdown that invades "Anti Pope" or the prim piano figure that begins "Melody Lee."

The Damned stray further off the punk rails with their first great horror cartoon "These Hands" (which uses circus sounds much more effectively than "Sunday's Best" had on Elvis's *Armed Forces*), the gothic dirge "Plan 9, Channel 7" (which rhapsodizes over the rumored relationship between James Dean and Vampira), and the magnificent and layered "Smash It Up," which is far poppier than its riotous title suggests. *Machine Gun Etiquette* is punk played with skill, inventiveness, wit, and imagination—all the things that critics claimed the genre lacks. This record would have shut those assholes up for good if they took the time to hear it.

FLEETWOOD MAC: *TUSK*

Rumours was a commercial monster that spent thirty-one nonconsecutive weeks at the top of *Billboard*'s album chart and supplied American radio with four top-ten hits. Naturally, the world couldn't wait to find out what Fleetwood Mac would deliver next. After the sometimes sunny, sometimes sour pop of *Rumours*, many fans didn't know what to do with *Tusk*, a sprawling double album's worth of paranoia, coke-fueled experimentation, chanting, and marching bands.

Tusk is generally remembered as the flop follow-up to *Rumours* (even though it went double platinum—not too floppy), but it is way more than that. *Rumours* is a good record, but "Go Your Own Way," "The Chain," and "Gold Dust Woman" are its only fairly adventurous numbers. On *Tusk*, Lindsay Buckingham fully indulged his studio geekery and imagination. Possibly liberated by the realization his band would never match the success of its previous album, he made beautiful and disorienting tracks such as "The Ledge," "What Makes You Think You're the One," "Not That Funny," and "That's Enough for Me." The title track, with its sinister chanting and marching band brass, is the single weirdest hit single ever released by a commercial pop band. "That's All for Everyone" is a ravishing homage to Buckingham's idol, Brian Wilson.

Elsewhere are some gripping slow burners from Stevie Nicks ("Sara," "Sisters of the Moon," "Storms"). Christine McVie composes one cutesy clunker ("Honey Hi"), but the rest of her tracks are pleasing enough, and in the case of "Brown Eyes," she delivers an ominous work worthy of Nicks. Still, *Tusk* is Lindsay Buckingham's show, and he makes it a spellbinding one.

JOE JACKSON: *LOOK SHARP!*

Joe Jackson started his career barking from the throat about sexual and social politics over jagged backing that was too clean for punk and too nasty and organic for New Wave. So did Elvis Costello, and Jackson was regularly dismissed as a mere Costello clone at the start of his career. The critics had a point. "Happy Loving Couples" and "Fools in Love" are outtakes from *My Aim Is True* in everything but copyright. He taps into bitter Elvis insight to decry the inequity and deceptiveness of romance and wins himself a signature song: "Is She Really Going Out with Him." When he hired Graham Maby, Jackson even copied Costello's great taste in bass players!

But as far as Costello clones go, Joe Jackson is the best. He shows that he is a formidable songwriter in his own right on *Look Sharp!* as he directs his sights at contemporary society beyond relationships, spitting at

According to photographer Brian Griffin, Joe Jackson hated Griffin's iconic cover because it did not spotlight the singer's face. Author's collection.

the media ("Sunday Papers") and fashion (the title track). Jackson would assert his originality a bit more on his superior second album, but for sheer bite, thrust, and unadulterated Costelloizing, he never bested *Look Sharp!*

I'M THE MAN

I'm the Man is still deep in Costello country, but nothing on it is as blatant as "Happy Loving Couples." Jackson's sounds are more varied and his songwriting is more reliably sharp than they'd been on *Look Sharp!* "On the Radio" gets things off to a stormy start, and it's just great song to great song until "Friday" shuts it all down. As Jackson messes with spine-tingling reggae ("Geraldine and John"), perky pop ("Kinda Kute"), tart ballads ("It's Different for Girls," "Amateur Hour"), and revved-up pop punk ("Don't Wanna Be Like That"; the uproarious title track), the band keeps things coherent with riveting, flawless performances. Graham Maby fingers some of the most exciting bass work on wax.

THE JAM: *SETTING SONS*

The Jam never really sounded as much like the Who as journalists wanted you to believe, but the Who had been a primary influence on the band ever since Paul Weller fell in love with *My Generation*. Along with the occasional storm of drums, plectrum scrape down guitar strings, or flicker of pickup, Weller derived his surly attitude and mod image from the early Who. For 1979's *Setting Sons*, he picked up on another important Who calling card. He intended the record to be a concept album with a story about three childhood friends whose wartime experiences divide them as adults. As so often happened to the Who, the realities of the record-making business meant the Jam had to abandon their conceptual ambitions to rush new product into stores. So like *The Who Sell Out* or *Lifehouse/Who's Next*, *Setting Sons* is really half a concept album. Also like those albums, it's great.

Setting Sons draws on the best elements of the Jam's punk and proto-Britpop phases with some of the hardest-hitting and loveliest music of their career. In the former camp is "Eton Rifles," a classic statement of righteous outrage against privileged military cadets, and the incendiary "Private Hell." In the latter is the ultramini mini-opera "Little Boy Soldiers," the stripped-down Motown vibe "Girl on a Phone," and the orchestrated rere-cording of Bruce Foxton's "Smithers-Jones."

The only track to miss the boat is a cover of "Heat Wave," though this is interesting because it reveals the Who's influence on two levels: it's clearly patterned on their version and not the Vandellas' original, and it serves the exact same filler purpose on *Setting Sons* as it did on the Who's own semi-conceptual second album, *A Quick One*. Like the Who's version, the

Jam's is not bad; it's just out of place among such an exceptional selection of original songs.

LED ZEPPELIN: *IN THROUGH THE OUT DOOR*

After the all-electric guitar onslaught of *Presence*, Led Zeppelin returned as a very different band in 1978. Jimmy Page's heroin problems and John Bonham's alcoholism forced John Paul Jones and Robert Plant to pick up the slack. As a result, *In Through the Out Door* is the most keyboard-heavy Zeppelin album, and it suggests that the group may have made the transition into the eighties relatively smoothly.

Jones cowrote all but one of the tracks (the electrified hoedown "Hot Dog," which doesn't belong on this record) and brings a nice variety of sounds to the studio floor: the sexy synths of "In the Evening," the pumping barrelhouse piano of "South Bound Suarez," the salsa polyrhythms of "Fool in the Rain," and the burbling synths of "Carouselambra," a murky, swirling, ten-minute-and-thirty-two-second puzzle that hints at how a Led Zep New Wave record might have sounded. Robert Plant brings back the more personal emotions of *Presence* as he mourns his son Karac on "All My Love" and shrieks his guts out at the climax of the Otis

In Through the Out Door was released with six distinct sleeves, each featuring a different shot from the same photo session. The covers were secreted in brown paper bags so dedicated collectors would have to buy multiple copies in order to obtain each cover. Author's collection.

Redding homage "I'm Gonna Crawl." With its new technology and unprecedented reliance on keyboards, *In Through the Out Door* seems to suggest that Led Zeppelin was turning some kind of corner, but John Bonham's death the following year and the band's wise decision to call it quits left all questions about what they might do next permanently unanswered.

TOM PETTY AND THE HEARTBREAKERS: *DAMN THE TORPEDOES*

Adversity often inspires great art. After Shelter Records handed Tom Petty and the Heartbreakers off to MCA Records without his consent, Petty fought to free himself from the label, declaring bankruptcy after MCA sued him for breach of contract. By the time he settled with MCA subsidiary Backstreet Records, he needed to scramble to build on the momentum of his first two albums. Petty revived some songs from his pre-Heartbreakers group Mudcrutch and dashed off some new ones. That isn't exactly the formula for creating a cohesive classic, but that is surely what *Damn the Torpedoes* is. It is the Heartbreaker's best album, indebted to the sixties rock they love but fresh enough for the New Wave.

Petty gets a little punky with the slashing "Refugee" and a little poppy with the piano-driven "Don't Do Me Like That," but the rest of the album just delivers more of the garage guitar rock of the band's first two albums. However, Petty's songs had never been so uniformly strong. "Even the Losers," "Here Comes My Girl," "Shadow of a Doubt (Complex Kid)," and "What Are You Doing in My Life" are as good as those punky and poppy singles. "Even the Losers" is his crowning achievement, one of the ultimate expressions of the desire and ability to rise above one's limitations. It's a complete lyrical and musical fulfillment of everything rock and roll had been promising since Elvis wiggled himself out of Tupelo poverty.

PINK FLOYD: *THE WALL*

Pink Floyd started thinking conceptually almost as soon as Syd Barrett was out of the band in the late sixties. Their most successful and original conceptual experiment was *The Dark Side of the Moon*'s thematic and sonic framework. Their clearest is *The Wall*, which invests more in story line. The blockbuster double album actually feels more like the successor to *Tommy* than *The Dark Side of the Moon*. Like the Who's rock opera, Roger Waters' tells the tale of a young boy emerging from a shattered childhood with profound emotional blockage, only to find his shaky place in the world as a worshipped star. Unlike *Tommy*, *The Wall* is without fancy. Its antihero, Pink, is no sense-deprived pinball wizard but a standard-issue, asshole rock star. His followers do not succumb to religious fervor before rejecting their idol; they devolve into a fascist mob like that one that stormed Comiskey Park the previous summer.

The Wall is remarkably ill-humored and cynical for such a popular record. With its biographical/autobiographical baggage (Barrett is generally believed to be the main inspiration for Pink, but the character also parallels its creator, who'd lost his own dad in World War II before becoming a rock star), it's hard not assume the lyrics don't reflect Waters's own dim views of his fans and fame. His portrayal of the women in Pink's life is equally dismal.

There are certainly a lot of good songs. The unlikely hit chant "Another Brick in the Wall (Part 2)" and "Young Lust" integrate rock and disco more organically than anything else of their era. "Comfortably Numb" is a worthy stoner anthem. Waters pushes his compositional abilities to full capacity with "The Trial" and scales them back to their most effectively skeletal with "Is There Anybody Out There?" and "Don't Leave Me Now." However, *The Wall* mostly feels like an end—a weighty, weary, and painfully self-aware final sneer from some of the original classic rockers. None of those classic rockers—not the ex-Beatles, not the Stones, not the Who, not Led Zeppelin—would ever have an impact on the kids like this again.

THE POLICE: *REGATTA DE BLANC*

Some have dismissed *Regatta de Blanc* as a sophomore slump with its overreliance on awkward Stewart Copeland songs, but those goofy tunes are a large part of what makes it such a fantastic album and helps it build a personality distinct from *Outlandos d'Amour*'s. Copeland's "Contact," "Does Everyone Stare," and "On Any Other Day" are three of the funniest, oddest songs the Police recorded. His vocal on "Does Everyone Stare" is charming in its tunelessness and conveys his lyrics' pre–"Every Breath You Take" obsessiveness well.

Otherwise, the Police deliver more of what fans loved about the first album with the tough pop of "Message in a Bottle," the psychedelic reggae of "Walking on the Moon," the rhythmically relentless "No Time This Time," and the smoldering "Bring on the Night." Like Elvis and the Attractions, the Police have outgrown punk labels on their second album, so it doesn't burn like *Outlandos d'Amour*, but the band's pop craft is advancing. *Regatta de Blanc* is a clear stepping-stone to *Zenyatta Mondatta*, the album that made the Police stars.

SQUEEZE: *COOL FOR CATS*

One of the wittiest and most organic groups to emerge from the earliest days of the United Kingdom's burgeoning New Wave, Squeeze started their career clumsily. John Cale commanded bandleaders Glenn Tilbrook and Chris Difford to chuck all the songs they'd been perfecting onstage and write all new ones for their eponymous debut album. They ended up with a record more representative of Cale's random power plays (one directive: write songs about musclemen) than Tilbrook and Difford's unique point of view.

Produced by the band and seasoned British studio man John Wood, *Cool for Cats* is unmistakably Squeezed. You'd have to put on a Cars record to hear pop as effortlessly fresh in 1979, and no one was writing such uncomplicatedly wry lyrics about sex with partners ("Slap and Tickle," "It's Not Cricket," "It's So Dirty," "Hop, Skip, and Jump," "Hard to Find") and without ("Touching Me, Touching You"). "Slightly Drunk" and "Goodbye

The cover of *Cool for Cats* was available in green, blue, yellow, pink, or purple, which is the color of my own copy. They're all totally boss. Author's collection.

Girl" deal with the complications that arise when lust blurs with love, while the title track and "The Knack" look beyond sex and behind the obnoxious poses of macho British lad culture, which is really the album's main underlying theme.

DONNA SUMMER: *BAD GIRLS*

Ever since it became a commercial juggernaut in the mid-seventies, disco had been influencing rock and yielding hits like "Miss You" and "Da Ya Think I'm Sexy." *Bad Girls* shows that the influence could move in the other direction too.

Donna Summer had actually gotten her professional start as a rock singer when she quit high school to front a band called the Crow (not to be confused with the Crow that recorded "Evil Woman"). She then got the role of Sheila in a traveling production of the rock musical *Hair*. Summer's career changed drastically after she hooked up with producer Giorgio Moroder. The two collaborated on "Love to Love You Baby," an orgasmic epic that coaxed all of disco's "let's dance then fuck" promise out to the surface. An incredible string of disco hits followed, including the hypnotic "I Feel Love," "Last Dance," and an unthinkably successful disco version of Jimmy Webb's bizarre mini-opera "MacArthur Park."

Summer and Moroder built their ultimate machine in 1979. The double LP *Bad Girls* yielded three huge hits. It's first two—the title track and "Hot

Stuff"—draw an explicit line from disco back to its rock roots with heavy guitar licks and Jagger-esque attitude. The pure disco "Dim All the Lights" is Moroder and Summer's most extraordinary creation, a dramatically structured smash climaxing with overdubbed, overlapped vocal harmonies that swoop and dart at each other like a flock of drunken sparrows.

Bad Girls is also structured like a classic rock concept album. Each of its four sides sticks to a different sound: guitar tracks on side A, disco on side B, torch songs on side C, and a return to the bubbly synth style of "I Feel Love" on side D. The side C ballads are strictly for the dentist's office, but the rest of *Bad Girls* is the hardest-hitting, most creative disco on disc.

TALKING HEADS: *FEAR OF MUSIC*

Transitional albums tend to be awkward but necessary markers in a band's development. *Fear of Music* is an exception: a transitional record that sounds more assured than anything else in the band's discography. Talking Heads had made two rhythmically and intellectually complex New Wave records that made the most of the limitations of their four pieces. Taking the next logical step for a clearly ambitious band, they started expanding that lineup on their third album, inviting guest stars such as King Crimson's Robert Fripp to assist on the African pop–influenced "I Zimbra," the ecologically minded "Air," and "Life During Wartime," a timely takedown of late seventies superficiality sung from the perspective of a revolutionary that became a dance-floor classic.

Talking Heads had yet to allow outside musicians to overwhelm, so *Fear of Music* is denser than '77 or *More Songs* and breathes more than their next two albums will. It is the ideal balance between both eras, and songs such as "Life During Wartime," "Mind," "Cities," "Heaven," and "Air" are some of the best Talking Heads would ever do.

THE UNDERTONES: *THE UNDERTONES*

If the Undertones were nothing more than one-hit (underground) wonders who wrote and recorded "Teenage Kicks"—the song with the impressive distinction of being revered DJ John Peel's favorite ever—they'd be among the greats. However, every song on their debut is a jolt of pop-punk euphoria. *The Undertones* pushes track after track of jittery rhythms, snappy melodies, and Feargal Sharkey's shaky vocals. Their songs may delve into dicey subject matter like incest ("Family Entertainment"), suicide ("Jimmy, Jimmy"), failure ("I Gotta Getta"), and jerking off ("Teenage Kicks," which joined the lineup on a rereleased edition in late 1979), but not a single track fails to supply sweet hooks.

For the most part, the Undertones deal with the tribulations of teenager-hood, though there are none of Tom Petty's victories in such portraits of unrequited frustration as "Girls Don't Like It," "Jump Boys," "Here Comes the Summer," and "Get Over You." The Undertones' searing performances provide all the release their characters never enjoy.

XTC: *DRUMS AND WIRES*

XTC started out as a New Wave band in a punk rock world, disfiguring their angular pop songs into compact shards of lean rock to fit in with the prevailing style. As New Wave pulchritude began displacing punk pugnacity in 1979, XTC found a more sympathetic pro-ducer in Steve Lillywhite and began explor-ing a more complementary sound on *Drums and Wires*. Most importantly, Andy Partridge and Colin Moudling's songs started con-sistently living up to the promise of early successes like "This Is Pop" and "Statue of Liberty." For the first time, they composed an entire album of top-tier material.

Andy Partridge conceptualized the memorably graphic cover of *Drums and Wires*. Author's collection.

As would often be the case, Moulding supplies the record's most out-right catchy numbers, including the evergreen "Making Plans for Nigel" (a top-twenty hit in the United Kingdom) and the woozy love song "Ten Feet Tall." Partridge brings the modern art, with sweaty, delirious, dancey dynamos like "Helicopter," "When You're Near Me I Have Difficulty," and "Scissor Man." "Complicated Game" is the culmination of the underlying anxiety running through even the poppiest numbers on *Drums and Wires*.

1980

As a new decade dawned, guitar-based rock and roll found itself sharing the airwaves a lot more than it had at the beginning of the previous decade. The year began with antiseptic adult contemporary pop production washing over records by soul (Stevie Wonder, Smokey Robinson), country (Kenny Rogers, Eddie Rabbit), and even rock (Styx, Cliff Richard) artists. All were rewarded in the charts. Disco was still kicking around as the year began with K.C. and the Sunshine Band's "Please Don't Go" at the top position, but punk started seeming as though it had no staying power outside of alarmist editorials in the mainstream media.

Most significantly, a new form of music was rising up from the American East Coast that allowed creative wordsmiths with nothing more than a turntable to make their own music without ever having to touch an instrument at all. The previous August, Englewood, New Jersey's, Sugarhill Gang let loose a stream of merry boasts over a copy of Chic's "Good Times" and scored the first rap single to peak into *Billboard*'s top-forty chart. It was the opening salvo in a new movement that would leave the importance, commerciality, and rebellious credibility of rock and roll badly shaken by the end of the decade and all but stone cold dead by the end of the century.

But that's the story of rock and roll on the radio, which the genre had been increasingly leaving over the course of the previous decade. By 1980, AOR radio was the genre's last radio refuge. Classic rock and rollers such as Pink Floyd, Heart, Tom Petty and the Heartbreakers, Rush, and the

Rolling Stones spent a lot more time in the upper regions of the album charts than the singles ones. New strains of rock were emerging too as punk found a second wind and an even harder edge at the other end of the American continent, the sounds that would define indie rock and Britpop in the nineties began to take shape, and New Wave made the synthesizer every bit as integral to popular music as the electric guitar.

ADAM & THE ANTS: *KINGS OF THE WILD FRONTIER*

Between making super-abrasive, Banshees-esque noise while playing a superficial punk pretty boy in *Jubilee* and becoming an actual superficial New Wave pretty boy with 1982's *Friend or Foe*, Adam Ant hit the perfect balance between those two leanings with *Kings of the Wild Frontier*. A lot of the lyrics are splendidly silly stuff about dancing ants and pirates, but there are also more pointedly satirical pieces about critical flavors of the moment, being a victim of your own emotions, and all other stripes of paranoia. But let's be honest: no one listens to Adam & the Ants for their lyrics. No worries, mate, because *Kings* is rich in royal melodies, glammy guitar lines, and dance-inducing Burundi beats. The catchy sweetness of anthems like "Feed Me to the Lions," "The Magnificent Five," "Dog Eat Dog," and "Press Darlings" are balanced by the discordance of "Ants Invasion," the brooding "Killer in the House," and the brooding of "Physical (You're So)." And the clattering "Antmusic" gets my vote for the single greatest single of the eighties. This may be the only pop song that uses tapping for its central hook. I'm surprised every other New Wave band didn't jump on the tapping bandwagon because it's so infectious on this track. Marco Pirroni's glam guitar harmonies and Adam's hiccups about an infectious new musical craze are brilliant too. I used to watch hours of MTV just waiting for this video to come on. It never came on often enough for me.

DAVID BOWIE: *SCARY MONSTERS (AND SUPER CREEPS)*

The classic rockers of the seventies who recognized the changing landscape of the new decade made some effort to move with the times. The Rolling Stones and Pink Floyd were mixing disco beats with their usual riffs. Paul McCartney was experimenting with synthesizers. Rush wholeheartedly embraced New Wave's synths and pop structures.

Their fellow old-timer David Bowie never moved with the times. He created them. Of all the elder statespeople who released a new record in 1980, none made an album as ahead of its time as Bowie did. *Scary Monsters (and Super Creeps)* does not merely use New Wave's glassy sounds as decorations signaling relevance. He builds a world out of them, and he does not reserve his more oblique ideas for the deep cuts. The queasy yet indescribably catchy tracks "Ashes to Ashes" (a sequel to "Space Oddity" that replaces sixties-style wonder with eighties-style complacency), "Fashion" (a fractured disfiguration of disco), "It's No Game," and "Scary Monsters (And Super Creeps)" were all released as singles—and all failed miserably in the United States.

As challenging as the songs on *Scary Monsters* are, they're all proper songs. There are none of the amorphous instrumentals of the Brian Eno period Bowie had just left behind. So the album shapes the illusion that he had resolved to rejoin the commercial crowd. Its super-freak sound reveals a more artistically minded reality.

ELVIS COSTELLO AND THE ATTRACTIONS: *GET HAPPY!!*

While touring the United States in 1979, Elvis Costello had an infamous encounter with Stephen Stills and singer Bonnie Bramlett that nearly destroyed his career. In a drunken, dumb-punk attempt to offend artists he regarded as aging hippies, Costello made ugly, obnoxious comments about James Brown and Ray Charles. When Bramlett went to the press with Costello's remarks, the media understandably branded him a racist.

Many believed his decision to next release an album of Tamla-Motown and Stax-inspired rave-ups to be his way of apologizing and proving the insincerity of his rant. As a public relations move, it was pathetic. As a montage of twenty short, sharp rockers in the soul mode, *Get Happy!!* is magnificent.

Elvis's earlier albums contained ample hints that sixties soul played a major role in his music, but never would he focus so directly on the music as he did on *Get Happy!!* The sparse arrangements ultimately make the record sound more in line with soul-inspired British bands like Small

The cover of *Get Happy!!* came with pre-applied coffee cup stains to give it that vintage look. Author's collection.

Faces and the Action than the lushly orchestrated American originals, but the decision not to overproduce *Get Happy!!* was a smart one. This is a mixture of punk and soul so perfectly blended that it must have made Paul Weller jealous. "Love for Tender," "The Imposter," "High Fidelity," "Beaten to the Punch," and an amphetamine-fueled reading of Sam & Dave's "I Can't Stand Up (For Falling Down)" blaze by in a streak of sweaty fury and rhythmic accuracy. Bassist Bruce Thomas and drummer Pete Thomas are the underrated heroes of *Get Happy!!*, while Steve Nieve's organ and piano lines—creepy crawly one moment, stately and bold the next—shimmer.

But this is Elvis's circus, and he gets off a lot of his best songs here and not just when he's burning down the barn. "Clown Time Is Over," "Opportunity," and "Motel Matches" explore soul's more sensual side. The two non–soul-inspired songs are among the album's greatest: "New Amsterdam," a woozy waltz on which Elvis supplies all the instruments, and the Procol Harum swirl of "Riot Act," on which he bitterly defends himself against the post-Stills/Bramlett flack.

THE CURE: *SEVENTEEN SECONDS*

The Cure would become one of the eighties' unlikeliest success stories: a group of pasty, glum dead-end kids who teased their hair up like tangled thorns and made deeply despairing songs for their fellow futureless youth. While heavy metal and punk tapped into the anger of having no future, the Cure's music was the sound of the depression that sets in next. Without the danciness, overt artiness, or exoticism of Siouxsie and the Banshees' early records, the Cure became the most credible poster kids for goth rock and ended up selling tons of albums.

There was little of all that on *Three Imaginary Boys*, a debut album that slipped out without the band's green light and found them in an awkward punk adolescence despite a few superb sides such as "10:15 Saturday Night," "Accuracy," and "Grinding Halt." With their second album, the Cure truly became the Cure. The foot-dragging instrumental "A Reflection" sets the tone for a gloomy disc that sounds like a poppier take on *The Marble Index* but with a more relatable point of view than Nico's blitzed poems. Robert Smith moans his romantic ennui, selfishness, and unrequited despair in plain language. "Three" is an even truer portrait of generational conflict than "Summertime Blues" and a far more authentic depiction of depression than "Paint It Black." Many rock and rollers became stars by speaking the language of their hopeless teenage audience. The Cure actually communicated with the kids.

THE DAMNED: *THE BLACK ALBUM*

Having expanded punk as far as it could go and creating its finest work with 1979's *Machine Gun Etiquette*, the Damned could only move beyond the genre with their next record. That means *The Black Album* is something of a transitional record, neither as ferocious as the one that preceded it nor as accomplished as the one that followed.

The Damned play with a lot of different styles as they search for their new sound, which only once leads them into sketchy territory: the infamously overproduced synth popper "History of the World, (Part 1)." Otherwise, the Damned get damned daring while making some of their best music. "Wait for the Black Out," "Drinking about My Baby," and "Hit or Miss" are the only tracks that fully acknowledge their punk past. "Lively Arts" comes close, but the shivery synth on the chorus nudges the track further into the goth direction the band first set its sights on with "Fan Club" from their debut album and would become more integral to their sound as the eighties progressed. Halloweeny ballads "Dr. Jekyll and Mr. Hyde" (featuring exceptional work by new bassist Paul Gray), "Twisted Nerve," and "12th Floor Vendetta" drift deeper into gothic forests. The crazed "Therapy" smacks of prog, and Captain Sensible's "Silly Kids Games," a swipe at game shows, is sunny pop complete with Beach Boys harmonies.

Vampiric singer Dave Vanian makes his most profound impression on "Curtain Call," which sweeps all the disparate styles on *The Black Album* into a spellbinding, seventeen-minute epic that would have gotten the Damned's punk membership card revoked had they recorded it two years earlier. Loaded with darkly atmospheric verses, deliriously catchy choruses, Captain Sensible's dreamy bridge, a plethora of sound effects and synthesizer experiments, and a chilling tape loop of Rimsky-Korsakov's "Scheherazade," "Curtain Call" couldn't be more at odds with punk ethos, yet it's a divine piece of music and my personal favorite song of the eighties. "Curtain Call" was a casualty in the United States, where the British double LP was snipped to a single (a side of manic live numbers was lost too), but all necessary elements of the *Black Album* have been restored on most subsequent reissues, so this great record can once again be heard just as Satan intended.

DEVO: *FREEDOM OF CHOICE*

No group that ended up crossing into the mainstream had more difficult origins than Devo. The group began as a put-on by a bunch of Kent State students who satirized the surrounding culture's "de-evolution" with nigh-unlistenable avant-garde rock like "Jocko-Homo" and "Mongoloid," made bizarre experimental films featuring their music, and wore plastic "energy domes" that looked like flowerpots on their heads.

What started as one of the less typical college lampoons got serious when David Bowie convinced Warner Bros. to sign Devo in 1977 and the band released their break-through album *Freedom of Choice* in 1980. For their third LP, Devo refined their geeky New Wave into a dozen totally focused potential singles. The freaky yet outrageously hummable "Whip It" scored them an actual hit and became one of the weirdest things to invade *Billboard*'s top twenty in 1981. The stuttering rhythms, funky synths, fuzzy riffs, and attitude-spitting vocals of "Girl U Want," "Gates of Steel," "Cold War," "Mr. B's Ballroom," and "That's Pep!" would have sounded just as radical and refreshing com-

The inner sleeve of *Freedom of Choice* is also an order form for those who choose to transition to a total Devo lifestyle. Among the items you could order are postcards ($2.50), 3D glasses ($1.25), and Devo's official yellow radiation suit ($10.95). Sadly, the energy domes were not included in the offer. Author's collection.

ing out of radios. And at the dawn of a decade when the prevailing ethos were superficiality, conformity, and nationalism, Devo arrived with a genuine point of view challenging such things with lyrics as digestible as a bowl of Froot Loops. The positivity of "Whip It," "Gates of Steel," "Planet Earth," and "That's Pep" caused Devo's visions of what the world and the human race could be to contrast with the often defeated and dejected stance of topical songs, making *Freedom of Choice* both musically and philosophically uplifting. Only in the eighties could five guys with flowerpots on their heads be their generation's voices of reason.

THE JAM: *SOUND AFFECTS*

The Beatles and the Kinks may have planted the movement's roots fifteen years earlier, but Britpop's true ground zero is *Sound Affects*. With their fifth album, the Jam fully shed their previous reliance on punk's speed and lack of adornment. Paul Weller's songs are more crafted than vomited forth, the arrangements more varied and subtle. "Monday" sparkles with baroque keyboard flourishes. Folky acoustic guitars drive "That's Entertainment!," a grim portrait of life in a Council estate where one can only fantasize about taking a break from exhaust fumes, construction noise, and inane pap on the telly. Even a romantic snog must be snatched in the center of extreme squalor and depression.

Brass fanfares explode at the conclusion of "Start!" Both "Monday" and "Man in the Corner Shop" pick up on Ray Davies's fascination with dreary Englishness, but this is no laid-back affair. "But I'm Different Now," the boiling "Set the House Ablaze," and "Boy About Time" can hardly be confused with punk, yet they all bounce with as much energy as the Jam's early records. Even the acoustic "That's Entertainment!" is muscular and mean. "Start!" may be one of rock's most egregious rip-offs, yet it's still imminently likable on its own terms, and on a thematic level, it pays all due respect to Britpop's past while forging its future simultaneously. *Sound Affects* is for past fans of *Face to Face* and future fans of *Parklife* alike.

JOHN LENNON AND YOKO ONO: *DOUBLE FANTASY*

After a long period of self-imposed house arrest, John Lennon made a last-minute return in 1980 with his second proper collaboration with Yoko Ono. Considering what happened a few weeks after its release, *Double Fantasy* is painful to criticize, though Lennon's post-rocker complacency is very evident in songs such as "(Just Like) Starting Over," "Watching the Wheels," "Beautiful Boy," and "Woman." They're perfectly professional, perfectly listenable pieces of work, but John's rebel fire is entirely absent. In contrast, Yoko's spectacular New Wave rave "Kiss Kiss Kiss," disco-punk fusion "Give Me Something," and enchanting "Beautiful Boys" and "Yes, I'm Your Angel," which Snow White could have covered convincingly, swirl with inspiration.

While Lennon's songs lack fire, they are clearly the work of a longtime peace champion who has finally found a bit of peace for himself. The abandoned child and angry young man who'd brought so much happiness into the world with his incomparable body of work and did so much to turn the rock LP into a legitimate art form finally seemed happy too. A sick loner pumped up with self-righteous religious delusions ended it on December 8, cutting through the extreme sweetness of *Double Fantasy* with unintended bitterness.

THE POLICE: *ZENYATTA MONDATTA*

After a debut album intended to establish them among the punks (it didn't work) and a quirky sophomore effort, the Police fully found themselves on their third album. Slick and flawlessly professional, *Zenyatta Mondatta* is not as primal as the band's first two albums, but it hangs together as a consistent work better. Getting the big hit pop single out of the way with its first track, the zingy Nabokov riff "Don't Stand So Close to Me" (which Sting insists was *not* inspired by his own days as a hunky schoolteacher), *Zenyatta Mondatta* then gets on with its essential agenda: pop reggae with spacey guitar spiraling out over a rhythm section crisper than an Arctic morn.

Elsewhere, Sting reaches into new directions as he strews political subjects ("Driven to Tears," "Bombs Away"), road laments ("Man in a Suitcase"), and character pieces ("When the World Is Running Down, You Make the Best of What's Still Around," "Shadows in the Rain") among his usual love songs. Despite its aspiration toward profundity, the album's other hit, "De Do Do Do, De Da Da Da," is pretty mind numbing, though. The Police would chase their ambitions more audaciously on their next two albums and become megastars in the process, leaving *Zenyatta Mondatta* feeling like the last chapter of the first phase of a way-too-short career.

THE PRETENDERS: *PRETENDERS*

Akron, Ohio, expatriate Chrissie Hynde had already established herself as a top rock journalist, the paramour of one of the genre's most revered artists (Ray Davies), and a fixture of the London punk crowd. None of these achievements indicated she'd turn out to be a rocker to challenge any other.

Pretenders is one of the all-time great debut albums. The band is white hot throughout, even on ballads like "Up the Neck" and the strikingly mature "Kid," but Hynde's too-cool snarl and extraordinary songs are what really make the LP a classic. "Precious," "The Wait," and "Tattooed Love Boys," a disturbingly ambivalent account of Hynde's own rape at the hands of an Ohio biker gang, are unhinged yet wildly melodic and, in the case of "Love Boys," as rhythmically complex as your average prog-rock song. The hit "Brass in Pocket" is a yearning, sexy Motown homage.

This is Hynde's record, but the rest of the band all make major contributions, from Martin Chambers's tom-tom attack that launches it all to James Honeyman-Scott's squealing guitar solos on "Tattooed Love Boys" to Pete Farndon pounding the album to it its conclusion with a bass line for the ages on "Mystery Achievement." Even the throwaway instrumental by Farndon and Honeyman-Scott is terrific.

PRINCE: *DIRTY MIND*

Ever since those primordial days when Jackie Brenston warned you ladies he was going to introduce you to his "Rocket 88," rock and roll has had a very dirty mind. In the sixties, guys like Mick Jagger and Lou Reed upped rock's pornography quotient, but none of them had the sheer audacity to do what Minneapolis multi-instrumentalist, multi-octave screamer, multidimensional genius Prince did. Beginning as the most audacious funk-rock-soul fuser since Sly Stone, Prince proceeded to sculpt a completely distinctive career with his dazzling originality and expertise, his addiction to the recording studio, and his outrageous persona that was one part purple harlequin and one part walking erection.

Prince on his way to do his weekly grocery shopping. Author's collection.

Prince somehow also became a superstar while trafficking in borderline-porno decades before the internet made such stuff as common as cola ads. *Dirty Mind* pirouettes over a series of sexual practices and taboos. "When You Were Mine" explains the aftermath of a ménage à trois gone wrong. "Dirty Mind" and "Head" are self-explanatory. "Sister" is an ode to incest that not only memorializes losing one's virginity to a sibling but also tosses in references to S&M, blow jobs, blue balls, and getting one's underwear caught in one's pubes.

The sound is just as out there as the words as Prince takes the communal big band spirit of funk and crushes it down to the insular, thin sound of a one-man band's basement demo, which is essentially what *Dirty Mind* is. It was as if Prince wanted to separate the straights who'd wandered into his world after hearing the comparatively mundane "I Wanna Be Your Lover" from the real freaks who would follow him down any dark alley he chose. Those who did would be rewarded a hundredfold.

QUEEN: *THE GAME*

Throughout the seventies, Queen were the kings of outrageous bombast. They took the ridiculousness of heavy metal that always writhed under the surface of Led Zeppelin's records and set it free with songs of operatic nonsense, bicycles, and big butts. They were Spinal Tap if David St. Hubbins had a sense of humor, Nigel Tufnel had a brain, and the two of them harmonized like a choir of Valkyries.

Queen's wit was still intact in the new decade, but their bombast and sheer absurdity had evaporated a bit. That may have disappointed some original fans, but it probably also won Queen some new ones, at least in America, where they had their greatest success yet with *The Game*. It was their first album to occupy *Billboard*'s number one spot. Its two singles, the charming Elvis pastiche "Crazy Little Thing Called Love" and the sincerely funky "Another One Bites the Dust," also went to the top, and both feature outstanding bass work from John Deacon, who wrote the latter smash. On "Crazy Little Thing," writer Freddie Mercury gives one of his most restrained performances, and he sings just as marvelously when he's pushing into a Presley baritone as when he's going for the top on the classic Queen power ballad "Save Me" or the sensitive title track. On "Don't Try Suicide," he shows he can still slash through the envelope of good taste with an absolutely uproarious satire of brain-dead message songs. I'm sure Big Fun was listening.

THE ROLLING STONES: *EMOTIONAL RESCUE*

After the relative creative success of *Some Girls*, the Stones are back to treading water with *Emotional Rescue*. "Indian Girl" is an oddly misguided and seemingly insincere stab at political commentary that pairs pseudo-Latin Muzak with an explicitly ugly lyric about the atrocities the Nicaraguan dictatorship was committing against its people with the U.S. government's assistance. "Send It to Me" is a halfhearted reggae. "Down in the Hole" is boring blues. "She's So Cold" is a monotonous and generic rocker. "All About You" is Keith Richards's dreariest and most shapeless solo number.

The rest of *Emotional Rescue* is pretty neat, though. The title track is the band's hilarious last word on disco, and Mick's Micky Mouse falsetto finally pulls the curtain back on how the Stones really felt about the genre. Ron Wood's bass line is great too. All three dips into watered-down punk are good, and "Let Me Go" is both funny and fairly fierce music. *Emotional*

Rescue finds the Stones beyond the point where they were making essential albums, but it shows that they could still make pretty good ones.

RUSH: *PERMANENT WAVES*

Rush painted themselves into a prog corner with *Hemispheres*. The title track was their prettiest long-form experiment, but its lyrics are gobbledygook, and none of its sections sound like a hit. So the guys refurbished their act and were rewarded with genuine stardom south of the border. "The Spirit of Radio," "Entre Nous," and "Freewill" are compact songs fit for mainstream radio that don't scale back Rush's convoluted time signatures and showy musicianship. Neil Peart's lyrics are just as cerebral as ever but far more lucid as he champions critical thinking, open communication, and radio's potential to progress with the times. There are still a couple of proggy suites, but "Jacob's Ladder" and "Natural Science" are more concise than the similar excursions on the band's earlier records. *Permanent Waves* became Rush's first major international hit album, and it's still just about their best.

SIOUXSIE AND THE BANSHEES: *KALEIDOSCOPE*

Beginning their career with an infamous gig that consisted of an endless improvisation on the "The Lord's Prayer," Siouxsie and the Banshees seemed born to make off-putting music. Their debut album kept that notion alive with its spooky, crazed noise. That format hit a dead end with their second album, which was so bereft of ideas that it actually included a studio attempt to re-create that rambling version of "The Lord's Prayer." Siouxsie and the Banshees desperately needed to take a fresh approach to their music, and they did so by following the poppier inclinations of singles such as "Hong Kong Garden" and trading in metallic guitars for icy synthesizers.

No one would mistake the resulting album for *Herman's Hermits' Greatest Hits*, but *Kaleidoscope* is certainly the most accessible Banshees album yet, even as the band doesn't sacrifice their eeriness or edginess. Losing guitarist John McKay and drummer Kenny Morris and welcoming in the far more subtle and artful players John McGeoch and Budgie had a lot to do with the refinement, but so did the maturing songwriting of Siouxsie and Steve Severin. "Christine" and "Happy House" are catchy singles about mental illness and the violence lurking behind the suburban ideal, respectively. For "Desert Kisses," the band develops the sweeping, darkly romantic sound that would sweep over their mid-eighties records. Punk spirit still haunts dissonant pieces "Trophy," "Hybrid," and "Skin," an ahead-of-its-time indictment of fur wearers. The *Scream* sounded like the work of a band that was ready to implode at any minute, and that band did. *Kaleidoscope* is the sound of a band reborn and showing that they've figured out how to stick around.

THE SOFT BOYS: *UNDERWATER MOONLIGHT*

Violent surrealism and gorgeous power pop consummate their forbidden relationship on the Soft Boys' *Underwater Moonlight*. Wildly imaginative rock history student Robyn Hitchcock marries his grotesque imagery—

bones being picked on, insects of love hatching under skin, old perverts under bridges, horrible ages of abuse and decay—with jangling guitars and sunny harmonies making it all sound like a collaboration between Hieronymus Bosch and the Byrds. Each track is a power-pop powerhouse, from the Swiftian antiwar tirade "I Wanna Destroy You"; to the hyped-up, sitar-sweetened "Positive Vibrations"; to the lewd come-ons "I Got the Hots" and "Old Pervert." The twin masterpieces of *Underwater Moonlight* are saved for the end: "Queen of Eyes" is a wondrously surreal

Enjoy your nightmares! Author's collection.

neo-psychedelic jewel, and the title track tells a nightmarish tale of a pair of statues who escape a rotten world to seek refuge under the sea, only to find it worse than their former pedestals.

SPINAL TAP: *SHARK SANDWICH*

Shit sandwich.

TALKING HEADS: *REMAIN IN LIGHT*

By the end of the seventies, most of the original punks—the Clash, the Damned, the Adverts—had moved on to more expansive worlds. Not surprisingly, the most radical record of the new decade by a band originally labeled "punk" came via Talking Heads. Not only were the African polyrhythms bubbling beneath earlier songs like "Tentative Decisions" and "I Zimbra" allowed to fully flourish on *Remain in Light*, but the core band also welcomed a dense ensemble of supporting percussionists, backup singers, and horn players. Producer Brian Eno layered on some icy synths, and guest guitarist Adrian Belew discharged ray-gun screeches and bleeps.

Remain in Light is split between a quartet of caffeinated, neurotic grooves and a run of low-key dirges. Those first four tracks—"Born under Punches (And the Heat Goes On)," "Crosseyed and Painless," "The Great Curve," and "Once in a Lifetime"—constitute the finest sequence on any Talking Heads record. With the latter song, Talking Heads' defining one, David Byrne defined the eighties' suffocating air of conservative complacency just when the decade had barely begun. A family man realizes how alienated he is from his beautiful wife, beautiful car, beautiful house, and beautiful money. Byrne sweats hard to express the man's anguish and confusion. Jerry Harrison's bubbling synth and Tina Weymouth's rippling bass line are the waters that will keep on flowing with or without him.

The relatively indistinct mood pieces that conclude the album are not as instantly appealing, but they take the most risks and sound nothing like anything else Talking Heads ever attempted. That these sounds sneaked into Talking Heads' first top-twenty album underscores what a weird year 1980 was.

TELEVISION PERSONALITIES: *AND DON'T THE KIDS JUST LOVE IT*

Without any record label interest, the Buzzcocks self-financed their first release and put it out on their own label they dubbed New Hormones in 1977. The following year saw the debut of *CMJ*, the college media journal that took the kind of off-the-grid music college radio stations played as seriously as *Billboard* took the mainstream airwaves. Thus was the independent rock business model born. However, the sound associated with indie rock took a few more years to materialize.

Perhaps the first truly important indie label, Rough Trade grew out of the London record store of the same name a year after the Buzzcocks' experiment. Initially releasing singles by punk and reggae artists, Geoff Travis's label hit on something else after signing local trio Television Personalities.

If eighties pop is defined by over-glossy production and fancy haircuts, there's no evidence of that on *And Don't the Kids Just Love It*. Low-fi to the core, Television Personalities' debut LP is a cavalcade of shambling playing and off-key cockney squawking. It's also utterly charming. Sporting a cover that unites sixties icons Twiggy and John Steed, as well as a cuckoo pastoral called "I Know Where Syd Barrett Lives," Television Personalities make their intentions very clear. Moon-eyed worshippers of mod and psych rock with a shaky grasp of recording technology, they pay tribute to the Who on fiery stuff like "This Angry Silence" and "Look Back in Anger," space off into Floydian dreamland on "A Family Affair," summon spaghetti-western psych worthy of Love on "Diary of a Young Man," and stomp out an *Aftermath*-era Stones tribute called "Silly Girl" and the Ray Davies–esque character studies "World of Pauline Lewis" and "Geoffrey Ingram."

As clearly indebted to their influences as Television Personalities are, they still sound unlike any other group because of their uniquely rough-hewn approach and recording quality. That sound would become less odd as artists such as Guided by Voices, Sebadoh, and Liz Phair picked up on that magical combination of retro spirit and homemade production. The sound of indie rock starts here.

PETE TOWNSHEND: *EMPTY GLASS*

Pete Townshend suggested to the press that the Who might actually be rejuvenated by Keith Moon's death, but his behavior and work told another story. If fans were taken aback by his seeming insensitivity to a fallen friend, the truth was that Townshend was devastated by the loss of his band's inimitable drummer. What followed was a great big leap into the void. When Pete wasn't messing with heroin, he was obliterating himself with drink, one time actually waking up in the bear pit of a London zoo, an incident he'd commemorate on the Who's "Cache Cache." Although he did continue to contribute such uncompromisingly personal songs to his band, he started saving his best ones for himself.

They can be heard on the devastating *Empty Glass* (as in "The glass is neither half-empty nor half-full"). The album got a big push from the joyous, devotional pop song "Let My Love Open the Door," but the rest of it is far more introspective. Townshend explores his increasingly complex sexuality on "And I Moved," on which he rhapsodizes about being seduced by a man, and "A Little Is Enough," on which he rhapsodizes about reuniting with his estranged wife. On the minor hit "Rough Boys," he uses sexual threats as a means to intimidate and emasculate male rivals—or is it an S&M confession? "I Am an Animal" is a delirious exploration of his innumerable contradictions—a sort of less despairing update of the Who's "However Much I Booze." With "Jools and Jim," he takes on the journalists who waxed indifferent to Moon's death while finally acknowledging the punk movement he helped create.

Townshend being Townshend, he saves some of that loathing for himself, and Townshend being Townshend, he voices all this bile, love, and self-analysis through songs of audacious power and beauty. The Who's final two albums of the early eighties lack the band's former fury. Townshend's first proper solo record reveals that he was far from finished.

U2: *BOY*

As the focus of rock and roll grew fuzzy in the eighties, critics hailed U2 as the genre's great hope. Initially a sort of Christian rock group out of Dublin, U2 would broaden their scope to tackle world politics and up the bombast of their new-wavy sound until it was suitable for arenas. Subtlety was never their strong suit, especially when they had such a big mouthpiece in lead singer Bono, but their hearts were generally in the right place, and they did make some excellent records along the way.

In light of the pomposity that defines U2, their first album is completely refreshing. They owed too much to seventies-era Who to qualify as a punk band, but U2 got as close to punk as they ever would with *Boy*. "I Will Follow," "Out of Control," and "Stories for Boys" are furious, strident, and electrifying. "Twilight," "The Ocean," and "An Cat Dubh" are spookily atmospheric. "A Day Without Me" is twinkling, lurching pop. The Edge may be rock's most limited guitar hero, but

The smeary image of U2 replaced the original cover of *Boy*, which depicted a shirtless boy (Peter Rowen) that the American label considered to be too distastefully suggestive. The picture of that same kid with a black eye and split lip on the cover of 1983's *War* was a-okay though. Author's collection.

you can't say he doesn't make the most of his delay pedal. Bassist Adam Clayton and drummer Larry Mullen Jr. make the most of their own technical limitations by locking together with strength-in-numbers force. U2 would make more earthquaking records than *Boy*, but as it captures the band during that brief moment in their career before the world started scrutinizing their every move, it is their least self-conscious and most fun record.

X: *LOS ANGELES*

The punk flame had all but gone out in London and New York, the cities that originated it. No matter. It soon reignited in Los Angeles, and just as *Never Mind the Bollocks, Here's the Sex Pistols* is the poster child for London punk and *The Ramones* defines the New York City equivalent, *Los Angeles* is the crucial album of the escalating L.A. punk scene. Almost journalistic in the way it chronicles the smack fiends, racists, girlfriend beaters, and decadent richies prowling Hollywood Boulevard, *Los Angeles* is coyote mean and junkie lean. That X hijacked Ray Manzarek to produce and add the odd keyboard and covered "Soul Kitchen" indicates that they intended to present themselves as the next step in a sort of local lineage that began with the Doors. Yet this music is so much more vital and authentic than Jim Morrison's gang ever was. Billy Zoom whips out high-speed Chuck Berry riffs as John Doe and Exene Cervenka's voices careen around each other like a pair of hot rods dragging down the Sunset Strip, never quite getting neck and neck enough to qualify as harmonies. At well under half an hour, *Los Angeles* blitzes by at equal velocity, leaving the listener panting, perspiring, and psyched to spin it again.

XTC: *BLACK SEA*

A year after releasing their first great album, XTC made an even better one with *Black Sea*. This isn't a concept album, but it is a singular piece in which all of the parts contribute immeasurably to the whole. XTC's social commentaries ("Respectable Street," another of this chapter's many Ray Davies homages), antiwar protests ("Generals and Majors," "Living Through Another Cuba"), love songs ("Love at First Sight," "Burning with Optimism's Flame"), and odes to inarticulateness ("No Language in Our Lungs") have little to do with each other, except for when all these themes convene on "Sgt. Rock (Is Going to Help Me)." The unity of *Black Sea* has more to do with the performances, writing, and recording. The sound is thick, Andy Partridge and Colin Moulding's songs are uniformly excellent, and their singing and playing are astoundingly confident. The variety of *Black Sea* is also remarkable, as African polyrhythms, British Invasion melodiousness, psychedelic nuances, and post-punk noise flow together into a wholly unique body of water.

When they aren't recording intellectual yet tuneful albums like *Black Sea*, XTC enjoys going deep-sea diving in the nineteenth century. Author's collection.

1981

On August 1, 1981, a magnitude 8.1 earthquake shook rock and roll. Image had been important to the genre since the days when multitudes swooned over Elvis's sneer. The way rock and rollers looked was always nearly as important as the way they sounded. Image threatened to supersede sound once and for all when Music Television debuted.

The first twenty-four-hour music channel began as the brainchild of one of TV's original rock stars. In 1979, Mike Nesmith produced a program called *Pop Clips* for Warner Cable's kid's channel Nickelodeon. The show featured video promos by artists such as the Rolling Stones, Rush, the Police, the Pretenders, Split Enz, Madness, Toto, and many of the others who would become MTV fixtures. The clips weren't too different from the musical "romps" that were the centerpieces of Nesmith's old series *The Monkees*. Artists would lip-sync along to their latest single or engage in nonsensical activities with the assistance of primitive camera tricks.

Nesmith schemed to expand *Pop Clips* into a full-fledged channel and approached Warner's John Lack with his idea. Lack loved the concept and ran with it. When MTV hit the air in 1981, it almost immediately reshaped popular music. The way artists looked took on greater significance than ever before. A lack of clips from major artists early on forced MTV to air what they had: a bevy of videos from obscure, weird, British New Wave artists. Without the channel running their clips on a constant loop, U2, Duran Duran, Annie Lennox, Tears for Fears, Human League, and many of the other artists who defined the eighties may not have done that. MTV also helped metal go mainstream when it began playing videos by Def Leppard and Quiet Riot and turned the already very popular Michael Jackson into a veritable pop god once the channel began loosening up its dedication to white rock bands.

MTV took a lot of knocks for encouraging what critics attacked as a new vapidness overtaking rock and roll, but critics always found fault with the corporate-determined media that conveyed rock and roll. As MTV was blamed for ruining rock in the eighties, many of the artists the channel promoted made some of the decade's most forward-thinking albums. However, it did pull focus from the kinds of deliberately constructed art albums that dominated the seventies and place it back on the single, which would have a detrimental effect on the LP in the end.

ELVIS COSTELLO AND THE ATTRACTIONS: *TRUST*

After four thematically consistent albums, Elvis Costello seemed to be either prepping a major career shift or reaching an impasse when he and the Attractions assembled the meandering *Trust*. The album is a summation of much of what he and the Attractions had already explored. "You'll Never Be a Man," "Pretty Words," and "Watch Your Step" recall the polished pop of *Armed Forces*. "Clubland" and "Strict Time" pound with *Get Happy!!* soul power, and Costello made "Big Sister's Clothes" in the one-man-band style of that album's "New Amsterdam." "Luxembourg" is a rockabilly number with some of the punk fury of *This Year's Model*, while "Shot with His Own Gun" displays the pre-rock craftsmanship of "Allison" on *My Aim Is True* while inching further from Cole Porter and closer to Kurt Weill.

Because *Trust* wanders where those earlier records walked narrow paths—a possible side effect of Elvis's prodigious chemical consumption—it feels like a lesser album, yet all the songs bear Costello's stamp of quality. His lyrics are some of his most cutting. On "Clubland," he aims his poison pen at the elitism of club culture and the vacuous dopes who've come to "shoot the pony" and "do the jerk" (why do I think he isn't referring to a couple of groovy sixties dance fads here?). The Attractions play with their usual precision though not always with their usual fire. A jumble of styles and sounds realized with varying levels of intensity, *Trust* may have seemed like a misstep in 1981. In light of the similarly eclectic records Elvis would produce after his work with the Attractions, it now sounds like the forerunner of *Spike*, *All This Useless Beauty*, and *When I Was Cruel*.

THE GO GO'S: *BEAUTY AND THE BEAT*

The Go-Go's rose from the same L.A. punk scene that spawned hard-core groups like the Germs (for whom singer Belinda Carlisle briefly drummed) and Fear, but their earliest recordings indicate that their punk predecessors were more likely the Shangri-La's than the Sonics. When they made their debut album for I.R.S. in 1981, Richard Gotteherer and Rob Freeman had basically shaved off the stubbly rawness of those demos.

The producers still could not tame the five women whom VH-1 documentaries remind us were completely out of control. Tracks like "Lust to Love," "This Town," "Tonight," "We Got the Beat," and "Can't Stop the World" are desperately passionate. The slick and poppy production utterly fails to reign in Gina Schock's tom-tom clobbering and Belinda Carlisle's over-the-edge yowling.

Not that pop was the wrong direction for the Go-Go's. "Our Lips Our Sealed" and "How Much More" are utterly perfect pop

I always assumed that the decision to depict the band doing "girly" things like wearing mud masks and towels on the cover of their first album was some sexist label exec's idea, but it was actually the Go-Go's'. The band supposedly returned those towels to Macy's after the cover shoot, which means some unsuspecting shopper ended up drying off with Belinda Carlisle's sloppy seconds. Author's collection.

classics. Attitudinal lyrics about lust, love, and roaming and ruling the streets like panthers prove that no production could sanitize the Go-Go's.

JOAN JETT AND THE BLACKHEARTS: *I LOVE ROCK 'N ROLL*

The Runaways made history in the late seventies as the first all-female rock and roll band to achieve some level of success. Most of that success was limited to Japan, but the band still had a far-reaching and lingering effect. Along with inspiring many young women to pick up the electric guitar, the Runaways launched some successful solo careers when they splintered. The most successful was that of guitarist Joan Jett, who kicked off with an eponymous old-fashioned patchwork of covers and originals in 1980 and scored.

I Love Rock 'n Roll from 1981 follows that formula with a new band called the Blackhearts and even better results. The title track, a much-improved cover of a flop single by the Arrows, became a heavy number one hit at a time when featherlight fare floated the airwaves. Her cover of Tommy James's "Crimson and Clover" doesn't best the original, but it became another hit. A version of the Dave Clark Five's "Bits and Pieces" was another worthwhile cover (much more so than the rendition of "The Little Drummer Boy" that capped off early editions of the album), but *I Love Rock 'n Roll* gets much of its punch from Jett's tough originals, especially "Love Is Pain," "Victim of Circumstance," the Diddley-ized "Be Straight," and a faster, less fussy remake of her old Runaways number "You're Too Possessive."

LYRES: *AHS 1005*

Glossy, soulless pop production had barely begun ruining many an eighties album when Boston-based Lyres were already in revolt. *AHS 1005* is impossible to place as a record released in 1981. The snarling attitude and raw production are pure 1965. Jeff Conolly put together Lyres after his even more brutish group, DMZ, went extinct in the late seventies. The new combo allowed more breathing space for his throaty grunt and squealing Farfisa, but he'd hardly been tamed. Neo-nuggets such as "Buried Alive" and "100 CC's (Pure Thrust)" burn with all the cro-mag fury of the Sonics, the Shadows of Knight, Question Mark & the Mysterians, and the rest of the mop-topped, one-hit horde. "High on Yourself," "She Pays the Rent," "Help You Ann," and "100 CC's (Pure Thrust)" are garage-rock gems with all the catchiness and pure thrust of the oldies that inspired them. Released as a 45-RPM twelve-inch LP, *AHS 1005* shreds by in under twenty-five minutes. Another minute may have caused listeners' heads to cave in.

TOM PETTY AND THE HEARTBREAKERS: *HARD PROMISES*

Tom Petty and the Heartbreakers solidified their reputation as the best neo-classic rockers of their day with 1979's *Damn the Torpedoes*. That album's success imbued the band with a cool confidence that caused them to goof off a bit on their next album. *Hard Promises* doesn't have the urgency of the record that preceded it. "Nightwatchman," a funky little toss-off about a night watchman, never would have made the cut on *Damn the Torpedoes*, but its lighthearted tone is what makes *Hard Promises* a pleasure. "Something Big" and "The Criminal Kind" are superficial by *Torpedoes* standards, but they still smolder, and their ornery southwestern tang is a nice new ingredient in the Heartbreakers' retro gumbo.

The rest of the album requires no buts or howevers. "The Waiting" is the band's most dedicated Byrds homage and arguably their best song. The Heartbreakers let it rip on "King's Road" and "A Thing About You" and settle into moody angst on "A Woman in Love." Stevie Nicks repays Tom and the guys for their work on her hit "Stop Draggin' My Heart Around" by lending her bleat to the bitter "Insider" and the delicate "You Can Still Change Your Mind."

THE POLICE: *GHOST IN THE MACHINE*

The Police had the world's ear after *Zenyatta Mondatta* went top five. They built on that success when they expanded their core sound on *Ghost in the Machine*. Sting almost single-handedly transforms the band by dubbing huge saxophone sections and keyboards over Stewart Copeland's ever-intricate drumming, Andy Summers's squalling guitar, and his own boinging bass. A clutch of ominous songs set the tone for the Police's darkest record. "Spirits in the Material World," "Secret Journey," and "Darkness" are intoxicating amalgamations of reggae and goth spookiness. The hopeful refrain "There has to be an invisible sun" does little to lift a grim depiction of survival amid the twin blights of war and poverty. "Demolition Man," "Rehumanize Yourself," and "Too Much Information" are nerve-wracking depictions of emotional and physical violence with jittery rhythms that up the anxiety. "Ωmegaman" is a discordant tale of technological and urban isolation and Andy Summers's best song.

The three little digital figures on the cover of *Ghost in the Machine* are supposed to represent each member of the Police. You can tell the one in the middle is supposed to be Sting either because of its "spiky hair" or the fact that it's in the middle. You just know Sting *had* to be in the middle. Author's collection.

Such tracks cast shadows over some of the Police's lightest work. With its steel drums, swirling Pete Townshend–style synthesizers, balmy steel drums, and message of elated awe, "Every Little Thing She Does Is Magic" is one of the eighties' most irresistible love songs. The vamping ska "Hungry for You (J'aurais Toujours Faim de Toi)" is a much more limited composition, but its jubilant tone is nearly as enthralling. "One World (Not Three)" is a sweet plea for global unity. Nice as those numbers are, the discontented majority is what makes *Ghost in the Machine* so affecting.

PRINCE: *CONTROVERSY*

From the synth croak that kicks it off, *Controversy* never lets up, and Prince never breaks character. Funk royalty, sexual messiah, tiny dancer in platforms, preacher of peace and love—the Prince persona coalesces on his fourth record, and it is awesome. He'd already shed all shades of conventional soul on the experimental *Dirty Mind*. *Controversy* is the "professional" realization of Prince's newfound individuality. The record sounds big and polished compared to *Dirty Mind*, which sounds like the work of a one-man band holed up in his basement studio that it is. *Controversy* sounds as though a proper group recorded it even though Prince personally handles most of its parts again.

The material hits new highs too. "Controversy" is an outrageously confident mission statement on which Prince releases his self-mythologizing from Pandora's Box. Was anyone really debating whether he was "straight or gay" before he'd even released a major hit record? No matter because they certainly would be now. He continues to freak out the straights and stir controversy with the hopped-up, hilarious "Jack U Off," but there's less shock value here than on *Dirty Mind*. Prince even dabbles in above-the-waist issues on "Ronnie, Talk to Russia," a zippy plea for Cold War resolution, and the more muddled, headline-referencing "Annie Christian."

Of course, Prince does most of his thinking with Little Prince, and there's plenty of unambiguous hip grinding on "Sexuality," "Do Me Baby," and "Private Joy." Party record, orgy sound track, and compendium of current affairs, *Controversy* heralded the coming of the new decade's resident pop genius at his full powers.

THE RAMONES: *PLEASANT DREAMS*

The Ramones' formula—a few words shouted over a couple of power chords in under two minutes—is responsible for a lot of amazing music, but it is also incredibly limiting. After four great records, the band recruited Phil Spector to develop their sound on *End of the Century* with unspectacular results. Instead of accepting that minor failure and retreating to raw simplicity, the Ramones gave progress another shot by having Graham Gouldman produce *Pleasant Dreams*. Gouldman may be best known as a member of mock poppers 10cc, but the Ramones were likely more impressed with the songs he wrote for the Yardbirds, the Hollies, Herman's Hermits, and other sixties favorites.

Not surprisingly, the band was again disappointed with an overly slick record. Graham's compressed, smooth production doesn't have the raw power of Tommy Ramone's work on those first four records, yet *Pleasant Dreams* is a lot better than its reputation suggests. The indifference of the songs on *End of the Century* is gone in the wake of Joey and Johnny Ramones' deteriorating relationship. Joey's pain over losing the woman he loved and his anger about being stuck in a band with the guy who was now groping her in the back of their tour van rip through "Don't Go" and "The KKK Took My Baby Away," which also references Johnny's well-documented conservatism and bigotry.

Despite Gouldman's attempts to domesticate them, the Ramones sounds savage on "You Sound Like You're Sick," "You Didn't Mean Anything to Me," and "All's Quiet on the Eastern Front," which features one of Dee Dee's best vocal counterpoints. Joey and Dee Dee's songs are as catchy as ever, often favoring a poppier sound than the speedy punk of their earlier work. If not for Gouldman's glossy production, *Pleasant Dreams* could have rated alongside the Ramones' best records.

THE ROLLING STONES: *TATTOO YOU*

Faced with a rapidly approach tour and not really getting along, Mick Jagger and Keith Richards had neither the time nor the inclination to cook up enough material for a new Rolling Stones LP to promote on the road. They compromised by asking producer Chris Kimsey to sift through leftovers cut since the *Goat's Head Soup* sessions way back in 1972 and select some decent ones so the Stones could give them a fresh coat of grease. The band also recorded two new numbers: "Neighbors" and "Heaven." Ironically,

Tattoo You wound up sounding fresher than most of the new albums the Stones had released over the past decade. The tediously generic "Start Me Up" has aged poorer than any of the band's other classics, but most of the record is up to their usual standards. There's little of the forced cynicism of *Some Girls* or the laziness of *Black and Blue* and *Emotional Rescue*. How did the charming, uncharacteristically sincere "Waiting on a Friend" take nearly a decade to see release? Why did the guys sit on the hypnotic groove "Slave" and the breathtaking soul ballad "Worried About You" for so long?

"Hang Fire" captures the voices of those who found themselves out of work but were more than happy to spend their days on the dole, drinking and partying—a most Stones-like solution to a very real problem. While it easily could be misinterpreted as a sour piece of classist mockery, Keith Richards insisted it is a satirical middle finger held aloft to politicians like Thatcher who were allowing such conditions to persist. "Little T&A" is a bit tougher to defend as Keith "extols" his new girlfriend Patti Hansen in insulting, sexist terms, but its riffing and rhythm are the hottest on the album. The wonderful soul pleader "No Use in Crying" requires no disclaimers.

The album's categorized structure—rockers on side A, make-out ballads on B—draws attention to its function as a clearinghouse, yet it makes for a pleasing listening experience. That function also indicated that the World's Greatest Rock and Roll Band might be winding down. Although they weren't even halfway through their record-making history in 1981, the Rolling Stones' most inspiring moments were undeniably in the past.

RUSH: *MOVING PICTURES*

Rush doubled down on the successful formula of *Permanent Waves* with *Moving Pictures*. There is only one lengthy track this time— the catchy "Camera Eye"—and a whole lot of prog pop. "Tom Sawyer," "Limelight," "Red Barchetta," and the fusiony instrumental "YYZ" all became signature songs on the strengths of their melodiousness, complexity, and virtuosity. The guys were listening to contemporary artists like the Police and Talking Heads, and such hip influences helped bring their rock into the New Wave eighties. *Moving Pictures* expanded Rush's palette

Rush's love for a good old pun informs the cover of their biggest album. Author's collection.

with more extensive use of the synthesizers and reggae by way of Sting that frilled *Permanent Waves*. "Tom Sawyer" and the fizzy "Vital Signs" would be unthinkable without Geddy Lee's keys. Rush was justly rewarded with their first number one album in Canada and their biggest yet in the United States and United Kingdom. That taste of commercial and artistic success further propelled them away from prog and toward New Wave on their next album.

SIOUXSIE AND THE BANSHEES: *JUJU*

Beginning as an abrasive excuse for terrorizing audiences with bizarre improvisations and Siouxsie Sioux's forward fashion sense, Siouxsie and the Banshees rapidly developed their craft to become one of their era's most distinctive, artful, and tuneful groups. Much progress was evident on 1980's *Kaleidoscope*, but the band's first truly great album is its fourth.

The group compositions are startlingly strong. "Spellbound" and "Arabian Nights" were British hit singles that still incorporated a good deal of the icy exoticism of the Banshees' earlier records. These tracks, along with "Into the Light" and "Monitor," also bear a strong whiff of mid-sixties psychedelia spurred by Steve Severin and guitarist John McGeoch's love for *Their Satanic Majesties Request*. "Halloween" marries the discordance of the band's first two albums to propulsive dark pop. "Sin in My Heart," "Night Shift," and "Voodoo Dolly" are scary mood pieces.

Throughout the record, Siouxsie masters a croon that could veer off course in the past. McGeoch keeps the songs from straying too far into conventional New Wave with his flickering fireballs of affected noise, and Budgie braces with drumming no longer constricted by the previous album's more metronomic rhythms. The way he throws "Spellbound" down the stairs makes me nuts. Siouxsie and the Banshees would tidy up their sound even more on their next album and continue to develop it in varying directions from there, but *Juju* marks the moment that the band first harnessed their dark powers.

THE WHO: *FACE DANCES*

Losing Keith Moon meant the Who was no longer *The Who*. Rock's most distinctive drummer played an integral role in his band's sound. It was Moon who brought the chaos, but the noise and amphetamine energy had already been draining out of the band's music for a while as the drummer self-destructed. The relative sedateness of *Who Are You* indicated that the Who's mightiest days were behind them.

So it is slightly unfair that *Face Dances* received the brunt of so much venom when it appeared a couple of years after Moon's passing. Critics lambasted the album as Muzak-Who and foisted much of the blame on producer Bill Szymczyk. Granted, the band's first album with former Small Face/Face Kenney Jones behind the kit is tame even by *Who Are You* standards. Szymczyk polished away all edges. The group's always-impeccable harmonies sounded perhaps a bit too flawless.

The placidity of the music is a weak reflection of Townshend's personal crisis in the wake of Moon's death, which found his marriage in shambles and himself swirling in a maelstrom of hard drugs, booze, and suicidal thoughts. That he'd released one of rock's great solo records a year earlier just made *Face Dances* seem tamer. Townshend's bandmates accused him of keeping his best material for himself (they had a point). But they weren't exactly pulling their own weight either. John Entwistle, who could usually be counted on to contribute a dark jewel or two, managed only a nice riff with some overly on-the-nose lyrics about his role in the band ("The Quiet One") and a heavy-metal drag that may be the worst thing in the entire Who discography ("You").

A rogue's gallery of fine artists contributed portraits to the cover of *Face Dances*. Among them are David Hockney, Richard Hamilton, David Inshaw, Colin Self, Clive Barker (not the horror writer/filmmaker, FYI), and Peter Blake, who also designed the whole package. Author's collection.

Face Dances may not be a great Who album, but it would be a good album by any other group without the Who's baggage. This is the work of a mature, professional band. Well into their thirties and having lived through all they'd lived through, the Who could hardly be expected to continue playing the snarling punks forever. "You Better You Bet," "Cache Cache," and "Another Tricky Day" are adult rock and roll songs groaning with Townshend's diary-like confessions. "Don't Let Go the Coat" is a lovable psalm to Meher Baba that never flirts with sanctimoniousness. "Daily Records" is a pretty meditation of the drudgery of playing rock and roll past one's prime.

Daltrey took some heat for bellowing Townshend's personal lyrics, but listen to his nuanced, confidential vocal on "How Can You Do It Alone," an aching look at sex, masturbation, and loneliness. Entwistle may have failed as a composer this time, but his bass playing is as intricate as ever. His upward spiraling lines on "Cache Cache" dazzle. *Face Dances* is not in the same league as the Who's best albums. How many albums are?

X: *WILD GIFT*

Wild Gift picks up right where *Los Angeles* left off, with Ray Manzarek once again producing and X bolting through another set of corrosive social commentaries and ruminations on sex and death. Manzarek's work is smoother, yet X is still an album away from settling into a more sedate sound. "We're Desperate," "I'm Coming Over," and "It's Who You Know" are unhinged punk rock.

There is still greater diversity here than on *Los Angeles*. An undercurrent of fifties rock and roll swims throughout *Wild Gift*, boogying to the surface atop Billy Zoom's muted arpeggios and Bigsby bending on "Adult Books," the sock-hop-gone-wild vibe of "In This House That I Call Home," the souped-up rockabilly rhythms of "Beyond and Back," and the Chuck Berry jive of "Year 1." Exene Cervenka and John Doe's tales of smut and street life aren't quite as potent as things like "Johnny Hit and Run Pauline" or "Los Angeles" were on the first album, but their intertwining howls make even trifling lyrics like "I'm Coming Over" disquieting. *Wild Gift* strikes the right balance between the rabid ferocity of the record that came before it and the polish of the one that followed, and for that, it might be X's best.

1982

On August 2, 1982, the *New York Times* officially declared MTV a hit, and its influence was very apparent to anyone paying even cursory attention to popular music. Perhaps eccentric artists such as the Clash, Human League, Men at Work, Duran Duran, the Motels, and Toni Basil would have had their first major American hits in 1982 without seemingly unlimited airtime for their videos but probably not. MTV certainly cannot be credited with making a star of Michael Jackson, but the images of him moon walking in his floods and single, spangly glove certainly played a tremendous role in his transformation from lovable young pop star to deluded and allegedly monstrous pop-culture deity.

Thriller would not be released until the very end of 1982, and its influence would not truly overwhelm the pop scene until "Billie Jean" debuted on MTV the following March. So the album's influence does not hover over its release year the way *Sgt. Pepper's* did back in 1967. The year 1983 would be that of the blockbuster LP; 1982 was a year of quieter classics.

KATE BUSH: *THE DREAMING*

Kate Bush is the kind of artist whose vision is so singular, so peculiar, that the only person capable of fully realizing that vision is the artist herself. After a debut full of interesting songs captured with unsympathetic seventies pop clichés (did "The Saxophone Song" really need that saxophone solo?), Bush got more involved in the productions of *Lionheart* and *Never for Ever*. But it still wasn't enough, and she took total control on her fourth LP.

The Dreaming is Kate Bush coming into her own with remarkably strong songs and creative, thoughtful—even mad—production to match. Each song is like a little film that not only tells a story but also sets the mood with music and sonic touches that fully support the theme. So "Sat in Your Lap," which deals with humankind's impatient quest for knowledge, spools out with the freneticism

The cover photo of *The Dreaming* illustrates the lyrics of "Houdini." Putting a key in your mouth is still very unsanitary. Author's collection.

of a computer spewing data. She brings "There Goes a Tenner"—a funny portrait of thieves getting cold feet in the middle of a big heist—to life as a cockney oompah. The title track, an indictment of white weapons-grade uranium miners ravishing land belonging to indigenous Australians, is all didgeridoos and chanted choruses.

Elsewhere, Bush tackles topics as varied as the Vietnam War ("Pull Out the Pin," featuring mentor David Gilmour), Bess Houdini's attempt to contact her dead husband via séance ("Houdini"), and *The Shining* ("Get Out of My House"). She voices her characters by taking fearless vocal chances (her desperate screams of "I love life!" in "Pull Out the Pin," her crazed "hee-hawing" in "Get Out of My House") and paints the scenery by making the most of the limitations of brittle eighties production techniques. She would take such sounds even further on her next album and most complete flowering of her genius.

ELVIS COSTELLO AND THE ATTRACTIONS: *IMPERIAL BEDROOM*

After making five powerful albums with producer Nick Lowe, Elvis Costello switched producers and put together a borderline antiseptic collection of country covers with Billy Sherill. It was a weird move no fan could have predicted and few likely appreciated, but it was momentous in that *Almost Blue* was the first real sign that Elvis Costello was an artist never content to stick with one thing for too long.

Almost Blue doesn't hold up very well, but it must have cleared out some cobwebs because Elvis and the Attractions were back the very next year with top material and a fresh sound. The sound can be attributed to producer Geoff Emerick, the guy who engineered *Revolver*, *Sgt. Pepper's*, and *Abbey Road*. There is a noticeable Beatles influence on *Imperial Bedroom*, particularly in the brass and strings that add regality to ". . . And in Every Home" and "Town Cryer." Yet no one but Elvis Costello could write songs as dense with wordplay and anxiety as "Man out of Town," and the Beatles never wrote anything as unfancifully impenetrable as "Beyond Belief" or as adult as "The Long Honeymoon" or as consciously sophisticated as "Almost Blue" (a torch song that has no relation to the C&W LP of 1981). "Man out of Time" is like an encyclopedia of Costello's best lines (when I was in my cups, the line "Love is always scarpering or cowering or fawning, you drink yourself insensitive and you hate yourself in the morning" always resonated with me).

Elvis Costello, the master pop craftsman with utter respect for the verse/chorus/bridge/chorus structure, tossed that shit right out the window when he wrote "Beyond Belief." The song unfolds gradually, crawling through a couple of taut verses, then hinting at climax with a brief sparkling interlude before snapping shut like a bear trap for another verse that finally explodes into an exhilarating repeated refrain (and it explodes quite literally—listen for that "bomb" blast!). The genius of the nontraditional structure of "Beyond Belief" is the way it builds suspense; instead of scattering little payoffs throughout the piece, as most writers use choruses, Elvis saves it up for the end, and it's well worth the wait. If Alfred Hitchcock had written a pop song, it would have been "Beyond Belief."

Imperial Bedroom does share the Beatles' predilection for extreme eclecticism and rule-defying songwriting, but the Attractions' instantly identifiable playing makes the album sound much more unified than, say, *Revolver* or "The White Album." And their playing is absolutely astounding as bassist Bruce Thomas strangles wiry riffs at the tail of "Shabby Doll," Steve Nieve ripples glinting piano triplets throughout "The Loved Ones," and the entire band bashes the death-metal din that bookends "Man out of Time." The Attractions would soon tumble into the über-slick arms of top-forty production team Clive Langer and Alan Winstanley. The resulting collaboration would be nearly disastrous for the band, leaving *Imperial Bedroom* as the closing chapter in the Attractions' first fabulous phase.

THE DAMNED: *STRAWBERRIES*

You probably haven't heard it, you may not have heard of it, you may even be a Damned fanatic who thinks its subpar, but *Strawberries* is my selection for the best Damned album and the best album of 1982. Each spin of this electrifying potion of punk, psych, Goth, and pop raises the same baffling question: how is *Strawberries* not universally regarded as a classic? At a time when more and more bands were moving in the painfully polished direction that Langer and Winstanley's work exemplified, the Damned released one last mighty howl from a more organic age. As was the case with Costello's work before he said "farewell"(temporarily) to tactile production, *Strawberries'* touchstone is the sixties. So there's a bit of Stooges fury ("Ignite"), a bit of garage-rock mania and Kinky character study ("Dozen Girls"), a bit of Motown stomp ("Stranger on the Town"), a bit of Doors dourness ("Gun Fury," "The Dog"), a bit of Left Banke–style baroque pop ("The Pleasure and the Pain"), a bit of raga rock ("Under the Floor Again"), and a bit of political protest ("Generals," "Bad Time for Bonzo").

You know what's the most Goth of all animals? The pig. Author's collection.

   The band shadows all of this with their punk and goth leanings, so *Strawberries* never sounds like anyone but the Damned. Their left-wing politics ("Gun Fury" is a righteous jab at the Police Support Unit's abuse of power; "Bad Time for Bonzo" takes a swipe at Reagan), silly humor, iconoclasm ("Don't Bother Me" skewers the Rolling Stones), and horror fixation ("The Dog" is based on *Interview with the Vampire*) are all accounted for too. Dark numbers sit alongside the light and colorful, sometimes blending together in anthems such as the alternately hopeful and cynical "Life Goes On" and "Under the Floor Again."

   The title refers to Captain Sensible's feeling that putting out records like this for an unappreciative audience was like "giving strawberries to pigs." In light of this album's magnificence and its almost nonexistent reputation, he has a point.

BILLY IDOL: *BILLY IDOL*

It didn't really matter what tube you were in. In the eighties, you could grock Billy Idol if you were a metalhead, a top-forty fluff head, a New Waver, or even a less dogmatic goth or punk, especially if you'd been following him since his days in the early British punk group Generation X. With his crossover appeal, personal style that felt more like a personal brand (the bleached spikes, the leather wardrobe, the Elvis sneer), and a sound that was really more pop than anything else, Billy Idol could have been little more than a generic rocker for the eighties if he and his hits didn't exude so much personality.

Idol's eponymous debut doesn't give us much of a peek at his punk roots. The hit "White Wedding" is fairly sinister, but the rest of the album is straight pop. Choruses of "If you wanna rub-a-dub, rub-a-dub" help build a case that Idol needed to tap more into the darkness of "White Wedding."

MICHAEL JACKSON: *THRILLER*

In the seventies, Michael Jackson became the most credible child pop star since Brenda Lee. As the front kid for his brothers' group the Jackson 5, he had the voice, energy, charisma, dance moves, and smile to make him a pop star as legit as Jagger, Brown, Turner, or any of his other elders. The group's songs were frothy, but they had enough appeal to become huge hits and beloved by listeners of all ages.

The Jackson 5 were big enough to star in their own Saturday morning cartoon, just as the Beatles did in the decade before, and Michael enjoyed a great deal of success when he split from the group to record solo sides such as "Rockin' Robin," "Ben," "Don't Stop 'Til You Get Enough," and "Rock with You." The latter two tracks were from his smash 1979 album *Off the Wall*, his first collaboration with producer Quincy Jones and his biggest LP to date, going to number three in early 1980.

Impressive achievements all, but nothing could have prepared Jackson or the world for the epochal success of *Thriller*. With his second Quincy collaboration, Michael Jackson made the album that defined the eighties. It spent 448 weeks on *Billboard*'s album charts and eventually sold more than 65 million copies throughout the world. As of this writing, it is the all-time top-selling record in the world. Seven of its nine songs were top-ten singles.

Because of its influence and success, this book could not have been written without giving *Thriller* its due. Without question, it is an iconic pop record with a clutch of excellent singles. With its Eddie Van Halen solo, "Beat It" is a legit rock and roll track from an artist who'd never rummaged in that bag before. "Billie Jean" and the best of them, "Wanna Be Startin' Somethin'," find Jackson in his more familiar discothèque, but both are more lyrically and musically mature than his earlier work in that mode.

However, *Thriller* is a hugely uneven album with flaws that will be glaring to all but the most fanatical Jackson apologists. "The Lady in My Life" and the Paul McCartney collaboration "The Girl Is Mine" sound out of place anywhere but a dentist's office. "P.Y.T." is a "Rock with You" retread. The title track is an amazing video, but as a song, it's mostly just a catchy, repetitive riff. Its creator's odd, purportedly despicable behavior will also taint the music for anyone who believes his possible child victims' allegations of calculated sexual abuse.

All that being said, *Thriller* remains impossible to ignore when discussing the music of 1982, and its mega success would cast a shadow over eighties pop. Artists from Prince to the Police to Def Leppard to Madonna would quickly follow it with their own extroverted packages of radio-ready singles, and though many of these albums would stand as strong unified works in and of themselves, the fact that so many singles were pulled from them was another blow to the art of album making. Crowding albums with singles had been a practice of the pre-LP era. When the Beatles started taking a more artistically minded approach to LP making and refusing to even place one single on most of their albums, most albums started featuring a single or two at most, and many featured none at all. After *Thriller*, that would be economically unthinkable as corporations began eating up record labels to the point where the industry was dominated by just six companies by decade's end. As far as such major labels were concerned, a new album should function more like a greatest-hits compilation with plenty of fodder for top-forty radio than another *Sgt. Pepper's* or *Dark Side of the Moon*.

However, that attitude also helped spark a rebellion of independent labels and college radio stations that would deliver some of the least marketable yet most interesting music of the eighties, and when an album by a grungy trio of underground leaders from Aberdeen, Washington, displaced Michael Jackson's album *Dangerous* from *Billboard*'s number one spot in early 1992, many critics and artists viewed it as a symbolic victory against the commercialism consuming rock and roll.

THE JAM: *THE GIFT*

The Jam's final record is the one that most delivers on their mod image. *The Gift* is rhythmically tight, with Rick Buckler slapping out the kinds of Benny Benjamin beats dapper modernists shimmied to in 1963. Paul Weller and Bruce Foxton's songs are pure pop in the mode of the English groups that worshipped American soul in the salad days of the Vespa and the Baracuta G-9 Jacket. At times, the Jam betrays their fealty to their favorite era, as when Weller skids out *Shaft* wah-wah licks on "Precious," but "Trans-Global Express," "Running on the Spot," and the phenomenal Motown paean "Town Called Malice"—an outraged portrait of National Front violence—find these mods at their most modish.

Because it doesn't peel the paint like *In the City* and *All Mod Cons* and doesn't supply nonstop classics like *Sound Affects*, *The Gift* tends to get marginalized. Without a doubt, the Jam's most electrifying days did lie in the past. The road ahead was a path of maturity Paul Weller preferred to travel with his more far-out soul ensemble the Style Council. However, *The Gift* is a terrific album, heavier of beat and lighter of heart (musically if not lyrically) than the Jam of old.

THE MISFITS: *WALK AMONG US*

After five years of putting out singles and EPs—those punkest of punk formats—hard-core cult creeps the Misfits finally got around to cutting an LP in 1982. Clocking in at under twenty-five minutes, *Walk Among Us* feels no more long-winded than the group's previous releases. The Misfits almost sound like they're trying to outrun the listener in an attempt to slip their abundant hooks past the most obstinately antipop punks. On that account, they fail. It takes no more than one listen to catch all the catchy melody that billows behind these thirteen tracks like exhaust from the Munster Mobile. And for all the Misfits' fealty to evil, there is innocent charm in Glenn Danzig's nostalgic odes to horror hosts ("Vampira"), retro sci-fi ("I Turned into a Martian"), grade-A horror classics ("Night of the Living Dead"), and grade-Z horror classics ("Astro Zombies"). The Misfits were highly inspired by the United Kingdom's most lovable horror punks, the Damned, and Dave Vanian's influence is obvious in Danzig's own dark croon. Not that the Misfits can't be legitimately scary. The album's centerpiece, "Mommy, Can I Go Out and Kill Tonight?," is as disturbed as that title sounds. "Rip the veins from human necks until they're wet with life," Danzig bellows. With muscles like his, you know he can do it.

MISSING PERSONS: *SPRING SESSION M*

New Wave had a reputation for being superficial music played by pretty boys and girls who got by on their looks and their ability to locate the "on" switches of their drum machines. At first blush, Missing Persons supported this stereotype. Their music sounded robotic, and bleeping, blooping lead singer Dale Bozzio looked striking with her cotton-candy hair and mirror-ball bikini.

Anyone who took the time to listen to *Spring Session M* knew there was a lot more going on with this band. Dale's then husband Terry Bozzio is the kind of drummer who runs clinics, and he brings jazz precision and

Many people have suggested that Lady Gaga copped Dale Bozzio's look. You can't say they don't have a point. Author's collection.

prog rock complexity to Missing Persons' New Wave. The singles "Words," "Windows," "Destination Unknown," and "Walking in LA" are as sugar catchy as anything else on 1982 radio, but they're also smarter and tougher in lyric and sound. Album tracks such as "U.S. Drag," "Tears" (which could have been on Rush's *Signals*), "No Way Out," and "Rock and Roll Suspension" are as byzantine as New Wave got.

NINE BELOW ZERO: *THIRD DEGREE*

In the late seventies, Nine Below Zero drummed up local interest as one of London's top pub bands. They drew sweat like their punk peers while mimicking the attitudinal blues of the early Stones and Yardbirds. Mark Feltham did things to his harp Jagger never dared.

By their third album, they had transferred the wild energy they put into the Motown covers that made up their stage sets (captured on their debut LP, *Live at The Marquee*) to a serrated lineup of all-original material. It was no hollow gesture that the band chose Swinging London icon David Bailey to shoot the cover of *Third Degree*. Nine Below Zero is tight, taut, modish. With only the thinnest 1982 sheen, the album stirs memories of circa-1965 Small Faces and Who. "Wipe Away Your Kiss" is a tantalizing homage to the Jam playing homage to the Beatles. "Why Can't We Be What We Want to Be" slows the pace without letting up on the intensity. "Egg on My Face" is a vain attempt to temper the band's fire by swapping acoustics for the usual electric attack. "Sugarbeat (And Rhythm Sweet)" is freaky soul spotlighting Brian Bethell's wiry bass, and the pile-driving leadoff track, "Eleven Plus Eleven," would deserve classic-single status even if it hadn't helped launch the eighties' key rock and roll sitcom, *The Young Ones.*

Although they never had much impact in the United States, Nine Below Zero is well worthy of discovery by anyone who digs their ties as skinny as their drainpipe trousers, realizes Pete Townshend was always at his best when thrashing a Rickenbacker, and understands that Elvis Costello would have been a lot better off had he never met Langer and Winstanley.

PRINCE: *1999*

Just one month before Michael Jackson made his checkmate grab for the Prince of Pop's crown, another member of the funky royal family took pop a lot further out. On *Controversy*, Prince had ironed out the weird, homemade wrinkles of *Dirty Mind* with a polished, radio-ready production. On *1999*, he refunkifies his sound for a series of extended experiments. This is one of the weirdest hit albums of the eighties.

1999 is officially a solo Prince album, but he sneaked the name of his new band (written backwards) into that eye shape over the "I" in his name. He also made the "I" in *1999* look like a dick. Both are very Prince things to do. Author's collection.

While the sexy "Little Red Corvette" and the catchy rockabilly of "Delirious" hooked *1999* for radio listeners, Prince spends the rest of this ambitious double album following his quirkier impulses. The title track was chopped down for radio and MTV, but on the LP, it's a restless, relentless rumination on nuclear apocalypse beginning with a demon's creepy—and rather unconvincing—reassurance and ending with a child's creepier query: "Mommy, why does everybody have a bomb?" And who but Prince (and Stevie Wonder) had the nerve to begin a major statement with other singers? These singers are Dez Dickerson, Lisa Coleman, and Jill Jones, members of Prince's new group the Revolution. Despite Prince inviting these folks to his party and secreting the words "and the Revolution" on the album cover, *1999* feels like an even more insular project than the almost totally solo *Controversy*. "Something in the Water (Does Not Compute)," "All the Critics Love You in New York," and the orgiastic "Automatic" are projections from the darkest corners of Prince's brain. The constant jamming can get monotonous, and that's something Prince would scale back on his next album, but for immersion into the most unfiltered recesses of a genius's mind, *1999* cannot be equaled.

RUSH: *SIGNALS*

Moving Pictures was a smash blend of prog rock and New Wave. Rush moved deeper into contemporary territory when they completely jettisoned the prog epics of yore and cemented synthesizers as an essential element of their current sound on *Signals*. The album rounds off Rush's strongest trio of albums as it moves deeply enough into New Wave to sound like an authentic product of its time and tricky enough to still sound like a Rush record. The Police-worshipping "New World Man" gave the band their biggest hit single, but the doleful "Subdivisions" and the roiling "Weapon" endeared them more to longtime fans while still supplying catchy tunes and some of Neil Peart's most insightful and accessible words about local and global politics.

As synthesizers started to overwhelm the arrangements, Alex Lifeson was beginning to feel sidelined, but his contributions to all of these songs are still crucial, and he gets at least one old-fashioned outlet for his hard riffing with "Analog Kid." As synths almost completely consumed Rush on their next couple of records, Lifeson and the band's fans would get more disgruntled, and Rush would stop producing the quality material to support their experiments.

SIOUXSIE AND THE BANSHEES: *A KISS IN THE DREAMHOUSE*

By their fifth album, *A Kiss in the Dreamhouse*, Siouxsie and the Banshees had fully worked their original abrasiveness out of their system and matured in every way a group should. The band is more confident and on target than ever before. Siouxsie Sioux's voice is strong throughout, eliminating any need to mask its limitations with over-the-top stridency, and everyone's writing is spectacular. *A Kiss in the Dreamhouse* collects a variety of inventive songs drawing inspiration from such unlikely sources as Rod Serling and Jerzy Kosinski. Forceful tracks such as "She's a Carnival," "Cascade," and the dance-floor magnet "Slowdive" (the record's first single) are as ear catching as anything else on early eighties New Wave radio. The eerie psychedelic loops "Circle" and "Obsession," the jazzy "Cocoon," and the S&M Latin swirl "Melt!" (the second single) reveal an experi-

Siouxsie Sioux finally meets the woman of her dreams. Author's collection.

mentalism more musical and focused than anything the group tried in the past. "Painted Bird" gets my vote for the band's best track. The way its spinning verses blow up into choruses crowded with Siouxsie's contrapuntal vocals, the way John McGeoch's ascending riff pushes up beneath them, launching those voices into the sky, drives me mad. This is the song I want to hear the next time a million sparrows burst out of my skull.

PETE TOWNSHEND: *ALL THE BEST COWBOYS HAVE CHINESE EYES*

Pete Townshend had a lot of baggage to deal with as the leader of one of rock's biggest and brashest bands. What did the thugs and punks who adored the Who think of this very synthesized, very sensitive, very—according to numerous irritated/irritating critics—*pretentious* eighties pop record? Townshend had developed a love of "streamed poetry," which informs his half-spoken deliveries of "Stop Hurting People," "Communication," and "Uniforms" (which are all a lot more structured than "Body Language," a track Townshend wisely left off the record).

The most devoted Pete worshipper may feel uncomfortable listening to him confess his sexual failures and existential angst on "Somebody Saved Me." But such matters are what make *All the Best Cowboys Have Chinese Eyes* a fascinating listen. Pete is giving us access to his personal flaws and his flawed ideas, making for the kind of intimate experience one almost never gets from such a big star. And the difficulty of his ideas are never let down by difficult music. "Face Dances Part Two," delivered in jerky 5/4 time, is as catchy as his songs get—"The Sea Refuses No River" and "Somebody Saves Me" are as beautiful. "Slit Skirts" is an invigorating triumph of not going gently into that dark night. Even the record's most pompous numbers are full of energy, emotion, and enough sincerity to contradict those charges of pretentiousness.

THE WHO: *IT'S HARD*

A lot of the frustration that inspired Pete Townshend to create one of 1982's most compelling solo albums also caused him to take part in one of the year's most disappointing ones. Aggravated with the lack of support for *Face Dances* without and within the Who, Townshend called on his bandmates to get more involved for *It's Hard*. He had them suggest topics for songs and put a greater deal of the songwriting burden on John Entwistle. The band sacked producer Bill Szymczyk, whose slick production of *Face Dances* was widely ridiculed, and rehired Glyn Johns, who'd helped produce the Who's most beloved album, *Who's Next*. With such historically minded attention to the creation of their latest album, what Who fan wouldn't love it?

All of them. Despite the band's good intentions, *It's Hard* is a waste. It barely sounds like the Who at all as they trudge through weak material overburdened with dated synthesizers. Entwistle's songs are dire. Townshend's are often dispiriting. Hearing him express embarrassment over his opposition to nuclear arms in his younger years on "Cry If You Want" is depressing and very in keeping with the stridency of the era's conscience-challenged world leaders, American President Reagan and British Prime Minister Thatcher.

More often his songs are regrettable because of their lack of strong melody or structure. They tend to meander rather than punch. Johns's production is frigid. "I've Known No War" (a taut yet strangely resigned expression of nuclear-age anxiety), "Athena" (Townshend's jubilant but inscrutable confession of lust for actress Theresa Russell), and "Eminence Front" (a hypnotic and jazzy repudiation of Reagan-era decadence that sounds nothing like the Who) are the only salvageable tracks on *It's Hard*. A clearly exhausted Who called it quits after a "farewell" tour in support of the album. Despite that hype, the Who would tour again and even record again, but they'd never make another album in the twentieth-century rock album era that they did so much to enliven.

X: UNDER THE BIG BLACK SUN

After two thrashing constitutionals on the independent Slash Records label, X took their enterprise to producer Ray Manzarek's old label, Elektra. During their move to the majors, X shed a few of their punk scales and allowed their fifties influences to shine through on *Under the Big Black Sun*. There's a lot of Bo Diddley rolling in "The Hungry Wolf" and "Motel Room in My Bed." "Come Back to Me" is lush, Flamingoes-style balladry. The psycho rumba "Dancing with Tears in My Eyes" and the surfy title track extend the retro vibe.

X jets back to their high-velocity roots on "Because I Do" and "Real Child of Hell," but *Under the Big Black Sun* is powerful less for its aggression and more for its maturity. And though the record is not as rabid as the ones it followed, the emotions are rawer. Exene Cervenka addresses the death of her sister Mirielle in "Riding with Mary," which unflinchingly re-creates the moment she died in a car accident. "Come Back to Me" painfully recounts the funeral and the aching need to see Mirielle one last time. Always iffy when it comes to pitch, Exene sounds particularly close to cracking on this track, undermining the polish of X's bid for mainstream success and maximizing the real emotions behind their music.

XTC: ENGLISH SETTLEMENT

XTC had never been a crowd-pleasing hit machine, but there is a sense of chin-to-the-chest inwardness on *English Settlement* not present on the group's previous records. While the other albums opened with big, brisk pop numbers like "Making Plans for Nigel" and "Respectable Street," *English Settlement* starts with the moody, misty "Runaway." XTC get dreamy on "All of a Sudden (It's Too Late)" and disorienting on "Jason and the Argonauts." Even the more traditionally poppy tracks like "Ball and Chain" and "Senses Working Overtime" sound mildly weary, but rather than sapping the listener's interest, they draw us in closer.

English Settlement is an intellectual experience rather than a visceral one, even as the material is as melodious as ever. Andy Partridge and Colin Moulding composed a cerebral yet creative selection of lyrics. "Snowman" uses seasonal imagery as a simile for romantic frustration. "Jason and the Argonauts" uses mythology as a metaphor for the oppressiveness of Western ideology. There are antiwar statements ("Melt the Guns"), sketches of familial discord ("Runaways," "No Thugs in Our House"), and a look at the injustice of unfettered consumption ("Sense Working Overtime"). At double-LP length and loaded with unusually lengthy songs, *English Settle-ment* sucks the listener into its murky depths with all the undertow of the surf zone.

1983

The year 1983 is one of blockbuster albums, many of which are hard not to view as self-conscious responses to the smash status of *Thriller*. Long-standing artists such as David Bowie and the Police seemed intent on dethroning Michael, and both made better albums than the self-appointed Prince of Pop ever did. An audacious newcomer in a pink tutu gave those seasoned old boys a run for their money with her own hit-bursting debut. Smaller acts from Dublin, Milwaukie, and Athens suggested that high-art content was still possible in the year of leg warmers, Cabbage Patch Kids, SDI, and Mario Bros.

However, the art of the rock LP also faced a new challenge as the cassette outsold the vinyl LP for the first time. With its compact size that could be popped into a dashboard stereo or portable player and its inferior sound quality and packaging, the cassette became popular because of its convenience rather than its audio quality. Attempts to improve that sound with Dolby B noise-reduction technology introduced to consumers in 1968 cut down on the persistent hiss that defines the cassette-listening experience, but it also dulled the overall sound. With twice the capacity of a vinyl LP, the cassette was still attractive to buyers because it made room for bonus tracks, which some of the year's artists took advantage of, as when the Police included the B-side "Murder by Numbers" on the cassette edition of *Synchronicity*. However, the plastic-shelled medium with the easily damaged and quick-to-deteriorate tape implied that rock music was becoming more disposable. The first appearance of the digital compact disc (CD) late in the previous year set events in motion that would change rock music even more radically by the end of the decade.

The CD's great selling point was squeaky-clean sound free of vinyl's pops and crackle or the hiss and murkiness of a deteriorating cassette. Although it could house more music than a single vinyl LP or prerecorded cassette, with its eighty-minute capacity, the very format made the music it contained more disposable. Sure, a listener could lift stylus off vinyl before an offending track or hit the "fast-forward" button on a cassette player, but neither action was as effortless and instantaneous as hitting the "skip" button on a CD player, thus messing with the artist's vision for their carefully constructed album. The "shuffle" button, which randomizes tracks during play, obliterates that vision completely and got album buyers used to listening to music on their own terms regardless of the artist's intentions. In essence, the new features of the CD were priming music listeners for the greater media changes to come at the end of the century that would further degrade the very concept of the album.

The CD and the cassette also degraded the value of vinyl records, which could be purchased for peanuts as sales dropped. Although it was less expensive to manufacture than the vinyl LP (in 1983, it cost $3 or $4 to produce a single disc), the CD initially retailed for about $15.99 at a time when a new release on vinyl could be had for a mere $8.99 or so. With the rise of the used record shows that started popping up in convention halls across America with greater frequency, a collector could show up with a pocketful of crumpled George Washingtons and return home with a pirate's booty of wax discs. I can still vividly recall my first trip to the Long Island record convention where I picked up three albums—*The Monkees*, *More of the Monkees*, and the Beach Boys' *Endless Summer*—for that many dollars and the one where I scored five Beatles albums for whatever pittance a middle-class thirteen-year-old has in his wallet. Such events would keep the fires of used record collecting stoked well into the future even as the purchase of new vinyl was flickering out.

DAVID BOWIE: *LET'S DANCE*

David Bowie was one of the most popular artists of the seventies, but he was not a consistent maker of hit singles in the United States. That changed in 1983 when his photogenic puss was all over MTV and he released *Let's Dance*, the most commercially savvy album of his career. The title track, his serpentine cover of Iggy Pop's "China Girl," and the Motown hom-age "Modern Love" put him over like nothing before. While this more commercially minded Bowie would see his artistry suffer over the course of the decade (that Motown affinity would go horribly awry when Jagger jumped into the mix a couple of years later), *Let's Dance* hits a good bal-ance between both branches of success. None of its material has the jagged edges of "Ashes to Ashes" or "Fashion"—the two singles from Bowie's pre-vious album—but both "China Girl" and "Let's Dance" sport a thick layer of sweat and grit that masks the polish. "Modern Love" wears its polish proudly in keeping with its inspiration. The rest of the album is similarly catchy and slightly quirky, and at just eight tracks, there isn't room for a dud. *Let's Dance* may not be Bowie's most challenging work, but it is one of the eighties' most artistically satisfying mainstream pop albums.

DEF LEPPARD: *PYROMANIA*

When Led Zeppelin and Black Sabbath molded heavy metal, they seemed intent on pleasing kids and scaring off parents and pop radio. As metal continued along as a primarily British form, bands sold plenty of albums but few singles. *Pyromania* changed that.

Students of Slade, Queen, T. Rex, and other glammers, Def Leppard did not like to think of themselves as progeny of Sabbath or Iron Maiden. The Sheffield quintet thought of themselves as a rock and roll band, not necessarily a metal one, but their heaps of hair, horn-ball moron lyrics, razor riffs, and Joe Elliott's sing-scream got them lumped in with the metallurgists.

What Def Leppard lacked was metal's gloominess, grunginess, and disdain for pop hooks. *Rumours* sounds like musique concrète compared to Def Leppard's third album. Producer Mutt Lang labored the record into anodyne perfection. There is not

The first album I ever got was *Pyromania*, which was a co-Christmas gift for my sister and me. We had to share it because I didn't own a record player and had to ask permission to use hers whenever I wanted to listen to the album. My dad made an 8-track copy of the record for me, but I didn't have a proper 8-track player either. So I had to listen to the tape on my 2-XL, which was a robot-shaped trivia game that used 8-track tapes. Since responding to questions involved pressing a button to select a particular track, 2-XL did not automatically change tracks, so I had to change tracks manu-ally, sometimes in the middle of a song. That sure is a lot of trouble to go to for the pleasure of hearing "Rock! Rock! (Till You Drop)." Author's collection.

a guitar lick out of place, not an imprecise drum strike, not a vocal harmony that doesn't sound like it was filtered through a supercomputer. The production's soulessness can't tamp down the irresistible choruses of "Photograph," "Foolin'," and "Rock of Ages," all of which became some of the biggest hits often categorized as metal in the early eighties. Album tracks "Rock! Rock! (Till You Drop)," "Stagefright," and "Action! Not Words" are pretty catchy too. The lyrics are uniformly stupid calls to rock in both senses. On the surface, they're not necessarily any sillier than early R&R or blues songs that first made the connection between getting off to music and getting off in bed. The metaphors just taste extra stale this time because Def Leppard came to them third hand—and because these blow-dried guys are a lot less cool than Muddy Waters. The rest of the album is pretty blah, but there's no point in suggesting that *Pyromania* is anything but a success.

As the eighties trudged on, Def pretenders such as Bon Jovi, Poison, Warrant, and White Lion would double down on *Pyromania*'s pop-metal formula. They sprayed their hair higher, glossed their riffs shinier, and poured more sugar on their choruses, selling millions of albums and dragging rock and roll's good name through the Aqua Net.

BILLY IDOL: *REBEL YELL*

Billy Idol's second album is easily his best. *Rebel Yell* is both atmospheric and tirelessly catchy. Idol's eternal compadre Steve Stevens, who'd been pretty restrained on *Billy Idol*, gets to show off his six-string flamboyancy as Idol gets to do some legitimate sneering on the bourbon-soaked title track and the appealingly sleazy "Flesh for Fantasy." For "Eyes Without a Face," Billy Idol doesn't just borrow the title of George Franju's horror masterpiece *Les Yeux sans Visage*, he also nicks the film's gothic beauty. Billy Idol being Billy Idol, he is unable to keep his silliness completely at bay (hence the mid-song rap about taking a "psychedelic trip" and reading "murder books" in Las Vegas), but the track is all the more endearing for it and Idol's best in my opinion.

Those are the hits, but album tracks such as the desolate "Daytime Drama," the crazy catchy "(Do Not) Stand in the Shadow," and the celestial "Dead Next Door" are excellent too. The only faux pas is some farty sax on the flop single "Catch My Fall," but cut him some slack. It was the eighties.

CYNDI LAUPER: *SHE'S SO UNUSUAL*

For some whacko reason, *She's So Unusual* somehow doesn't have the same enduring influence as *Purple Rain, Thriller, Synchronicity, Born in the USA, Like a Virgin*, or any of the other blockbuster albums of the early eighties. Yet it's better than most of those albums, and it still has the power to knock your Starry Night soles off with its unbelievable string of hits. Everyone remembers the deliriously cheerful "Girls Just Want to Have Fun" (a song Lauper deemed "chauvinistic" before rewriting Robert Hazard's lyrics from a more feminist perspective), so inescapable in 1983, but the others are even better. Lauper lets her quirk flag fly musically and lyrically on the mastur-bation ode "She Bop," goes full melodrama yet totally earns your tears with "Time After

Annie Leibovitz shot this iconic album cover in Coney Island. Author's collection.

Time," hits the hard rock on her cover of the Brains' "Money Changes Everything," and swirls and twirls through Jules Shear's "All Through the Night."

But that's not all, as she somehow successfully covers the uncoverable Prince with a boffo version of "When You Were Mine" and ends the LP with a string of superb album cuts that find her dittoing Two Tone Records ("Witness"), Devo ("I'll Kiss You"), Betty Boop (the legit 1920s artifact "He's So Unusual"), and Yoko Ono ("Yeah Yeah") all while retaining her own inimitable unusualness. *She's So Unusual* is as much a sign of its times as a bowl of Pac-Man Crunch, as timeless as *The Wizard of Oz*, and as col-orful and kooky as both.

MADONNA: *MADONNA*

Madonna seemed like something of a pop alien when she pirouetted out of New York City's club scene and onto MTV in 1983. She wrote alarmingly catchy songs, styled herself like a punk who'd just been shoplifting at Fred-erick's of Hollywood, made the most of her limited voice whether dropping into a throaty croon or swooping up into Minnie Mouse territory, and pre-sented herself as defiantly self-possessed and unapologetically sexy. She was the mighty role model girls had been craving, and her instantly recognizable style inspired the coining of the term "wannabe." Snobby rock critics dismissed her as facile, but Madonna ultimately emerged as the defining pop star of her decade just as Elvis, the Beatles, and Elton John defined theirs. Prince wasn't as consistently popular. Michael Jackson wasn't as prolific or forward thinking.

Madonna's carefully cultivated image has often overwhelmed her music, though she had a remarkable run of hits. She's been pretty innovative too, especially considering the restrictions of the top-forty pop world that has always been her playground despite her nods to the underground, New Wave, and club cultures.

As far as pop albums go, you'd be hard pressed to find one loaded with more smashes than Madonna's debut. Six of the eight songs are bona fide classics, all of which are among Madonna's very best: "Lucky Star," "Burning Up," "Holiday," "Physical Attraction," "Everybody," and "Borderline" (my pick for her best song). There aren't many albums with that kind of hit ratio and fewer on which all the hits are so eternally effervescent. Both of the two lesser-known numbers, "I Know It" and "Think of Me," are good, and Madonna never cops out with drippy adult contemporary ballads as she would on future releases. *Madonna* is the most convincing evidence that she had some cool New Wave cred before she went supernova.

NEW ORDER: *POWER, CORRUPTION, & LIES*

Joy Division grew out of British punk but had more in common with the dour tone and minimalism of the burgeoning goth scene. After making just two albums and 45-RPM history with "Love Will Tear Us Apart," an early anthem for that gloomy new movement, Joy Division came to an abrupt end when front man Ian Curtis took his own life in 1980.

New Order is the band that grew out of the ruins. Their first album, *Movement*, has the air of unfinished business flowing through songs that reference Curtis and songs such as "Ceremony" that could pass for lost Joy Division tracks. The music is good, but New Order no longer had to settle for being the Artist Formerly Known as Joy Division when they found their own voice with their second album.

The most immediately striking thing about *Power, Corruption, & Lies* is how joyful it feels after Joy Division's joylessness. This temper is obvious from the first few guitar plucks of "Age of Consent." Even when the mood settles down on "We All Stand," the rhythm and production spark. "586" merely dupes us into thinking it will return to the gloominess of *Movement* before it explodes into a swirling cousin of New Order's dance-floor classic "Blue Monday." "Your Silent Face" brings the tempo down, but the mood is sweepingly romantic, not dejected. Its hilariously tart closing couplet raises both the gaze from the footwear and two defiant fingers in the air. The other striking things are how well New Order has incorporated synths into their sound and how strong their songwriting has become. Nothing on the album had the massive influence of "Blue Monday," but the burbling "The Village" is single-worthy and the best of both organic and synthetic instrumentation. *Power, Corruption, & Lies* is the sound of a great career kicking into gear.

THE POLICE: *SYNCHRONICITY*

The Police expanded their sound with horns and keyboards on *Ghost in the Machine*, but even that album sounds underdeveloped next to *Synchronicity*. The band and Hugh Padgham's production is as plush as they come, and with less of a reliance on reggae rhythms, the music is the most eclectic the Police would ever collect on a single disc. They seem intent on drawing the cinema out of their songs, so when Sting laments how humans are walking in the soon-to-be-extinct footsteps of the dinosaurs, you can just about see the volcanic steam rising from the Earth and the immense sauropods lumbering toward their doom. When he sings of sharing tea in the Sahara with a pair of sisters, you can see the vastness of a barren, sandy world beneath a limitless, sheltering sky. You can see all color drain from the album's otherwise vivid world as Sting casts himself as some sort of gothic depression king against a potpourri of bizarre imagery. He illustrates his lost soul with an album of surreal snapshots: a dead salmon frozen in a waterfall (that's his soul up there), a spotty sun (that's his soul too), a skeleton choking on bread (ditto), and so on.

Even when the perspective passes to Stuart Copeland on the wacky jungle romp "Ms. Grendenko" or Andy Summers on the deranged paranoia Looney Tune "Mother," the music continues to be incredibly visual. Too much of the album's reputation hangs on the huge hit "Every Breath You Take." Rest assured that nothing else on *Synchronicity* could have been pulled from it and slapped onto one of Sting's boring solo albums. For one last time, Copeland and Summers prod him into making forceful, dark music, and the results are a great album that richly deserves its era-defining success.

R.E.M.: *MURMUR*

Synchronicity is audacious in its invention and scope. The product of an inscrutable quartet from bohemian Athens, Georgia, *Murmur* is defiantly small. Michael Stipe's voice is hardly ever understandable above Peter Buck's jangle or Mike Mills and Bill Berry's swampy backbeat. "Talk About the Passion" never lifts its gaze from the floor. "We Walk" is a chaste stroll. "Perfect Circle" is a whisper. But in creating this music, R.E.M. crafts a cinematic world as assuredly as the Police do, but while the Police made a blockbuster, R.E.M. put out a little indie sleeper. As such, it sounds eternally fresh despite its tenebrous atmosphere. And the energy of a lot of these songs helps it to rise above early R.E.M.'s introverted reputation. "Moral Kiosk," "Catapult," "Sitting Still," and "Radio Free Europe" are instant pop parties (though the latter is not nearly as powerful in its remade form on *Murmur* as the original Hib-Tone single version was).

The kudzu festooned cover of *Murmur* completes the album's Southern Gothic vibe. Author's collection.

Incredibly, one day many years from 1983, R.E.M. would give in to swaggering, rock star confidence and make such extroverted moves as *Monster* and *Reveal*. Michael Stipe would become a strong, political voice. However, the bigger, bolder R.E.M. was never as alluring and enchanting as the guys who seemed like strange wood sprites murmuring among the kudzu in an Athenian garden.

U2: *WAR*

The U2 phenomenon starts here, and it never gets better. After an electrifying start with *Boy*, U2 skidded past *October* to land on their most striking and consistent album (though I still prefer *Boy* for its energy). On *War*, U2 unveiled their first major anthems. "Sunday Bloody Sunday," an account of Ireland's troubles at the hands of British imperialists, makes no effort to contain its outrage. A portrait of Lech Walesa's worker's strike in Poland, "New Year's Day" swells with hope. Both sounded like daggers slashing across a terrain of sugar-crusted cake knives on 1983 radio and MTV. The atmosphere is icy and desolate, and that empty feeling caused some critics to dismiss *War* in 1983. How could they be dismissive of tracks as fierce as "Two Hearts Beat As One" or "Like a Song . . ." or as eerie as "Seconds" or "Drowning Man" or as groovy as "Red Light" or "The Refugee" or as heavenly as "40"? How could they be dismissive of Bono's expressive wail or the Edge's lacerating sci-fi transmissions? Today, *War* is rightly regarded as one of the most important albums of the eighties, and it catches U2 at that prime moment when they were at their peak powers and not yet self-conscious about them.

VIOLENT FEMMES: *VIOLENT FEMMES*

Milwaukee's Violent Femmes did nothing less than invent a new genre with their eponymous debut. On one end of the musical spectrum are Gordon Gano's acoustic guitar, Brian Ritchie's acoustic bass, and Victor Delorenzo's spare drum kit mostly limited to the snare. On the other end are Gano's Pete-Shelley sneer and the band's malicious, speedy attack. This was something new that could be defined as "acoustic punk," but even that pat definition ignores the deep subtleties in the music: Ritchie's machine-gun leads and a drift into rapt elegance with "Good Feeling." Gano's words are as laser-focused as the music as he spits spite over being a teenager in unrequited love and lust. *Violent*

The CD edition of *Violent Femmes* includes two bonus tracks, one of which isn't as good as the songs on the proper album and one of which is the super-catchy "Ugly." Author's collection.

Femmes wallows in rejection, envy, and frustration. Gano's tunefulness is equally arresting. "Blister in the Sun," "Please Don't Go," "Gone Daddy Gone," and much of the rest could be playground sing-alongs in some twisted parallel universe. The counting chant of "Kiss Off" and the concluding shout of "Add It Up" seem consciously designed for a taunt around the merry-go-round. This is one of those albums so bloated with definitive classics that one can easily forget that it was only the beginning of a long, fruitful career and ignore the rest of Violent Femmes' work. That is probably a bit of a burden for the band, but as burdens go, *Violent Femmes* is one of the best.

TOM WAITS: *SWORDFISHTROMBONES*

After *Heart Attack and Vine*, Tom Waits jumped ship from Asylum and boarded Island. In the transition, the singer-songwriter's already weird take on beat poetry, jazz, blues, and circus music tumbled overboard, got all caked up with mud and seaweed, and slithered back on deck.

The result, *Swordfishtrombones*, is pretty uncategorizable. Tom Waits goes totally off the wall with his awkward, lurching rhythms, his growling vocal Muppetry, his demented song structures, and his lapses into pure cacophony—dig him stabbing an organ to death on "Dave the Butcher." The flashes of regularity among all the irregularity will draw you in more assuredly than any of the conventional stuff on his early staid albums like *The Heart of Saturday Night* could have. Waits follows the torture of "Dave the Butcher" with a pretty, smoky ballad called "Johnsburg, Illinois," which he then follows with the rocking clitter-clatter of "16 Shells from a Thirty-Ought Six," which gets my vote for his most divine moment. "In the Neighborhood" will have you and your drunken cronies singing around the bar as assuredly as "Down Down Down" will get you doing a mad rumba and "Soldier's Things" will leave you sobbing in your Schlitz. The invention across these fifteen tracks is stunning, as the songs slobber with everything from vibes to banjo to brass bands to bagpipes to—perhaps most off-the-map of all for Waits—some basic, gritty rock and roll guitar. But it's the terrific songs and that voice pitched somewhere between a banshee and Cookie Monster that draw it all together into a package pitched dead center between the absurd and the sublime.

X: *MORE FUN IN THE NEW WORLD*

After two albums of lean, seventies-style punk and one with a twist of fifties rock and roll, X started exploring the decade in between on *More Fun in the New World*. "Hot House" is an ace Stones homage, and there is a Motown undercurrent to the bouncing beat of "We're Having Much More Fun" and a Leslie Gore shuffle in "New World." The chorus of "True Love" is pure bubble gum, and the album's most striking track. "I Must Not Think Bad Thoughts," jangles like folk rock while displaying the subtler dynamics of the more progressive later sixties. Billy Zoom zooms surfy guitar lines through a lot of this stuff.

X still rages through this more varied and nuanced material, and they still give it up for their fifties and seventies influences with a great cover of

Jerry Lee Lewis's "Breathless," the Bo Diddley–meets–Ricky Nelson bop of "Poor Girl," and the pure punk assault of "Devil Doll" and "Painting the Town Blue." The album ends on a truly far-out note with a didn't-see-that-coming exercise in disco funk called "True Love Part 2." So, while *More Fun in the New World* may not be as consistently vicious as *Los Angeles* or as emotional as *Under the Big Black Sun*, it delivers fully on its title, making it the best X album to reach for no matter what mood you're in.

1984

The year 1984 was a rough one. Ronald Reagan got reelected. AIDS was on the rise amid the apathy of people in power like Reagan. The famine that started sweeping Ethiopia the previous year worsened.

More on topic, future Second Lady Tipper Gore brought a lot of unwanted publicity to the record industry when she rallied a bunch of officious ninnies to wage war against pop music with her Parents Music Resource Center (PMRC), which she formed in 1984. The following year, she successfully lobbied to get the Recording Industry Association of America to slap "Parental Advisory" stickers on albums containing "pornographic " content (it would be another five years before the first album to sport the iconic black-and-white sticker, *2 Live Crew's Banned in the U.S.A.*, was released with all due fanfare). The so-called Filthy 15 the PMRC selected as evidence of suggestive content in 1984 was a laughable assortment of Satanic Panic fuel (Mercyful Fate's "Into the Coven," Venom's "Possessed"), generic rock and booze lyrics (Def Leppard's "High 'n' Dry," Black Sabbath's "Trashed"), generic rebellion (Twisted Sister's "We're Not Gonna Take It"), PG (Madonna's "Dress You Up") and PG-13 sex stuff (Cyndi Lauper's "She Bop," Mary Jane Girls' "In My House"), more R-rated fare (W.A.S.P.'s "Animal [Fuck Like a Beast]"), and MOR chanteuse Sheena Easton ("Sugar Walls"). That last song shared a composer with the song that sparked all this hysteria when Gore heard her daughter grooving to Prince's "Darling

Nikki." That track also happened to appear on the year's most artistically audacious commercial sensation.

Judged solely on the quality of its music, 1984 wasn't the best year of the eighties, but it did have an unusually high number of blockbuster releases. While 1982 could claim *Thriller* and 1983 had *Synchronicity*, *An Innocent Man*, and *Pyromania*, 1984 was the year of such single-spewing juggernauts as the *Footloose* sound track, *Born in the U.S.A.*, *Eliminator*, *Sports*, *Can't Slow Down*, *Like a Virgin*, *Private Dancer*, *She's So Unusual*, *Purple Rain*, and, yes, *1984*. It was a year of commercial breakthroughs and an artistic demarcation line at the dead center of the decade. If 1984 didn't produce as much great pop as 1982 or 1983, it certainly had more than 1985 or 1986. Certainly the work the Smiths, Siouxsie and the Banshees, Echo & the Bunnymen, R.E.M., the Replacements, and Mr. Controversy himself—Prince—produced that year is among the decade's best.

THE BANGLES: *ALL OVER THE PLACE*

The Bangles was the only band to climb out of Los Angeles's sixties-fetishizing Paisley Underground to become zillion-selling pop superstars. However, when they hit big in 1986 with *Different Light*, there was a mere dusting of paisley atop the drum machines, synthesizers, and other heavy-handed eighties production signatures. "Manic Monday" is a really good record, but the original fans the Bangles had won by doing time on the Sunset Strip were probably left wondering what happened to the organic, no-frills band they loved.

At least they still had their copies of *All Over the Place*. As organic as the later albums would sound overprocessed, *All Over the Place* is a vital, harmony-hugged throwback to the best of mid-sixties West Coast pop. The Bangles make their roots and great taste clear with a faithful cover of the Merry-Go-Round's sunny "Live," but they also show that they're plugged into the current scene with a version of Katrina and the Waves' "Going Down to Liverpool" that is the album's best track. But everything on *All Over the Place* is a winner, and though the Bangles could have been boxed in by their retro ethos, they

Rickenbacker guitars, portable record players, and a great big garage: the Bangles are very up front about what makes them cool on their first album cover. Author's collection.

sound both distinctive and unfettered as they explore graceful chamber pop ("More Than Meets the Eye"), straight-for-the-jugular garage punk ("Silent Treatment"), and a flurry of the jangle pop that was their true specialty.

JULIAN COPE: *WORLD SHUT YOUR MOUTH*

As a member of the Teardrop Explodes, Julian Cope was an important figure in the neo-psychedelic scene (had his band hailed from Los Angeles instead of Liverpool, they surely would have gotten boxed into the Paisley Underground with the Bangles). A cocktail of drugs and aggression exploded the group before they could make a third LP, and Cope was left to run off to a wonderland of his own. His was no hippie nursery of tangerine trees and plasticine porters, though, which you could probably tell from his debut's title. However, *World Shut Your Mouth* is not a flood of negativity. "Sunshine Playroom" soothes the terror of fleeing the nest with the joyous discovery of oral sex. "Pussyface" is not an insult but a weird term of affection for another thrilling lady. Although that song was actually intended for the Teardrop Explodes, it fits perfectly with the free-spirited yet totally crazy vibe of *World Shut Your Mouth*. So does the music, which is both lovingly evocative of the sixties pop Cope adores without being self-consciously retro, as the pounding, thoroughly modern "Kolly Kibber's Birthday" makes clear.

THE CURE: *THE TOP*

Through *Seventeen Seconds*, *Faith*, and *Pornography*, the Cure went from creepily minimalistic to tormented, but the sounds were all steel gray. As great as all those albums are, they might leave one feeling the Cure needed to start juggling up their sound or risk landing in a rut. Robert Smith and Lol Tolhurst tested out a sweeter approach on a trio of delightful singles ("Let's Go to Bed," "The Walk," "The Love Cats") before folding that approach in with the darker style they'd already perfected on LP. This gave the Cure a refreshed sound even if *The Top* ends up sounding a bit messy. Dark, "classic Cure" type things like "Wailing Wall," "Give Me It" (which is more hard core than anything on *Pornography*), and the churning title track don't sound like they belong on the same record as light pieces like the romantic "Bird Mad Girl" (which I like to believe was inspired by Siouxsie Sioux, with whom Smith was currently moonlighting), the bubbly

"Dressing Up," "Piggy in the Mirror," or the whimsical "Caterpillar." But that blend of sweet and somber would be a cardinal component of the band that would butt "Catch" against "Torture" or "Friday I'm in Love" against "Trust" in the coming years.

ECHO & THE BUNNYMEN: *OCEAN RAIN*

Grand imagery and weirdness get swept up in the grand vision of Echo & the Bunnymen's fourth album. *Ocean Rain* brings to mind images of bracing storms and vast seas: a sort of New Wave *Salty Dog*. The Bunnymen's masterpiece is also similar to Procol Harum's in its use of elaborate orchestrations. A thirty-five-piece ensemble swoops over "Silver," chugs behind the shivering "Nocturnal Me," plucks icily across the divine "Killing Moon," discharges discordant lightning bolts on "Thorn of Crowns." Buoys poppy, morose, psychedelic, sweet, folky, and waltzing bob on its dark waters. Despite the elegance of the arrangements, *Ocean Rain* is very much a rock and roll record. Check out the psycho-Diddley raver "Thorn of Crowns," which makes even crazier use of vegetable imagery than Syd Barrett's "Vegetable Man."

MADONNA: *LIKE A VIRGIN*

Madonna piled many of her best and best-known songs on her first album, but *Madonna* did not become the blockbuster phenomenon her second LP did. Like *Thriller*, *Synchronicity*, *Purple Rain*, or *Pyromania*, *Like a Virgin* is an album that defines the eighties. The title song was shocking on release because of the frankness of its sexual metaphor, but it became a hit on its melodic merits and because of how well Madonna sold it. "Material Girl" is a tongue-in-check anthem of eighties self-absorption but also a production as sweet and fizzy as a flute of champagne and an important building block in Madonna's self-mythologizing. "Angel" and "Dress You Up" are more forceful hits that don't skimp on the sexiness. The hits are so impactful that the ordinariness of the schmaltzy ballads and passable pop that make up the rest of the album is a little surprising. That willingness to iron out her quirks when it suited her would help Madonna cross over. She could raise legit controversy with things like "Erotica" and "Like a Prayer" (well, she could raise it with the cross-burning video if not the splendiferous song) while also playing to the dentist's-office chair with "This Used to Be My

Playground" or "Take a Bow." That made her future work interesting in fits and starts (though the zesty *True Blue* is totally fab from start to finish), and a lot of her more daring moves seem like a put-on, but it also made her a superstar who could have her cake and eat it too, which had clearly been her goal since *Like a Virgin*.

THE PRETENDERS: *LEARNING TO CRAWL*

I believe lazy rock critics have overexaggerated the existence of the "sophomore slump"—the theory that second albums tend to be weak because artists expend all of their best material on their debuts—though *Pretenders II* is a pretty good example of this alleged phenomenon. It isn't a bad album—certainly not with very good songs like "Message of Love," "Talk of the Town," "Waste Not Want Not," and "Pack It Up"—but it too often plays like a lesser version of the band's first album. They even cover another Ray Davies song, though Chrissie Hynde's relationship with him probably accounts for that.

Then came two tremendous shake-ups: both guitarist James Honeyman-Scott and bassist Pete Farndon died of overdoses. Hynde and drummer Martin Chambers took two years to mourn and rebuild their band. The title of *Learning to Crawl* implies that they needed to learn how to be a band again, and this exuberant album does sound like it could have been another group's debut. Instead of letting those tragedies turn her bitter or dour, Hynde sounds as if she has embraced life anew, even when dealing with Honeyman-Scott's death on the brisk "Back on the Chain Gang" or surveying disturbingly changed landscapes on "Time the Avenger" and "My City Was Gone." On that track, new bassist Malcolm Foster makes his presence felt with the Pretenders' best bass line since "Mystery Achievement." The real star of *Learning to Crawl* remains Hynde, whose songwriting has matured richly on "Chain Gang," "Time the Avenger," "Show Me," and the modern holiday standard "2000 Miles." On dynamite like "Middle of the Road" and "Watching the Clothes," the new Pretenders show they can rock almost as hard as the old one.

PRINCE AND THE REVOLUTION: *PURPLE RAIN*

Everyone likes to rhapsodize about how Michael Jackson was the most spectacular male all-around entertainer of the eighties, but as far as I'm concerned, no one could touch Prince. He could sing like he had a built-in pitch wheel, play guitar that would give Hendrix the heebie-jeebies, and dance like James Brown and Plastic Man's baby. No artist burned with as much creativity. That guy loved to sing about sex, but a glance at his schedule during his most vital years makes one wonder if he ever even had the time to take off his purple pants. Prince recorded not only his greatest album and another pretty terrific one during that time but also a wealth of unreleased music and B-sides, mounted a meticulously choreographed tour, and masterminded side projects for the Time, Sheila-E, Vanity 6, Apollonia 6, and the Family. All that makes James Brown sound like the Godfather of Slacking.

In 1984, Prince even starred in his own movie. In *Purple Rain*, he plays "The Kid," a wunderkind musician who lives in his parents' basement and creates music deemed too weird for First Avenue, the Minneapolis club where Morris Day and the Time draw huge crowds by playing music almost exactly like that of The Kid and his band, the Revolution. Except it's not as good. The Kid meets aspiring singer Apollonia, falls in love with her, and lets her know this by tricking her into jumping naked into a lake. In Minneapolis. In the winter. Despite The Kid's sadism, Apollonia is unable to resist his brilliance, so she buys him a guitar. When Morris Day gets wind of the budding ingenue, he swoops in to turn her into his personal protégé. The Kid reacts to this news by punching Apollonia in the face.

Back at home, trouble is brewin' as The Kid's equally personable dad slaps around his mom before jamming out on an upright piano that sounds like a $35 Casio keytar. There is also discord in The Kid's band, where Revolutionaries Wendy Melvoin and Lisa Coleman must contend with their leader's massive ego to convince him to play a new song they wrote—a new song called "Purple Rain," that is!

Will The Kid win back the love of Apollonia by making her leap into a bonfire while wearing nothing but a Richard Nixon mask? Will The Kid turn into his evil father, fulfilling his worst nightmares and risking a lawsuit from George Lucas? Will he best Morris Day and the Time at the big Battle of the Bands? Will the water be warm enough for Wendy and Lisa? All this and so much more is revealed 2 U in *Purple Rain*.

So a certain taste for so-bad-it's-good movies is necessary to fully appreciate *Purple Rain*. With the exceptions of Melvoin and Day, whose charm manages to shine through his character's nastiness, the acting is uniformly awful. The script is amateur hour, and the film is twenty minutes too long. The Kid's bedroom, with its porcelain drama masks and satin-clad harlequins, is creepier than any the set in *The Texas Chainsaw Massacre*. There's also that discomfiting misogynist streak. Like the scene where The Kid humiliates Apollonia at the lake, the one where Day asks his crony, Jerome, to body slam a girl into a dumpster is played for laughs. Such mean-spirited moments aren't fun, but Prince acting out a psychodrama with a puppet is. So is the ridiculous dialogue (Morris Day: "I wish you could see my home, it's so exciting. In my bedroom . . . I have a brass . . . waterbed.").

Oh, Prince . . . take me with U. Author's collection.

On the plus side, *Purple Rain* is one of the very few feature films to benefit from being shot and edited like a music video, and all of those stunning performance sequences can be thoroughly enjoyed without a wisp of irony. Prince really was the greatest all-around entertainer of his generation. The guy had a forty-octave vocal range and could make his guitar sound like a crash-landing UFO just by licking it.

That brilliance is behind the most deservedly enduring product of *Purple Rain*: its spectacular sound track. Prince ships us to the top floor of rock and roll heaven with "Let's Go Crazy," straps us to the back of his Princecycle for a pastoral ride with "Take Me with U," puts our hearts through a paper shredder as he screams purple murder on "The Beautiful Ones," bends our brains with "Computer Blue," gives us a one-way ticket to erotic city with "Darling Nikki" (the song that inspired the PMRC) and a guided tour of his familial pains with "When Doves Cry," drops us to the stage boards with "I Would Die 4 U," picks us back up again with "Baby I'm a Star," and blows us away once and for all with the extravagant epic title track of his masterpiece.

Although *Purple Rain* is very much an expression of Prince's genius—and he is one of the very, very few pop people I believe deserves to be called a genius—the other members of the Revolution deserve credit for its perfection. Guitarist Wendy Melvoin painted the complex chord voicing that elevates the title track, and keyboardist Lisa Coleman scored its majestic string arrangement. Along with keyboardist Matt Fink, they helped write "Computer Blue," and Fink sets fire to his synth on "Baby I'm a Star" ("Doctor!"). A stunning statement from its central artist and a true band effort, *Purple Rain* is one of the most perfectly conceived and executed albums ever made and that rare album that was both the biggest and best of its year.

R.E.M.: *RECKONING*

So much for the sophomore slump. *Reckoning* is R.E.M.'s second album, and it might also be their best one. *Murmur* was terrific, but some of the songwriting was slightly unformed. Not so with *Reckoning*. R.E.M. was never really an innovative band, and *Reckoning* isn't either. Peter Buck's Rickenbacker work still owes everything to the Byrds. Mike Mills and Bill Berry still don't do anything that Tom Petty's rhythm section wouldn't. Michael Stipe is still mumbling surrealist imagery that Leonard Cohen could have devised. Yet there is indefinable magic in "7 Chinese Bros." and "Time After Time," incomparable gravitas in "So. Central Rain" and "Camera," unparalleled energy in "Pretty Persuasion" and "Harborcoat" and "Second Guessing" and "Little America." As is true of all the best basic rock and roll bands, all the ingredients of R.E.M. are familiar, but they blend together in an instantly identifiable and totally unique brew.

THE REPLACEMENTS: *LET IT BE*

A sloppy drunk quartet of Minneapolis dirt bags, the Replacements pursued fame with one hand and scorned it with the other, winning a following because they were unpredictable, outrageous, loutish, and quite mad. That human nicotine stain Paul Westerberg emerged as a tremendous power-pop composer in the tradition of Pete Townshend, Alex Chilton, and Rick Nielsen is beside the point.

That combination of stage infamy—Westerberg deciding his band would eschew their greatest hits in favor of appalling Chuck Berry covers, guitarist Bob Stinson lifting his skirt to present his balls to the audience or shower them with his piss poured from a shoe some dickhead had lobbed at him, teen brother bassist Tommy Stinson dropping jaws simply by being so young—and spectacularly ragged records made the Replacements cult heroes. They could get prestigious opening tour slots for Keith Richards and Tom Petty but couldn't bring themselves to appear in anything as crass as a music video.

On paper, the Replacements' story is not much different from any other band's: they rose from middle-class ennui to enjoy a degree of popularity, engaged in heated rock and roll rivalries with other local groups (particularly Hüsker Dü), overindulged in a variety of substances, and didn't all live to tell the tale. The big differences are the vehemence with which they refused to play the rock and roll success game, the respect and loathing they earned, and their confounding paradoxical status as ordinary legends. Punks like Joe Strummer, Johnny Rotten, and even Joey Ramone were larger than life, either as cartoon characters or as political guiding lights. The Replacements were the cretins demolishing classic rock and roll tunes in the garage next door, and like Spinal Tap's keyboardist, they just wanted to have a good time all the time, often at the expense of their fans, their critics, and themselves. They weren't gods. They were me, and they were you. You can't say that about many rock stars at their peak popularity, can you?

The Replacements got started as a defiantly sloppy Minneapolis hardcore group. They started deviating from that path with 1983's *Hootenanny*. *Let It Be* diluted their punk past even further with its pianos, acoustic guitars, and mandolins. The slop remains in full effect. This record makes Keith Richards seem as polished as Jeff Lynne and Dee Dee Ramone as sweet voiced as Joni Mitchell. Chris Mars's drumming is more all over the beat than behind it. Paul Westerberg and Bob Stinson's guitars flap around like flags in a hurricane. Westerberg always sounds like he might puke mid-song.

The revelation is Westerberg's songwriting. The twisty "I Will Dare" (featuring Peter Buck on guest guitar and Westerberg, himself, on mandolin years before Buck gave that instrument pride of place in many an R.E.M. recording) and gut-shredding "Unsatisfied" are rock and roll classics from a time when this kind of stuff barely existed anymore. You certainly couldn't find any on the Stones' recent records, and "Unsatisfied" is the flip side of Mick Jagger's loquacious complaint of dissatisfaction from two decades prior. Paul Westerberg is barely able to repeat more than "Look me in the eye and tell me I'm satisfied . . . I'm so unsatisfied." Yet his ravaged, wrecked, raging delivery says everything Mick did. Music to claw your own eyes out to.

The stuttering speed boogie "Favorite Thing," the frenzied-punk-morphs-into-barroom-blues "We're Comin' Out," the hilarious "Tommy Gets His Tonsils Out" and "Gary's Got a Boner," the uplifting and ahead-of-its-time "Androgynous," and the profoundly simple/simply profound "Answering Machine" are not too shabby either, even though they're all totally shabby.

SIOUXSIE AND THE BANSHEES: *HYAENA*

Siouxsie and the Banshees hit a creative pinnacle with 1982's *A Kiss in the Dreamhouse*. That inspiration was still in full effect when *Hyaena* arrived a

year and a half later. These two albums may
be the most perfect of the Banshees' career,
though *Hyaena* is more of a challenge than
Dreamhouse, which kept things very accessible across nine compact songs. "Blow the
House Down," the violent epic that closes
Hyaena, is nearly as hard on the ears as anything on *The Scream* or *Join Hands*. It's the
last time the Banshees would really do that
sort of thing, though. The rest of the album
is more pop, even if its icy sheen doesn't
make most of the cuts that much cuddlier
than "Blow the House Down." The band
surely doesn't go soft and warm on the angsty

Maria Penn's painting made the
cover of *Hyaena* one of the coolest and most timeless of 1984.
Author's collection.

"We Hunger," the spaghetti western "Bring Me the Head of the Preacher
Man," or "Running Town," which lashes out to a tortured guitar riff. Yet
there are glimmers of light reflecting off the glacier with the elegant "Take
Me Back" and the irresistible "Belladonna." The two singles may be the
Banshees' most enchanting: "Dazzle," with its Disney movie orchestrations
and relentless beat, and the spooky, surrealist "Swimming Horses." Over a
backing track that shimmers like the reflection of stars on a wading pool,
Siouxsie Sioux paints surrealistic images that barely mask the song's erotic
topic. "He gives birth to swimming horses" is probably the loveliest way one
can say, "He spurts sperm out of his penis." Trippy and frosty as a spiked
sno-cone, *Hyaena* would make great listening for the next time you find
yourself in the Arctic with nothing but a tab of acid.

THE SMITHS: *THE SMITHS*

There is no doubt that the most momentous debut of 1984 was that of
four Manchester boys with a slanted reverence for pop's past and a total
commitment to irreverence. The Rolling Stones and Motown-worshipping
Johnny Marr best represents the former with his arpeggios like sheets of
falling rain. Pompadoured Steve Morrissey embodies the latter with his
songs celebrating apathy and taking advantage of the dole, lamenting how
love and beauty lead to death, or whispering nightmarish tales of child
murdering and molesting. There is so much cynicism, so much darkness, so
much evil in Morrissey's words that a lot of critics and fans miss the humor.
How can you mope along to lines like "Hand in glove, the sun shines out

of our behinds"? And for those who find his delivery monotonous, consult his wild whoops on "Miserable Lie."

Yet the dominant allure of the band's first and finest album is its antiqued exquisiteness, its shimmering guitars and pianos and mournful vocals and how they offset the uncomfortable empathy Morrissey plugs into his tales of sex, violence, gleeful indolence, and shiny behinds. *The Smiths* is a delicate work of art that sacrifices none of what makes rock and roll vital and electrifying.

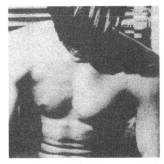

Every Smiths album cover is bold and stylish. Morrissey selected this image of Joe Dallesandro from *Andy Warhol's Flesh* for their debut. Author's collection.

U2: *THE UNFORGETTABLE FIRE*

U2 had done their best work on their first few albums when there was still some punk spirit behind their righteousness. After the smash success of *War*, the pomposity that would make them pretty insufferable by the time they put out the overrated *Joshua Tree* and the boring *Rattle and Hum* was beginning to leak into their music. So *The Unforgettable Fire* is not as good as *Boy* or *War*. Songwise, the lazily vague "Pride (In the Name of Love)" and the repetitious "Bad" aren't much, but you'll rarely hear this much uninhibited passion outside of an opera house. The album is even better when Bono doesn't step on the Edge, Larry Mullen, and Adam Clayton as they kick it out on "Wire" and "Indian Summer Sky." Not everything here works. "MLK" sounds like a shapeless attempt to rewrite the beautiful "40" while going to the Martin Luther King well once too often. The endless "Elvis Presley and America" is a poorly sung six-and-a-half-minute wank. But when U2 is on fire, they make *The Unforgettable Fire* worthwhile.

VAN HALEN: *1984*

Van Halen had squeaked into *Billboard*'s top twenty a couple of times with "Dance the Night Away" in 1979 and their cover of "Oh! Pretty Woman" in 1982, and they always sold plenty of LPs, but they could not have been prepared for the rocket success of *1984*. The band had vetoed a catchy Eddie Van Halen synth lick back in 1981. When they revived it at the behest of producer Ted Templeman three years later, "Jump" became the first song by a band as heavy as Van Halen to go to number one on the singles chart. The song isn't remotely metal, but it did clear the way for the more characteristic Van Halen bluster "I'll Wait," which matches another synth line to harder rock, and "Panama" to go top twenty too. "Hot for Teacher" wasn't a chart hit, but its memorably asinine video was an MTV staple. With so many radio and TV hits, *1984* became one of the biggest hit-generating machines of 1984. That success also apparently swelled David Lee Roth's already sizable head, and his decision to commit to a solo career while blasting Eddie

Van Halen was a terrible influence on babies. Author's collection.

for his own extracurricular activities heightened tensions in the band. Roth abandoned Van Halen in 1985, Sammy Hagar joined the band, and Van Halen became just as generic as any other eighties hair band.

1985

Released on compact disc in late 1984, *Peter Gabriel IV* (aka *Security*) was the first album made with digital recording, mixing, and mastering equipment. The sound was slick, clean, flawless, and lacking the atmosphere of old-fashioned analogue recording. DDD became a CD selling point for some. For others, it encapsulated the issues plaguing pop music in general in the mid-eighties.

Recording was becoming sterile. Record making was becoming a race to make the next *Thriller*, *Synchronicity*, *Like a Virgin*, or *Purple Rain*. The soul had dripped out of pop radio. Bland pretty boys Bryan Adams and soap opera actor Jack Wagner became pop stars. Mick Jagger abandoned the Rolling Stones to make a soulless solo debut, and David Lee Roth abandoned rock and roll altogether to become a clownish lounge lizard. The blandest musicians of the seventies were rewarded in the eighties when Phil Collins, Chicago, Glenn Fry, Don Henley, REO Speedwagon, Foreigner, and Starship, who released what has sometimes been called the worst pop song of all time ("We Built This City"), scored huge hits. The year's defining song was "We Are the World," a well-meaning effort to raise money to relieve starvation in Ethiopia but an utterly insipid song that was inescapable on radio.

The long player was barely a refuge in a year that saw a great dip in the overall quality of popular music. While the quantity of great albums was lower than it had been in the decade thus far, new albums by Kate Bush,

Killing Joke, Tears for Fears, and others made the most of mid-eighties production values. New artists such as the Jesus & Mary Chain and the Dentists made great albums by ignoring the decade altogether.

KATE BUSH: *HOUNDS OF LOVE*

Kate Bush had been a singular artist from the very start, but she only fully fulfilled her potential when she took complete command of her music with 1982's *The Dreaming*. On *Hounds of Love*, she commanded the greatest bundle of songs she ever composed and assembled them with intricate care and staggering vision. Side A plays like a mini–greatest-hits comp as classic singles leap for attention like puppies. How the hell can anyone choose just one to take home? The throbbing "Running Up That Hill (A Deal with God)"? The irresistible title track? I'd probably choose "The Big Sky," a track as expansive and overwhelming as its title, but then I'd have to leave behind the icy "Mother Stands for Comfort" and the elegant "Cloudbusting."

On side B, Bush eliminates any such choices by building a mini-concept, each track an essential yet individual brick in its structure. It's a tale of someone adrift at sea, staying alive by poring over life events. Like any pop concept worth hearing, "The Ninth Wave" consists of songs that stand on their own perfectly, and each one stretches beyond the grandiosity of side A to soothe ("And Dream of Sheep"), chill ("Under Ice," "Watching You Watch Me"), terrify ("Waking the Witch"), invigorate ("Jig of Life"), spellbind ("Hello Earth"), and console ("The Morning Fog"). Bush plays mad scientist, electronically manipulating "Waking the Witch" and "Watching You Watch Me" to unsettling effect. She drops all the synths and drum machines and icy sound effects for "Jig of Life," a stunning piece of organic music making. Bush's mum was a traditional Irish dancer, and daughter keeps that tradition alive with sawing fiddles and River Dance stomping. Brother John delivers the Brogue-thick rap that climaxes the most muscular track on Kate Bush's masterpiece. However,

Kate Bush

Hounds Of Love

Those who screw around with reissues of beloved albums must tread carefully or risk pissing off longtime fans, but Kate Bush's decision to replace the original album version of "Big Sky" with the superior single mix for this reissue of *Hounds of Love* on her own Fish People label was a great one. Author's collection.

the album's most extraordinary instrument is its mistress's voice, which Bush layers all over her masterpiece with abandon. "She abandons herself completely on "The Big Sky," her shrieks easily ranking alongside such scream-sterpieces as Daltrey's on "Won't Get Fooled Again" and Lennon's on "Mother." My spine vibrates just thinking about it.

THE CURE: *THE HEAD ON THE DOOR*

The Cure was caught between their doomiest and most delicious impulses on *The Top*. The *Head on the Door* sees them coming through the other end of the portal and clutching their best record yet. With the exception of the darkly alluring "Kyoto Song" and "Sinking," Robert Smith leaves his angst on the lyric sheet, allowing the band to whip up a string of tracks that at least sound jolly. "In Between Days" is the long-overdue resurrection of "Boys Don't Cry"–style rush, and its successful revival would make this kind of track an essential component of many Cure albums to come. "The Blood," "The Baby Screams," and the fuzz-bass frothing "Screw" were made to get goth kids' blood circulating. The album's twin gems are its twin centerpieces: the clap-happy "Close to Me" (though I prefer the horn-embellished single mix) and "A Night Like This," a rare 1985 sax song that doesn't totally abuse the instrument. As great as *The Head on the Door* is, it is actually just the beginning of a stellar new phase of the Cure's career. Their greatest work is coming soon.

THE DAMNED: *PHANTASMAGORIA*

With their 1985 album, *Phantasmagoria*, the Damned fully succumb to Dave Vanian's fascination with the goth movement he helped create and bad eighties production. There are some very good songs on the record that must struggle to overcome the decade's digital studio crimes. The best of these songs are "There'll Come a Day," "Is It a Dream," "Edward the Bear," and The Eighth Day," and all find the Damned welcoming straight pop with more brio than ever before.

The Damned went full Goth with *Phantasmagoria*. That's model Susie Black on the cover. She'd later marry Nick Cave. Author's collection.

The one track that emerges completely unscathed is the best on the record and the best of the Damned's psych tributes. The clear influence is the Who circa 1967. The monster-mash lyric inspired by a British comic book villain could have been John Entwistle's follow-up to "Boris the Spider." The old Edwardian vibe recalls his "Silas Stingy." The "bad lad, bad boy" chorus is lifted straight out of Townshend's "Our Love Was." The definitive version is the "Bad Trip Mix" from the extended twelve-inch single, which features a fabulous Peter Lorre impression.

THE DENTISTS: *SOME PEOPLE ARE ON THE PITCH THEY THINK IT'S ALL OVER IT IS NOW*

The ghosts of American West Coasters like Love, the Beau Brummels, and the Byrds haunt the Dentists retro psych, though their own countryman Syd Barrett is huddling in the briars too (and on the phenomenal title track of their inaugural EP, *Strawberries Are Growing in My Garden [And It's Wintertime]*, so are the Beatles). With a completely organic sound alien to the year it was made, *Some People Are on the Pitch They Think It's All Over It Is Now* may as well have been time-machined from 1967 to 1985. Sincerely great songs and a refusal to indulge in Naz Nomad (the Damned impersonating a sixties psych band) or Dukes of Stratosphear (XTC doing the same) types of masquerading prevent the Dentists' debut from sounding parodic or absurdly indebted to past heroes. These guys pitch perfectly conceived firebombs ("Tony Bastable v. John Noakes," "I Had an Excellent Dream," "Back to the Grave"), ballads ("Mary Won't You Come Out and Play," "Kinder Still"), and eerily biting mood pieces ("Flowers Around Me," "I'm Not the Devil," "You Make Me Say It Somehow") that would bewitch in any era.

DIRE STRAITS: *BROTHERS IN ARMS*

Seven years had passed since square British blues combo Dire Straits had a hit in the United States with the superb "Sultans of Swing." That changed most assuredly when they dropped the ultraslick, DDD monster *Brothers in Arms* in 1985. That year, you couldn't blow your nose without having "Money for Nothing" blare out of your nostrils. The sports-rock staple "Walk of Life" would become big the following year. However, the truly great single from the band's comeback triumph was its first and least commercially successful. "So Far Away" barely sneaked into the top twenty, but it's as hooky and alluring as anything Dire Straits ever did. Mark Knopfler's six-string impersonates a Hawaiian pedal steel and fools me completely.

Otherwise, *Brothers in Arms* is hit or miss, though mostly hit. The ballads walk the middle of the road, but the album comes to life in its second half, which seems to foretell the Vietnam-era nostalgia that would soon sweep America. It's an Englishman's travelogue of war as Mark Knopfler sings "Ride Across the River" from the point of view of a soldier of fortune in Southeast Asia and plays an executioner's drummer with a nagging conscience in the excellent folk-rock "The Man's Too Strong." With the title song, Knopfler does a much better job of sifting through the complexities of wartime bonds than Billy Joel did on his vapid "Goodnight Saigon." "One World" personalizes such conflicts in a zippy casing.

The flying dobro that launched the CD into dominance. Author's collection.

Brothers in Arms was a major flagship release for the CD age. With its full-digital presentation, it showed off the pristine possibilities of digital recording. With the extra space a seventy-four-minute CD allotted, it featured considerably longer versions of "So Far Away," "Money for Nothing," "Why Worry," and "Your Latest Trick" than the edits on the vinyl edition. *Brothers in Arms* was the first CD that outsold its vinyl equivalent. Robert Simonds of the first CD-only label, Rykodisc, claimed that demands for *Brothers in Arms* had so overwhelmed CD manufacturers that he had trouble getting his own titles produced. Dire Straits may have been an old-fashioned band, but their success in 1985 was tightly entwined with new technology.

THE JESUS & MARY CHAIN: *PSYCHOCANDY*

At a time when even former underground artists like Elvis Costello and the Damned were succumbing to mid-eighties production bloat, a new breed of bands was galvanizing the organic, grimy sounds that would define alternative rock in the next decade. On their debut, the Jesus & Mary Chain blowtorched through all of the era's saxes, drum machines, and Casio keyboards by shotgun marrying two key sixties artists. From the

Velvet Underground comes flaming onslaughts of feedback. From Phil Spector comes retro teen-pop hookiness and puppy lovesickness—as well as a couple of nods to Hal Blaine's "Be My Baby" intro.

Psychocandy may require a few listens to suss it out, but underneath the pandemonium are some really good songs. "Just Like Honey" can go toe-to-toe with Greenwich and Barry's greatest hits. There is jingly beauty in the rusty outer shell of "The Hardest Walk." Toss "Never Understand" into the dishwasher, and it will come back out as one of Brian Wilson's best early creations. "Cut Dead" is simply beautiful. The album's chainsaw aesthetic might leave you with a severe migraine by the time you get to "Inside Me," but I'm not sure Jesus & Mary Chain would consider that to be a bad thing.

KILLING JOKE: *NIGHT TIME*

In the late seventies, Notting Hill's Killing Joke fused the aggression of punk, the dancebility of funk, and the gloom of goth to forge a new form of music that pointed to the industrial sounds that artists like Al Jourgensen developed in the eighties. Eighties production conventions smoothed out some of Killing Joke's edges, but they used the decade's sheen to their advantage almost as well as artists like Kate Bush and Prince did. Rarely has an album been so dark and so stirring in such equal proportion as *Night Time*. With drummer Paul Ferguson's racing tempos, guitarist Geordie Walker's swooping shadows, and bassist Paul Raven's funky grind, *Night Time* is powerful yet lean, bleak yet eminently enjoyable. Even slower pieces like the British hit "Love Like Blood" and "Multitudes" pulse propulsively. The entire album feels like a 3 a.m. highway drag with the headlights off. Behind the wheel, Jaz Coleman maintains control of his croon, neither spilling into the feral scream of his early work nor letting up on the anguish.

I always thought this album would be the perfect background music for a Goth aerobics class. Author's collection.

PRINCE AND THE REVOLUTION: *AROUND THE WORLD IN A DAY*

Prince had made one of *the* massive smash eighties pop albums with *Purple Rain*. On his next album, he consciously changed direction to avoid comparison with the album he seemed to realize he'd never top. Critics, who did not gush over Prince's latest as they had his last, assumed he was also consciously blending his signature brand of syncopated pop with that of pop's most untoppable group by dressing up his songs in multicolored *Sgt. Pepper's* uniforms. Prince claimed to have little interest in the Beatles and insisted they had no influence on his neo-psychedelic *Around the World in a Day*. Its title track (a collaboration with Lisa Coleman's brother David) sounds like it owes more to *Satanic Majesties*–era Rolling Stones than the Beatles, with its spiraling arabesques and "Sing This All Together" community vibe, though he probably wasn't spinning that disc much either. In fact, Prince didn't spend a lot of time listening to anyone's music but his own once he became a superstar. The concept of "a government of love and music boundless in its unifying power" is still one of the most perfect (if unintentional) summations of Beatles 1967 imaginable. It's one of the most perfect summations of Prince 1985 too.

Prince continues that flower-power spirit on the Utopian "Paisley Park" (which would be the name of his recording complex and record label) and the celestial "Condition of the Heart." With the magical mystery megahit "Raspberry Beret," Prince's genius fully flowers with his most refreshing pop melody and an absolutely splendid arrangement that introduces Beatlesque strings to the Revolution's mix. The lyric has a Summer of Love freshness and color that never falls into retro pastiche because Prince maintains his signature sexiness ("If it was warm she wouldn't wear much more . . ."). The bridge is just as grand as the unforgettable verses and choruses and may actually provide the most inventive moment in the song as those strings really spring out of the mix.

However, most of *Around the World in a Day* sticks to Prince's usual funky formula with uneven results. "Tambourine" is one of his best deep cuts, and "Pop Life" is a wiry, percolating single, but its finger wagging also reveals a certain conservatism rising in Prince's dirty mind. It festers into outright jingoism in the simple-minded "America" and sanctimoniousness on "The Ladder." Prince's pornographic and prayerful poles engage in outright war on "Temptation," but anyone who sits through all eight minutes of this self-indulgent dreck is the loser. *Around the World in a Day* is the first album of Prince's classic period with poor tracks, but the great ones still make it essential.

R.E.M.: *FABLES OF THE RECONSTRUCTION/ RECONSTRUCTION OF THE FABLES*

R.E.M. debuted with their two best albums, so it's easy—and not uncommon—to view their third as a disappointment. The *Trouser Press Record Guide* wrote off *Fables of the Reconstruction* or *Reconstruction of the Fables* as "colorless and dull," and the band's own Bill Berry told *Rolling Stone* the album "sucked." Its moodiness is easy to mistake for exhaustion. The guys couldn't even be bothered to settle on a title!

Fables of the Reconstruction! Reconstruction of the Fables! Fables of the Reconstruction! Reconstruction of the Fables! is to the rock album what "My daughter! My sister! My daughter! My sister!" is to cinema. Author's collection.

For those who stumbled on the grouchy press before the music, *Fables of the Reconstruction* (really the better title) should come as a delightful surprise. Well, maybe "delightful" is not the right word, as this is a pretty dark album, hooking into the somber mood of "Perfect Circle" and dragging it across most of the LP. There are exceptions (the peppy pop-funk classic "Can't Get There from Here," the pogoing "Life and How to Live It," cheerless yet up-tempo pieces like "Driver 8" and "Auctioneer"), but even if there weren't, R.E.M. always wore moody well. *Fables* shows off some of their most mesmerizing glum moods: "Maps and Legends," the gorgeous labor lament "Green Grow the Rushes," "Feeling Gravity's Pull," and "Old Man Kinsey." The latter two cuts find Peter Buck experimenting with dissonant riffs that put paid to *Trouser Press'* allegation of colorlessness. *Fables of the Reconstruction* may not be as immediate as *Murmur* or *Reckoning*, but allowing it to grow on you reaps long-term rewards.

THE REPLACEMENTS: *TIM*

The Replacements seesawed between hard-core hysteria and Stonesy shamble rock on *Let It Be*. Their next record found the band's punk past mostly purged and the shambling grooves scrubbed with slick eighties production courtesy of Tommy Ramone of all people. But you just can't clean these boys up too much. The Replacements fight through Tommy's overly compressed sounds with what may be the most consistent run of songs they ever dumped onto a single platter. Perhaps there isn't anything as powerful as "Unsatisfied" or as beautiful as "I Will Dare," but there are no Kiss covers or "Gary's Got a Boner"–style goofs either. There's just a barrage of great pop pieces puked up from the most unabashed romantic on the barroom floor. "Hold My Life," "I'll Buy," "Swingin' Party," and "Kiss Me on the Bus" will weaken the knees of the toughest thug. "Left of the Dial" and "Bastards of Young" are outstanding outsider anthems. "Dose of Thunder" shows the guys could still rage, and "Waitress in the Sky" demonstrates they could still talk shit without sacrificing their new full-time commitment to classic pop melodiousness.

THE SMITHS: *MEAT IS MURDER*

Rough Trade felt it necessary to fill time with the first of many Smiths compilations as the band worked on their second proper record. *Hatful of Hollow* was a smashing collection of singles and tracks recorded for the British Broadcasting System that was surely exchanged among many Anorak wearers on Christmas 1984. *Meat Is Murder* isn't as immediately satisfying as that comp or the Smith's eponymous debut. "I Want the One I Can't Have" and "Nowhere Fast" are a touch generic. I'm on board with the message of the title track, but its lugubrious non-melody, endlessness, and kitschy slaughterhouse sound effects make it go down uneasily.

The rest of the record has all the strength, variety, and glistening atmosphere that make all Smiths records great. Morrissey's fanged humor and Marr's rainy strumming drive "The Headmaster Ritual," while touches of Presley ("Rusholme Ruffians"), noise rock ("What She Said"), and funk ("Barbarism Begins at Home") expand the Smiths' palette. Morrissey was a master of conveying teenage lovesickness for his own smirking amusement, and the hilarity of his lyrics tended to be lost on the lovesick teens who were his primary audience, but the joke in "That Joke Isn't Funny Anymore" really isn't very funny. This unlikely single is a crushing tale of cruel rejection that morphs from swooning romanticism to lights-out hopelessness without undergoing any major changes in arrangement. It's Morrissey's voice that transforms. His shift from breeziness in the song's opening passages to the lump-throated despair of the repeated refrain "I've seen this happen in other people's lives and now it's happening in mine" is devastating.

In the United States, the addition of another towering single, the swampy wallow "How Soon Is Now?," added additional substance. The genesis of "How Soon Is Now?" is kind of funny: it is Johnny Marr's idea of how he imagined Creedence Clearwater Revival after reading about their music but before actually hearing much of it. In a way, it is similar to "Born on the Bayou," with its murky production, lethargic rhythm, and heavily tremeloed guitars, but the Smiths achieve something darker and grander on the song Seymour Stein, the legendary founder of Sire Records, believed to be the eighties' own "Stairway to Heaven." Morrissey's dourness often comes off as parody, but "I am human and I need to be loved, just like everybody else does" is such a nakedly primal plea that it's understandable why so many people take this song dead seriously.

TEARS FOR FEARS: *SONGS FROM THE BIG CHAIR*

The year 1984 was the one of blockbuster albums, but 1985 yielded few. In fact, only two of the top ten albums on Billboard's year-end album chart weren't released in 1984: Phil Collins's *No Jacket Required* and Tears for Fears' *Songs from the Big Chair*. While *No Jacket Required* exemplified much about what was going wrong in rock in 1985—the middle-of-the-road attitude, the by-numbers songwriting, the impotent production values—*Songs from the Big Chair* showed how to move with the times by exploiting new tech for its weirdness value, blasting through the gloss with big emotions, and building perfect pop songs like the clanging "Shout" and wistful "Everybody Wants to Rule the World." "Head Over Heels" may be the finest love song of the eighties. Its construction is perfect: the dramatic opening, the brilliantly arranged call-and-response of Roland Orzabal's throaty gale and Curt Smith's teary falsetto, the powerful chorus, and the fantastically phased, elliptical finale. Roland Orzabal then deconstructs pop conventions into the fragments that form the forward-thinking pop mosaics of "Broken" and the trippy atmospheres of "Listen." Prince was the only other major artist of the time so intent on conquering the arts as well as the charts.

SUZANNE VEGA: *SUZANNE VEGA*

Suzanne Vega seems forever painted as a bookish New York City folky, but she's always shared too much of Bowie's restless image metamorphosing for that stereotype to hold true. Her only album that suits it is her first, and even here it's a bit reductive. No one is going to mistake the relatively rocking "Neighborhood Girls" for Joan Jett's latest, but Vega curls her lips around its streetwise lyric with the cool sexiness that makes even her most restrained work electrifying.

Suzanne Vega's lyrics are way more imaginative than the cover A&M slapped on her first album. Author's collection.

That coolness registers on the thermometer too. *Suzanne Vega* is a really wintery album. "Cracking" and "Freeze Tag" whip up images of snow-blocked city blocks and January's abandoned playgrounds. Joe Gordon's shudders of electric guitar on "Small Blue Thing" crystallize icicles at the track's edges. Such musicianship is fine throughout the album, yet *Suzanne Vega* is more of a vehicle for Vega's impressionistic lyricism than anything else. Producers Lenny Kaye and Steve Addabbo keep the arrangements watercolor thin. On subsequent LPs, Vega would plunge into more radical arrangements, experimenting with synthesizers and industrial beats with thrilling results. *Suzanne Vega* is low key in comparison, but it is a fine debut from one of the best and most underappreciated artists of her generation.

1986

By 1986, the eighties seemed like they couldn't get any more *eighties*. Naturally, there was a pushback, and fighting against the tide of Reagan-era conservatism, MTV's image mongering, synthesizers, and sanitized production techniques came a wave of sixties nostalgia that manifested in the year's big Monkees revival and the wave of Vietnam-era movies that began with Oliver Stone's *Platoon*. Within a year or two, there'd be a host of new TV shows (*The Wonder Years, China Beach, Tour of Duty*) and movies (*Full Metal Jacket, 1969, Hamburger Hill, Casualties of War*, even *Batman*) indebted to or focused on the sixties, but the decade's influence was already in full force on wax as touches of Byrdsy jangle and psychedelia could be heard in the grooves of new records by everyone from the Bangles to Prince to XTC to R.E.M. to the Smiths to Love and Rockets. Even the decade's freshest new music form, rap, started looking back by working some old-fashioned rock guitar into the mix. Phil Collins, Starship, Lionel Richie, Peter Cetera, and Mr. Mister may have ruled the charts with pop pap fit for Ronnie and Nancy, but the charts were rarely the place to find great rock and roll in the eighties.

ELVIS COSTELLO AND THE ATTRACTIONS: *BLOOD & CHOCOLATE*

After five years of formal experiments (*Almost Blue, Imperial Bedroom*) and unsympathetic, bloodless productions (*Punch the Clock, Goodbye Cruel World*), Elvis Costello and the Attractions finally got back to the raw record making that caused a lot of punters to mistake *Get Happy!!!* and *This Year's Model* for punk. The title suggests a dollop of sweetness to make the assault more palatable, and there are a few Hershey's kisses sprinkled on side B of *Blood & Chocolate*. First, you must endure the raging come-on "Uncomplicated," the poison-spitting kiss-off "I Hope You're Happy Now," the Dylan-trapped-in-a-tornado chaos of "Tokyo Storm Warning," the frothingly desperate "Home Is Anywhere You Hang Your Head," and the creepily obsessed "I Want You."

Despite the clashing "Honey Are You Straight or Are You Blind" and the weary "Battered Old Bird," the rest of *Blood & Chocolate* is poppier or prettier, but each track is a superb example of songwriting and performing. Costello sometimes has the tendency to conceal his intentions under tarps of clever wordplay and obscure imagery, but with the exception of "Tokyo Storm Warning" and "Crimes of Paris," *Blood & Chocolate* is completely direct and utterly affecting. I've never heard a song that captures the mania of a man head over heels in unrequited love as authentically as "Home Is Anywhere You Hang Your Head" does. The other tracks deal with relationships from emotional ("I Want You," "I Hope You're Happy Now") or novel ("Honey Are You Straight or Are You Blind?," in which the singer wonders if his lust object shares his own sexual inclination) angles. *Blood & Chocolate* really feels like we have the good old Elvis and the Attractions back, though it was more of a last roll in the hay than a happy reunion. After this, they basically split for good, only to make one more record on which, once again, their unique band identity would be muted by a producer's personality (though *All This Useless Beauty* is a hell of a lot better than *Goodbye Cruel World*). For all intents and purposes, *Blood & Chocolate*

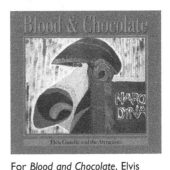

For *Blood and Chocolate*, Elvis Costello developed the alter ego "Napoleon Dynamite," a name he also included in his not-at-all-hideous painting on the album cover. The guy who made that *Napoleon Dynamite* movie insists he knew nothing about this, which would mean that two people came up with the name "Napoleon Dynamite" totally independent of each other, which is pretty rich. Author's collection.

is the last album by Elvis Costello and the Attractions. At least they went out making the best album of 1986.

LOVE AND ROCKETS: *EXPRESS*

Siouxsie and the Banshees took the sepulchral noise that Procol Harum and Nico invented in the sixties and sculpted the sounds and sights most associated with gothic rock, but they always rejected that label as reductive. Heavily influenced by Siouxsie, Peter Murphy's Bauhaus became one of the defining goth groups of the eighties despite not accepting the label either. That Bauhaus' hearts were not in gothic despair was never clearer than when Daniel Ash, David Haskins, and David J split from Murphy to blow the cobwebs out of their systems with Love and Rockets.

Express, their second album, reflects only passing vestiges of the defining Bauhaus sound. Darkness hovers over the proceedings, but those proceedings are psychedelic, wildly heavy, and rather cheerful. "Kundalini Express" is a nutty gob of trippy, bubble-gummy pseudo-metal fit for college radio with a chorus fit for a *Sesame Street* sing-along. "It Could Be Sunshine" somehow layers sixties-style backward loops over eighties-style synth marimba as jazz sax bellows in the distance. "All in My Mind" would be a piece of pop refreshment if it weren't so fuzzy and murky. Yet even as all the influences and arrangement elements clash each track into oblivion, the unmissable melodiousness never gets buried in the muck.

METALLICA: *MASTER OF PUPPETS*

Heavy metal attracted multitudes of disaffected fans, but those fans rarely included "serious" rock critics. Perhaps the critics had trouble taking metal seriously because most of its highest-profile bands—from Black Sabbath to Iron Maiden to Van Halen—didn't seem to take it very seriously.

Metallica was a different story. Shedding the cartoonishness of Black Sabbath and rejecting the humor of Van Halen, they seemed truly convinced that the whole house of cards would crumble at any moment and we'd all be fucked. They didn't dress their songs or selves in Halloween costumes. They were a bunch of greasy-haired, denim-clad, beer-guzzling louts. In other words, they were the first major metal band made up of genuine metal fans. As the teenyboppers were chasing Mötley Crüe, Bon Jovi, and Def Leppard to the upper regions of the pop charts in the second half of the eighties, Metallica fans were happy to consider themselves hard-core cultists of a "real" metal band.

Eventually, the top forty would catch up with Metallica (or vice versa), but in 1986, their major-label debut *Master of Puppets* was pretty uncompromising. While most earlier metalheads like Ozzy Osbourne, David Lee Roth, and Bruce Dickinson sang in an upper-register howl that sometimes bordered on the operatic, James Hetfield dropped his voice to a monster growl and favored low-end, palm-muted, downstroking riffs. Lead guitarist Kirk Hammett took the upper register with Eddie Van Halen–indebted leads, but the long, proggy, miserable songs on *Master of Puppets* are nothing like Van Halen's horny, compact pop. Hetfield's lyrics about the horrors of violence ("Battery"), drug addiction (the title track), war ("Disposable Heroes"), madness (the Ken Kesey–inspired "Sanitarium"), and, well, horror (the Lovecraftian "The Thing That Should Not Be") are more literary than Ozzy's empty songs on similar subjects. Ozzy and Diamond Dave's sense of fun is utterly absent.

There's also subtlety as Metallica breaks up the assault with acoustic guitars, vocal and guitar harmonies, and some pretty potent melodies. Such elements would help them become unlikely top-forty chart mates of Milli Vanilli, Roxette, and Debbie Gibson before the end of the decade.

PRINCE AND THE REVOLUTION: *PARADE*

Despite being a mess, Prince's first movie was a huge success. *Purple Rain* made a lot of money at the box office and yielded one of the great and iconic albums of the eighties. You can't blame the guy for trying to capture another bit of purple lightning in a bottle, but the completely misguided period rom-com *Under the Cherry Moon* was a commercial disaster. Fortunately, Prince's unparalleled musical artistry was still in effect. In one of his classically offhand feats of musical bravado, he cut the drum tracks for the first four songs on the sound track straight through in single takes, only pausing between them as bands of silence would on the completed album. Then he rolled the tape back and did the same thing with his bass. Everyone who was ever present in the studio with him must have been perpetually agape.

Although *Parade* isn't nearly the tour de force *Purple Rain* is, Prince's second sound track LP is still a grand statement and surely his most romantic record with the Revolution. There's still some horny toad funk in "New Position," "I Wonder U" (adapted from a letter a fan gave him in Rio de

Janeiro), "Girls & Boys," and the hit "Kiss," but "Under the Cherry Moon," "Do U Lie?," "Venus de Milo," and "Sometimes It Snows in April" are strictly for a hand-in-hand swoon under a June moon. Prince has also retained traces of his previous record's *Magical Mystery Tour* swirl for the nouveau-psych numbers "Christopher Tracy's Parade" and "Life Can Be So Nice," which is the hardest piece of rock and roll he'd done since "Let's Go Crazy." "Mountains" and "Anotherloverholeinyohead" are anthemic shoulda-been hits. Once again, Wendy Melvoin and Lisa Coleman make a great piece of work even better with their harmonic vocabulary that is somewhat beyond Prince's, and his songs

PRINCE AND THE REVOLUTION / PARADE
MUSIC FROM THE MOTION PICTURE UNDER THE CHERRY MOON

Prince once said that "Kiss" is the only track on *Parade* that he was proud of, but the album's sound engineer, Susan Rogers, has speculated that Prince was just taking out his displeasure with *Under the Cherry Moon* on its soundtrack. Author's collection.

would never be quite so nuanced again after he dismissed the Revolution. Warner Bros. pictures may disagree, but Warner Bros. music has to admit that *Parade* made Prince's $12 million turkey well worth the unrecouped budget.

R.E.M.: *LIFE'S RICH PAGEANT*

A year after releasing their moodiest record to date, R.E.M. put out their happiest, and though they have a renowned knack for brooding, they're just as convincing when bouncing off the ceiling on sonic pogo sticks like "Hyena," "Just a Touch," and "Begin the Begin." They get downright silly on the mock tango "Underneath the Bunker" and the Mike Mill's adrenaline-shot cover of the Clique's "(I Am) Superman."

Mills, Stipe, Buck, and Berry still hadn't mailed their brains to Krypton, as they expressed a strong environmental conscience on "Fall on Me" and "Cuyahoga" and mapped out the ominous acoustic folk rock that would define their sound in the early nineties on the faux–Civil War ballad "Swan Swan H." On "These Days" and "I Believe," there is an implied threat that the guys are saying good-bye to the kinds of goofs they drop elsewhere on the record to devote themselves to pop activism permanently. They never did that completely, even if they never made a record as completely or sincerely fun as *Life's Rich Pageant* again.

RUN-DMC: *RAISING HELL*

Since it first infiltrated the charts in 1979, rap became an increasingly powerful force in popular music, but it seemed to have as much in common with guitar-based rock as jazz has with baroque music. That means there are similarities—the cockiness, the heavy beats—but they seemed to appeal to different audiences and originate from artists who weren't too interested in what was happening in the other guy's camp. Blondie became the first rock band to acknowledge a deeper connection when they incorporated a rap into their 1981 single "Rapture" and got a number one hit in the deal. Debbie Harry was no Grandmaster Flash, but this fairly silly stab at marrying the budding genre to the old one suggested that there were untapped possibilities.

Hollis, Queens, trio Run-DMC realized these possibilities with their very first album. While earlier rap records had been fairly minimalistic, Run-DMC enjoyed a fuller sound thanks to producer Larry Smith, who imagined Joseph "Run" Simmons and Darryl "DMC" McDaniels rapping over metal guitar riffs. The results, "Rock Box," became the first rock-rap crossover from a genuine rap artist, and the results were so revolutionary that DMC was declaring himself the "King of Rock" on their second album.

However, it was Run-DMC's third LP that really crossed over. There hadn't been a ton of overlap between the kids who dug rap and the burnouts who banged their heads before producer Rick Rubin mashed Run and DMC's lyrics and Jam Master Jay's turntable skills with grinding guitars cribbed from the Knack's "My Sharona" or provided live by classic rock hero Joe Perry on *Raising Hell*. Tackling "Walk This Way" was a move ripe to happen since Aerosmith's original was already a proto-rap, but the remake smashed the original on the charts and single-handedly plugged rap into the mainstream. Just as good were monsters like "Peter Piper," "It's Tricky," and "My Adidas," all heavier than the heaviest metal but a hell of a lot funkier.

On the strength of such tracks, *Raising Hell* became the first rap record to sell more than a million units and spawn four genuine Hot 100 hits singles. Its smash synthesis of rock and rap became highly influential as

Janet Perr designed the cover of *Raising Hell* using two different color schemes for two different versions. One featured Caroline Greyshock's photo of the group tinted purple with green lettering and the other featured it with a green tint and magenta lettering. Author's collection.

artists from Sonic Youth to R.E.M. to Ice-T's Body Count to the Beastie Boys worked to unlock its formula with varying degrees of success. The success of rap on its own would be undeniable despite increasingly irrelevant naysayers like Keith Richards, Gene Simmons, and John Entwistle insisting it took no musical skill to speak lyrics and that hip-hop was a fad doomed to fade. Soon enough, they would see their precious rock and roll on the fade as rap usurped it in terms of influence and popularity.

THEY MIGHT BE GIANTS: *THEY MIGHT BE GIANTS*

There'd been nerdy rockers before They Might Be Giants, but as intellectual or inclined to eat paste as people like Elvis Costello or Devo seemed, you probably wouldn't be advised to steal their lunch money or cheat off their math exams. John Flansburgh and John Linnell, two totally geeky Brooklyn Matheletes, were the real deal. You know you weren't going to catch the jock or the glue-sniffing punk in your class toting around their eponymous first album, which abounds in bespectacled cleverness, such as the tooty hoedown "Number Three" and the Poindexter weirdness of "Put Your Hand Inside the Puppet Head." Too bad for those jocks and punks because they were missing out on some wonderful songs, eclectic synthy arrangements, genre dabblings, and mad humor.

SIOUXSIE AND THE BANSHEES: *TINDERBOX*

Siouxsie and the Banshees had gone through a couple of radical shifts in their first eight years, transitioning from nightmarish grind rock to synthesizer-soaked fever dreams, but the band's most surprising change occurred on their seventh album. For the first time, the Banshees sound like they are lightening up and looking for a hit. They'd already done catchy singles like "Hong Kong Garden," "Slow Dive," and a surprisingly sincere cover of the Beatles' "Dear Prudence," but they'd never done so with the chart-ready polish of *Tinderbox*. Although this was a much poppier Banshees than before, they continued to mine dark stuff in their lyrics. Themes of a pedophiliac predator ("Candy Man"), natural disasters (the dance-club classic "Cities in Dust"), and everyday discomfort ("92 Degrees") can't tamp down the big sounds and big hooks of these tracks. Things only get discordant on "This Unrest." Otherwise, *Tinderbox* is an incredibly accessible record and one that shows what expert craftspeople Siouxsie and the

Banshees had become since they first assaulted ears with twenty appalling minutes of "The Lord's Prayer."

THE SMITHS: *THE QUEEN IS DEAD*

It's clear the Smiths are out for blood even before the regicidal lyrics sink in. As soon as they rip out the title track like Zeppelin pounding "Achilles Last Stand," we're off with *The Queen Is Dead*. From there, moods change like the wind: a jolly yet withering look at long-term employment ("Frankly Mr. Shankly"), a zany cry of irritation at one's own flapping jaw ("Bigmouth Strikes Again," which now feels like Morrissey's definitive song in light of his incorrigible spew of idiotic opinions), a cheeky portrait of a man of the cloth who likes to express himself by dressing like a ballerina ("Vicar in a Tutu"), an expres-

No, that isn't the queen in her coffin. It's actor Alain Delon in the movie *L'Insoumis*. Author's collection.

sion of stark romantic self-pity and self-annihilation ("I Know It's Over"), a couple of hilarious shouts of romantic glee and self-annihilation ("Cemetery Gates," "There Is a Light That Never Goes Out"), Morrissey's barb for a music industry he felt didn't have his back ("The Boy with the Thorn in His Side"), and whatever the hell "Some Girls Are Bigger Than Others" is. Unlike the tracks on the first Smiths record, which form a consistent mood, there's nothing to musically link those on *The Queen Is Dead* aside from their quality, which is as high as Morrissey's pompadour.

THROWING MUSES: *THROWING MUSES*

There had never been a band quite like Throwing Muses. Their structures are unpredictable and bizarre. Their lyrics are disjointed and disturbing. Their interplay is inimitable, as bandleader Kristin Hersh and sister Tanya Donnelly's guitars chime against Leslie Langston's remarkable jazz bass and David Narcizo's precise drumming. Hersh's voice is a constant dare unleashing goat bleats and banshee shrieks.

The Rhode Island quartet's antipop was never starker than on their debut. On later records, Kristin Hersh started playing with more recognizable rock forms, but here she is scratching at walls in a dark room, etching out sounds you'd expect from someone who's never even heard pop music. Yet there are ways into this challenging music, and even the most frightening pieces, such as "Hate My Way," have passages of extraordinary beauty. The rockabilly rave-up "Rabbit's Dying" is downright catchy. *Throwing Muses* isn't the most enjoyable Throwing Muses LP, but it is a debut that announces the band's intentions to follow their own muse completely.

XTC: *SKYLARKING*

Skylarking exudes the sunnier sides of sixties pop in composition, production, and outlook. Andy Partridge, Colin Moulding, and David Gregory basically commit to their Dukes of Stratosphear alter egos without the jokiness. And instead of drawing on the weirder strains of mid-sixties psych as the Dukes did, our psychedelicized XTC is clearly under the sway of the era's cleanest productions, namely, *Sgt. Pepper's* and *Pet Sounds*. *Skylarking* is intoxicating, full of details and joy, but smart enough to include the year's most pointed, courageous, and confrontational single, "Dear God," which was left off initial pressings of the album because Partridge was dissatisfied with the song and Virgin Records got cold feet about its agnostic message.

Todd Rundgren's production is a work of George Martin–worshipping art as the tracks swirl into a kaleidoscopic whole while each maintains its own distinct persona: the folky slam of "Dear God," the goo-goo-g'joob strings of "1000 Umbrellas," the lush "Grass," the airy "Summer's Cauldron," the stately "Sacrificial Bonfire," the jazzy "Man Who Sailed Around His Soul," and so on into the psychedelic sun. Before recording had even begun, Rundgren sequenced the songs, envisioning the album as a day-of-hope to night-of-death song cycle. When the band balked at the producer's takeover of their work, Rundgren advised XTC to "dick around with if for a few hours your way if you like" (as Partridge told *Spin* magazine in 1989) while he went home. Wisely, they ultimately came around and saw it Rundgren's way.

1987

Much of the fun of eighties music had already been crushed under the studded boots of hair metal and big-haired pop, which weren't nearly as much fun as Bon Jovi and Taylor Dane would have you believe. What 1987 lacked in the kinds of wonderful one-hit wonders we most associate with the decade, it made up for in the serious art new and old artists brought to the mixing console. To toss a floodlight on that fact, two of the best albums of 1987 use art rock's favorite format: the double album.

Art and fun don't have to be mutually exclusive, and some of the decade's most serious artists actually seem to be loosening up in bids for big eighties success. If there's one thing that binds most of the eclectic albums that follow together, it's their danceability. So put on your studded dancing boots and blast another coat of Aqua Net at your head. We're about to dive into the LPs of 1987.

THE CURE: *KISS ME, KISS ME, KISS ME*

Kiss Me, Kiss Me, Kiss Me shows off everything that is fabulous about its band, which is something all double albums must do. The gloomy crawl of the Cure's first major phase is apparent in "If Only We Could Sleep Tonight" and "The Snakepit," even if those tracks' raga sparkles sprinkle them with more color than you'll find on *Seventeen Seconds* or *Faith*. For the poppier, more romantic side the Cure uncovered on *The Top* and *The Head on The Door*, you'd do no better than the smash "Just Like Heaven," the love-drunk "Catch," and the ecstatic "Perfect Girl." For the hard-core side the band chiseled out on *Pornography*, there are the somewhat more controlled variations in "The Kiss," "Torture," "All I Want," and "Shiver and Shake."

All of those classic styles are not merely paraded out one more time on *Kiss Me, Kiss Me, Kiss Me*—they are perfected. More perfection awaits in the self-contained dance party "Why Can't I Be You?," the gusty "How Beautiful You Are," the gorgeous "One More Time," the tense and towering "Like Cockatoos," and the graceful yet impassioned "A Thousand Hours." Two years later, *Disintegration* would be heralded as the Cure's masterpiece, but that album simply does not host the sheer versatility, beauty, and mastery of *Kiss Me, Kiss Me, Kiss Me*, an album that is also the very best of 1987 as far as I'm concerned.

DUKES OF STRATOSPHEAR: *PSONIC PSUNSPOT*

The mid-1980s: a barren wasteland of antiseptic record production distinguished by harsh, gated drum sounds, tinny horns, and synthesizers. Aside from the most low-fi college bands, no one came out unscathed. Elvis Costello and the Attractions put out *Goodbye Cruel World* (1984), a record that kicks off with a Darryl Hall duet complete with blurting sax solo. The Damned also got saxy on *Phantasmagoria*, their over-polished, synth-swathed bid for mainstream success. Even the filthy Replacements broke out some flatly recorded horns on the otherwise fierce *Pleased to Meet Me*. The real tragedy of such records is that they often contained a good deal of excellent songs that could have really shined in a less shiny setting. But labels remained convinced that their acts had to delve into DDD flawlessness in order to compete with the likes of Phil Collins and Lionel Richie. Consequently, sixties holdovers like the Stones, Pete Townshend, and George Harrison were among the worst offenders, probably because they had to struggle the hardest to remain relevant.

Some of the cagier groups skirted contemporary production trends by releasing one-off "novelty" records credited to some long-lost, fabricated sixties band. They put together collections of organic retro rock that stood in warm contrast to the icy sounds of the day. In 1984, the Damned masqueraded as Naz Nomad and the Nightmares to release *Give Daddy the Knife, Cindy*, a phony sound track to a phony Roger Corman–esque psychedelic horror movie containing gritty covers of American psych and garage classics, such as the Human Beinz's "Nobody but Me," Paul Revere and the Raiders' "Kicks," and the Electric Prunes' "I Had Too Much to Dream (Last Night)." It wasn't anything incredibly essential, just a fresh palette cleansing before they mounted *Phantasmagoria*.

XTC didn't succumb to the trappings of eighties production as severely as many of their contemporaries, but an album like 1983's *Mummer* still displayed a slightly off-putting sheen. But the sixties-psych enthusiasts yearned for that era's organic creativity enough to feel the need to retreat into their own pseudonymous project. Thus, Partridge transformed into "Sir John Johns," bassist/ singer Colin Moulding was now "The Red Curtain," keyboardist Dave Gregory became "Lord Cornelius Plum," and drummer Ian Gregory was now "E.I.E.I. Owen," and XTC was reborn as the Dukes of Stratosphear.

Unlike the Damned/Naz Nomad, XTC/ the Dukes of Stratosphear composed original music, making their ruse a bit more convincing and a lot more artistically significant. In fact, the records XTC released as the Dukes of Stratosphear rate as some of the best music they produced and some of the most successful and accurate homages to sixties

This 2001 CD compilation includes both Dukes of Stratosphear releases: the excellent E.P. *25 O'Clock* and the LP *Psonic Psunspot*. Author's collection.

psychedelia ever recorded. Partridge would later consider *Psonic Psunspot* to be an official XTC LP that functions as the missing link between *Skylarking* and *Oranges and Lemons* and credit the entire Dukes project with refreshing XTC creatively by giving them the "excuse to dress up crazy and not be (ourselves)," as he told the *Chicago Tribune* in 2009.

The Dukes' first release, the 1985 EP *25 O'Clock*, puts a very fine point on their intentions, with each song serving as a specific takeoff on a specific classic of the original psychedelic era. "25 O'Clock" is a ringer for "I Had Too Much to Dream," "Bike Ride to the Moon" is a poppier rewrite of Pink Floyd's "Bike," and not only does "The Mole from the Ministry" sound like the Beatles' "I Am the Walrus," but its fabulous music video also reinterprets the "Walrus" sequence from *Magical Mystery Tour*. Such specificity makes *25 O'Clock* sound a bit too much like a Rutles-style novelty albeit a superb one.

The Dukes of Stratosphear relaxed a bit on their one and only LP. With *Psonic Psunspot*, they crafted a neo-psychedelic classic that still pays all due tribute to Floyd, the Beatles, the Beach Boys, the Kinks, and other behemoths of the mid-sixties while still sounding quite like XTC (by this point, they'd fessed up about the Dukes' true identity). By parading out all the essential tropes of psychedelia—satires of the military and straight society, drug songs, music hall, backward tape loops, Mellotrons, ostentatious surrealism, half-baked conceptual devices—XTC essentially created the ultimate album of 1967 twenty years after the fact.

ECHO & THE BUNNYMEN: *ECHO & THE BUNNYMEN*

So what does a culty college rock band do after making their universally acclaimed masterpiece? Naturally, they attempt to go for the big commercial gold. And so Echo & the Bunnymen followed the moody and experimental *Ocean Rain* with the bright and bubbly *Echo & the Bunnymen*.

Echo & the Bunnymen could actually be an acceptable party album. As soon as "The Game" rips in, you know it's not time to usher everyone out the door, turn off the lights, and slip on the headphones for some intense private listening. That does not mean the album is devoid of atmosphere. With Ray Manzarek pressing the keys, "Bedbugs and Ballyhoo" recalls the Doors at their most serpentine without skimping on the catchy chorus (and Ian McCullough's repetition of "That's the way the bee bumbles" may make you crack your first mid–Bunnymen album smile). "Bombers Bay" is lyrically dark yet sonically uplifting. "Lips Like Sugar," "All in Your Mind," and "New Direction" show off the band at their sexiest and danciest. The moodiest thing on here, closing track "All My Life," is also the most musically mundane. But after the forty-something minutes of sexy partying that precede it, it can only pale.

GUIDED BY VOICES: *DEVIL BETWEEN MY TOES*

Fourth-grade teacher Robert Pollard had been spending his free time penning weird little songs reflecting his eclectic tastes in pop since he was a teenager. At a time when the Dayton, Ohio, scene was mainly fixated on metal, the locals thought Pollard was out of his mind when he started performing his fractured homages to the Monkees, King Crimson, Wire, and R.E.M. with Guided by Voices. That band would swap members regularly over the years, but Pollard's dedication to making music has been alarmingly consistent. As of this writing, he has written or cowritten more than

2,700 songs according to the Guided by Voices database (https://gbvdb.com).

Pollard's showmanship is nearly as legendary as his ability to crank out material. Guided by Voices shows boast the length and mass inebriation of a Grateful Dead festival, the manic energy of a Who bash, and the bizarre nonsequiturs of a 3 a.m. phone call from your alcoholic best buddy. Most of all, they are inspirational. Seeing this ordinary-looking, middle-aged fourth-grade teacher standing center stage, mimicking his idol Roger Daltrey, and clearly having the most fun he's ever had in his life made everyone in the audience feel like they could do that too. So what if they couldn't crank out five songs "while sitting on the pot," as a DJ once claimed of Pollard during an interview ("and three of them are good!" Pollard clarified).

GBV would later immortalize Bob Pollard's ill-tempered pet rooster Big Daddy and the accompanying phrase on the cover of their debut album in their song "Don't Stop Now," which Pollard often referred to as "The Ballad of Guided by Voices." Author's collection.

Guided by Voices was just as potent on disc. They recorded song after song on chintzy home four-track recorders. Pollard carefully selected the best for his band's albums and was always left with a wealth of leftovers for single B-sides, EPs, and outtake compilations. Guided by Voices have released a staggering four *box sets* of outtakes. There's surely a ton of unreleased material still in the vaults.

While low-fi recordings of high-fi melodies define Guided by Voices' discography, the band didn't settle on that approach right out of the gate. After a super-polished debut mini-album that cast them as Dayton's answer to R.E.M., Guided by Voices moved from the apparently lush confines of Group Effort Studios in Kentucky to Steve Wilbur's 8-Track Garage in their hometown. The fruits of those sessions, the band's debut LP *Devil Between My Toes*, gave the first real taste of the band's low-fi ethos, though the song selection is uneven with too many sketchy instrumentals. Fully formed songs, such as the Who-esque "Captain's Dead," the Herman's Hermits–like "Hank's Little Fingers," "Hey, Hey Spaceman," and "Dog's Out," showed what Pollard was really capable of.

SANDBOX

Also recorded at the 8-Track Garage, *Sandbox* sounds significantly slicker than *Devil*, and the song selection is stronger without any of the first album's instrumentals. Perhaps nothing on Guided by Voices' second LP is as rousing as "Captain's Dead" or as playground hummable as "Hank's Little Fingers," but *Sandbox* is Guided by Voices' first album that proved that Bob Pollard could dish up a consistent set of distinctive pop and that— perhaps most importantly of all—he and Guided by Voices could do it with relative high fidelity without sounding like poseurs. "Serious" (translation: "tiresome") fans would fall out of their basements to argue against that point a dozen years later when the band moved to TVT, but even those dogmatic types should have no beef with the awesome riffing of "A Visit from the Creep Doctor," the resolute "Everyday," the can-hoisting/Beatle-quoting "Barricade," the rumbling "Can't Stop," the perfect miniature "Long Distance Man," and the lurching "I Certainly Hope Not." As most of those relatively ordinary titles indicate, Guided by Voices had yet to fully embrace their wonderful weirdness on *Sandbox*, but they'd correct that too on their next album.

INXS: *KICK*

Kick is a prime example of how 1987 tried to oppress traditional bands and how certain bands didn't fight their era one iota. INXS was clearly taking its core cues from the sixties. With his leather pants, wild tresses, perpetual pout, perpetually bare chest, and "Touch me, I'm Jesus" stage moves, Michael Hutchence couldn't have patterned himself on Jim Morrison more if he'd crowned himself Lizard King of Australia. "Mediate" apes Dylan both musically and videoly. "New Sensation" and "Need You Tonight" try some James Brown moves, and the atmospheric "Never Tear Us Apart" draws from the more pleading and elegant strain of sixties soul. Yet the gated-drum/farty-sax/swaths-of-synth production is so eighties that I expect a packet of Garbage Pail Kids stickers to plop out of the speakers whenever I spin *Kick*. Yet it still works. "Mediate" and the strident opening track "Guns in the Sky" haven't aged well, but the other aforementioned tracks, "Devil Inside," "Wild Life," and "Calling All Nations" are as catchy and fun as any pop music of an era in which most artists seemed to be having a lot more fun than their audiences.

THE PIXIES: *COME ON PILGRIM*

I first became aware of the Pixies after reading an article about them in *Rolling Stone* magazine at the height of my unimaginative immersion in classic rock. I could not fathom how the almost vengefully ordinary quartet pictured on the page could qualify as a, in *Rolling Stones'* words, "thrash band." Where were the bales of hair, the tattoos, the all-black wardrobes, the sneers, the Ibanezes? All I saw was a woman who looked like she may have missed her last weekly shampoo, a somewhat corpulent bald guy, and two other fellows too plain to even describe.

A few years later, I found myself playing bass in a vengefully ordinary band (every song sounded like Eddie Vedder and Anthony Kiedis dueting on a cover of "Hey Bulldog"). During a rehearsal in the lead singer's bedroom, I noticed a Pixies poster on the wall. This was less ordinary than that photo in *Rolling Stone*. It depicted a naked corpulent bald guy giving the old Roman thumbs-down who looked like he'd been forced to the ground by cops. Above his prostrate figure read "Death to the Pixies." The unsettling image and zingy motto only made the various details about the Pixies I'd acquired harder to puzzle together. It also heightened my curiosity, and when I started to pick the singer's brain about the Pixies, he figured it would just be easier to lend me a Pixies mix tape he'd compiled than bury me in effusive rap.

The next day, as I drove to my friend Phil's house, I popped the tape into the deck. It was only a five-minute drive to Phil's, but I probably would have popped the cassette back out of the deck after five minutes even if the trip was longer because what I heard utterly revolted me: a clearly psychotic man screaming in Spanish over Dexedrine power chords one would not be out of line to describe as "thrash."

After arriving at Phil's, I asked him, "Have you ever heard the Pixies? It is the worst garbage I've ever heard in my life." We then turned on MTV and zoned out for an hour or two. Every five minutes or so, I was compelled to exclaim, "Jesus, I just can't believe how horrible the Pixies are!"

On the drive home, I popped the tape back into the deck. Now the raving maniac was giggling about being "the son of incestuous union." This was too much. Out came the tape again. "I hope I never have to hear this shit again."

As soon as the five-minute drive home was over, I raced up to my bedroom and put the Pixies tape on my stereo. The raving maniac now raved about his greatest fear: losing his "penis to a whore with disease" ("just kidding," he said). The worst.

After listening to the rest of the tape, I rewound it to the beginning and listened again. And again.

What was happening to me was after five solid years of listening to nothing but the Beatles, the Stones, and the Who, the Pixies were now rearranging my brain. They were making me think differently about music, and by the dozenth or so listen, I'd become a different person. I was not just in love with the Pixies; I wanted to *become* the Pixies. I soon quit that lousy band I was in (the singer never did get his mix tape back) and formed my own lousy band. The first songs I "wrote" for my new band were basically Pixies songs with my own (inferior) lyrics pasted on top. I put my Beatles, Stones, and Who albums aside for a solid year and immersed myself in everything the Pixies wrought: Nirvana, the Breeders, Daisy Chainsaw, Shudder to Think, and so on. The Pixies changed the way I thought about music. A good song didn't have to have a catchy melody (though the Pixies' songs were often deliriously catchy) or a rockin' beat (although their beats often rocked) like some audio blockbuster flick. It could also be disjointed and disturbing like a David Lynch midnight movie. The Pixies changed the way I made music. They even changed the way I thought about what makes an album an album.

Do eight tracks running for twenty minutes qualify as an album? It's certainly too long for an EP. So what is the Pixies' debut? Its unconventional length may not be the only thing that gets you asking that particular question while taking in *Come On Pilgrim*. Is this pop? Is it punk? Is it thrash as *Rolling Stone* averred? Is it some loony's idea of Mexican folk music? Yes, yes, yes, and yes.

The late Vaughan Oliver was 4AD's distinctive house artist. For *Come On Pilgrim*, he presented the band with this guy's hairy back. Author's collection.

Such identity confusion is built into the Pixies music and mythos. Singer/guitarist/ malevolent despot Charles Thompson IV (aka Black Francis; aka Frank Black; aka corpulent bald guy) advertised for a partner in crime with an infamous classified ad looking for a "bassist into Hüsker Dü and Peter, Paul, and Mary." He got Kim Deal (aka Mrs. John Murphy; aka woman who may have needed a shampoo), a sweet-voiced foil to his primal shrieking. Artful noisemaker and nonsequitur spouter Joey Santiago supplied lead guitar, and eccentric David Lovering supplied the beat. The Pixies' patented loud–quiet–loud dynamics, Francis Bacon grotesqueries, college-boy cleverness, and zesty tunefulness would reverberate tremendously through rock in the years to come, not least of all giving the band that would be to the nineties what the Beatles were to the sixties a firm sense of direction.

As the opening salvo in a new age of alternative rock and roll nirvana, *Come On Pilgrim* has great historical value. That wouldn't mean a thing if it didn't also have the songs, and it has eight magnificent, gore-splattered ones: the psycho dirge "Caribou," the screeching throb "Vamos," the neck-breaking "Isla De Encanta," the asymmetrical pure poppers "Ed Is Dead" and "The Holiday Song," the manically catchy and just plain maniacal "Nimrod's Son," the new-wavy pogo "I've Been Tired," and the rumbling, horny "Levitate Me." It also has words—words like "you are the son of incestuous union," "losing my penis to a whore with disease," and "she's just rotting in stupid bliss." Is this nightmare or guffaw fuel? There's another question to ponder while bashing your skull along to *Come On Pilgrim*.

PRINCE: *SIGN O' THE TIMES*

After several albums with the Revolution, Prince was once again occupying his palace alone, though the material on his second double album is sourced from several aborted projects with and without the Revolution. He commits acts of aural female impersonation on the deliciously filthy "If I Was Your Girlfriend," the highly disfunktional "Strange Relationship," and the party anthem "Housequake," which are all remnants of a project called "Camille" that would have had Prince speeding up his voice to voice that title character for the duration of an entire LP. He dabbles with children's music on the charming "Starfish and Coffee," deals with social issues (albeit it in an outrageously alarmist way) on the ghostly title track, and jams for the long haul on "It's Gonna Be a Beautiful Night," a live track that displays the presence of a working band more explicitly than anything on the Revolution albums. In perhaps his most far-out, most "what was he thinking?" stroke, Prince takes the absurdly white-bread pop chanteuse Sheena Easton under his wing and showcases her on the hit "U Got the Look."

More importantly, *Sign O' the Times* is an eclectic, kingly mess housing buried gems

According to photographer Jeff Katz, all this junk on the cover of *Sign O' the Times* came straight out of Prince's apartment. Author's collection.

waiting to be uncovered on repeated listens. Spin side A again to really appreciate the wall-rattling "Play in the Sunshine" and the intoxicating "Ballad of Dorothy Parker." Revisit side B for the crazy-making "It" and side D for the enthralling, slow-burn psychedelics of "The Cross" complete with synth sitar. *Sign O' the Times* is a big, jam-packed gift to fans and a beacon that things were going to be alright even without the Revolution.

R.E.M.: *DOCUMENT*

A lot of critics rate *Document* as one of R.E.M.'s very best, if not their very best of all. It was certainly a commercial breakthrough. *Document* was the band's first album to crack *Billboard*'s top ten and a vessel for two of their best-known songs, one of which was their first single to crack the American top ten.

To my ears, *Document* sounds a bit transitional, caught between the magic murk of R.E.M.'s first phase and the radio-song success of their second. Producer Scott Litt gives the band a bigger sound that unfortunately mutes the muted mystery of their earlier albums. Each of their earlier albums came wrapped in timelessly organic texture that bucked the worst tendencies of mid-eighties production. That is not so with much of *Document*. "Finest Worksong" is downright overbearing. From a compositional standpoint, several of the songs on side B are a bit underwhelming.

Still, this is the album with the irresistible verbal avalanche "It's the End of the World as We Know It," the impassioned (and serially misunderstood) hit "The One I Love," the classically moody "Welcome to the Occupation," the classically power-poppy "Disturbance at the Heron House," and the gleeful, almost Motown-esque "Exhuming McCarthy." The quality of those tracks would carry over to R.E.M.'s next album.

THE REPLACEMENTS: *PLEASED TO MEET ME*

The year 1987 had its share of great albums, but there wasn't much happening that was as raw, as alive, as *Pleased to Meet Me*, even as it does suffer a bit from antiseptic mid-eighties production syndrome. The Replacements fight against that slickness on the opening cut, "I.O.U.," but when they give in on "Alex Chilton," they actually manage a genuine eighties power-pop classic worthy of its namesake. Even the brass on "I Don't Know" can't sink the Replacements because they overpower the grungy sax with their drunkenly garbled backing vocals and herky-jerky rhythms. One might be a bit skeptical of the lounge jazz of "Nightclub Jitters" if it wasn't so clearly a parody and so clearly a well-conceived little number that contributes to the anything-and-everything climate of *Pleased to Meet Me*. The 'Mats (a nickname bestowed by sozzled fans who'd mispronounced the band's name as the "Placemats") then storm through cranky, R.E.M.-style pop ("The Ledge"), Stonesy rock and roll ("Valentine"), sleazy cock rock ("Shooting Dirty Pool"), lovely folk rock ("Skyway"), and yet another decade-defining classic only to be found left of the dial ("Can't Hardly Wait") before slumping out the door.

SIOUXSIE AND THE BANSHEES: *THROUGH THE LOOKING GLASS*

Through the Looking Glass is one of those time-filling covers that album bands manufacture when their compositional coffers are empty. Siouxsie and the Banshees make even this kind of disc an essential occupant of their discography with lush arrangements of classics by Iggy Pop, the Doors, Roxy Music, Billie Holiday, the snake from *The Jungle Book*, and Dylan. (Siouxsie was allegedly horrified when she discovered who'd written that old Julie Driscoll hit she loved, "This Wheel's on Fire." She thinks he'd be no fun at a party.) *Looking Glass* has some of the best use of harp on a pop album, but with choices such as Television's "Little Johnny Jewel" and John Cale's towering "Gun," the band also relocates a bit of their punk fury.

THE SMITHS: *STRANGEWAYS HERE WE COME*

Final albums often find bands losing the plot or running low on ideas. This is clearly not the case with *Strangeways Here We Come*, even if it may not quite live up to Morrissey and Johnny Marr's opinion that it is the Smiths' finest album. It does find the band fattening their sound with horns, mallets, synth strings, and other interesting bits that bring the production to life. The diamond-brilliant "Stop Me If You Think You've Heard This One Before" is the only *Strangeways* single that really rises above and beyond. The album's other hits—the glammy "I Started Something I Couldn't Finish," the droll lite reggae "Girlfriend in a Coma"—are minor compared to the Smiths' earlier staples, while the listless, shapeless "Last Night I Dreamed That Somebody Loved Me" is arguably one of the weakest things in their catalog and ample fodder for anyone who derides Morrissey as a humorless mope mop (a charge so many of his other songs blow away).

Strangeways deserves to be heard because of its wonderful obscurities. "Rush and a Push and the Land Is Ours" is a subtle yet absorbing opener. "Death of a Disco Dancer" is a hunk of majestic, 1987-by-way-of-1967 psychedelia. "Death at One's Elbow" is a classic piece of Manchester rockabilly, and "I Won't Share You with Anybody" is a chilling, elegant finale that allegedly speaks volumes about why Morrissey and Marr parted strangeways. The relentlessly bitter "Paint a Vulgar Picture," a bullet for disrespectful record companies, may say even more.

SUZANNE VEGA: *SOLITUDE STANDING*

Solitude Standing feels like Suzanne Vega's attempt to break big with bigger production values, but that may just be because that is precisely what happened when "Luka," a catchy number sung from the point of view of an abused boy, became a hit in the summer of 1987. As strong as that song is, it's the rest of *Solitude Standing* that makes the album hold up, though the maternally warm "Gypsy" is the only song that is as hooky as "Luka." Even that "da-da-da-da" bit that DNA looped to make "Tom's Diner" a massive 1990 dance hit barely makes an appearance at the end of Vega's decidedly uncommercial a cappella original.

The mood across *Solitude Standing* is alluring and never trampled under its slick, electrified, and synth-heavy arrangements. "Ironbound/Fancy Poultry" is a riveting vignette. "In the Eye" is a clattering laser-focused pop tune far more danceable than anything on Vega's debut. The title track is even more intense. Critic Billy Altman described Zeppelin's "Kashmir" as "a masterpiece of controlled tension" in the *Rolling Stone Record Guide*; that phrase applies just as well to "Solitude Standing." "Night Vision," "Calypso," "Language," and "Wooden Horse (Caspar Hauser's Song)" are four more subtly restless yet masterfully controlled pieces. Vega's finest work still lies before her at this point, but *Solitude Standing* clinched her commercially and stands up as a strong artistic statement.

1988

The return to a more organic sound that would define the best nineties rock still seemed like a distant dream by 1988, and some regarded the situation in nearly apocalyptic terms. The previous year, rock critic Simon Frith warned in his essay "The Industrialization of Popular Music" that "we've come to the end of the record era now (and so, perhaps, to the end of pop music as we know it)" because of the contemporary emphasis on pop as commodity rather than art. In 1988, the commoditization of rock and roll reached a startling milestone when just six companies, known as the "Big Six," remained after consuming all other majors to monopolize the record industry: Capitol-EMI, CBS, BMG, PolyGram, Warner Music, and MCA.

Yet there is a sense of new birth and rebirth in the best music of the year that saw the digital CD outsell the analogue vinyl LP for the first time as automation of the production process helped lower the retail prices of many CDs (it now cost just $1 to manufacture a single disc), and older albums marketed in budget series, such as CBS's Nice Price and BMG's Best Buy, might sell for as little as $7.99, fueling sales of classic rock albums to kids like me who were unmoved by top-forty radio in 1988. Perhaps not coincidentally, the reign of the Big Six arrived just as small independent labels, such as Sub-Pop in Seattle, 4AD in London, Matador in New York, and Bar/None in Hoboken, were attracting forward-thinking young artists sick of the majors' way of doing business and determined to reach listeners weary of the top forty. Morrissey and Keith Richards stepped outside of bands either seemingly dead or most sincerely dead to make worthwhile solo debuts. Jane's Addiction slithered out of the sleazy Sunset Strip scene that gave us the hair bands polluting the era and put a scary, junkie spin on the metal revival that felt far less mannered than Axl Rose's whining. Both the Pixies and My Bloody Valentine—perhaps the two bands that would have the most profound influence on the coming decade—released striking albums too.

Meanwhile, two of the most influential rock bands of the waning eighties released LPs that found them inching closer toward genuine superstardom (though only one would truly snatch the coveted ring), and two of the most influential rap groups ever released albums that would make rock seem increasingly safe and irrelevant. So for a year oppressed by the likes of Def Leppard, Tiffany, Debbie Gibson, Rick Astley, and White Snake, 1988 still managed its share of important and excellent discs.

ROBYN HITCHCOCK AND THE EGYPTIANS:
GLOBE OF FROGS

Former Soft Boy Robyn Hitchcock frankensteined crazed songwriting, lugubrious singing, and pop hooks better than anyone since Syd Barrett. His mad-scientist skills are fully evident on *Globe of Frogs*. With guest spots for Glen Tilbrook's dulcet voice and Peter Buck's chiming Rickenbacker, *Globe of Frogs* feels like Hitchcock's bid for the big time, and the success of "Balloon Man" (a song originally composed for the Bangles) got him about as close as he'd ever come. Yet as catchy and impeccably produced as "Balloon Man," "Vibrating," "Sleeping with Your Devil Mask," "Unsettled," "Flesh Number One (Beatles Dennis)," and the concert staple "Chinese Bones" are, it's tough to feature what radio listeners would have made of such ghastliness as "Their rotting brains fell to the floor and crawled away towards the door" or "her eyeballs had rolled up so her pupils had vanished."

JANE'S ADDICTION: *NOTHING'S SHOCKING*

In the late eighties, the hairspray-splattered Sunset Strip scene seemed less likely to produce challenging music than Phil Collins did. Then came Jane's Addiction. In contrast to the forced decadence of Guns N' Roses or Mötley Crüe, Jane's Addiction reeked of authenticity, stripping away all the cock-rock posturing and tacky glamour of their neighbors. While Vince Neal and Axl Rose were screeching about screwing strippers, Perry Farrell was spitting bitterness about the nonexistence of God and the idiocy of politicians, surveying the wasteland of televised terror, and meditating on the hollowness of masculinity while pissing down his leg and whacking off in the shower. Guitarist Dave Navarro and bassist Eric Avery discharged riffs reminiscent of Led Zeppelin at their funkiest. While the poseurs were branching out with power pap like "Sweet Child O'Mine" and "You're All I Need," Jane's Addiction was shaping "Jane Says," a touching and melodic pre-eulogy to a junkie girlfriend with a charming arrangement of acoustic guitars and steel drums, and the sumptuous and nostalgic "Summertime Rolls."

The arresting sculpture on the cover of *Nothing's Shocking* was clearly intended to shock with its "sex is violence" imagery. Needless to say, major American retailers made a stink about it, so Perry Farrell proposed sending them copies of the album in brown-paper bags as if they were pornography. This would not be the last time Jane's Addiction ran aground of censorious types. Author's collection.

LIVING COLOUR: *VIVID*

Despite their well-oiled machinery and well-crafted songs, Living Colour did not have an easy time finding a record label in a music industry unsure of what to do with an African American group. As bassist Muzz Skillings told the *Washington Post* in 1989, "The official line was, 'We like the songs, but . . .' Some just said, 'We don't know what to do with you,' or with the political undercurrent of the songs." This is ironic, insulting, and sad considering that African American artists invented rock and roll. Some radio listeners assumed Buddy Holly was black just because he rocked and rolled.

Record and radio industry racism resulted in the segregation of white rock and roll and black soul in the sixties, after which black artists who played guitar-based rock were rare, and all-black bands were even rarer. The Jimi Hendrix Experience, Love, the Chambers Brothers, Sly and the Family Stone, and Prince and the Revolution were all biracial groups.

It is infuriating that their race has to be an issue at all because Living Colour should be a noteworthy band just because they made powerful, catchy, socially conscious hard rock. Vernon Reid is a versatile and technically impeccable guitarist, and his interplay with Skillings on *Vivid* is rejuvenating. Their riffing is as responsible for the breakthrough popularity of "Cult of Personality" as the song's pointed lyric and Cory Glover's elastic voice are. I love how much Reid's guitar solo breathes on that track and "Desperate People" as Skillings is left to carry the riff without superfluous rhythm guitar. On the lighthearted "Glamour Boys," Living Colour gives themselves over to pure pop and scored another hit, while the only marginally less catchy yet much more purposeful "Open Letter (To a Landlord)" performed even more successfully on *Billboard*'s mainstream rock chart. On "I Wanna Know," Living Colour mixes things up with angular funk and guest spots for Chuck D. and Flavor Flav of Public Enemy. They even reserve a spot for a creative Talking Heads cover. Living Colour would expand their sound further on their next album, *Time's Up*, but it was their debut that made them stars.

PAUL McCARTNEY: *CHOBA B CCCP*

Decadent American and British rock and roll had long been off limits in the Soviet Union. Of course, you can't tame teens even if they live under strict communist rule, and a pipeline of bootlegs and imports existed in the USSR as early as World War II. The bootleggers often had to get pretty creative to smuggle their wares into Russia. They'd sometimes repurpose used X-rays by etching music into them as they would into a standard vinyl disc.

When Mikhail Gorbachev became the general secretary of the Communist Party of the Soviet Union in 1985, the USSR began to undergo an ideological makeover. Gorbachev was more tolerant of capitalist decadence than his predecessors had been. He loosened the government's tight controls over freedom of speech. By 1990, Russian fans of rock and roll no longer had to pass around copies of *Sgt. Pepper's* in secret.

As a show of support for the age of glasnost ("openness and transparency") Gorbachev ushered in, Paul McCartney ensured that his latest album would be released in the Soviet Union. It was a live-in-the-studio recording of rock and roll classics he had already planned to put out in the United Kingdom with an album cover inspired by those that adorned rock albums bootlegged for the underground Russian market. He and a pickup band that included Mick Green of original British rockers Johnny Kidd and the Pirates fire through classics made famous by Elvis Presley, Bo Diddley, Eddie Cochran, Fats Domino, Wilbert Harrison, Sam Cooke, and Paul's idol Little Richard intended as a sort of rock and roll primer, as was Mick

Carr's liner notes explaining the origins of each song. McCartney titled it *Choba B CCCP*, Russian for "Back in the USSR."

As a historical document, the album is pretty interesting. The introduction of what could be the greatest artistic product of capitalist society to the communists is a charming project, and at age forty-six, Paul proved he could still rip it up pretty well—though one hopes the folks who bought this disc were inspired to root out the original versions of its songs. *Choba B CCCP* is best when not inviting unfavorable comparisons with original versions, as when Paul transforms Duke Ellington's jazz-pop standard "Don't Get Around Much Anymore" into a chunky New Orleans–style rocker.

MORRISSEY: *VIVA HATE*

Just days after the release of *Strangeways, Here We Come*, Morrissey was already at work on his solo debut. *Viva Hate* is a different beast from the final Smiths record. While the Smiths' sound was always distinct from contemporary trends, *Viva Hate* and its gated, glossy Stephen Street production is pure eighties and completely lacks the distinct musicianship that Johnny Marr and Andy Rourke brought to every Smiths session. *Viva Hate* sounds like Morrissey's attempt to achieve solo stardom, but his writhing discontent and all-around disagreeableness could never have put him in competition with Rick Astley.

Take the utterly sweet-sounding "Bengali in Platforms," which can be interpreted as either an in-character snapshot of Thatcher-era racism or just an honest expression of Morrissey's own shitty opinions about immigration and race, which he has become more comfortable expressing in recent years. "Everyday Is Like Sunday," Morrissey's definitive solo number, is less distasteful and more melodious, though his wish to see a dull seaside holiday town nuked into oblivion seems like curmudgeonliness for the sake of curmudgeonliness.

Morrissey's anger is most justified on "Margaret on the Guillotine," though the lyric is devoid of insight (he wants her executed because she makes him feel old and tired—not because of her policies that caused a rise in unemployment and hostility toward immigrants?), and the airy music never touches ground. With "Angel, Angel Down We Go Together," Morrissey finally reveals a degree of humanity by offering some very Morrissey comfort to a suicidal friend, and Street lays on a string arrangement owing more to "Eleanor Rigby" than to "The Long and Winding Road." "Suedehead" is the most Smiths-like number on the disc and arguably the finest.

Now if only Morrissey would shut up so I could still enjoy listening to his music.

MY BLOODY VALENTINE: *ISN'T ANYTHING*

Shoegaze was an offshoot of early Britpop known for musicians more concerned with manipulating their multitudinous guitar pedals than directly engaging with audiences. Dublin's My Bloody Valentine was the genre's flagship band, and they would go on to make the album that defined the genre's neo-psychedelic noise, *Loveless*.

My Bloody Valentine was much more conventional in their early days when they were putting out slightly generic but tuneful indie pop records on Alan McGee's Creation Records. When McGee encouraged bandleader Kevin Shields to probe beyond the jangle of their singles, Shields started to allow dissonance to seep into the songs on his band's debut LP.

Isn't Anything is not as legendary as the band's next album would be, but it is a better entryway into My Bloody Valentine's work. The noise has not yet gotten so dense that you have to grope for the hooks. The stop-starting "Soft as Snow," the ominous and acoustic "Lose My Breath," the sneering strut "Cupid Come," the cosmic debris–trailing "(When You Wake) You're Still in a Dream," and nearly everything else would hold up as great songs regardless of arty production. About halfway through the album, Shields starts dropping in tracks such as "No More Sorry" and "All I Need" that are as dramatic, demanding, and delirious as anything on *Loveless*, so *Isn't Anything* still provides newcomers with a complete idea of what My Bloody Valentine was about.

N.W.A.: *STRAIGHT OUTTA COMPTON*

Members of N.W.A. were still in their teens when they recorded their breakthrough *Straight Outta Compton*, and it shows in the album's juvenile misogyny, homophobia, and posturing. However, the hard-won wisdom that made the album a revelation in 1988—and a smash success despite a complete lack of radio play—contradicts Ice Cube and MC Ren's years.

Unlike the Rolling Stones, whose violent undertaste was always as fake as Mick Jagger's Chicago inflections, N.W.A. lived the nightmare they rap about. Ice Cube's sister was murdered when he was twelve. Eazy-E and MC Ren dealt drugs to get by. Music was an escape from their rough lives in Compton, but there's little escapism on *Straight Outta Compton*. The lyrics and voices are violent. The simple on-the-beat rhymes keep the words clear, and the super-spare tracks force them to punch out of the mix. Dr. Dre, MC Ren, and the D.O.C. write about what they see. Cops are racist assholes who harass them and kill their neighbors. Life offers few opportunities. They fight back. They make a living where they can. The compassionate "Express Yourself" and "Quiet on the Set" and "Something 2 Dance 2," both of which take the former track's advice, are the only respites from the grind.

That "Parental Advisory" sticker was the PMRC's way of letting kids know which records they should definitely, definitely buy. Author's collection.

Musical and lyrical starkness rules *Straight Outta Compton*, but choppy voice samples and wiggly James Brown and P. Funk samples rescue the record from monotony. The hatred of women and LGBTQ people was always rotten, and it's especially tough to take in light of the abuse allegations against Dr. Dre. That element of the album is prehistoric. Infuriatingly, the need for groups like N.W.A. to speak out against the harsh authoritarianism engulfing them is just as relevant as ever.

THE PIXIES: *SURFER ROSA*

Just twenty minutes long, *Come On Pilgrim* was almost an album. There is no question what *Surfer Rosa* is, even as anything that dumps together all the shrieking, bopping, melodicizing, feedbacking, surfing, and sloppy Spanish of the Pixies' first long-playing long player is still indefinable. *Surfer Rosa* is actually just thirteen minutes longer than *Come On Pilgrim*, but it sounds huger, packing in nearly twice as many songs and thundering with Steve Albini's production, which would make a Celesta sound like a herd of rampaging mastodons.

Surfer Rosa is a more powerful production than *Come On Pilgrim*, though a few underdeveloped songs make the album feel less substantial in some ways. Yet even the lesser songs like "Something Against You" and "Broken Face" leave stains. When Black Francis's songwriting is sharp, it is a stiletto in the eyeball. "Bone Machine," "Break My Body," and "Where Is My Mind?" are as important to their era and the era around the bend as anything on R.E.M.'s *Green* or Jane's Addiction's *Nothing's Shocking*. So is "Gigantic," the first taste of the songwriting powers that would give Kim Deal the serious case of the George Harrisons that would soon prod her to breed with a kindred spirit from Throwing Muses.

PUBLIC ENEMY: *IT TAKES A NATION OF MILLIONS TO HOLD US BACK*

While *Straight Outta Compton* felt straight from the streets with its young-ster artists, sparse arrangements, and often puerile messaging, Public Ene-my's second album sounds like the work of self-possessed pros. Chuck D.'s lyrics are pointed from "go" as he questions the loyalty of black radio ("They call themselves black, but we'll see if they play this"), calls out rock and roll for denying its black roots, and shuts down the old-timers who dismiss rap in one of the genre's most mature statements of purpose, "Bring the Noise." Chuck D.'s push for black nationalism and keen knowledge of world politics and world history reveals the brain behind a genre some critics painted as mindless (unfortunately, Professor Griff's extracurricular slurs against gays and Jews threatened to unravel some of that good work).

With tracks like "Bring the Noise" and the expressly militant "Black Steel in the Hour of Chaos," which reads like a classic outlaw ballad updated for 1988, the album's modus operandi seems primarily political, but *It Takes a Nation of Millions to Hold Us Back* is also a great dance album and a resource for such disparate rock detritus as the beat from James Brown's "Funky Drummer" and the chorus from Queen's "Flash." "Bring the Noise," "Don't Believe the Hype," and "Louder Than a Bomb" are as fun as any of those songs Public Enemy sampled. Chuck D. twists his tongue around his verbiage effortlessly. Producer Hank Shocklee's sounds are full, furious, and incredibly energized. Recurring nails-on-the-chalkboard siren and teakettle shrieks underscore the lyrics' urgency and push the funk into avant-garde territory. Flavor Flav's keening asides spray cartoon comedy all over Chuck D's truth, and he gets to freak out completely on the Looney Tunes–surreal "Cold Lampin' with Flavor."

With its fun, chaos, attitude, and intelligence, *It Takes a Nation of Mil-lions to Hold Us Back* became an instant classic and is widely considered one of the greatest albums in any genre. Few rock and roll records from 1988 could keep pace with it energy, and few were so influential.

R.E.M.: *GREEN*

With their clean tunefulness and traditionally structured songwriting, R.E.M. only had to want it to hit the big time. By *Green*, they clearly wanted it. The U2-like "Orange Crush" and the ear-worming "Stand" and "Pop Song 89" all went top twenty on one *Billboard* chart or another (somehow, the equally perfect "Get Up" didn't manage to chart anywhere). These are all punchy, extroverted tracks, yet the heart of *Green* lies in its smaller tracks. Reflecting the rusticity implied in the album title, Peter Buck sets aside his Rickenbacker to pick his mandolin on "You Are the Everything," "The Wrong Child," and "Hairshirt," creating a new R.E.M. sound as defining as the electric jangle still evident in "World Leader Pretend" and "Untitled." Michael Stipe continues to focus and clarify his lyric writing. Sometimes this works, as when he plays a self-doubting politician stumbling into destruction on "World Leader Pretend." Sometimes it doesn't, as when he plays a little boy taunted for his mental disabilities on "The Wrong Child." Nevertheless, *Green* is still the most consistent album of R.E.M.'s new mandolin phase.

KEITH RICHARDS: *TALK IS CHEAP*

Even the most loyal Stones fan had to admit that things were getting really embarrassing in the eighties. Releasing fairly undistinguished albums like *Emotional Rescue* and *Undercover* was one thing. Accepting the worst tendencies of eighties production while tossing off utterly worthless material was another. Strangely, *Dirty Work*, the nadir of the Rolling Stones' career, was more Keith Richards's doing than Mick Jagger's. Maybe Keith was trying to compete with Mick's insipid solo album *She's the Boss*. The one clear thing in the mid-eighties mire is that the Stones had reached a dead end and needed to refresh.

Keith cleared out the cobwebs by doing something he always promised he'd never do: he went solo. This was more like it: the loose riffs, the grime, the songs built more on grooves than bogus melodic, lyrical, or production concepts. *Talk Is Cheap* sounds a lot more like a Rolling Stones album than anything the Stones had done in years, and in light of middle-aged Jagger's unnatural vocal mannerisms, Keith's grungy growl was like a breath of air both fresh and stinking of Marlboros and screwdrivers. There is even a degree of diversity as Keith messes with fifties boogie on "I Could Have Stood You Up," funk (complete with Bootsy Collins and Maceo Parker) on

"Big Enough," luxurious Al Green soul on "Make No Mistake," and earnest balladry on "Locked Away." Much of the other material is indistinct, but it still sounds good.

SIOUXSIE AND THE BANSHEES: *PEEPSHOW*

Siouxsie and the Banshees abandoned the abrasiveness that defined their early work for good with *Tinderbox*. *Peepshow* doubles down on that move toward a more marketable sound with out-and-out opulence. Mike Hedges and the band's production are like jewels: rich, multicolored, polished, and cold. And there's as much variation between tracks as there is between an emerald and an amethyst. "Peek-a-Boo," a big spew of disgust at the dubious entertainment name checked in the LP's title, is serpentine psychedelic swing, all backward tapes and automaton accordion. "The Killing Jar" is a race across verdant panoramas. "Scarecrow" is spindly, moonbeam-stabbed trees. "Carousel" is malevolent circus music. "Burn Up" is a demonic hoedown. "The Last Beat of My Heart" takes the deluxe production to extremes with palatial orchestrations. "Rawhead and Bloodybones" is the closest *Peepshow* comes to revisiting the old avant-gardism, though even this freak show has an underlying sweetness.

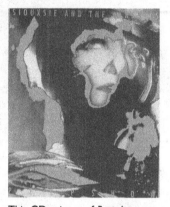

This CD reissue of *Peepshow* from 2014 had to be repressed because initial copies went out with a mastering error: there is an unnaturally long silence after "Rawhead and Bloody Bones" and a few extra stray seconds of "Rawhead" after that silence. Whoops. Author's collection.

THROWING MUSES: *HOUSE TORNADO*

House Tornado is the greatest statement from Throwing Muses' original lineup, and though I personally prefer *The Real Ramona*, much was lost when Leslie Langston and her pirouetting bass left the fold. It dances all over *House Tornado*. The torrential strumming of Kristin Hersh and Tanya Donelly flood the ground as Hersh's gale wail rains above. The combined noise is vicious yet elegant, violent yet soothing, thoroughly modern yet as eerily antiqued as a torn sepia photo trapped under an eiderdown of cobwebs. *House Tornado* secrets the chilly joy of "Colder," the angularity of "Mexican Women," the sunny break of "Juno," the sugar rush of Donelly's "The River," the runaway shadows of "Saving Grace," and the sheer magic of "Walking in the Dark," the finest song of Throwing Muses' career and 1988 as far as I'm concerned. It evokes images of an attic empty aside from a grand piano, a single naked lightbulb, and a ghost wailing of death dreams. Then in comes the rhythm section, and jewels of every color drop from the ceiling. Lights whirl. Brains get buzzed from some concoction served in a round-bottom beaker. Kristen Hersh recites pure poetry that evokes a faded, fantastical childhood long gone. So do her piano riffs, which recall "Linus and Lucy."

Vaughan Oliver's work on the cover of *House Tornado* was replaced with a more convention band photo for the sleeve of the American edition. Author's collection.

1989

Guitar-based rock music was on the verge of a breaking point in 1989. Mainstream rock went downy soft as dismal hair bands figured out that the best way to sell albums was to suppress the metal and hack out insipid "power ballads." Thus, Poison broke through with the rancid faux-country ballad "Every Rose Has Its Thorn," Warrant did the same with "Heaven," Bon Jovi followed along with "Born to Be My Baby," Sheriff did too with "When I'm with You," and Bad English did so with "When I See You Smile." They all ranked among the top-selling singles of the year, and they were all rank.

Meanwhile, ex-Chicago singer/bassist Peter Cetera scored the top-selling single of the year with the instantly forgettable "Look Away," and similar seventies holdovers Phil Collins, Don Henley, Rod Stewart, and Donny Osmond of all people also had hits big enough to place among the year's biggest sellers and worst sounders.

Yet, interesting things were also afoot as several of the underground's elder statespeople—including Elvis Costello, the B-52's, and the Cure—broke through with their first major hit singles. Relative newcomers like the Stone Roses, the Pixies, and Nirvana didn't have hits in 1989, but all shook up the scene with seismic power that reverberated into the next decade.

KATE BUSH: *THE SENSUAL WORLD*

Kate Bush hit a career peak that couldn't be followed when she unleashed *Hounds of Love* in 1985. Four years later, she followed it with *The Sensual World*, a less consistently adventurous record but a well-crafted and thematically tight one. Bush immerses herself in the title realm, ruminating on love and lust for everything from the usual sex partners to her computer. *The Sensual World* is home to such essential songs as the *Ulysses*-inspired title track and "This Woman's Work," a startling piece some have interpreted as the fear of a new father whose wife and child face life-threatening difficulties in the delivery room and others as the regrets of a man who has already lost his wife.

Because the sounds are so in line with those of *Hounds of Love*—tempestuous drumming, quilts of overdubbed vocals, squealing guitars (occasionally supplied by her mentor, Dave Gilmour), and free-form structures—*The Sensual World* feels like a belated sequel to that album though without the earlier records' uniformly superb songwriting and weirdness.

ELVIS COSTELLO: *SPIKE*

After the Attractions era shuddered in 1986 with *Blood & Chocolate*, Elvis Costello found himself a new label, Warner Bros., and a new writing partner. Paul McCartney helped Elvis get the biggest American hit of his career with their collaboration, "Veronica," a song about Elvis's grandmother's bout with Alzheimer's. The accompanying album, *Spike*, extends such unusual concerns across songs that deal with capital punishment, the treachery of Margaret Thatcher and her dedication to privatization, and the almighty's disappointment with all the crap his spawn created. The diverse concerns of Elvis's lyrics are matched in songs that ping-pong from the Byrdsy jangle of "This Town" (with Byrdsy guest star Roger McGuinn), the Kinky gloom of "Let Him Dangle," the Beatlesque "Veronica," the jazzy "God's Comic," the funky "Chewing Gum," the folky "Tramp the Dirt Down," and the very-late-eighties adult pop "Satellite."

All of this lyrical and musical flittering results in an album of songs that don't sound like they belong on the same album. Costello and T-Bone Burnett's production approaches are equally inconsistent. The musicians mess with synths one moment and acoustic arrangements the next. *Spike* hangs together strangely—and, going on for more than an hour, it is also a victim of early compact disc–era sprawl—but the individual songs are mostly great. It might take a few listens to digest, but it's worth the effort.

JULEE CRUISE: *FLOATING INTO THE NIGHT*

As part of his first gig scoring *Blue Velvet* for all-American surrealist David Lynch, composer Angelo Badalamenti had to find a vocalist with feathery enough technique to do justice to an ethereal ballad called "Mysteries of Love." Badalamenti asked his friend Julee Cruise, a self-proclaimed "belter" who'd played Janice Joplin in a revue on the New York City stage, if she knew of anyone who fit the bill. When the search turned out to be fruitless, Cruise suggested she give it a whirl. Coming down from her comfort zone, she discovered she could do dreamy as well as mighty. This led to a fruitful relationship between Cruise, Badalamenti, and Lynch that culminated in another New York City stage production, *Industrial Symphony #1*, in which Cruise dangled from wires in a prom dress while singing half a dozen remarkable songs with music by Badalamenti and lyrics by Lynch.

Plain Recordings' 2014 vinyl reissue of *Floating into the Night* includes a hidden bonus track (a few seconds of industrial noise and whispering) at the end of side A. Author's collection.

That same year, the trio gathered all that material and more onto *Floating into the Night*, the starkest and most sincerely beautiful record of 1989. Much like the films Lynch was making at the time, the album is an uncanny collision of fifties pastiche (recalling the square pop of people like the Fleetwoods and Shelley Fabares), eighties fashions (synthesizers hold sway), and the avant-garde. Hear how dissonant, jarring passages invade otherwise placid pieces such as "I Remember," "Rockin' Back inside My Heart," and "Into the Night." Lynch's lyrics are skeletal forests of the most direct sentiment and the most teasingly spare poetry. The record reaches a draining climax with "The World Spins," which would be used to devastating effect on a pivotal episode of *Twin Peaks*. Several other songs on *Floating into the Night* would also be used on Lynch and Mark Frost's landmark TV series in the early nineties (scrubbed of Cruise's vocal, "Falling" would be its theme song), but these songs first found a home on one of the most underrated albums of the late eighties. Isn't it too dreamy?

THE CURE: *DISINTEGRATION*

Poor Robert Smith. He seemed to be doing so well. After a run of unbelievably gloomy albums in the early eighties, the seemingly incurable mope suddenly started infusing some color into *The Top*, *The Head on the Door*, and *Kiss Me, Kiss Me, Kiss Me*. You'd think his increased use of hallucinogens might have kept the rainbow arcing. Instead, Smith disappeared into himself and came up with a dozen dark, languid demons guaranteed to doom his unwanted newfound success.

The plan backfired, and *Disintegration* became the Cure's biggest smash yet and their defining statement. This does not necessarily mean it is their best album, though many Cure fans do testify that it is. I personally find the musically and tonally varied *Kiss Me, Kiss, Me, Kiss Me* to be the top Cure album, but it just doesn't define the band's dark rep as thoroughly as *Disintegration* does. The album does wander more into commerciality than bleak early records from *Seventeen Seconds* through *Pornography* did. The Cure even accomplished the unthinkable by coming just one spot shy of the top of *Billboard*'s charts with the atypically contented "Lovesong." That song's romance is less of an anomaly on *Disintegration*, which swoons even when shuffling through emotional muck. The burst of synths and wind chimes that launches the album is enchanting. Then follows the record's most concise and accessible numbers, four of which became big hits on the modern rock charts. The back end of *Disintegration* is more samey, logged up with long dirges, but even these feature interesting elements to keep the ears dazzled: the relatively upbeat tunefulness of the title track, the bluesy piano licks of "Homesick," and the funereal harmonium of "Untitled."

DE LA SOUL: *3 FEET HIGH AND RISING*

A year after Public Enemy and N.W.A. reclaimed the threat from rock and roll and left it bleeding in the gutter, De La Soul sneaked up on pop and absorbed its sunshine. With more merry spirit than Sugar Hill Gang and wilder mosaic imaginations than Public Enemy, De La Soul injected hip-hop with the healthy spirit of psychedelia that was a cornerstone of their "D.A.I.S.Y. Age" philosophy. The songs are kooky fragments espousing ideas that would have come off as hopelessly unhip by less crafty, witty artists. Posdnuos, Trugoy, and Maseo celebrate high school romance ("Jenifa Taught Me"), warn against drugs ("Say No Go") and gangs ("Ghetto Thang"), and preach positivity in a world of talking storybook animals

("Tread Water"). They sample Johnny Cash,
Sly Stone, Steely Dan, the Monkees, the
Turtles, Hall & Oates, and, most radically of
all, Public Enemy themselves. All of these
elements tossed in the same soup could have
been choppy or jarring, but De La Soul is so
immutably smooth that 3 Feet High and Rising is totally wholesome. *The Village Voice*
famously called it "the *Sgt. Pepper's* of hip
hop," but with its overt humor, surreal skits,
montage anti-structure, and cartoon freakiness, it's more like hip-hop's *Head*.

"D.A.I.S.Y." is an acronym for
"da inner sound, y'all!" Your
guess is as good as mine.
Author's collection.

GUIDED BY VOICES: *SELF-INFLICTED AERIAL NOSTALGIA*

It took a few goes for Guided by Voices to become Guided by Voices. On
their debut mini-album, *Forever Since Breakfast*, they were R.E.M.—all
jangly guitars, twangy accents (by way of Dayton rather than Athens), and
slick studio polish. On *Devil Between My Toes*, they were groping for consistently fine material. On *Sandbox*, they lapsed back into over-polish. All of
those albums had their great moments (and despite not sounding at all like
GBV, *Forever Since Breakfast* is pretty much all great).

  Self-Inflicted Aerial Nostalgia gets everything right. Robert Pollard and
the gang accept their low-fi destiny and roll out enough pristine pop to
let you know they could be very good at being normal if they wanted to
("The Great Blake Street Canoe Race," "White Whale," "Crux"), enough
pure weirdness to let you know they'd rather not be ("Slopes of Big Ugly,"
"The Qualifying Remainder"), and an onslaught of the twain meeting to let
you know what they're best at. "Navigating Flood Regions," "An Earful of
Wax," the Sabbath-esque "Chief Barrel Belly," and "Radio Show (Trust the
Wizard)" are quintessential fist-and-Rolling-Rock-hoisting anthems. "Paper
Girl," "Trampoline," "Short on Posters," "Dying to Try This," and "Liar's
Tale" are among Pollard's prettiest miniatures. Man, can that guy write a
song! He'd write more. Lots and lots and lots and lots and lots more. He'd
written his share before *Self-Inflicted Aerial Nostalgia*, but this is the album
that marks the beginning of Robert Pollard and Guided by Voices' golden
age.

NIRVANA: *BLEACH*

What Elvis Presley was to the fifties, the Beatles were to the sixties, Led Zeppelin was to the seventies, and U2 was to the eighties, Nirvana would be to the nineties. Although they were part of the larger movement that developed in and around Seattle that the media labeled "grunge," Nirvana surpassed any of the genre's other bands in terms of influence, commercial success, and ability. No other grunge group had a songwriter as pop-savvy as Kurt Cobain (Mark Lanegan came close, but frankly, I always saw Screaming Trees as more of a nouveau garage-psych band than grunge group) or a musician as distinctive as drummer Dave Grohl. The mid-paced, sludgy guitars and self-loathing lyrics that defined Nirvana and other grungies would seemingly sweep away the vapid melodies, boasting, and production of hair metal overnight. Not yet, though. Grunge and Nirvana gestated for a few years before becoming phenomena in late 1991.

Released on the definitive grunge indie Sub-Pop, *Bleach* certainly doesn't sound like the arrival of a generation-defining band. The playing is stiff, largely due to original drummer Chad Channing. The songwriting is not yet there either, and it's telling that most of Kurt Cobain's efforts are outclassed by a Shocking Blue cover that isn't even "Venus." That he would put together an LP's worth of material as strong as *Nevermind* just two years later is unbelievable. Yet there are indications of Nirvana's greatness here. After wearing out a copy of *Meet the Beatles!*, Cobain had unlocked the secrets of pop songwriting effectively enough to write the disarmingly simple "About a Girl." He hadn't yet figured out how to marry that sensibility to the squall that consumes the rest of *Bleach*. Krist Novoselic snakes out his first great bass line in the opening moments of the record, and "Blew" is further indication that Cobain could really write a song. His obsessions raise their misshapen heads often in the ones that follow: the hateful underbelly of Small Town USA (darkly hilarious "Floyd the Barber"), the crushing of teen spirits ("School"), his own perceived freakishness ("Negative Creep"), and his troubled upbringing ("Mr. Moustache," a bitter ode to his dad). This is the raw material of a really important and really good band. The pieces haven't been fastened together yet, but they would be soon enough.

THE PIXIES: *DOOLITTLE*

There isn't a damn thing about the Pixies that makes sense. Four unbelievably ordinary people make nightmare music. Black Francis's primal screams don't seem to rip from a place of anger, as they did for John Lennon or Pixie-worshipping Kurt Cobain. They seem to stem from insanity, though Francis, for all his mercurial behavior, seems relatively sane, even academic, as when he shrieks about the Cinema 101 staple *Un Chien Andalou*. So are these screams of irony? Maybe mischievousness is closer to the mark, because even though the seer violence and decaying imagery might be the first things about the Pixies that hit you (and as I explained in my entry on *Come On Pilgrim*, I found them really, really off-putting at first), their humor soon becomes apparent. So do Francis's pop powers, which transformed *Come On Pilgrim* and *Surfer Rosa* from endurance tests into compulsively listenable classics and make *Doolittle* one of *the* greatest rock albums, period.

The original title of *Doolittle* was *Whore*, but Black Francis was afraid the image of this monkey (who has clearly gone to heaven) paired with that title might give the impression that he was a lapsed Catholic, so he changed it. Author's collection.

One incredible song follows another, each in line with the Pixies' unique arena but dashing from a different edge of the field. "Debaser" is dance-club music for drooling nimrods, and I have never been at a party that didn't go nuts when it jittered onto the sound system. "Tame" is New Wave for serial killers. "Wave of Mutilation" is surf music for cretins who've never stepped into the sun. "I Bleed" is a power ballad for the vampiric. "Here Comes Your Man" is Beatle-esque pop for those who think "I know the dirty beard hangs" is a perfectly acceptable pop lyric.

Everything that follows is equally fractured and equally fabulous super-ball bouncing off the jaws of biblical anthems (the sublime "Monkey Gone to Heaven"), spaghetti western sound tracks ("Mr. Grieves"), punk ("Dead"), smarmy lounge-lizard rap ("La La Love You"), and prog meter shifting ("No. 13 Baby"). "Hey" has particularly resonated with fans, quite possibly because it finds Francis dropping some of his most direct and relatable missives ("If you go I will surely die!") in the middle of his usual weird imagery ("The whores like a choir. . . . This is the sound that the mother makes when the baby breaks!"). "Silver" is music for descending a canyon on muleback.

Doolittle is *Revolver* for kids with cracks in their skulls. It's a tasty treat for coprophagists. It's abnormal, asymmetrical perfection, and the greatest album of 1989 and plenty of other years too.

PRINCE: *BATMAN*

When director Tim Burton got the gig directing what would be the biggest blockbuster of 1989, he wanted his usual partner, Danny Elfman, to write the score. Producer Jon Peters had a more original idea. He wanted Prince. Burton and Peters compromised: Elfman would write the proper score, and Prince would contribute a couple of pop songs.

Prince, however, does not know what a compromise is, and when he wrote an entire album's worth of songs, *Batman* found itself with two tie-in albums. Prince's LP may not be as fondly remembered as *1999* or *Purple Rain*, and its smash single "Batdance" tends to get thought of as a novelty today, but *Batman* actually has its share of excellent songs: the grinding "Electric Chair" and "The Future," both of which end up getting ground up and sprinkled into "Batdance," and the frothy "Party Man." "Batdance" itself is the most bizarre and experimental song to ever take *Billboard*'s top spot.

THE STONE ROSES: *THE STONE ROSES*

The Stone Roses is an album with such a looming reputation that it's a little surprising to hear what a slow burn it is on first listen. Just as "I Wanna Be Adored" takes its time creeping up from total silence, *The Stone Roses* may take some time to creep into your consciousness. Ian Brown is not an especially distinctive singer, and his totally offhand delivery is initially underwhelming. The hooks bob up and down in a sea of ghostly atmosphere. The songs tend toward the repetitious.

The album's influential nature, however, is immediately apparent. This is the true birth of Britpop. It is the missing link between the Kinks and Blur, the Beatles and Oasis, the Rolling Stones and the Charlatans (UK). And with repeated listens, the beauty—most of it tripping off John Squire's guitar strings—snuggles more and more under your skin. The offhand becomes the cool. The underwhelming becomes the overwhelming. The hooks start to hook you. The repetitious becomes the anthemic. The idea that this is the best British album ever made—or the best *album* ever made (as *NME* voters crazily voted it in 2006—though to put some perspective on this poll, they also voted albums by Oasis, the Sex Pistols, and the Arctic Monkeys ahead of *Revolver!*)—will probably be hard to swallow for anyone who didn't spend 1989 playing "I Am the Resurrection" and "Fool's Gold" on repeat at raves. Taken under more reasonable consideration, *The Stone Roses* still stands as a transportive and genre-defining album.

THROWING MUSES: *HUNKPAPA*

The common take on *Hunkpapa* is that it's a letdown after Throwing Muses' first two albums. Yes, it's a bit poppier than the abrasive eponymous debut and the askew architecture of *House Tornado*. What *Hunkpapa* may lack in freaky adventurousness it makes up for with strong songwriting and full-tilt energy. "Bea" and "Mania" are explosive excuses for Dave Narcizo to pummel his kit and Kristin Hersh to howl.

The major revelation of *Hunkpapa* is Kristin Hersh's comfort with more conventional pop styles. The single "Dizzy" probably could have been a hit with a major-label push. "No Parachutes," "Fall Down," and "Santa Claus" (a B-side exclusive to the CD edition) are further evidence of Hersh's growing knack for pop songwriting, while the more naturally pop-inclined Tanya Donelly keeps developing the skills she'd fully exploit in a few years with Belly on her two fine contributions.

If there's anything to gripe about with *Hunkpapa*, it's that "Take" doesn't really go anywhere over five minutes, that its horns don't really belong on a Muses record, and that phenomenal bassist Leslie Langston doesn't get as many moments to break out and blister as she did on the previous albums. She'd be gone before the next one, where Hersh and Donelly's pop sensibilities bloomed fully, winning over even the blinkered critics who dismissed *Hunkpapa*.

THE VASELINES: *DUM-DUM*

A lot of the best records of 1989 tended toward the doomy and epic. The Vaselines did not. Former BMX-Bandit Eugene Kelly and new cohort Frances McKee played pithy, peppy pop with touches of punk speed and psychedelic baubles. After a couple of excellent EPs (which is where you'll find all those songs Nirvana covered), they made an LP almost as succinct and just as delectable though not with any shortage of feedback floods and provocative topics. On *Dum-Dum*, diabolical cats, assholey friends, addiction, head-in-the-sand conservatives, stupidity, Jesus' uptight attitude toward sex, and big

This compilation of the Vaselines' first E.P. and LP was a must-have for alterna-kids once Kurt Cobain started championing the band. Author's collection.

motherfuckin' acid trips are fair game for the gleeful twosome, who receive exciting support from rhythm section Charlie Kelly and James Seenan. Eugene and Frances's exorbitant melodic gifts keep these out-there songs totally within reach. The climactic masterwork of *Dum-Dum* kind of flies in the face of all these positive attributes. "Lovecraft" is epic, not particularly melodic, and lyrically obscure. It's ostensibly a tribute to the purple prose of horror writer H. P. Lovecraft. What the sparse words have to do with him are lost on me. The track still pushes forward like a psychedelicized rocket ship. A big motherfuckin' trip.

1990

Popular myth tells us the nineties arrived when Kurt Cobain first struck the opening riff of "Smells Like Teen Spirit" in 1991. A look over the previous year's best albums may tell us otherwise. Much of what would define nineties rock—its Grrl power, grunge, Britpop, angst, irony, do-it-yourself inventiveness, and uncommercial commerciality—were already brewing while Phil Collins and Bon Jovi were still dominating the charts. Really, the best nineties rock—Nirvana notwithstanding—never dominated the charts, so that may be an irrelevant distinction to make.

Never mind all that, though, because even if the term "alternative rock" was not yet on the lips of every trend-hopping A&R turkey, 1990 was still when MTV dropped groups as weird as They Might Be Giants and Jane's Addiction into regular rotation. Branching further into the pop-culture landscape, it was also when television finally got cinematic and profoundly artistic, as one of the decade's best albums commemorates. All this innovation started well before *Nevermind*. It started in 1990.

AFGHAN WHIGS: *UP IN IT*

After self-releasing their debut, *Big Top Halloween*, Cincinnati's Afghan Whigs landed with Sub Pop and put out the album that saw at least half of their persona in place. By melting grunge into the seemingly antithetical sounds of Philly soul, Afghan Whigs created a unique new monster. The half still missing was consistently great songwriting, though some of the material on *Up in It* is definitely memorable: the boiling "Retarded," the lurching "Southpaw," the grinding "Hey Cuz," the stumbling "You My Flower," the bluesy and groovy "Son of the South," and the almost Byrds-like "In My Town," which is especially cool since the band would never do anything so jangly again. When the songs aren't great, the Whigs slather on enough intensity that it almost doesn't matter. Even though he had yet to transition from cutoff sweats and combat boots to three-piece suits and wingtips, singer Greg Dulli already had his Bad Motherfucker act down, talking shit on "Retarded," waxing inelegantly wasted on "Hated" and "Hey Cuz," calling out good ol' boys on "White Trash Party," and, of course, engaging in stormy sexual politics on "You My Flower," "Son of the South," and "Sammy."

Afghan Whigs put arresting and unsettling images on their album covers. Well, at least until that album with the astronaut on it. That cover sucked. Author's collection.

ANGELO BADALAMENTI (WITH JULEE CRUISE): *SOUNDTRACK FROM* TWIN PEAKS

Break *Twin Peaks* into its components, and it doesn't seem like a show that would revolutionize TV. It's a bit of a cop show, a bit of a soap opera, a bit of a sitcom, a bit of a who-done-it, a bit of a high school drama, a bit supernatural—nothing uncommon to the small screen. However, the way David Lynch and Mark Frost assembled the series disassembled the vast wasteland.

The same could be said of the series' sound track, which toyed with such boring genres as cocktail jazz, MOR fifties, white blues, and New Age. The way Angelo Badalamenti executes this music—with its eerie melodies (sometimes cooed by Julee Cruise) and unexpected developments—subverts the genres it simulates. Superimpose that incredible music over Lynch and Frost's incredible images, and you have two incredible entities inseparable from each other. Hearing "Laura Palmer's Theme" without picturing the doomed character grinning back from her prom photo is just as unthinkable as watching Audrey Horne sway around the Double R Diner without hearing "Audrey's Dance."

Badalamenti got his start scoring Ossie Davis's *Gordon's War* (1973) and a cop movie with Carroll O'Connor and Ernest Borgnine called *Law and Disorder* (1974). His most fruitful collaboration began in 1986 when David Lynch hired him to coach Isabella Rossellini as she prepared to play a nightclub singer in *Blue Velvet*. Lynch and Badalamenti forged a quick friendship and wrote the meterless, new-wavey "Mysteries of Love" for the film together. Lynch then hired Badalamenti to write the jazzy, noirish *Blue Velvet* score. That same sensibility infused his work on *Twin Peaks*. The three-note synthesized bass line of "Falling" kicked off the show each week, masterfully setting the tone for all the off-kilter crime, romance, comedy, and dreaminess to follow. Each episode closed with the gorgeously creeping piano-and-synth duet "Laura Palmer's Theme." In between was a symphony of chromatic jazz bass lines, brushed drums, squealing saxophones, echoing clarinets, and, occasionally, the ethereal voice of Julee Cruise singing under Badalamenti's direction. Its sound track came two spots shy of *Billboard*'s top twenty and resonated with listeners as disparate as ambient Moby and thrashing Anthrax. No nineties show changed television the way *Twin Peaks* did, and Angelo Badalamenti's music played a starring role in that development.

THE BREEDERS: *POD*

So Kim Deal was getting antsy under the Black Francis regime and decided she needed a break from being a Pixie. Meanwhile, Tanya Donelly was having similar feelings in fellow New England combo Throwing Muses. Sharing their frustrations while touring Europe with their bands, Deal and Donelly decided to start up a side project. Oddly, Tanya was less committed to it than Deal was, and she ended up contributing less material to the Breeders' first album than she did to the Muses' records. She'd ultimately return to her original band to contribute two of her— and their—best songs before going off on her own commercially successful path with Belly.

Vaughan Oliver was the creative mastermind behind the covers of so many 4AD albums. For the cover of the Breeders' *Pod*, he is the subject. Kevin Westenberg photographed Oliver with eels strapped to his underwear. Author's collection.

But first came *Pod*. Disturbed and sugary sweet, this is a worthier successor to *Doolittle* than the Pixies' own *Bossanova* would be. Deal's writing can be fragmented, but it is never shapeless. In fact, the most fractured thing on the record is a cover of the Beatles' "Happiness Is a Warm Gun." The original songs are bubble-gum–pop singles through a fish-eye lens, sometimes shadowy ("Metal Man," "Lime House," "Glorious," "Oh!," "Iris"), sometimes bouncy ("Hellbound," "Doe," "Fortunately Gone," the Donelly-cowritten "Only in 3's") but always spot on. Steve Albini's bottomless production gives it elephantine power.

On their next album, the Breeders would shoot pop through a Cuisinart and end up with a hit record shocking even in the anything-can-happen days of 1993. However, the Breeders' first album is their most consistently great one.

GUIDED BY VOICES: *SAME PLACE THE FLY GOT SMASHED*

As far as a lot of people are concerned, the Guided by Voices story doesn't really start until 1992's *Propeller*—or even 1994's *Bee Thousand*. Those folks are missing out on one of the band's greatest achievements. In 1990, Robert Pollard (often with help from little brother Jim) composed a song cycle that is disturbing and depressing—a couple of descriptors not usually used for the fun-loving beer guzzler. On *Same Place the Fly Got Smashed*, Bob took a much darker view of alcohol, crafting a shattered song cycle about a drinker's degrading descent and ultimate death.

It all starts with a fleeting sound collage that vomits into two minutes of crazed bellowing and screaming. From there, *Same Place the Fly Got Smashed* starts folding some treats into the mix: the popped-up "Pendulum" and "The Hard Way," the prayer-like "Drinker's Peace," the hammering "Mammoth Cave," the emancipatory "How Loft I Am?," and "When She Turns 50," a ballad that—no exaggeration—should have placed Robert Pollard in the same league as Paul McCartney and Brian Wilson. Interspersed among these shards of pop perfection are more uncompromising numbers like the groggy "Ambergris," the chilling "Star Boy," and the black-hearted epics "Local Mix-Up/Murder Charge" and "Blatant Doom Trip." *Same Place the Fly Got Smashed* is one of the finest albums Guided by Voices ever made, which means it's one of rock and roll's finest albums.

JANE'S ADDICTION: *RITUAL DE LO HABITUAL*

Jane's Addiction crept out of the same Sunset Strip scene that farted out its share of devil-horns-waving hair bands. Unlike those poseurs, Jane's Addiction exuded real danger with the creepy, drugged out, and weirdly hippie-ish *Nothing's Shocking*. That debut also showed that Perry Farrell, Dave Navarro, Eric Avery, and Stephen Perkins could write something as traditionally catchy as "Jane Says" without clearing their air of decay. On their second album (and last before an extended breakup), they limited their established funky hard rock to an opening run of brief songs as good as anything on *Shocking*. The second side is totally different: a suite of extended tracks about personal loss. This is the greatest stretch of Jane's Addiction music on disc and some of the most dramatic music by any nineties artist. With its enthralling lick and commanding string arrangement, "Then She Did" is a landmark, though the throbbing "Three Days" and Eastern-psych–influenced "Of Course" are fantastic as well. Aside from being a great musical achievement, *Ritual de lo Habitual* was also a massive success, penetrating the *Billboard* Hot 100 and going double platinum in the United States, proving that alternative rock was already a prominent stone in the mainstream in 1990.

If record stores thought that sculpture of the naked conjoined twins with flaming heads on the cover of *Nothing's Shocking* was a bit much, they must have simultaneously messed their pants when Janes's latest arrived with Perry Farrell's art depicting a nude *ménage a trois* inspired by the song "Three Days." To appease the Walmarts and other such family-friendly retailers that have no compunctions about selling semiautomatic weapons, Perry provided an alternative cover with the First Amendment printed on it. Author's collection.

THE LA'S: *THE LA'S*

Britpop became a post-grunge phenomenon throughout the world in the mid-nineties. It had really been around before the decade began in the form of Pulp, who brought the wit and detached cool; Stone Roses, who brought the drugginess; and the La's, who brought the sixties influences. In 1988, the latter band released their most famous single, and "There She Goes" covers all those bases with a lyric that might have been about a girl and might have been about heroin and a melody that might have been lifted off *Rubber Soul*.

Two years later, that song found a home on *The La's*, which also cut bits of the Kinks ("Son of a Gun"), the Who ("I Can't Sleep"), and the Smiths ("Timeless Melody") into the blend without diluting the La's' own distinctive features—namely, Lee Mavers's dirty rasp and immaculate songwriting. Every song on *The La's* is excellent, though bassist John Power's irritation with playing these songs caused him to leave the group, which pulled the bricks from the band's foundation. They never made another record, though the one they did has had serious legs. It would be hard to imagine the most identifiable Britpop sounds without *The La's*. Oasis never did anything one-tenth as good.

THE PIXIES: *BOSSANOVA*

The Pixies ended the eighties with a true masterpiece, but real tensions were starting to grow in a band that always seemed to be feigning intensity. Kim Deal was irked that Black Francis was getting all the CD space and went off to form her own group in the wake of *Doolittle*. The Pixies were not over yet, but Francis and Deal's relationship pretty much was. When the band reconvened to make their fourth album, Francis was basically running the show unchallenged, but he didn't really have the material.

That is apparent on the written-in-the-studio *Bossanova*, which is a significant step down from the greatness of *Doolittle*. Let's not forget that *Doolittle* sits on a very high step. Greeted as a bit of a disappointment, *Bossanova* is actually an excellent record despite some bits of filler toward the end ("Blown Away," "Hang Wire"). Some of Francis's best songs are here. "Velouria," "Allison," and "Is She Weird" drag the Pixies' core weirdness into the pop toy box as assuredly as "Here Comes Your Man" did on *Doolittle*. *Bossanova* also contains the Pixies' two prettiest songs, "Ana" and "Havalina," as well as one of their most assaultive, though "Rock Music" does feel a little lazy compared to earlier terrors like "Tame," "Something Against You," and "Nimrod's Son." *Bossanova* isn't very intent on being scary, though. It feels more like the Pixies' effort for wider popularity. Considering that they tried to break big with songs about aliens, pigs, and jazzman Mose Allison, they weren't exactly selling out.

SONIC YOUTH: *GOO*

Defiantly discordant, existentially experimental, New York City's Sonic Youth was
an unlikely major-label signee. But 1990 was
when this kind of move, which would define
nineties rock, really started happening. Sonic
Youth played the game with a set of songs
commercial enough for the major label
DGC—well, commercial for Sonic Youth.
"Dirty Boots" is tuneful, but its feedback
torrents weren't going to get it played alongside "Cherry Pie" on Z100. The single "Kool
Thing" is even more immediately appealing,
its bendy riff exerting more gravity than Jupi-
ter, but Kim Gordon sneering "Hey, Kool
Thing . . . are you gonna liberate us girls from
male white corporate oppression?" wasn't
the kind of thing the audiences that Wilson
Phillips and Roxette numbed could digest.
And what the hell would anyone make of
Gordon's hypnotic take on "Rock and Roll

Geffen gave Sonic Youth some
guff over Robert Pettibon's cartoon on the cover of the band's
major-label debut. Apparently,
the suits thought its suggestion
of violence would not go over
well at Walmart. The band dug in
their heels, and the two Walmart
shoppers who like Sonic Youth
were rewarded with an art-
fully packaged CD. Author's
collection.

Heaven": "Tunic (Song for Karen)"? Ironic subject matter, relentless noise,
and confrontational politics would become more accepted after Nirvana
blew open the doors in 1991, but Sonic Youth set the stage with *Goo*.

THEY MIGHT BE GIANTS: *FLOOD*

Flood is the album that introduced non-cultists to the quirky work of They
Might Be Giants. In the final year that hair metal was rock's unchallenged
moron champion, there was nothing on MTV like "Birdhouse in Your Soul"
and "Istanbul (Not Constantinople)." They were children's songs for adults
(and possibly some children). The refreshing nerdishness of these two hits
flows all the way through *Flood*, a kooky composite of genre parodies and
teacher's-pet lyricism. History, science, and civics lectures are all on the
lesson plan. Great tracks rule—the singles "Twisting in the Wind," "Particle
Man," "We Want a Rock," "Someone Keeps Moving My Chair"—though
John Flansburgh and John Linnell's attempts to work in R&B forms don't
work, especially when they try to force heavy-handed social commentary

into phony funk on "Your Racist Friend" or lounge-lizard crooning over awkward reggae in "Hearing Aid." Much more interesting is the inclusion of a series of wacky miniature themes that show off what a fount of ideas these guys are.

SUZANNE VEGA: *DAYS OF OPEN HAND*

Suzanne Vega was branded an insular folkie after her debut album and had a huge pop hit about child abuse on her second. She continued to shape-shift with her third album, which often sidelined her trademark acoustics and storytelling for mystical songwriting and trippy synthesizer space-scapes. Because of those synths, *Days of Open Hand* might seem a little too trapped in its era at first blush, but like *Purple Rain* or *Hounds of Love*, it is an album that makes the most of its seemingly dated arrangements and is unimaginable any other way. Banks of pre-*Nevermind* synths are as integral to these songs as Vega's cool voice and canny words about prognostication or the dehumanizing experience of voting are. She also takes advantage of more organic sounds on the revolutionary romance "Room Off the Street," the cheerfully macabre "Men in a War," the snapshot of the aftermath of a suicide attempt "Fifty-Fifty Chance," and "Tired of Sleeping," a song to which any new parent can relate. Whether trafficking in guitars or Fairlights, *Days of Open Hand* is always a transporting experience, especially once it soars past its poppy opening quartet of tracks to rocket into the depths of space with "Institution Green," "Those Whole Girls," "Big Space," "Predictions," and "Pilgrimage."

1991

And so, as every boilerplate VH-1 documentary about hair metal or the nineties or music or whatever reminds us, "then everything changed." Cue Kurt's guitar riff and the gym full of rioting grunge puppies. The year 1991 was that of Nirvana, flannel shirts, and a liberating cry of disdain for all the hairspray, leather, and cock waving of the previous half decade. Grunge may not have been as gross as hair metal, but it was ultimately just as limited, and Nirvana stands greasy head and slumped shoulders above most of their peers because Kurt Cobain possessed a way with a pop hook that very few other Seattle groups did. And when surveying 1991, the other pop adepts and not the grungies are the artists who still hold up today.

Yet, because 1991 is the year that guitar-based rock found a sound to replace the main one of the previous decade, it also feels like the year the nineties really began. It is the first year the CD outsold the cassette. Such decade-defining bands as Pearl Jam and Smashing Pumpkins released their debuts that year. The decade-defining festival, Perry Farrell's Lollapalooza, first hit the road in 1991 with an eclectic lineup that included Jane's Addiction, Siouxsie and the Banshees, rapper Ice-T, industrialists Nine Inch Nails, the funky Fishbone, the shouty Rollins Band, the shouty and political Rage Against the Machine, and a hipster freak show. That communal, cross-cultural spirit was also alive in the ethos of a new generation that unconsciously took a lot of its cues from the hippies of their parents' day. Kurt Cobain would famously tell his fans in the liner notes of Nirvana's

Incesticide compilation, "If any of you in any way hate homosexuals, people of different color, or women, please do us a favor—leave us the fuck alone! Don't come to our shows and don't buy our records." The genre that gave us "Brown Sugar" and Axl Rose would begin moving away from overtly misogynistic lyrics, and women with guitars would start gaining greater opportunities to express themselves to larger audiences. Sadly, rock musicians "of different color" would remain rare.

MY BLOODY VALENTINE: *LOVELESS*

For psychedelic intoxication in unmeasured proportions, nothing came close to *Loveless* in 1991. It's the sound of a brain drugged beyond functionality. That makes the album an acquired taste and possibly a listen appropriate only for very specific moods (or activities) despite often sitting at the top of lists of 1991's best albums. You may not always feel like listening to *Loveless*, but when you do, it will immobilize you quicker than an overdose of STP. From those swooping, thick streaks of absurdly affected guitar that begin "Only Shallow," *Loveless* is a scary, overwhelming experience. The incongruent sweetness and calm of Bilinda Butcher's vocals makes the experience all the more unsettling. Kevin Shields seems intent on disorienting the listener with his dense production and queasy "let's clear the uncommitted from the room" pieces like "Touched." Those who stick around and pay attention will detect great beauty glimmering out of the viscous "To Here Knows When" and "I Only Said" and vigorousness in "Loomer," "When You Sleep," and "What You Want."

NED'S ATOMIC DUSTBIN: *GOD FODDER*

Ned's Atomic Dustbin may owe their unique version of punk to having two bass players (Alex Griffin leads high up on the neck; Matt Cheslin holds down the bottom), but strong songs and kinetic energy make *God Fodder* exceptional. Even with those two basses—and added touches of percussion and keyboards—the band's self-production is thin, but Dan Worton's detailed, tireless drumming makes tracks like "Grey Cell Green," "Throwing Things," and "Capital Letters" powerful. The band's attitude also elevates *God Fodder* far above the mass of the class of 1991; their joyful performances contrast the prevailing grumpy mood, and even if the title of the frustrated "Happy" is meant to be ironic and singer Jonn Penney always sounds like he's purposely holding back, the song *sounds* like a complete expression of pure happiness created to send hordes of kids pogoing to the heavens.

NIRVANA: *NEVERMIND*

I was sitting on the sofa at Phil's house and watching MTV (see the entry on *Come On Pilgrim* a few chapters back) when I first felt the earthquake that rattled so many other teenagers in 1991. At the time, you rarely saw a guitar band on Music Television that didn't purse its lips and whip around its bleached locks. This guitar band was decidedly different. Phil described them as "Metallica with the lead singer from R.E.M." With their self-directed gaze, grotty guitars, and primally screaming singer, they reminded me of Plastic Ono Band–era John Lennon. They certainly didn't have a thing in common with Poison or Warrant, and those superstars would soon find themselves on the incline as droves of young people wandered away from such fantasies and toward the tough yet surreal realities of Kurt Cobain and Nirvana. I soon found myself doing the nearly unimaginable: buying an album that came out more recently than 1979.

An album as over-discussed as *Nevermind* is hard to discuss from a fresh perspective and tempting to criticize. The idea that it "changed everything" seems irrelevant today, especially since the alternative window it opened closed after just five or six years despite indie bands and labels claiming victory when Nirvana's second album displaced *Dangerous* by commercial juggernaut Michael Jackson from the top of *Billboard*'s album chart in January 1992. Like any blockbuster record by Jackson, Madonna, or Def Leppard, *Nevermind* spewed a series of singles, although only "Smells Like Teen Spirit" was a significant mainstream hit. *Nevermind*'s success sparked a major-label signing frenzy that saw former underground groups such as Shudder to Think (Epic), Urge Overkill (Geffen), and Afghan Whigs (Elektra) end up with Big Six–owned labels only to put out an album or two—shedding a good deal of their indie-era eccentricity in the process—before collapsing within the system. Meanwhile, the door that subsequently let in mainstream pop superstars such as Britney Spears, the Spice Girls, and the Backstreet Boys is still wide open today (and doesn't that image-focused pop scene have a lot in common with the hair metal scene Nirvana was supposed to have vanquished?). Released on the major label DGC (owned by MCA at the time), *Nevermind* wasn't an independent record anyway, and, frankly, it didn't really sound like one. Butch Vig's production is too slick by several quarts, and that isn't a minor flaw. *Nevermind* also popularized the most overused prank of the CD era: the hidden bonus track. After a ten-minute silence following the final song listed on the CD case, "Something in the Way," you'd hear an unlisted track known as "Endless Nameless"—at least you would if you happened to purchase the second pressing of *Nevermind* (it was accidentally left off the first pressing). When Phil and I went to Caldor together to buy *Nevermind*, his copy had "Endless Nameless," and mine didn't. No biggie. It's not much of a song.

Nevermind still remains a powerful, emotional, and, perhaps most significantly of all, musical experience. Kurt Cobain's love of the Beatles didn't exactly produce a lovably poppy album, but it did inspire the strong melodies that make "Come As You Are,"

Geffen once again got skittish about a cover selected by one of their hip new signees when Nirvana submitted this photo of a—*gasp!*—naked baby. As the company began planning alternate artwork, Kurt Cobain suggested they just label his preferred cover with a sticker reading "If you're offended by this, you must be a closet pedophile." Check mate. Author's collection.

"Drain You," "In Bloom," "Something in the Way," and "On a Plain" timeless songs.

It's also tempting to give Kurt Cobain all the credit, as he wrote the mass of the material that makes *Nevermind* feel like a greatest-hits comp and delivered it with an emotional intensity that seemed to be missing from rock since Lennon died (perhaps since he'd released *Plastic Ono Band*). Yet so much of the album's might booms off of Dave Grohl's drum skins. Ultimately, *Nevermind* is best appreciated not as some sort of game-changing, era-defining historical document but as a dozen tracks composed with true craftsmanship that create a sustained mood and are played and sung with whopping commitment. Isn't that true of all great albums?

PEARL JAM: *TEN*

Pearl Jam was the band that came closest to competing with Nirvana during 1991's grunge boom. They helped yank Seattle into the pop limelight when surfer Eddie Vedder caught the wave of dreary self-examination that defined the town's scene. *Ten* just missed the top spot of *Billboard*'s album chart, and two of its singles landed in the top five of that magazine's mainstream rock singles. A number of groups rushed to cop the album's sound.

Ten was successful, but it failed to deliver a fresh sound or a bunch of great songs. Where Nirvana zipped, Pearl Jam dragged. *Ten* was incredibly influential, but it didn't influence much good unless you're so addicted to Vedder's mumbly vocal style and the band's sludgy characterless licks that you're willing to endure Stone Temple Pilots or Bush. "Jeremy," "Black," "Even Flow," and "Oceans" are pretty good adolescent angst odes, but *Ten* is not an album that rises to its reputation. Pearl Jam would do more interesting things on their subsequent albums and develop a more cult-like following, but because they became increasingly unwilling to play the industry's standard promotional games, their wide influence peaked with their first album.

THE PIXIES: *TROMPE LE MONDE*

"Happy" probably isn't a word anyone would use to describe the Pixies' first albums, even if stormy stuff like "Isla de Encanta," "Tony's Theme," and "Debaser" are elating. *Trompe le Monde* is what it sounds like after those clouds break and the sun blazes through. That L.A.-day sound is ironic considering how relationships in the band had deteriorated, leaving *Trompe le Monde* as the band's final album for more than two decades and their last one ever with Kim Deal. Gil Norton's clean, bright production makes rabid stuff like "Planet of Sound," "The Sad Punk," "Space (I Believe In)," and "Distance Equals Rate Times Time" sound as playful as puppies. So do Francis's funny missives about the superficiality of campus life and underground cultures, architecture, aliens, and sea monkeys in paradise. On "Palace of the Brine," "Motorway to Roswell," and "The Navajo Know," the Pixies embrace the kind of uncomplicated pop they'd dallied with on "Dig for Fire." This may not have been what a lot of fans wanted from such an edgy group, but at least it gives the comforting impression that the Pixies went out a lot happier than they actually did.

R.E.M.: *OUT OF TIME*

After years as college radio stars, R.E.M. started popping up elsewhere on the dial with *Document* and *Green*. By *Out of Time*, they were full-blown stars. The album was a Grammy-devouring, number one smash. "Losing

My Religion" scored a scene on *Beverly Hills 90210* that was the talk of high school halls. Michael Stipe sang "Shiny Happy People" with the Muppets.

Twenty-five years after the hype, the album feels a bit inconsistent because of some misplaced ambitions. R.E.M.'s folky pop and hip-hop are a terrible match, and "Radio Song" is an awkward attempt to funk up the band's usual sound as KRS-One performs a rap better suited to Fred Flintstone in a Fruity Pebbles commercial. The unpalatably cloying "Shiny Happy People" should not have gone farther than that performance on *Sesame Street*.

The excellent tracks—of which there are many—make it impossible to dismiss *Out of Time*. The band's effervescent joyousness fully matures on "Near Wild Heaven" and "Me in Honey" (a much tastier duet with fellow Athenian Kate Pierson than "Shiny Happy People"), while their moodiness does the same on "Low," "Texarkana," and "Country Feedback." Peter Buck's percussive mandolin brings out new textures in the material. The inconsistency of *Out of Time* will continue to be an issue on most of R.E.M.'s megastar albums of the nineties, but as will be the case on *Automatic for the People*, *Monster*, and *New Adventures in Hi-Fi*, the journey is still worth taking.

SMASHING PUMPKINS: *GISH*

It was easy to lump Smashing Pumpkins in with the grunge crowd. They looked like they pulled their togs from the same Salvation Army bin that the Sub Pop bands did. Their guitars were sludgy, their lyrics humorless, self-obsessed, and self-loathing.

However, there was something else going on with this band from the very beginning. Sludgy and sloppy are not the same thing, and Billy Corgan is a studio perfectionist who often dubbed most of the instruments on his records himself. This is less of an issue on *Gish*, which reveals more of a band spirit than the group's later albums would. Jimmy Chamberlain is a seasoned timekeeper as indebted to Gene Krupa as he is to John Bonham. With her lead vocal on the haunting "My Daydream," D'arcy Wretzky crystallized her icy persona even if it wasn't always her on bass. While Corgan's whiney persona would soon overcome his music to a degree that it's hard to feel much true love for his project, he and his words are obscure enough on the first Pumpkins LP to vaporize that issue. Nothing on *Gish* is as tiresomely "woe is me" as "Disarm" or self-consciously cutesy as "Today" would be on the band's next album. *Gish* is a collection of somewhat gothy, somewhat metallic, somewhat psychedelic tracks that are heavy and dreamy in just the right proportion.

MATTHEW SWEET: *GIRLFRIEND*

Simple, Beatle-esque pop was a rarity in both the alternative and the non-alternative top forties of 1991, making Matthew Sweet's breakthrough a tough album to categorize and a bracing gust of fresh air. There was nothing like his trend-damning stew of jangling guitars, multitracked harmonies, and Liverpool-meets-L.A. melodies at the time. *Out of Time* is the only other album from 1991 with love songs as uncomplicated and irresistible as "I've Been Waiting," "I Wanted to Tell You," and the title track, none of which are delivered with shiny happy sarcasm. Sweet could sulk with the best of them, but none of his peers had the guts to do so with the tenderness he displays in "Nothing Lasts," "You Don't Love Me," or "Winona." This is no twee fest, though, and tracks such as "Holy War," "Thought I Knew You," and "Does She Talk?" bite, as does the ravaged guitar work of Television's Richard Lloyd. On "Divine Intervention" and "Holy War," Sweet tackles big issues with a clarity that seemed lost amidst grunge's random surrealism and muddled pseudo-poetry.

This vintage photo of Tuesday Weld signals Sweet's sixties obsession. Author's collection.

THROWING MUSES: *THE REAL RAMONA*

Perhaps it was the departure of Leslie Langston, whose superb yet angular bass helped shift Throwing Muses music off kilter. Perhaps it was the growing confidence of sidekick Tanya Donnelly. Whatever the reason, Throwing Muses achieved the ultimate balance between their pop inclinations and artier tendencies with *The Real Ramona*. I wonder if Kristin Hersh was moved to compose such delectables as "Counting Backwards," "Him Dancing," "Golden Thing," and "Graffiti" after Tanya presented "Not Too Soon," which is as brilliantly bouncy as Belly's best and as aggressively tuneful as a carousel calliope. I wonder if Kristin then hated herself so much for treading so deeply into pop territory that she felt compelled to write the raving, terrifying "Hook in Her Head." I wonder if "Not Too Soon" also inspired Tanya to build on her accomplishment by grabbing new bass player Fred Abong and rushing off to form Belly. No matter what the circumstances were that inspired Throwing Muses to create these songs, *The Real Ramona* is their most perfect album and, to my ears, the very best of 1991.

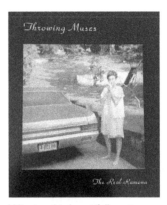

Winning this beautifully maintained copy of *The Real Ramona* for a reasonable price on ebay was one of my greatest coups as a vinyl hunter. Author's collection.

U2: *ACHTUNG BABY*

In 1987, U2 completed their transition from being a particularly successful college rock band that had not yet cracked the top ten of *Billboard*'s album charts to the biggest band in the world. *The Joshua Tree* went to number one in almost every major market in the world, U2 filled stadiums and ruled MTV, and Bono became rock's hunky conscience. Yet the edge of a band once edgy enough to deserve a member called the Edge had gone blunt. The punky energy that made *Boy* and *War* so keen was softening into a sound more befitting top-forty radio, and by the time U2 released the bluesy, snoozy sound track for their major motion picture *Rattle & Hum* in 1988, they were as edgy as a beach ball. Yet they still sold millions of albums, so it is to U2's credit that they then started fucking with their formula at the height of their popularity.

U2 wasn't the first minister to marry rock and roll and club-based dance music (that kind of thing had already been happening in the Madchester scene for a few years), but they were certainly the biggest. So new recordings such as "Mysterious Ways" and "Even Better Than the Real Thing" sounded fairly radical when they commandeered the video waves in 1991. Digging deeper into *Achtung Baby*, there are somewhat more out-there things such as the sensual "The Fly," the surging "Acrobat," and the pounding "Zoo Station," all of which hint at what U2 could do when they let their imaginations go wild.

1992

In the year that the effects of *Nevermind* really rippled through rock, "grunge" was the industry's favorite buzzword. The year's most prominent modern rock bands were Nirvana, Pearl Jam, Alice in Chains, Soundgarden, Screaming Trees, Soul Asylum, and the Pearl Jam/Soundgarden supergroup Temple of the Dog. The year 1992 began with *Nevermind* bumping Michael Jackson's *Dangerous* off of the top spot of *Billboard*'s album charts, which a lot of commentators took as symbolic of something or other. That same year, filmmaker Cameron Crowe cashed in on the craze with *Singles*, a grunge rom-com of all things. Designer Marc Jacobs presented a grunge fashion show. Yeesh.

Yet the less grungy sounds that would soon be championed as "alternative" by a press desperate to put some sort of label on all the eclecticism were already in effect. Many makers of the best albums of 1992 may have had a pair of Doc Martens in their closets, but their music drew on a wide variety of sources: the girl-group sound of the sixties, punk, folk, twee pop, industrial, blues, and hip-hop.

AFGHAN WHIGS: *CONGREGATION*

There are germs of Afghan Whigs' roguishness and soul leanings on *Up in It*, but the unique approach that separated them from the generic grunge scene didn't crystallize until *Congregation*. The band's third album is not only focused in vision with its fixation on back-alley sexual politics, self-loathing, and chemically induced surrender, but it's also consistent in quality. *Up in It* offset great songs with forgettable ones. *Congregation* shuffles really good tracks ("Kiss the Floor," "This Is My Confession," "Let Me Lie to You") with really great ones. Greg Dulli lets himself go completely with "I'm Her Slave," the piano-pumped "Turn on the Water," "Conjure Me," "Dedicate It," and the rabid bonus track "Miles Iz Ded." You can practically hear his drool splattering the mic. On the acoustic "Tonight," the mania lets up, but the intensity doesn't. It's a bit of a preview of the more textured tone to come on the Whigs' next album, and there is a bit of a transitional flavor to *Congregation*, but the album still holds up as an intense experience on its own. Plus a cover of "The Temple" is the most listenable thing *Jesus Christ Superstar* ever spawned.

ARRESTED DEVELOPMENT: *3 YEARS, 5 MONTHS, AND 2 DAYS IN THE LIFE OF . . .*

De La Soul brought Technicolor positivity to hip-hop, but their wackiness tended to mute their more pointed political positions. Arrested Development took that stance a lot more seriously. They celebrate and support humanity in a wide range of scenarios across *3 Years, 5 Months, and 2 Days in the Life Of* . . . . "Mama's Always on Stage" is a moving show of support for single mothers. "Mr. Wendal" is an equally inspiring lesson on how to treat homeless people. "Children Play with Earth" is a call for kids to quit staring at that damn TV and get outside and enjoy nature. "Raining Revolution" does the same for adults regardless of weather conditions. The sweet life lessons get less universal when Speech starts preaching Christianity, but like George Harrison on *All Things Must Pass*, he never gets so sanctimonious or finger waggy that the music loses its cool. An atheist may roll eyes at the lyrics of "Man's Final Frontier," but the beat is as hard as anything NWA hit. "Fishin' for Religion" also recalls Harrison's attitude toward spirituality, voicing the frustration that comes with believing in God but mistrusting organized religion. The hit "Tennessee" expresses the pain of enlightenment in a country with a history of injustice of which many people would rather remain in ignorance.

Arrested Development's intelligence and complexity made them striking if not necessarily unique in hip-hop, but what made them really stand out was their revolutionary musicality. Although they did their share of sampling the usual suspects (Sly Stone, James Brown), they also used drummer Rasa Don, guitarist Brother Larry, and saxophonist Larry Jackson to bring their music to life. This, along with their unthreatening messaging and eclectic style, helped Arrested Development to become the first major alternative–hip-hop crossover group. They were also the first hip-hop band to appear on MTV's live acoustic showcase *Unplugged*, and their videos for "Tennessee," "Mr. Wendal," and "People Everyday" went into rotation as part of the channel's "Buzz Bin" alternative showcase.

ANGELO BADALAMENTI: *TWIN PEAKS: FIRE WALK WITH ME (ORIGINAL SOUNDTRACK)*

Fans were furious when ABC gave *Twin Peaks* the axe in 1991. Many were flummoxed when David Lynch released its feature-film prequel/sequel the following year, though critical assessment of the cryptic and brutal *Twin Peaks: Fire Walk with Me* has improved dramatically in recent years. Less controversial is its sound track album, which has even been called the "best ever" by *NME*. Maestro Angelo Badalamenti revisits and expands some themes used in the series, taking the simple synthesizer pieces "New Shoes" and "Audrey's Prayer" and swelling them into the sensuous pure-jazz title theme and the achingly beautiful "Questions in a World of Blue" featuring Julee Cruise's sad serenade, respectively.

Beyond similar jazzy ("The Pine Float," "Don't Do Anything [I Wouldn't Do]," "Moving Through Time") and somberly synthy (the spellbinding "Voice of Love") pieces, Badalamenti and Lynch add colors new to the *Peaks* palette. There's Lynch's punishing blues "The Pink Room," which pulses on a sneering string bass riff, Badalamenti's own manic beatnik vocal on the hip-hop–influenced "A Real Indication," and the label-defying horror show "The Black Dog Runs at Night." A mind-bending medley feels like a mini–Badalamenti's *Greatest Hits* by morphing from nostalgic fifties pop to one of his saddest synth themes to a particularly tear-jerking take on "Laura Palmer's Theme" to the familiar yet still grand TV theme song. As the cherry on this slice of pie, the Little Jimmy Scott–crooned "Sycamore Trees," one of Badalamenti and lyricist Lynch's most mysterious concoctions, gets a second life after its use in the gob-smacking final episode of the TV series. You may hate the film, but *Twin Peaks: Fire Walk with Me* is an irresistibly dreamy slice of music.

DAISY CHAINSAW: *ELEVENTEEN*

Daisy Chainsaw's influences are recognizable—the grinding riffs of metal, the velocity and ferocity of punk, the flightiness of psychedelic—but the London quartet used those influences in a totally bizarre synthesis. Daisy Chainsaw got a lot of their personality from their freaky lead singer. KatieJane Garside presents herself as a sort of mud faerie, a waif splattered in filth whose cute coos and girly giggles inevitably froth over into serial-killer shrieks. Opening tracks "I Feel Insane" and "You Be My Friend" are her manifesto: she is crazy, and you will be her friend, like it or not. From there, Daisy Chainsaw is either slashing out outrageous riffs (the metal-mania "Dog with Sharper Teeth," the ass-wagging "Love Your Money") or freaking you out with aural nightmares (the queasy "Waiting for the Wolves" and "Everything Is Weird"). With "Hope Your Dreams Come True," Daisy Chainsaw shoot out of both sides of their double-barrel with a single show-stopping bullet. With "Natural Man," they do the truly unthinkable by whipping off a catchy little acoustic pop tune unlike anything else on the record. Set in a bathtub, "Natural Man" also ends with rock's best fake-out fart joke.

This surreal cover is not as cuckoo as the music on *Eleventeen*. Author's collection.

FRENTE!: *MARVIN THE ALBUM*

At a time when thick, swampy guitars brewed in Seattle were the major rage, Frente! must have seemed as though they came from another place. For we Americans, they did come from another place—Australia—and I say "must have" because the band wasn't really known in the United States until their debut album was finally released (with the addition of their cover of New Order's "Bizarre Love Triangle" and the moving "No Time" and the loss of a couple of minor tracks) in 1994. That's when there was more of a framework for their sunny, Kinky pop within the more expansive "alternative" scene, and *Marvin the Album* does feel perfectly in tune with the multicolors of 1994 when like-minded artists such as the Cardigans, *Parklife*-era Blur, and ¡Simpatico!-era Velocity Girl did their thing. So in its way, *Marvin the Album* both looks back to fresh sixties pop and forward beyond grungy 1992. Each track is a lovely lit- tle gem, and though Angie Heart's mile-wide smile is audible across most of them, *Marvin* is no village idiot. It begins on a melancholic note with the dusky "Girl," revisits that mood on "Pretty Friend" and the breakout single "Labour of Love," mourns on "Reflect," and expresses outrage while playing the roles of El Salvadorians amid a civil war on the jazzy "Cuscatlan." Yet the prevailing mood is happy. "Accidentally Kelly Street," "Most Beautiful," "See/Believe," "Ordinary Angels," and "Dangerous" could be prescribed as mood-altering drugs.

Considering the title of their debut album and its cover image of some sort of parallel universe of fish and broccoli, it is clear that Frente! took their work very seriously. Author's collection.

GUIDED BY VOICES: *PROPELLER*

Guided by Voices hit their first major artistic peak in 1990 with the conceptual *Same Place the Fly Got Smashed*, but that didn't matter much when Robert Pollard was in debt from self-financing albums too few people bought. Having lost core members Mitch Mitchell and Kevin Fennell, Bob suspected that his band was coming to an end and resolved to make one final Guided by Voices disc. This fond farewell would blossom into a true labor of love. The guys individually custom- ized each of its 500 LP sleeves, and Pollard selected some of the best from his bottomless barrel of tunes.

Since there wasn't the controlling feel of the basic indie rocker *Self-Inflicted Aerial Nostalgia* or the doomy *Same Place*, *Propel- ler* ends up as the most eclectic Guided by Voices release yet, highlighting everything the band did so well and often with nothing more sophisticated than a cheap cassette four-track machine. There are takeoffs of big

Guided by Voices and friends custom designed all 500 sleeves for the original run of *Propeller*. By the end, they were just glu- ing scraps of cardboard from beer cases onto the sleeves. This 2021 reissue of *Propeller* on Skat Records uses one of the more artful designs. Original copies have sold for as much as $6,200, but I got this reissue on Deep Discount for a very reasonable $17. Author's collection.

arena rock ("Over the Neptune"), psychedelia ("Mesh Gear Fox," "Weed King"), heavy metal ("Lethargy," "Some Drilling Implied"), and hot-rod rock ("Quality of Armour," "Exit Flagger") as well as classic Guided by Voices power pop ("Unleashed! the Large Hearted Boy") and pure weirdness ("Particular Damaged," the odds-and-sods medley "Back to Saturn X Radio Report," "Ergo Space Pig"). There are even moments of beauty with "Red Gas Circle" and "14 Cheerleader Coldfront," a collaboration with prodigal bandmate Tobin Sprout. And so the album that was to be Guided by Voices' good-bye pulled the unexpected trick of setting all the essential elements of the band's "classic" era—ultra–low-fi recording, unfettered eclecticism, Tobin Sprout—into place. *Propeller* ended up vivifying interest in the band, which would go on to make the string of albums that launched them into low-fi legend.

JULIANA HATFIELD: *HEY BABE*

While a lot of independent groups were getting grungy or disturbingly surreal or aping the Smiths in the late eighties, Boston's Blake Babies were a fresh breath of pure pop. As soon as the trio split in 1992, bandleader Juliana Hatfield didn't waste a second getting her solo career started, and she did so with her most Blake Babyish disc. *Hey Babe* is a smashing solo debut with all the sweet-pop melody and power-pop guitar work of the Babies' best. Yet on tracks like "Nirvana" (about Hatfield's infatuation with the band with which everyone was infatuated in 1992), "Get Off Your Knees," and "No Outlet," she gets heavier on her own than she ever did with her old band. I love it when an artist drops the album title in a song that isn't named after the album, and I get chills every time Juliana breaks that lulling, droney guitar break in "No Outlet" by sneering "Hey babe, there's something I can keep."

Some critics sneered at Hatfield's girlish voice and accused her of being either too self-deprecating or too self-aggrandizing, failing to realize how patronizing the former gripe is and how shortsighted the latter one is. Just as a lot of critics missed the humor in Morrissey's tales of woe, they also let the subtle funniness of "Ugly" ("I'm ugleeeeee with a capital U") and the knowingly absurd self-aggrandizements of "Everybody Loves Me But You" soar over their heads. As over-the-top as these songs are, there is still a layer of true woe beneath them that makes them work as humor and weepy diary entries.

PJ HARVEY: *DRY*

In 1992, Polly Jean Harvey punctured the grunge lethargy like a razor through a dingy flannel. She neutered most of her guitar-wielding peers with legit rage and a distressingly expressive voice weaned on Siouxsie Sioux and Captain Beefheart. That voice and her filthy guitar work led the eponymous trio PJ Harvey (Steve Vaughn: bass; Rob Ellis: drums) through eleven bluesy blades on their debut *Dry*. Her lyrics are cast in Black Francis shadows but with a keen feminist message that stands her apart from the Pixies' surrealism for the sake of surrealism. She decries male expectations of female beauty ("Dress") and propriety ("Sheela-Na-Gig") and celebrates the least celebrated aspects of the female body ("Happy and Bleeding").

DRY DEMOS

Dry is so unhinged, so genuinely scary, that it can be easy to lose sight of how good songs such as "O Stella," "Oh My Lover," and "Water" are (standouts like "Dress," "Happy & Bleeding," "Victory," and the heady "Sheela-Na-Gig" are tougher to mask). The eleven demos included on a limited, double-disc edition of *Dry* on the Too Pure label brought Harvey's skills into clear focus, revealing the traditional craft, even prettiness, of songs that would sound monstrous on *Dry*. Although demo discs tend to be historically interesting yet ultimately disposable, *Dry Demos* actually enhances the proper album. It's also a unique and rewarding listen on its own merits.

R.E.M.: *AUTOMATIC FOR THE PEOPLE*

While *Green* and *Out of Time* have their dusky moments, R.E.M. balanced them with a lot of shiny, happy pop tunes. Aside from the giggly Dr. Seuss/Tokens tribute "The Sidewinder Sleeps Tonight" and the oddly romantic Andy Kaufman memorial "Man on the Moon," *Automatic for the People* keeps its chin down and its brow furrowed. This is even true when lyrics about the naked bliss of swimming at night ("Nightswimming") or fucking ("Star Me Kitten") don't reflect such

R.E.M. made great records, but their album covers sure are ugly. Author's collection.

grimness. That dark tone makes *Automatic for the People* enchanting as a whole, even if its relentless pop-culture referencing is too cute and its centerpiece "Everybody Hurts" is a lyrically and musically insipid ball of corn that demands a sprint to the "next" button on your CD player. When it's at its best—as it is with the elegant "Nightswimming," the clashing "Ignoreland," the bitter "Monty Got a Raw Deal," and the woozy "Sweetness Follows" (a far less cloying boost of encouragement than "Everybody Hurts")—*Automatic for the People* is automatically one of R.E.M.'s best albums.

SHUDDER TO THINK: *GET YOUR GOAT*

By welding hard rock and indie rock to angular prog artiness and Craig Wedren's otherworldly wailing, Shudder to Think forged one of the most unique sounds of the late eighties (Wedren's predilection for performing naked with a banana balanced on his shoulder gave them a pretty unusual look too). It took them several tries to figure out the best way to use that sound. Neither of the band's first two albums had the consistently great material of the *Ten Spot* EP released between them. Shudder to Think finally produced an album's worth of awesomeness with *Get Your Goat*. Anyone could probably stitch together a bunch of disparate and difficult influences, but not every band can do it while delivering the hooks of glammy tracks such as "Love Catastrophe" and "Shake Your Halo Down." "Pebbles" shows just how much pop mileage they could get out of a single, bizarre line. I defy anyone to hear it and not spend the next week hiccupping "Poor little girl screaming traffic in her hair."

Shudder to Think did not go easy on their audience, and both Wedren's voice and fractured pieces such as "Rain-Covered Cat" and "Funny" seem designed to clear out the uncommitted. The committed should probably be committed, but they will also find themselves obsessed with a band unlike any other. Poor little girl screaming traffic in her hair.

SLOAN: *SMEARED*

Although a cult band outside of Canada, Sloan became superstars at home because of their effortless way with a pop hook and their individual distinctiveness. Guitarist Patrick Pentland is a masterful dispenser of magnetic hard-rock riffs. Bassist Chris Murphy brings the shiny, extroverted power pop. Guitarist Jay Ferguson's pop is more introverted and twee. Drummer Andrew Scott supplies the quirk. Each member is a virtuosic musician, a singer, and a songwriter.

Anyone who came to the Sloan party a little late might be surprised by the band's beginnings. While Cheap Trick–meets–the Beatles power pop ruled the mass of Sloan's future recordings, they entered the Halifax scene with a noisier, indier sound deeply indebted to *Isn't Anything*–era My Bloody Valentine. The band's melodiousness was not exactly absent in songs too catchy for the real Valentine. In fact, if you drain off the rivers of feedback that drown "Underwhelmed," "I Am the Cancer," and "Take It In," those tracks would be fit for Sloan's poppier sophomore LP *Twice Removed*. You wouldn't even have to strip much from the appropriately sweet "Sugartune," the dreamy "What's There to Decide?," or the rapturous "500 Up." "Raspberry," "Marcus Said," "Left of Center," "Lemonzinger," and "Two Seater" are edgier, more innately dissonant, and further removed than twice from subsequent Sloan discs. These are the tracks that make *Smeared* cool and unique, though the poppier ones are what make it and the rest of Sloan's career worth your attention.

THEY MIGHT BE GIANTS: *APOLLO 18*

Despite all the styles They Might Be Giants run through over nineteen tracks of *Flood*, noisy guitar rock is on short order. They made up for that in 1992 with *Apollo 18*. Although it lacks an indelible anchor like "Birdhouse in Your Soul" and it's grunge-era arrangements deprive it of *Flood*'s sonic diversity, *Apollo 18* is another terrific album. The opening track, "Dig My Grave," is as intense as these intellectuals ever got, but an intrusive violin is an early indication that predictability still isn't on Flansburgh and Linnell's to-do list. The single "I Palindrome I," "My Evil Twin," the fifties-ish "Narrow Your Eyes," and "See the Constellation" are standout rockers, though esoteric weirdness has not been left out on the porch completely. The disjointed "Spider" weaves a retro-horror vibe, and the single "The Guitar" deconstructs conventional pop, leaving shards of "The Lion Sleeps Tonight" among the debris. The strangest stroke of *Apollo 18* is a cluster of seconds-long mini-songs called "Fingertips," which was intended to provide zillions of possible listening experiences to listeners comfortable with the "shuffle" button on their CD players.

SUZANNE VEGA: 99.9F°

Suzanne Vega had already shown she was much more than some wan New York City folkie when she made the mysterious, multilayered *Days of Open Hand* in 1990, but not enough people heard that record for it to really change her reputation. Then a few months later, the production team known as DNA created a dance remix of the a cappella "Tom's Diner," which became a huge hit and a surprisingly successful marriage of Vega's literacy with a hard dance sound.

Perhaps that is what inspired her to go further out on a limb with her next personal project. With the assistance of producer Mitchell Froom, Vega created a near-industrial landscape totally distinct from any of her previous sounds and received her sharpest support yet from such aces as Richard Thompson, Los Lobos' David Hidalgo, and Attraction Bruce Thomas, who contributes some of the most memorable bass lines of his career, which is saying a lot.

Vega puts such collaborators to good use with her best selection of songs. While *99.9F°* is not exactly a concept album, there is a running theme of the body running off course as she tells tales of a patient dizzy after receiving a traumatizing diagnosis ("Blood Makes Noise"), a woman coolly noting the feverishness of her lover (the title track), a woman imagining the object of her desire is addicted to diagnosis ("([If You Were] In My Movie"), a child examined for sexual abuse ("Bad Wisdom"), and former golden boys and girls finally hitting bottom ("When Heroes Go Down"). In the twisty "As Girls Go," she stands back in amused confusion as a male takes full control of his body by slipping into a more suitably feminine skin. With "In Liver-

pool," she creates her masterpiece, a blissful showcase of production grandeur, *Abbey Road* arpeggios, gothic-romance poetry, and intense longing.

The overheated bodies often at the center of such lyrics receive complementary textures and temperatures in a record that sounds as fiery as its flame-engulfed cover image due to Froom's steam-works production and Vega's exploitation of her voice's latent sexiness. All of this makes for not just the best album of 1992, and one of the best albums of the 1990s, but one of the best albums of the entire pop era too.

High temperatures are a running theme of *99.9F°*, and its cover picks up on that theme. Author's collection.

1993

The relative success of Nirvana (whose revolutionary "Smells Like Teen Spirit" was only the thirty-second-best-selling single of 1992), Pearl Jam, Alice in Chains, and their ilk jolted record execs into signing other guitar-based bands that weren't necessarily fashion plates fit for MTV. And this was not limited to Seattle-style sludge. While the grunge years were rendered in shades of plaid and gray, the expanded palette of 1993 is vibrantly varied. The influence of sixties psychedelia and British Invaders, seventies punk and hard rock, and even country, experimental music, and jazz were apparent in the seemingly noncommercial groups that suddenly found themselves signed to indies and majors alike. The pundits scrambled for an umbrella term for these eclectic new artists and settled on "alternative," implying that specimens as disparate as Björk and Urge Overkill were on the same team simply because neither of them sounded like Janet Jackson, Garth Brooks, or Kenny G.

AFGHAN WHIGS: *GENTLEMEN*

One of the most interesting consequences of Kurt Cobain's stardom was that a whole generation of new rockers tuned into his politics, particularly his feminism. Nirvana didn't just do away with hair metal's cod swagger; they also diluted its misogyny. Almost overnight, it became painfully unhip to regurgitate the sexism that had been one of rock's favorite ingredients since its beginnings. A lot of musicians became so self-conscious about coming off as cock rockers that they avoided rock's swagger altogether, opting to hunch at center stage while staring down at their Converse All-Stars.

The one group of young bucks who really bucked this trend was Afghan Whigs. Having started as another bunch of grungy scruffs with flannel shirts tied around their cutoff sweatpants, the Whigs had evolved into R&B-worshipping slick-o's in baggy black suits and two-tone wingtips by 1993. Their glamour was as antithetical to their peers' images as their willingness to get their hands dirty in the muckiest aspects of sex was. In 1993, no rocker but Greg Dulli would have warbled anything as caked in machismo cheese as "Ladies let me tell you about myself; I've got a dick for a brain and my brain is gonna sell my ass to you."

That line also betrays the self-loathing that distinguishes *Gentlemen* from the cock-rock records that preceded it. Jagger and his progeny displayed little remorse when using women and throwing them away like yesterday's papers. It's not so easy for Dulli, who gets entangled in a relationship that inevitably hits a brick wall in this despondent song cycle. There is no joy in his sex, no confidence

Afghan Whigs even courted controversy with their cover art. The implications of this photo are . . . well . . . pretty unsettling. Author's collection.

in his swagger, and no macho escape hatch from the feelings that get in the way of his penile escapades. On "What Jail Is Like," "Debonair," "Gentleman," and "Fountain and Fairfax," the music is as tumultuous as the messages are dejected. On "When We Two Parted," the instrumental "Brother Woodrow/Closing Prayer," and "My Curse," on which guest vocalist Marcy Mays gives voice to Dulli's opponent in romance, it is transcendent. With *Gentlemen*, the Afghan Whigs became one of the few male alternative bands of 1993 to deal with sex directly and admit how complicated it can be.

BELLY: *STAR*

Although *Pod* reflected Tanya Donelly's preference for perky pop, she didn't have much input into that album. Having left Throwing Muses because she knew she'd always play second fiddle to stepsister Kristin

Hersh, Donelly ended up basically playing that same instrument behind Kim Deal in the Breeders. So she split to form Belly, a revolving-door band of which she was the one stable member.

There is little that is stable about the death-obsessed surrealism she unleashes on her band's debut record. *Star* balances Donelly's witchy atmosphere and pop adeptness across a hefty fifty minutes and fifteen songs that never feel like the usual CD-age overkill. That's because each one of these songs is perfect, from "Someone to Die For," the creeping miniature that opens the set, to "Stay," the twilighty ballad that closes it. Belly whips up torrents on "Angel" and "Dusted," gets the legs swinging with "Slow

When I was 19, I threw a crazy *Sixteen Candles*–type house party while my parents were away. That's when someone spilled something or other on my precious copy of *Star*, hence the wrinkles on the CD booklet pictured here. Author's collection.

Dog," frightens with "Low Red Moon," and enchants with "Untogether." When I first heard "Feed the Tree" on New York's WDRE in 1993, I fell in love. I was elated that I could finally enjoy some music from my own generation. Donelly makes the most of her dodgy pitch with seductive coos, tortured wails, and joyous whoops. *Star* is resplendent in the influence of the trippy pop that returned in the nineties, but its pervasive darkness and occasional dissonance keep it completely contemporary.

BJÖRK: *DEBUT*

Few artists have followed their muse like Björk Guðmundsdóttir. She got her start as a child singer in her native Iceland and achieved international success with her band the Sugarcubes in the eighties. After that band disbanded in 1992, Björk revived her solo career with an eclectic mix of dance music, jazz, and pop. Whether she is performing to drum machines and synths or live drums and saxophones moaning diminished chords, Björk's voice is always the most expressive instrument on *Debut*. She might manipulate it into wildly different places from phrase to phrase, but whether she's wailing, whispering, or crooning, she is almost always exuding joy. Almost. Björk conveys angst in the confounded and pounding "Human Behavior" and melancholy in "Anchor Song"—the two songs that bookend *Debut*. In between, she celebrates the perfect mate in "Venus as a Boy" and what she gets up to with him in "Big Time Sensuality." When self-doubt and cynicism were the most fashionable postures, Björk was a rush of sunshine, and *Debut* was one of the most inspirational albums of 1993.

BLUR: *MODERN LIFE IS RUBBISH*

The sounds that would come to define Britpop had been in the airwaves since the days of the Jam and Madness. However, the term was specific to nineties bands that took their cues from such artists and the ones that inspired them, most obviously the Kinks, the Who, and Small Faces. They were groups that never tried to hide their cockney accents, sang of English mundanities, and styled themselves like the mods of yore.

The best and most unabashed of the Britpop bands, Blur began their career more under the influence of dance groups like the Happy Mondays than Ray Davies. Blur's debut, *Leisure*, was a decent but fairly undistinguished effort in that area. They fully resigned themselves to the artists they love most on their second album. Damon Albarn shared Ray Davies's very British mode of satire and social commentary. His distinctively unrefined cockney inflection unifies an eclectic platter of hippity-hoppity anthems ("For Tomorrow), noisy rockers (the jolting "Advert"), twitchy retro New Wave ("Pressure on Julian"), sparkling pop ("Star Shaped"), wistful ballads ("Blue Jeans"), music hall ("When the Cows Come Home"), power pop ("Turn It Up"), and psychedelia (the single "Chemical World," "Oily Water," "Miss America").

The one downside of *Modern Life Is Rubbish* is that it's a bit unwieldy, a problem not unique in the CD age when groups were too eager to take advantage of all seventy-five minutes the medium afforded. Blur take the CD's capacity to absurd heights by ending their album with fifty tracks of four seconds of silence. They'd get that tendency under control on their next album.

THE BREEDERS: *LAST SPLASH*

Tanya Donelly's pop sensibilities are apparent on the Breeders' first album even though *Pod* has few of her songs. After she left the band, Kim Deal let weirdness take off completely. The weirdest thing about *Last Splash* is that it became a big crossover hit on the strength of "Cannonball." Kim Deal takes the classic pop song, smashes it with a sledgehammer, and puts the pieces back together in a pot-reeking mosaic. "Cannonball" is a bunch of disparate shards that don't belong together. Josephine Wiggs's Bootsy bass line. Kelley Deal's Tiki slide guitar. Kim Deal's garage-brewed power chords. Obscure lyrics about how the Marquis de Sade is not all that. A special spotlight for mic feedback. Yet "Cannonball" became one of *the* signature alterna-pop hits. It just goes to show that a stellar tune is a stellar tune no matter what angle you shoot it from.

"Cannonball" and the rest of *Last Splash* exemplify how marvelously upended the pop scene had become in 1993. Before that year, it was absurd to think that a band could break out with such angular avant-gardism, which bubbles through on a kick line of oddball album tracks: "No Aloha," "Roi," "Mad Lucas," "Hag." The Breeders had not totally leaned away from their sweeter inclinations. They make perfectly accessible pop of the sighing "Do You Love Me Now?," the Beatlesque "Invisible Man," the Who-esque "Divine Hammer," the hard-riffing "Saints," and the country-time whimsical "Drivin' on 9." Deal's kooky humor still keeps these songs well clear of normalcy.

GRANT LEE BUFFALO: *FUZZY*

By adopting a southern persona despite a Northern California origin, Grant Lee Buffalo could have been the Creedence Clearwater Revival of the nineties, but their music is much closer to the rustic spaciousness of the Band. Grant Lee Phillips is a masterful storyteller though a more abstract one than Robbie Robertson. The aching "Fuzzy," the rousing "Shining Hour," the lurching "Wish You Well," the playful "Dixie Drug Store," and the surly "Stars N' Stripes" are all literate and moving. Phillips possesses the best male voice of his era: velvety in its low range, ghostly in its falsetto, a crescendo in its howling middle. Rock and roll hadn't produced a singer of such depth since Van Morrison (one of Phillips's idols). Bassist, keyboardist, and producer Paul Kimble works the echo knob like Phil Spector, but *Fuzzy* is still a spacious and crisp production. Kimble would muddy up that clarity a bit on Grant Lee Buffalo's next album and produce a masterpiece of American rock.

NIRVANA: *IN UTERO*

Although it wouldn't be known for several months, 1993 was the year that the poster boys for nineties rock released their final studio album. Everyone knew Kurt Cobain had problems, but even as desperately as he flaunts them on *In Utero*, few could imagine things would end as they did on April 8, 1994, when he succumbed to depression and killed himself.

In 1993, it was fashionable to cry out from the abyss, but Cobain's scream was authentic, and authenticity is paramount on *In Utero*. Here Nirvana fully realized their arty noise without compromise. Cobain said the band's management and label hated the abrasive record and wanted "another *Nevermind*," but Butch Vig's pseudo-metal production did a disservice to *Nevermind*'s raging songs. Steve Albini produces *In Utero* with mid-fi ferocity. Dave Grohl's drums never sounded so gargantuan. Grohl beats the blood out of his kit on "Scentless Apprentice" and the stop-start nightmare "Milk It." Cobain screams them like he only did in fits on *Nevermind*.

Yet he had too much love for pop to exclusively fill *In Utero* with noise bombs. "Serve the Servants" sounds like "Help!" blasted through a blownout woofer. "Heart Shaped Box," "Pennyroyal Tea," and "Rape Me" would have fit well on *Nevermind*. "All Apologies" and "Dumb" are pretty songs that showcase the extent of Cobain's talent. The guy was a great songwriter, able to tap into the simplicity that made John Lennon's early songs so instantly pleasurable and the emotional rawness that made his later ones so real. How Kurt Cobain might have developed that talent beyond *In Utero* is one of rock's saddest unanswered questions.

LIZ PHAIR: *EXILE IN GUYVILLE*

When sex seemed like it was off the table for male groups in 1993, no one seemed happier to pick that topic up and claim it for women than Liz Phair. Her debut double album *Exile in Guyville* could have been read as a response to *Gentlemen* if it wasn't already intended to be a response to the Stones' *Exile on Main*. Or was it? In truth, Phair did not compose *Guyville* as a track-by-track answer to *Main Street*. She used the Stones' album only as a template to help her arrange her songs. Parallels between the albums don't hold up well under scrutiny. Phair didn't need gimmicks anyway because her record—as Stonesy as the mesh of guitars and producer Brad Wood's behind-the-beat drumming are—is utterly unique. Wood's production is low-fi, only a bit more sonically plush than Phair's "Girly

Sound" demo tapes that made her name in the underground.

When *Exile in Guyville* was released, Liz Phair became an alternative It Girl, and the *Guyville*–as–response–to–*Main Street* connection made nearly as good copy as her outrageously frank lyrics did ("Fuck and run—even when I was twelve," "I can be a real cunt in spring," "I want to be your blow job queen," and so on). However, the "potty mouth" label trivialized her talent. Phair used odd chords creatively, possessed an unrefined yet poignant voice, and wrote lyrics with more humor than a lot of her devotees recognized. While her tales of sexual and romantic woe can stir the emotions—especially when set against such gorgeously lilting tunes as "Dance of the Seven Veils," "Canary," "Explain It to Me," "Shatter," and "Gunshy"—there is wonderful exuberance in the defiant single "Never Said," "Help Me Mary," "Soap Star Joe," "Strange Loop," and the thoroughly empowered "6'1"." Even when her heart's getting broken, Phair doesn't want anyone thinking she's a victim.

I once woke up to find a bunch of my records sitting in a puddle of water on my bedroom carpet. My most prized album suffered the worst cover damage—I couldn't even bring myself to open the shrink wrap of *Exile in Guyville* for about ten years, which is very out of character for me. In any event, I chucked the fucked cover and illustrated my own one on a blank white sleeve. I still have no idea where the water came from. Author's collection.

PJ HARVEY: *RID OF ME*

PJ Harvey's second album is one of the worst-sounding great albums. Steve Albini's productions could be overpowering (see *In Utero*), but *Rid of Me* is tinny, hissy, overly compressed, and claustrophobic. In a way, this is fitting, because *Rid of Me* is one jaw-clenching record, even when drummer Robert Ellis breaks out of his shackles on the title track and Polly Jean starts bellowing. Albini mixed the album to sneak attack listeners lulled by nearly silent passages with sudden explosions of volume. The band's chaotic blues and the violently sexual imagery of "Rub 'Til It Bleeds," "Legs," and "50 Foot Queenie" are just as assaultive. Most of *Rid of Me* sticks to a monochromatic guitar/bass/drums grind, but the *Psycho*-string arrangement of

"Man-Size Sextet" is an early indicator of the eclecticism that will make the rest of PJ Harvey's career even more interesting.

MATTHEW SWEET: *ALTERED BEAST*

When critics fell over themselves to praise Matthew Sweet's breakthrough, *Girlfriend*, they tended to focus on the music's sweetness: his glimmering overdubbed guitars, the comforting retro-ness of his Beatles and Byrds references, the classic concision of his songs, the lushness of Fred Maher's production. So when Sweet followed that big hit with the deliberately messy and acidic *Altered Beast*, a lot of the critics were baffled. Perhaps they hadn't been listening close enough to the underlying nastiness of *Girlfriend* tracks such as "Thought I Knew You," "Does She Talk?," and "Holy War." If they had been, *Altered Beast* would have seemed like a more logical progression as Sweet builds on the bitterness of such songs with production to match. Yes, Richard Dashut is best known as Fleetwood Mac's smash-era producer, but Sweet didn't hire Dashut for his pristine work on *Rumours*. Sweet was more interested in channeling the sloppy derangement of *Tusk*, and just as *Tusk* was more fascinating and challenging than *Rumours*, *Altered Beast* is—in my perhaps unpopular opinion—a similar improvement over *Girlfriend*.

The cover of *Altered Beast* was released in five different covers: blue, green, purple, orange, and yellow. If this book wasn't in black and white, you'd see that I own the blue one. Author's collection.

The polish flakes away as rusty guitars roar, well-deep drums bash, and Sweet sneers and spits. "Dinosaur Act," "Devil with the Green Eyes," "Ugly Truth Rock," "In Too Deep," and especially "Knowing People" are straight-up mean, and their loathing feels more authentic than the mass of Sweet's grungier contemporaries because of his pop rep. It sounds like he was willing to burn down his critical goodwill for the sake of getting something toxic off his chest. He did make room for some of the more soothing pop styles of *Girlfriend*, though "Life Without You," "Time Capsule," "What Do You Know?," and "Someone to Pull the Trigger" do not skimp on the despair. So while the production sounds messy, the vision is actually quite focused, and for my money, *Altered Beast* is Matthew Sweet's underappreciated peak.

U2: ZOOROPA

Zooropa is divisive not only because Bono's new yen for adopting obnoxious, ironic personas wore out some less committed fans but also because the music is so weird. The thing is, U2 could do weird very well. If "Mysterious Ways" was a bit of a welcome change after the tedium of "Angel of Harlem," then "Numb" is a revivifying plunge into an icy stream. It takes everything we came to know about U2—including Bono's bombastic pipes—and wipes them away.

That's the most revolutionary cut on *Zooropa*, but the title track, the hilariously discofied "Lemon," the trashy smash "Daddy's Gonna Pay for Your Crashed Car," and "The Wanderer"—starring guest vocalist Johnny Cash and guest instrument, a $20 Casio keyboard—are just as far out. Bono's withering perspective of contemporary life goes down more pleasantly with a less hectoring tone and more humor. Only "Stay (Far Away So Close)" doesn't try to rise to the rest of the album's experimentalism.

URGE OVERKILL: *SATURATION*

When Nirvana banished the hair metalists, the leftover poses of seventies hard rock went with them. In their place was a new air of enlightenment. While one might not lament the reduction of Stones- and Zeppelin-style misogyny in rock and roll, the embarrassment that now came with tossing off a big riff or tossing one's long, luxurious hair around was kind of an unfortunate trade-off. Most bands now felt they could really traffic in that stuff only ironically. This resulted in a lot of bad music and a lot of twee popsters flashing the devil horns to get a giggle out of their shoe-gazing fans.

Irony threatened to turn formerly vital rock and roll into a joke once and for all and may partially account for the near death of the genre by the end of the nineties. Yet Cobain was also a big fan of Urge Overkill, whose big riffs harkened back to the days of Boston and Bad Company and whose hair was simply grown for flipping. That's probably because corporate rockers like Boston and Bad Company were really dumb, but Urge Overkill wielded wit like a hidden stiletto in James Bond's boot heel.

The key to Urge's greatness is their genuine love of the music they seem to be parodying (seventies corporate rock), their punk roots evident in their early releases for Touch and Go Records, and their supersharp wit. The baker's dozen tracks on *Saturation* aren't funny because they sound like Boston send-ups; they're funny because chief writers Nash Kato and "Eddie" King Roeser are funny guys who mine Fidel Castro, daytime and evening soap operas, and pickups halted by misread sexual proclivities for song lyrics.

Saturation is not a comedy album, though. The bizarrely titled ballad "Bottle of Fur" homes in on the ache of lost love with absolute sincerity (despite Nash's knowingly seventies use of the term "make it"). "Crackbabies" and Roeser's monstrous "Stalker" revive the guys' Touch-and-Go–era punk power. Drummer Blackie O.'s "Drop Out" is a peek at the loser teens still lurking somewhere under Urge's designer sunglasses and velvet smoking jackets. Once you get past the surface humor of *Saturation*, the sincerity of a great rock and roll band playing sincerely great rock and roll is what sets it apart from the ironists with nothing going on below the surface.

US3: *HAND ON THE TORCH*

Rock and hip-hop had collided like chocolate and peanut butter in a Reese's cup as far back as mid-eighties Run-DMC records. Groups like Body Count and Arrested Development made rap fundamentally organic by using live instruments. Us3 took it even deeper into the essentials by fusing it with bebop. Producer Geoff Wilkinson conceived of Us3 as a mash of classic jazz samples, live jazz instrumentation, and Rahsaan Kelly's cool wordiness, which he delivers with all the effortless aplomb of a Freddie Hubbard solo. Samples come exclusively from the Blue Note archives, and in a breakthrough move, *Hand on the Torch* was the first hip-hop release on jazz's definitive label. That was a heartwarming olive branch passed between an old guard that often failed to recognize rap's artistry. It also made sense because Us3's debut is a legit jazz article—and a totally intoxicating one at that. Anyone who doesn't want to move to the Herbie Hancock–sampling smash "Cantaloop (Flip Fantasia)," "I Got It Goin' On," "It's Like That," "Just Another Brother," or "Lazy Day" is just being stubborn.

1994

When the term "alternative" went into wide use to encompass not just the Seattle grunge scene but also indie bands throughout the country, major labels went into a short-lived frenzy to sign any group with shaggy hair and six strings. Groups with decidedly low commercial potential like Tad, Boredoms, Melvins, Ween, Royal Trux, Shudder to Think, and Butthole Surfers went from indie to major. Groups that had previously recorded on shitty four-tack cassette machines were gaining access to relatively plush studios and making bigger and often better albums (though, as we'll see, some decided to keep the fi low—*very* low).

Instead of quashing artists' creativity, the widened spotlight and higher stakes of the major-label era forced them to perfect their work. Consequently, 1994 was an even better year than 1993 as original alternative acts developed their voices in bold ways, excellent new groups entered the ring, and alt grand-parents did some of their best work in years. The year 1994 was the peak for nineties rock and possibly the finest for guitar-based rock since 1968.

THE BEASTIE BOYS: *ILL COMMUNICATION*

The Beastie Boys took off with *License to Ill* in 1986, drawing a huge new fan base that probably had no idea that the wiseass New York City hip-hop trio got their start as a wiseass New York City hard-core punk trio almost a decade earlier. Their work was eclectic and did not totally eschew their beginnings, as anthems such as "No Sleep Till Brooklyn" and "Fight for Your Right" mixed dumb metal riffs and dumb raps. However, the Beasties didn't actually play the guitars on the album, and the way they mocked hair in their videos gave the whole thing the whiff of a grand piss take.

License to Ill was a lunkheaded celebration of all the things white kids love: boasting, partying, getting into trouble at school, running from cops, getting alcohol poisoning, belittling females. Mike D., Ad-Rock, and MCA grew up considerably with their second album, *Paul's Boutique*, which ran with De La Soul's sound collage style, and their third, *Check Your Head*, on which they started revisiting their punk past, playing all the instruments on the aggressive "Gratitude."

Their next album, *Ill Communication*, was the Beastie's Boys' most organic record since their punk days, as the Beasties revisit those roots with much-improved songcraft and less obnoxious humor. Their winking, Quentin Tarantino–era fixation on seventies postures feels kind of puerile today, but everyone sure loved that video for "Sabotage" in 1994, and it was refreshing to hear them thrash their instruments on it and the hard-core "Tough Guy" and "Heart Attack Man." "Sure Shot," "Root Down," and "Get It Together," featuring the sweet slur of A Tribe Called Quest's Q-Tip, are some of their most mature hip-hop tracks.

BLUR: *PARKLIFE*

Parklife was Blur's breakthrough album on a number of levels. They shored up their songwriting, tidied up their production, and scored a crossover hit with the discofied opening track "Girls and Boys." The rest of the album falls in line with the British mod-psych bug that bit Blur before they made *Modern Life Is Rubbish*. Track after track, they wear their influences on their Ben Sherman–tailored sleeves: the Kinks, the Beatles, Scott Walker, Syd Barrett, the Jam, the Clash, and the Stone Roses. They hired *Quadrophenia* star Phil Daniel's to monologue the title track.

In 2010, *Parklife* was one of ten British albums the Royal Mail selected to appear on a series of British stamps. The other selectees that also receive entries in this very book are *Let It Bleed*, Led Zeppelin's fourth album, *The Rise and Fall of Ziggy Stardust and the Spiders from Mars*, *London Calling*, and *Power, Corruption, and Lies*. Author's collection.

Blur's debt to past heroes could have reduced them to a sort of cover band that plays original material if that material wasn't so well crafted. Track after track, lyricist Damon Albarn just keeps hitting it across the pitch. He introduces a neighborhood of citizens colorful in their grayness: the rut-stuck couples of "End of a Century"; Tracy Jacks, who attempts to escape his own rut with a bit of impromptu streaking; the wasted weekend revelers of the punked-up "Bank Holiday"; the misguided Yank-o-phile of "Magic America"; the obnoxious people watcher of "Parklife." Guitarist Graham Coxon and bassist Alex James fashion a forward-thinking edge that demolishes any accusations that Blur offers nothing more than retro caricature.

THE CARDIGANS: *EMMERDALE*

It took some unlikely materials to knit the Cardigans (pun!). Guitarist Peter Svensson and bassist Magnus Sveningsson had a background in the Swedish heavy-metal scene. Singer Nina Persson tended to whisper confidentially. The group's touchstones are the lighter, lusher side of sixties pop: think *Pet Sounds*–era Beach Boys, *Village Green*–era Kinks, Brigitte Bardot, and Sérgio Mendes. Their lyrics are often dour and disturbed or so gleefully twee that they border on the deranged.

Originally released exclusively in the Cardigans' native country (and later given a *Yesterday and Today*–style butchering so it could be merged with their second album, *Life*, for international release), *Emmerdale* is the freshest debut of 1994. It is humorous and conscious of its own pop roots without lapsing into dismal derision even when the group lounges their way through an unrecognizable cover of "Sabbath Bloody Sabbath." "Sick & Tired" has the best flute riffing outside of a Tull album. The bleak "Black Letter Day," the breezy "Over the Water," and the joyous "Rise & Shine" are also remarkable. Each song is a little treasure played by a rhythm section as crisp as a December morning and sung in a voice cool, cute, and commanding.

ELVIS COSTELLO: *BRUTAL YOUTH*

Elvis Costello seemed to lose direction when he stopped working with the Attractions after *Blood and Chocolate* in 1986. There were still lots of great songs, great performances, and interesting ideas, but they did not coalesce into perfect wholes on *Spike* or *Mighty Like a Rose*.

In 1994, Elvis once again called on the assistance of Steve Nieve, Pete Thomas, and even archenemy Bruce Thomas, and when he didn't use Bruce, he used another longtime collaborator, Nick Lowe. Perhaps this is what brought some clarity back to Elvis's vision because *Brutal Youth* is his best album since *Blood and Chocolate* and his best album to not feature the words "and the Attractions" on its cover, even if it probably should have. The band doesn't deserve all the credit, as Elvis brought his strongest batch of songs in years to the project. He regains his old punk pugnacity on "Pony St.," "13 Steps Lead Down," "My Science Fiction Twin," and the skull-crushing "20% Amnesia" (that cold open makes me nuts). The ballads "You Tripped at Every Step," "London's Brilliant Parade," "Still Too Soon to Know," and "Favorite Hour" are some of the most poignant of his career. That clarity extends to his lyrics as he deals with self-help programs, hell, his hometown, his dark side, military rape, and the usual romantic complications in ways that are accessible without sacrificing his intricate wordplay and wordiness.

GRANT LEE BUFFALO: *MIGHTY JOE MOON*

Grant Lee Buffalo debuted with *Fuzzy*, a terrific album with really good songs and a really good sound grounded by Grant Lee Phillips's distorted acoustic guitar and majestic voice. *Mighty Joe Moon* magnifies those strengths a hundredfold. The group dusts off pump organs, Dobros, mandolins, marimbas, banjos, and tablas to animate Phillips's superb songs. You'd have to go back to *All Things Must Pass* or *Surf's Up* to find a composition as perfectly conceived as the aching, soaring, meditative "Mockingbirds." Phillips casts his visionary net widely enough to cover America's history of violence and narrowly enough to ensnare his own dark moods. Paul Kimble's production is not as clear as it was on Fuzzy, but it is considerably more atmospheric. Grant Lee Buffalo sounds like a folk ensemble using the Grand Canyon as an echo chamber. Everything sounds large no matter if it's the sinister onslaughts of "Sing Along" and "Demon Called Deception" or the delicate whispers of "It's the Life" and "Rock of Ages." *Mighty Joe Moon* is a classic of American rock and roll in the tradition of *Blonde on Blonde*, *The Band*, and *After the Gold Rush* and every bit as good as those classics.

GUIDED BY VOICES: *BEE THOUSAND*

Discouraged by a lack of support from their families and the world outside of Dayton, Ohio, Guided by Voices almost called it quits after making 1992's *Propeller*. Response to that album was so strong that it gave their career an adrenaline shot, and they started the whole damn thing up again. *Propeller* was a mix of proper studio recordings and ones they cut on four-track cassette. Although they'd gained wider attention, Guided by Voices decided to stick with no-fi cassette recording and made *Vampire on Titus*, an album as monochromatic as *Propeller* is motley.

For their next album, Guided by Voices continued to strip away all fidelity but returned to the variety of *Propeller*. The resulting album is the favorite of many a Guided by Voices hot freak and one of the nineties' greatest. *Bee Thousand* is like a thirty-six-minute "White Album" recorded in McCartney's basement if he and the other Fabs spent their days guzzling MGD instead of licking LSD. There's so much going on—pseudo-Merseybeat and synth pop, raga and prog rock, avant noise and folk, metal and

The vinyl-only "Director's Cut" of *Bee Thousand* expanded the package to three LPs, which include material that Bob Pollard considered for the album but chose not to include, a few demos, and everything from the *Grand Hour* and *I Am a Scientist* E.P.'s. Author's collection.

weirdo soul, torch balladry and drones, elves, demons, robot boys, buzzards, dreadful crows—and it all goes by so quickly under such a dense layer of white fuzz that it's easy to miss the craftsmanship on first listen. That it requires true immersion to fully appreciate is one of the coolest things about *Bee Thousand* and a key explanation for the cult it developed. I don't necessarily think that it's the greatest Guided by Voices album, but there is no better example of what makes them great.

KRISTIN HERSH: *HIPS AND MAKERS*

After spending the eighties as one of college rock's best and most criminally underrated bands, Throwing Muses entered the nineties in a constant state of upheaval. First to go was Leslie Langston. Tanya Donelly left next. And so, Throwing Muses was now two, and 1992's *Red Heaven* found Kristin Hersh and drummer Dave Narcizo working a bit too hard to make up for their diminished numbers with overwhelming productions of often underwhelming material.

No doubt, Kristin Hersh needed to refresh her creativity. She did so by expanding the gloomy acoustic flavors of "Pearl," the most mesmerizing track on *Red Heaven*, into a whole record. The brilliance of Hersh's first solo album is that she forfeited none of her innate electricity when working solely with acoustics. Take "A Loon," a performance as terrifying as any you'll hear on those terrifying early Muses albums. Her whoops are strokes of pure madness and pure inspiration. But then listen as the track soothes itself into a temple-massaging lullaby. Hersh explores all the possibilities of her voice and guitar.

The rest of *Hips and Makers* presents similar variety even as the mood always suggests thunderheads are rolling in. Hersh cries a haunted duet with Michael Stipe on "Your Ghost," gets plaintive at the piano on "Beestung," rages through "Teeth," exhilarates on "Sundrops," and turns breathlessly desperate on "The Letter" and frisky on the title track. *Hips and Makers* gave the impression that Kristin Hersh might not need a band at all, but it actually provided a more positive function by inspiring her to reinvigorate the Muses to make a couple of superb new albums. Fortunately, she didn't give up on her solo career either, which continues to surprise and thrill.

NIRVANA: *MTV UNPLUGGED IN NEW YORK*

Nirvana's appearance on MTV's *Unplugged* series was the final creative statement from the nineties' defining band and a pop star whose terrible exit from this world swelled his mystique. Kurt Cobain's performance on *Unplugged* has been analyzed like some sort of rock and roll Zapruder film, but such morbid hullaballoo misses the real value of the TV special and its accompanying sound track.

Rather than a sad epitaph, *MTV Unplugged in New York* is a surprise celebration of the best songwriter to emerge from that thing called "grunge," which tended to value sonic sludge over quality tunes. Stripped of their feedback squalls, presented with acoustic

There are those who'd have you believe that every aspect of Nirvana's *Unplugged* appearance—right down to the set design—bore some sort of profound and tragic significance. I'm pretty sure the guys just thought all those candles looked cool. Author's collection.

instrumentation and brushed drums, "All Apologies," "About a Girl," "Pennyroyal Tea," "Come As You Are," and "On a Plain" fully shine as simple pop melodies and chord structures spiced with Cobain's evocative Sylvia Plath–meets–Francis Bacon lyricism. Twenty-five years after all the tragedy and controversy, Cobain's songs are what remain, and they were never given a more naked or elegant presentation than on *Unplugged in New York*.

The album is also significant as a testament to Nirvana's great taste in songs and ability to put their own stamp on diverse selections from David Bowie, the Vaselines, Leadbelly, and the Meat Puppets (that band's Kirkwood brothers accompany Nirvana on three performances here and pull no attention from the show's stars). Cobain's lighthearted, self-effacing between-song banter further deflates the show's reputation for funereal heaviness, but its candlelit atmosphere still leaves *Unplugged in New York* feeling like a fittingly somber final chapter.

PAVEMENT: *CROOKED RAIN, CROOKED RAIN*

The slacker—that unique breed of beflanneled twenty something who uses irony as a smug substitute for sincerity—was a favorite Generation X stereotype. Get used to that word "irony" because we're in the nineties now, and you're going to be seeing a lot of it in the coming pages. Perhaps it was because we were jaded from the cynicism and greed of Reagan's eighties or the fatuousness of that decade's most popular music. Perhaps we white kids who bought and made the rock and roll of the Clinton era no longer had a focused target for our naturally rebellious impulses and simply needed an outlet. We tossed our disdain at everything in sight in the hopes that some of it might stick. Rebels without a clue, as Tom Petty said. And oh, isn't Tom Petty "soooo cool?"

Whatever the cause, those of my generation began seeing everything—as has so often been observed—through quotation marks such as the ones above. (Forgive me, Petty. I legit think you're cool. Sincerely.) Sometimes we'd make them in the air with our fingers for maximum bluntness. We'd praise that thing that corporations or the media or *the man* wanted us to think was cool and spend our disposable incomes on—how about Zima, for another random example—while clawing the air with our air quotes. "Zima is soooo cool," we'd sneer. We'd probably go out and buy a six-pack of it anyway.

That disdain for everything and the inability to recognize our own hypocrisies were chief traits of slackers. And as the nonjudgmental joys of praising the simple freedoms and pleasures that Chuck Berry raved about curdled into Poison's greasy take on them in the eighties, all musicians who did not position themselves behind a riot shield of irony risked looking—in the insensitive parlance of the time—"lame." Some artists, such as Urge Overkill, so committed themselves to the ironic lifestyle that they made a sort of entertaining absurdist theater of it (more on that to come). Some—such as those middle-aged guys in Guided by Voices who'd grown up with a sincere love of Alice Cooper and King Crimson or even younger artists like Juliana Hatfield who would decry "the irony that's ruining rock and roll" without a trace of irony—resisted.

Stephen Malkmus did not resist, though his Slacker supreme act also seemed more self-aware than that of a lot of the kids he serenaded. With his sloppy hair and dress, his sloppy voice, and the sloppy band backing him up, Malkmus seemed like the quintessential slacker, but he was a tough read. Did he sincerely think everything was lame? Or was he putting on his own fans?

With matters of sincerity less relevant after the passing of decades, Pavement rises above a lot of the other groups who struck similar poses with their strong grip on pop songwriting, genuinely funny humor, and willingness to get grueling. They won over critics with their 1992 debut *Slanted and Enchanted*, released on the coolest indie label, Matador, but as many times as I've spun that particular album, none of it has ever taken root in my brain. As far as I'm concerned, they really earned the raves with *Crooked Rain, Crooked Rain*, which contains their most assured run of songs. The singles "Cut Your Hair" and "Range Life" look askance at the contemporary rock scene with withering wit and sharp tunes. They either consciously or unconsciously recycle the rock detritus of more sincere days (the melody of "Silence Kit" pulled right out of Buddy Holly's "Every Day," the lazy Flying Burrito Brothers' back-porch strum of "Range Life"). They play and sing as an apparent afterthought. The rhythm of "Stop Breathin'" is initially so slack that it practically floats off into free time. But then the band tightens up and gets sincerely furious. Anything that hits as hard as that or "Unfair" or that scrawl of dissonance "Hit the Plane Down" can't be a total put-on. Can it?

LIZ PHAIR: *WHIP SMART*

In 1994, I was obsessed with Liz Phair. I'd preach to anyone in earshot that they had to own *Exile in Guyville*. When her second album was scheduled for release on September 20, 1994, I put in a time-off request at work so I could hole up in my room and spin *Whip Smart* over and over. Two things struck me on the first of those spins: I loved it, and I was surprised by how quickly it went by compared to the double length *Guyville*. If that debut was a big bed of emotion to sink into, this new one felt like a scrumptious piece of candy to pop into your mouth.

Actually, *Whip Smart* is only fourteen minutes shorter than *Exile in Guyville* with just four fewer songs. Plus, there are fewer miniature pieces and more epics. Phair stretches some of these tracks with hypnotic, lyrical chants. "I won't decorate my love," "You gotta have fear in your heart," "When they do the double-dutch, that's them dancing." These lines sum up where she's at on *Whip Smart*. The album is uncompromising, even as Phair flirts with more polished pop production (almost every song features bass guitar this time!). It can be paranoid (see "Jealousy"). It also has a wonderful knack for transforming simple memories and nostalgia into something mythic. The opening track reworks "Chopsticks," the first song all piano students learn, into a ribald memoir about summer camp and one-night stands. "Dogs of LA" places Buddha among the California detritus she remembers roaming through, casting a spiritual aura over a song of coming-of-age bonding. The enchanting title track portrays children's games as ritualistic dances while also imparting some exceptionally healthy and heartwarming parenting advice from someone who'd yet to even become a parent. *Whip Smart* is the sound of Liz Phair reaching a bit beyond the low-fi textures of *Exile in Guyville* and getting it just right.

SHUDDER TO THINK: *PONY EXPRESS RECORD*

Good luck trying to define Shudder to Think. Their guitars hit with hardcore impact. Their structures and meters shift like King Crimson's. Their lyrics would confound William Burroughs. And then there's Craig Wedren's voice: keening, falsettoing, hiccupping, whispering, husking, screaming. That voice may be at home in a haunted house, but it has no place in rock and roll. New guy Nathan Larson's sharp riffs on tracks such as "Gang of $," "Nine Fingers on You," and "Chakka" are the best explanation for the stranger-than-fiction fact that Shudder to Think got signed to major-label Epic Records.

Shudder to Think responded to their rising prospects with an all-around first-class product. Ted Nicely's production is thicker and shinier than Eli Janney's brittle work on *Get Your Goat*. The vamping chant of "X-French T Shirt" is pop catchy, and the track went into rotation on alternative and college radio. *Pony Express Record* is still way too bizarre for the big leagues, though. Challenging things like "Sweet Year Old," "Trackstar," and "Full Body Anchor" would have given the grunge puppies hives, and the decision to release the jarring "Hit Liquor" as the album's first single was a veritable act of self-sabotage. It's also a credit to how committed Shudder to Think was to their muse in 1994. They'd make an outrageous grab for mainstream success with their next album.

VERSUS: *THE STARS ARE INSANE*

I discovered Versus when they opened for Liz Phair at the Academy the same day we all found out what happened to Kurt Cobain. It was one of the best shows I've ever attended, partly because the terrible news drew the individuals in the audience together, partly because Guyville's exile was playing songs from such an amazing album, and partly because the opening act was great. Screaming his brains out on the blood-curdling "I'll Be You," Richard Baluyut offered the catharsis we couldn't really expect from someone as low key as Liz.

I then went on the hunt for Versus's debut album, and when I finally tracked down a copy of *The Stars Are Insane*, I learned that their fire and moodiness transferred from the stage to digital disc very well. The songs are gloomy, the production is murky, and the vocals are buried down deep, but that's all part of Versus's allure. Baluyut and bassist Fontaine Toups pack the disc with excellent tracks that transcend their sometimes dated obsessions. "River" deals with the death of River Phoenix. "Solar Democrat" rages about mid-nineties politics vaguely (that vagueness probably reflects the fact that things were

In the pre-ebay age. you had to do some legwork to find certain albums. *The Stars Are Insane* is one I expended a lot of energy on. Others included Team Dresch's *Personal Best* and the Blue Up?'s *Spool Forka Dish*. They were all worth the effort. Author's collection.

actually relatively good in America in 1994). There are indie anthems (the ghostly "Thera"), minimalist drones ("Deseret"), punk screeds ("Solar Democrat"), long fuse ballads ("Janet"), and straight poppers ("Wind Me Up"). The *Stars Are Insane* established Versus as a band to watch, and they fulfilled that promise with their excellent second album, *Secret Swingers*. I'm so glad I didn't stay home to mourn Cobain that April 8.

VERUCA SALT: *AMERICAN THIGHS*

Veruca Salt was a rare real-deal overnight success. They barely had any gigs under their belts when indie label Minty Fresh offered them a deal. That origin is unimaginable when hearing how seasoned Veruca Salt sounds on their debut. Nina Gordon and Louise Post's voices blend like they'd been harmonizing since kindergarten. Their songs are consistently excellent, Gordon handling the more pop-oriented material and Post supplying the heavy rock. Gordon's brother Jim Shapiro and Jim Lack are a granite-solid rhythm section.

Although small-minded critics hacked out comparisons to the Breeders and Liz Phair, Veruca Salt was their own thing—neither as arty as the Breeders nor as light as Liz. They were as committed to hard rock as Urge Overkill but without any of their fellow Chicagoans' irony. There's an evil undercurrent to their music whether they're kicking out the jams or establishing mood with whispery pieces like "Fly" and "Sleeping Where I Want." Their pop sensibilities are fang-sharp too, and they won a big hit on alternative radio with the insidiously catchy "Seether." Although Veruca Salt failed to get as much play with any of the album's follow-up singles, tracks like "Number One Blind," "Victrola," "All Hail Me," and "Wolf" are just as strong.

1995

The year 1995 continued the strong streak begun on the college airwaves two years before. This year, there were few monumental newcomers, but the artists who had been at it since the beginning of the decade produced some of their most mature work to date, and it was those discs that constituted the year's best. Little did most of them know that the craze for guitar-based rock was about to peak, that girls from the spice shelf and boys from the backstreet were lurking around the corner on the precipice of walloping success and walloping influence, primed to limit popular music to pop once and for all.

BELLY: *KING*

Liberated from playing second fiddle in Throwing Muses and the Breeders, Tanya Donelly ran the first Belly album as a virtual one-woman show, and its creepy intimacy made *Star* one of the best discs of 1993. The album also had the hit-worthy material to help it rise up from the underground. Donelly capitalized on the success of "Feed the Tree" and "Gepetto" by writing even bigger hooks for the second Belly album.

King has more of a band feel than its predecessor due to a more stable lineup featuring new bassist Gail Greenwood and flawless production from old pro Glyn Johns, whose résumé includes work with the Beatles, the

Rolling Stones, Bob Dylan, the Who, Led Zeppelin, and many other artists well out of Belly's alternative league. Consequently, *King* isn't as uniquely enchanting as *Star*, but it still boasts great songs and great sound. Tracks like "Puberty," "Silverfish," and "The Bees" show that Donelly hadn't curbed her strange lyricism for Belly's stab at stardom, while "Super-Connected" reveals that she might not have been 100 percent happy that she'd taken that stab. Unfortunately, it failed to pay off when the album didn't do a fraction of the business *Star* did, which led to Belly's demise (though the King-era lineup would reunite for another disc in 2018). At least Belly went out with an excellent album. The enthralling title track alone would make *King* transcend its time.

BETTIE SERVEERT: *LAMPREY*

On *Palomine*, Bettie Serveert introduced a brand of indie rock that could be cuddly as the big-eyed puppy on the cover or noisy as a pit bull fight. Their second album, *Lamprey*, arrived with much slicker production. That may have violated some statute in the indie law book, but the wildness of Peter Visser's guitars and the boom of Berend Dubbe's drums, so up front in the mix, retained the raw power of *Palomine*. Carol van Dijk's red wine voice has grown even richer with age.

Like *Palomine*, *Lamprey* consists of dirges and sparkling pop sweets, but it goes out of its way to emphasize the contrast between those styles by interspersing them throughout the record, so the emotionally bare epic "Keepsake" leads into the sparkling single "Ray Ray Rain," which lurches into the groaning "D. Feathers," which gives way the pounding and uplifting "Re-Feel-It," and so on. The format may have been devised to keep listeners engaged. They would have been anyway with so many terrific songs in order.

BLUR: *THE GREAT ESCAPE*

Parklife helped define the sound, style, and attitude of Britpop, and critics lined up to acknowledge its achievements and quality. A backlash followed when Blur followed it with *The Great Escape*. Although it still received its share of accolades, some commentators found the album cynical, posturing, and empty. They accused Damon Albarn of doing more to celebrate Britain's lad culture than criticize it, especially after lazily provocative It

Boy artist Damien Hirst directed a video for "Country House" that featured Blur in a *Benny Hill*–esque frolic with scantily dressed models. Graham Coxon grew weary of the music's Kinks-isms, and even Albarn, the album's chief architect, would disown it in later years.

This is an unfair legacy for an album with the breadth and detail of *The Great Escape*. While "Tracy Jacks" was a pretty empathetic character portrait, most of *Parklife* was actually pretty cynical, certainly more so than "Best Days," which perfectly picks up on Ray Davies's insightfulness and melodic skills. Albarn's skewering of materialism, advertising culture, and lad culture is sharp in "Top Man," "Globe Alone," "Entertain Me," "He Thought of Cars," and "The Universal." Musically, the album is a lusher, more eclectic dish than *Parklife*. "The Universal" is majestically orchestrated. "Entertain Me" is a tough piece of organic disco with Alex James's most limber bass line. Blur would never again write material as tuneful and well structured as "Best Days," "The Universal," "Charmless Man," and "Mr. Robinson's Quango" after they decided to follow the more experimental path Radiohead laid after 1995.

THE CARDIGANS: *LIFE*

The Cardigans heighten the cheerily daffy retro pop sounds they introduced on *Emmerdale* on their second album. The swirling Studio 54 dance "Carnival," the cheeky cocktail party sound track "Gordon's Gardenparty" (which shamelessly cribs the tune of Nick Drake's "Bryter Layter"), the cuckoo children's song "Pikebubbles" (a crazed skit about a severely paranoid father), the plucky "Tomorrow," the spy flick–theme spoof "Travelling with Charley," and the loony epic "Closing Time" all smack of straight-up parody, but they are also brilliantly conceived pop productions, as tuneful as the best of the Beach Boys and the Kinks.

Life also recalls sixties pop in the shoddy way the album was treated outside the band's native Sweden. The four craziest tracks were clipped and replaced with songs from *Emmerdale* in the United States, while *Life* lost three of those songs and gained five *Emmerdale* tracks elsewhere in the world. When the Cardigans returned the following

The Cardigans presented themselves in a very ironic package, but their songcraft, production, and musicianship are sincerely great. Author's collection.

year and released a genuine international hit, no record company treated their extraordinary pop art so frivolously again.

CORNERSHOP: *WOMAN'S GOTTA HAVE IT*

The Britpop groups fetishized sixties rock, so one might assume Cornershop was just doing the same by playing a form of music that would be easy to shorthand as "indie raga rock." For this group, led by brothers Tjinder and Avtar Singh, the Indian elements were not merely the "exotic" decorations they were in the Beatles' and Stones' raga rock dalliances. Cornershop's sitars and tablas are part of the fundamental foundations of the dance-party grooves "6 A.M. Jullander Shere" and "My Dancing Days Are Done." Tracks such as "Hong Kong Book of Kung Fu" and "Roof Rack" drone indie style without the raga instrumentation. So do "Wog" and "Jansimram King," but Tjinder Singh's culture remains an important factor as he ponders his status as a "western oriental" and slips into Punjabi. The face-melting "Call All Destroyer" drops everything but a few pointed words and a gnarly riff. It's as explosive as rock got in 1995. *Woman's Gotta Have It* is as diverse, uncompromising, and fun.

GUIDED BY VOICES: *ALIEN LANES*

After nearly a decade as Dayton's best and weirdest local band, Guided by Voices finally grabbed national attention with 1994's *Bee Thousand*. The recording's ultra–low-fi fuzz, Robert Pollard's random way with words, and his tendency to wrap up songs after a single verse and chorus couldn't mute the supreme craftsmanship of the record's twenty tiny tracks.

On *Alien Lanes*, Pollard and company loaded a marathon twenty-eight songs onto a single album, and his pop mastery was even sharper than it had been on *Bee Thousand*. A wiser bandleader probably would have taken delicious morsels like "A Salty Salute," "As We Go Up, We Go Down," "Game of Pricks," "Closer You Are," "Blimps Go 90," "Always Crush Me," and "My Son Cool," then padded them past the two-minute mark and kept some of them in reserve for the next album. Bob, of course, always had another twenty-eight tunes in the pipeline (maybe another 128 is more like it). He never wasted time overworking songs that were already perfect. Balancing such mid-length miniatures are transitional crumbs like "Hit," "Gold Hick," "Big Chief Chinese Restaurant," and "Pimple Zoo" and two-minute-plus epics like "Watch Me Jumpstart," "Motor Away," "My Valuable Hunting Knife," and "Chicken Blows."

Whether they are super short, medium short, or long short, the songs on *Alien Lanes* are consistently marvelous, each one exactly as it should be. One more second of the spine-chilling "Auditorium" is totally unnecessary when it explodes into the liberating "Motor Away" at just the right moment. When you hear that song's simple message of finding freedom behind a steering wheel, escaping all the bad relationships and fake friends, you know you're not sitting in the lap of some guy playing intellectual games with pop conventions. Pollard is clearly sincerely in love with the basic joys and power of rock and roll. *Alien Lanes* is a work of total joy and inspiration. Drag-ass critics often whine that "Bob needs an editor," but you'd deserve to get your hands edited off your wrists if you tried editing one tune off of *Alien Lanes*.

P.S. Tobin Sprout's songs are great too.

PJ HARVEY: *TO BRING YOU MY LOVE*

PJ Harvey's first two albums were powerful but constricted, particularly the Steve Albini–produced *Rid of Me*. Flood, who'd abated U2's world domination when he engineered *The Joshua Tree*, hooks up with John Parrish and Harvey to open up her sound and decorate it with more varied arrangements and approaches. *To Bring You My Love* is the first PJ Harvey album that actually breathes, though she sounds less liberated here because there are fewer opportunities for her to cut loose than there were on *Dry* and *Rid of Me*. That's because the music is more polite, the songs are more tightly constructed, and the production is a far cry from Steve Albini's mid-fi hubbub. Harvey even managed to reach a wider audience when the minimalistic blues "Down by the Water" got some mainstream play and went to number two on *Billboard*'s Alternative chart—pretty unusual for a song about drowning one's daughter. The intensity is still high, as Harvey and her two coproducers warp the blues into simmering production pieces. Her voice is just as fearsome when she restrains it as it is when she lets her inner Doberman off its

The woman who named her debut *Dry* placed photos of herself in or alongside water on the covers of each of her first four albums. Author's collection.

leash. "Down by the Water" resolves in intimate whispers quite unlike her signature howl but a lot scarier.

HELIUM: *THE DIRT OF LUCK*

Mary Timony grew up in a household where she mostly heard classical music and her older brother played jazz guitar. Having her mind blown at a show by fellow Washington, D.C., natives Fugazi, Timony began imagining a new form of music that was as cerebral and traditionally musical as the stuff she heard as a kid and the grinding noise she heard at that Fugazi show. In effect, she devised a sort of indie prog rock far less fussy and technically pristine than that of another fellow D.C. band, Shudder to Think (whose Nathan Larson would later play with Timony in Mind Science of the Mind, which is literally the proggiest band name that will ever be). That sound got its first airing with her early band Autoclav and went nuclear with Helium.

The first extended blast of Helium came in 1994 with their doomy EP *Pirate Prude*, a short story in half a dozen tracks about vampires and prostitution. Mary Timony's lurid tales fit for a Halloween night flowered on her band's first LP the following year. *The Dirt of Luck* is populated with skeletons, gorgons, and other damaged creatures. The music growls like a dragon, whispers like a ghost, clatters and clangs like bones doing the Hully Gully, and whooshes and whistles like a psychedelic UFO. Imagine if Sonic Youth and the Groovie Goolies formed a supergroup. Timony's trad craftspersonship is obvious in songs such as "Superball," "Oh the Wind and the Rain," and "Honeycomb," but she is at her most bewitching when bashing a few fissures in her pop craft, sculpting gnarled pieces like "Trixie's Star," "Medusa," "Skeleton," and "Pat's Trick." Everything about that last track is just so damn dirty: from lyrics that snarl "it's dirty and I'm so dirty too") to guitars and bass that sound like they just stepped out of a mud bath to Mary Timony's super-sexy delivery, which one might mistake for a come-on if she didn't clearly want to slash your face with a broken bottle. And why hasn't a filmmaker scored a creepy, retro sci-fi movie with the shivery instrumental "Comet #9" yet?

Mary Timony's very own artwork adorns *The Dirt of Luck*. Author's collection.

PAVEMENT: *WOWEE ZOWEE*

After defining themselves as *the* ramshackle, irony-peddling, genre-dabbling indie rock band of the nineties with *Slanted and Enchanted* and *Crooked Rain, Crooked Rain*, Pavement perfected each of those elements on their follow-up.

Wowee Zowee was not as well received as *Crooked Rain* at the time, perhaps because there's so much of it to absorb before turning in that witty record review before deadline. *Rolling Stone* deemed it "scattered and sloppy." The *Los Angeles Times* called it "lazy and unfinished." *The Guardian* found it fit for no one but fifteen-year-old boys.

Exile on Main Street had the same problem. In both cases, a bit of time and attention revealed greatness. Pavement sometimes seems as though they're riffing on other artists across their album's eighteen tracks: Bowie's grand space folk on "We Dance," *Village Green*–era Kinks on "Brinx Job" and "Grave Architecture," Nirvana on "Flux = Rad," the Muppets on "Serpentine Pad." Its best tracks are so immediately striking that patience seems unnecessary to appreciate *Wowee Zowee*, but if that is what it takes, then it is worth it because it is Pavement's eclectic best. Stephen Malkmus's wacko way with words, which tended to change each time he recorded a vocal take, rewards close listening.

Percussionist Bob Nastanovich wanted to call Pavement's latest album *Dick-Sucking Fool at Pussy-Licking School*. For some reason, the rest of the band vetoed this idea. Author's collection.

PULP: *DIFFERENT CLASS*

Jarvis Cocker was the urbane face of Britpop, waxing wiseass about sex and social class. He cooed, purred, and occasionally broke a sweat over Pulp's cool and clever concoctions. The seventeen years of work Pulp had put into their act is evident in the masterful *Different Class* (that was not a typo—this principal nineties Britpop group had been at it since the days when *Fawlty Towers* was still airing on BBC Two).

Different Class may take a while to warm up to because Cocker initially seems to be putting us on. When we get comfortable with the fact that he is, we can move on and sink into Pulp's plush songs. The next thing likely to slap you is the relentlessly mounting excitement of dance-floor crowders like "Common People" (in which a pampered toff schemes to slum it in bed with some schmo beneath her station) and "Disco 2000" (in which a loser dreams of reconnecting with a former girlfriend now settled and out of his league). The message of "Mis-Shapes" may interrupt the grooving with more revolutionary thoughts, while you may stop swaying to "Underwear" and double over as Cocker describes the awkward underbelly of seduction. Producer Chris Thomas shapes *Different Class* with all the polish he'd buffed onto "The White Album" and *Country Life*, both albums I'd find it very hard to believe aren't on the jukebox in Pulp's salon. Anne Dudley's string arrangements are indispensable to this triumph of attitude, withering wit, and old-fashioned professionalism rare in the scabby world of nineties rock.

RADIOHEAD: *THE BENDS*

Radiohead seemed like a pretty typical nineties indie band when they released their first album in 1993. The over-the-top self-loathing and loud–quiet–loud dynamics were requirements in Nirvana's wake. Although it had its share of excellent songs and one massive college radio smash, there was nothing on *Pablo Honey* that really suggested a band with the staying power and influence of the Radiohead we now know.

That changed with *The Bends*, which pours over with the confidence of a band that has just discovered who they are. And who is Radiohead at this point? Well, they aren't quite the abandoned, borderline proggy experimenters they'd become with *OK Computer*, but they are a guitar group that works with less traditional electronic noises, views their contemporary world as alien and chaotic, and sets brilliant melodies sail on a noisy and chaotic sea. For wall-to-wall excellent songs, *The Bends* beats all other Radiohead albums. Radiohead slams out chorus-driven anthems like the title track, "Bones," "Black Star," and "Just"; stop the show with magically moody mopers like "Fake Plastic Trees," "Bullet Proof . . . I Wish I Was," and "Street Spirit (Fade Out)"; and toss out a superb Beatles replicant with "My Iron Lung."

The fact that great songwriting isn't necessarily the most exceptional thing about this exceptional band means it also isn't necessarily their best album, but *The Bends* proved Radiohead was more than another whiney bunch of creeps who could locate the "on" switches of their Big Muff peddles. Its success made it possible for them to do anything they wanted to do, and that's exactly what Radiohead has been doing ever since.

SMASHING PUMPKINS: *MELLON COLLIE AND THE INFINITE SADNESS*

In the midst of what may be the best period for rock albums since the sixties, few artists really set out to make major rock albums. Discs such as *The Great Escape* and *Exile in Guyville* were intrinsically strong and consciously conceptual, but they didn't exactly have the ambition or grandeur of a *Wall* or a *1999*, probably because Damon Albarn and Liz Phair didn't have the ego of Roger Waters or Prince. Billy Corgan did, and he very self-consciously set out to make Smashing Pumpkins' third album capital-A Art. In the run-up to its release, he reveled in describing it as a double-disc concept album (though he later denied that there was a concept).

In the vinyl era, it would have actually required three LPs to contain all two hours of *Mellon Collie and the Infinite Sadness*. There's not much concept, but there's a whole lot of material to wade through. Impressively, the songwriting is a lot stronger than it was on Smashing Pumpkins' commercial breakthrough, 1993's *Siamese Dream*, but *Mellon Collie* is fabulously undisciplined as an album. It bounces from style to style like an alt-rock "White Album." Smashing Pumpkins delve into metal ("Where Boys Fear to Tread," "An Ode to No One," "Jellybelly," "Bodies," "Tales of Scorched Earth"), dreamy orchestrated pop ("Tonight, Tonight"), grunge ("Zero," "Bullet with Butterfly Wings"), glam ("Muzzle," "Here Is No Why"), electronic ("Love") and organic ("Cupid De Locke," "Thirty-Three) psychedelia, delicate moods ("To Forgive," "Galapagos," "Take Me Down"), neo-prog rock ("Porcelina of the Vast Oceans," "Thru the Eyes of Ruby"), folk rock ("In the Arms of Sleep"), dance pop ("1979," "Beautiful"), solo showcases ("Stumbeline"), and low-key bubble gum ("We Only Come Out at Night," "Lily," "Farewell and Goodnight"). It's best to ignore Corgan's lyrics, which tend to be

The woman in John Craig's collage on the cover of *Mellon Collie* is a composite of Jean-Baptiste Greuze's painting *The Souvenir (Fidelity)* and Raphael's portrait of Saint Catherine of Alexandria. Author's collection.

whiney, precious, or pretentious, but he handles the challenges of grand album making in an era of self-effacement masterfully.

ELLIOTT SMITH: *ELLIOTT SMITH*

On his 1994 debut, former Heatmeiser guitarist Elliott Smith mapped out the hushed acoustic approach he would perfect with his second record the following year. Smith's tales of isolation and addiction are so chilling on his self-titled disc because there's none of the Stones' zonked smirking behind the scoring and shooting. He sounds backed into a corner without an ounce of fight left in him. He renders strong statements like "No bad dream fucker's gonna boss me around" weak. His voice and picking are too delicate for the forcefulness of his words to register. That chilling weariness seems to undermine the idea that Smith was not really in dire shape and merely creating characters and reporting on the things he saw around him, which is the common story told by those closest to him. Even if they are right—and one can only hope they are—the songs on *Elliott Smith* create such a clear image that this music would lose none of its power even if it had been made by a happy-go-lucky jokester.

MATTHEW SWEET: *100% FUN*

Matthew Sweet is the extrovert flip side to Elliott Smith's blend of British Invasion melody and alternative-rock self-loathing. Smith probably would not have sang anything as up front as "Sick of Myself," and though his later solo records had music as raucous, he'd never belt like Sweet. Yet as nasty as viewpoints of "Sick of Myself," "Not When I Need It," and "We're the Same" are, the delivery is always as sweet as the man's name. So the intentionally ironically titled *100% Fun* is an album that may endure better than—forgive me—*Nevermind* or *In Utero* for us current grown-ups long removed from spending the mid-nineties moping around college campuses. Because even as we may have grown out of that very-nineties "everything is shit" attitude, we will never grow out of loving the kind of timeless power pop Sweet rolls out on *100% Fun*.

TEAM DRESCH: *PERSONAL BEST*

With members who'd done time in Dinosaur Jr., Screaming Trees, Hazel, and Calamity Jane, Team Dresch was a sort of indie-punk supergroup. That novelty and their stance as leaders in the homocore movement were not as arresting as the sheer power of the music they made together. *Personal Best* is one of the great nineties punk albums, a triumph of viciousness and superb musicianship. The complex guitar interplay of "She's Crushing My Mind" is as beautiful as the screaming chorus is terrifying. While tracks such as "Fagetarian and Dyke," "Hate the Christian Right," and "#1 Chance Pirate Radio" (which celebrates Sinead O'Connor's famed *Saturday Night Live* appearance) make the band's politics explicit, love songs actually rule *Personal Best*. They can be incensed wails ("She's Crushing My Mind"), rollicking kiss-offs ("Freewheel"), or romantic reveries ("She's Amazing"). "Fake Fight" and "Growing Up in Springfield" draw the two main themes together as the simplicity of love is complicated in a world that demonizes LGBTQ people. That situation is not quite as horrible today as it was in 1995, but the power of *Personal Best* has not changed one pinch.

The cover of *Personal Best* was inspired by Robert Towne's 1982 film of the same name. Author's collection.

THROWING MUSES: *UNIVERSITY*

With Tanya Donnelly's departure after 1991's *The Real Ramona*, Throwing Muses was reduced to a duo, and Kristin Hersh and David Narcizo did their best with the tough but unfocused *Red Heaven*. After recruiting their former roadie Bernard Georges to pick up the bass, the Muses really became a band again. They sound utterly revitalized on *University*. Hersh's material matches the group's regained strength. The firm lineup delivers an assortment of accelerated rock ("Bright Yellow Gun," "Shimmer"), dizzying funhouse rides ("Calm Down, Come Down"), mood pieces (the magical "Crab Town," the stormy "No Way in Hell," the spooky title track), pop desserts ("That's All You Wanted"), and intense dirges ("Flood," "Fever Few") with a pro polish their earlier albums shunned. While Georges's driving bass work doesn't have the dazzling quirk of ex-Muse Leslie Langston's asymmetrical slapping and plucking, his solidity gives the band a thicker sound that helps Hersh's more traditionally structured material retain the power of her more eccentric earlier work.

URGE OVERKILL: *EXIT THE DRAGON*

Saturation exuded ironic joy. For *Exit the Dragon*, Nash Kato, Eddie "King" Roeser, and Blackie Onassis drop the James Bond–meets–Boston act and awaken to a hangover of despair. The band's real-life drug issues and interpersonal problems steer a record that seems to consciously try to recapture the dark decadence of *Exile on Main Street* without resorting to Urge's usual parodic kitsch. Even the nearly nine-minute tribute to murdered pop singer Selena feels heartfelt. Forget the velvet jackets and comedy code names; *Exit the Dragon* is a sincerely powerful rock and roll album and a sincerely harrowing one too. It was also Urge Overkill's last album for sixteen years, but the band's own issues were probably as much to blame for their dissolution as the public's indifference to a wealth of songs that still deserve to be discovered.

1996

A few years into the frenzy to sign alternative bands, groups were starting to enjoy their heightened positions and pursue higher levels of success. Kurt Cobain's "I hate myself and want to die" attitude ran its course in a way too horrible and real for most of the artists who'd jumped on the self-loathing gravy train. As their stations improved, they found themselves with less to rail against, and only the cheesiest grunge poseurs like Sponge, Moist, and Bush kept up the act. The era's best bands found other routes of expression, many of them embracing a glammy outlook and style antithetical to the grunge atmosphere of a couple of years earlier.

Meanwhile, the very way people listened to music was on the verge of changing. On November 26, 1996, the Fraunhofer Institute in Germany was granted a patent for a new music medium called the MP3. It would be the first major nonphysical format and make it possible to purchase any song from any album without having to splurge for the whole platter. Not only was rock nearing obsolescence, its main medium was too.

AFGHAN WHIGS: *BLACK LOVE*

If any band was going to resist lightening up in the 1996 style, it was Afghan Whigs, and *Black Love* sounds like an alternate title for the relationship-in-ruins song cycle that was their previous album. However, the album is costumed as a crime concept set in the seventies, so though its songs are as moody and menacing as those on *Gentlemen*, *Black Love* skirts that album's personal nature. So in its way, it is as frivolous as much of 1996's rock.

The project began life as a film, but by the time it was reduced to a sound track without pictures, whatever story line Greg Dulli intended was impossible to detect. In the debris are his usual themes of deception, self-destruction, and romantic angst. His words are weakest when some sort of plot seems to be skulking in the shadows without really revealing itself. On the singles "Going to Town" and "Honky's Ladder," he slips into groan-inducing blaxploitation clichés.

There may not be much actual storytelling in "Step into the Light" and "Night by Candlelight," but these atmospheric pieces are dramatic and cinematic. "Summer's Kiss" makes astounding use of tension and release and the rhythmic chaos learned from listening to *Quadrophenia* on repeat. "Faded" is an epic, entrancing finale, and "My Enemy" and "Double Day" are rabid in the usual Whigs way. *Black Love* may be a failure as a concept album, but it is a smashing success as the latest collection of Afghan Whigs tracks.

BECK: *ODELAY*

Beck Hansen got his start strumming fractured folk songs but seemed to be having his requisite fifteen minutes of fame when he toyed with hip-hop and captured the slacker zeitgeist. "Loser," a collage of irony and nonsense, became a sort of novelty hit in 1993. There was a swift and really ruthless backlash. In a tasteless and heartless article about Kurt Cobain's suicide in *Spin* magazine, writer Gina Arnold wished Beck had met Cobain's end instead.

Like Radiohead, Beck bounced back from dismissals of his early work to be hailed as one of the most innovative artists of his time. His fifth album, *Odelay*, builds on and refines the quirky hip-hop noise and cut-up nonsense of 1993's *Mellow Gold*. The project started as a return to Beck's folkish beginnings but spun out of control as he abandoned his work with *Mellow Gold* producers Tom Rothrock and Rob Schnapf and moved over to the Dust Brothers, who played on a more electronic field. Hip-hop moves to the fore again, but there are still callbacks to Beck's origins with the folk guitars of "Lord Only Knows," "Ramshackle," and "Jack-Ass." He zings out raga rap with "Derelict," punks out with "Minus," and freaks out with "High Five (Rock the Catskills)," but the essential sound of *Odelay* is a collision of hip-hop, retro-seventies sarcasm, the essential pop songwriting that makes Beck's songs stick, and the production weirdness that makes them artful.

BELLE & SEBASTIAN: *TIGERMILK*

Belle & Sebastian began as a project in a music business course at a Glasgow college. For his final assignment, Stuart Murdoch recorded an almost absurdly sensitive debut album steeped in the most delicate sixties pop (think *Village Green* Kinks and *Odyssey and Oracle* Zombies) and droll eighties British pop (think the Smiths). Murdoch shared Morrissey's ability to weave the painfully personal with the preposterous, but he does so with the empathy and humanity Moz always lacked and displays a true gift for intricate storytelling. "The State I Am In" and "She's Losing It" could be treatments for short films. Belle & Sebastian printed only 1,000 copies of *Tigermilk*, but this extraordinary debut landed in the right hands, and a fruitful career began.

IF YOU'RE FEELING SINISTER

If You're Feeling Sinister is a continuation of *Tigermilk*'s echoing, multilayered sound (think *All Things Must Pass*), but consistently stronger material makes it feel like a massive leap forward. The way Stuart Murdoch superimposes sexually frank lyrics over sweetly elegant music is disquieting yet beguiling. "The Stars of Track and Field," with its deliberate build from near silence; "Seeing Other People," with its magical Vince Guaraldi–like arpeggios; and the title track are instant classics. "The Fox in the Snow" and "The Boy Done Wrong Again" are unbearably tender. "Me and the Major,"

A very consistent and evocative aesthetic links the covers of all of Belle & Sebastian's albums. Author's collection.

"Like Dylan and the Movies," "Get Me Away from Here, I'm Dying," and "Mayfly" race along with the heady giddiness of a heart bursting with new love. *If You're Feeling Sinister* is an album to fall in love to and an album to fall in love with. There were arguably better ones in the nineties, but there were none more beautiful.

THE CARDIGANS: *FIRST BAND ON THE MOON*

As sincerely great as their pop had been from the beginning, the Cardigans always had more than a whiff of irony with their lounge Black Sabbath remakes, album covers depicting happy puppies or Nina Persson in wholesome pinup pose, and songs about garden parties and circuses. The moroseness at the heart of many of these songs always felt a bit ironic too, but ironically, that started to change with *First Band on the Moon*, the album with that song that became a massive hit despite everyone assuming it had nothing but wind between its ears. Of course, "Love Fool" is one of the Cardigan's darkest songs yet, and that same darkness permeates the rest of the album, which only really leans on the cheekiness of *Emmerdale* and *Life* when the band turns "Iron Man" into cocktail treacle complete with Sinatra-style dooby-dooing. *First Band on the Moon* never exactly sounds like a dark album even when things get misty on the Sabbath-quoting "Heartbreaker" or "Happy Meal II." However, its songs are all about romantic subservience, degradation, rejection, self-deception, and the death of communication. So while the rest of the indie world was grinning in 1996, the Cardigans of all people were beginning to turn their smiles upside down, and they'd complete that descent with their next album.

GRANT LEE BUFFALO: *COPPEROPOLIS*

Two years after releasing *Mighty Joe Moon*, Grant Lee Buffalo seemed reinvigorated on *Copperopolis*. That may seem odd since *Mighty Joe* is their best album, but like most every other group in 1996, they sound sunnier than ever on their latest release. Paul Kimble's production—so dense on *Fuzzy* and *Mighty Joe Moon*—has opened up considerably to allow sunrays to beam through expansive pieces like "Homespun," "Arousing Thunder," and "Bethlehem Steel." Grant Lee Phillips still takes some hard looks at America on "Homespun," "Crackdown," "Even the Oxen," and "Comes to Blows," and he does so with greater clarity than before, but he also allows himself to revel in pure romanticism on the heavenly "Arousing Thunder" without the underlying doubt of "Honey Don't Think" on the previous album. "The Bridge," "All That I Have," "Better for Us," and "Hyperion and Sunset" are delicate productions that ease their troubled messages down like caramel syrup. Phillips reminds us that he possesses the most expressive and beautiful voice in nineties rock.

GUIDED BY VOICES: *UNDER THE BUSHES, UNDER THE STARS*

Under the Bushes, Under the Stars didn't turn out as originally intended. The sessions began with Kim Deal at the producer's helm and the ambition to make the slickest Guided by Voices album since *Sandbox*. Artistic differences and some complex feelings between Deal and Robert Pollard ended the collaboration. The resulting album is a mixed bag of tracks recorded by Deal, Steve Albini, John Shough, Doug Easley, and Davis McCain, but it all sounds like a singular sprawling piece, more refined than *Bee Thousand* and *Alien Lanes* but far from the polish of future albums like *Do the Collapse*, *Isolation Drills*, or even *Mag Earwhig!*

So *Under the Bushes* is either the final low-fi or final mid-fi Guided by Voices album in their first phase. It's also the final one with the "classic" Guided by Voices lineup of Tobin Sprout, Mitch Mitchell, and Kevin Fennell, and there is a bit of an elegiac feel to some of the material, such as Sprout's glam-warp "To Remake the Young Flyer" and the moving anthem "Don't Stop Now," which Pollard would sometimes introduce onstage as "the ballad of Guided by Voices." There are also some of the jolliest ("Office of Hearts," "Your Name Is Wild," "Underwater Explosions"), nastiest ("Cut-Out Witch"), noisiest ("The Official Ironmen Rally Song"), and cloudiest ("No Sky," "Lord of Overstock") rock and roll of Guided by Voices' classic era, as well as an EP's worth of additional first-rate material cut from the feature presentation.

For some fans who were not able to accept the more buffed band Guided by Voices soon became, the Guided by Voices story ends here. Those people are missing out on some stupendous music, but they at least received a fittingly fine farewell from "their" Guided by Voices.

LUSCIOUS JACKSON: *FEVER IN, FEVER OUT*

Coming from the same scene as the Beastie Boys, Luscious Jackson shared the Beastie's undogmatic love of hip-hop and desire to cross-pollinate with other genres. They also shared a label (the Beastie Boys' own Grand Royal) and Kate Schellenbach, who'd drummed on the Beasties' *Pollywog Stew* EP. Luscious Jackson were more committed to live instrumentation and pop hooks than the Beastie Boys, which gave them a distinct personality, as did the fact that they were four women in a male-dominated, highly sexist scene.

While their first LP, *Natural Ingredients*, didn't fully live up to the promise of their debut EP *In Search of Manny*, Luscious Jackson poured all their powers into *Fever In, Fever Out* and made what may be the finest hip-pop LP. It's a slumpless sophomore album showcasing the band's coolness in every way. Jill Cunniff's vocals are smooth and controlled throughout, and Daniel Lanois's production seems to use Brian Wilson's "Wind Chimes" as a sort of atmospheric template. Hook-heavy singles like "Naked Eye" and "Under Your Skin" sound breezy and balmy even as Kate Schellenbach's rhythms push hard in the undercurrent. "Don't Look Back," "Mood Swing," "Water Your Garden," and "Faith" ease back into psychedelic repose. Self-examining lyrics lend the tracks weight, but the sentiments are more mature and nuanced than the kind of boloney angst that had been passing for insight in the first half of the nineties. Positions like "live slow, die old" or "Soothe Yourself" were ripostes to grungy self-pity. On the flip side, the winsome yet unsparing "Why Do I Lie?" is as refreshingly clear as Gavin Rosdale pseudo–self-loathing is messy and meaningless. This is what it sounds like when adults address their demons.

Fever In Fever Out was the first Luscious Jackson album the band did not totally self-produce. Quintessential late-nineties producer Daniel Lanois helped out with this one. Author's collection.

SLOAN: *ONE CHORD TO ANOTHER*

Sloan had made a great album of noisy, My Bloody Valentine–type indie menace and a very good though inconsistent straight indie sophomore album. They fully came into their own with *One Chord to Another*. The band who'd gotten anthemic without losing their cool on stuff like "I Am the Cancer" and "500 Up" were primed to lose it and go full power pop. The production is as retro organic as that of *If You're Feeling Sinister*. The songs sparkle from start to finish, channeling Cheap Trick, Wings, and Chicago but doing what those bands did with greater finesse. The hard and glammy "The Good in Everyone," the brassy romp "Everything You've Done Wrong," the blazing "G Turns to G," the snaky and shaky "The Lines You Amend," the word-twisting "Autobiography," and the psychedelicized march "Anyone Who's Anyone" (a replica of the Who's

"Armenia City in the Sky") are standouts on an album of standouts. More than ever before, each member of the band asserts his personality through the distinctive singing, playing, and songwriting that make Sloan the year's only band that requires you to know exactly who each guy in the group is: power-popping Chris Murphy, hard-rocking Patrick Pentland, sweet and sensitive Jay Ferguson, and off-kilter and martini-dry Andrew Scott. A friend and I once got into a debate over who is the most essential member of Sloan, prompting another friend to remark that it sounded like we were arguing about our favorite dreamboat in a boy band. If only there was a boy band as deserving of that much spit as Sloan is.

Sloan were almost vengefully unfashionable in the nineties. When it was coolest to put some ugly, out-of-focus photo of a random object on one's album cover, the guys always put themselves on theirs. I think this one is their most stylish. Author's collection.

THROWING MUSES: *LIMBO*

Throwing Muses were always dark and off kilter, whether screeching through their terrifying debut, blending their mania with sugary pop to perfection on *The Real Ramona*, or bellowing with a fat new sound on *University*. *Limbo* skates off of that album's polish, but it leaves the darkness behind. For the first time in her career, Kristin Hersh sounds happy, and even when *Limbo* dials down the tempo with "Serene" or "White Bikini Sands," it does so with a newfound contentment. When the beats per minute picks up and she unlocks her Pandora's voice box on things like "Ruthie's Knocking," "Freeloader," "Tar Kissers," and "Cowbirds," she sounds giddy without the manic edge of her early work. This might not have been what longtime fans wanted from the Muses, and reviews tended to be unenthusiastic. Those who couldn't handle a happier Hersh had to hang on to numbers like the title track and "Shark," which tease

I've always found Gilbert Hernandez's illustration on the cover of *Limbo* quite striking. Hernandez is most famous for co-creating the cult comic *Love and Rockets* with his brothers Jaime and Mario. Author's collection.

the band's past viciousness while still sounding pretty jovial underneath the teeth gnashing. Perhaps that contentment is what made Hersh hang her band in the closet after *Limbo*, and it gave the Throwing Muses story a sense of serene—though temporary—closure.

SUZANNE VEGA: *NINE OBJECTS OF DESIRE*

Suzanne Vega had gone out on a limb by toughening her sound with industrial rhythms on 1992's *99.9F°* with the assistance of producer Mitchell Froom. The experiment was a success in more ways than one. She had married and had a child with Froom before making *Nine Objects of Desire*. He returned to produce and play a starring role in Vega's most personal and romantic lyrics yet. She sings a song of love's sweet distractions on "Caramel" and ups the eroticism on "My Favorite Plum." "Honeymoon Suite" is a piece of straight reportage about their first night as a married couple. Their daughter, Ruby, is the subject of the tumbling "Birth-Day (Love Made Real)" and the gorgeous "World Before Columbus."

In keeping with Vega's bliss, the music is less feverish than that of *99.9F°*, but what *Nine Objects* lacks in intensity it makes up for in variety. Vega and Froom dabble with bossa nova ("Caramel"), a Zeppelin-esque string arrangement ("Stockings"), burbling pop ("No Cheap Thrill," which sports the catchiest chorus Vega ever wrote), woozy waltz time ("Honeymoon Suite"), and rubber-legged ("Thin Man"), bouncy ("Tombstone"), and seductive ("My Favorite Plum") jazz. Sadly, the domestic ecstasy would not last, and Vega's next album would be full of references to her and Froom's divorce. It's appropriate, though, that she seemed to be at the height of her joy in the joyful pop landscape of 1996.

1997

Whatever claws underground rock seemed to have in the mainstream since the beginning of the nineties were effectively dislodged by 1997. Guitar-based bands such as Bush and Matchbox 20 sold well by appropriating the music of the era's more vital artists and polishing it into anodyne irrelevance. Elton John and Sean Combs scored the year's two biggest hits by recycling a couple of old hits for smarmy eulogies. No Doubt got play on *120 Minutes* with the Miami Sound Machine–soundalike "Don't Speak" and became one of the year's biggest sellers along with other sensations such as Celine Dion, the Spice Girls, and Hanson. Their pop influence would ultimately be more profound and long lasting than that of the bands that initially seemed to define the decade.

HOLLY GOLIGHTLY: *PAINTED ON*

On her fourth solo album, former leader of the Kent garage band Thee Headcoatees, Holly Golightly, made the ultimate neo–garage-rock record. With its organic production, raw performances, and raw language, *Painted On* is retro without resorting to burlesque. Golightly's anger makes this an authentic A-bomb of self-expression, but fans of the Stones, the Sonics, and the Seeds could still be fooled into thinking *Painted On* came out in 1965—at least until they hear her stream of "fucks."

Although Golightly takes her sonic and rhythmic cues from old bands, monsters such as "Run Cold," the swaggering "For All This," the lethal title track, the hip-shaking instrumental "Snake Eyed," and the mesmerizing closer "Anyway You Like It" still vibrate with originality. So does Golightly's defiantly cockney intonation laid over decidedly American-style blues, country, and rock and roll. *Painted On* would be simply cool if Golightly's nastiness weren't so superheated.

GUIDED BY VOICES: *MAG EARWHIG!*

Aside from high-kicking mainstay Bob Pollard, the Guided by Voices that made *Mag Earwhig!* is a completely different band from the one we last saw in *Under the Bushes, Under the Stars*. Gone are Tobin Sprout, Mitch Mitchell, and Kevin Fennell after rough going during their final sessions— though a few tracks featuring the newly departed members ("Are You Faster?" "I Am Produced," "Knock 'Em Flyin'") made the cut of *Mag Earwhig!* In are Cobra Verde from Cleveland.

Also in is the high-polished sound that began the process of alienating some of Pollard's more doctrinaire fans. Those who could not let the Devo-like mechanisms of "Can't Hear the Revolution," the Stonesy "Bulldog Skin," the dreamy psychedelia of "Learning to Hunt," the metal chant "Little Lines," the agitated punk of "Bomb in the Bee-Hive," or the space-age power pop of "Jane of the Waking Universe" into their hearts lost out big time. Such fans made the mistake of concluding that Guided by Voices' greatest asset was the way they recorded their music. It had always been Pollard's songs. That being said,

Guided by Voices' homemade ethos extended to their album covers, which usually featured Robert Pollard's nifty collages. This one's my fave. Author's collection.

one of *Mag Earwhig!*'s finest moments—the towering "I Am a Tree"—is the work of new boy Doug Gillard, the only Cobra Verde member who'd stick around for Guided by Voice's next and most controversial album.

HELIUM: *THE MAGIC CITY*

On Helium's debut, the Boston trio painted a work of art with globs of oily noise. The smears of feedback and fuzz were not thick enough to smother Mary Timony's innate tunefulness, which made every track scary and pleasurable in equal proportion—like curling up on the couch to watch *Frankenstein*. Appropriately, *The Dirt of Luck* also gave Timony an outlet for her fixation on monsters and mythical creatures at odds with the stark realism of nineties rock, though she always used her gorgons and skeleton people for personal metaphorical purposes.

On *The Magic City*, Timony and producer Mitch Easter (who'd produced R.E.M.'s first two records) take a turpentine-soaked rag to the thick oils of *The Dirt of Luck*, drawing her melodies closer to the surface and pulling the shroud off her fantasies. *The Magic City* is home to castles and dragons and astronauts and medieval people gamboling along oceans of wine. Timony complements her idiosyncratic fancies with the baroque keyboards and melodies that would take full flight at the

Mary Timony was subsisting on a diet of King Crimson, Yes, and the Zombies when she made *The Magic City*. Shocker! Author's collection.

outset of her solo career. Helium still whips up some hurricanes on their final album, working hard dance and electronic influences into things like "Medieval People" and "The Revolution of Hearts, Pts. 1 & 2," on which Mary Timony comes out of the closet as a prog acolyte once and for all.

RADIOHEAD: *OK COMPUTER*

Radiohead began as a weedy British offshoot of what Nirvana started. They found a voice of their own with their second album. On their third, they rebuilt contemporary rock using some unexpected tools. *OK Computer* is a neo-progressive rock album waving around all of prog's trademark idiosyncrasies: big concepts, science fiction, creative chording, and tricky time signatures. Yet no one would mistake *OK Computer* for *Closer to the Edge*. Radiohead explore the synthesizers, hip-hop rhythms, and heavily treated drum, vocal, and guitar sounds that the band that made *Pablo Honey* wouldn't have entertained.

Fellow artists got in line behind *OK Computer*'s sonic futurism as dutifully as they'd gotten behind *Nevermind*. Also like Nirvana's milestone, Radiohead's exploded with songs that defined their era. Where were you in 1992? Watching "Smells Like Teen Spirit," "In Bloom," "Come as You Are," and "Lithium" on MTV. Where were you in 1997? Strapped into headphones, marveling to the Lennon-esque "Karma Police," the celestial "No Surprises," and the surging "Let Down."

"Paranoid Android," my choice for the greatest song of the nineties, accurately predicted where we'd end up in the coming century: a computerized society would leave us empty and vulnerable in the worst way. It is also harrowing, dramatic, and packed with great stuff melodically, instrumentally, and productionally (that's a word!). One may argue that "Paranoid Android" is not the greatest song on *OK Computer*, but there's nothing else on the CD that gives you more bang for your buck. Plus there are Jonny Greenwood's bludgeoning riffs, Phil Selway's tom-tom machine gunning, and Thom's angel-to-demon dynamics. "Paranoid Android" leaves me flawed, stunned, shaken, stirred, and feeling a whole lot more human than I felt before it started.

In between the singles lurk the soaring "Subterranean Homesick Alien," the suitably dramatic "Exit Music (For a Film)," the gnarly "Electioneering" (Radiohead's last traditional guitar-based rock song for a long time), and the aching, crawling "Tourist." With its recurring themes of unchecked consumerism metastasizing into existential alienation, *OK Computer* crystallized ideas that had been swirling through the Britpop world since Blur put out *Modern Life Is Rubbish* in 1993, but Radiohead did it in a way that seemed to rocket beyond the quotidian social observation of that genre.

SHUDDER TO THINK: *50,000 B.C.*

If ever there was a band for which the rock star brass ring seemed unattainable, it's Shudder to Think. Or is it? After all, beneath Craig Wedren's unearthly wail and choppy surrealism, there are plenty of riffs fit for a Queen album. On *50,000 B.C.*, Shudder to Think shed much of their prog angles and slither out in a spangly, glam skin. While that cost them a good deal of what made them unique, they emerge as a fabulous rock and roll band that still has enough vocal and lyrical weirdness to remain distinct from any other. What other band would coo "Naughty, naughty, naughty, can't steer so sexy in a war" or "My teeth are fit with mandibles and a dangled fig"? Wedren gets less obscure and even sweet on the love songs (Love songs! From Shudder to Think!) "Beauty Strike," "All Eyes Are Different," and "You're Gonna Look Fine, Love." They also play with soul and make an accessible rock anthem of "Red House," an old track from 1991's *Funeral at the Movies* EP rerecorded with heightened slickness and power in a crazy bid for a hit single. Alas, it was too good for all the chumps wagging their empty heads to "Semi-Charmed Life."

Even the most rigid fans have to forgive the newfound joy in Shudder to Think's music considering how *50,000 B.C.* came on the heels of a serious cancer scare for Wedren. One of the main virtues of Shudder to Think had always been their ability to shock, and hearing them court traditional beauty and adult contentment may be their most shocking move of all.

SLEATER-KINNEY: *DIG ME OUT*

Sleater-Kinney became one of the most worshipped bands of the nineties on the strength of their songs, musicianship, feminist messaging, and refusal to play the usual objectification games that the music industry usually foists on female artists. The third album by the Olympia, Washington, trio continues the double-six-string/double-voice attack of *Call the Doctor* with the new addition of Janet Weiss's crisp drumming. The sour and sweet counterpoint between Corin Tucker's anguished bleat and Carrie Brownstein's controlled speak-singing continues to be the most exciting musical element, and it reaches

The cover of *Dig Me Out* is a kool homage to the cover of *The Kink Kontroversy*. Author's collection.

a toe-tingling peak on "Little Babies." With its sneering satire of the traditional female role in the patriarchy, it is also the most explicitly feminist song on *Dig Me Out*. Its songs mainly mine more typical pop themes of romantic relationships healthy and otherwise and the recuperative powers of playing and hearing great rock and roll. With its wild, liberating guitars and voices, *Dig Me Out* has its own recuperative powers.

ELLIOTT SMITH: *EITHER/OR*

Elliott Smith's third album builds a bit on the skeletal acoustic sounds of his eponymous second album. There are more drums, more up tempos, and occasionally even electric guitars in tracks such as "Alameda," "Ballad of Big Nothing," the thumping "Pictures of Me," and the venom-spitting "Cupid's Trick," on which Smith seethes with near-silent intensity, leaving the livid volume to the instrumental accompaniment. Allegedly written in a heavy chemical stupor, "Cupid's Trick" seems to defy interpretation. Its writer couldn't even remember what it meant. Anything this intense can only mean nothing and everything.

Smith seemingly made *Either/Or* to rise above the insularity of *Elliot Smith*, yet this is still dark and depressing music despite the extra lift of the new arrangements and rhythms. Acute emotions even infuse the moments of relative light. Closing track "Say Yes" twists the smitten opening line "I'm in love with the world through the eyes of a girl who's still around the morning after" with a litany of bitterness, and if it doesn't make you weep, you should probably report your soul stolen.

SUPERGRASS: *IN IT FOR THE MONEY*

Following a fat, stripped-down rock and roll debut, Oxford's Supergrass broadened their sound in wonderful ways. The *Rubber Soul*–esque "Late in the Day" would have been out of place on *I Should Coco*, but it finds a complementary home on an album that welcomes big horn arrangements, acoustic guitars, synthesizers, pianos, and the wicked weirdness of "Sometimes I Make You Sad." There's still a glut of Supergrass super rock on the thrashing "Richard III," the Chuck Berry–subverting "Tonight," the spacious and borderline psychedelic "Sun Hits the Sky," and "Cheapskate," but the band's employment of more colorful arrangements and textures gives each its own discrete personality. "Late in the Day," "It's Not Me," and the smoky "Hollow Little Reign" are prettier than anything on *I Should Coco*. *In It for the Money* deserves a place in the Britpop pantheon alongside *Parklife* and *Different Class*.

VERUCA SALT: *EIGHT ARMS TO HOLD YOU*

Producer Brad Wood shot Veruca Salt's *American Thighs* through an evocative layer of mid-fi indie gauze, and the result was arguably the strongest debut album since Wood's production of Liz Phair's *Exile in Guyville* the year before. Yet gnarly beasts like "All Hail Me," "Victrola," and their definitive hit "Seether" suggested that Veruca Salt might be happier to rock without the indie part (so did the disc's AC/DC-referencing title).

Eight Arms to Hold You seems to confirm that. It is a rock album as full throttle as any by the Young Brothers. With tungsten-weight production from Bob Rock—who'd worked with such hairspray enthusiasts as Bon Jovi and Mötley Crüe—tracks such as "Straight," "Volcano Girls," the lethal "Don't Make Me Prove It," and "Shutterbug" hit harder than anything on *American Thighs*. Even poppier numbers such as "With David Bowie" and ballads such as the rapturous "Benjamin" are thicker than the mass of Veruca Salt's first album.

The title of Veruca Salt's second album was the working title of the Beatles' second feature film, *Help!* I really dig this cover design. Author's collection.

Consequently, Veruca Salt's recordings have lost a good deal of their atmospheric allure, but they gained a lot of power. Although the band's first and final major-label disc was commercially successful for an alternative album, frictions began forming between Post and Gordon, and the latter would depart for a solo career as Post carried their band into the twenty-first century.

YO LA TENGO: *I CAN HEAR THE HEART BEATING AS ONE*

Yo La Tengo from Hoboken, New Jersey, had been a banner band for indie kids since 1986's *Ride the Tiger*. Their mixture of Velvet Underground squall and detached vocals was hip, but on *I Can Hear the Heart Beating as One*, the material really justifies the presentation. There are explicit Velvets references ("Moby Octapad" cops the bass line of "European Son"), but other tracks wander into more pastoral glades. The beautiful "Autumn Sweater" draws up images of leaves drifting down on country lanes. The instrumental mood setter "Green Arrow" is a firefly-flecked summer night.

"Damage" is a deep trek into Lynchian woods. "Stockholm Syndrome" recalls that most pastoral of all pop discs, *The Kinks Are the Village Green Preservation Society*. Yo La Tengo cranks up the noise with the driving "Sugarcube," a punk cover of "Little Honda," and the overwhelming "Deeper into Movies," but *I Can Hear the Heart Beating as One* gets more of its power from the band's heart than their biceps.

1998

If there's any doubt that *OK Computer* was the most influential album of 1997, just look to the albums of 1998. With a single flip of the calendar, artists responsible for some of the most organic music of the nineties suddenly adopted Radiohead's synthesized, sci-fi textures. They still used their guitars, but they tended to costume those guitars in heavy effects or bury them deep in the mix.

As was the case with the post-*Pepper's* psychedelia craze thirty years before, all this bandwagon hopping resulted in some mediocre music, but it also inspired some really great stuff. Yet artists who stayed true to their more organic principles—and one defiant artist who turned his back on his own zanier progressive tendencies—made some of the best music of 1998. Hurtling to the end of the century, many rock bands' decision to ditch or disguise their guitars may have played a role in weakening the genre's status and influence in the next century.

BECK: *MUTATIONS*

Despite his folky origins, Beck made his name beyond a mini-cult by cutting together hip-hop, electronic, and Dadaist tomfoolery. So with no small amount of his trademark drollness, Beck made his most organic disc since his pre-fame days in the year of electric tomfoolery. *Mutations* doesn't lack weird decorations, but the overall effect of the music is more psychedelic 1967 than computerized 1998.

The real revelation of *Mutations* is not Beck's ability to reject trends he helped create but how great a songwriter and singer he is once he drops his hipster act. As excellent an album of its type as it is, *Odelay* didn't have a single song as perfect as the majestic "Lazy Flies," the loopy "Tropicalia," the mournful "We Live Again," or the elegant "Dead Melodies." With "Canceled Check," "Bottle of Blues," and "Sing It Again," he brings the acoustic blues into the present as spectacularly as PJ Harvey had revised the electric blues a few years earlier. With "Nobody's Fault but My Own," he resuscitates that most exquisitely dated of all pop forms, raga rock. *Mutations* wasn't particularly influential, but it was the first meaningful evidence that Beck is not only a master prank puller but also one of the most classically skilled and versatile artists of his generation.

BELLE & SEBASTIAN: *THE BOY WITH THE ARAB STRAP*

Belle & Sebastian crafted two brilliant albums in 1996, so the slight listlessness that creeps into their third album could be expected. Some of Stuart Murdoch's songs aren't as inspired as the ones on *Tigermilk* or *If You're Feeling Sinister*, and he relies on bandmates Isobel Campbell and Stevie Jackson, whose quaky voice lacks the finesse of Stuart and Isobel's, to contribute material. As the focus falls off Murdoch a bit, the band gets to show that they can do a convincing Motown takeoff ("Dirty Dream Number Two") or get trancey ("A Space Boy Dream"). Belle & Sebastian's next two albums would be less consistent and contain several songs that feel like retreads of their earlier work, and the next after that would find them accepting a bigger, less complementary sound with producer Trevor Horn (Yes, Buggles). This leaves *The Boy with the Arab Strap* as their last album to fully harness their antiqued magic.

The title of Belle & Sebastian's third album is not exactly a reference to the sexual device designed for erection maintenance and clitoral stimulation known as the Arab strap. Arab Strap is the name of a fellow Scottish group . . . who were not super-jazzed about Belle & Sebastian using their name without their consent. So no matter which Arab strap you plan to use, please always remember to ask for consent first! Author's collection.

THE CARDIGANS: *GRAN TURISMO*

Perhaps no post–*OK Computer* album seemed as wrong as *Gran Turismo* did in 1998. The Cardigans had been a cheeky, cheerful group that dressed up their songs of hurt as sunny, mid-century lollipop pop. Now they were swept up in a tidal wave of homesick-alien electronics and totally unironic misery. Nina Persson stopped singing her songs of rejection through dimples. The seriousness of *Gran Turismo* made the Cardigans feel like the first sad casualty of pop's latest progression.

Revisiting *Gran Turismo* decades after its release, the jading of the Cardigans no longer matters as much, and the album's strength becomes instantly apparent. Its darkness, spacey arrangements, and utter lack of humor are all sympathetic to its specific tracks, which are consistently excellent. Loungey vibes or Muzak French horns would be totally out of place on mirthless things like "Erase/Rewind," "Explode," "Higher," and "Junk of the Hearts." Up-tempo tracks like "Hanging Around," "Do You Believe," and the hit "My Favorite Game" mix up the disc with fuzzy aggression rather than the sugar high of old. Drums and guitars are still prominent in each track even if they are processed beyond recognition. *Gran Turismo* isn't superior to the early Cardigans albums, but there may be room enough in the world for an *Emmerdale* and a *Grand Turismo* just as there's room for Adam West and Christian Bale.

PJ HARVEY: *IS THIS DESIRE?*

PJ Harvey was another artist who tossed aside organic record making for heavily effected sounds in 1998. On *Is This Desire?*, Harvey sieves her bluesy rage and swagger through the synths, drum machines, and electronic effects fashionable in 1998. The extra textures expanded PJ Harvey's art immeasurably and helped make *Is This Desire?* her finest album yet as far as I'm concerned. Despite the emphasis on weird production touches, the music is raw and real. "The Sky Lit Up," "Joy," "A Perfect Day Elise," "My Beautiful Leah," and "No Girl So Sweet" are as authentically aggressive and scary as anything on Harvey's more explicitly guitar-centric albums. "The Wind," "Catherine," "Electric Light," and the title track settle to a spooky hush. Perhaps the album's most brilliant track, "The Garden," matches the airy yet ominous arrangements of those tracks with one of the most propulsive and magnetic drumbeats on disc. "The River" mostly eschews synthesized trickery for a baleful foghorn that chills to the core.

Although Flood and BAFTA-winning Marius de Vries had their hands in producing *Is This Desire?*, they didn't bring too much to the project that Polly Jean hadn't already brought during the demo phase. The progressive textures and perfectly sustained mood of *Is This Desire?* are already in place on her demos. In fact, the completed tracks of "Joy," "No Girl So Sweet," "Electric Light," and "Catherine" are nearly identical to the demos, which put PJ Harvey's mastery of her art in stark relief.

KRISTIN HERSH: *STRANGE ANGELS*

There are some synthesizers on Kristin Hersh's spellbinding second album, but they are never used to approximate alien worlds. *Strange Angels* is a dusty nook of spiderweb acoustic strings, veils of cellos and violins, and dancing-skeleton pianos and tambourines. The album itself was something of a forgotten item too, rarely receiving the glowing reviews it deserved. Hersh's evocative, surreal imagery, delicate melodies, and spare, refined arrangements are her prettiest on disc. She awakens her inner banshee only with the tempestuous "Gazebo Tree," but even at her most seemingly serene, Hersh's inferno is always lit.

LIZ PHAIR: *WHITECHOCOLATESPACEEGG*

With her *Girly Sound* tapes and *Exile in Guyville*, Liz Phair exploited the atmospheric possibilities of low-fi recording. She and producer Brad Wood polished up her sound significantly for *Whip Smart*. And then they went all in on the long-delayed *Whitechocolatespaceegg*. The electronic spaciness of 1998 floods into the title song (an awed tribute to her newborn son), "Headache," and the album's best track, the dizzying mother/daughter dialogue "What Makes You Happy."

Whitechocolatespaceegg basically holds on to organic arrangements for the majority of its fifty-one minutes. That length, put to such great use on the nearly flawless *Exile*, is a bit much this time since there are a few

Liz Phair continues her gradual move toward the mainstream by posing for her first cover photo that is actually in focus. Author's collection.

songs that could have been pruned. To my ears, the weakest of the bunch is Phair's would-be hit single. The singsongy melody of "Polyester Bride" is trite, and her hesitant vocal makes the track sound less finished than most of its disc mates. The final track, "Girl's Room," has similar issues. These subpar pieces are masterpieces compared to the stuff Phair was poised to make in the wake of the success of "Polyester Bride" when she decided to remake herself in the image of her buddy Sheryl Crow and rendered her career arc the most baffling and disappointing one of the nineties.

ROBERT POLLARD: *WAVED OUT*

Released just as Guided by Voices were transitioning into their high-fi phase, *Not in My Airforce* gave Robert Pollard a solo outlet for his low-fi impulses. This was necessary, but *Airforce* also hinted that Pollard might have even more trouble reigning himself in as a solo artist than he had as leader of Guided by Voices. Fortunately, his second album refuted that assumption, if only temporarily. *Waved Out* is one of Pollard's most concise records as a solo artist or a bandleader. Not everything will take up residence in your brain, but *Waved Out* still contains several of his best songs as it breathlessly rushes through "Make Use" and "Subspace Biographies," stutters with the title track and "Whiskey Ships," soars with "Wrinkled Ghost," and slows down to reflect with "People Are Leaving," an emotionally stunning rumination on death initially concocted by composer/multi-instrumentalist Stephanie Sayers. These songs are the most convincing examples of Bob the Pop Craftsman, though he still gets weird with "Showbiz Opera Walrus," which out-freaks the freaky Beatles song that clearly inspired it, and "Pick Seeds from My Skull," which is actually a bit tedious but is mercifully saved for the end, so it's a breeze to skip. Pollard's solo records would eventually catch up with Guided by Voices' new studio shine, but none of them would surpass the quality of *Waved Out*.

KID MARINE

The possibility that solo Pollard might continue the progress of *Waved Out* fell apart with that same year's *Kid Marine*. The music isn't bad. The new backing band that would help him make *Do the Collapse* crackles. However, the songs don't display Pollard's usual golden ear. The lack of structure can be expected from the guy who created all those fantastic fragments on *Bee Thousand* and *Alien Lanes*. The lack of hooks is much less forgivable. There are some pretty good songs, such as "Far Out Crops" and "White Gloves Come Off," but there's nothing in the realm of the previous albums' "Psychic Pilot Clocks Out" or "Subspace Biographies." "Town of Mirrors" boasts a big shout-along chorus perfect for band/audience communion in concert, but that chorus isn't very catchy, and the rest of the track barely qualifies as a song.

R.E.M.: *UP*

R.E.M's shift away from the organic sounds of *Automatic for the People* and *Monster* could have more to do with a major upset in the band than post–*OK Computer* bandwagon hopping. Drummer Bill Berry split after *New Adventures in Hi-Fi*, necessitating all the drum machines and loops that give *Up* its futuristic sound. Yet the club-bound "Leave" on *New Adventures* suggests that R.E.M. was already headed in this direction before Berry headed off.

While "Leave" uses electronics to pounding, dissonant effect, the fourteen tracks on *Up* are whispery, meditative little machines. This is R.E.M.'s quietest album. It's even more somber than *Automatic*, which couldn't resist throwing in booming stuff like "Ignoreland" and cheery stuff like "The Sidewinder Sleeps Tonight." *Up* floats above its low energy bar only once with the glammy "Lotus," though even that is pretty laid back. The lingering vibe of *Up* is the musical weightlessness and emotional heaviness of tracks such as "Suspicion," "The Apologist," "Sad Professor," "You're in the Air," "Diminished," and "Parakeet." The numbers that refuse to mope, such as the Brian Wilson tribute "At My Most Beautiful," "Why Not Smile," and "Daysleeper," are too tightly controlled and low key to achieve "Sidewinder" levels of joy. So *Up* is not R.E.M.'s most pleasurable album, but it is their most perfect mood piece.

SLOAN: *NAVY BLUES*

Sloan's completely assured fourth LP is an old-fashioned, capital-R-O-C-K Record, totally and unabashedly devoted to the days when Kiss and Cheap Trick wailed from the airwaves. Unlike a band like Urge Overkill, who slammed home the irony like a self-aware Spinal Tap, Sloan work in subtler shades, so you never feel as though they're taking the piss with old-fashioned arena rock like "She Says What She Means," "Iggy & Angus," "On the Horizon," and the in-joke anthem "Money City Maniacs," which is my choice for Sloan's greatest. As soon as those air-raid sirens rev up, you know you're in for something serious. This is the kind of getting-down-to-business hard rocking that most nineties bands were too self-conscious to attempt sans irony. Sloan says, "Fuck irony," and slams out the power chords like they're discharging A-bombs by the dozen. Had "Money City Maniacs" been about the kind of stuff that one usually sings about while playing this kind of music (screwing), it would be bullshit. But it's about spraying Coca-Cola on some sleeping guy. That is the antithesis of bullshit.

Sloan's inventiveness shines when they step off the fuzz boxes for Jay Ferguson's slippery "C'mon C'mon," Chris Murphy's comical "Chester the Molester," and Patrick Pentland's sincerely aching "I'm Not Through with You Yet." Drummer Andrew Scott wins the inventiveness sweepstakes with "Sinking Ships" and "Seems So Heavy," two sweeping mini-epics that sound unlike anything in rock's trope sack. They sure don't sound like anything Gene Simmons would pound out while dribbling fake blood down his chin.

ELLIOTT SMITH: *XO*

Screaming rock and weepy gloom are rock's two go-to styles for expressing extreme misery. Elliott Smith used mostly the latter to get his emotional state across on *Elliott Smith* and *Either/Or*. With *XO*, he flipped conventions, using the lush production and glistening pop of the Beatles as a ramp for dumping his guts on the ground. *XO* never recalls those very few instances when the Beatles actually allowed their personal emotions free reign (I'm thinking of things like "Yer Blues" and "I Want You"). It recalls the stylishness and craft of *Rubber Soul* and *Revolver*. That combination of very personal pain and shimmering pop is initially jarring because it is such a rare combination. On further listening, the combination makes the sweet production and the sour emotions more rewarding. The most gruelingly personal track is "Waltz #2 (XO)," a sad and angry letter to Smith's troubled

I'll always associate this album with the Christmas my wife and I spent listening to it while drinking and doing a jigsaw puzzle. That's the kind of thing that makes an album's significance transcend the kind of crap critics blab about in album reviews. Author's collection.

mother, who completely upset his life when she took up with an abusive asshole. That kind of message is not usually material for perfectly manicured, Beatlesque pop.

"Waltz #2" is a standout, but every ingredient on *XO* is superb. What's your favorite? The whispers that explode into mighty crescendos on "Sweet Adeline"? The sugar bounce of "Baby Britain"? The skipping "Independence Day"? The heady slam of "Bled White"? The left-field funk of "A Question Mark"? The dreamy minimalism of "Tomorrow, Tomorrow," "Pitseleh," "Waltz #1," or the a cappella "I Didn't Understand"? They're all stupendous pieces of pop self-exorcism, and they all add up to the best album of 1998 as far as I'm concerned.

1999

And so we reach the end of our trip, the end of a century, and a seismic shift in the music business on a number of levels. The year 1999 was the one in which pop music took control in a specifically definable way as Britney Spears and Christina Aguilera became the year's breakout artists. Boy bands that had been kicking around for a few years, such as Backstreet and Boys 'N Sync, took over. Old-timer Cher earned the biggest hit of the year by playing into the pop landscape and distorting her naturally strong voice with new tech called Auto-Tune, which is capable of making the most off-key warbler fit for prime time.

Much of the guitar-based rock that had the biggest commercial impact in 1999 was as indebted to mainstream pop as Shania Twain's and Garth Brooks's takes on country were. Blink-182 made punk fit for teenyboppers. Former punk group Goo Goo Dolls made MOR rock fit for your parents. The year's biggest guitar-oriented albums came from groups such as Korn, the Offspring, Limp Bizkit, and Kid Rock, all of whom fused hard rock and hip-hop with all the authenticity of the suburban mall kids who ate up their product.

Perhaps most importantly, the fundamental way people consumed music was changing. MP3 music files posed the first major challenge to physical media when file-sharing site Napster went online on June 1, 1999. An estimated 80 million users were taking advantage of the site by early 2001. In 1999, the Recording Industry Association of America recorded $14.6 billion in revenue. It was down to a mere $6.97 billion by 2014. The home computer's ability to burn CDs allowed downloaders to make their own physical media for the trifling cost of a blank CD-R (compact disc–recordable). As music became so easily and instantly attainable, downloaders heard a lot more artists but often listened with less attention. A lot of people amassed hours of music they didn't even bother to listen to. In essence, music was becoming disposable.

File sharing also changed the way people listened to music as they picked and chose the songs they wanted as opposed to consuming albums in their entireties as the artists intended. In June 1999, rock critic Greg Kot noted in a *Chicago Tribune* article titled "R.I.P. 33 R.P.M." how the album has "been made obsolete by MP3 downloads, movie soundtracks and CD shufflers." He explained that "listening to entire rock albums has become a lost leisure-time activity, particularly among a younger generation of consumers and music-makers who have grown up in a quick-cut world ruled by their channel changers and computer mouses," and that "the shifting tastes of the marketplace have reduced the incentive for rock artists to focus on the album as a coherent, self-contained work of art." By 2006, downloads of single songs were outnumbering CD sales nineteen to one, so if the album era appeared to be essentially kaput at the end of the twentieth century, the tag was now officially on its toe. The immense popularity of pop, the dire quality of mainstream guitar rock, and the intangible nature of new media and lazy listening habits seemed to signal an end of more than the century. Rock and roll, which had been a consistent pop-cultural force for nearly half a century, was not only flirting with irrelevance—it seemed to be on the verge of extinction. Yet there were still great rock albums in the final year of the twentieth century, new artists who pointed out alternative paths for guitar-based rock in the early twenty-first century, and old-timers who still managed to surprise, delight, and anger longtime fans.

BECK: *MIDNITE VULTURES*

In 1999, some of us were scrambling to our bunkers before the Y2K apocalypse—that elusive bug that conspiracy theorists insisted would cause banks, power plants, transportation systems, and sex organs to simultaneously self-destruct because computer programs were unprepared for the flip from 1999 to 2000. Others were gearing up for the biggest party in a century. Beck consciously set out to make the ultimate sound track for that shindig with *Midnite Vultures*, and in my circle, the thump of "Sexx

Laws," "Nicotine & Gravy," "Mixed Bizness," and the rest was inescapable as the twentieth century wound down.

Consequently, it feels a little trapped in time today, and after the depth of the more timeless *Mutations*, *Midnite Vultures* also feels like a slight step backward. Yet it also reveals how much Beck had refined his songwriting since his prankster days. "Mixed Bizness" is superb contemporary R&B, "Hollywood Freaks" cannot be beat for well-informed late-nineties hip-hop parody, "Broken Train" is a wiggly heap of junkyard percussion, and "Get Real Paid" is the only Prince pastiche that matters and indispensable to the ultimate party-like-its-1999-

Beck's idea of the ultimate party apparently involves pleather pants and some sort of human blow-up doll. Thanks for the invite, Beck, but I think I'm washing my hair that night. Author's collection.

because-it-really-is CD. "Beautiful Way" is pretty enough to deserve a spot on Beck's previous disc. These are all great songs, though listening to most of them outside of a party is a bit like watching *The Rocky Horror Picture Show* on TV by yourself.

THE FLAMING LIPS: *THE SOFT BULLETIN*

Oklahoma City's Flaming Lips had been perpetrating bizarre production monkeyshines since they sampled the Beatles on their debut album. They pulled the ultimate one with 1997's *Zaireeka*, a four-CD set that demanded all four discs be played simultaneously on different sound systems to puzzle together a sort of octophonic sound. In light of such crazed experimentation, the band's most overt overture to mainstream success since lip-syncing on *Beverly Hills 90210* sounds positively mundane. Compared to the work of other bands, *The Soft Bulletin* remains an audacious world of majestic strings, massive drum sounds, choirs of overdubbed vocals, and futuristic textures.

That's beat generation figure Neal Cassady in a photo by Lawrence Schiller on the cover of *The Soft Bulletin*. Cassady is on acid in that picture. So is everyone who loves *The Soft Bulletin*. Author's collection.

The Soft Bulletin never buries its melodiousness under the bells and whistles, and it never flinches from dark subject matter as bandleader Wayne Coyne deals with death in "Feeling Yourself Disintegrate" and drummer Steven Drozd's drug problems in "The Spiderbite Song." This marks a big turn after the bizarre fantasy/sci-fi surrealism of Coyne's earlier words. Songs such as "Race for the Prize" and "Buggin'" are breakthroughs on the basic pop-songwriting level. The "Nobody Home"–like "What Is the Light?," the "I Am the Walrus"–like "The Gash," and the "Expecting to Fly"–like "Feeling Yourself Disintegrate" are in the same psychedelic grade as the songs they emulate.

GUIDED BY VOICES: *DO THE COLLAPSE*

Boy oh boy, did Guided by Voices fans hate this album when it appeared on major-label (major label! Blasphemy!) TVT. The band's low-fi production had been washed out to sea on a wave of slickness courtesy of producer Ric Ocasek. The songs were mostly longer than two minutes with multiple verses and choruses. There was even a power ballad with violins. All of this amounted to a betrayal of everything for which Guided by Voices stood.

I can see how someone raised on the low-fi gunk of *Bee Thousand* and *Alien Lanes* would bristle at the crisp sounds of *Do the Collapse*. I, however, was not raised on those albums. *Do the Collapse* was actually my introduction to Guided by Voices. When I first heard the album, I did not hear it as a sellout. I heard what might be the best power-pop album I'd ever heard. I heard a collection of perfect songs with lyrics such as "I'm a born again, boot stomping, witch humper." When I heard "Hold on Hope," I did not hear some mawkish piece of mainstream piffle; I heard something beautiful that could have been on *Abbey Road*—or at least Matthew Sweet's *Girlfriend*. I heard an irresistible pop song about the time Mr. Pollard's fourth-grade class caught him picking his nose. I heard the June-day folk of "Dragon's Awake," the racing rock of "Surgical Focus" and "Strumpet Eye," the heart-aching arpeggios of "Wrecking Now," and the all-out weirdness of "Liquid Indian," "Optical Hopscotch," and "In Stitches." I heard *Do the Collapse* free of baggage, which is the ideal way to hear any music. And I didn't stop loving it after I fell in love with *Bee Thousand* and *Alien Lanes* because its songs are so well conceived, produced, performed, and odd. I love *Do the Collapse* because it is the record that made me fall in love with Guided by Voices, because its songs became such an inseparable part of my life, because I cannot cross the threshold from spring to summer without hearing "Dragons Awake!" in my head, because I can't forget the night I first got a copy of "Teenage FBI" on a CD comp and met a woman who would become one of my best friends (Hi, Sarah!). It is that personal significance that can never be expressed in some academic, pros-and-cons record review. It's what really makes us fall in love with the music that means the most to us.

LE TIGRE: *LE TIGRE*

Bikini Kill was one of the most influential and high-profile punk bands of the nineties, and their explicit feminist philosophy was just as integral to the band as their fierce music. When Bikini Kill ended in 1997, leader Kathleen Hannah got to work on a new project more in line with the rising electro-clash movement, which used retro synths and drum machines as a foundation for the kind of toothy aggression Hannah used to express with Bikini Kill.

For *Le Tigre*, that retro sensibility is also evident in a band name pulled from silly eighties fashion trends and the pop-cultural junk she references in her songs. So *Le Tigre* is both a crash course in feminism and a pocket-sized party. The trio shouts the praises of great women artists and activists, questions patriarchal cinema, mocks the apolitical and apathetic, and reminds us that Rudy Giuliani sucked even before he got in bed with America's biggest villain of the twenty-first century.

Le Tigre candy-coat their messages with sixties pop beats, irresistible hooks, wacky pop-cultural references ("Phanta" toys with the main riff of Darth Vader's march and R2-D2 sound effects, "Deceptacon" takes its title from *Transformers* cartoons, "Hot Topic" references both a punk-appropriating mall store and, seemingly, Stevie Wonder's "Black Man") and genuinely funny humor, which is a really hard thing to pull off in rock music. So after you've freed your mind, your ass will follow it onto the dance floor as great stuff like "My My Metrocard," "Deceptacon," "Let's Run," and "Friendship Station" reminds us that being politically aware can be a blast.

ROBERT POLLARD AND DOUG GILLARD: *SPEAK KINDLY OF YOUR VOLUNTEER FIRE DEPARTMENT*

In 1998, the ever-changing Guided by Voices received its greatest shake up yet when Bob Pollard turned over the "classic" lineup of Tobin Sprout, Kevin Fennell, and Mitch Mitchell and hired Cobra Verde to back him on *Mag Earwhig!* By 1999, he'd let go most of that band and put together a whole new Guided by Voices, retaining only the invaluable Doug Gillard. If Gillard's contribution of the sublime "I Am a Tree" to *Mag Earwhig!* wasn't proof enough of his worth, then *Speak Kindly of Your Volunteer Fire Department* will be the final word. Gillard dubbed on all the instrumentation himself, which is not only musically flawless (never a Pollard hallmark) but also as vigorous as that of any "real" band. Pollard's songs are some of his best. The anthems "Do Something Real" and "Tight Globes" became fixtures of Guided by Voices' live marathons. "Pop Zeus" and "Messiahs" are intricate and vitalizing. "Same Things," "Soul Train College Policeman," and "And My Unit Moves" are fine mini-tunes. *Speak Kindly of Your Volunteer Fire Department* is one of Pollard's few extracurricular albums that is as good as his best work with Guided by Voices.

THE ROOTS: *THINGS FALL APART*

The Roots had been around for a decade when they created the album that most commentators agree was the one on which things fully came together. *Things Falls Apart* is an album with enough distance from alt hip-hop's first wave to have a perspective on what that movement meant, what has transpired since then, and where it was headed. Like first wavers Us3 and Arrested Development, the Roots are a proper hip-hop *band*, featuring Hub Hubbard on bass and Questlove on drums and an ensemble of guest musicians. Unlike those groups, their productions are much sparer, and their mood is much more melancholic. Although "Step in the Realm" offers a really catchy chorus, the opening few tracks are not as melodic or inventive as the earlier alt-rap bands were, so in essence, they are truer to

The terribly disturbing image on the cover of *Things Fall Apart* depicts riot cops chasing an African American teenager during a civil rights protest. Author's collection.

rap's original austere spirit. By track 5, "Dynamite!," the Roots are loosen-
ing up with flowing jazz rhythms, and things start getting really interesting.
Tinkling percussion jerks "Without a Doubt" from side to side. "Ain't Sayin'
Nothin' New" stands on a heavier jazz foundation. "Act Too (The Love of
My Life)" updates a doo-wop vibe for the twenty-first century without a
single "doo" or "wop." For "The Return of Innocence Lost," guest speaker
Ursula Rucker layers a horrifically disturbing account of the world's worst
father over a spacey track that does away with hip-hop's essential beat completely. "You Got Me" draws on seventies soul with a lilting Erykah Badu
chorus and seems to single-handedly force the love song into maturity with
a detailed, personal, literate lyric. *Things Fall Apart* is a starkly mature
album with arrangements stripped to the essentials, precise musicianship,
and clear vision.

SLOAN: *BETWEEN THE BRIDGES*

Sloan mastered the art of rock songwriting with *One Chord to Another*
and *Navy Blues*. *Between the Bridges* perfects their album craft. While the
individual songs have no more in common than the ones on their previous
records did, the band give their latest batch a sense of unity with recurring
musical themes and segues that harkens back to the conceptual LP making
of the seventies.

That period aura extends to the music as the guys layer on lush *Rumours*
harmonies, get a lot of mileage out of their Fender Rhodes, reference Television, and even go full prog with Andrew Scott's "Sensory Deprivation."
Patrick Pentland grinds out two of his most inviting pithy rockers with "Losing California" and "Friendship." Jay Ferguson contributes his most consistent and eclectic selection of songs with the springy "Don't You Believe
a Word," the twinkling "Waiting for Slow Songs," and the atypically tough
"Take Good Care of the Poor Boy." Chris Murphy's "The Marquee and the
Moon" is elegance worthy of the band to which it pays tribute. While the
different songwriting styles of Sloan's four engines can make their albums
sound a bit disjointed, the quality of the songs, the equality of the contributions (each band member brings in precisely three songs each), and the
segues make *Between the Bridges* one of Sloan's most wholesome albums.

THE WHITE STRIPES: *THE WHITE STRIPES*

As rock and roll nearly flickered out in 1999, the White Stripes released their first album. This is significant because they were to be the last major rock and roll band—the kind of group your grandpa has heard of. Jack and Meg White brought it all back home to the essentials that made the genre as fresh and feral as it had been forty-five years earlier. Brewed in blues, sporting a true guitar hero, emphasizing the most primal beat, the White Stripes could have shared a bill with Little Richard and Eddie Cochran if not for Jack White's metallic warble, post-Hendrix fretting, and unusual lyricism. Such things made the White Stripes unique, as did such cheeky, blatant gimmicks as their Starlight Mint imagery and Jack and Meg's creepy siblings/married-couple mystery relationship. While their debut album neither broke the White Stripes into the mainstream nor boasted the superb songwriting that would make *White Blood Cells* and *Elephant* the kinds of albums that top lists, *The White Stripes* is still a strong sampler of the stuff the duo would soon perfect. Both pay tribute to and modernize trad blues, compose some catchy tunes, punish their instruments, strum some acoustic numbers and savvy covers, and look supercool.

In the next decade, the White Stripes would be at the forefront of a new "garage-band" movement that seemed poised to rescue rock and roll from the cemetery, but the simple fact that bands such as the Strokes, the Hives, and the Vines couldn't measure up to Jack and Meg in terms of songwriting or originality brought that wave to a swift end. The much-discussed garage-band revival would be over faster than punk or grunge and had zero lasting impact on pop music. The White Stripes broke up, Meg went into hiding, and even the once-ubiquitous Jack White keeps a relatively low profile these days. RIP White Stripes. RIP rock and roll.

The White Stripes' Starlight mint iconography was in place from the very start. Author's collection.

BACK COVER

Rock and roll did not experience some sort of Y2K moment, melting down as soon as the ceremonial ball touched ground on January 1, 2000. The garage-rock band revival of 2002 that the White Stripes and New York City's the Strokes set off gave the media one final rock and roll movement to champion. Alas, it was over almost as soon as it began as fellow movement leaders the Vines offered nothing more than warmed-over Nirvana choruses and Sweden's the Hives took their sixties-worshipping act over the parody line. Between the Hives' pseudo-sixties garage rock, the White Stripes' seventies-style heavy blues rock, the Strokes' eighties-style New Wave, and the Vine's nineties-style pseudo-grunge, each band embodied a specific decade in rock and roll history, suggesting that rock and roll had hit a wall. With nowhere left to progress, guitar-based rock bands were doomed to flame out.

The 2000s did see a number of guitar bands, such as New Pornographers, the Arctic Monkeys, the Soundtrack of Our Lives, Franz Ferdinand, the Arcade Fire, the Shins, the Killers, Spoon, Interpol, and Kings of Leon, achieve various degrees of indie-level success and make some excellent music, but none became household names. Retro-soul belter Amy Winehouse did become phenomenally famous on the strength of her powerful contralto but also because of the serious personal problems that brought a tragically early end to her career on July 23, 2011.

Established rock and roll artists such as Radiohead, PJ Harvey, Guided by Voices, Juliana Hatfield, Kristen Hersh, Sloan, Helium's Mary Timony, Elvis Costello, and Beck continued to produce fine work into the new century. Hell, even a few old-timers, such as Brian Wilson and the Who (reduced to a duo after the 2002 death of John Entwistle), put out their best albums in decades in the 2000s. There wasn't much actual innovation, though. Indeed, *Brian Wilson Presents SMiLE*—a career-rejuvenating solo revival of his abandoned *SMiLE* project—did sound like nothing before it, but Wilson had imagined its innovations nearly four decades earlier. That 1966–1967 period remained a high-water mark for the rock and roll album never surpassed as far as I'm concerned.

In the 2010s, a number of factors further weakened guitar rock's influence. The economic collapse of 2008 forced 80 percent of public schools to slash their budgets. Music education was an all-too-common victim, depriving the world of a lot of would-be Hendrixes. Popular video games such as Guitar Hero and Rock Band allowed a lot of them to get their ya-ya's out without having to ever learn to play an actual instrument. Music software was a standard feature on a lot of home computers, and with tools such as GarageBand loops (which could authentically reproduce everything from drumbeats to bass lines) and Auto-Tune, the kind of musicianship necessary for live performance was no longer necessary to make music. Basically, musicians and singers lost pop to the producers. Skyrocketing rents in music epicenters such as New York City forced live venues from the grungiest (CBGB) to the most hipster fancy (Galapagos in Williamsburg, Brooklyn) to shut down, leaving the remaining musicians with fewer places to gig.

Meanwhile, the overall attitude toward rock music began to shift. The genre's appropriation of black music and rejection of black and female artists caught up with it as the term "rockist," which equates a preference for rock and roll with racism and sexism, became an internet buzz term. So did "poptimist," which indicates the kind of person who views the new breed of pop by stars such as Beyoncé and Taylor Swift as welcome and positive alternatives to the rock and roll that older critics such as myself insisted was the only popular music worth a damn. The kids who spent their teen years listening to Britney Spears and Christina Aguilera grew up to be the music critics of the twenty-first century, and they are now calling the shots regarding what is and isn't in. The earlier arbiters of taste fell in line largely with a more inclusive definition of what constitutes good music. In 2009, rock's most narrow-minded institution, the Rock and Roll Hall of Fame, inducted its first hip-hop group: Run-DMC. Subsequent years saw the induction of artists such as ABBA, Hall & Oates, Linda Ronstadt, Bon

Jovi, Def Leppard, Janet Jackson, and Whitney Houston, all of whom would have been far too pop for the Hall of Fame a decade earlier. Jann Wenner's *Rolling Stone* magazine even gave the Monkees—those prefab pop boogiemen he allegedly vowed to never allow into his Hall of Fame—a rave notice for their 2016 reunion album, *Good Times!*

At the same time, it has become common, perhaps even expected, for commentators to deride rock's most formerly unimpeachable artists from the Beatles to the Rolling Stones to Led Zeppelin. Citations of these artists' sexism and cultural appropriation make it harder for we older fans to defend them to a new generation more sensitive to such issues than mine was. Ambivalence becomes unavoidable. When I used to hear songs such as "Under My Thumb," I paid little mind to their issues and just tuned into the fabulous music or wrote off the nastiness as "it's only rock and roll." In a more enlightened age, it's a lot harder to stomach Mick Jagger's gloating about how he has reduced his girlfriend to a squirmy dog, yet I still can't resist Charlie Watts's mesmerizing beat and Brian Jones's cool marimba. To paraphrase one of Mick's more fair-minded songs, it's very complicated.

As the rock stars of old lost much of their significance, the very term "rock star" has too. Today, you can respond to a help-wanted ad looking for a "rock star accountant" or a "rock star human resources coordinator." Roll over, Chuck Berry.

In early 1958, Danny & the Juniors declared that rock and roll is here to stay just three years into the existence of a form of music anyone older than seventeen dismissed as a passing fad. Rock and roll exercised godlike influence over popular culture for the next four or five decades, dictating or influencing fashions, lingo, and political and cultural ideas and attitudes for better and worse, but I like to think mostly for the better. Rock and roll's artists inspired us to dress, think, and express ourselves without limits or regret, even if we were at odds with the ethos of our parents' generations. Its clubs and concert halls gave us places to convene and commune. Its albums gave us the most potent and meaningful symbols, texts, and artworks we could imagine. Rock and roll wielded such influence for more than half a century. Not bad.

But were Danny & the Juniors wrong? Is rock and roll really dead? Several commentaries on this very topic in sources ranging from *Vice* to the *New York Times* to the *New Republic* to *Forbes* of all things have officially pronounced it dead or nearly dead with varying degrees of melancholy and glee. Such articles often compared the status of rock in the 2010s to that of jazz in the second half of the twentieth century. There were still a lot of guitar-playing bands in the decade, but they generally didn't have the cultural influence the twentieth century's bands enjoyed.

But rock may just be merely dead and not most sincerely dead. Look at all the cemetery soil the vinyl LP has been displacing. As recently as 2011, the cheeky twentieth-century pop-culture survey *Whatever Happened to Pudding Pops?* declared the phonograph "gone for good." Over the next decade, vinyl albums made a comeback that would have been unimaginable a few years earlier: 2.1 million vinyl records were sold in in the United States in 2009. That figure hit 9.2 million in 2014, and that figure tripled by 2020, which saw the sale of 27.54 million vinyl albums according to *Billboard*. In just the first six months of 2021, 17 million had sold to Americans. By October, vinyl had usurped the CD as the best-selling physical music format, and orders for new discs were causing "production logjams" and overwhelming the "balky, decades-old pressing machines" used to manufacture them, according to a *New York Times* article titled "Vinyl Is Selling So Well That It's Getting Hard to Sell Vinyl."

And what was the top-selling vinyl album of the 2010s? The Beatles' *Abbey Road*. What were the other top sellers? Pink Floyd's *The Dark Side of the Moon*, the seventies-centric *Guardians of the Galaxy* sound track, Bob Marley's *Legend*, Amy Winehouse's *Back to Black*, Michael Jackson's *Thriller*, the Beatles' *Sgt. Pepper's Lonely Hearts Club Band*, and Fleetwood Mac's *Rumours*. And who is buying these rock albums? According to 2019 statistics, 38 percent are Generation Xers. However, a sizable 35 percent fall into the eighteen-to-thirty-four age bracket, and 7 percent are younger than that. New media from Queen's big-screen jukebox musical *Bohemian Rhapsody* (its sound track was the seventeenth-biggest seller of 2020) to that 2020 viral video of skateboarder Nathan Apodaca lip-syncing to Fleetwood Mac's "Dreams" have kept the old classics in the pop-cultural collective consciousness. America's top-selling vinyl LP of 2020 was not by one of those old-timers, but Harry Styles's *Fine Line* (232,000 vinyl copies sold in the year) is still an organic signpost that young people could work with the stringed tools of yore. Today, we may not know how many of the more than 2 million people who bought his album as of this writing were inspired to try making a little rock and roll of their own, but we might find out in the years to come.

Somewhere, a kid slips on a pair of headphones and drops a stylus on *Rumours* or *Abbey Road* or *Fine Line*. She grabs a guitar and strums the chords of "Dreams" or picks out the fuzzy riffs of "Come Together" or "Watermelon Sugar." A new rock LP era starts to take shape.

A TIME LINE OF ROCK
ALBUM MILESTONES

1931: RCA Victor releases the first twelve-inch LPs. They are made of an easily destroyed vinyl compound called Victorlac. RCA quickly pulls its albums off the market and shelves LP production because of the Great Depression.

1932: Columbia Records attempts to market similarly flawed ten-inch LPs.

1948: Engineer Peter Goldmark perfects the long-playing record for Columbia Records. The twelve-inch disc can house twenty-one minutes of sound on each side and spins at 33⅓ RPM. The previous format was a ten- or twelve-inch disc that spun at 78 RPM. Twelve-inch 78s could hold five minutes of music per side. Ten-inch ones could only hold three.

April 1951: As "Jackie Brenston & His Delta Cats," Ike Turner & His Rhythm Kings release the 78-RPM single generally regarded as rock and roll's first record: "Rocket 88."

1954: The first rock and roll album, *Rock with Bill Haley and His Comets*, is released. However, the LP is most popular as a classical music medium throughout the fifties. The 45-RPM seven-inch disc, introduced shortly after Goldmark's LP, will be the main rock and roll format for the next twelve years.

1955: Columbia Records introduces the Columbia House Record Club, a mail-order music club famous for offering eight albums for a penny with the only catch being that members then have to purchase an additional four albums at absurdly inflated prices and field monthly deliveries of unrequested, undesired albums.

March 4, 1957: *Gene Vincent and His Blue Caps* is likely the first American rock and roll album to not include any singles.

March 23, 1956: Elvis Presley releases his eponymous debut album.

May 1, 1957: Chuck Berry's debut album, *After School Session*, is released.

October 15, 1957: Elvis Presley's *Elvis' Christmas Album* is most likely the first rock and roll album in a gatefold sleeve.

November 27, 1957: Buddy Holly releases his first album with his band, *The "Chirping" Crickets*.

July 1958: Little Richard releases his eponymous debut album.

1959: The Teddy Bears release *The Teddy Bears Sing!*, the first album produced by group member Phil Spector. It is also one of the first albums to be mixed in stereo, which is ironic considering Spector's reputation as a mono purist.

1959: LPs sell more units than singles for the first time, though most of these LPs neither rock nor roll.

1960: Retailer Russ Solomon opens major record retail chain Tower Records in Sacramento, California.

June 16, 1961: The first album on Motown/Tamla, the Miracles' *Hi . . . We're the Miracles*, is released.

March 19, 1962: Bob Dylan's eponymous debut album is released.

December 9, 1962: The Supremes release their debut album, *Meet the Supremes*.

May 1963: James Brown's *Live at the Apollo* is released. It is likely the first live rock album.

March 22, 1963: The Beatles' first album, *Please, Please Me*, is released.

August 1963: Bootleggers rejoice! The Phillips electronics company introduces a portable alternative to reel-to-reel tapes called the cassette tape at the *Funkausstellung* (radio exhibition) in Berlin, Germany.

November 22, 1963: Phil Spector releases *A Christmas Gift for You from Philles Records* on the same day President John F. Kennedy is assassinated. The nation's dour mood following that tragedy is sometimes blamed for the album's commercial failure, but it will go on to become a holiday classic.

January 10, 1964: The Beatles' American debut LP, *Introducing . . . The Beatles*, is released.

April 16, 1964: The Rolling Stones' self-titled debut album is released.

October 1, 1964: *The Beatles vs. The Four Seasons*, a twofer package consisting of Vee-Jay Records' *Introducing . . . The Beatles* and *Golden Hits of the Four Seasons*, is rock and roll's first double-album release.

October 2, 1964: The **Kinks** release their eponymous first album.

March 22, 1965: Bob Dylan goes electric with the release of *Bringing It All Back Home*. Cries of "Judas!" ensue.

September 15, 1965: Otis Redding releases the landmark album *Otis Blue/Otis Redding Sings Soul*.

1966: Prerecorded eight-track tapes become popular because of their portability rather than their sound quality, which is dreadful.

January 1966: Paul Williams publishes the inaugural issue of *Crawdaddy!*, the first serious rock magazine.

May 16, 1966: The Beach Boys release their landmark LP, *Pet Sounds*.

May/June/July 1966: The first deliberately recorded rock and roll double album is . . . well, there's some debate about this one, and it all depends on when precisely Bob Dylan's *Blonde on Blonde* was released. Some sources, such as *Rolling Stone* magazine, peg it as early as May 16. Dylan biographer Clinton Heylin says June 20. Jake Brown's fairly exhaustive quest to determine the date on gloriousnoise.com has him hypothesizing July 1 but refusing to insist that is the definitive date. Why this matters is that the Mothers of Invention's double disc *Freak Out!* was released right around this time as well, and it is possible that it beat *Blonde on Blonde* into shops.

August 5, 1966: The Beatles release *Revolver*, which is often rated as the best album they ever made.

October 22, 1966: *The Supremes A' Go-Go* becomes the first album by an all-female group to top the *Billboard* album chart.

1967: The rock LP outsells the single and the adult pop LP for the first time.

January 1967: The Beatles' renegotiated contract with Capitol Records stipulates that the label can no longer alter their LPs for the American market. The subsequent release of *Sgt. Pepper's Lonely Hearts Club Band* in nearly identical states in Great Britain and the United States will largely put an end to the practice of releasing albums with different tracks in different parts of the world.

January 9, 1967: *More of the Monkees* is released. It is the first rock and roll album to become the best-selling album of the year.

March 1967: The Velvet Underground release their landmark debut album *The Velvet Underground & Nico*.

March 10, 1967: Aretha Franklin releases the landmark album *I Never Loved a Man the Way I Love You*.

May 12, 1967: The Jimi Hendrix Experience's first album, *Are You Experienced?*, is released.

May 18, 1967: Brian Wilson holds the final recording session for the Beach Boys' much-anticipated *SMiLE*. He will abandon the album, which will remain unfinished and generate fervent cult fascination for decades to come.

May 22, 1967: The Monkees release *Headquarters*, the album they recorded as a band after wrestling control of their music from music supervisor Don Kirshner.

May 26, 1967: The Beatles' landmark LP *Sgt. Pepper's Lonely Hearts Club Band* is released in the United Kingdom on Parlophone records. It comes out in the United States on Capitol the following June 1. *Sgt. Pepper's* is the first rock album without bands of silence between its songs and the first packaged with its lyrics.

September 1967: *Procol Harum* is released in the United States. It is arguably the first progressive rock album, the first goth rock album, or both.

November 10, 1967: The Moody Blues release *Days of Future Passed*, which is sometimes considered to be the first progressive rock album because of the band's collaboration with the London Symphony Orchestra.

December 1967: Donovan's *A Gift from a Flower to a Garden* becomes the first rock box set when its two LPs are housed inside a box.

1968: Few albums are mixed in mono, as the stereo LP becomes the dominant rock format.

November 1, 1968: George Harrison releases *Wonderwall Music*. It is the first solo album by a Beatle and the first LP on the Beatles' own Apple Records.

November 22, 1968: The Kinks release the landmark album *The Kinks Are the Village Green Preservation Society*. It fails to make any impression on the *Billboard* album charts but will become one of the most beloved and influential albums ever made.

November 29, 1968: Van Morrison releases the landmark album *Astral Weeks*.

December 20, 1968: Rock's most likely candidate for first rock opera, the Pretty Things' *S.F. Sorrow*, is released.

January 12, 1969: **Led Zeppelin** release their eponymous debut album. It is arguably the first heavy-metal album.

May 17, 1969: The Who's landmark rock opera, *Tommy*, is released in the United States. It will be released in the United Kingdom on May 23.

July 1969: A two-LP collection of Bob Dylan outtakes known as *The Great White Wonder* is released. It is the first widely distributed rock bootleg album.

May 8, 1970: The Beatles release their final album, *Let It Be*.

February 10, 1971: Carole King releases *Tapestry*, which will become the first album by a woman to go "diamond," meaning it will sell more than 15 million units.

May 12, 1971: The Rolling Stones release the landmark album *Exile on Main Street*.

May 21, 1971: Marvin Gaye releases *What's Going On*, the first high-concept soul album. Motown's Berry Gordy calls it "the worst thing I ever heard in my life."

August 14, 1971: The Who releases the landmark album **Who's Next**.

1972: KGB-FM in San Diego, California, becomes the first radio station to switch to the album-oriented rock (AOR) format.

June 16, 1972: David Bowie releases his landmark concept album *The Rise and Fall of Ziggy Stardust and the Spiders from Mars*.

1973: According to an analysis on FiveThirtyEight.com, the albums released during this year will spawn more classic rock radio staples than any other year.

March 1, 1973: Pink Floyd release their landmark album *The Dark Side of the Moon*.

August 11, 1973: DJ Kool Herc starts freestyling over an extended beat break in James Brown's "Sex Machine" at a party in the Bronx, which may very well be the first public rap performance.

August 15, 1973: Norman Jewison's film of Andrew Lloyd Webber and Tim Rice's *Jesus Christ Superstar* is released. It is the first movie based on the plot and songs of a rock album.

October 5, 1973: Elton John releases the landmark album *Goodbye Yellow Brick Road*.

September 1974: Brian Bukantis publishes the first issue of *Goldmine*, a magazine devoted to record collecting that established a system for grading used records that sellers still use today.

November 10, 1975: Patti Smith releases the landmark album *Horses*.

April 23, 1976: The Ramones debut album, *Ramones*, is released. It is the first American punk LP.

September 28, 1976: Stevie Wonder releases the landmark album *Songs in the Key of Life*.

December 1976: Blondie releases their eponymous debut album, which is arguably the first New Wave LP.

1977: Album sales peak.

February 18, 1977: The Damned's debut album, ***Damned, Damned, Damned***, is released. It is the first British punk album.

July 22, 1977: Elvis Costello releases his debut album, ***My Aim Is True***.

October 28, 1977: The Sex Pistols release their landmark debut album ***Never Mind the Bollocks, Here's the Sex Pistols***. They never record another LP.

1978: Geoff Travis launches the groundbreaking indie rock label Rough Trade.

1979: Fatback's ***Fatback XII*** featuring the first rap track, "King Tim III (Personality Jock)," is released.

July 11, 1979: Ry Cooder's ***Bop till You Drop*** is the first American rock album recorded using digital equipment.

October 19, 1979: Prince releases his eponymous debut album. He plays all of the instruments on it.

December 14, 1979: The Clash releases the landmark album ***London Calling***. Ten years later, *Rolling Stone* magazine will name this 1979 release the best album of the eighties.

July 8, 1981: The Go-Go's release ***Beauty and the Beat***, the first LP by an all-female rock band to go to number one on *Billboard*'s album chart.

August 1, 1981: I want my MTV! Music Television debuts, introducing American kids to weird British New Wave artists they may have never heard of without it. MTV will also help draw public attention away from the album and back to the single.

October 1, 1982: The first album released on compact disc, Billy Joel's ***52nd Street*** debuts in Japan.

November 30, 1982: Michael Jackson releases his landmark album ***Thriller***, which ushers in a new era of blockbuster albums full of potential hit singles. It will become the best-selling album of all time and maintain that status until a new tally of sales figures in 2018 reveals that the Eagles' *Their Greatest Hits (1971–1975)* has usurped it.

1983: The cassette outsells the vinyl LP for the first time.

1983: Robert Simonds founds Rykodisc, the first CD-only record label.

June 17, 1983: The Police releases the landmark album ***Synchronicity***.

July 27, 1983: Madonna releases her self-titled debut album.

1984: Tipper Gore founds the Parents Music Resource Center (PMRC), which will successfully lobby to get "Parental Advisory" stickers slapped on albums containing "pornographic" content in August 1985.

1984: *Peter Gabriel IV* becomes the first DDD CD, as it is made with digital recording, mixing, and mastering equipment.

June 25, 1984: Prince and the Revolution release the landmark album *Purple Rain*.

May 13, 1985: Dire Straits release *Brothers in Arms*, which becomes the first compact disc to outsell its vinyl equivalent.

September 16, 1985: Kate Bush releases the landmark album *Hounds of Love*.

1986: Bruce Pavitt and Jonathan Poneman found Sub Pop, the independent label that will introduce the world to Nirvana and grunge in a few years.

May 15, 1986: Run-DMC releases *Raising the Hell*, the first rap record to sell more than a million copies.

1987: Rock critic Simon Frith warns that the end of the rock LP era is nigh in his essay "The Industrialization of Popular Music," which argues that the commoditization of the rock album will be its doom.

1988: Consolidation within the music industry leaves just six companies, known as "The Big Six," in charge of all major labels: Capitol-EMI, CBS, BMG, PolyGram, Warner Music, and MCA.

1988: The compact disc outsells the vinyl LP for the first time.

June 28, 1988: Public Enemy releases the landmark album *It Takes a Nation of Millions to Hold Us Back*.

April 17, 1989: The Pixies release the landmark album *Doolittle*.

July 24, 1990: 2 Live Crew's *Banned in the U.S.A.* is the first album slapped with the Recording Industry Association of America's iconic "Parental Advisory" sticker.

1991: The compact disc outsells the cassette for the first time.

September 24, 1991: Nirvana's landmark album, *Nevermind*, is released. Independent labels and underground musicians rejoice when it displaces Michael Jackson's *Dangerous* from *Billboard*'s number one, but this alleged victory against mainstream pop will not have long-term repercussions for nonmainstream rock. It will spark a major-label signing frenzy, but many of the formerly independent artists the labels sign will not have long-lasting careers.

March 24, 1992: Arrested Development releases *3 Years, 5 Months, and 2 Days in the Life Of . . .* , the first major alternative–hip-hop crossover album.

June 22, 1993: Liz Phair releases the landmark album *Exile in Guyville*.

November 26, 1996: The first major nonphysical music format, the MP3, is patented.

May 21, 1997: Radiohead releases their landmark album *OK Computer*.

June 1, 1999: MP3 sharing site Napster is launched.

June 15, 1999: The White Stripes release their eponymous debut album.
June 20, 1999: In his article "R.I.P. 33 P.P.M.," rock critic Greg Kot eulogizes the rock album, which he notes has "been made obsolete by MP3 downloads, movie soundtracks and CD shufflers."

SELECTED BIBLIOGRAPHY

BOOKS

Appleford, Stephen. *Rip This Joint: The Stories behind Every Song*. New York: Thunder's Mouth Press, 2000.

Atkins, John. *The Who on Record*. Jefferson, NC: McFarland, 2009.

Barnes, Richard, ed. *The Who Maximum R&B*. New York: St. Martin's Press, 1982.

Bronson, Fred. *The Billboard Book of Number One Hits*. New York: Billboard Publications, 1985.

Bukszpan, Daniel. *The Encyclopedia of New Wave*. New York: Sterling Publishing, 2012.

Cutter, Matthew. *Closer You Are: The Story of Robert Pollard and Guided by Voices*. Cambridge, MA: Da Capo Press, 2018.

Davies, Ray. *X-Ray: The Unauthorized Autobiography*. New York: Overlook Press, 1995.

Ennis, P. H. *The Seventh Stream: The Emergence of Rock 'n' Roll in American Popular Music*. Hanover, NH: Wesleyan University Press, 1992.

Fashingbauer Cooper, Gael, and Brian Bellmont. *Whatever Happened to Pudding Pops?* New York: Pedigree, 2011.

Garr, Gillian G. *She's a Rebel: The History of Women in Rock & Roll*. New York: Seal Press, 2002.

Giuliano, Geoffrey. *Behind Blue Eyes*. New York: Dutton, 1996.

Hepworth, David. *Never a Dull Moment: 1971—The Year That Rock Exploded*. New York: Henry Holt and Company, 2016.

Heylin, Clinton. *Babylon's Burning: From Punk to Grunge*. New York: Canongate US, 2007.

Hinman, Doug. *The Kinks All Day and All of the Night: Day-by-Day Concerts, Recordings, and Broadcasts, 1961–1996*. San Francisco: Backbeat Books, 2004.

Jackson, Andrew Grant. *1973: Rock at the Crossroads*. New York: Thomas Dunne Books, 2019.

Lefcowitz, Eric. *Monkee Business: The Revolutionary Made-for-TV Band*. Port Washington, NY: Retrofuture Products, 2010.

Levy, Shawn. *Ready, Steady, Go! The Smashing Rise and Giddy Fall of Swinging London*. New York: Doubleday, 2002.

Lewisohn, Mark. *The Complete Beatles Recording Sessions*. New York: Sterling Publishing, 1988.

Love, Darlene. *My Name Is Love*. New York: William Morrow Paperbacks, 1998.

Majewski, Lori, and Jonathan Bernstein. *Mad World: An Oral History of New Wave Artists and Songs That Defined the 1980s*. New York: St. Abrams Image, 2014.

Marsh, Dave. *Before I Get Old: The Story of the Who*. New York: St. Martin's Press, 1983.

Marsh, Dave, and John Swenson. *The New Rolling Stone Record Guide*. New York: Random House, 1982.

Matos, Michaelangelo. *Can't Slow Down: How 1984 Became Pop's Blockbuster Year*. New York: Hatchette Books, 2020.

McNeil, Legs, and Gillian McCain. *Please Kill Me: The Uncensored Oral History of Punk*. New York: Grove Press, 1996.

Morton-Jack, Richard. *Psychedelia: 101 Iconic Underground Rock Albums*. New York: Sterling Publishing, 2017.

Neill, Andy, and Matt Kent. *Anyway, Anyhow, Anywhere: The Complete Chronicle of The Who 1958–1978*. New York: Sterling Publishing, 2005.

Pendergrast, Sara, and Tom Pendergrast. *Bowling, Beatniks, and Bell-Bottoms: Pop Culture of 20th-Century America (Vol. 4 1960's–1970's)*. Santa Cruz, CA: Thomson/Gale, 2002.

Popoff, Martin. *Led Zeppelin: All the Albums, All the Songs*. Minneapolis: Quarto Publishing Group USA, 2017.

Priore, Domenic. *Smile: The Story of Brian Wilson's Lost Masterpiece*. London: Bobcat Books, 2005.

Riley, Tim. *Tell Me Why*. New York: Vintage Books, 1988.

Robbins, Ira A., ed. *The Trouser Press Guide to '90s Rock*. New York: Fireside/Simon & Schuster, 1997.

Rodriguez, Robert . *Revolver: How the Beatles Reimagined Rock and Roll*. Milwaukee, WI: Backbeat Books, 2012.

Sandoval, Andrew. *The Monkees: A Day-by-Day Story of the '60s TV Pop Sensation*. San Diego, CA: Thunder Bay Press, 2005.

Savage, Jon. *England's Dreaming: Anarchy, Sex Pistols, Punk Rock, and Beyond*. New York: St. Martin's Griffin, 2002.

Schaffner, Nicholas. *The Beatles Forever.* New York: McGraw-Hill, 1978.

————. *The British Invasion.* New York: McGraw-Hill, 1983.

Schuftan, Craig. *Entertain Us: The Rise and Fall of Alternative Rock in the Nineties.* Beaumont, TX: ABC Books, 2012.

Shea, Stuart, and Robert Rodriguez. *Fab Four FAQ: Everything That's Left to Know about the Beatles.* Milwaukee, WI: Backbeat Books, 2007.

Stubbs, David. *Jimi Hendrix: The Stories behind the Songs.* London: Wellbeck Publishing Group, 2020.

Townshend, Pete. *Who I Am.* New York: HarperCollins, 2012.

Turner, Steve. *Beatles '66: The Revolutionary Year.* New York: Ecco, 2016.

Unterberger, Richie. *Urban Spacemen and Wayfaring Strangers.* San Francisco: Miller Freeman Books, 2000.

————. *White Light/White Heat: The Velvet Underground Day-by-Day.* London: Jawbone Press, 2009.

————. *Won't Get Fooled Again: The Who from* Lifehouse *to* Quadrophenia. London: Jawbone Press, 2011.

Wells, Simon. *Butterfly on a Wheel: The Great Stones Drugs Bust.* New York: Omnibus, 2011.

ARTICLES

Anonymous. "'60 Looks Brightest Ever for Disks & Phonos." *Billboard*, September 26, 1960.

Caro, Mark. "Partridge Calls Reissues 'the Next XTC Records.'" *Chicago Tribune*, May 31, 2009.

Crowther, Bosley. "Screen: One-Track Film; 'Girl Can't Help It' Has a Mansfield Mania." *New York Times*, February 9, 1957.

Forde, Eamonn. "Oversharing: How Napster Nearly Killed the Music Industry." *The Guardian*, May 31, 2019.

Harrington, Richard. "Rock's Changing Colour." *Washington Post*, July 9, 1989.

Kot, Greg. "R.I.P. 33 R.P.M." *Chicago Tribune*, June 20, 1999.

Kozinn, Allan. "CD's: Too Much of a Good Thing?" *New York Times*, December 28, 1988.

Leeds, Jeff. "The Album, a Commodity in Disfavor." *New York Times*, March 26, 2007.

Ramone, Dee Dee. "My Life As a Ramone." *Spin*, April 1990.

Rolontz, Bob. "LP's Top Singles in Unit Sales for First Time." *Billboard*, February 15, 1960.

Sisario, Ben. "Vinyl Is Selling So Well That It's Getting Hard to Sell Vinyl." *New York Times*, October 21, 2021.

Strauss, Neil. "Pennies That Add Up to $16.98: Why CD's Cost So Much." *New York Times*, July 5, 1995.

United Press International. "Compact Disc Sales Booming." *Chicago Tribune*, December 7, 1986.

Wenner, Jann S. "Lennon Remembers, Part One." *Rolling Stone*, January 21, 1971.

Williams, Paul. "Village Green Preservation Society." *Rolling Stone*, June 14, 1969.

WEBSITES AND WEB ARTICLES

allmusic.com (accessed November 15, 2020–April 25, 2021).

Caulfield, Keith. "Harry Styles' 'Fine Line' Leads 2020's Record-Breaking Year for Vinyl Album Sales in U.S." *billboard.com*, https://www.billboard.com/index.php/articles/business/chart-beat/9509163/harry-styles-fine-line-2020-vinyl-album-sales-us#:~:text=Harry%20Styles'%20Fine%20Line%20helped,31%2C%20 2020, January 8, 2021.

Daley, Beth. "Gen Xers, Millennials and Even Some Gen Zs Choose Vinyl & Drive Record Sales Up." *theconversation.com*, https://theconversation.com/gen-xers-millennials-and-even-some-gen-zs-choose-vinyl-and-drive-record-sales-up-125541, November 3, 2019.

discogs.com (accessed November 15, 2020–April 25, 2021).

DMS. "Back in Time—A Brief History of the Vinyl Record." https://www.disc-manufacturingservices.com/blog/post/back-in-time-a-brief-history-of-the-vinyl-record, September 6, 2017.

Editors of Encyclopaedia Brittanica, The. "Peter Carl Goldmark." https://www.britannica.com/biography/Peter-Carl-Goldmark (accessed October 18, 2021).

Flanagan, Bill. "Is Rock 'n' Roll Dead, or Just Old?" *nytimes.com*, https://www.ny-times.com/2016/11/20/opinion/sunday/is-rock-n-roll-dead-or-just-old.html, November 19, 2016.Ozzi, Dan. "Rock Is Dead, Thank God." *vice.com*, https://www.vice.com/en/article/a3aqkj/rock-is-dead-thank-god, June 14, 2018.

Ross, Danny. "Rock 'N' Roll Is Dead. No, Really This Time." *forbes.com*, https://www.forbes.com/sites/dannyross1/2017/03/20/rock-n-roll-is-dead-no-really-this-time/?sh=582047d84ded, March 20, 2017.

Shephard, Alex. "What Happened to Rock and Roll?" *newrepublic.com*, https://newrepublic.com/article/139572/happened-rock-music, December 30, 2016.

Sterling, Scott T. "We Need to Unpack the Best-Selling Vinyl of the Decade." *floodmagazine.com*, https://floodmagazine.com/73172/we-need-to-unpack-the-best-selling-vinyl-records-of-the-decade, January 9, 2020.

Thill, Scott. "June 21, 1948: Columbia's Microgroove LP Makes Albums Sound So Good." https://www.wired.com/2010/06/0621first-lp-released, June 21, 2010.

ARTIST AND ALBUM INDEX

CPSIA information can be obtained
at www.ICGtesting.com
Printed in the USA
BVHW082340030522
635571BV00006B/3

9 781493 064595